X-FORCE

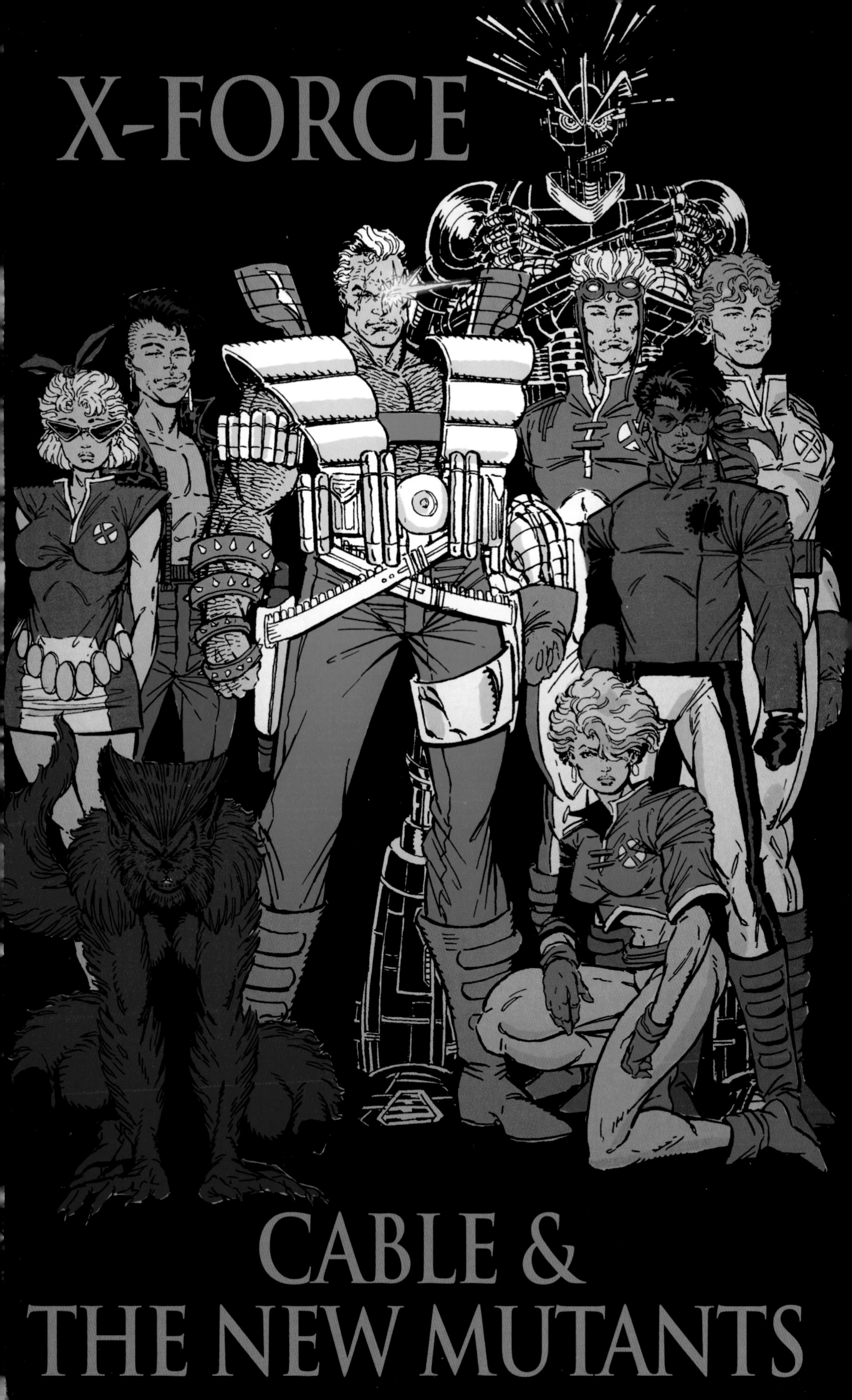

CABLE & THE NEW MUTANTS

X-FORCE

WRITERS
LOUISE SIMONSON,
FABIAN NICIEZA,
& DWIGHT ZIMMERMAN

PENCILERS
ROB LIEFELD
& BOB HALL

INKERS
HILARY BARTA,
BOB WIACEK,
JEFF ALBRECHT
& TIM DZON

COLORISTS
GLYNIS OLIVER,
BRAD VANCATA,
MIKE ROCKWITZ,
TOM VINCENT
& NEL YOMTOV

LETTERERS
JOE ROSEN,
MICHAEL HEISLER
& RICK PARKER

EDITOR
BOB HARRAS

COVER ART
ROB LIEFELD

FRONT COVER INKS
SCOTT WILLIAMS

COVER COLORS
THOMAS MASON

COLLECTION EDITOR
JOHN BARBER

EDITORIAL ASSISTANTS
JAMES EMMETT
& JOE HOCHSTEIN

ASSISTANT EDITORS
NELSON RIBEIRO
& ALEX STARBUCK

EDITORS, SPECIAL PROJECTS
MARK D. BEAZLEY
& JENNIFER GRÜNWALD

SENIOR EDITOR, SPECIAL PROJECTS
JEFF YOUNGQUIST

RESEARCH
JEPH YORK

SENIOR VICE PRESIDENT OF SALES
DAVID GABRIEL

EDITOR IN CHIEF
JOE QUESADA

PUBLISHER
DAN BUCKLEY

EXECUTIVE PRODUCER
ALAN FINE

X-FORCE: CABLE & THE NEW MUTANTS. Contains material originally published in magazine form as NEW MUTANTS #86-94 and ANNUAL #5. First printing 2010. ISBN# 978-0-7851-4970-5. Published by MARVEL WORLDWIDE, INC., a subsidiary of MARVEL ENTERTAINMENT, LLC. OFFICE OF PUBLICATION: 417 5th Avenue, New York, NY 10016. $24.99 per copy in the U.S. and $27.99 in Canada (GST #R127032852); Canadian Agreement #40668537. **Printed in China.** ALAN FINE, EVP - Office of the President, Marvel Worldwide, Inc. and EVP & CMO Marvel Characters B.V.; DAN BUCKLEY, Chief Executive Officer and Publisher - Print, Animation & Digital Media; JIM SOKOLOWSKI, Chief Operating Officer; DAVID GABRIEL, SVP of Publishing Sales & Circulation; DAVID BOGART, SVP of Business Affairs & Talent Management; MICHAEL PASCIULLO, VP Merchandising & Communications; JIM O'KEEFE, VP of Operations & Logistics; DAN CARR, Executive Director of Publishing Technology; JUSTIN F. GABRIE, Director of Publishing & Editorial Operations; SUSAN CRESPI, Editorial Operations Manager; ALEX MORALES, Publishing Operations Manager; STAN LEE, Chairman Emeritus. For information regarding advertising in Marvel Comics or on Marvel.com, please contact Ron Stern, VP of Business Development, at rstern@marvel.com. For Marvel subscription inquiries, please call 800-217-9158. **Manufactured between 8/11/10 and 9/15/10 by R.R. DONNELLEY ASIA PRINTING SOLUTIONS, DONGGUAN, GUANGDONG, CHINA.**

10 9 8 7 6 5 4 3 2 1

ABLE & THE NEW MUTANTS

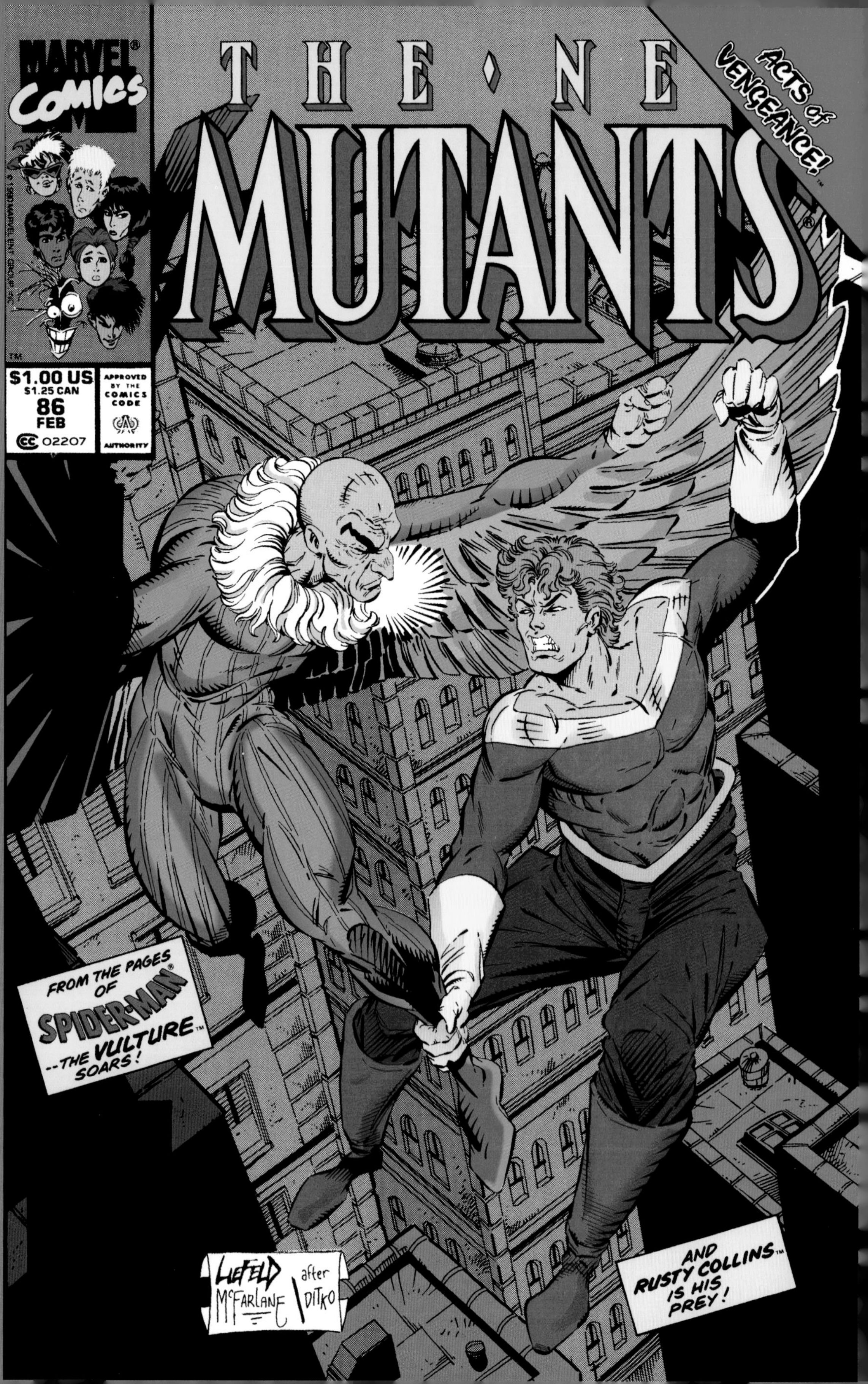
MARVEL COMICS
THE · NE
MUTANTS
ACTS of VENGEANCE!
$1.00 US
$1.25 CAN
86
FEB
02207
APPROVED BY THE COMICS CODE AUTHORITY
FROM THE PAGES OF SPIDER-MAN
--THE VULTURE SOARS!
LIEFELD McFARLANE after DITKO
AND RUSTY COLLINS IS HIS PREY!

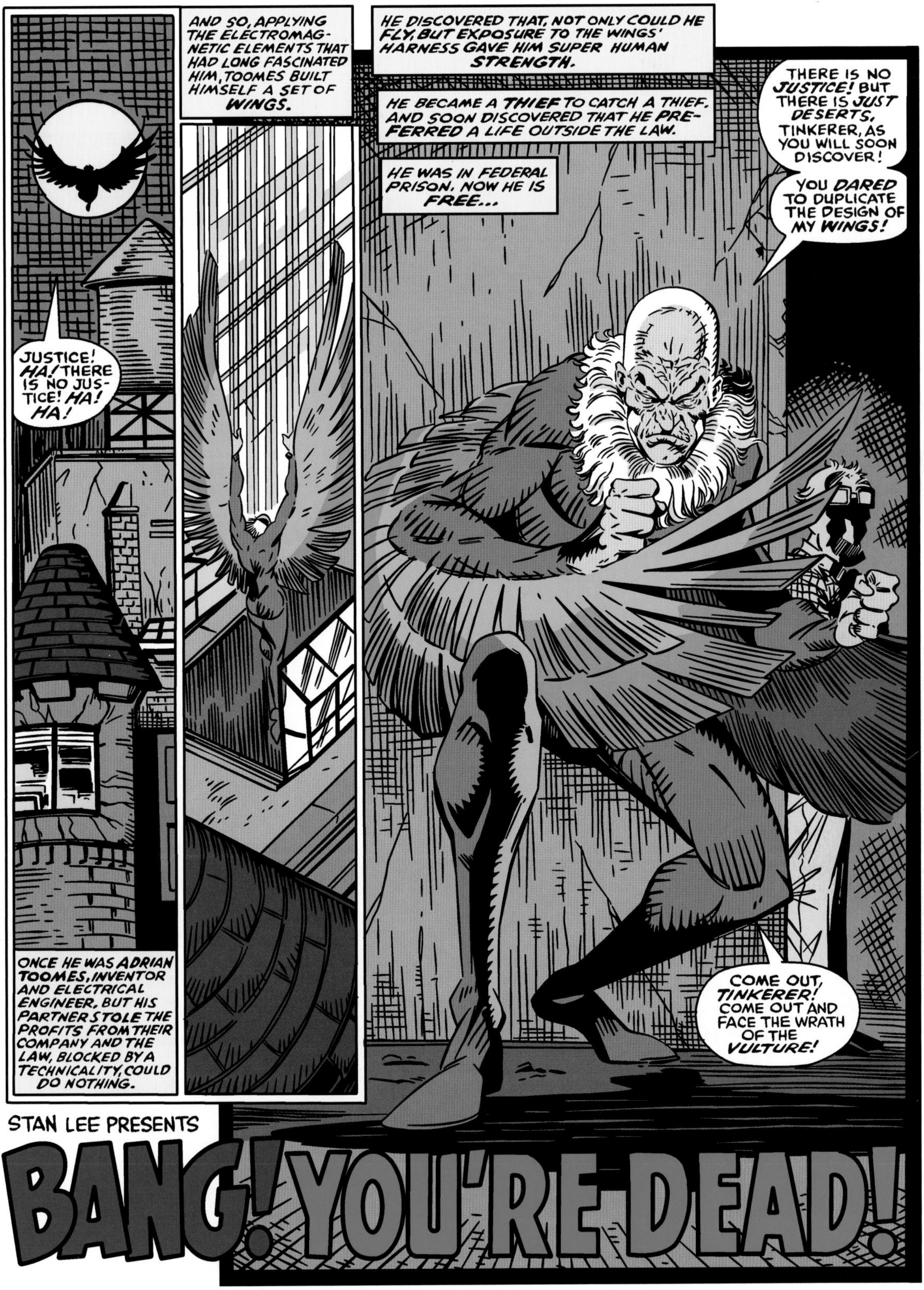
ONCE HE WAS ADRIAN TOOMES, INVENTOR AND ELECTRICAL ENGINEER. BUT HIS PARTNER STOLE THE PROFITS FROM THEIR COMPANY AND THE LAW, BLOCKED BY A TECHNICALITY, COULD DO NOTHING.
JUSTICE! HA! THERE IS NO JUSTICE! HA! HA!
AND SO, APPLYING THE ELECTROMAGNETIC ELEMENTS THAT HAD LONG FASCINATED HIM, TOOMES BUILT HIMSELF A SET OF WINGS.
HE DISCOVERED THAT, NOT ONLY COULD HE FLY, BUT EXPOSURE TO THE WINGS' HARNESS GAVE HIM SUPER HUMAN STRENGTH.
HE BECAME A THIEF TO CATCH A THIEF. AND SOON DISCOVERED THAT HE PREFERRED A LIFE OUTSIDE THE LAW.
HE WAS IN FEDERAL PRISON. NOW HE IS FREE...
COME OUT, TINKERER! COME OUT AND FACE THE WRATH OF THE VULTURE!
THERE IS NO JUSTICE! BUT THERE IS JUST DESERTS, TINKERER, AS YOU WILL SOON DISCOVER!
YOU DARED TO DUPLICATE THE DESIGN OF MY WINGS!

STAN LEE PRESENTS

BANG! YOU'RE DEAD!

LOUISE SIMONSON WRITER · ROB LIEFELD PENCILER · BOB WIACEK INKER · JOE ROSEN LETTERER · GLYNIS OLIVER COLORIST · BOB HARRAS EDITOR · TOM DEFALCO EDITOR IN CHIEF

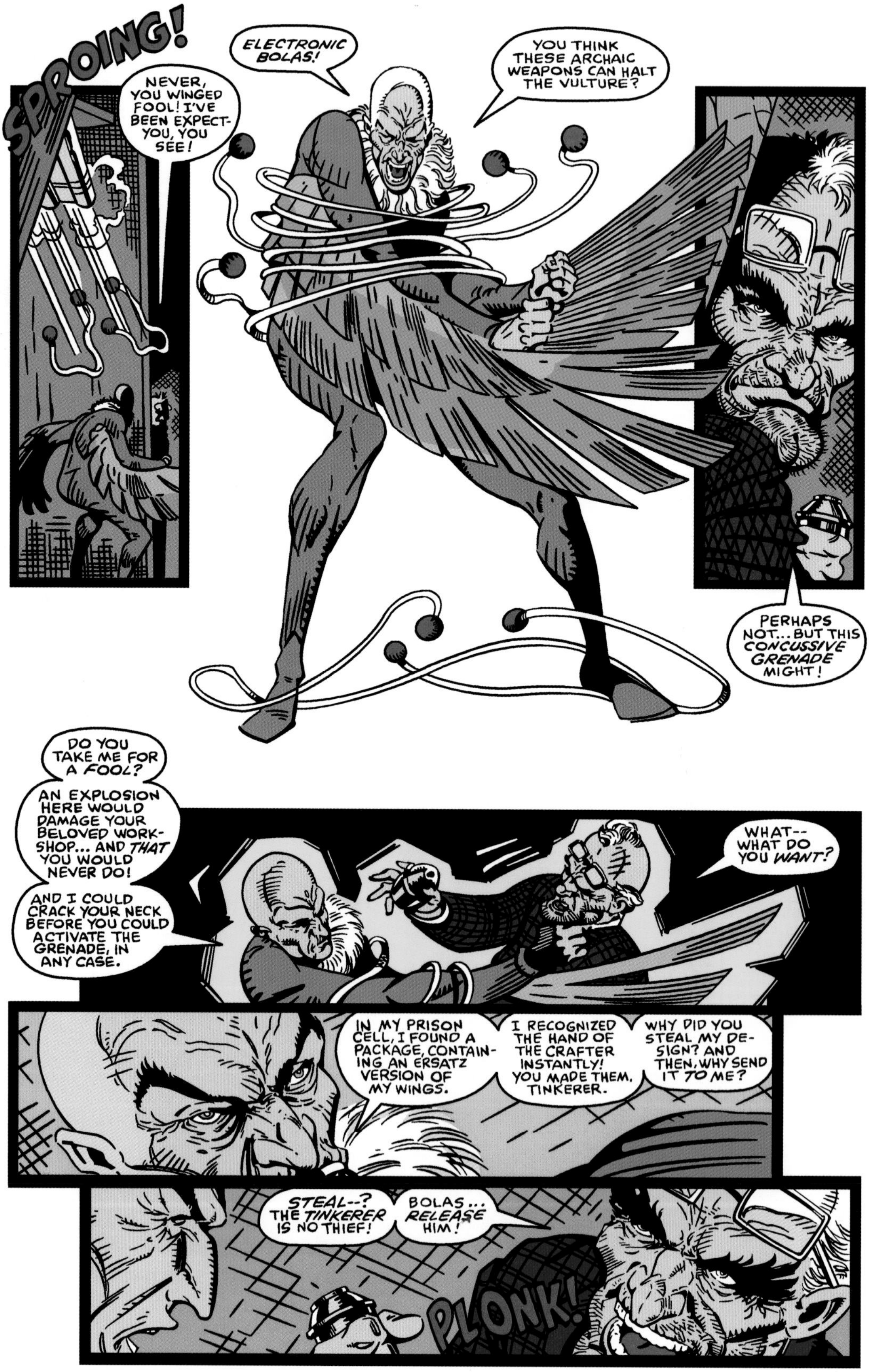
SPROING!
NEVER, YOU WINGED FOOL! I'VE BEEN EXPECT- YOU, YOU SEE!
ELECTRONIC BOLAS!
YOU THINK THESE ARCHAIC WEAPONS CAN HALT THE VULTURE?
PERHAPS NOT... BUT THIS CONCUSSIVE GRENADE MIGHT!
DO YOU TAKE ME FOR A FOOL?
AN EXPLOSION HERE WOULD DAMAGE YOUR BELOVED WORK- SHOP... AND THAT YOU WOULD NEVER DO!
AND I COULD CRACK YOUR NECK BEFORE YOU COULD ACTIVATE THE GRENADE, IN ANY CASE.
WHAT-- WHAT DO YOU WANT?
IN MY PRISON CELL, I FOUND A PACKAGE, CONTAIN- ING AN ERSATZ VERSION OF MY WINGS.
I RECOGNIZED THE HAND OF THE CRAFTER INSTANTLY! YOU MADE THEM, TINKERER.
WHY DID YOU STEAL MY DE- SIGN? AND THEN, WHY SEND IT TO ME?
STEAL--? THE TINKERER IS NO THIEF!
BOLAS... RELEASE HIM!
PLONK!

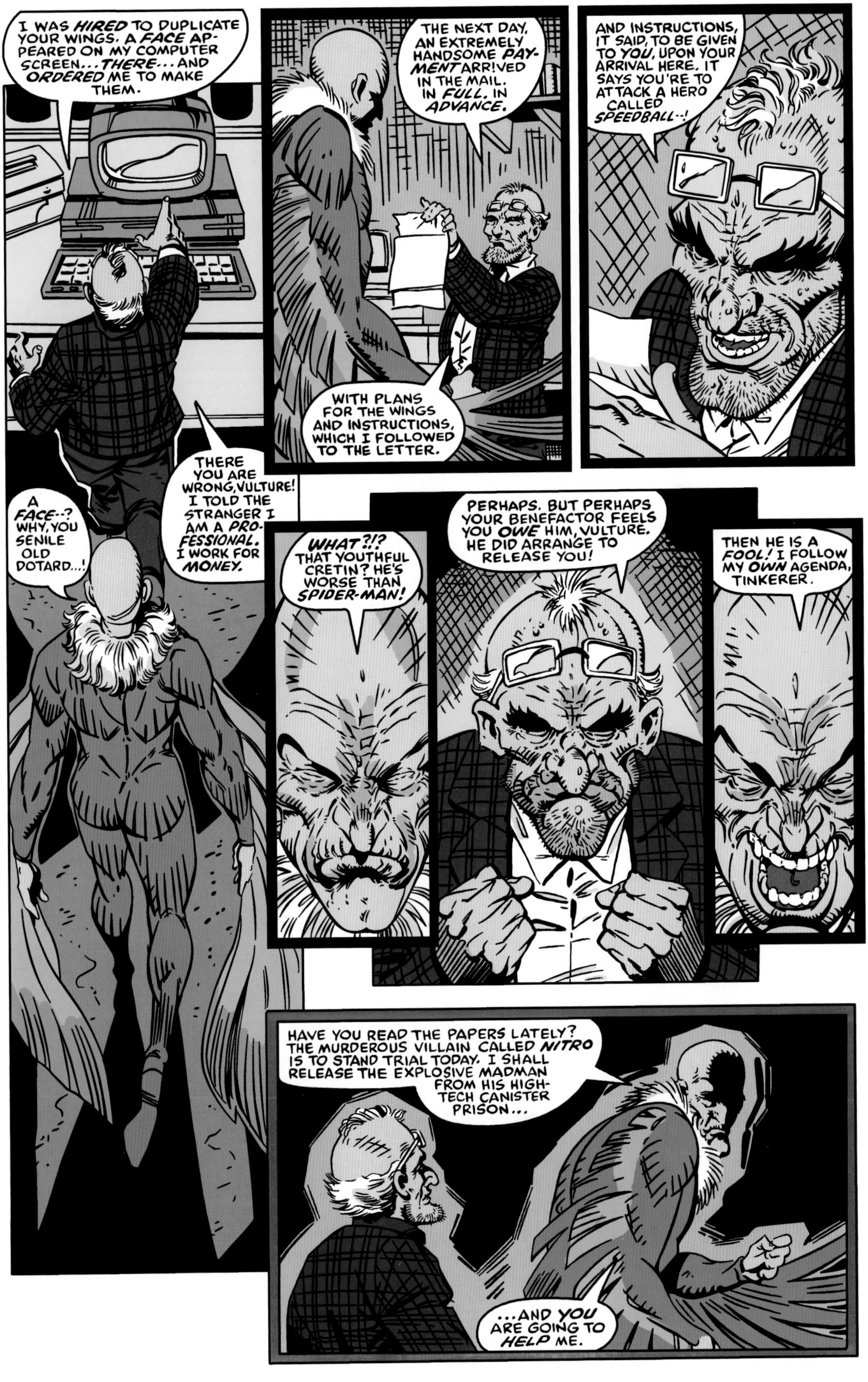
I WAS HIRED TO DUPLICATE YOUR WINGS. A FACE APPEARED ON MY COMPUTER SCREEN... THERE... AND ORDERED ME TO MAKE THEM.
THE NEXT DAY, AN EXTREMELY HANDSOME PAYMENT ARRIVED IN THE MAIL. IN FULL, IN ADVANCE.
WITH PLANS FOR THE WINGS AND INSTRUCTIONS, WHICH I FOLLOWED TO THE LETTER.
AND INSTRUCTIONS, IT SAID, TO BE GIVEN TO YOU, UPON YOUR ARRIVAL HERE. IT SAYS YOU'RE TO ATTACK A HERO CALLED SPEEDBALL--!
A FACE--? WHY, YOU SENILE OLD DOTARD...!
THERE YOU ARE WRONG, VULTURE! I TOLD THE STRANGER I AM A PROFESSIONAL. I WORK FOR MONEY.
WHAT?!? THAT YOUTHFUL CRETIN? HE'S WORSE THAN SPIDER-MAN!
PERHAPS. BUT PERHAPS YOUR BENEFACTOR FEELS YOU OWE HIM, VULTURE. HE DID ARRANGE TO RELEASE YOU!
THEN HE IS A FOOL! I FOLLOW MY OWN AGENDA, TINKERER.
HAVE YOU READ THE PAPERS LATELY? THE MURDEROUS VILLAIN CALLED NITRO IS TO STAND TRIAL TODAY. I SHALL RELEASE THE EXPLOSIVE MADMAN FROM HIS HIGH-TECH CANISTER PRISON...
...AND YOU ARE GOING TO HELP ME.

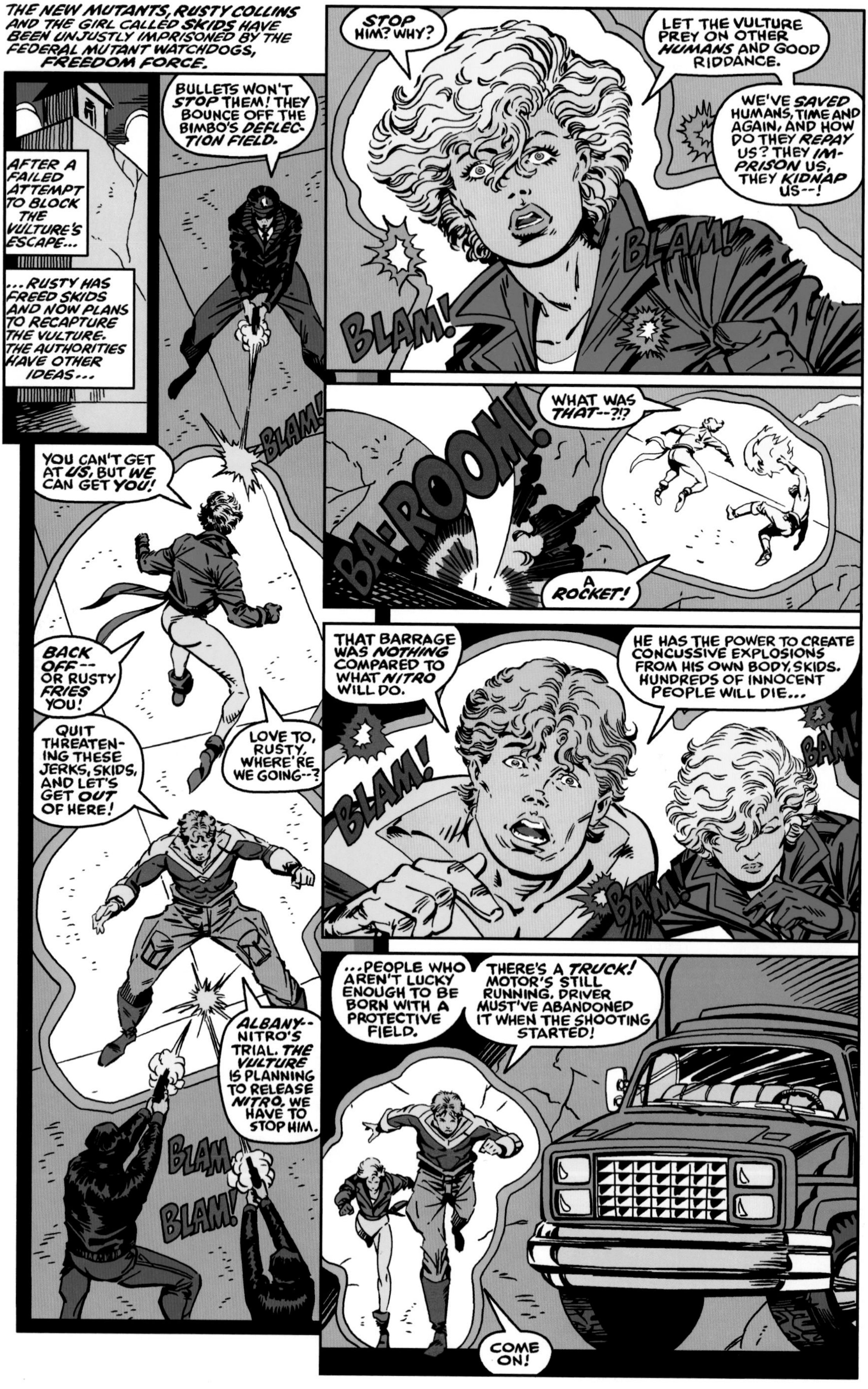
THE NEW MUTANTS, RUSTY COLLINS AND THE GIRL CALLED SKIDS HAVE BEEN UNJUSTLY IMPRISONED BY THE FEDERAL MUTANT WATCHDOGS, FREEDOM FORCE.
AFTER A FAILED ATTEMPT TO BLOCK THE VULTURE'S ESCAPE...
...RUSTY HAS FREED SKIDS AND NOW PLANS TO RECAPTURE THE VULTURE. THE AUTHORITIES HAVE OTHER IDEAS...
BULLETS WON'T STOP THEM! THEY BOUNCE OFF THE BIMBO'S DEFLECTION FIELD.
BLAM!
YOU CAN'T GET AT US, BUT WE CAN GET YOU!
BACK OFF--OR RUSTY FRIES YOU!
QUIT THREATENING THESE JERKS, SKIDS, AND LET'S GET OUT OF HERE!
LOVE TO, RUSTY. WHERE'RE WE GOING--?
ALBANY--NITRO'S TRIAL. THE VULTURE IS PLANNING TO RELEASE NITRO. WE HAVE TO STOP HIM.
BLAM
BLAM!
STOP HIM? WHY?
LET THE VULTURE PREY ON OTHER HUMANS AND GOOD RIDDANCE.
WE'VE SAVED HUMANS, TIME AND AGAIN, AND HOW DO THEY REPAY US? THEY IMPRISON US, THEY KIDNAP US--!
BLAM!
BLAM!
BA-ROOM!
WHAT WAS THAT--?!?
A ROCKET!
THAT BARRAGE WAS NOTHING COMPARED TO WHAT NITRO WILL DO.
HE HAS THE POWER TO CREATE CONCUSSIVE EXPLOSIONS FROM HIS OWN BODY, SKIDS. HUNDREDS OF INNOCENT PEOPLE WILL DIE...
BLAM!
BAM!
BAM!
...PEOPLE WHO AREN'T LUCKY ENOUGH TO BE BORN WITH A PROTECTIVE FIELD.
THERE'S A TRUCK! MOTOR'S STILL RUNNING. DRIVER MUST'VE ABANDONED IT WHEN THE SHOOTING STARTED!
COME ON!

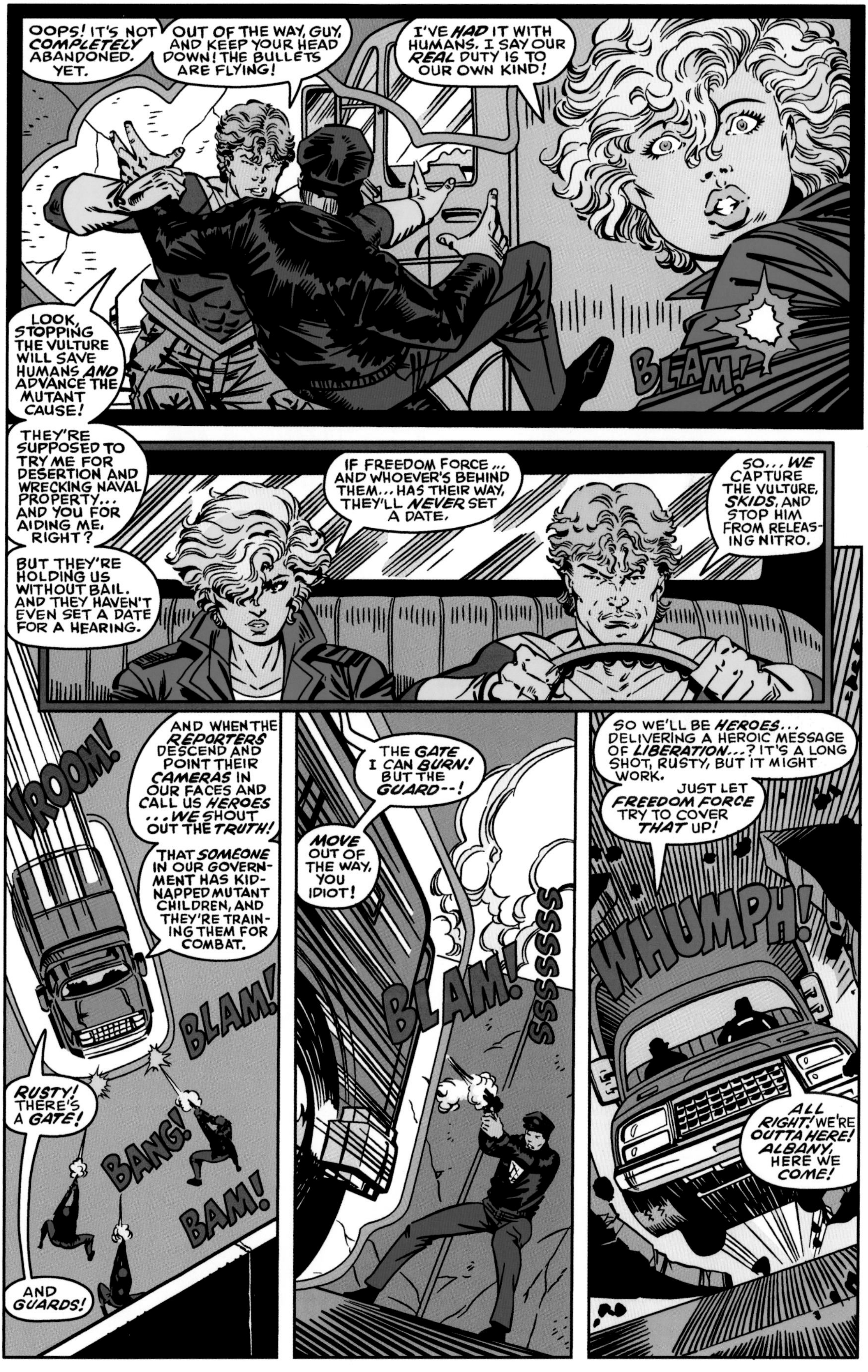
OOPS! IT'S NOT COMPLETELY ABANDONED. YET.
OUT OF THE WAY, GUY, AND KEEP YOUR HEAD DOWN! THE BULLETS ARE FLYING!
I'VE HAD IT WITH HUMANS. I SAY OUR REAL DUTY IS TO OUR OWN KIND!
LOOK, STOPPING THE VULTURE WILL SAVE HUMANS AND ADVANCE THE MUTANT CAUSE!
BLAM!
THEY'RE SUPPOSED TO TRY ME FOR DESERTION AND WRECKING NAVAL PROPERTY... AND YOU FOR AIDING ME, RIGHT?
BUT THEY'RE HOLDING US WITHOUT BAIL. AND THEY HAVEN'T EVEN SET A DATE FOR A HEARING.
IF FREEDOM FORCE... AND WHOEVER'S BEHIND THEM... HAS THEIR WAY, THEY'LL NEVER SET A DATE.
SO... WE CAPTURE THE VULTURE, SKIDS, AND STOP HIM FROM RELEASING NITRO.
VROOM!
AND WHEN THE REPORTERS DESCEND AND POINT THEIR CAMERAS IN OUR FACES AND CALL US HEROES ...WE SHOUT OUT THE TRUTH!
THAT SOMEONE IN OUR GOVERNMENT HAS KIDNAPPED MUTANT CHILDREN, AND THEY'RE TRAINING THEM FOR COMBAT.
BLAM!
RUSTY! THERE'S A GATE!
BANG!
BAM!
AND GUARDS!
THE GATE I CAN BURN! BUT THE GUARD--!
MOVE OUT OF THE WAY, YOU IDIOT!
BLAM!
SSSSSSS
SO WE'LL BE HEROES... DELIVERING A HEROIC MESSAGE OF LIBERATION...? IT'S A LONG SHOT, RUSTY, BUT IT MIGHT WORK.
JUST LET FREEDOM FORCE TRY TO COVER THAT UP!
WHUMPH!
ALL RIGHT! WE'RE OUTTA HERE! ALBANY, HERE WE COME!

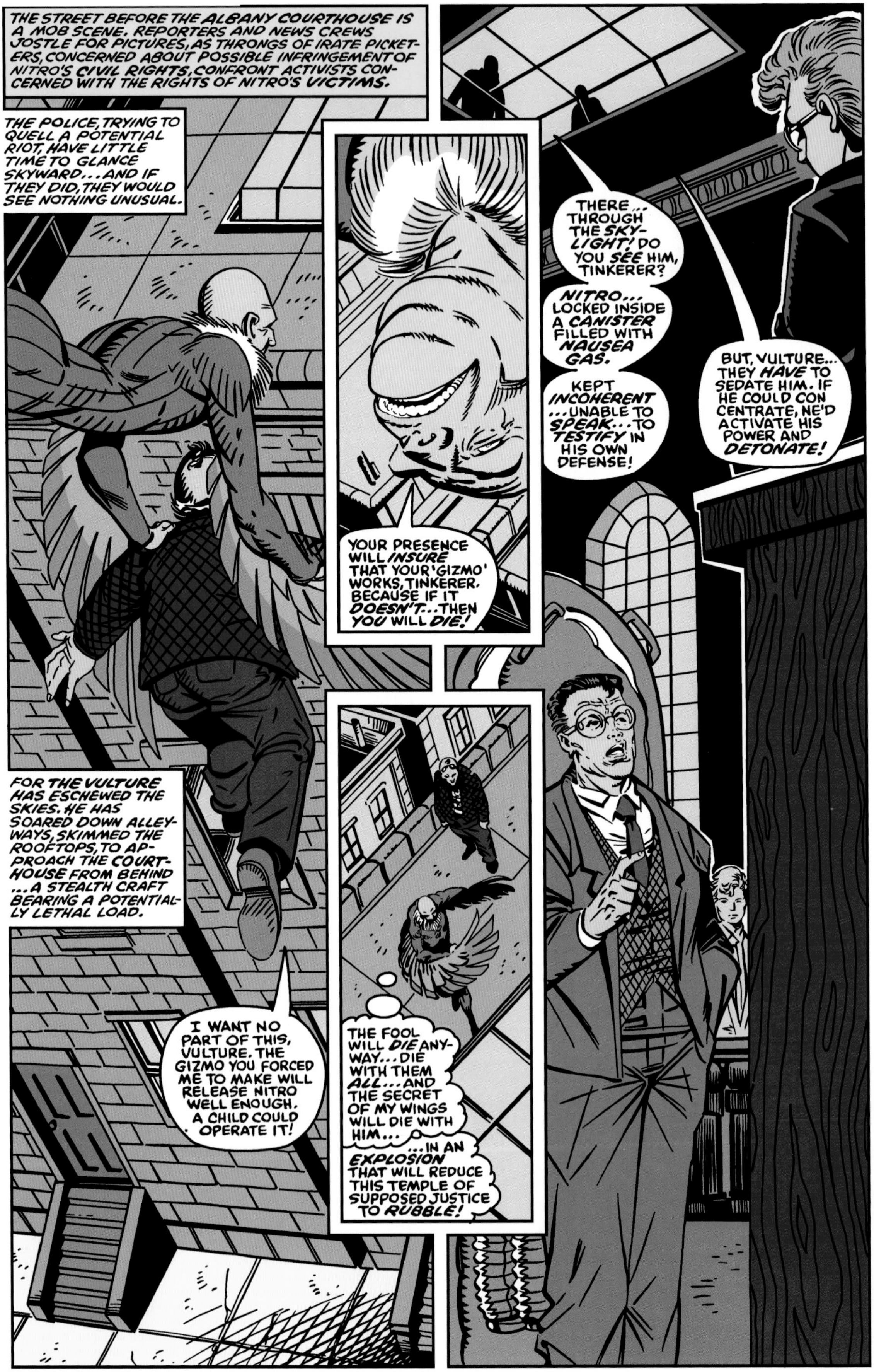

THE STREET BEFORE THE ALBANY COURTHOUSE IS A MOB SCENE. REPORTERS AND NEWS CREWS JOSTLE FOR PICTURES, AS THRONGS OF IRATE PICKETERS, CONCERNED ABOUT POSSIBLE INFRINGEMENT OF NITRO'S CIVIL RIGHTS, CONFRONT ACTIVISTS CONCERNED WITH THE RIGHTS OF NITRO'S VICTIMS.
THE POLICE, TRYING TO QUELL A POTENTIAL RIOT, HAVE LITTLE TIME TO GLANCE SKYWARD... AND IF THEY DID, THEY WOULD SEE NOTHING UNUSUAL.
FOR THE VULTURE HAS ESCHEWED THE SKIES. HE HAS SOARED DOWN ALLEYWAYS, SKIMMED THE ROOFTOPS, TO APPROACH THE COURTHOUSE FROM BEHIND ...A STEALTH CRAFT BEARING A POTENTIALLY LETHAL LOAD.
I WANT NO PART OF THIS, VULTURE. THE GIZMO YOU FORCED ME TO MAKE WILL RELEASE NITRO WELL ENOUGH. A CHILD COULD OPERATE IT!
YOUR PRESENCE WILL INSURE THAT YOUR 'GIZMO' WORKS, TINKERER. BECAUSE IF IT DOESN'T... THEN YOU WILL DIE!
THE FOOL WILL DIE ANYWAY... DIE WITH THEM ALL... AND THE SECRET OF MY WINGS WILL DIE WITH HIM...
...IN AN EXPLOSION THAT WILL REDUCE THIS TEMPLE OF SUPPOSED JUSTICE TO RUBBLE!
THERE... THROUGH THE SKYLIGHT! DO YOU SEE HIM, TINKERER?
NITRO... LOCKED INSIDE A CANISTER FILLED WITH NAUSEA GAS.
KEPT INCOHERENT ...UNABLE TO SPEAK... TO TESTIFY IN HIS OWN DEFENSE!
BUT, VULTURE... THEY HAVE TO SEDATE HIM. IF HE COULD CONCENTRATE, HE'D ACTIVATE HIS POWER AND DETONATE!

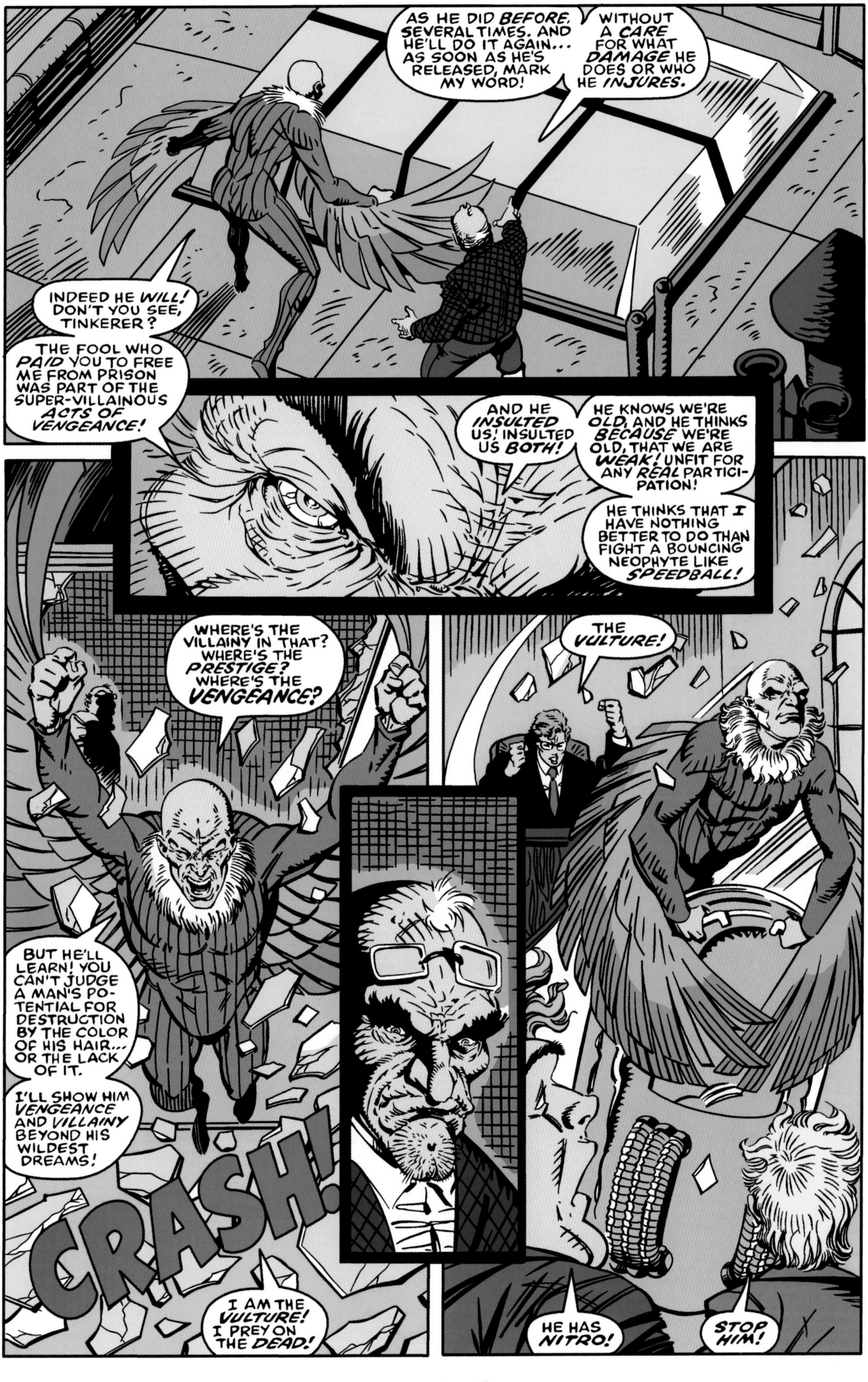
AS HE DID BEFORE, SEVERAL TIMES. AND HE'LL DO IT AGAIN... AS SOON AS HE'S RELEASED, MARK MY WORD!
WITHOUT A CARE FOR WHAT DAMAGE HE DOES OR WHO HE INJURES.
INDEED HE WILL! DON'T YOU SEE, TINKERER?
THE FOOL WHO PAID YOU TO FREE ME FROM PRISON WAS PART OF THE SUPER-VILLAINOUS ACTS OF VENGEANCE!
AND HE INSULTED US, INSULTED US BOTH!
HE KNOWS WE'RE OLD, AND HE THINKS BECAUSE WE'RE OLD, THAT WE ARE WEAK! UNFIT FOR ANY REAL PARTICI-PATION!
HE THINKS THAT I HAVE NOTHING BETTER TO DO THAN FIGHT A BOUNCING NEOPHYTE LIKE SPEEDBALL!
WHERE'S THE VILLAINY IN THAT? WHERE'S THE PRESTIGE? WHERE'S THE VENGEANCE?
BUT HE'LL LEARN! YOU CAN'T JUDGE A MAN'S PO-TENTIAL FOR DESTRUCTION BY THE COLOR OF HIS HAIR... OR THE LACK OF IT.
I'LL SHOW HIM VENGEANCE AND VILLAINY BEYOND HIS WILDEST DREAMS!
CRASH!
I AM THE VULTURE! I PREY ON THE DEAD!
THE VULTURE!
HE HAS NITRO!
STOP HIM!

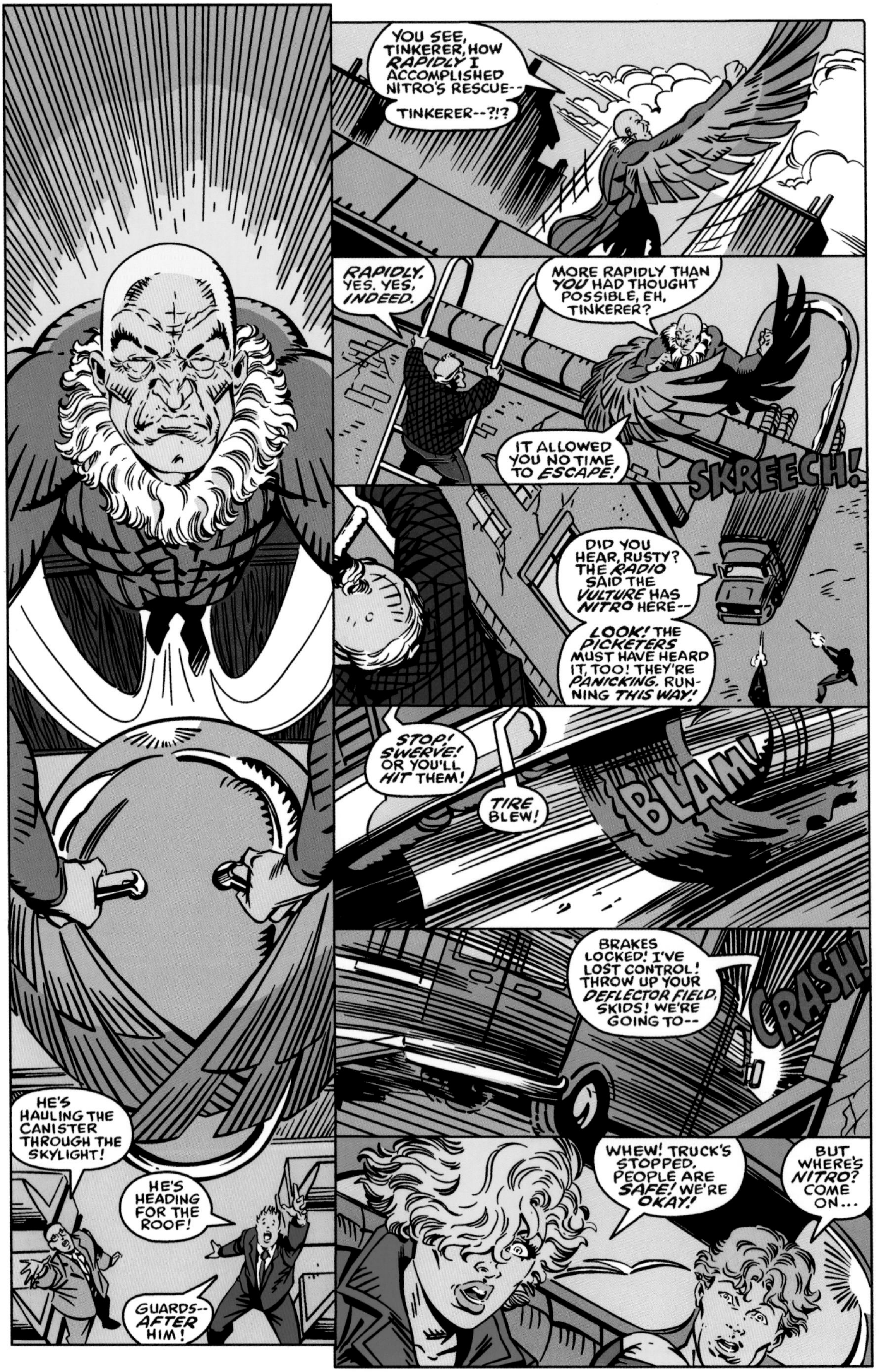
HE'S HAULING THE CANISTER THROUGH THE SKYLIGHT!
HE'S HEADING FOR THE ROOF!
GUARDS--AFTER HIM!
YOU SEE, TINKERER, HOW RAPIDLY I ACCOMPLISHED NITRO'S RESCUE--
TINKERER--?!?
RAPIDLY. YES. YES, INDEED.
MORE RAPIDLY THAN YOU HAD THOUGHT POSSIBLE, EH, TINKERER?
IT ALLOWED YOU NO TIME TO ESCAPE!
SKREECH!
DID YOU HEAR, RUSTY? THE RADIO SAID THE VULTURE HAS NITRO HERE--
LOOK! THE PICKETERS MUST HAVE HEARD IT, TOO! THEY'RE PANICKING. RUNNING THIS WAY!
STOP! SWERVE! OR YOU'LL HIT THEM!
BLAM!
TIRE BLEW!
BRAKES LOCKED! I'VE LOST CONTROL! THROW UP YOUR DEFLECTOR FIELD, SKIDS! WE'RE GOING TO--
CRASH!
WHEW! TRUCK'S STOPPED. PEOPLE ARE SAFE! WE'RE OKAY!
BUT WHERE'S NITRO? COME ON...

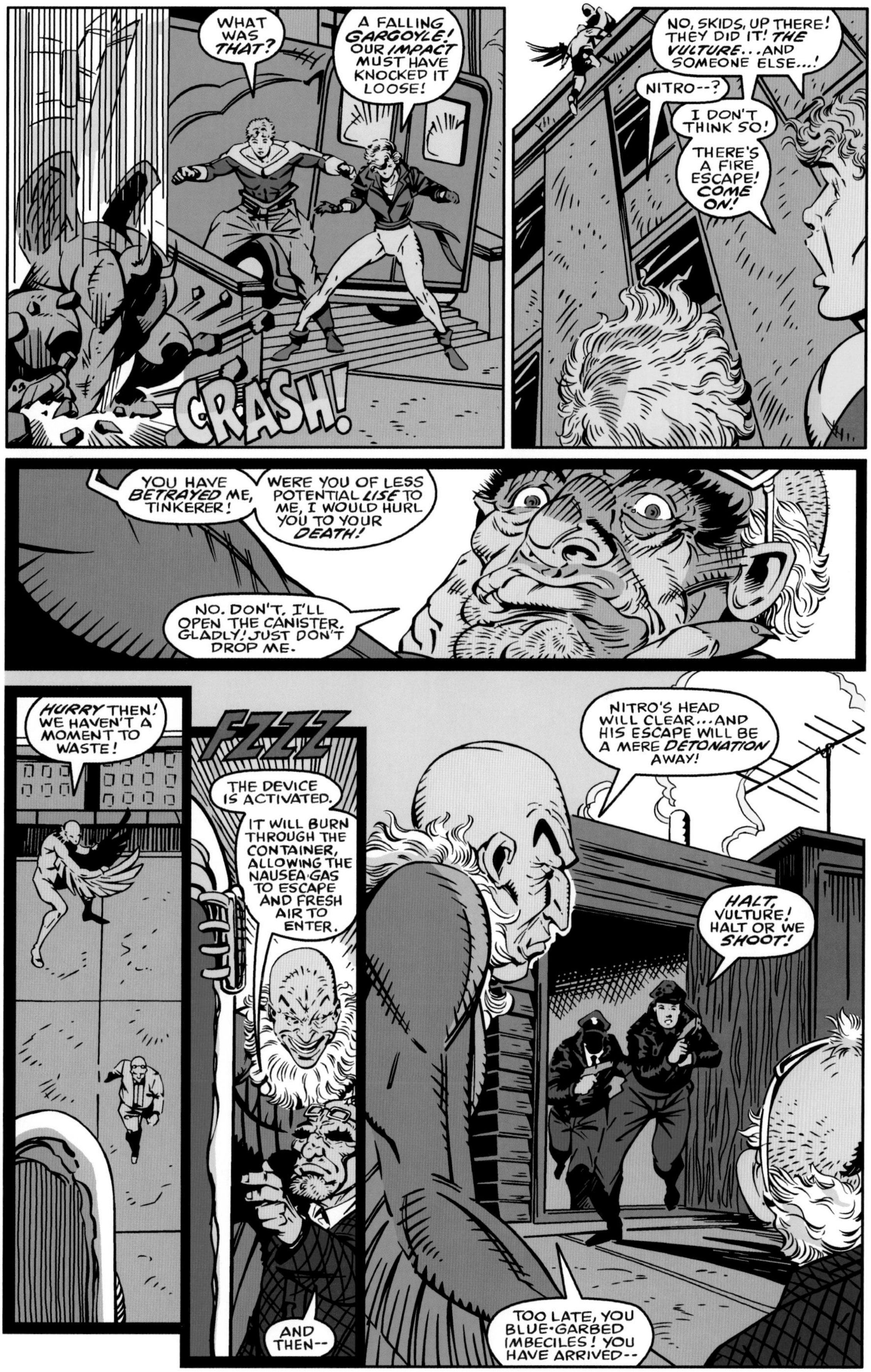

WHAT WAS THAT?
A FALLING GARGOYLE! OUR IMPACT MUST HAVE KNOCKED IT LOOSE!
CRASH!
NO, SKIDS, UP THERE! THEY DID IT! THE VULTURE...AND SOMEONE ELSE...!
NITRO--?
I DON'T THINK SO!
THERE'S A FIRE ESCAPE! COME ON!
YOU HAVE BETRAYED ME, TINKERER!
WERE YOU OF LESS POTENTIAL LISE TO ME, I WOULD HURL YOU TO YOUR DEATH!
NO. DON'T. I'LL OPEN THE CANISTER. GLADLY! JUST DON'T DROP ME.
HURRY THEN! WE HAVEN'T A MOMENT TO WASTE!
FZZZ
THE DEVICE IS ACTIVATED.
IT WILL BURN THROUGH THE CONTAINER, ALLOWING THE NAUSEA GAS TO ESCAPE AND FRESH AIR TO ENTER.
AND THEN--
NITRO'S HEAD WILL CLEAR...AND HIS ESCAPE WILL BE A MERE DETONATION AWAY!
HALT, VULTURE! HALT OR WE SHOOT!
TOO LATE, YOU BLUE-GARBED IMBECILES! YOU HAVE ARRIVED--

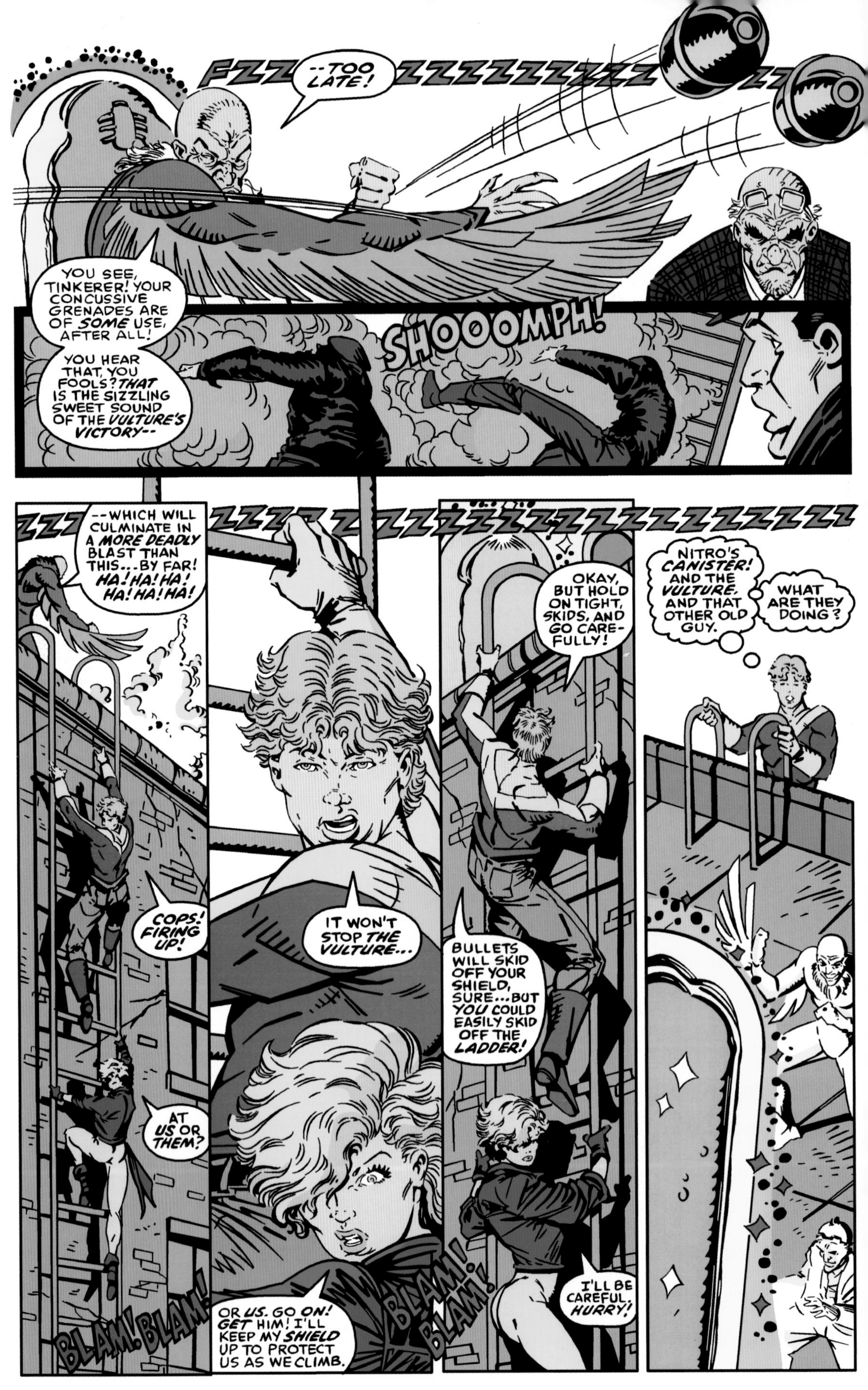
FZZ
--TOO LATE!
ZZZZZZZZZZZZ
YOU SEE, TINKERER! YOUR CONCUSSIVE GRENADES ARE OF SOME USE, AFTER ALL!
SHOOOOMPH!
YOU HEAR THAT, YOU FOOLS? THAT IS THE SIZZLING SWEET SOUND OF THE VULTURE'S VICTORY--
--WHICH WILL CULMINATE IN A MORE DEADLY BLAST THAN THIS... BY FAR! HA! HA! HA! HA! HA! HA!
COPS! FIRING UP!
AT US OR THEM?
BLAM! BLAM!
IT WON'T STOP THE VULTURE...
OR US. GO ON! GET HIM! I'LL KEEP MY SHIELD UP TO PROTECT US AS WE CLIMB.
BLAM! BLAM!
OKAY, BUT HOLD ON TIGHT, SKIDS, AND GO CAREFULLY!
BULLETS WILL SKID OFF YOUR SHIELD, SURE... BUT YOU COULD EASILY SKID OFF THE LADDER!
I'LL BE CAREFUL. HURRY!
NITRO'S CANISTER! AND THE VULTURE. AND THAT OTHER OLD GUY.
WHAT ARE THEY DOING?

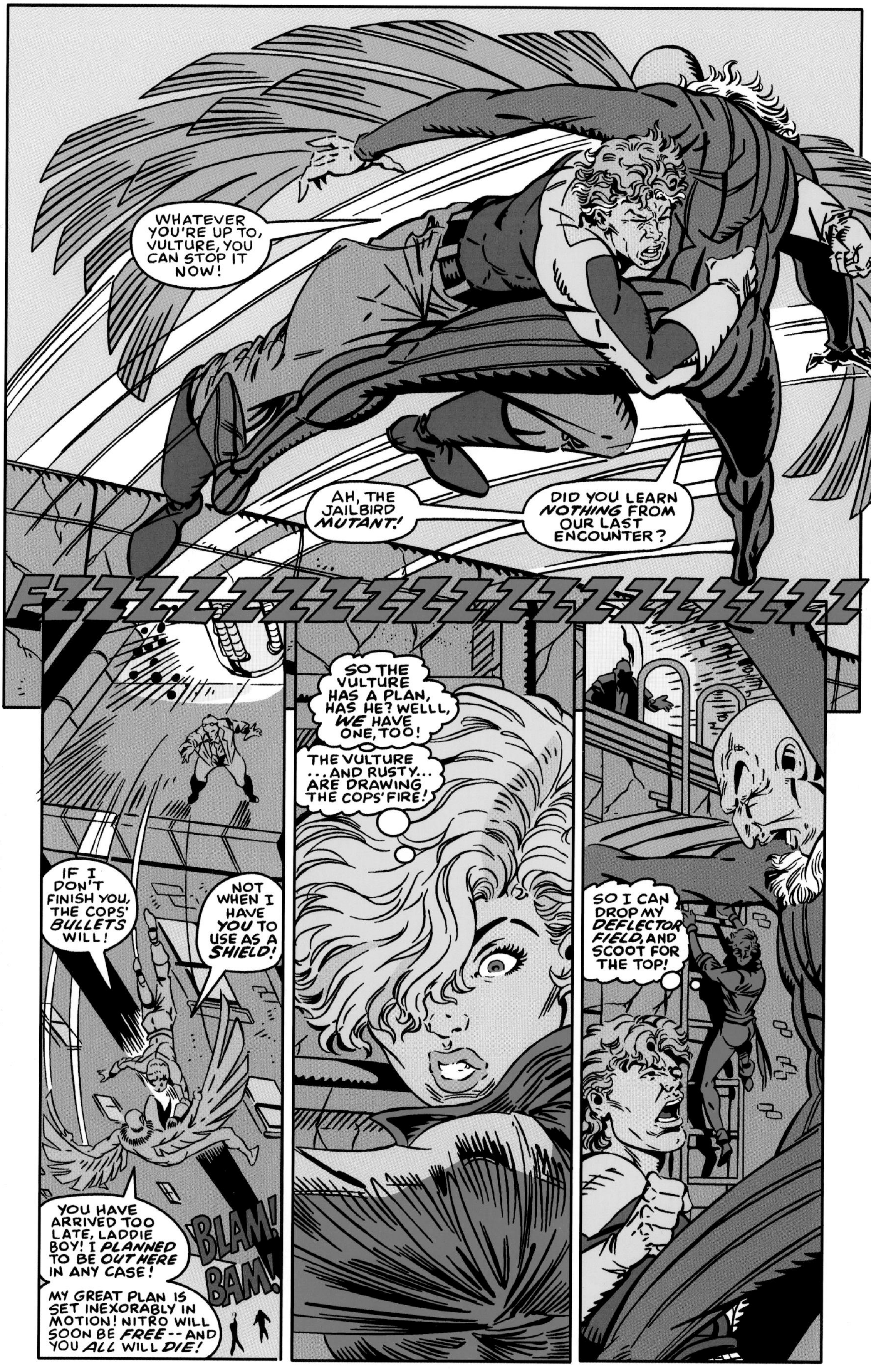
WHATEVER YOU'RE UP TO, VULTURE, YOU CAN STOP IT NOW!
AH, THE JAILBIRD MUTANT!
DID YOU LEARN NOTHING FROM OUR LAST ENCOUNTER?
FZZZZZZZZZZZZZZZZZZZZ
IF I DON'T FINISH YOU, THE COPS' BULLETS WILL!
NOT WHEN I HAVE YOU TO USE AS A SHIELD!
YOU HAVE ARRIVED TOO LATE, LADDIE BOY! I PLANNED TO BE OUT HERE IN ANY CASE!
MY GREAT PLAN IS SET INEXORABLY IN MOTION! NITRO WILL SOON BE FREE-- AND YOU ALL WILL DIE!
BLAM!
BAM!
SO THE VULTURE HAS A PLAN, HAS HE? WELLL, WE HAVE ONE, TOO!
THE VULTURE ...AND RUSTY... ARE DRAWING THE COPS' FIRE!
SO I CAN DROP MY DEFLECTOR FIELD, AND SCOOT FOR THE TOP!

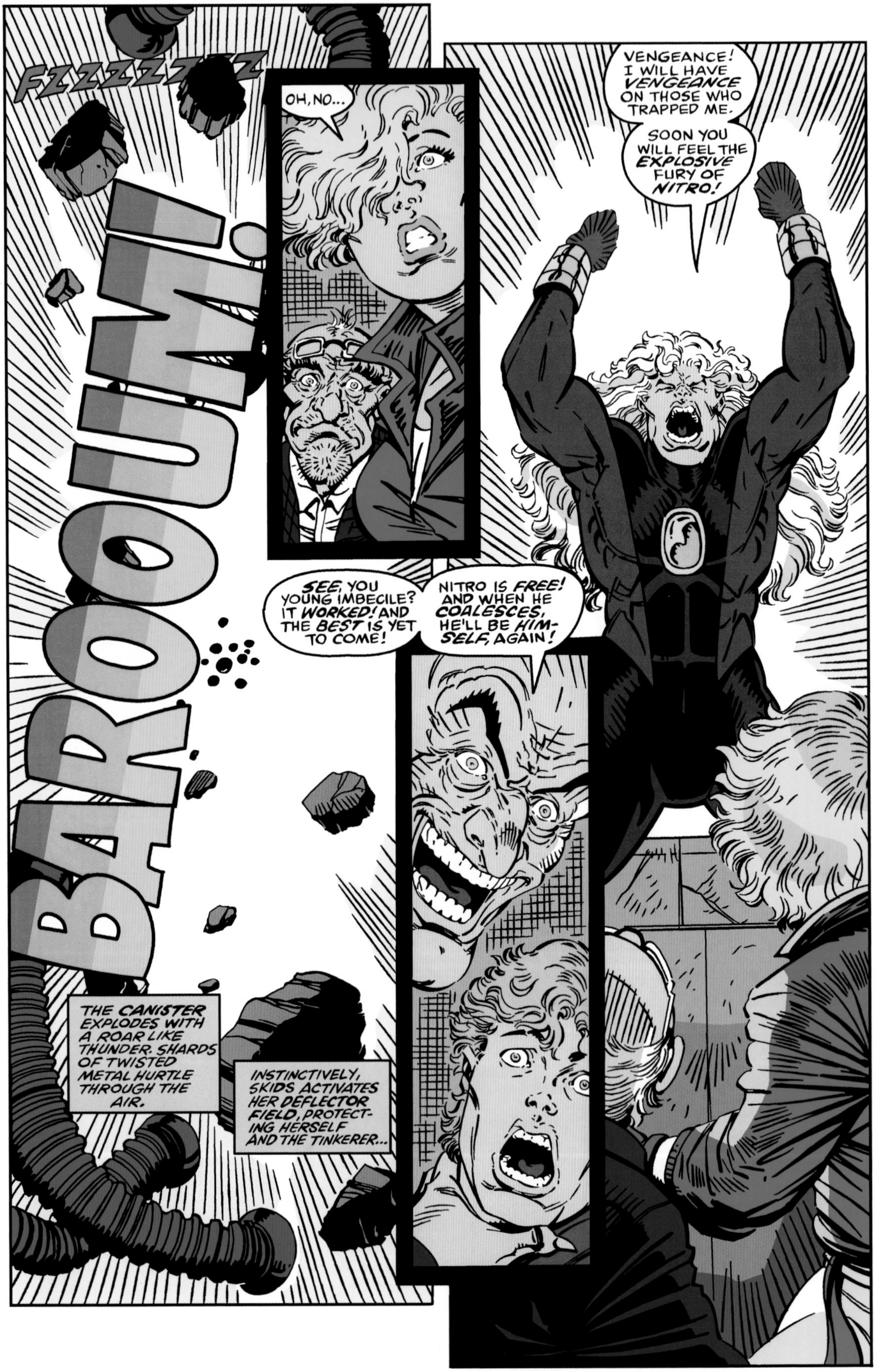
FZZZZZZZZ
OH, NO...
BAROOM!
VENGEANCE! I WILL HAVE VENGEANCE ON THOSE WHO TRAPPED ME.
SOON YOU WILL FEEL THE EXPLOSIVE FURY OF NITRO!
SEE, YOU YOUNG IMBECILE? IT WORKED! AND THE BEST IS YET TO COME!
NITRO IS FREE! AND WHEN HE COALESCES, HE'LL BE HIMSELF, AGAIN!
THE CANISTER EXPLODES WITH A ROAR LIKE THUNDER. SHARDS OF TWISTED METAL HURTLE THROUGH THE AIR.
INSTINCTIVELY, SKIDS ACTIVATES HER DEFLECTOR FIELD, PROTECTING HERSELF AND THE TINKERER...

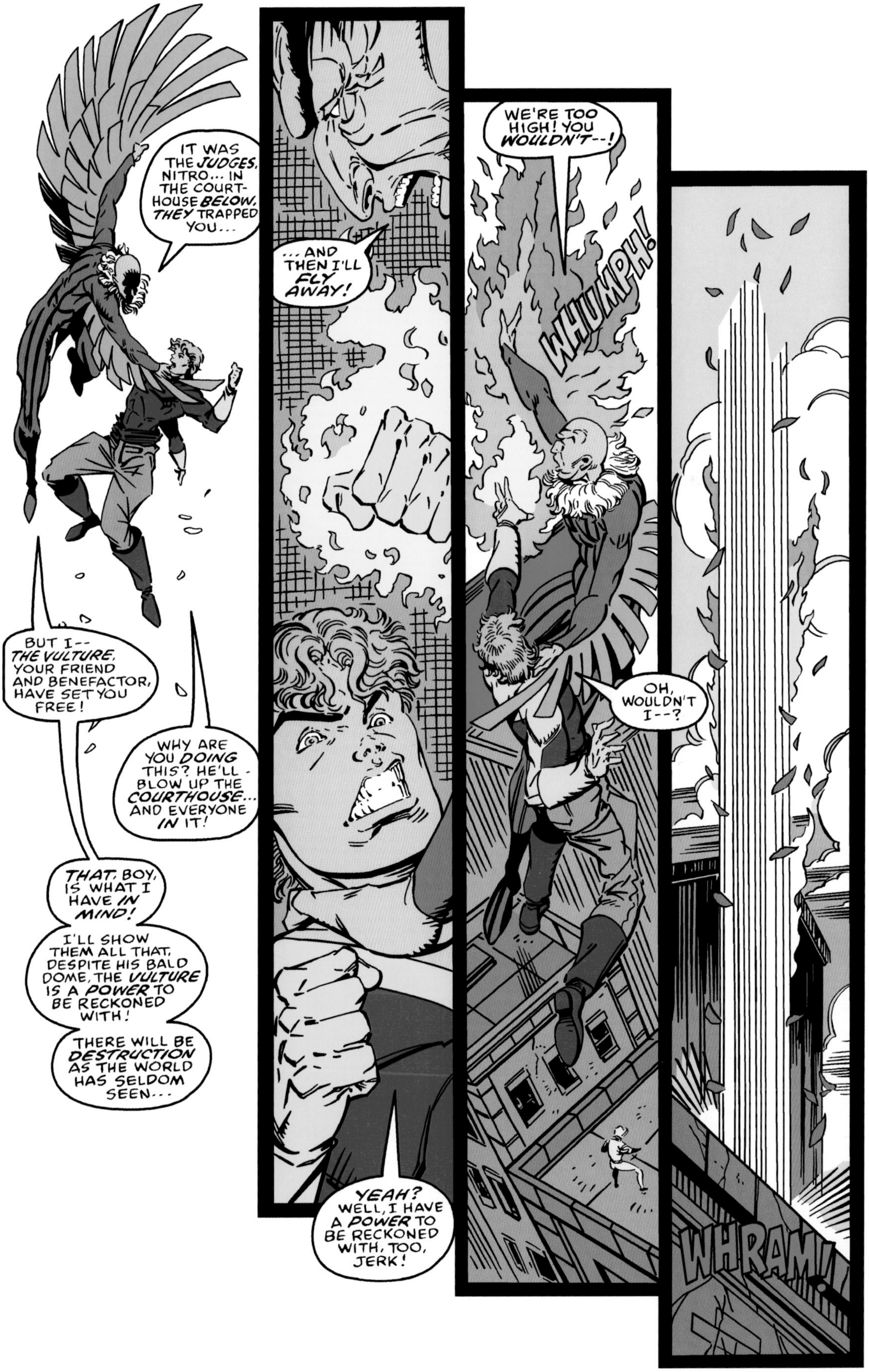

IT WAS THE JUDGES, NITRO... IN THE COURTHOUSE BELOW. THEY TRAPPED YOU...
BUT I-- THE VULTURE, YOUR FRIEND AND BENEFACTOR, HAVE SET YOU FREE!
WHY ARE YOU DOING THIS? HE'LL BLOW UP THE COURTHOUSE... AND EVERYONE IN IT!
THAT, BOY, IS WHAT I HAVE IN MIND!
I'LL SHOW THEM ALL THAT, DESPITE HIS BALD DOME, THE VULTURE IS A POWER TO BE RECKONED WITH!
THERE WILL BE DESTRUCTION AS THE WORLD HAS SELDOM SEEN...
...AND THEN I'LL FLY AWAY!
YEAH? WELL, I HAVE A POWER TO BE RECKONED WITH, TOO, JERK!
WE'RE TOO HIGH! YOU WOULDN'T--!
WHUMPH!
OH, WOULDN'T I--?
WHRAM!!

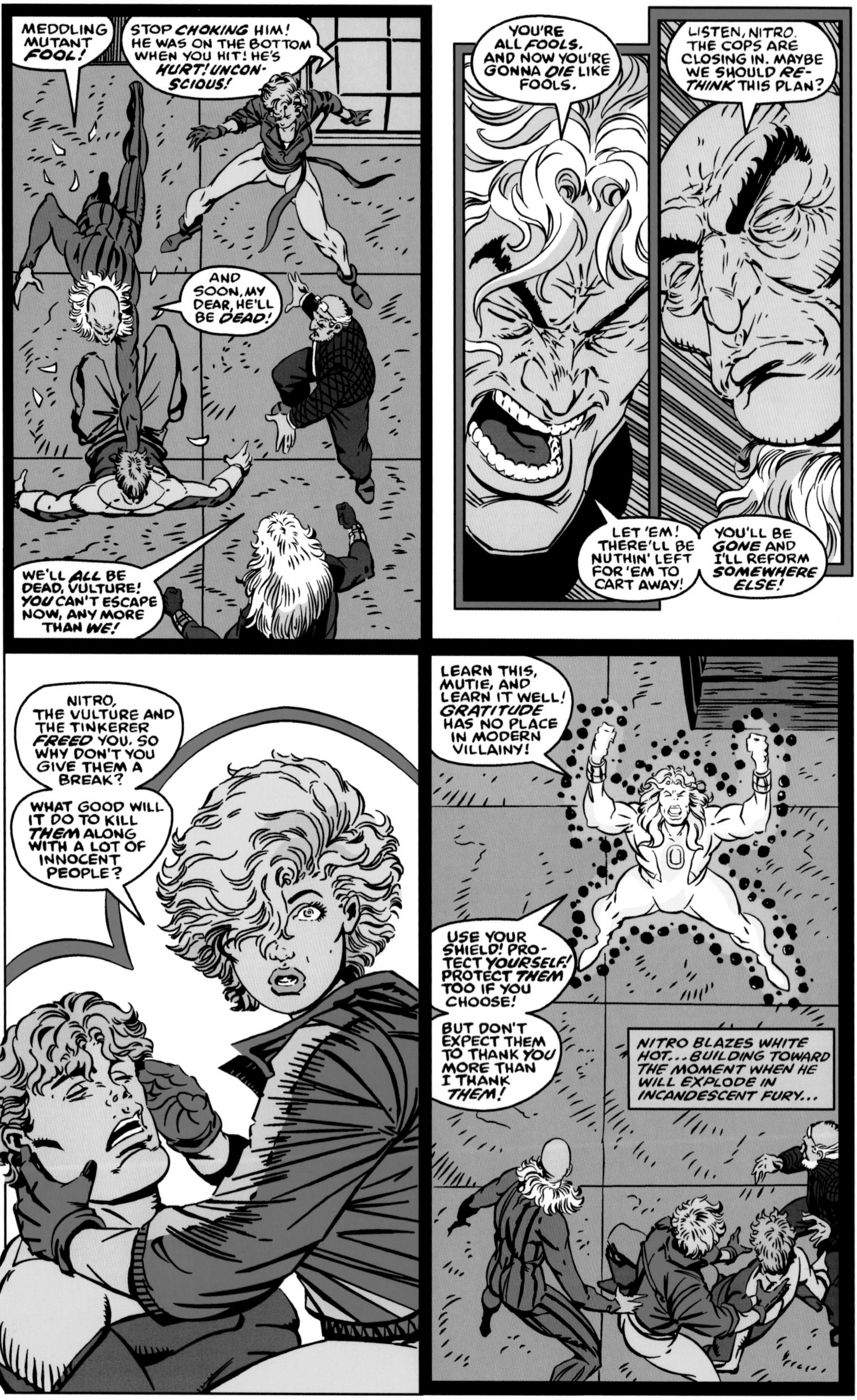
MEDDLING MUTANT FOOL!
STOP CHOKING HIM! HE WAS ON THE BOTTOM WHEN YOU HIT! HE'S HURT! UNCONSCIOUS!
AND SOON, MY DEAR, HE'LL BE DEAD!
WE'LL ALL BE DEAD, VULTURE! YOU CAN'T ESCAPE NOW, ANY MORE THAN WE!
YOU'RE ALL FOOLS. AND NOW YOU'RE GONNA DIE LIKE FOOLS.
LISTEN, NITRO. THE COPS ARE CLOSING IN. MAYBE WE SHOULD RETHINK THIS PLAN?
LET 'EM! THERE'LL BE NUTHIN' LEFT FOR 'EM TO CART AWAY!
YOU'LL BE GONE AND I'LL REFORM SOMEWHERE ELSE!
NITRO, THE VULTURE AND THE TINKERER FREED YOU, SO WHY DON'T YOU GIVE THEM A BREAK?
WHAT GOOD WILL IT DO TO KILL THEM ALONG WITH A LOT OF INNOCENT PEOPLE?
LEARN THIS, MUTIE, AND LEARN IT WELL! GRATITUDE HAS NO PLACE IN MODERN VILLAINY!
USE YOUR SHIELD! PROTECT YOURSELF! PROTECT THEM TOO IF YOU CHOOSE!
BUT DON'T EXPECT THEM TO THANK YOU MORE THAN I THANK THEM!
NITRO BLAZES WHITE HOT... BUILDING TOWARD THE MOMENT WHEN HE WILL EXPLODE IN INCANDESCENT FURY...

NO! DON'T!

SKIDS LEAPS TOWARD HIM, HER DEFLECTION FIELD FULLY EXTENDED.

THROWING HERSELF ONTO NITRO, EVEN AS HE BEGINS TO DISCORPORATE...

...DESPERATELY WRAPPING HER FIELD AROUND HIM, SKIDS COVERS THE MADMAN, HOPING AGAINST HOPE TO PREVENT DISASTER.

SHE BECOMES, IN EFFECT, A HUMAN CONTAINMENT VESSEL. BUT NITRO'S FURY CANNOT BE CONTAINED...

BOOM!

HE STILL DETONATES WITH ENOUGH FORCE TO DESTROY A CITY BLOCK.

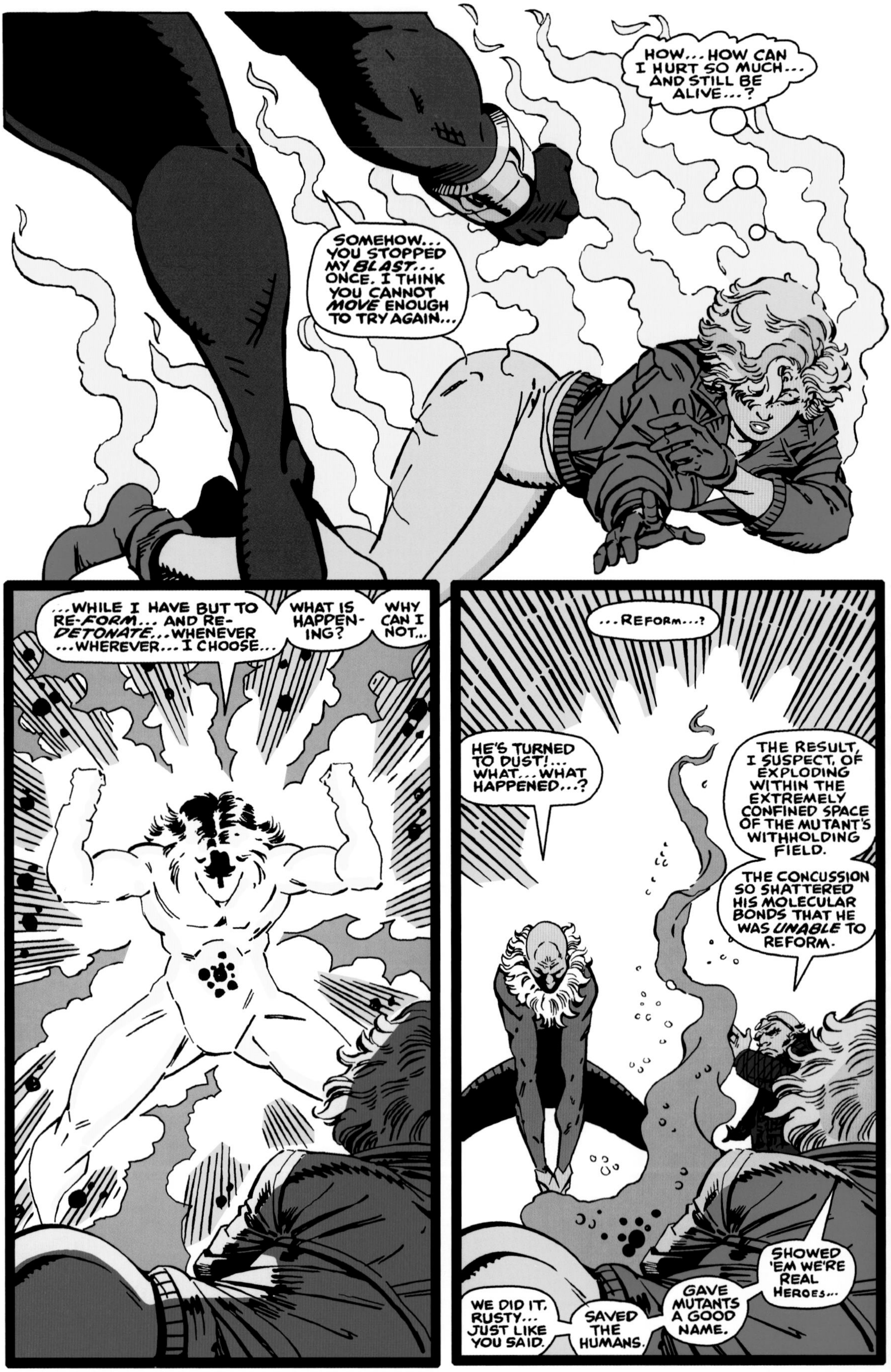
HOW... HOW CAN I HURT SO MUCH... AND STILL BE ALIVE...?
SOMEHOW... YOU STOPPED MY BLAST... ONCE. I THINK YOU CANNOT MOVE ENOUGH TO TRY AGAIN...
...WHILE I HAVE BUT TO RE-FORM... AND RE-DETONATE... WHENEVER ...WHEREVER... I CHOOSE...
WHAT IS HAPPEN-ING?
WHY CAN I NOT...
...REFORM...?
HE'S TURNED TO DUST!... WHAT... WHAT HAPPENED...?
THE RESULT, I SUSPECT, OF EXPLODING WITHIN THE EXTREMELY CONFINED SPACE OF THE MUTANT'S WITHHOLDING FIELD.
THE CONCUSSION SO SHATTERED HIS MOLECULAR BONDS THAT HE WAS UNABLE TO REFORM.
WE DID IT, RUSTY... JUST LIKE YOU SAID.
SAVED THE HUMANS.
GAVE MUTANTS A GOOD NAME.
SHOWED 'EM WE'RE REAL HEROES...

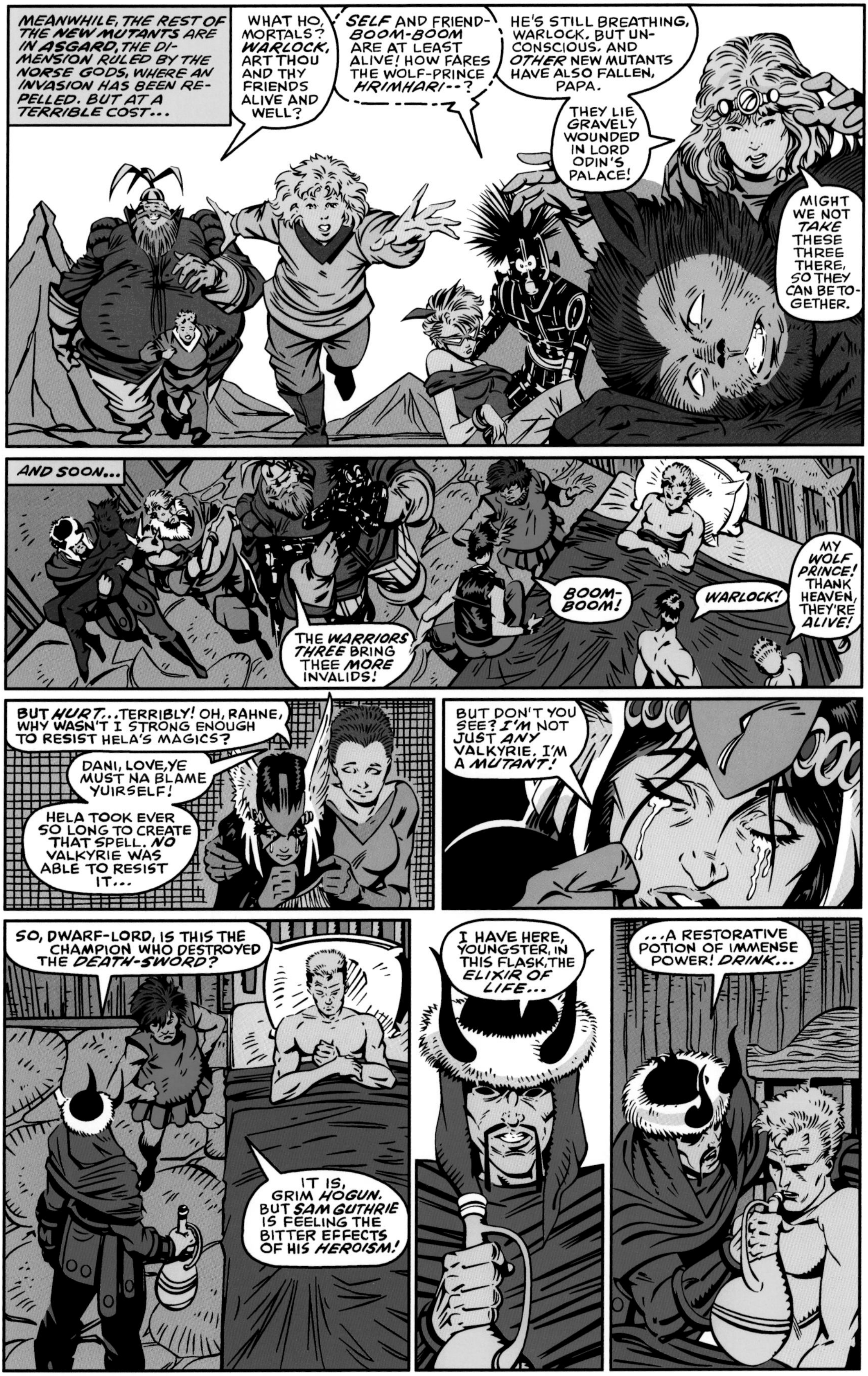
MEANWHILE, THE REST OF THE NEW MUTANTS ARE IN ASGARD, THE DIMENSION RULED BY THE NORSE GODS, WHERE AN INVASION HAS BEEN REPELLED. BUT AT A TERRIBLE COST...
WHAT HO, MORTALS? WARLOCK, ART THOU AND THY FRIENDS ALIVE AND WELL?
SELF AND FRIEND-BOOM-BOOM ARE AT LEAST ALIVE! HOW FARES THE WOLF-PRINCE HRIMHARI--?
HE'S STILL BREATHING, WARLOCK, BUT UNCONSCIOUS. AND OTHER NEW MUTANTS HAVE ALSO FALLEN, PAPA.
THEY LIE GRAVELY WOUNDED IN LORD ODIN'S PALACE!
MIGHT WE NOT TAKE THESE THREE THERE, SO THEY CAN BE TOGETHER.
AND SOON...
THE WARRIORS THREE BRING THEE MORE INVALIDS!
BOOM-BOOM!
WARLOCK!
MY WOLF PRINCE! THANK HEAVEN, THEY'RE ALIVE!
BUT HURT... TERRIBLY! OH, RAHNE, WHY WASN'T I STRONG ENOUGH TO RESIST HELA'S MAGICS?
DANI, LOVE, YE MUST NA BLAME YUIRSELF!
HELA TOOK EVER SO LONG TO CREATE THAT SPELL. NO VALKYRIE WAS ABLE TO RESIST IT...
BUT DON'T YOU SEE? I'M NOT JUST ANY VALKYRIE, I'M A MUTANT!
SO, DWARF-LORD, IS THIS THE CHAMPION WHO DESTROYED THE DEATH-SWORD?
IT IS, GRIM HOGUN. BUT SAM GUTHRIE IS FEELING THE BITTER EFFECTS OF HIS HEROISM!
I HAVE HERE, YOUNGSTER, IN THIS FLASK, THE ELIXIR OF LIFE...
...A RESTORATIVE POTION OF IMMENSE POWER! DRINK...

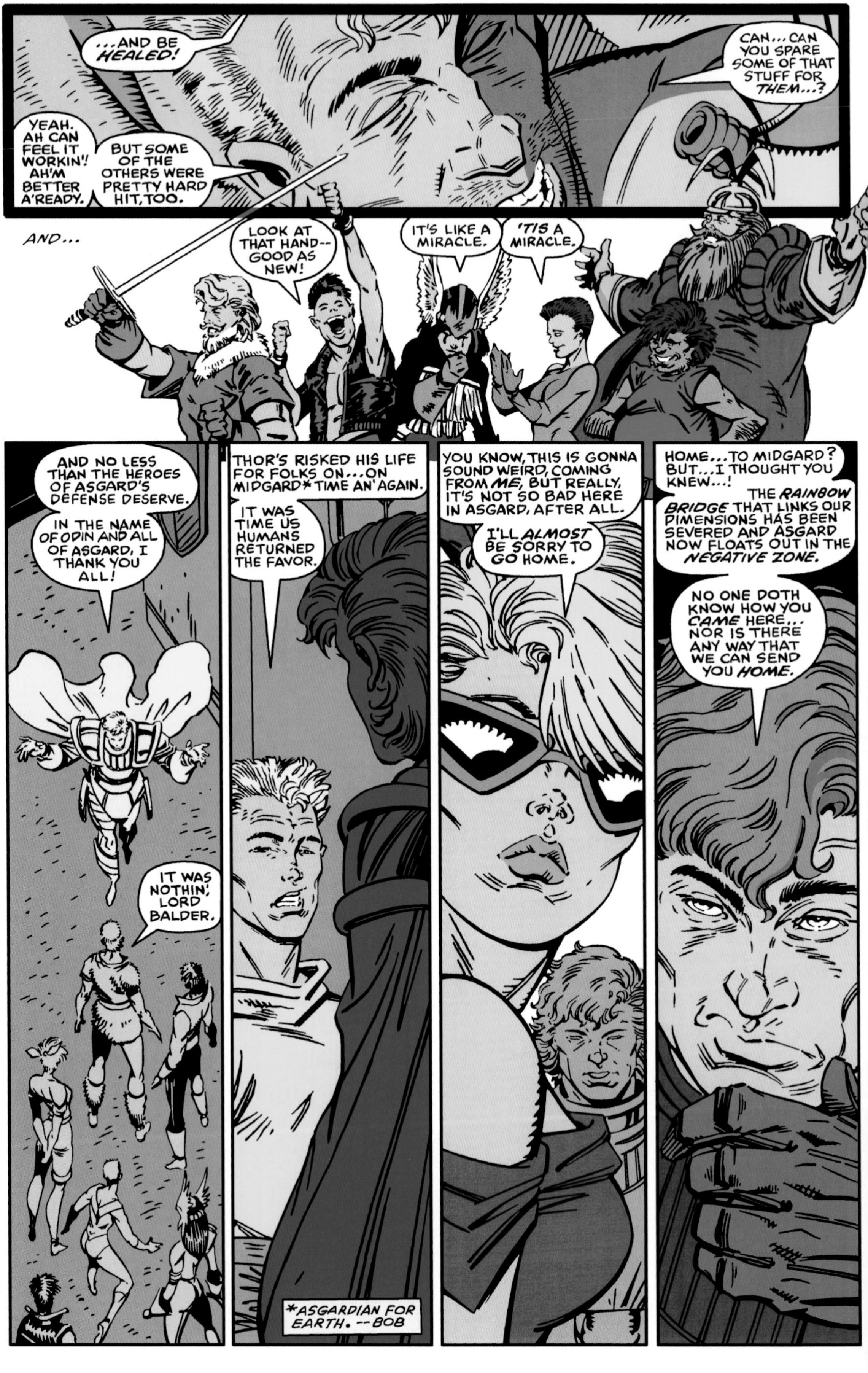
...AND BE HEALED!
CAN... CAN YOU SPARE SOME OF THAT STUFF FOR THEM...?
YEAH. AH CAN FEEL IT WORKIN'! AH'M BETTER A'READY.
BUT SOME OF THE OTHERS WERE PRETTY HARD HIT, TOO.
AND...
LOOK AT THAT HAND-- GOOD AS NEW!
IT'S LIKE A MIRACLE.
'TIS A MIRACLE.
AND NO LESS THAN THE HEROES OF ASGARD'S DEFENSE DESERVE.
IN THE NAME OF ODIN AND ALL OF ASGARD, I THANK YOU ALL!
IT WAS NOTHIN', LORD BALDER.
THOR'S RISKED HIS LIFE FOR FOLKS ON...ON MIDGARD* TIME AN' AGAIN.
IT WAS TIME US HUMANS RETURNED THE FAVOR.
*ASGARDIAN FOR EARTH. --BOB
YOU KNOW, THIS IS GONNA SOUND WEIRD, COMING FROM ME, BUT REALLY, IT'S NOT SO BAD HERE IN ASGARD, AFTER ALL.
I'LL ALMOST BE SORRY TO GO HOME.
HOME...TO MIDGARD? BUT...I THOUGHT YOU KNEW...!
THE RAINBOW BRIDGE THAT LINKS OUR DIMENSIONS HAS BEEN SEVERED AND ASGARD NOW FLOATS OUT IN THE NEGATIVE ZONE.
NO ONE DOTH KNOW HOW YOU CAME HERE... NOR IS THERE ANY WAY THAT WE CAN SEND YOU HOME.

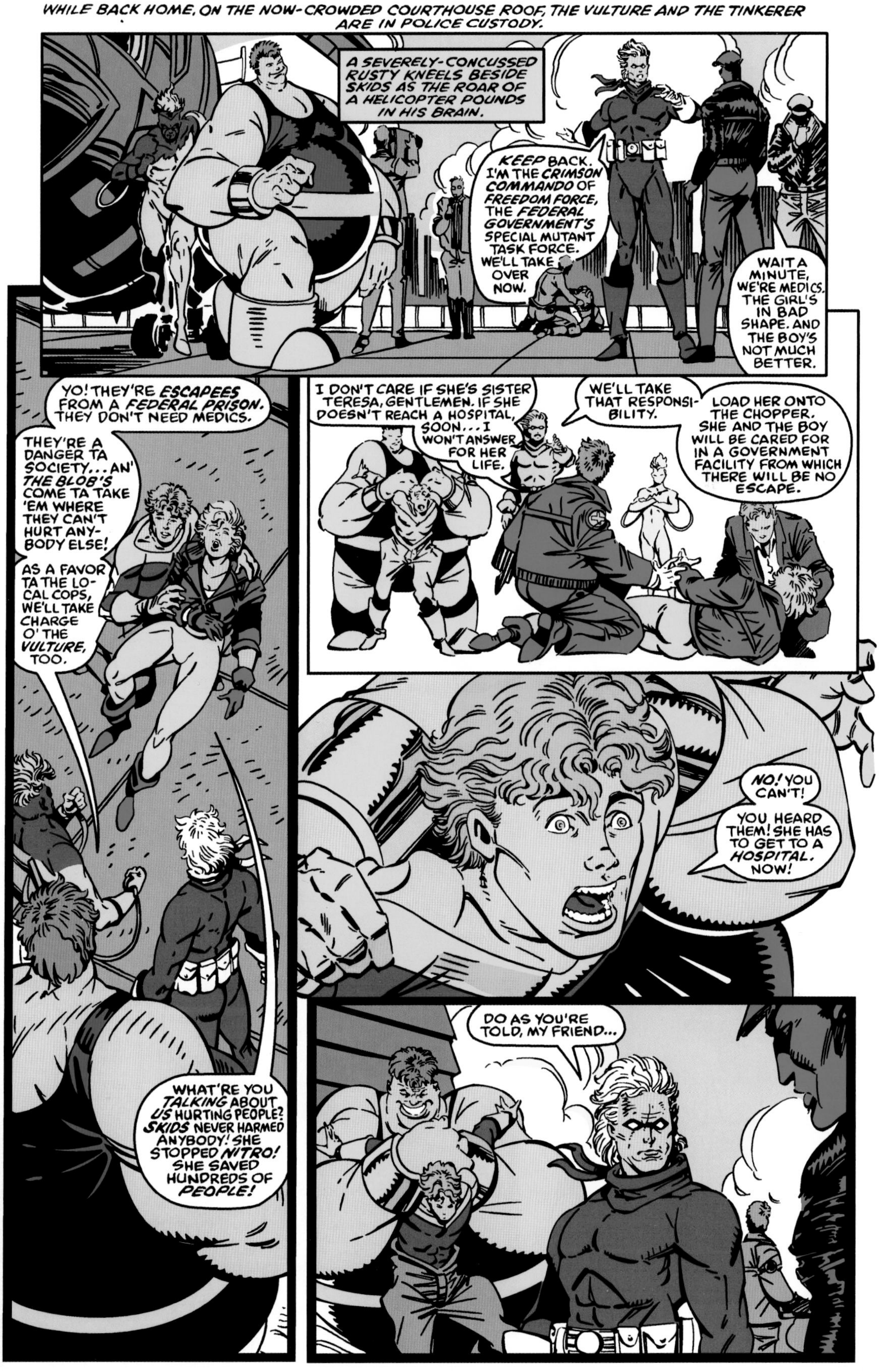
WHILE BACK HOME, ON THE NOW-CROWDED COURTHOUSE ROOF, THE VULTURE AND THE TINKERER ARE IN POLICE CUSTODY.
A SEVERELY-CONCUSSED RUSTY KNEELS BESIDE SKIDS AS THE ROAR OF A HELICOPTER POUNDS IN HIS BRAIN.
KEEP BACK. I'M THE CRIMSON COMMANDO OF FREEDOM FORCE, THE FEDERAL GOVERNMENT'S SPECIAL MUTANT TASK FORCE. WE'LL TAKE OVER NOW.
WAIT A MINUTE, WE'RE MEDICS. THE GIRL'S IN BAD SHAPE. AND THE BOY'S NOT MUCH BETTER.
YO! THEY'RE ESCAPEES FROM A FEDERAL PRISON. THEY DON'T NEED MEDICS.
THEY'RE A DANGER TA SOCIETY... AN' THE BLOB'S COME TA TAKE 'EM WHERE THEY CAN'T HURT ANYBODY ELSE!
AS A FAVOR TA THE LOCAL COPS, WE'LL TAKE CHARGE O' THE VULTURE, TOO.
WHAT'RE YOU TALKING ABOUT, US HURTING PEOPLE? SKIDS NEVER HARMED ANYBODY! SHE STOPPED NITRO! SHE SAVED HUNDREDS OF PEOPLE!
I DON'T CARE IF SHE'S SISTER TERESA, GENTLEMEN. IF SHE DOESN'T REACH A HOSPITAL, SOON... I WON'T ANSWER FOR HER LIFE.
WE'LL TAKE THAT RESPONSIBILITY.
LOAD HER ONTO THE CHOPPER. SHE AND THE BOY WILL BE CARED FOR IN A GOVERNMENT FACILITY FROM WHICH THERE WILL BE NO ESCAPE.
NO! YOU CAN'T!
YOU HEARD THEM! SHE HAS TO GET TO A HOSPITAL. NOW!
DO AS YOU'RE TOLD, MY FRIEND...

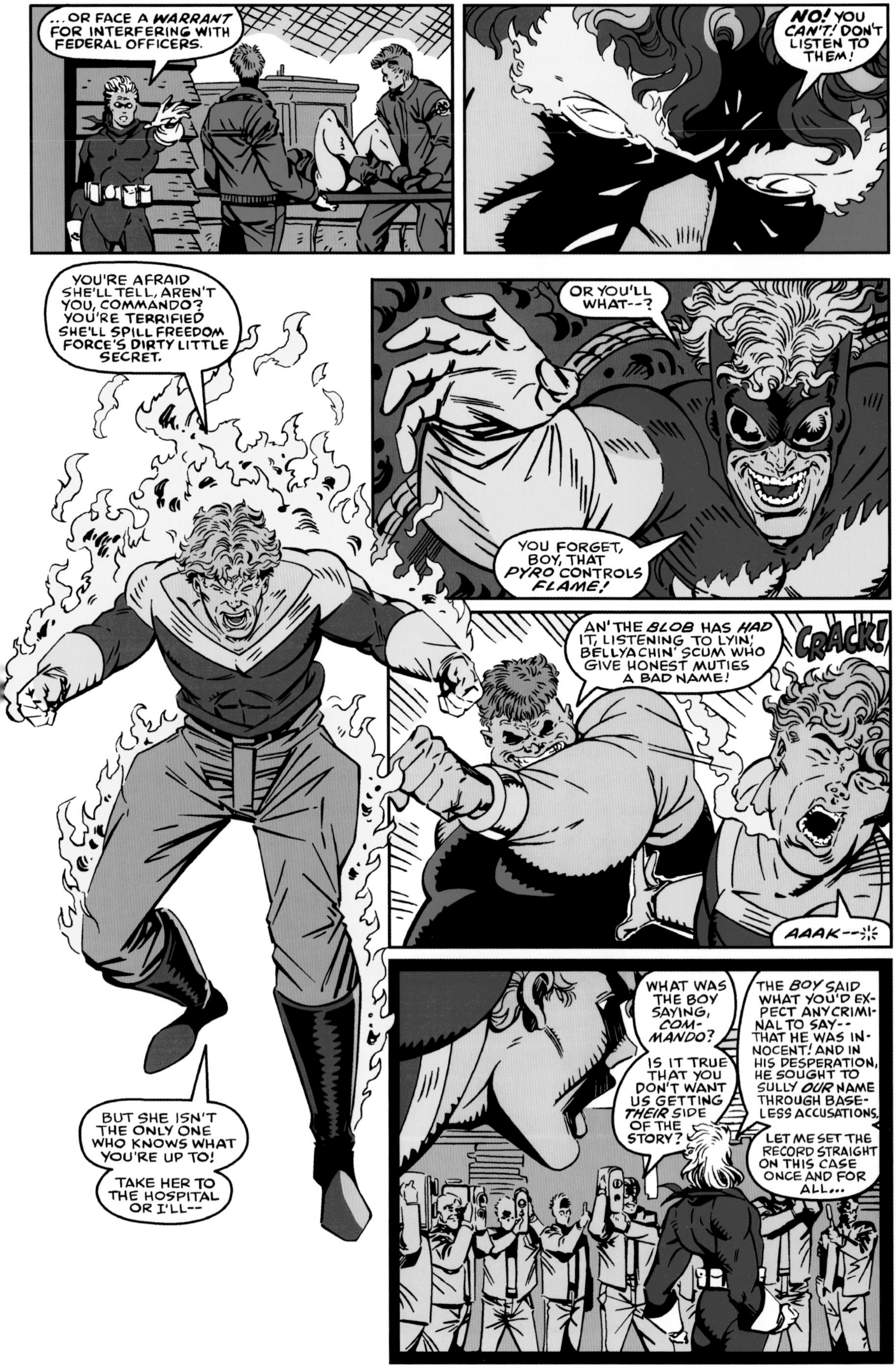
...OR FACE A WARRANT FOR INTERFERING WITH FEDERAL OFFICERS.
NO! YOU CAN'T! DON'T LISTEN TO THEM!
YOU'RE AFRAID SHE'LL TELL, AREN'T YOU, COMMANDO? YOU'RE TERRIFIED SHE'LL SPILL FREEDOM FORCE'S DIRTY LITTLE SECRET.
BUT SHE ISN'T THE ONLY ONE WHO KNOWS WHAT YOU'RE UP TO!
TAKE HER TO THE HOSPITAL OR I'LL--
OR YOU'LL WHAT--?
YOU FORGET, BOY, THAT PYRO CONTROLS FLAME!
AN' THE BLOB HAS HAD IT, LISTENING TO LYIN', BELLYACHIN' SCUM WHO GIVE HONEST MUTIES A BAD NAME!
CRACK!
AAAK--
WHAT WAS THE BOY SAYING, COMMANDO?
IS IT TRUE THAT YOU DON'T WANT US GETTING THEIR SIDE OF THE STORY?
THE BOY SAID WHAT YOU'D EXPECT ANY CRIMINAL TO SAY--THAT HE WAS INNOCENT! AND IN HIS DESPERATION, HE SOUGHT TO SULLY OUR NAME THROUGH BASELESS ACCUSATIONS.
LET ME SET THE RECORD STRAIGHT ON THIS CASE ONCE AND FOR ALL...

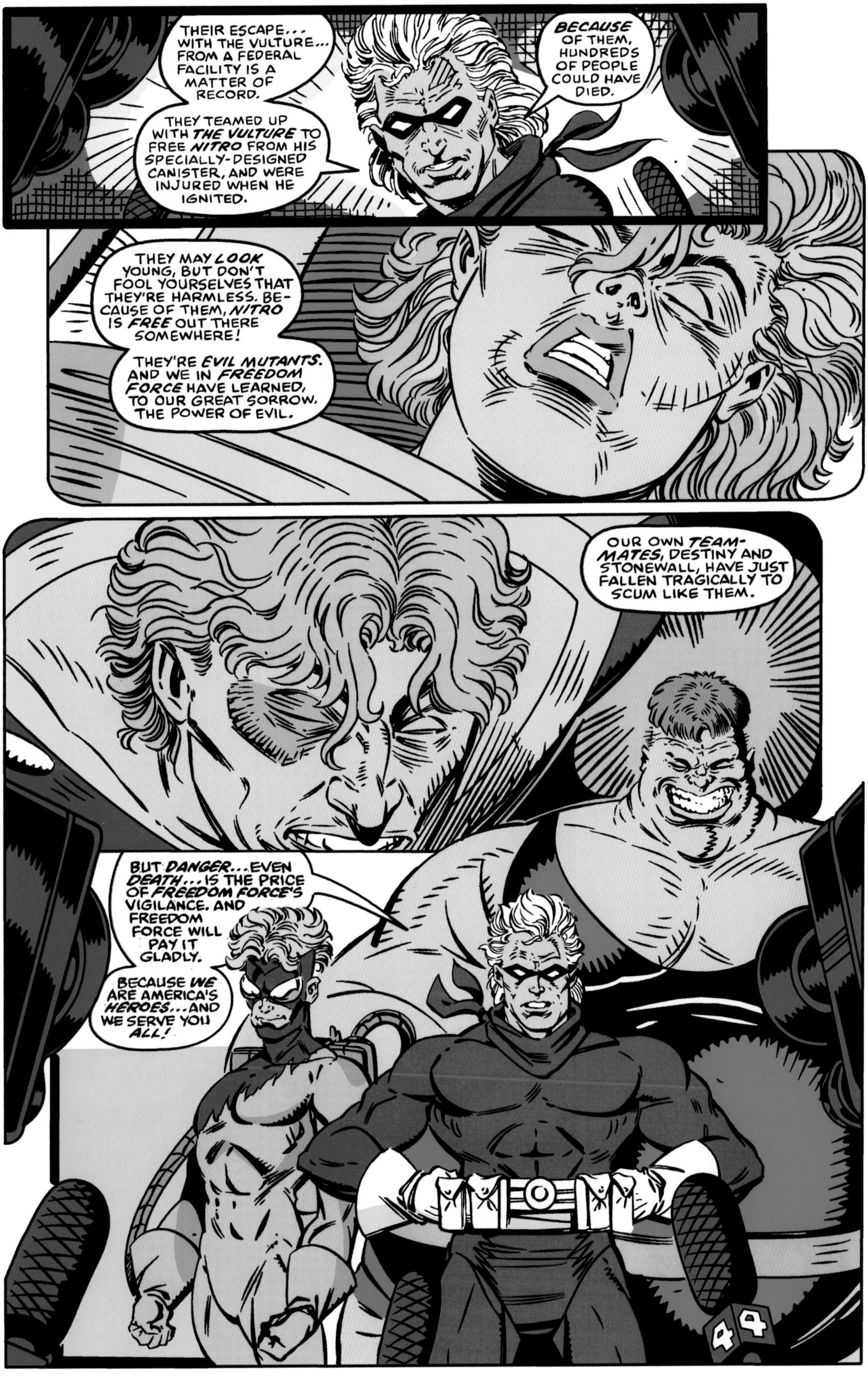
THEIR ESCAPE... WITH THE VULTURE... FROM A FEDERAL FACILITY IS A MATTER OF RECORD.
THEY TEAMED UP WITH THE VULTURE TO FREE NITRO FROM HIS SPECIALLY-DESIGNED CANISTER, AND WERE INJURED WHEN HE IGNITED.
BECAUSE OF THEM, HUNDREDS OF PEOPLE COULD HAVE DIED.
THEY MAY LOOK YOUNG, BUT DON'T FOOL YOURSELVES THAT THEY'RE HARMLESS. BECAUSE OF THEM, NITRO IS FREE OUT THERE SOMEWHERE!
THEY'RE EVIL MUTANTS. AND WE IN FREEDOM FORCE HAVE LEARNED, TO OUR GREAT SORROW, THE POWER OF EVIL.
OUR OWN TEAM-MATES, DESTINY AND STONEWALL, HAVE JUST FALLEN TRAGICALLY TO SCUM LIKE THEM.
BUT DANGER... EVEN DEATH... IS THE PRICE OF FREEDOM FORCE'S VIGILANCE. AND FREEDOM FORCE WILL PAY IT GLADLY.
BECAUSE WE ARE AMERICA'S HEROES... AND WE SERVE YOU ALL!

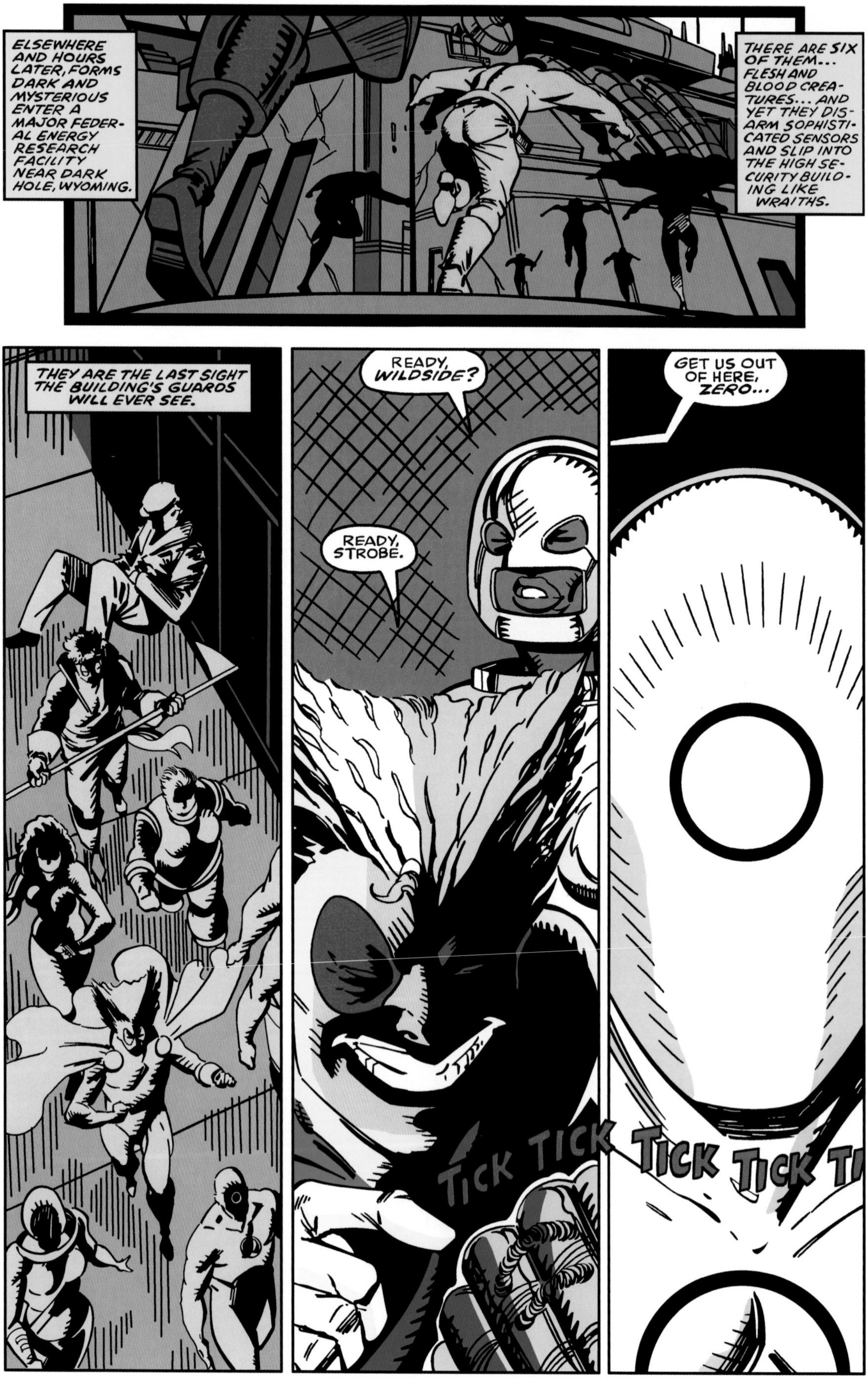
ELSEWHERE AND HOURS LATER, FORMS DARK AND MYSTERIOUS ENTER A MAJOR FEDERAL ENERGY RESEARCH FACILITY NEAR DARK HOLE, WYOMING.
THERE ARE SIX OF THEM... FLESH AND BLOOD CREATURES... AND YET THEY DISARM SOPHISTICATED SENSORS AND SLIP INTO THE HIGH SECURITY BUILDING LIKE WRAITHS.
THEY ARE THE LAST SIGHT THE BUILDING'S GUARDS WILL EVER SEE.
READY, WILDSIDE?
READY, STROBE.
GET US OUT OF HERE, ZERO...
TICK TICK TICK TICK

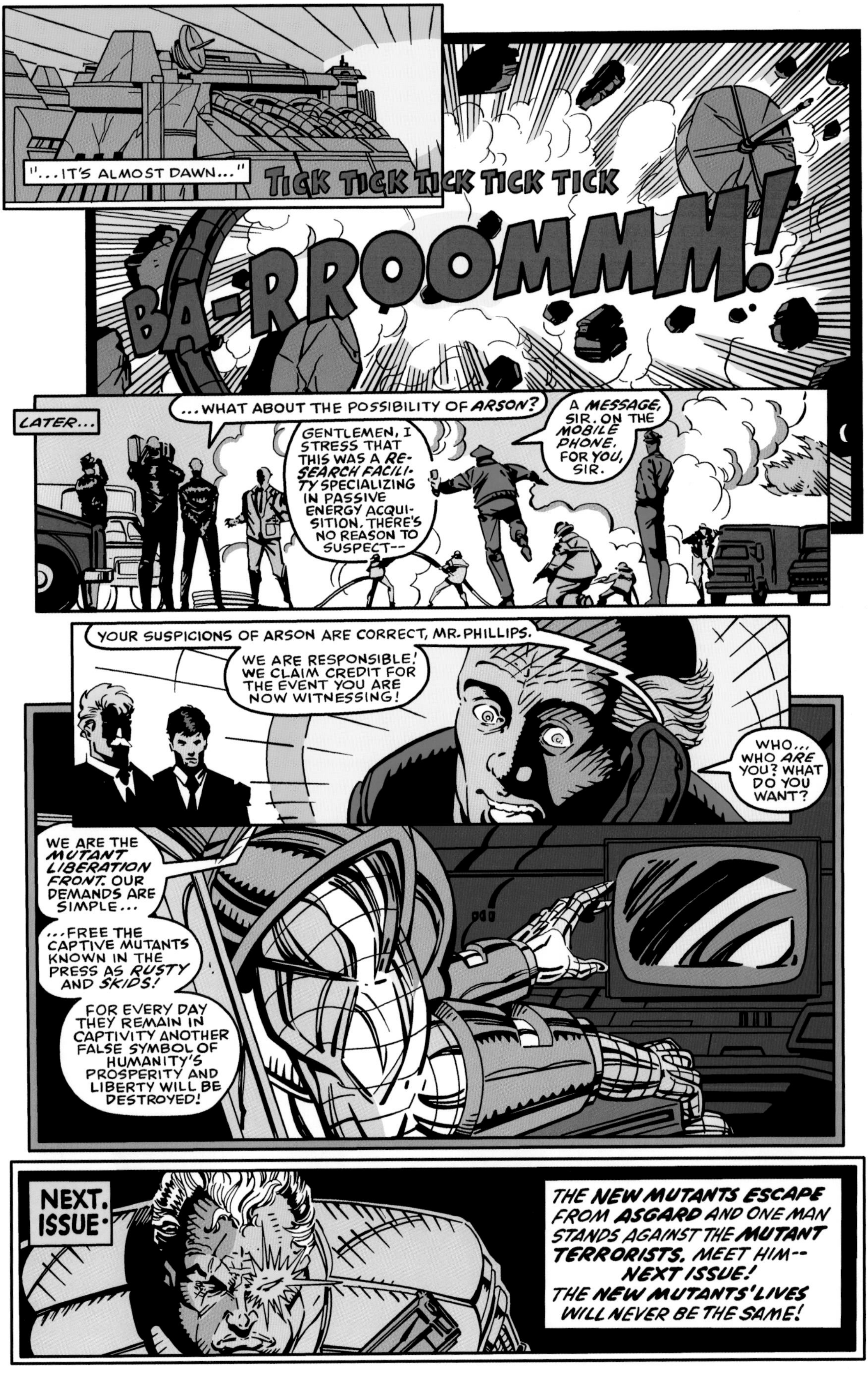
"...IT'S ALMOST DAWN..."
TICK TICK TICK TICK TICK
BA-RROOMMM!
LATER...
...WHAT ABOUT THE POSSIBILITY OF ARSON?
GENTLEMEN, I STRESS THAT THIS WAS A RESEARCH FACILITY SPECIALIZING IN PASSIVE ENERGY ACQUISITION. THERE'S NO REASON TO SUSPECT--
A MESSAGE, SIR. ON THE MOBILE PHONE. FOR YOU, SIR.
YOUR SUSPICIONS OF ARSON ARE CORRECT, MR. PHILLIPS.
WE ARE RESPONSIBLE! WE CLAIM CREDIT FOR THE EVENT YOU ARE NOW WITNESSING!
WHO... WHO ARE YOU? WHAT DO YOU WANT?
WE ARE THE MUTANT LIBERATION FRONT. OUR DEMANDS ARE SIMPLE...
...FREE THE CAPTIVE MUTANTS KNOWN IN THE PRESS AS RUSTY AND SKIDS!
FOR EVERY DAY THEY REMAIN IN CAPTIVITY ANOTHER FALSE SYMBOL OF HUMANITY'S PROSPERITY AND LIBERTY WILL BE DESTROYED!
NEXT ISSUE·
THE NEW MUTANTS ESCAPE FROM ASGARD AND ONE MAN STANDS AGAINST THE MUTANT TERRORISTS. MEET HIM-- NEXT ISSUE! THE NEW MUTANTS' LIVES WILL NEVER BE THE SAME!

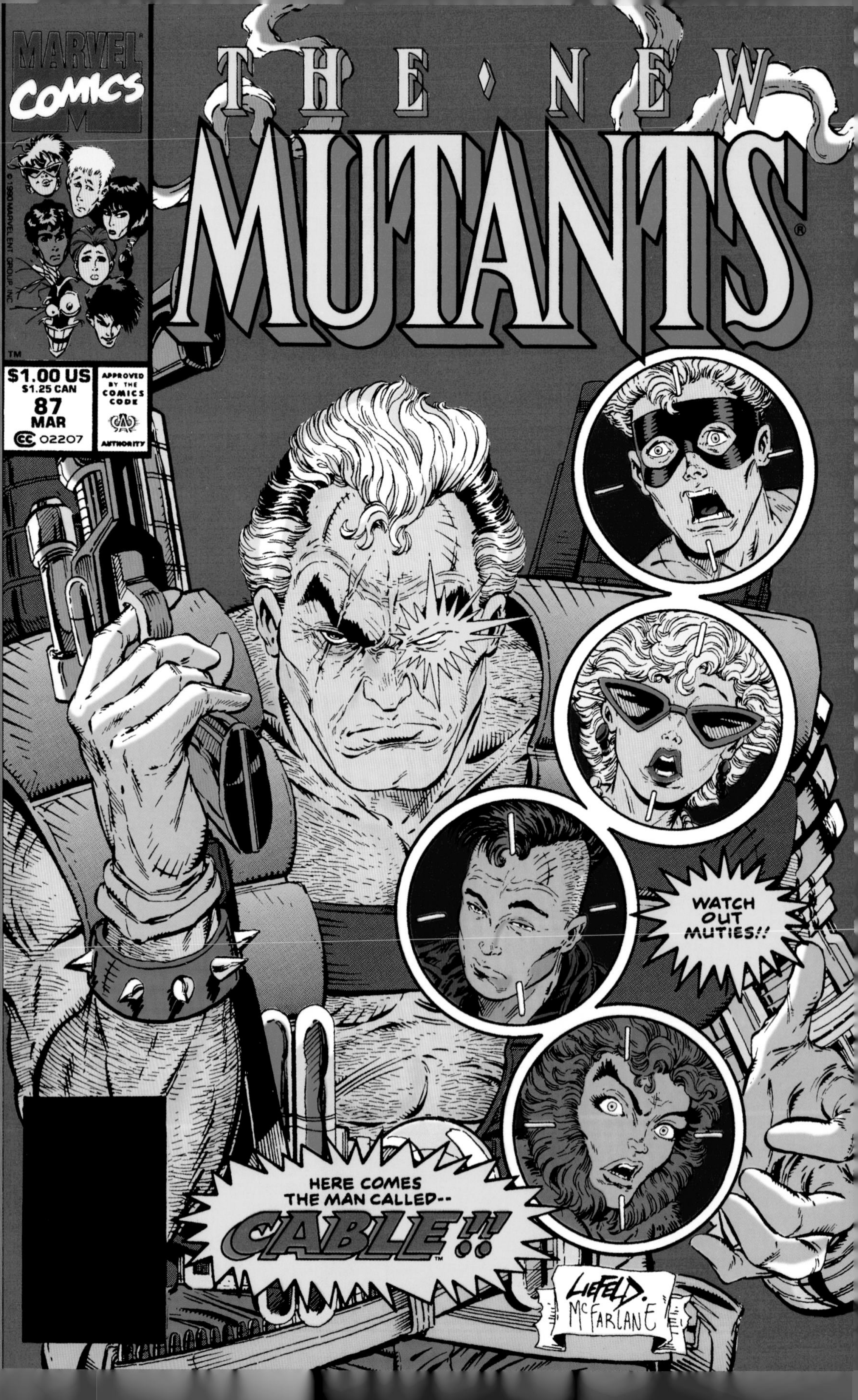
MARVEL COMICS
THE NEW MUTANTS
© 1990 MARVEL ENT. GROUP, INC.
$1.00 US
$1.25 CAN
87
MAR
02207
APPROVED BY THE COMICS CODE AUTHORITY
WATCH OUT MUTIES!!
HERE COMES THE MAN CALLED--
CABLE!!
LIEFELD.
McFARLANE

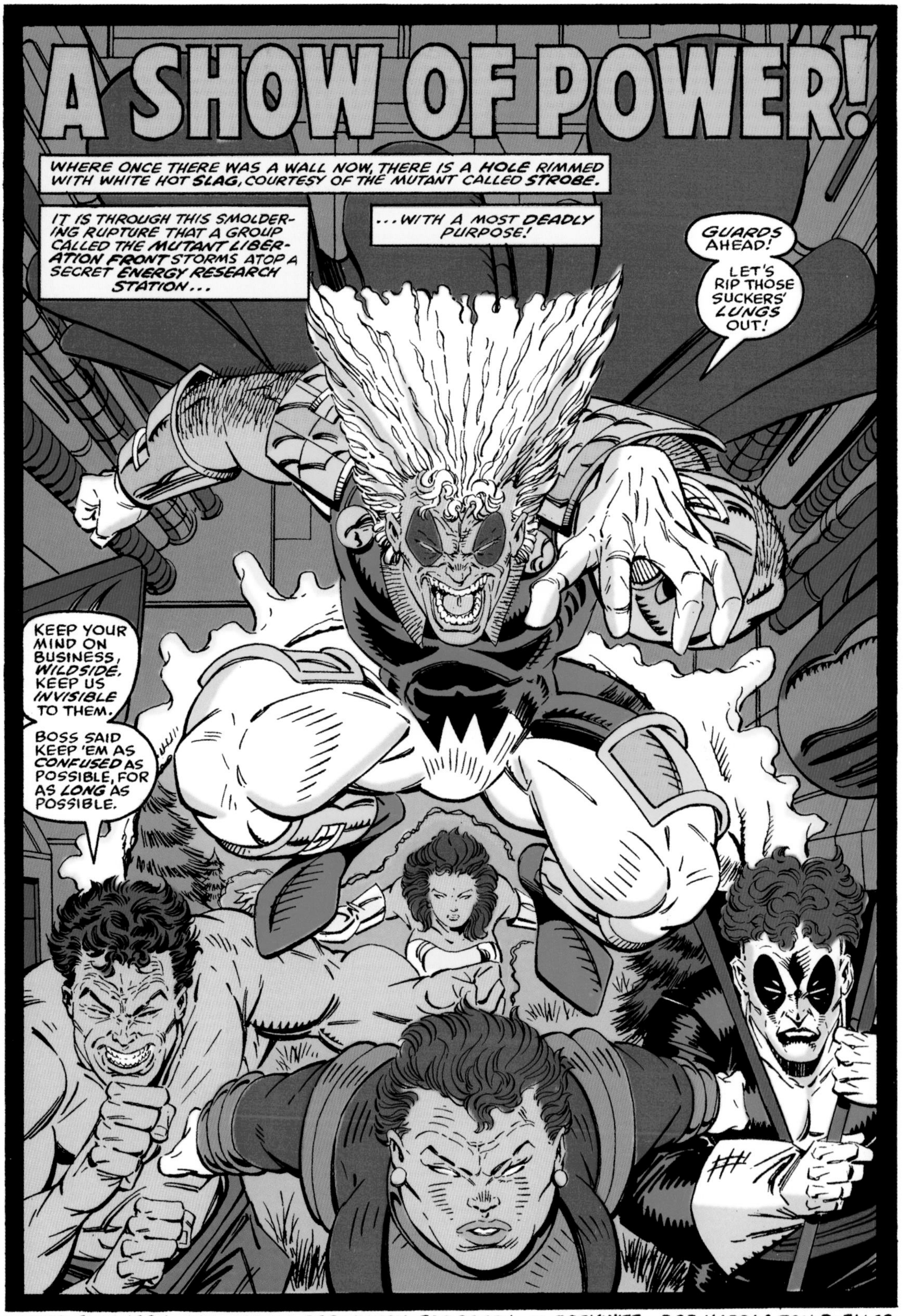
A SHOW OF POWER!
WHERE ONCE THERE WAS A WALL NOW, THERE IS A HOLE RIMMED WITH WHITE HOT SLAG, COURTESY OF THE MUTANT CALLED STROBE.
IT IS THROUGH THIS SMOLDERING RUPTURE THAT A GROUP CALLED THE MUTANT LIBERATION FRONT STORMS ATOP A SECRET ENERGY RESEARCH STATION...
...WITH A MOST DEADLY PURPOSE!
GUARDS AHEAD!
LET'S RIP THOSE SUCKERS' LUNGS OUT!
KEEP YOUR MIND ON BUSINESS, WILDSIDE. KEEP US INVISIBLE TO THEM.
BOSS SAID KEEP 'EM AS CONFUSED AS POSSIBLE, FOR AS LONG AS POSSIBLE.

LOUISE SIMONSON WRITER · ROB LIEFELD PENCILER · BOB WIACEK INKER · JOE ROSEN LETTERER · M. ROCKWITZ COLORIST · BOB HARRAS EDITOR · TOM DeFALCO EDITOR IN CHIEF

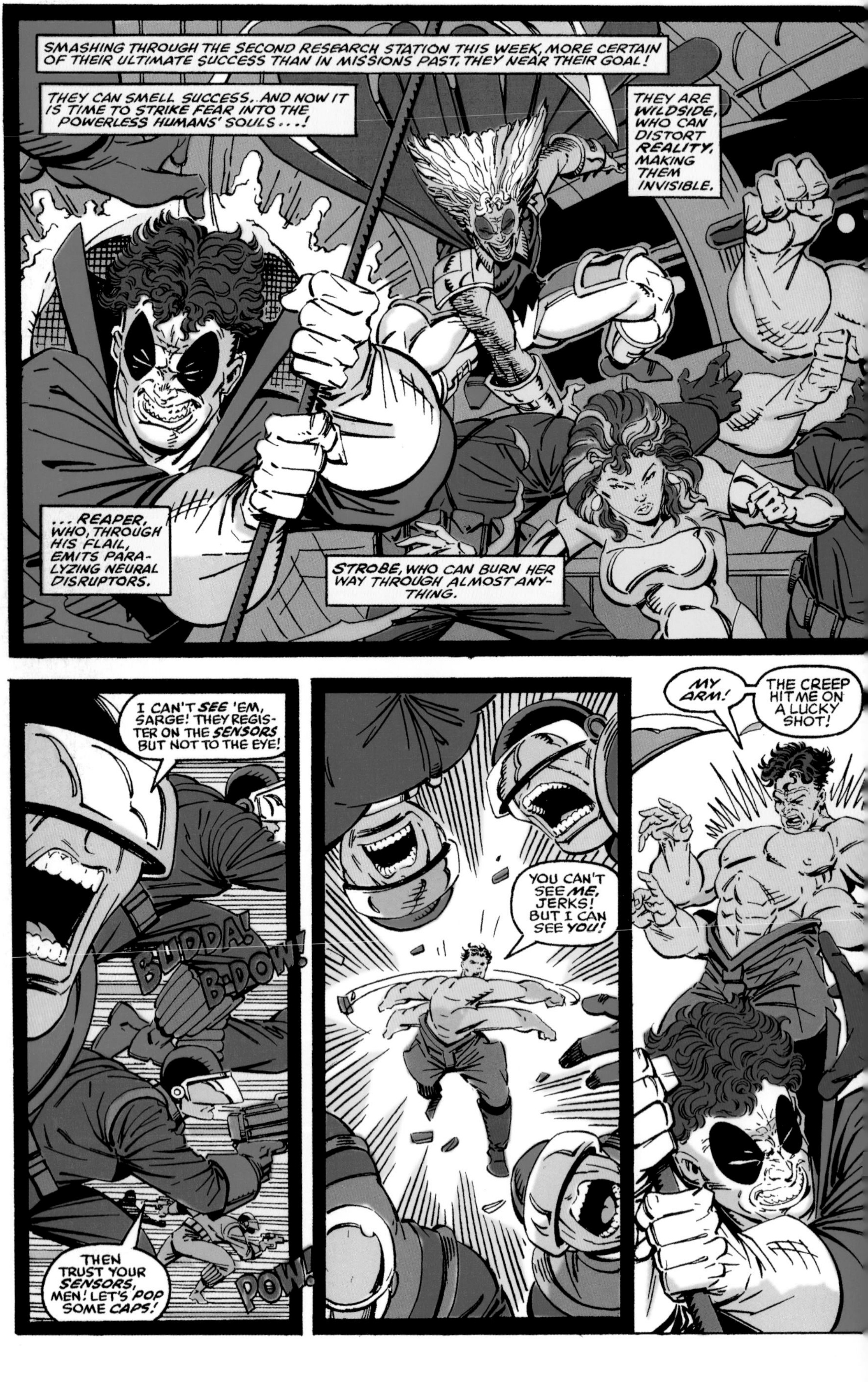
SMASHING THROUGH THE SECOND RESEARCH STATION THIS WEEK, MORE CERTAIN OF THEIR ULTIMATE SUCCESS THAN IN MISSIONS PAST, THEY NEAR THEIR GOAL!
THEY CAN SMELL SUCCESS.. AND NOW IT IS TIME TO STRIKE FEAR INTO THE POWERLESS HUMANS' SOULS . . .!
THEY ARE WILDSIDE, WHO CAN DISTORT REALITY, MAKING THEM INVISIBLE.
. . . REAPER, WHO, THROUGH HIS FLAIL, EMITS PARALYZING NEURAL DISRUPTORS.
STROBE, WHO CAN BURN HER WAY THROUGH ALMOST ANYTHING.
I CAN'T SEE 'EM, SARGE! THEY REGISTER ON THE SENSORS BUT NOT TO THE EYE!
BUDDA! B-DOW!
THEN TRUST YOUR SENSORS, MEN! LET'S POP SOME CAPS!
POW!
YOU CAN'T SEE ME, JERKS! BUT I CAN SEE YOU!
MY ARM!
THE CREEP HIT ME ON A LUCKY SHOT!

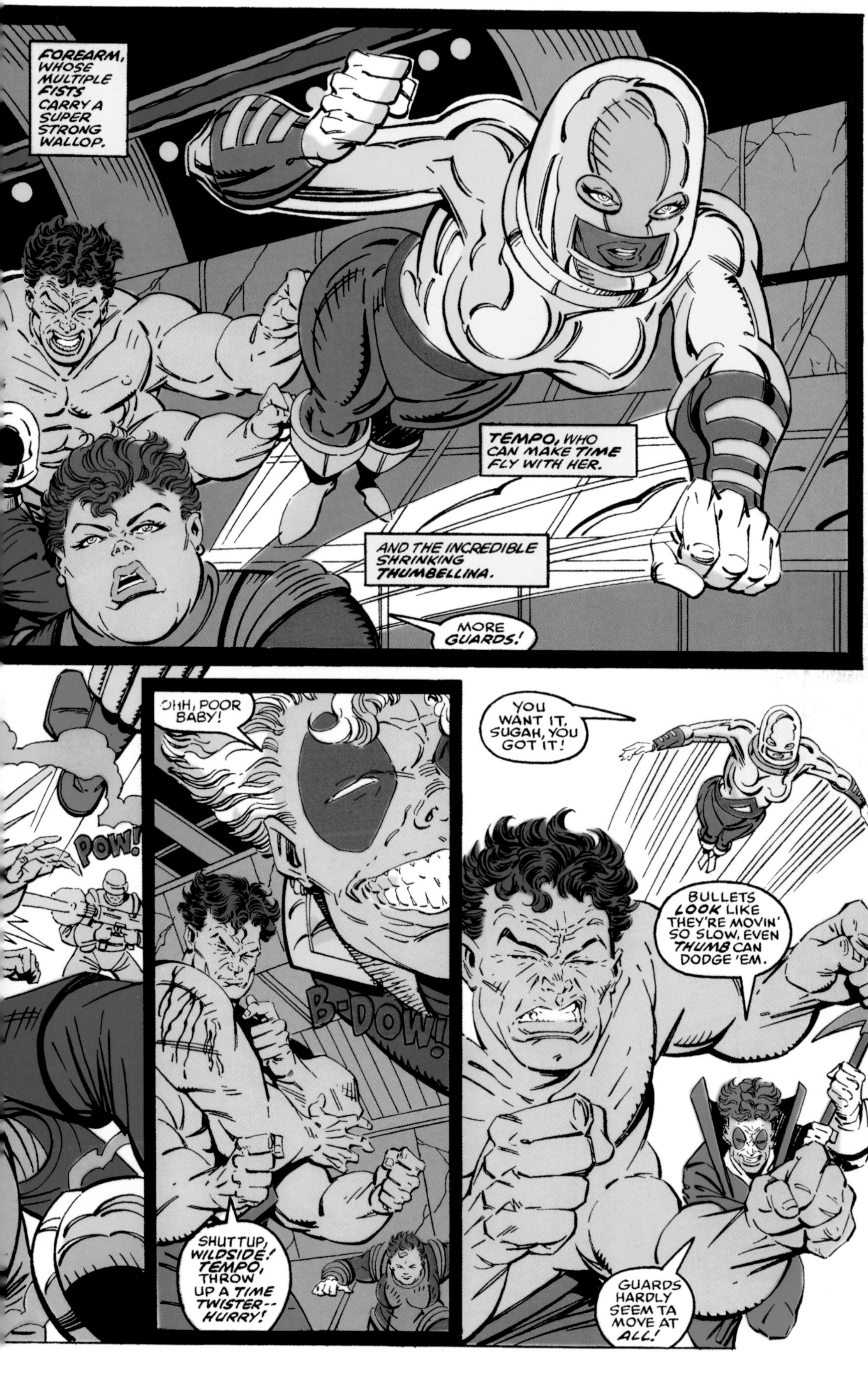
FOREARM, WHOSE MULTIPLE FISTS CARRY A SUPER STRONG WALLOP.
TEMPO, WHO CAN MAKE TIME FLY WITH HER.
AND THE INCREDIBLE SHRINKING THUMBELLINA.
MORE GUARDS!
POW!
OHH, POOR BABY!
B-DOW!
SHUTTUP, WILDSIDE! TEMPO, THROW UP A TIME TWISTER-- HURRY!
YOU WANT IT, SUGAH, YOU GOT IT!
BULLETS LOOK LIKE THEY'RE MOVIN' SO SLOW, EVEN THUMB CAN DODGE 'EM.
GUARDS HARDLY SEEM TA MOVE AT ALL!

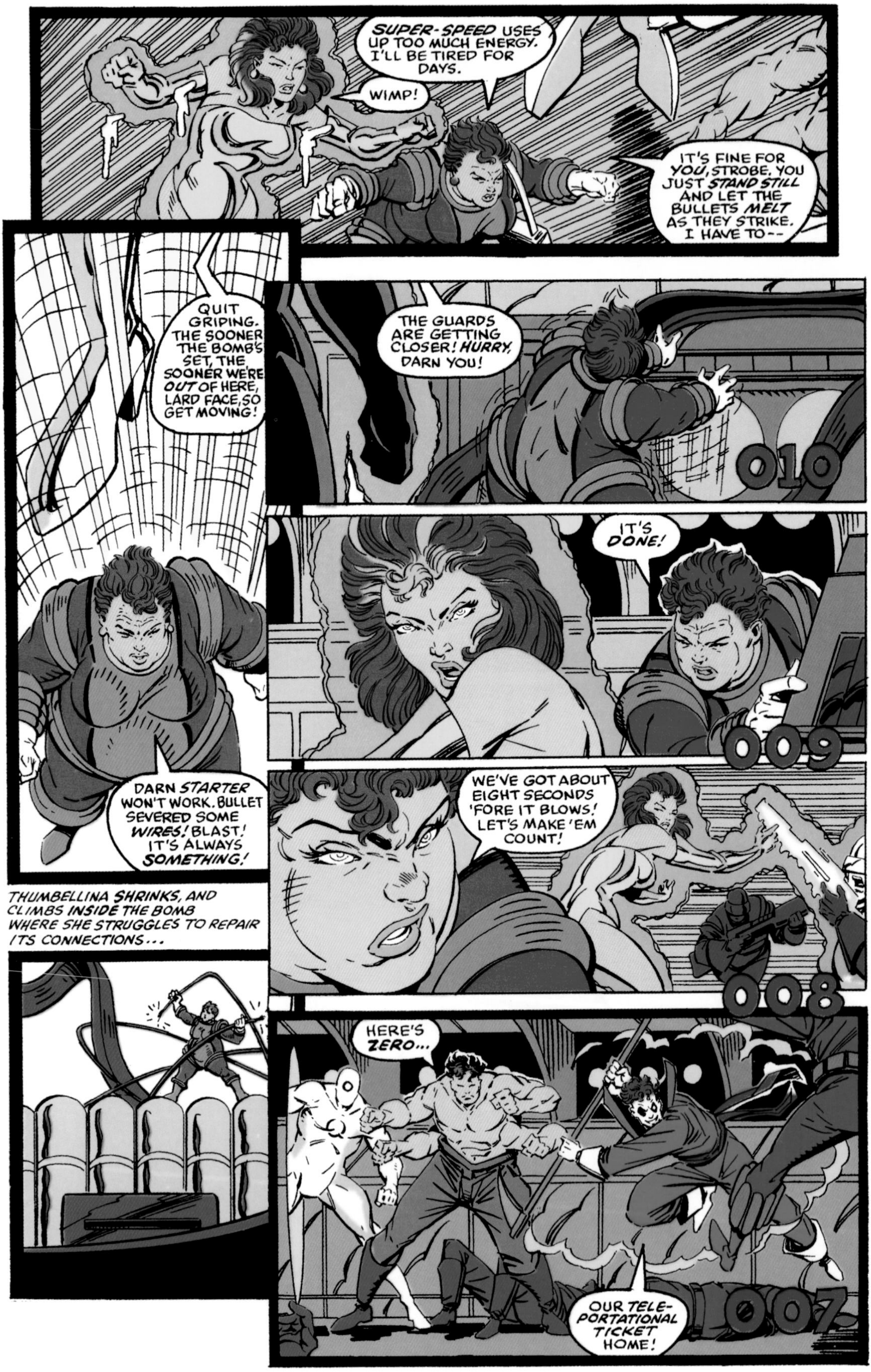
SUPER-SPEED USES UP TOO MUCH ENERGY. I'LL BE TIRED FOR DAYS.
WIMP!
IT'S FINE FOR YOU, STROBE. YOU JUST STAND STILL AND LET THE BULLETS MELT AS THEY STRIKE. I HAVE TO--
QUIT GRIPING. THE SOONER THE BOMB'S SET, THE SOONER WE'RE OUT OF HERE, LARD FACE, SO GET MOVING!
THE GUARDS ARE GETTING CLOSER! HURRY, DARN YOU!
010
IT'S DONE!
009
DARN STARTER WON'T WORK. BULLET SEVERED SOME WIRES! BLAST! IT'S ALWAYS SOMETHING!
WE'VE GOT ABOUT EIGHT SECONDS 'FORE IT BLOWS! LET'S MAKE 'EM COUNT!
THUMBELLINA SHRINKS, AND CLIMBS INSIDE THE BOMB WHERE SHE STRUGGLES TO REPAIR ITS CONNECTIONS...
008
HERE'S ZERO...
OUR TELE-PORTATIONAL TICKET HOME!
007

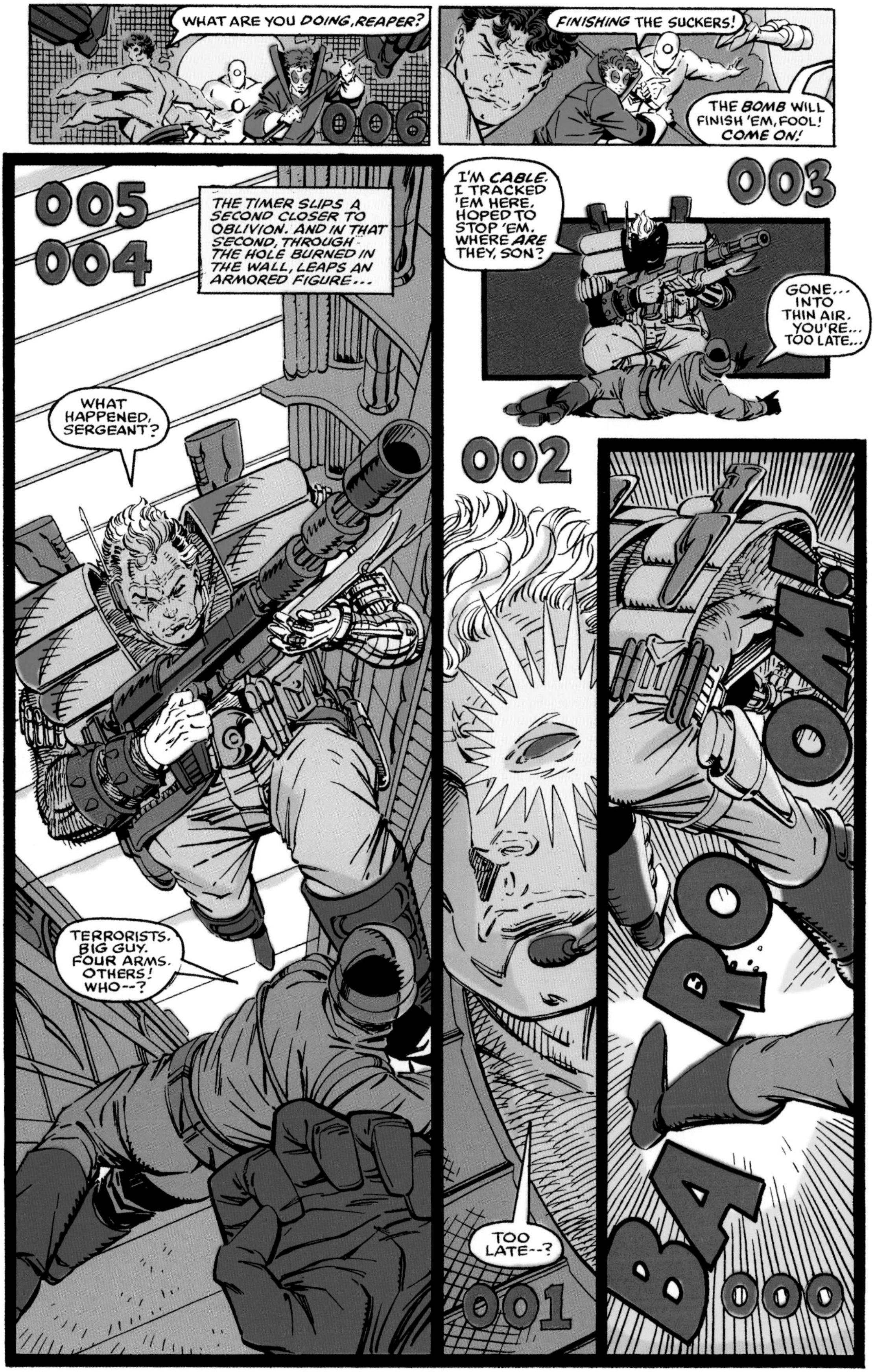
WHAT ARE YOU DOING, REAPER?
006
FINISHING THE SUCKERS!
THE BOMB WILL FINISH 'EM, FOOL! COME ON!
005
004
THE TIMER SLIPS A SECOND CLOSER TO OBLIVION. AND IN THAT SECOND, THROUGH THE HOLE BURNED IN THE WALL, LEAPS AN ARMORED FIGURE...
WHAT HAPPENED, SERGEANT?
TERRORISTS. BIG GUY. FOUR ARMS. OTHERS! WHO--?
I'M CABLE. I TRACKED 'EM HERE. HOPED TO STOP 'EM. WHERE ARE THEY, SON?
003
GONE... INTO THIN AIR. YOU'RE... TOO LATE...
002
TOO LATE--?
001
BAROOOM!
000

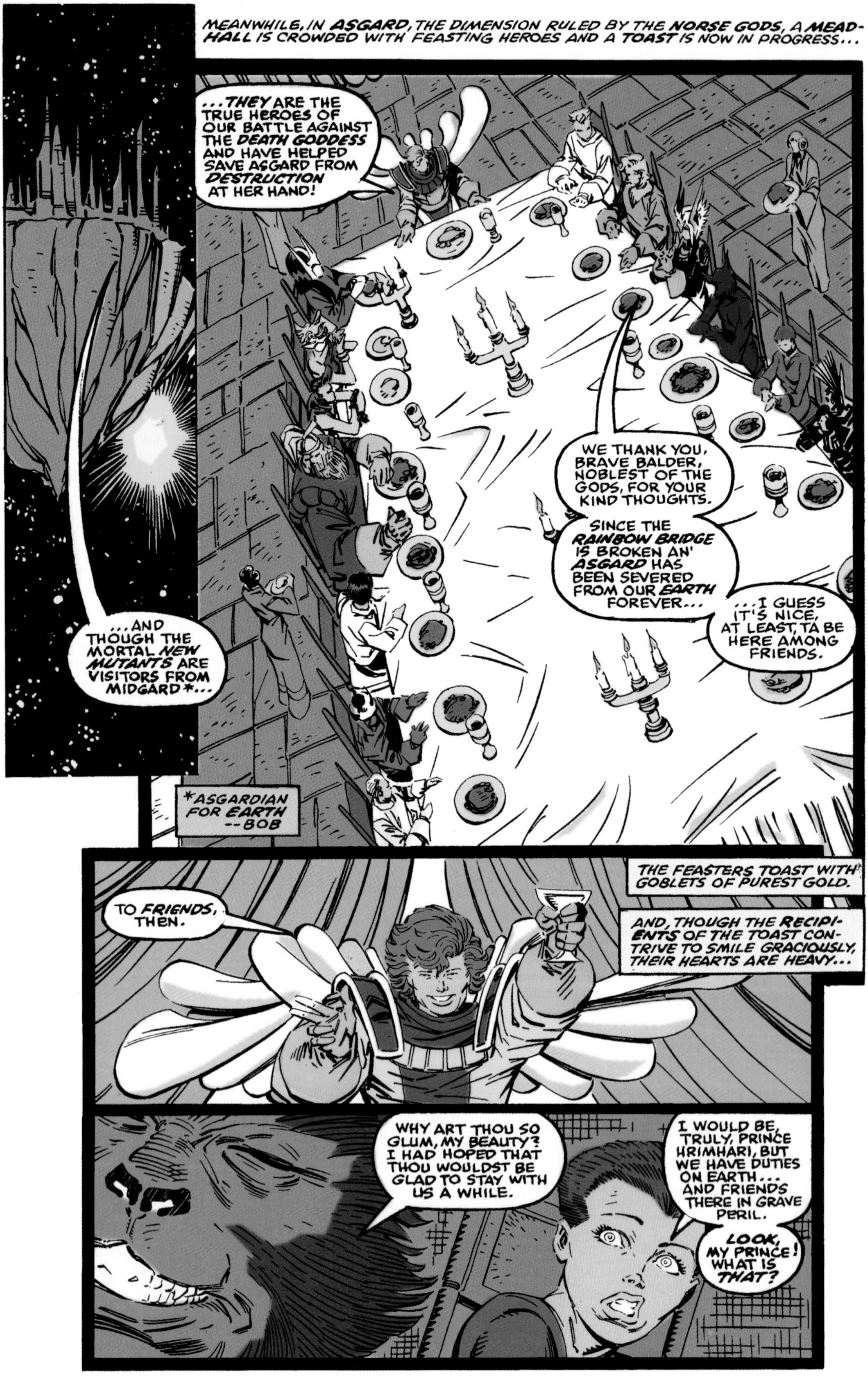
MEANWHILE, IN ASGARD, THE DIMENSION RULED BY THE NORSE GODS, A MEAD-HALL IS CROWDED WITH FEASTING HEROES AND A TOAST IS NOW IN PROGRESS...
...AND THOUGH THE MORTAL NEW MUTANTS ARE VISITORS FROM MIDGARD*...
...THEY ARE THE TRUE HEROES OF OUR BATTLE AGAINST THE DEATH GODDESS AND HAVE HELPED SAVE ASGARD FROM DESTRUCTION AT HER HAND!
WE THANK YOU, BRAVE BALDER, NOBLEST OF THE GODS, FOR YOUR KIND THOUGHTS.
SINCE THE RAINBOW BRIDGE IS BROKEN AN' ASGARD HAS BEEN SEVERED FROM OUR EARTH FOREVER...
...I GUESS IT'S NICE, AT LEAST, TA BE HERE AMONG FRIENDS.
*ASGARDIAN FOR EARTH --BOB
THE FEASTERS TOAST WITH GOBLETS OF PUREST GOLD.
TO FRIENDS, THEN.
AND, THOUGH THE RECIPIENTS OF THE TOAST CONTRIVE TO SMILE GRACIOUSLY, THEIR HEARTS ARE HEAVY...
WHY ART THOU SO GLUM, MY BEAUTY? I HAD HOPED THAT THOU WOULDST BE GLAD TO STAY WITH US A WHILE.
I WOULD BE, TRULY, PRINCE HRIMHARI, BUT WE HAVE DUTIES ON EARTH... AND FRIENDS THERE IN GRAVE PERIL.
LOOK, MY PRINCE! WHAT IS THAT?

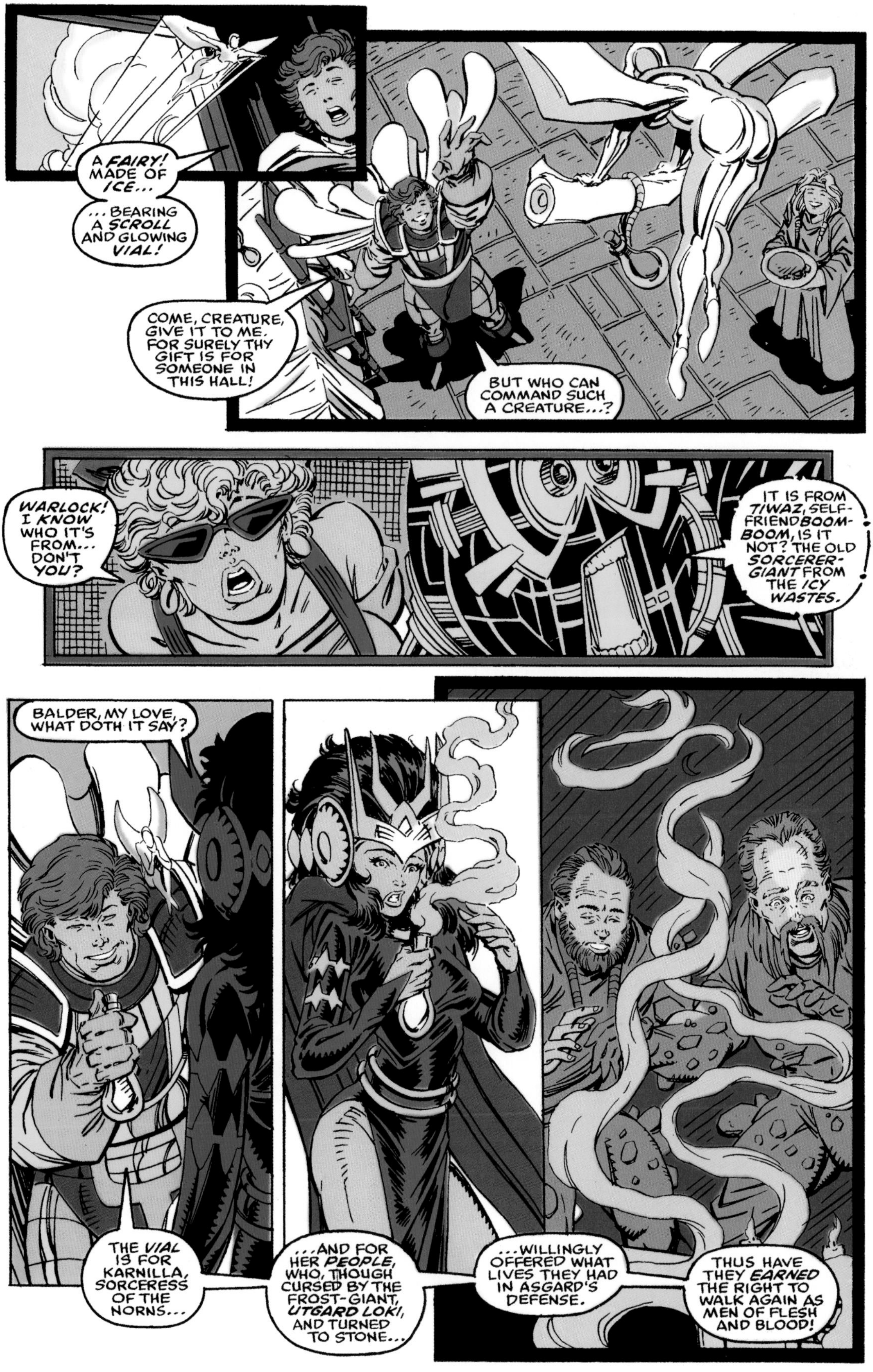

A FAIRY! MADE OF ICE...
...BEARING A SCROLL AND GLOWING VIAL!
COME, CREATURE, GIVE IT TO ME. FOR SURELY THY GIFT IS FOR SOMEONE IN THIS HALL!
BUT WHO CAN COMMAND SUCH A CREATURE...?
WARLOCK! I KNOW WHO IT'S FROM... DON'T YOU?
IT IS FROM TIWAZ, SELF-FRIENDBOOM-BOOM, IS IT NOT? THE OLD SORCERER-GIANT FROM THE ICY WASTES.
BALDER, MY LOVE, WHAT DOTH IT SAY?
THE VIAL IS FOR KARNILLA, SORCERESS OF THE NORNS...
...AND FOR HER PEOPLE, WHO, THOUGH CURSED BY THE FROST-GIANT, UTGARD LOKI, AND TURNED TO STONE...
...WILLINGLY OFFERED WHAT LIVES THEY HAD IN ASGARD'S DEFENSE.
THUS HAVE THEY EARNED THE RIGHT TO WALK AGAIN AS MEN OF FLESH AND BLOOD!

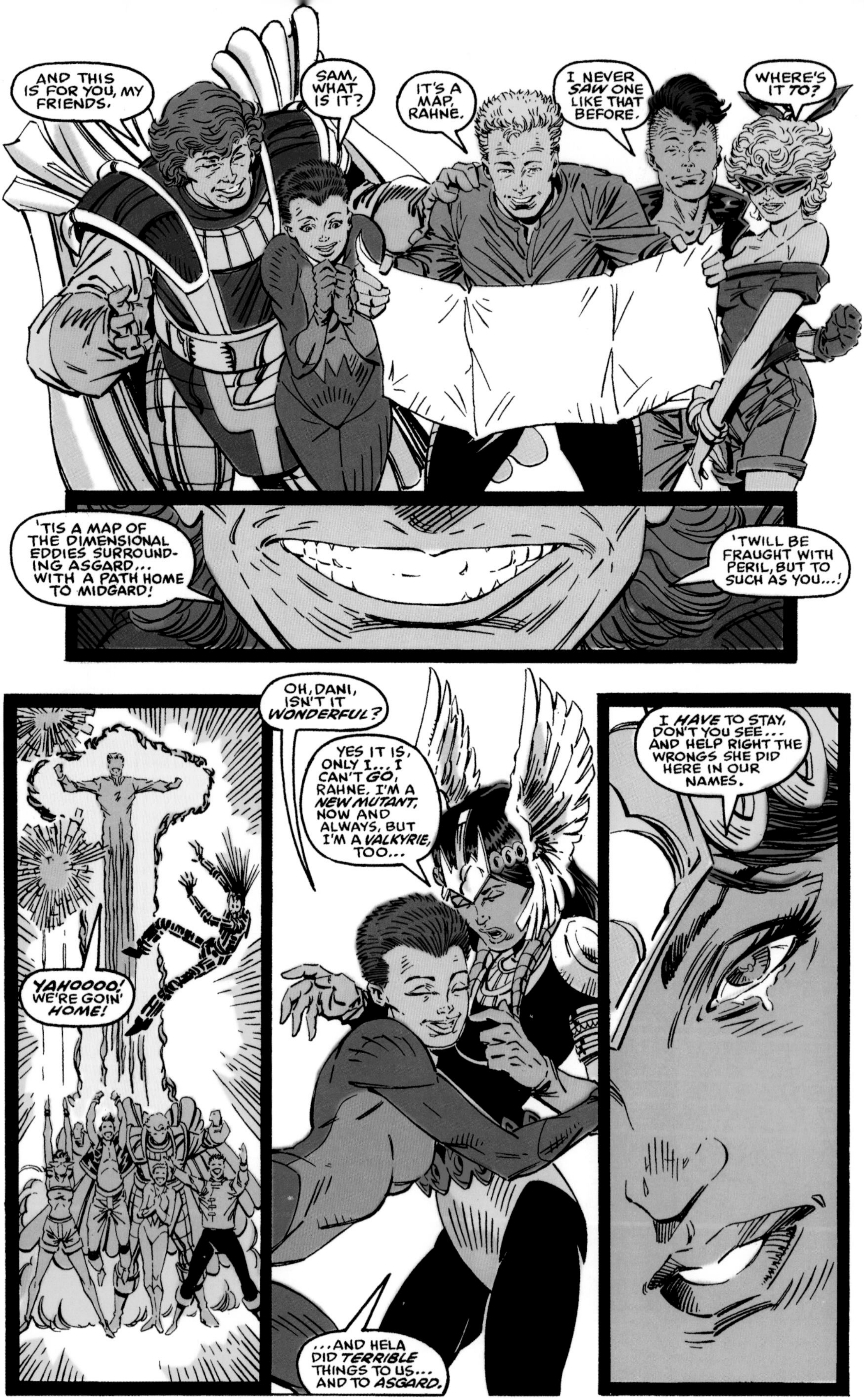
AND THIS IS FOR YOU, MY FRIENDS.
SAM, WHAT IS IT?
IT'S A MAP, RAHNE.
I NEVER SAW ONE LIKE THAT BEFORE.
WHERE'S IT TO?
'TIS A MAP OF THE DIMENSIONAL EDDIES SURROUNDING ASGARD... WITH A PATH HOME TO MIDGARD!
'TWILL BE FRAUGHT WITH PERIL, BUT TO SUCH AS YOU...!
YAHOOOO! WE'RE GOIN' HOME!
OH, DANI, ISN'T IT WONDERFUL?
YES IT IS, ONLY I... I CAN'T GO, RAHNE. I'M A NEW MUTANT, NOW AND ALWAYS, BUT I'M A VALKYRIE, TOO...
...AND HELA DID TERRIBLE THINGS TO US... AND TO ASGARD.
I HAVE TO STAY, DON'T YOU SEE... AND HELP RIGHT THE WRONGS SHE DID HERE IN OUR NAMES.

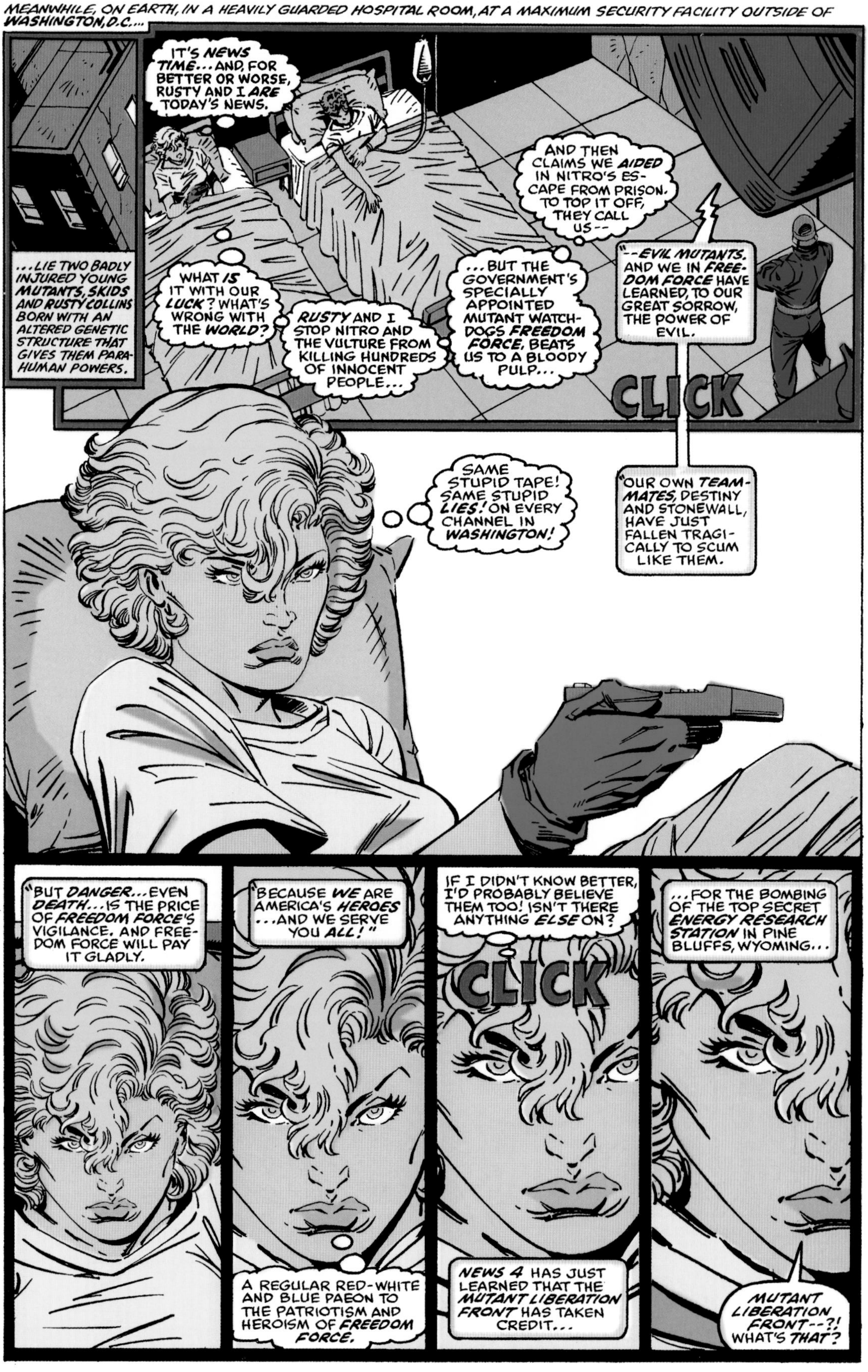

MEANWHILE, ON EARTH, IN A HEAVILY GUARDED HOSPITAL ROOM, AT A MAXIMUM SECURITY FACILITY OUTSIDE OF WASHINGTON, D.C....
...LIE TWO BADLY INJURED YOUNG MUTANTS, SKIDS AND RUSTY COLLINS BORN WITH AN ALTERED GENETIC STRUCTURE THAT GIVES THEM PARA-HUMAN POWERS.
IT'S NEWS TIME... AND, FOR BETTER OR WORSE, RUSTY AND I ARE TODAY'S NEWS.
WHAT IS IT WITH OUR LUCK? WHAT'S WRONG WITH THE WORLD?
RUSTY AND I STOP NITRO AND THE VULTURE FROM KILLING HUNDREDS OF INNOCENT PEOPLE...
...BUT THE GOVERNMENT'S SPECIALLY APPOINTED MUTANT WATCH-DOGS FREEDOM FORCE, BEATS US TO A BLOODY PULP...
AND THEN CLAIMS WE AIDED IN NITRO'S ES-CAPE FROM PRISON. TO TOP IT OFF, THEY CALL US--
"--EVIL MUTANTS. AND WE IN FREE-DOM FORCE HAVE LEARNED, TO OUR GREAT SORROW, THE POWER OF EVIL.
CLICK
SAME STUPID TAPE! SAME STUPID LIES! ON EVERY CHANNEL IN WASHINGTON!
"OUR OWN TEAM-MATES, DESTINY AND STONEWALL, HAVE JUST FALLEN TRAGI-CALLY TO SCUM LIKE THEM.
"BUT DANGER... EVEN DEATH... IS THE PRICE OF FREEDOM FORCE'S VIGILANCE. AND FREE-DOM FORCE WILL PAY IT GLADLY.
"BECAUSE WE ARE AMERICA'S HEROES ...AND WE SERVE YOU ALL!"
A REGULAR RED-WHITE AND BLUE PAEON TO THE PATRIOTISM AND HEROISM OF FREEDOM FORCE.
IF I DIDN'T KNOW BETTER, I'D PROBABLY BELIEVE THEM TOO! ISN'T THERE ANYTHING ELSE ON?
CLICK
NEWS 4 HAS JUST LEARNED THAT THE MUTANT LIBERATION FRONT HAS TAKEN CREDIT...
...FOR THE BOMBING OF THE TOP SECRET ENERGY RESEARCH STATION IN PINE BLUFFS, WYOMING...
MUTANT LIBERATION FRONT--?! WHAT'S THAT?

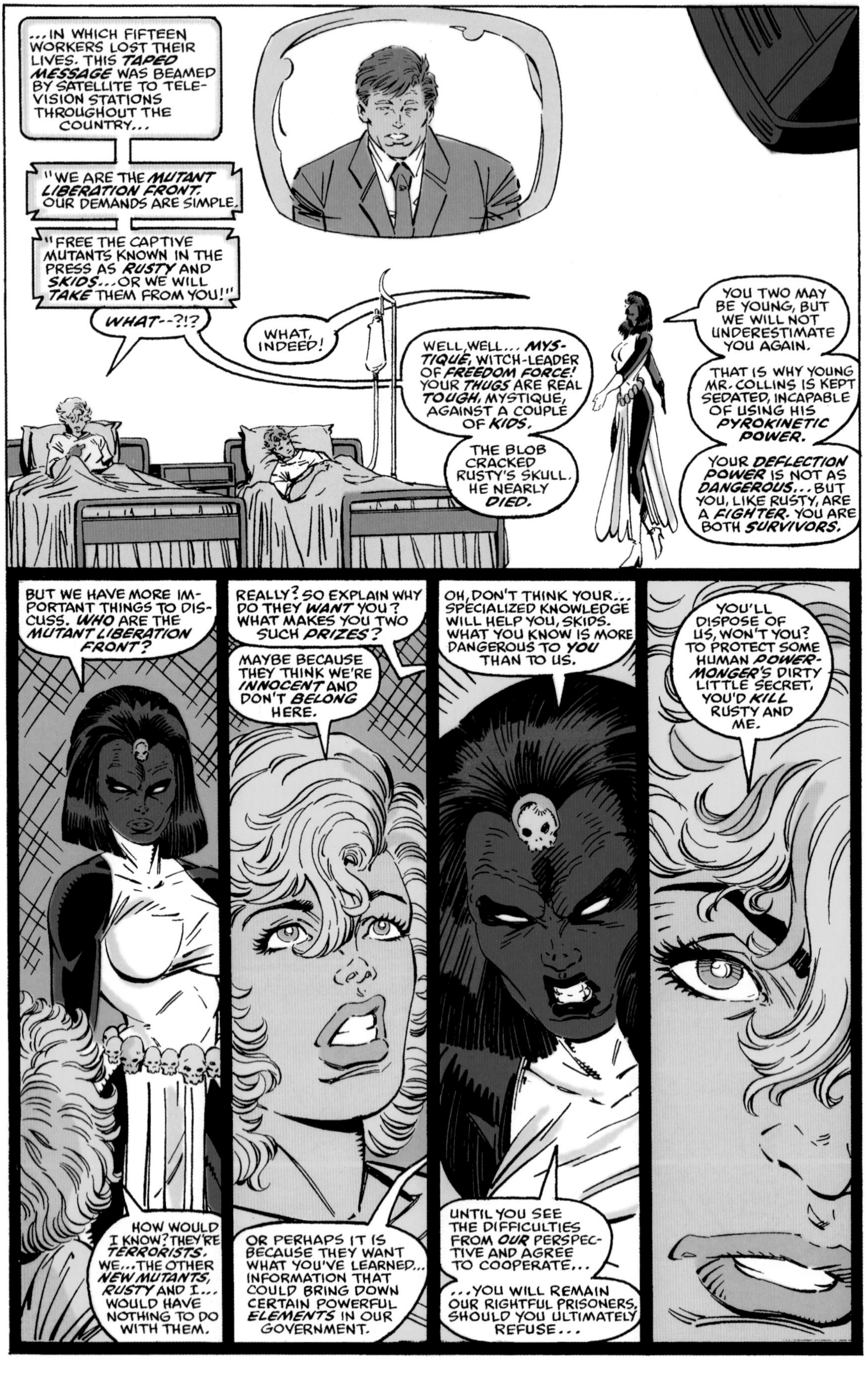
...IN WHICH FIFTEEN WORKERS LOST THEIR LIVES. THIS TAPED MESSAGE WAS BEAMED BY SATELLITE TO TELE-VISION STATIONS THROUGHOUT THE COUNTRY...
"WE ARE THE MUTANT LIBERATION FRONT. OUR DEMANDS ARE SIMPLE.
"FREE THE CAPTIVE MUTANTS KNOWN IN THE PRESS AS RUSTY AND SKIDS... OR WE WILL TAKE THEM FROM YOU!"
WHAT--?!?
WHAT, INDEED!
WELL, WELL... MYS-TIQUE, WITCH-LEADER OF FREEDOM FORCE! YOUR THUGS ARE REAL TOUGH, MYSTIQUE, AGAINST A COUPLE OF KIDS.
THE BLOB CRACKED RUSTY'S SKULL. HE NEARLY DIED.
YOU TWO MAY BE YOUNG, BUT WE WILL NOT UNDERESTIMATE YOU AGAIN.
THAT IS WHY YOUNG MR. COLLINS IS KEPT SEDATED, INCAPABLE OF USING HIS PYROKINETIC POWER.
YOUR DEFLECTION POWER IS NOT AS DANGEROUS... BUT YOU, LIKE RUSTY, ARE A FIGHTER. YOU ARE BOTH SURVIVORS.
BUT WE HAVE MORE IM-PORTANT THINGS TO DIS-CUSS. WHO ARE THE MUTANT LIBERATION FRONT?
HOW WOULD I KNOW? THEY'RE TERRORISTS. WE... THE OTHER NEW MUTANTS, RUSTY AND I... WOULD HAVE NOTHING TO DO WITH THEM.
REALLY? SO EXPLAIN WHY DO THEY WANT YOU? WHAT MAKES YOU TWO SUCH PRIZES?
MAYBE BECAUSE THEY THINK WE'RE INNOCENT AND DON'T BELONG HERE.
OR PERHAPS IT IS BECAUSE THEY WANT WHAT YOU'VE LEARNED... INFORMATION THAT COULD BRING DOWN CERTAIN POWERFUL ELEMENTS IN OUR GOVERNMENT.
OH, DON'T THINK YOUR... SPECIALIZED KNOWLEDGE WILL HELP YOU, SKIDS. WHAT YOU KNOW IS MORE DANGEROUS TO YOU THAN TO US.
UNTIL YOU SEE THE DIFFICULTIES FROM OUR PERSPEC-TIVE AND AGREE TO COOPERATE...
...YOU WILL REMAIN OUR RIGHTFUL PRISONERS, SHOULD YOU ULTIMATELY REFUSE...
YOU'LL DISPOSE OF US, WON'T YOU? TO PROTECT SOME HUMAN POWER-MONGER'S DIRTY LITTLE SECRET, YOU'D KILL RUSTY AND ME.

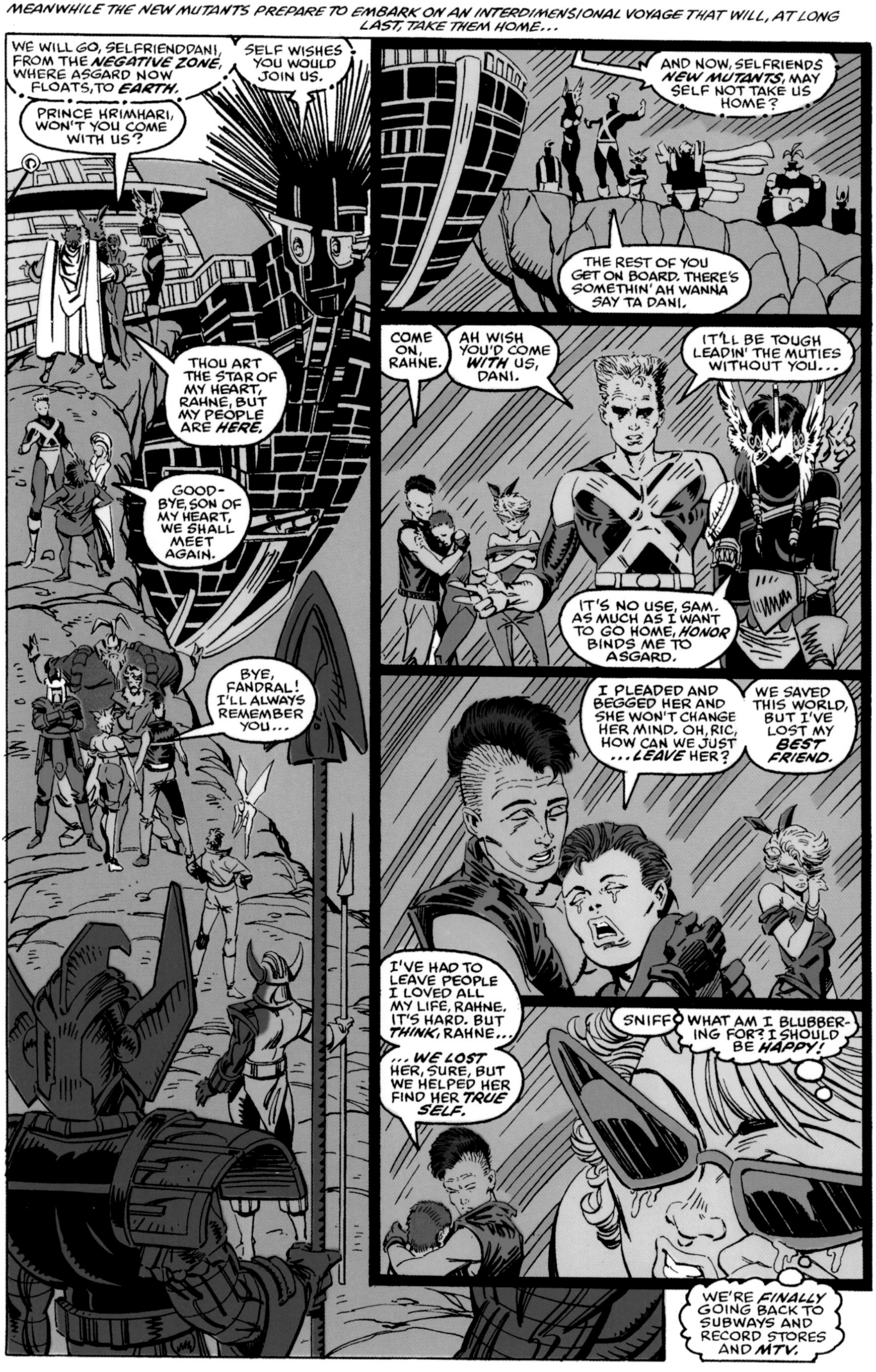
MEANWHILE THE NEW MUTANTS PREPARE TO EMBARK ON AN INTERDIMENSIONAL VOYAGE THAT WILL, AT LONG LAST, TAKE THEM HOME...
WE WILL GO, SELFRIENDDANI, FROM THE NEGATIVE ZONE, WHERE ASGARD NOW FLOATS, TO EARTH.
SELF WISHES YOU WOULD JOIN US.
PRINCE HRIMHARI, WON'T YOU COME WITH US?
THOU ART THE STAR OF MY HEART, RAHNE, BUT MY PEOPLE ARE HERE.
GOOD-BYE, SON OF MY HEART, WE SHALL MEET AGAIN.
BYE, FANDRAL! I'LL ALWAYS REMEMBER YOU...
AND NOW, SELFRIENDS NEW MUTANTS, MAY SELF NOT TAKE US HOME?
THE REST OF YOU GET ON BOARD. THERE'S SOMETHIN' AH WANNA SAY TA DANI.
COME ON, RAHNE.
AH WISH YOU'D COME WITH US, DANI.
IT'LL BE TOUGH LEADIN' THE MUTIES WITHOUT YOU...
IT'S NO USE, SAM. AS MUCH AS I WANT TO GO HOME, HONOR BINDS ME TO ASGARD.
I PLEADED AND BEGGED HER AND SHE WON'T CHANGE HER MIND. OH, RIC, HOW CAN WE JUST ...LEAVE HER?
WE SAVED THIS WORLD, BUT I'VE LOST MY BEST FRIEND.
I'VE HAD TO LEAVE PEOPLE I LOVED ALL MY LIFE, RAHNE. IT'S HARD. BUT THINK, RAHNE...
...WE LOST HER, SURE, BUT WE HELPED HER FIND HER TRUE SELF.
SNIFF
WHAT AM I BLUBBERING FOR? I SHOULD BE HAPPY!
WE'RE FINALLY GOING BACK TO SUBWAYS AND RECORD STORES AND MTV.

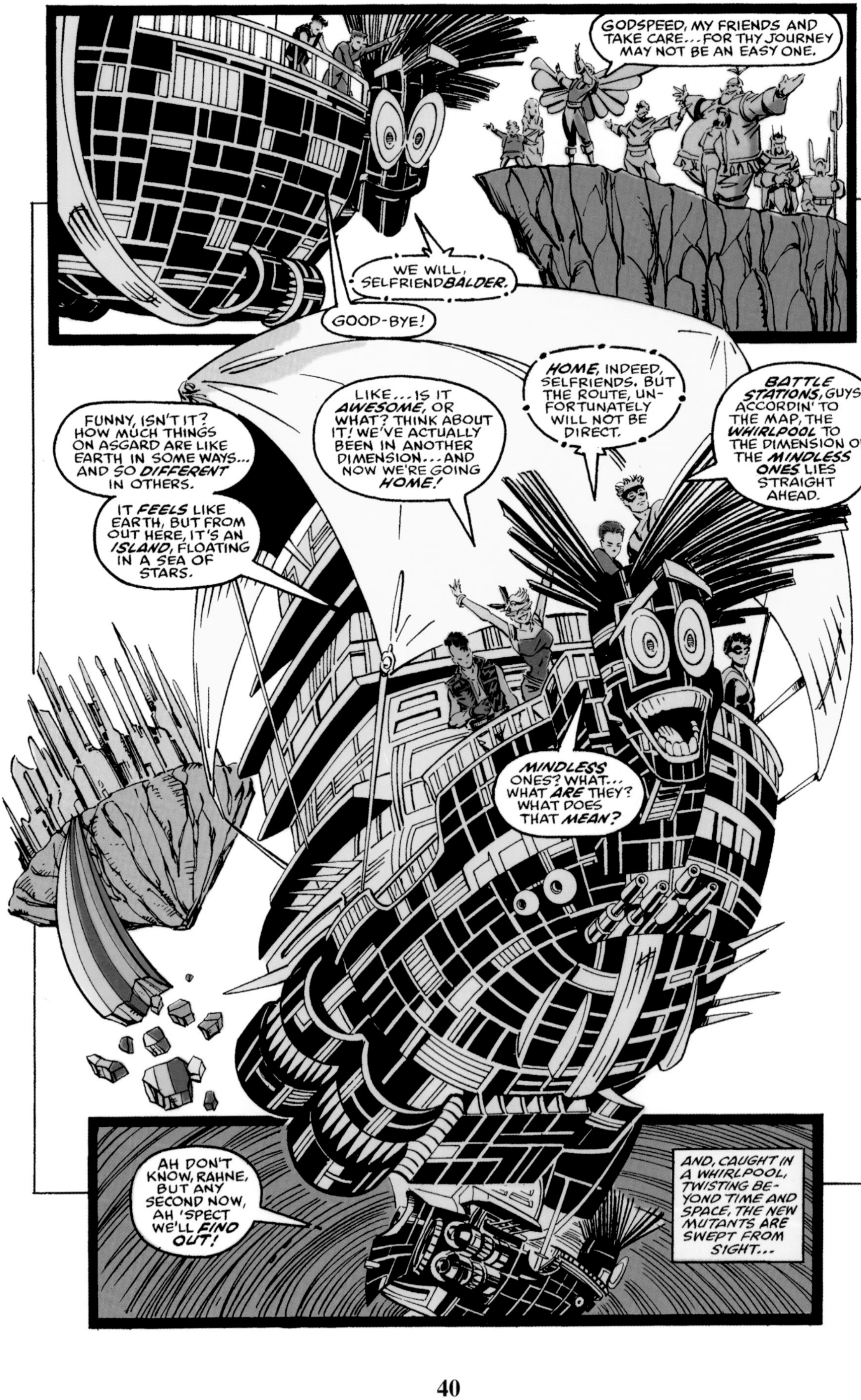
GODSPEED, MY FRIENDS AND TAKE CARE... FOR THY JOURNEY MAY NOT BE AN EASY ONE.
WE WILL, SELFRIEND BALDER.
GOOD-BYE!
FUNNY, ISN'T IT? HOW MUCH THINGS ON ASGARD ARE LIKE EARTH IN SOME WAYS... AND SO DIFFERENT IN OTHERS.
IT FEELS LIKE EARTH, BUT FROM OUT HERE, IT'S AN ISLAND, FLOATING IN A SEA OF STARS.
LIKE... IS IT AWESOME, OR WHAT? THINK ABOUT IT! WE'VE ACTUALLY BEEN IN ANOTHER DIMENSION... AND NOW WE'RE GOING HOME!
HOME, INDEED, SELFRIENDS. BUT THE ROUTE, UNFORTUNATELY WILL NOT BE DIRECT.
BATTLE STATIONS, GUYS. ACCORDIN' TO THE MAP, THE WHIRLPOOL TO THE DIMENSION OF THE MINDLESS ONES LIES STRAIGHT AHEAD.
MINDLESS ONES? WHAT... WHAT ARE THEY? WHAT DOES THAT MEAN?
AH DON'T KNOW, RAHNE, BUT ANY SECOND NOW, AH 'SPECT WE'LL FIND OUT!
AND, CAUGHT IN A WHIRLPOOL, TWISTING BEYOND TIME AND SPACE, THE NEW MUTANTS ARE SWEPT FROM SIGHT...

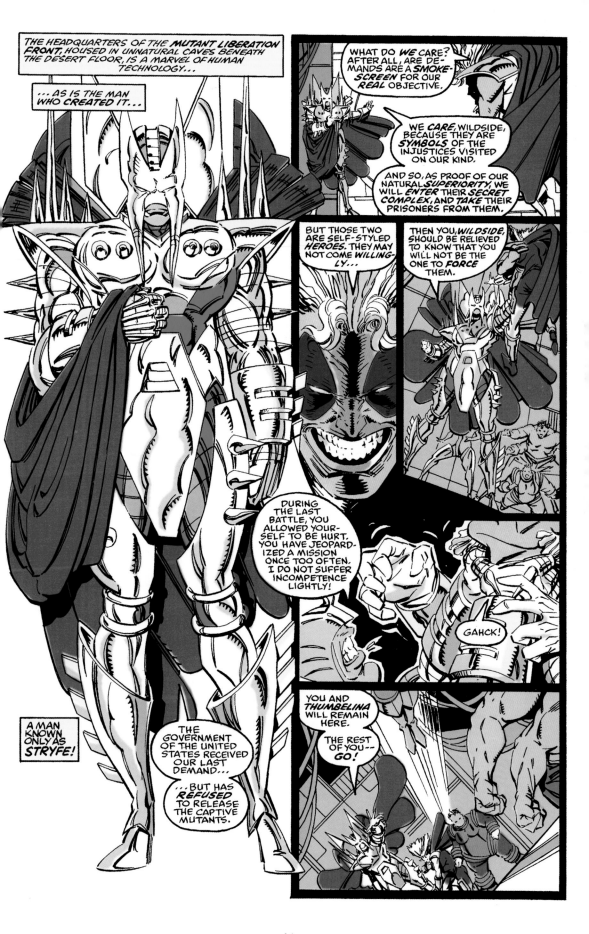

THE HEADQUARTERS OF THE *MUTANT LIBERATION FRONT*, HOUSED IN UNNATURAL CAVES BENEATH THE DESERT FLOOR, IS A MARVEL OF HUMAN TECHNOLOGY...

...AS IS THE MAN WHO *CREATED* IT...

WHAT DO *WE* CARE? AFTER ALL, ARE DE-MANDS ARE A *SMOKE-SCREEN* FOR OUR *REAL* OBJECTIVE.

WE *CARE*, WILDSIDE, BECAUSE THEY ARE *SYMBOLS* OF THE INJUSTICES VISITED ON OUR KIND.

AND SO, AS PROOF OF OUR NATURAL *SUPERIORITY*, WE WILL *ENTER* THEIR *SECRET COMPLEX*, AND *TAKE* THEIR PRISONERS FROM THEM.

BUT THOSE TWO ARE SELF-STYLED *HEROES*. THEY MAY NOT COME *WILLING-LY*...

THEN YOU, *WILDSIDE*, SHOULD BE RELIEVED TO KNOW THAT YOU WILL NOT BE THE ONE TO *FORCE* THEM.

DURING THE *LAST* BATTLE, YOU ALLOWED YOUR-SELF TO BE HURT. YOU HAVE JEOPARD-IZED A MISSION ONCE TOO OFTEN. I DO NOT SUFFER INCOMPETENCE LIGHTLY!

GAHCK!

A MAN KNOWN ONLY AS *STRYFE!*

THE GOVERNMENT OF THE UNITED STATES RECEIVED OUR LAST DEMAND...

...BUT HAS *REFUSED* TO RELEASE THE CAPTIVE MUTANTS.

YOU AND *THUMBELINA* WILL REMAIN HERE.

THE REST OF YOU-- *GO!*

41

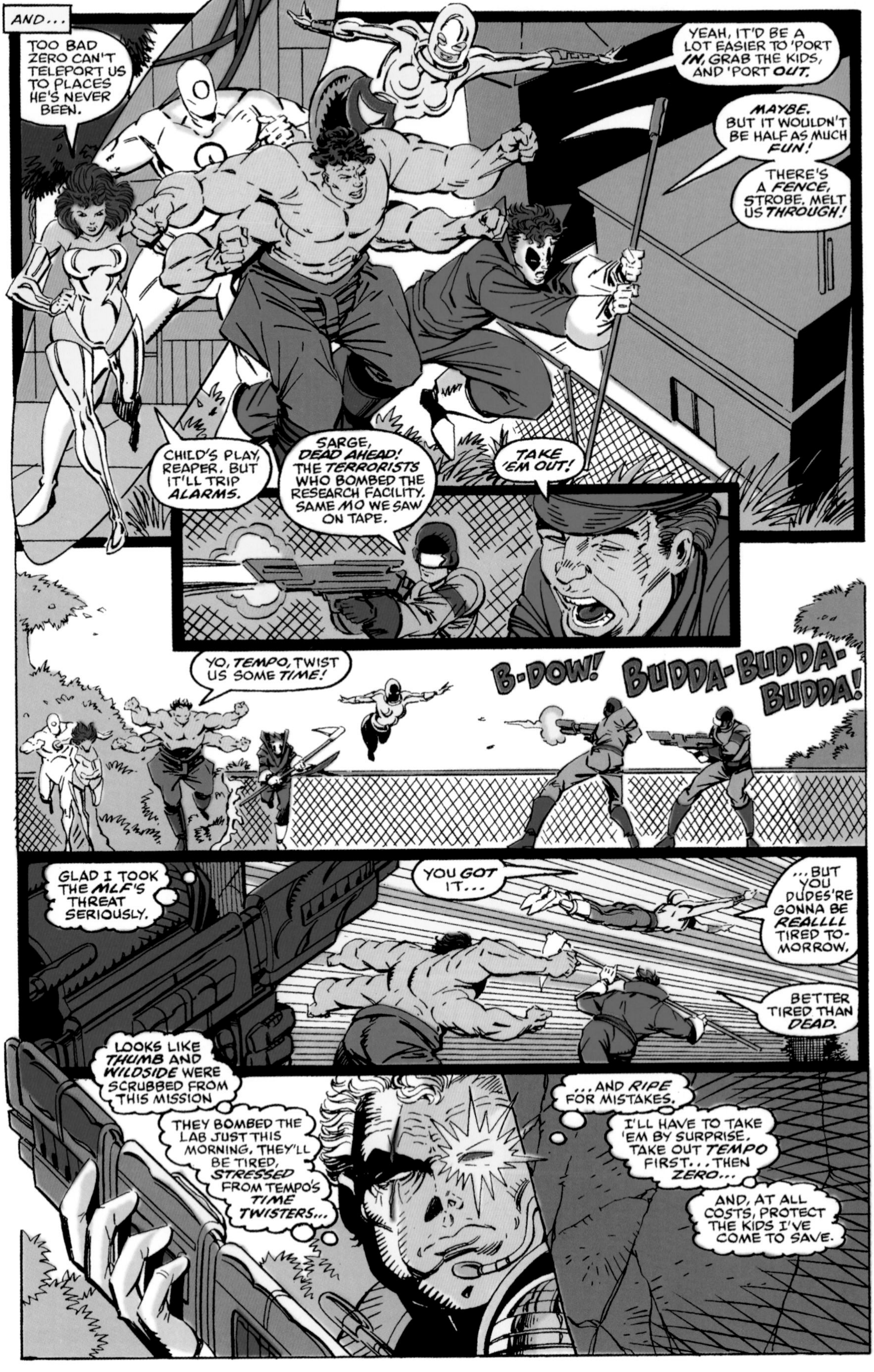
AND...
TOO BAD ZERO CAN'T TELEPORT US TO PLACES HE'S NEVER BEEN.
YEAH, IT'D BE A LOT EASIER TO 'PORT IN, GRAB THE KIDS, AND 'PORT OUT.
MAYBE. BUT IT WOULDN'T BE HALF AS MUCH FUN!
THERE'S A FENCE, STROBE. MELT US THROUGH!
CHILD'S PLAY, REAPER. BUT IT'LL TRIP ALARMS.
SARGE, DEAD AHEAD! THE TERRORISTS WHO BOMBED THE RESEARCH FACILITY. SAME MO WE SAW ON TAPE.
TAKE 'EM OUT!
YO, TEMPO, TWIST US SOME TIME!
B-DOW!
BUDDA-BUDDA-BUDDA!
GLAD I TOOK THE MLF'S THREAT SERIOUSLY.
YOU GOT IT...
...BUT YOU DUDES'RE GONNA BE REALLLL TIRED TO-MORROW.
BETTER TIRED THAN DEAD.
LOOKS LIKE THUMB AND WILDSIDE WERE SCRUBBED FROM THIS MISSION
THEY BOMBED THE LAB JUST THIS MORNING. THEY'LL BE TIRED, STRESSED FROM TEMPO'S TIME TWISTERS...
...AND RIPE FOR MISTAKES.
I'LL HAVE TO TAKE 'EM BY SURPRISE. TAKE OUT TEMPO FIRST... THEN ZERO...
AND, AT ALL COSTS, PROTECT THE KIDS I'VE COME TO SAVE.

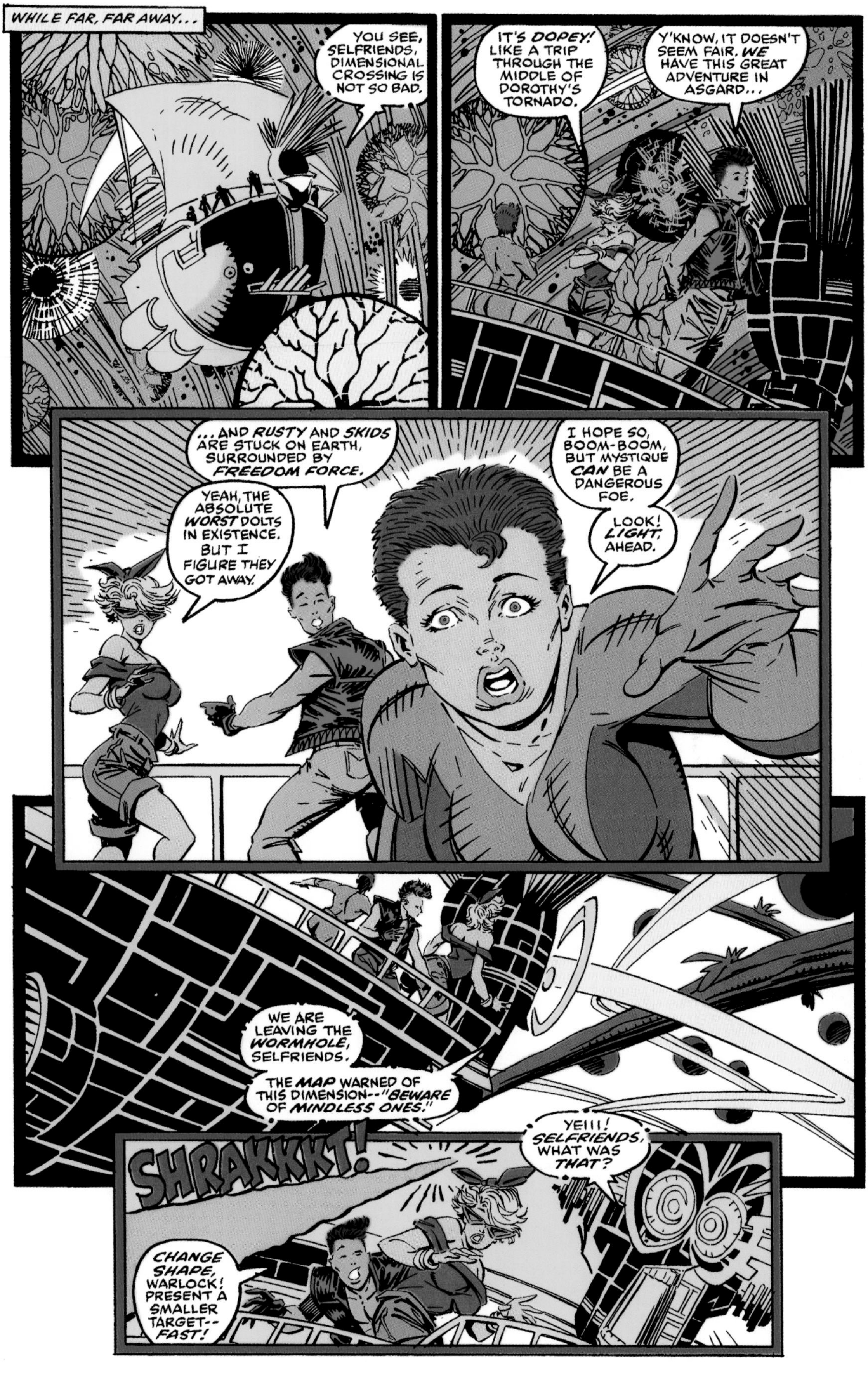
WHILE FAR, FAR AWAY...
YOU SEE, SELFRIENDS, DIMENSIONAL CROSSING IS NOT SO BAD.
IT'S DOPEY! LIKE A TRIP THROUGH THE MIDDLE OF DOROTHY'S TORNADO.
Y'KNOW, IT DOESN'T SEEM FAIR. WE HAVE THIS GREAT ADVENTURE IN ASGARD...
...AND RUSTY AND SKIDS ARE STUCK ON EARTH, SURROUNDED BY FREEDOM FORCE.
YEAH, THE ABSOLUTE WORST DOLTS IN EXISTENCE. BUT I FIGURE THEY GOT AWAY.
I HOPE SO, BOOM-BOOM, BUT MYSTIQUE CAN BE A DANGEROUS FOE.
LOOK! LIGHT, AHEAD.
WE ARE LEAVING THE WORMHOLE, SELFRIENDS.
THE MAP WARNED OF THIS DIMENSION--"BEWARE OF MINDLESS ONES."
SHRAKKKT!
YEIII! SELFRIENDS, WHAT WAS THAT?
CHANGE SHAPE, WARLOCK! PRESENT A SMALLER TARGET--FAST!

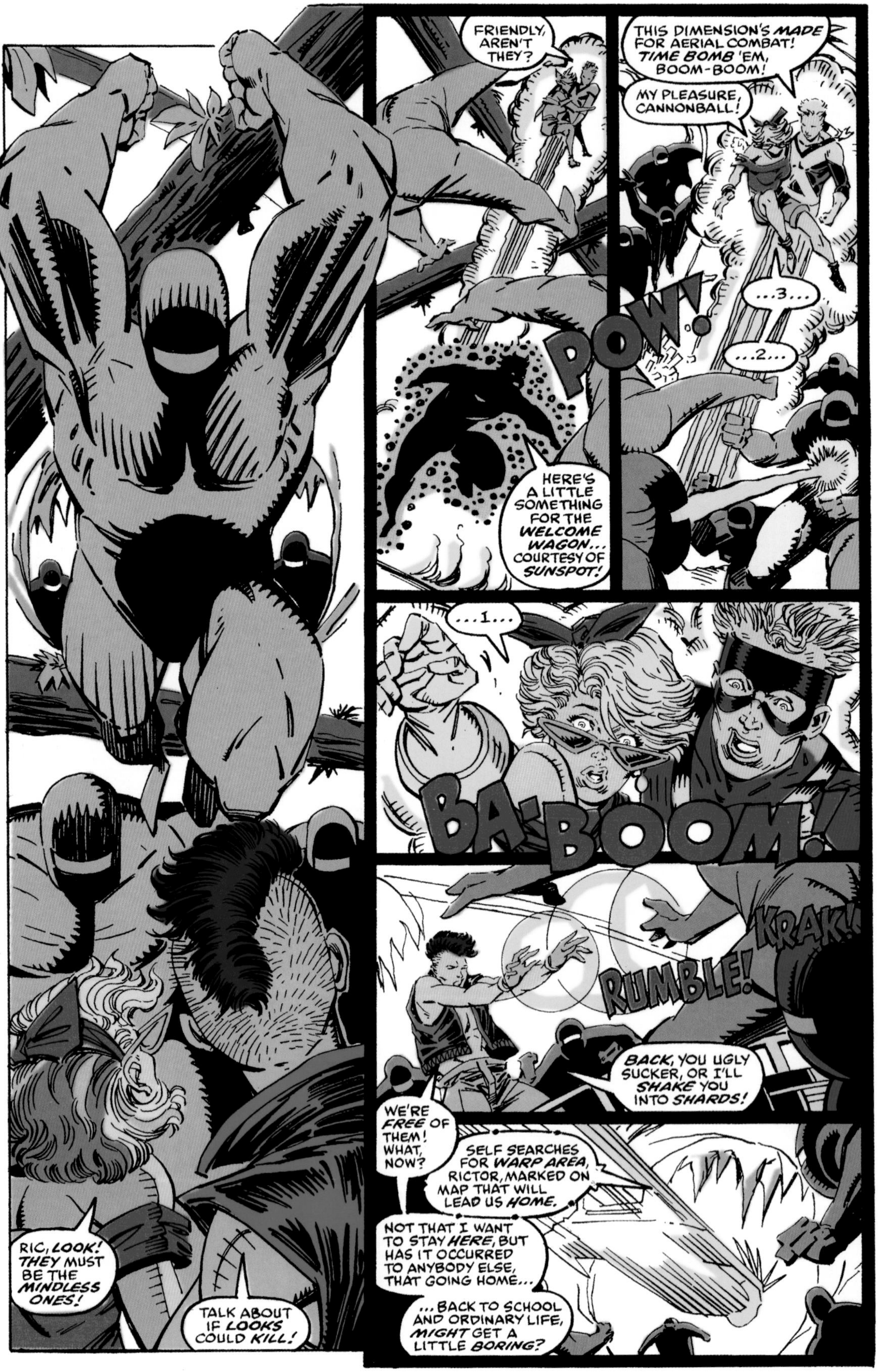

RIC, LOOK! THEY MUST BE THE MINDLESS ONES!
TALK ABOUT IF LOOKS COULD KILL!
FRIENDLY, AREN'T THEY?
POW!
HERE'S A LITTLE SOMETHING FOR THE WELCOME WAGON... COURTESY OF SUNSPOT!
THIS DIMENSION'S MADE FOR AERIAL COMBAT! TIME BOMB 'EM, BOOM-BOOM!
MY PLEASURE, CANNONBALL!
...3...
...2...
...1...
BA-BOOM!
KRAK!
RUMBLE!
BACK, YOU UGLY SUCKER, OR I'LL SHAKE YOU INTO SHARDS!
WE'RE FREE OF THEM! WHAT, NOW?
SELF SEARCHES FOR WARP AREA, RICTOR, MARKED ON MAP THAT WILL LEAD US HOME.
NOT THAT I WANT TO STAY HERE, BUT HAS IT OCCURRED TO ANYBODY ELSE, THAT GOING HOME...
...BACK TO SCHOOL AND ORDINARY LIFE, MIGHT GET A LITTLE BORING?

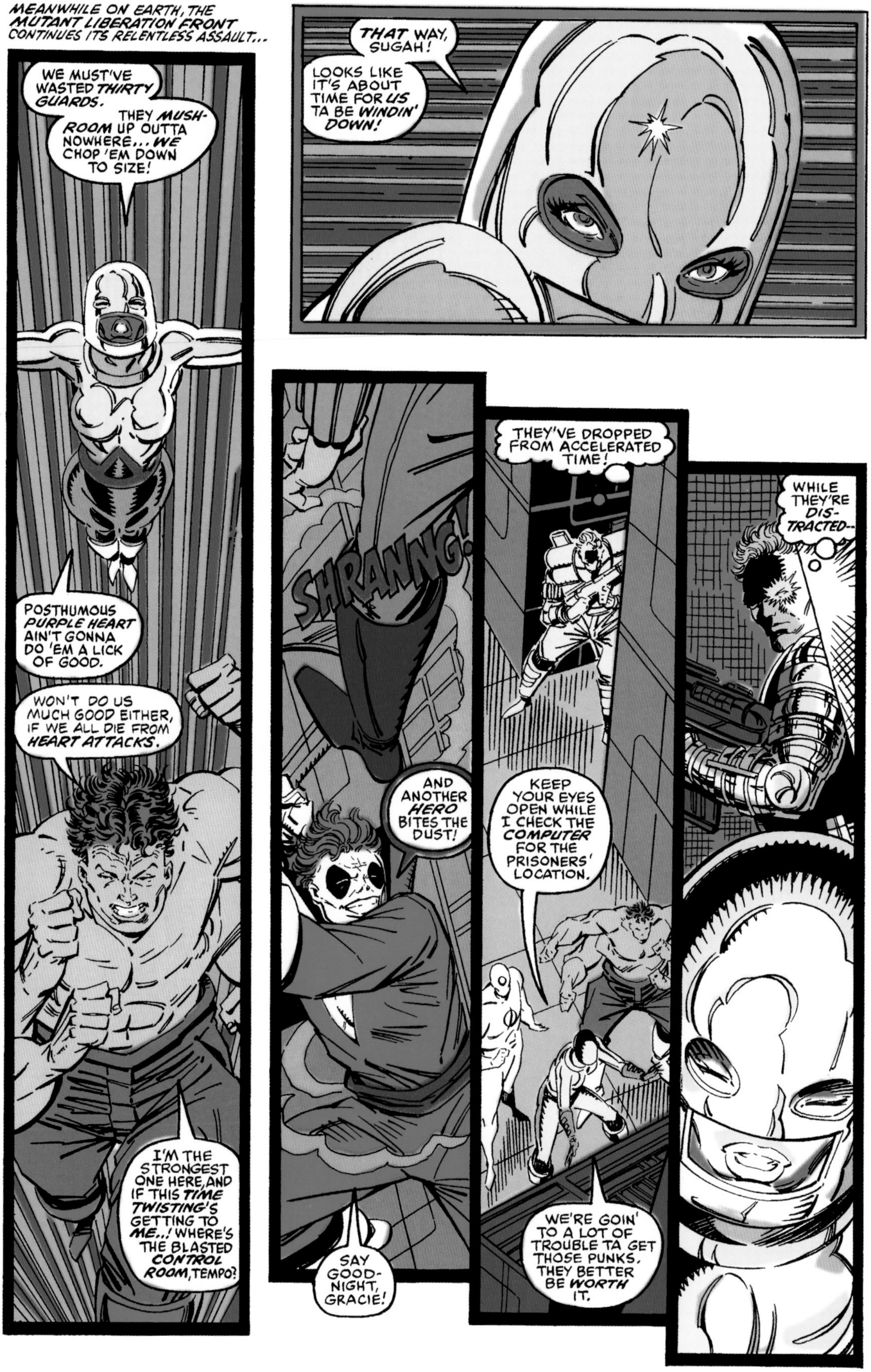
MEANWHILE ON EARTH, THE MUTANT LIBERATION FRONT CONTINUES ITS RELENTLESS ASSAULT...
WE MUST'VE WASTED THIRTY GUARDS.
THEY MUSHROOM UP OUTTA NOWHERE... WE CHOP 'EM DOWN TO SIZE!
POSTHUMOUS PURPLE HEART AIN'T GONNA DO 'EM A LICK OF GOOD.
WON'T DO US MUCH GOOD EITHER, IF WE ALL DIE FROM HEART ATTACKS.
I'M THE STRONGEST ONE HERE, AND IF THIS TIME TWISTING'S GETTING TO ME...! WHERE'S THE BLASTED CONTROL ROOM, TEMPO?
THAT WAY, SUGAH!
LOOKS LIKE IT'S ABOUT TIME FOR US TA BE WINDIN' DOWN!
SHRANNG!
AND ANOTHER HERO BITES THE DUST!
SAY GOOD-NIGHT, GRACIE!
THEY'VE DROPPED FROM ACCELERATED TIME!
KEEP YOUR EYES OPEN WHILE I CHECK THE COMPUTER FOR THE PRISONERS' LOCATION.
WHILE THEY'RE DISTRACTED--
WE'RE GOIN' TO A LOT OF TROUBLE TA GET THOSE PUNKS. THEY BETTER BE WORTH IT.

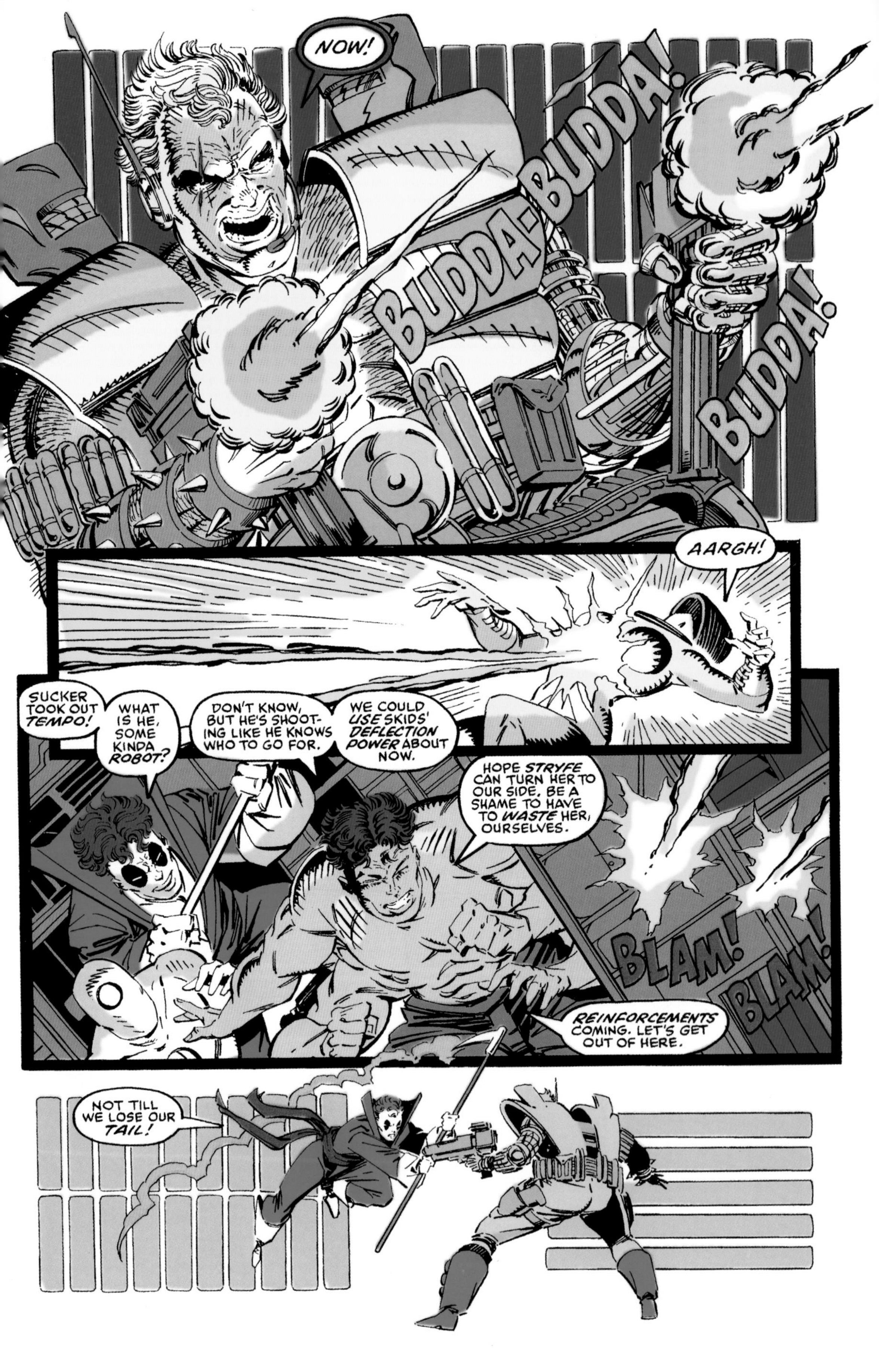
NOW!
BUDDA-BUDDA!
BUDDA!
AARGH!
SUCKER TOOK OUT TEMPO!
WHAT IS HE, SOME KINDA ROBOT?
DON'T KNOW, BUT HE'S SHOOTING LIKE HE KNOWS WHO TO GO FOR.
WE COULD USE SKIDS' DEFLECTION POWER ABOUT NOW.
HOPE STRYFE CAN TURN HER TO OUR SIDE. BE A SHAME TO HAVE TO WASTE HER, OURSELVES.
BLAM!
BLAM!
REINFORCEMENTS COMING. LET'S GET OUT OF HERE.
NOT TILL WE LOSE OUR TAIL!

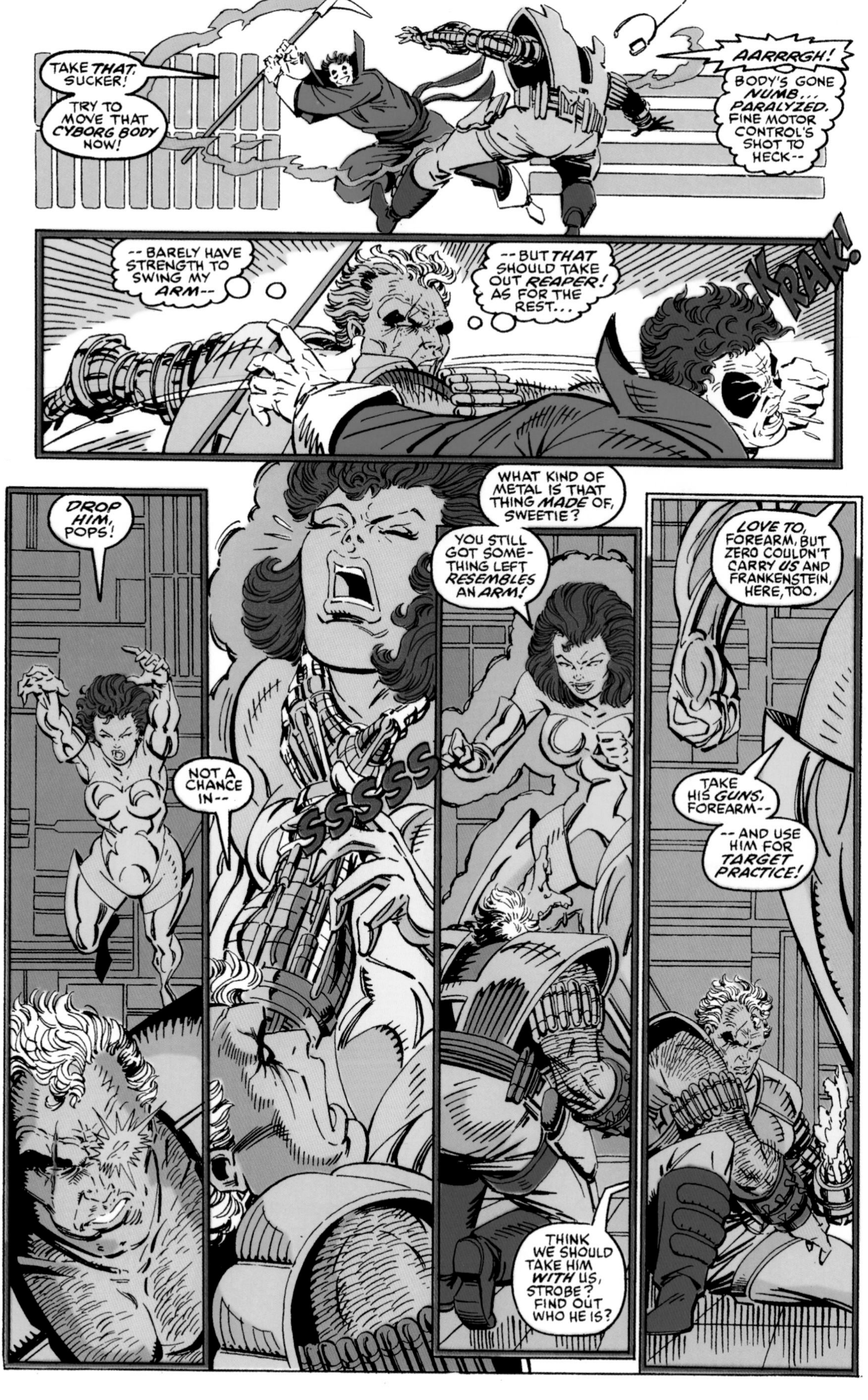

TAKE THAT, SUCKER!
TRY TO MOVE THAT CYBORG BODY NOW!
AARRRGH!
BODY'S GONE NUMB... PARALYZED. FINE MOTOR CONTROL'S SHOT TO HECK--
--BARELY HAVE STRENGTH TO SWING MY ARM--
--BUT THAT SHOULD TAKE OUT REAPER! AS FOR THE REST...
KRAK!
DROP HIM, POPS!
NOT A CHANCE IN--
SSSSSS
WHAT KIND OF METAL IS THAT THING MADE OF, SWEETIE?
YOU STILL GOT SOME-THING LEFT RESEMBLES AN ARM!
THINK WE SHOULD TAKE HIM WITH US, STROBE? FIND OUT WHO HE IS?
LOVE TO, FOREARM, BUT ZERO COULDN'T CARRY US AND FRANKENSTEIN, HERE, TOO.
TAKE HIS GUNS, FOREARM--
--AND USE HIM FOR TARGET PRACTICE!

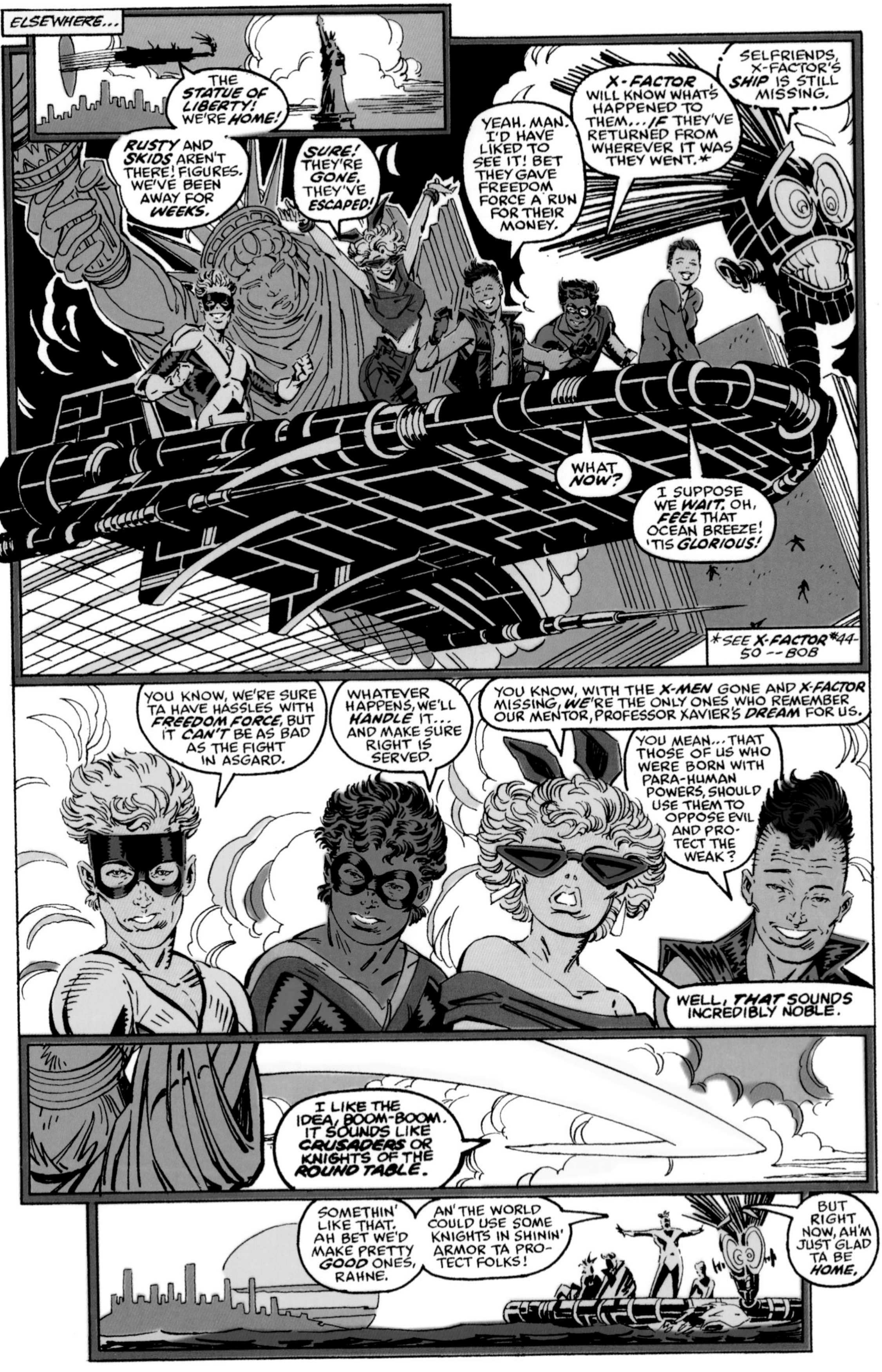
ELSEWHERE...
THE STATUE OF LIBERTY! WE'RE HOME!
RUSTY AND SKIDS AREN'T THERE! FIGURES. WE'VE BEEN AWAY FOR WEEKS.
SURE! THEY'RE GONE. THEY'VE ESCAPED!
YEAH. MAN. I'D HAVE LIKED TO SEE IT! BET THEY GAVE FREEDOM FORCE A RUN FOR THEIR MONEY.
X-FACTOR WILL KNOW WHAT'S HAPPENED TO THEM... IF THEY'VE RETURNED FROM WHEREVER IT WAS THEY WENT.*
SELFRIENDS, X-FACTOR'S SHIP IS STILL MISSING.
WHAT NOW?
I SUPPOSE WE WAIT. OH, FEEL THAT OCEAN BREEZE! 'TIS GLORIOUS!
*SEE X-FACTOR #44-50 -- BOB
YOU KNOW, WE'RE SURE TA HAVE HASSLES WITH FREEDOM FORCE, BUT IT CAN'T BE AS BAD AS THE FIGHT IN ASGARD.
WHATEVER HAPPENS, WE'LL HANDLE IT... AND MAKE SURE RIGHT IS SERVED.
YOU KNOW, WITH THE X-MEN GONE AND X-FACTOR MISSING, WE'RE THE ONLY ONES WHO REMEMBER OUR MENTOR, PROFESSOR XAVIER'S DREAM FOR US.
YOU MEAN... THAT THOSE OF US WHO WERE BORN WITH PARA-HUMAN POWERS, SHOULD USE THEM TO OPPOSE EVIL AND PROTECT THE WEAK?
WELL, THAT SOUNDS INCREDIBLY NOBLE.
I LIKE THE IDEA, BOOM-BOOM. IT SOUNDS LIKE CRUSADERS OR KNIGHTS OF THE ROUND TABLE.
SOMETHIN' LIKE THAT. AH BET WE'D MAKE PRETTY GOOD ONES, RAHNE.
AN' THE WORLD COULD USE SOME KNIGHTS IN SHININ' ARMOR TA PROTECT FOLKS!
BUT RIGHT NOW, AH'M JUST GLAD TA BE HOME.

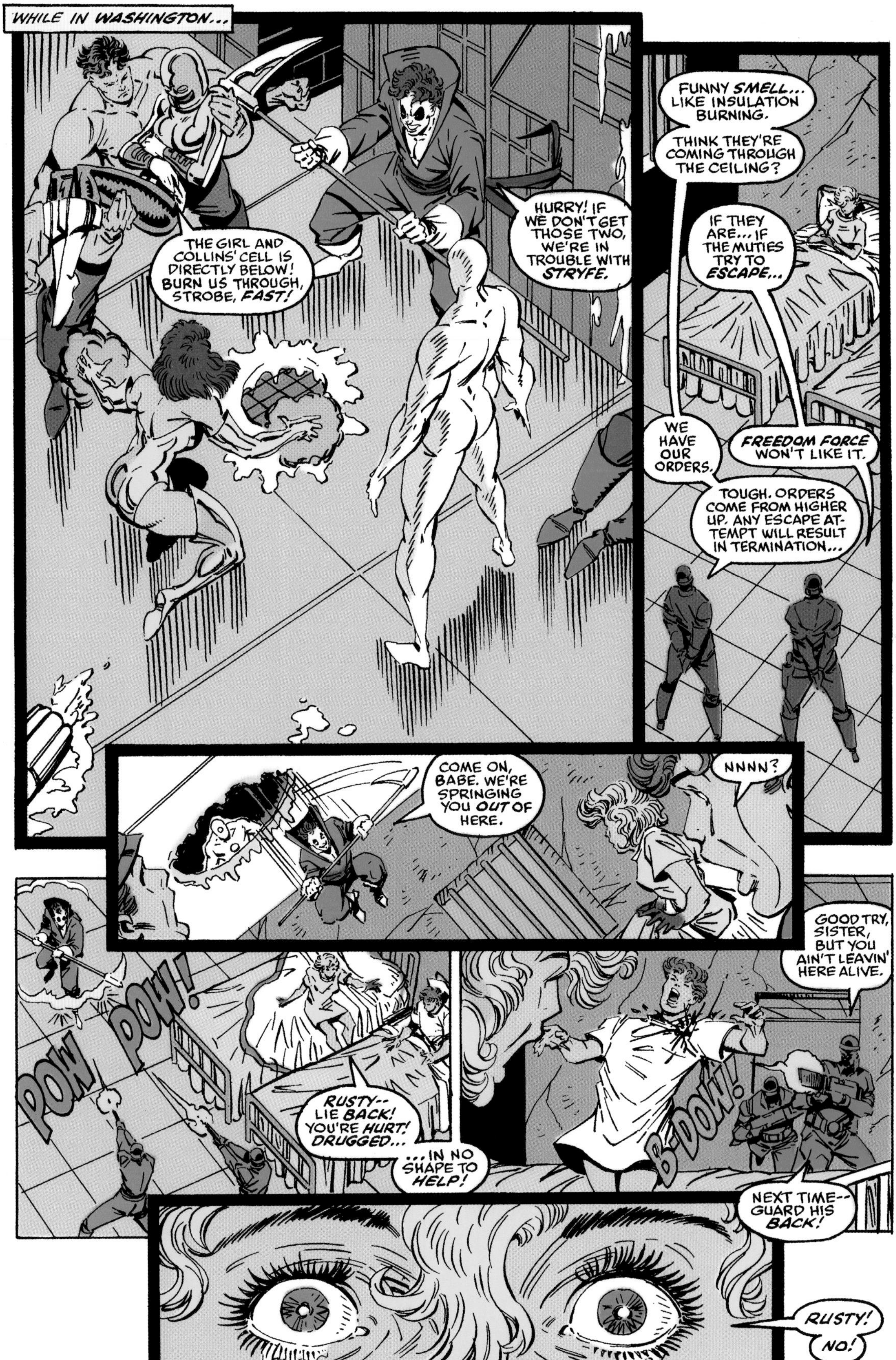
WHILE IN WASHINGTON...
THE GIRL AND COLLINS' CELL IS DIRECTLY BELOW! BURN US THROUGH, STROBE, FAST!
HURRY! IF WE DON'T GET THOSE TWO, WE'RE IN TROUBLE WITH STRYFE.
FUNNY SMELL... LIKE INSULATION BURNING.
THINK THEY'RE COMING THROUGH THE CEILING?
IF THEY ARE... IF THE MUTIES TRY TO ESCAPE...
WE HAVE OUR ORDERS.
FREEDOM FORCE WON'T LIKE IT.
TOUGH. ORDERS COME FROM HIGHER UP. ANY ESCAPE AT-TEMPT WILL RESULT IN TERMINATION...
COME ON, BABE. WE'RE SPRINGING YOU OUT OF HERE.
NNNN?
POW
POW
POW!
RUSTY-- LIE BACK! YOU'RE HURT! DRUGGED...
...IN NO SHAPE TO HELP!
GOOD TRY, SISTER, BUT YOU AIN'T LEAVIN' HERE ALIVE.
B-DOW!
NEXT TIME-- GUARD HIS BACK!
RUSTY!
NO!

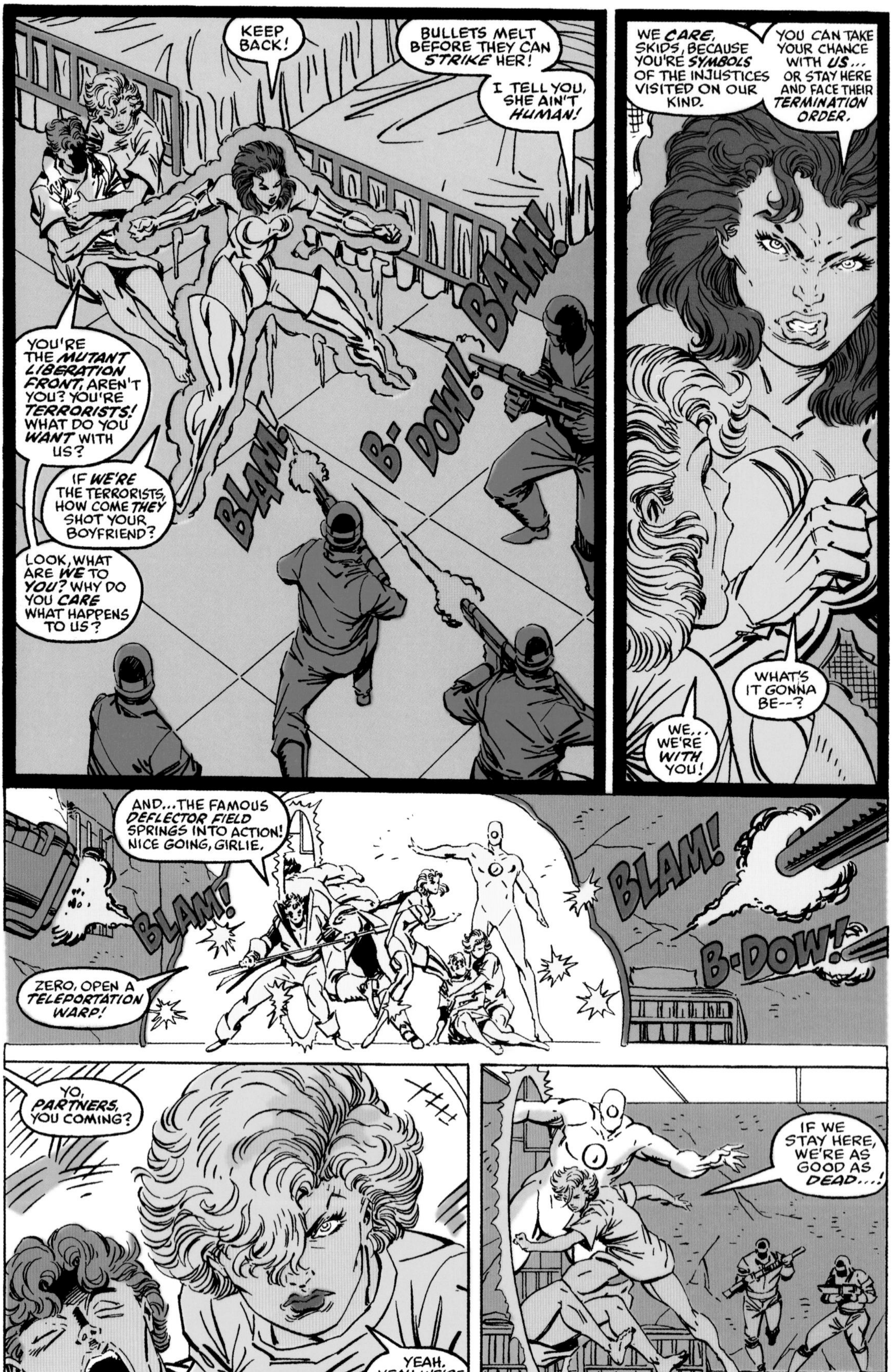
KEEP BACK!
BULLETS MELT BEFORE THEY CAN STRIKE HER!
I TELL YOU, SHE AIN'T HUMAN!
BAM!
B-DOW!
BLAM!
YOU'RE THE MUTANT LIBERATION FRONT, AREN'T YOU? YOU'RE TERRORISTS! WHAT DO YOU WANT WITH US?
IF WE'RE THE TERRORISTS, HOW COME THEY SHOT YOUR BOYFRIEND?
LOOK, WHAT ARE WE TO YOU? WHY DO YOU CARE WHAT HAPPENS TO US?
WE CARE, SKIDS, BECAUSE YOU'RE SYMBOLS OF THE INJUSTICES VISITED ON OUR KIND.
YOU CAN TAKE YOUR CHANCE WITH US... OR STAY HERE AND FACE THEIR TERMINATION ORDER.
WHAT'S IT GONNA BE--?
WE... WE'RE WITH YOU!
AND...THE FAMOUS DEFLECTOR FIELD SPRINGS INTO ACTION! NICE GOING, GIRLIE.
BLAM!
BLAM!
B-DOW!
ZERO, OPEN A TELEPORTATION WARP!
YO, PARTNERS, YOU COMING?
YEAH, YEAH, WE'RE COMING.
IF WE STAY HERE, WE'RE AS GOOD AS DEAD...!

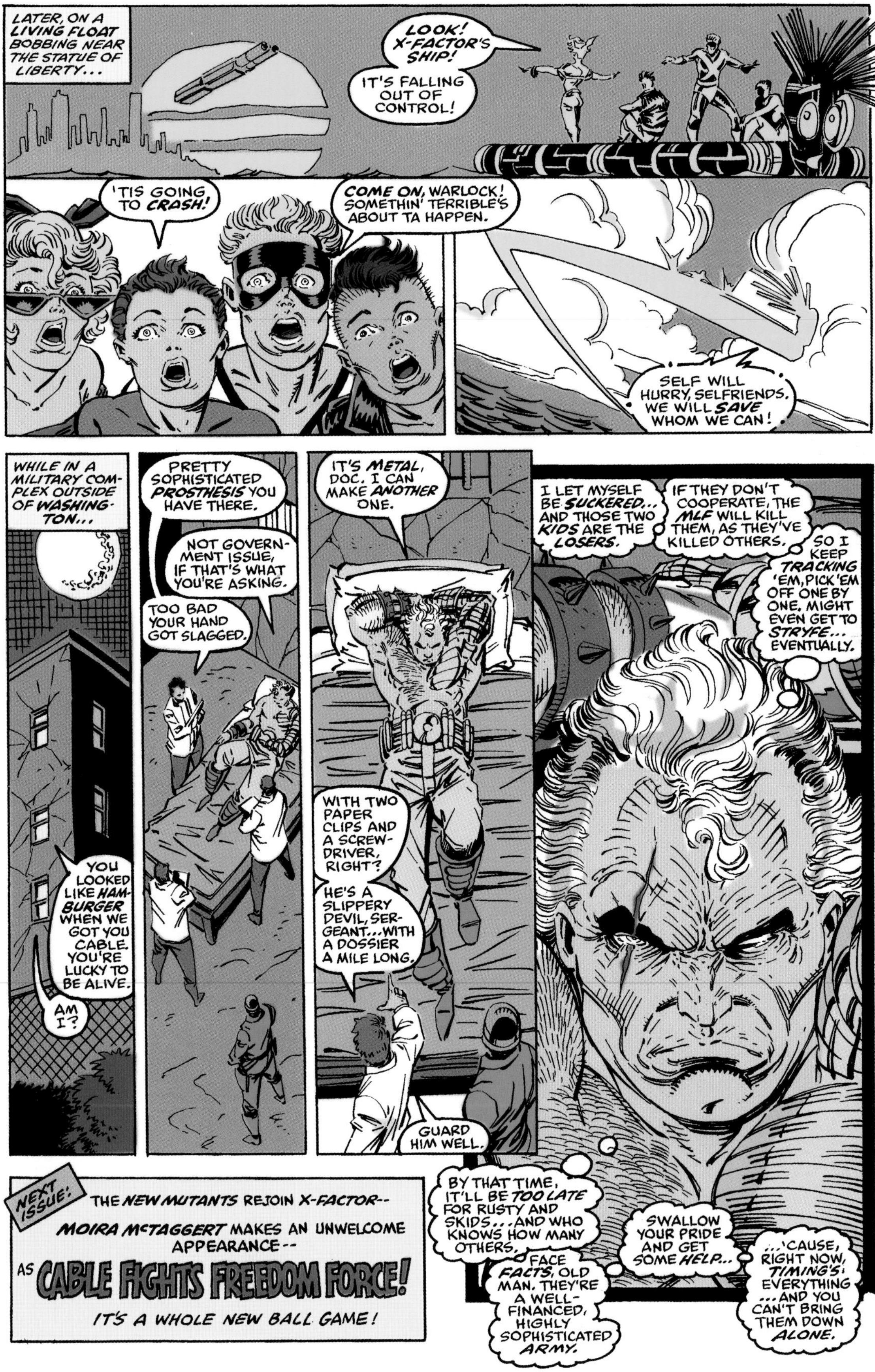
LATER, ON A LIVING FLOAT BOBBING NEAR THE STATUE OF LIBERTY...
LOOK! X-FACTOR'S SHIP!
IT'S FALLING OUT OF CONTROL!
'TIS GOING TO CRASH!
COME ON, WARLOCK! SOMETHIN' TERRIBLE'S ABOUT TA HAPPEN.
SELF WILL HURRY, SELFRIENDS. WE WILL SAVE WHOM WE CAN!
WHILE IN A MILITARY COMPLEX OUTSIDE OF WASHINGTON...
YOU LOOKED LIKE HAMBURGER WHEN WE GOT YOU CABLE. YOU'RE LUCKY TO BE ALIVE.
AM I?
PRETTY SOPHISTICATED PROSTHESIS YOU HAVE THERE.
NOT GOVERNMENT ISSUE, IF THAT'S WHAT YOU'RE ASKING.
TOO BAD YOUR HAND GOT SLAGGED.
IT'S METAL, DOC. I CAN MAKE ANOTHER ONE.
WITH TWO PAPER CLIPS AND A SCREWDRIVER, RIGHT?
HE'S A SLIPPERY DEVIL, SERGEANT...WITH A DOSSIER A MILE LONG.
GUARD HIM WELL.
I LET MYSELF BE SUCKERED... AND THOSE TWO KIDS ARE THE LOSERS.
IF THEY DON'T COOPERATE, THE MLF WILL KILL THEM, AS THEY'VE KILLED OTHERS.
SO I KEEP TRACKING 'EM, PICK 'EM OFF ONE BY ONE, MIGHT EVEN GET TO STRYFE... EVENTUALLY.
BY THAT TIME, IT'LL BE TOO LATE FOR RUSTY AND SKIDS... AND WHO KNOWS HOW MANY OTHERS.
FACE FACTS, OLD MAN. THEY'RE A WELL-FINANCED, HIGHLY SOPHISTICATED ARMY.
SWALLOW YOUR PRIDE AND GET SOME HELP...
...'CAUSE, RIGHT NOW, TIMING'S EVERYTHING ...AND YOU CAN'T BRING THEM DOWN ALONE.
NEXT ISSUE:
THE NEW MUTANTS REJOIN X-FACTOR--
MOIRA McTAGGERT MAKES AN UNWELCOME APPEARANCE--
AS CABLE FIGHTS FREEDOM FORCE!
IT'S A WHOLE NEW BALL GAME!

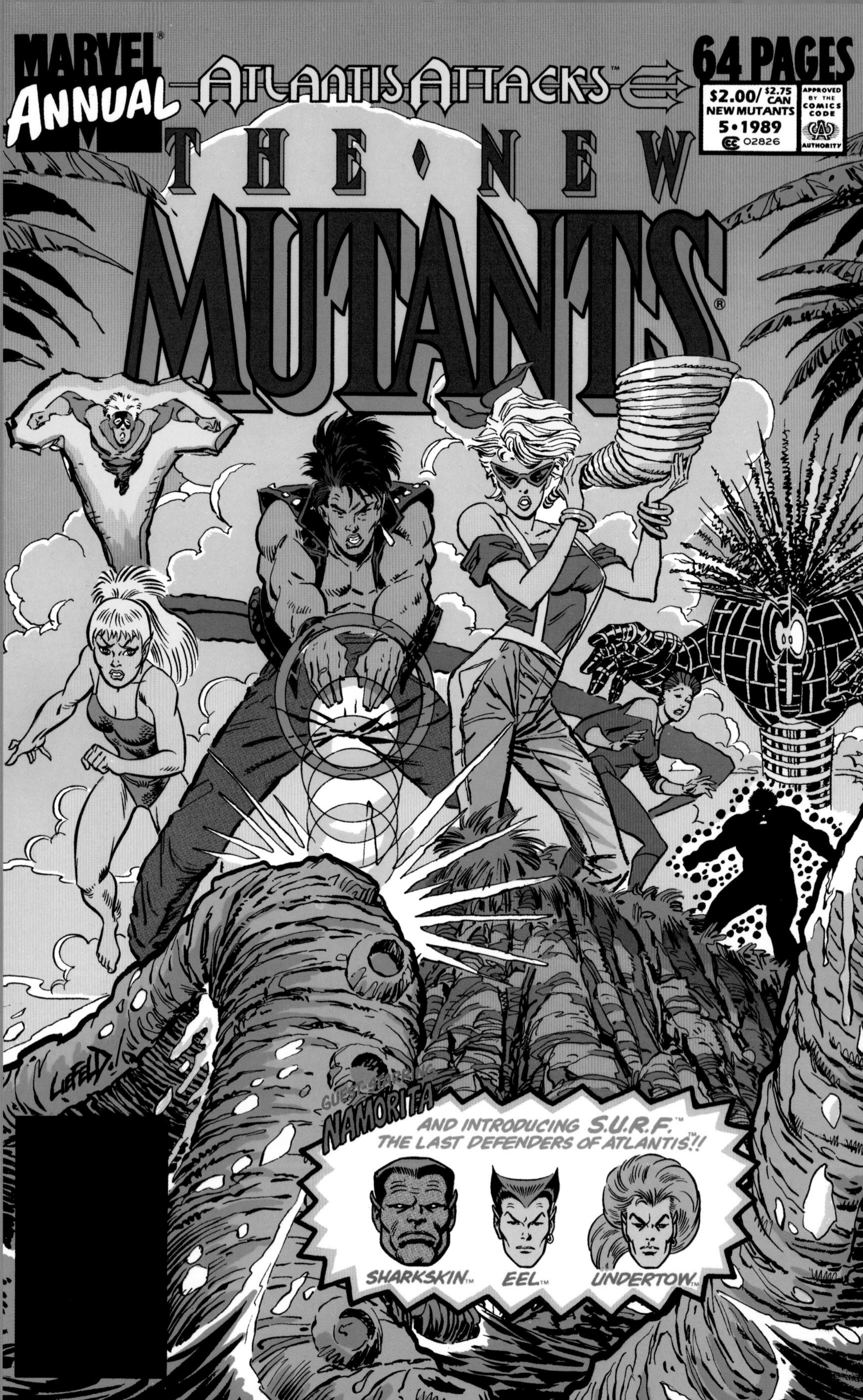
MARVEL®
ANNUAL
ATLANTIS ATTACKS™
64 PAGES
$2.00/ $2.75 CAN
NEW MUTANTS
5•1989
02826
APPROVED BY THE COMICS CODE AUTHORITY
THE NEW MUTANTS®
LIEFELD
NAMORITA
AND INTRODUCING S.U.R.F.™
THE LAST DEFENDERS OF ATLANTIS!!
SHARKSKIN™
EEL™
UNDERTOW™

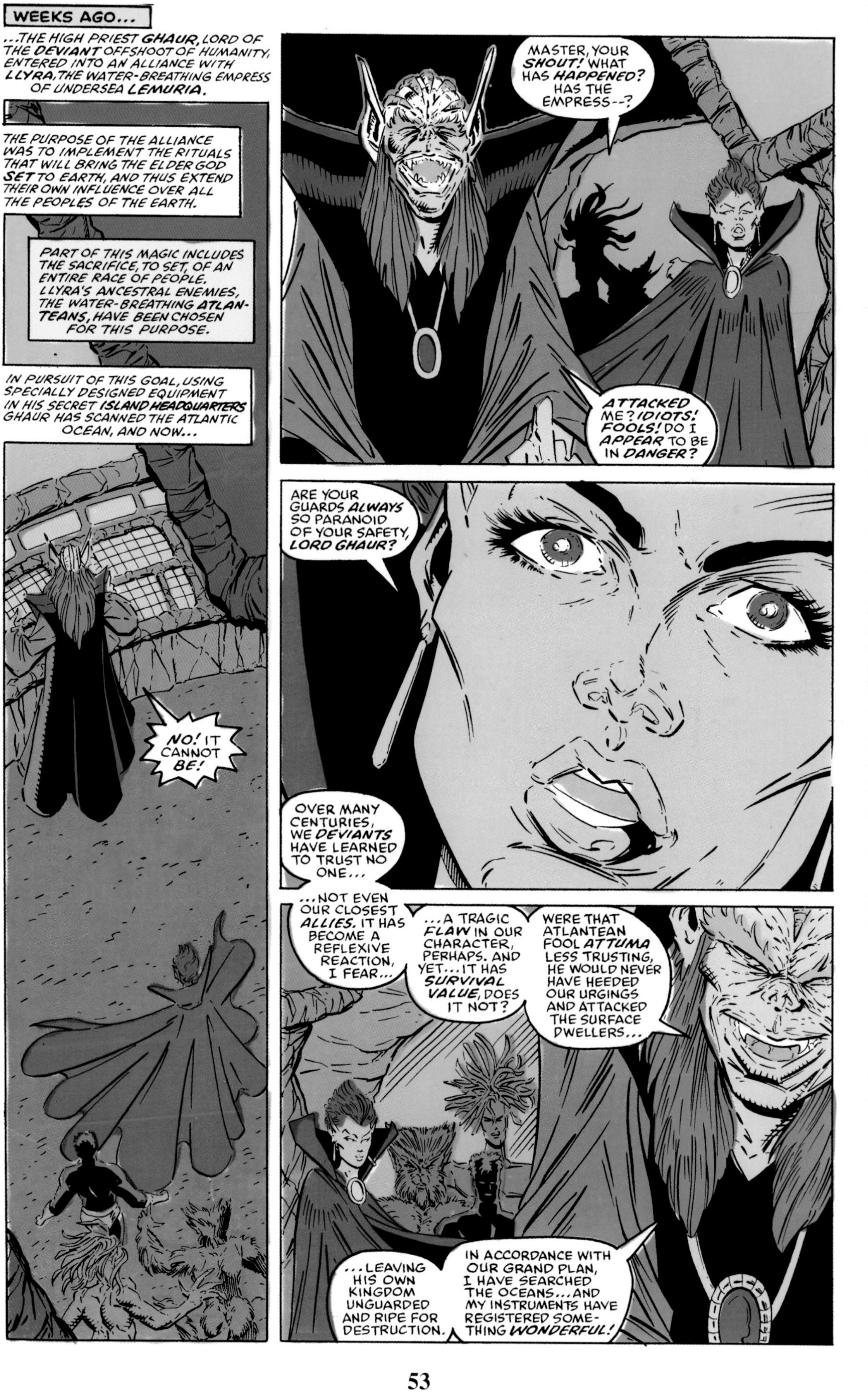
WEEKS AGO...
...THE HIGH PRIEST GHAUR, LORD OF THE DEVIANT OFFSHOOT OF HUMANITY, ENTERED INTO AN ALLIANCE WITH LLYRA, THE WATER-BREATHING EMPRESS OF UNDERSEA LEMURIA.
THE PURPOSE OF THE ALLIANCE WAS TO IMPLEMENT THE RITUALS THAT WILL BRING THE ELDER GOD SET TO EARTH, AND THUS EXTEND THEIR OWN INFLUENCE OVER ALL THE PEOPLES OF THE EARTH.
PART OF THIS MAGIC INCLUDES THE SACRIFICE, TO SET, OF AN ENTIRE RACE OF PEOPLE. LLYRA'S ANCESTRAL ENEMIES, THE WATER-BREATHING ATLANTEANS, HAVE BEEN CHOSEN FOR THIS PURPOSE.
IN PURSUIT OF THIS GOAL, USING SPECIALLY DESIGNED EQUIPMENT IN HIS SECRET ISLAND HEADQUARTERS GHAUR HAS SCANNED THE ATLANTIC OCEAN, AND NOW...
NO! IT CANNOT BE!
MASTER, YOUR SHOUT! WHAT HAS HAPPENED? HAS THE EMPRESS--?
ATTACKED ME? IDIOTS! FOOLS! DO I APPEAR TO BE IN DANGER?
ARE YOUR GUARDS ALWAYS SO PARANOID OF YOUR SAFETY, LORD GHAUR?
OVER MANY CENTURIES, WE DEVIANTS HAVE LEARNED TO TRUST NO ONE...
...NOT EVEN OUR CLOSEST ALLIES. IT HAS BECOME A REFLEXIVE REACTION, I FEAR...
...A TRAGIC FLAW IN OUR CHARACTER, PERHAPS. AND YET... IT HAS SURVIVAL VALUE, DOES IT NOT?
WERE THAT ATLANTEAN FOOL ATTUMA LESS TRUSTING, HE WOULD NEVER HAVE HEEDED OUR URGINGS AND ATTACKED THE SURFACE DWELLERS...
...LEAVING HIS OWN KINGDOM UNGUARDED AND RIPE FOR DESTRUCTION.
IN ACCORDANCE WITH OUR GRAND PLAN, I HAVE SEARCHED THE OCEANS... AND MY INSTRUMENTS HAVE REGISTERED SOMETHING WONDERFUL!

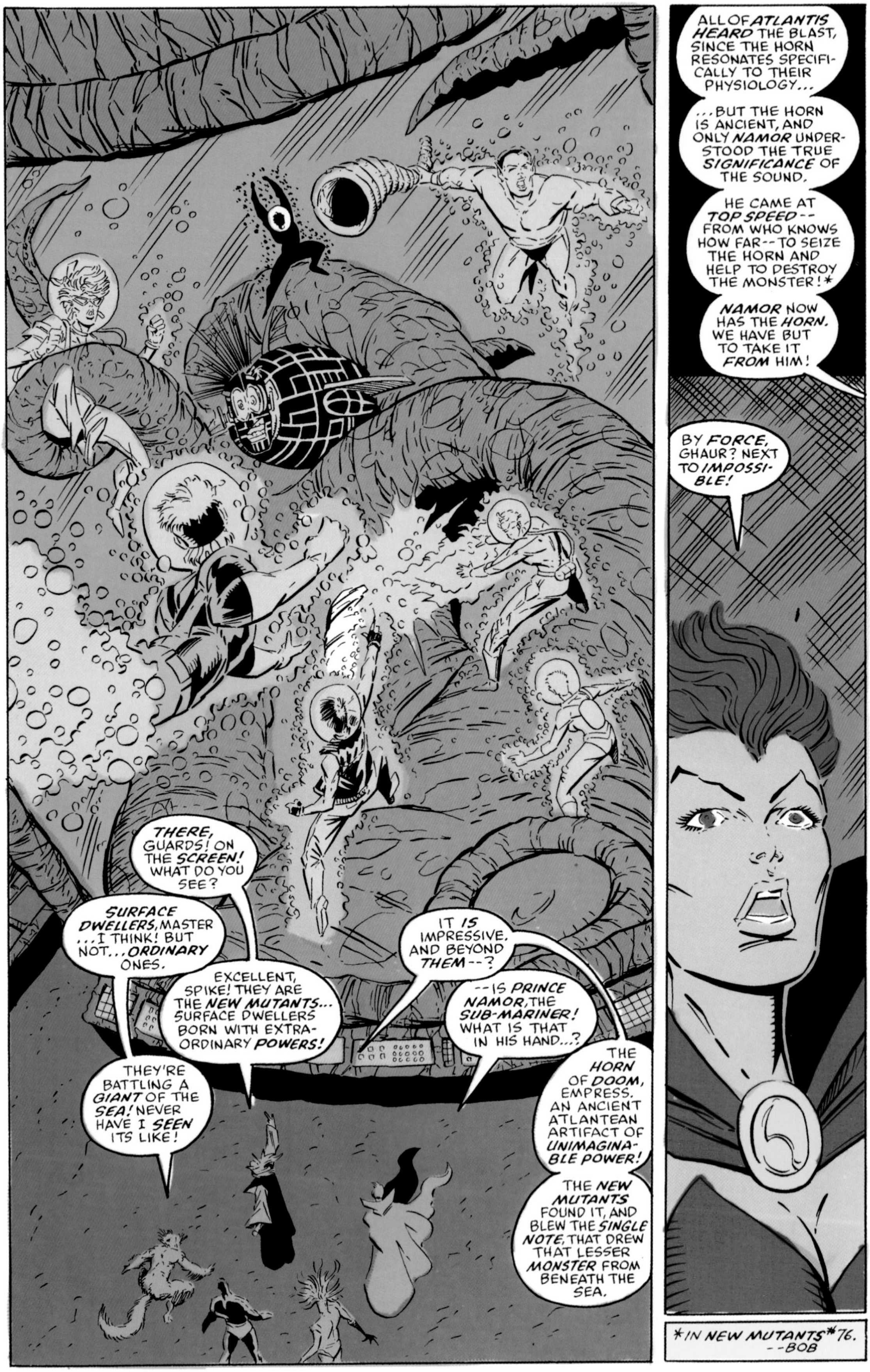
THERE, GUARDS! ON THE SCREEN! WHAT DO YOU SEE?
SURFACE DWELLERS, MASTER ...I THINK! BUT NOT... ORDINARY ONES.
EXCELLENT, SPIKE! THEY ARE THE NEW MUTANTS... SURFACE DWELLERS BORN WITH EXTRA-ORDINARY POWERS!
THEY'RE BATTLING A GIANT OF THE SEA! NEVER HAVE I SEEN ITS LIKE!
IT IS IMPRESSIVE, AND BEYOND THEM--?
--IS PRINCE NAMOR, THE SUB-MARINER! WHAT IS THAT IN HIS HAND...?
THE HORN OF DOOM, EMPRESS. AN ANCIENT ATLANTEAN ARTIFACT OF UNIMAGINA-BLE POWER!
THE NEW MUTANTS FOUND IT, AND BLEW THE SINGLE NOTE THAT DREW THAT LESSER MONSTER FROM BENEATH THE SEA.
ALL OF ATLANTIS HEARD THE BLAST, SINCE THE HORN RESONATES SPECIFI-CALLY TO THEIR PHYSIOLOGY...
...BUT THE HORN IS ANCIENT, AND ONLY NAMOR UNDER-STOOD THE TRUE SIGNIFICANCE OF THE SOUND.
HE CAME AT TOP SPEED--FROM WHO KNOWS HOW FAR--TO SEIZE THE HORN AND HELP TO DESTROY THE MONSTER!*
NAMOR NOW HAS THE HORN. WE HAVE BUT TO TAKE IT FROM HIM!
BY FORCE, GHAUR? NEXT TO IMPOSSI-BLE!
*IN NEW MUTANTS #76. --BOB

NOR DO WE WANT NAMOR TO BECOME AWARE OF OUR *DESIGNS* UPON HIS PRECIOUS *ATLANTIS!*

HE'S *SMARTER* THAN THAT BUNGLER ATTUMA. AND *STRONG.* YOUR *DEVIANTS* WOULD BE NO MATCH FOR HIM.

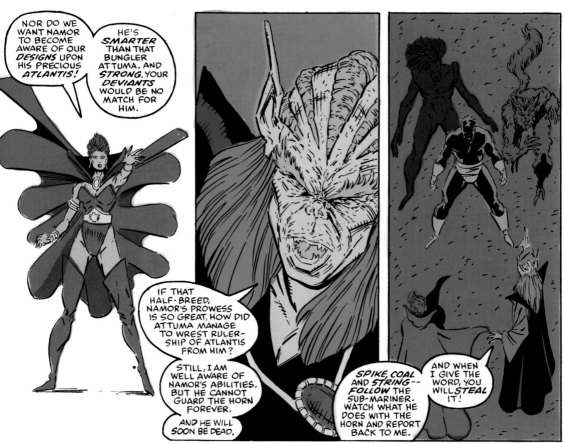

IF THAT HALF-BREED, NAMOR'S PROWESS IS SO GREAT, HOW DID ATTUMA MANAGE TO WREST RULER-SHIP OF ATLANTIS FROM HIM?

STILL, I AM WELL AWARE OF NAMOR'S ABILITIES. BUT HE CANNOT GUARD THE HORN FOREVER.

AND HE WILL SOON BE DEAD.

SPIKE, COAL AND STRING-- *FOLLOW* THE *SUB-MARINER.* WATCH WHAT HE DOES WITH THE HORN AND REPORT BACK TO ME.

AND WHEN I GIVE THE WORD, YOU WILL *STEAL* IT!

BUT...BUT *MASTER...* FROM THE *SUB-MARINER?!* PLEASE...!

SURELY *OTHERS* ARE BETTER EQUIPPED FOR DUTY *UNDERSEA!*

THE *LEMURIANS,* MASTER, ARE WATER BREATHERS. WHY NOT SEND *THEM,* INSTEAD?

I HAVE CHOSEN YOU THREE FOR A *REASON...* AND YOU WILL *OBEY!*

TAKE *OTHERS* WITH YOU IF YOU ARE AFRAID. BUT *YOU* MUST LEAD,...AND BE IN THE *FOREFRONT* OF ANY CONFRONTATION!

NOW *GO!* DO NOT RETURN WITHOUT *THE HORN!*

AND THEN--?

WHEN THE HORN IS MINE, WE WILL USE IT TO CALL UP ONE OF THE GREAT *SERPENTS* OF THE SEA. IT WILL DESTROY ATLANTIS...

...AND OUR *LORD SET* WILL BE ONE STEP CLOSER TO DOMINION OVER THE EARTH.

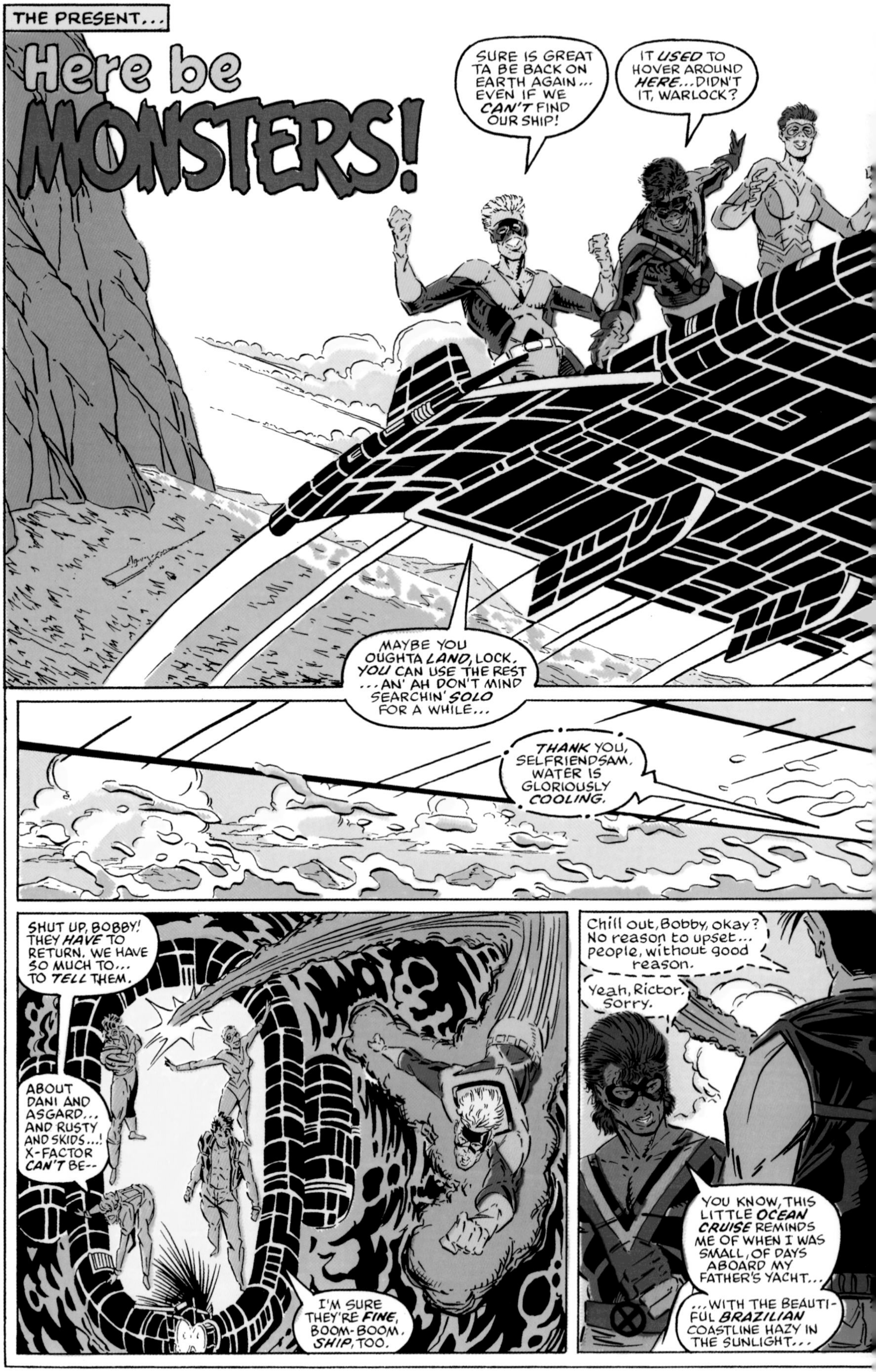

THE PRESENT...
Here be MONSTERS!
SURE IS GREAT TA BE BACK ON EARTH AGAIN... EVEN IF WE CAN'T FIND OUR SHIP!
IT USED TO HOVER AROUND HERE... DIDN'T IT, WARLOCK?
MAYBE YOU OUGHTA LAND, LOCK. YOU CAN USE THE REST ...AN' AH DON'T MIND SEARCHIN' SOLO FOR A WHILE...
THANK YOU, SELFRIENDSAM. WATER IS GLORIOUSLY COOLING.
SHUT UP, BOBBY! THEY HAVE TO RETURN. WE HAVE SO MUCH TO... TO TELL THEM.
ABOUT DANI AND ASGARD... AND RUSTY AND SKIDS...! X-FACTOR CAN'T BE--
I'M SURE THEY'RE FINE, BOOM-BOOM. SHIP, TOO.
Chill out, Bobby, okay? No reason to upset... people, without good reason.
Yeah, Rictor. Sorry.
YOU KNOW, THIS LITTLE OCEAN CRUISE REMINDS ME OF WHEN I WAS SMALL, OF DAYS ABOARD MY FATHER'S YACHT...
...WITH THE BEAUTIFUL BRAZILIAN COASTLINE HAZY IN THE SUNLIGHT...

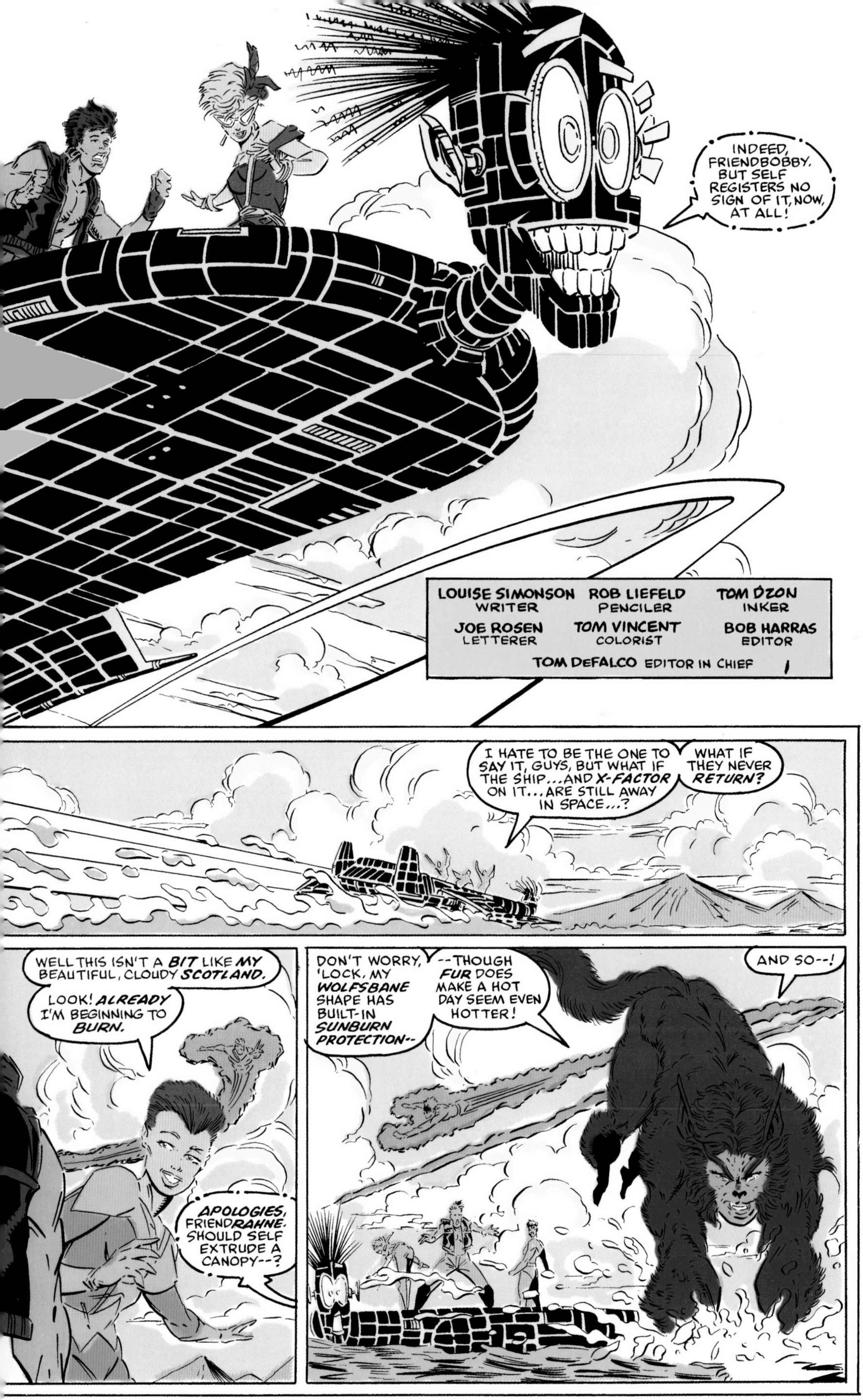
INDEED, FRIENDBOBBY. BUT SELF REGISTERS NO SIGN OF IT, NOW, AT ALL!
LOUISE SIMONSON WRITER ROB LIEFELD PENCILER TOM DZON INKER
JOE ROSEN LETTERER TOM VINCENT COLORIST BOB HARRAS EDITOR
TOM DeFALCO EDITOR IN CHIEF
I HATE TO BE THE ONE TO SAY IT, GUYS, BUT WHAT IF THE SHIP...AND X-FACTOR ON IT...ARE STILL AWAY IN SPACE...?
WHAT IF THEY NEVER RETURN?
WELL THIS ISN'T A BIT LIKE MY BEAUTIFUL, CLOUDY SCOTLAND.
LOOK! ALREADY I'M BEGINNING TO BURN.
APOLOGIES, FRIEND RAHNE. SHOULD SELF EXTRUDE A CANOPY--?
DON'T WORRY, 'LOCK, MY WOLFSBANE SHAPE HAS BUILT-IN SUNBURN PROTECTION--
--THOUGH FUR DOES MAKE A HOT DAY SEEM EVEN HOTTER!
AND SO--!

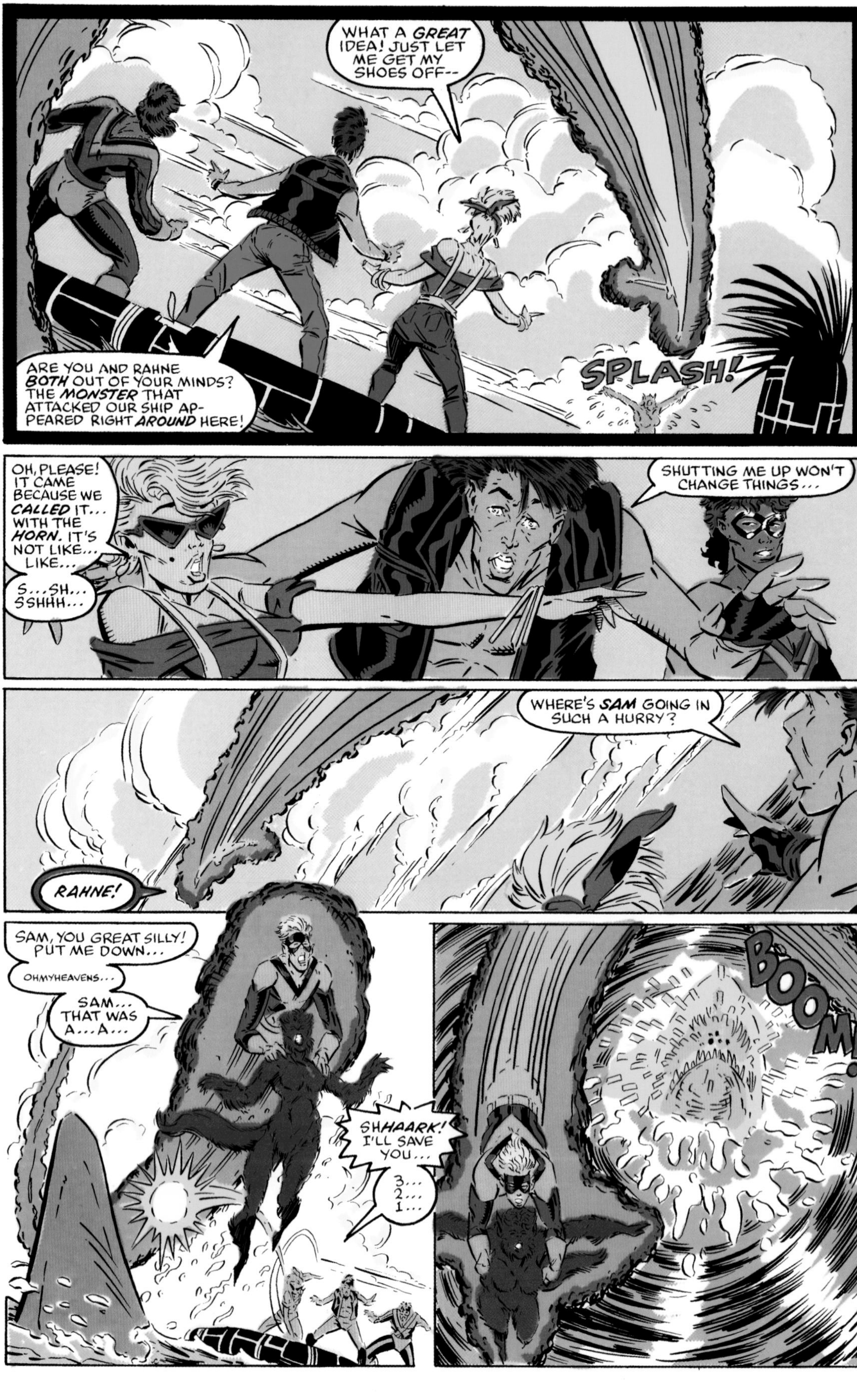
WHAT A GREAT IDEA! JUST LET ME GET MY SHOES OFF--
ARE YOU AND RAHNE BOTH OUT OF YOUR MINDS? THE MONSTER THAT ATTACKED OUR SHIP APPEARED RIGHT AROUND HERE!
SPLASH!
OH, PLEASE! IT CAME BECAUSE WE CALLED IT... WITH THE HORN. IT'S NOT LIKE... LIKE...
S...SH... SSHHH...
SHUTTING ME UP WON'T CHANGE THINGS...
WHERE'S SAM GOING IN SUCH A HURRY?
RAHNE!
SAM, YOU GREAT SILLY! PUT ME DOWN...
OHMYHEAVENS...
SAM... THAT WAS A...A...
SHHAARK! I'LL SAVE YOU...
3... 2... 1...
BOOOM!

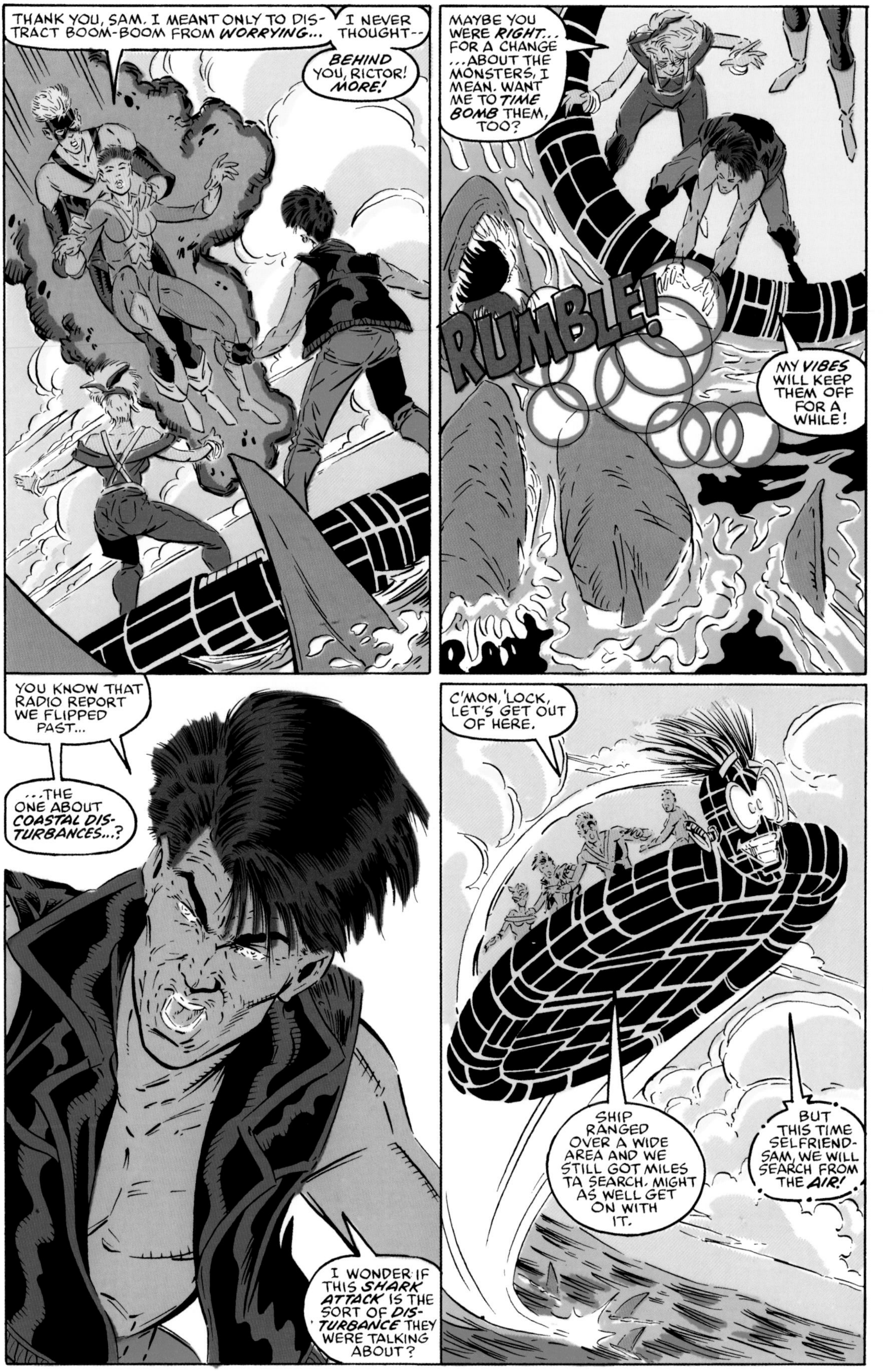
THANK YOU, SAM. I MEANT ONLY TO DISTRACT BOOM-BOOM FROM WORRYING...
I NEVER THOUGHT--
BEHIND YOU, RICTOR! MORE!
MAYBE YOU WERE RIGHT... FOR A CHANGE ...ABOUT THE MONSTERS, I MEAN. WANT ME TO TIME BOMB THEM, TOO?
RUMBLE!
MY VIBES WILL KEEP THEM OFF FOR A WHILE!
YOU KNOW THAT RADIO REPORT WE FLIPPED PAST...
...THE ONE ABOUT COASTAL DISTURBANCES...?
I WONDER IF THIS SHARK ATTACK IS THE SORT OF DISTURBANCE THEY WERE TALKING ABOUT?
C'MON, 'LOCK, LET'S GET OUT OF HERE.
SHIP RANGED OVER A WIDE AREA AND WE STILL GOT MILES TA SEARCH. MIGHT AS WELL GET ON WITH IT.
BUT THIS TIME SELFRIEND-SAM, WE WILL SEARCH FROM THE AIR!

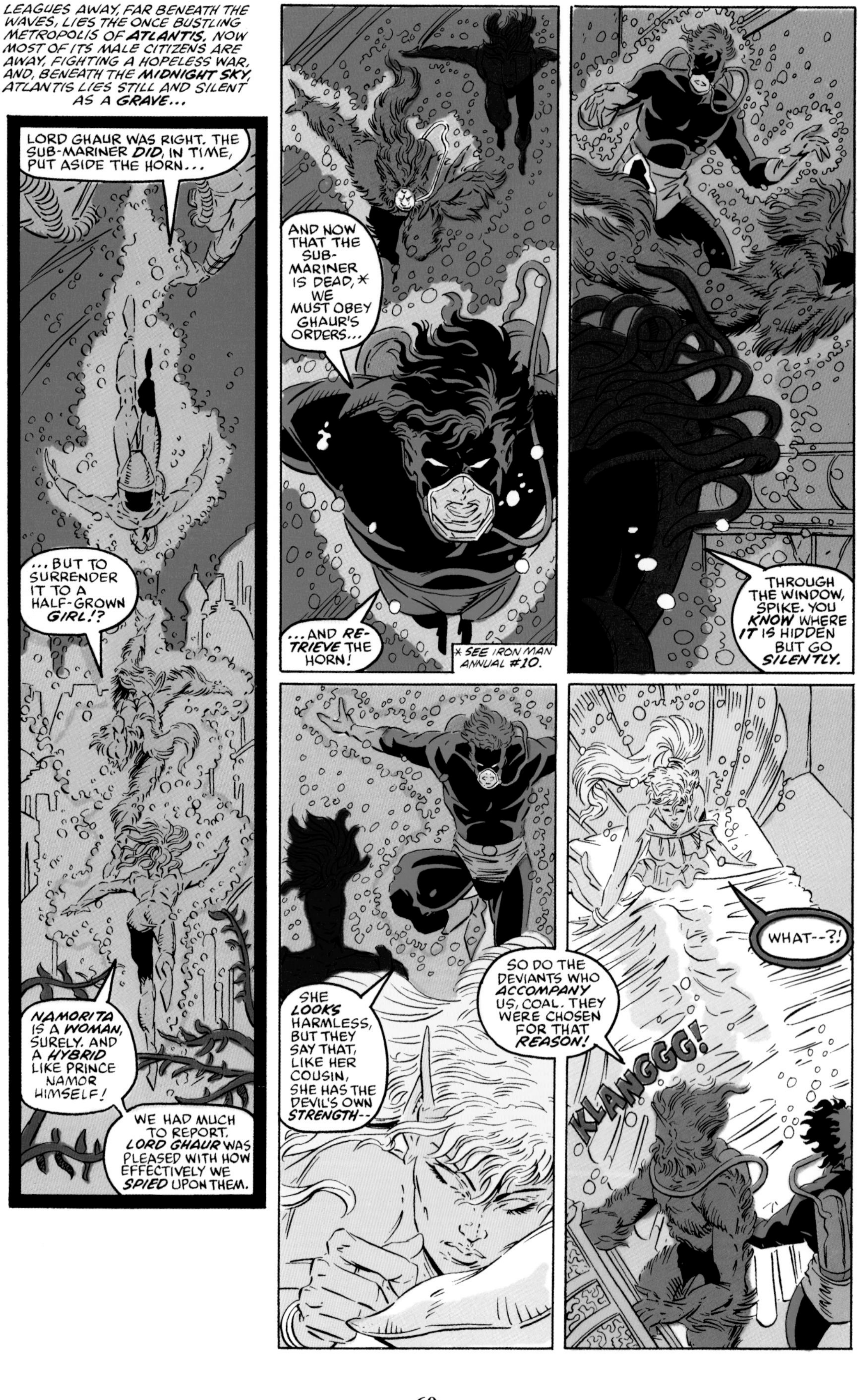
LEAGUES AWAY, FAR BENEATH THE WAVES, LIES THE ONCE BUSTLING METROPOLIS OF ATLANTIS. NOW MOST OF ITS MALE CITIZENS ARE AWAY, FIGHTING A HOPELESS WAR, AND, BENEATH THE MIDNIGHT SKY, ATLANTIS LIES STILL AND SILENT AS A GRAVE...
LORD GHAUR WAS RIGHT. THE SUB-MARINER DID, IN TIME, PUT ASIDE THE HORN...
...BUT TO SURRENDER IT TO A HALF-GROWN GIRL!?
NAMORITA IS A WOMAN, SURELY. AND A HYBRID LIKE PRINCE NAMOR HIMSELF!
WE HAD MUCH TO REPORT. LORD GHAUR WAS PLEASED WITH HOW EFFECTIVELY WE SPIED UPON THEM.
AND NOW THAT THE SUB-MARINER IS DEAD,* WE MUST OBEY GHAUR'S ORDERS...
...AND RETRIEVE THE HORN!
* SEE IRON MAN ANNUAL #10.
THROUGH THE WINDOW, SPIKE. YOU KNOW WHERE IT IS HIDDEN BUT GO SILENTLY.
SHE LOOKS HARMLESS, BUT THEY SAY THAT, LIKE HER COUSIN, SHE HAS THE DEVIL'S OWN STRENGTH--
SO DO THE DEVIANTS WHO ACCOMPANY US, COAL. THEY WERE CHOSEN FOR THAT REASON!
WHAT--?!
KLANGGG!

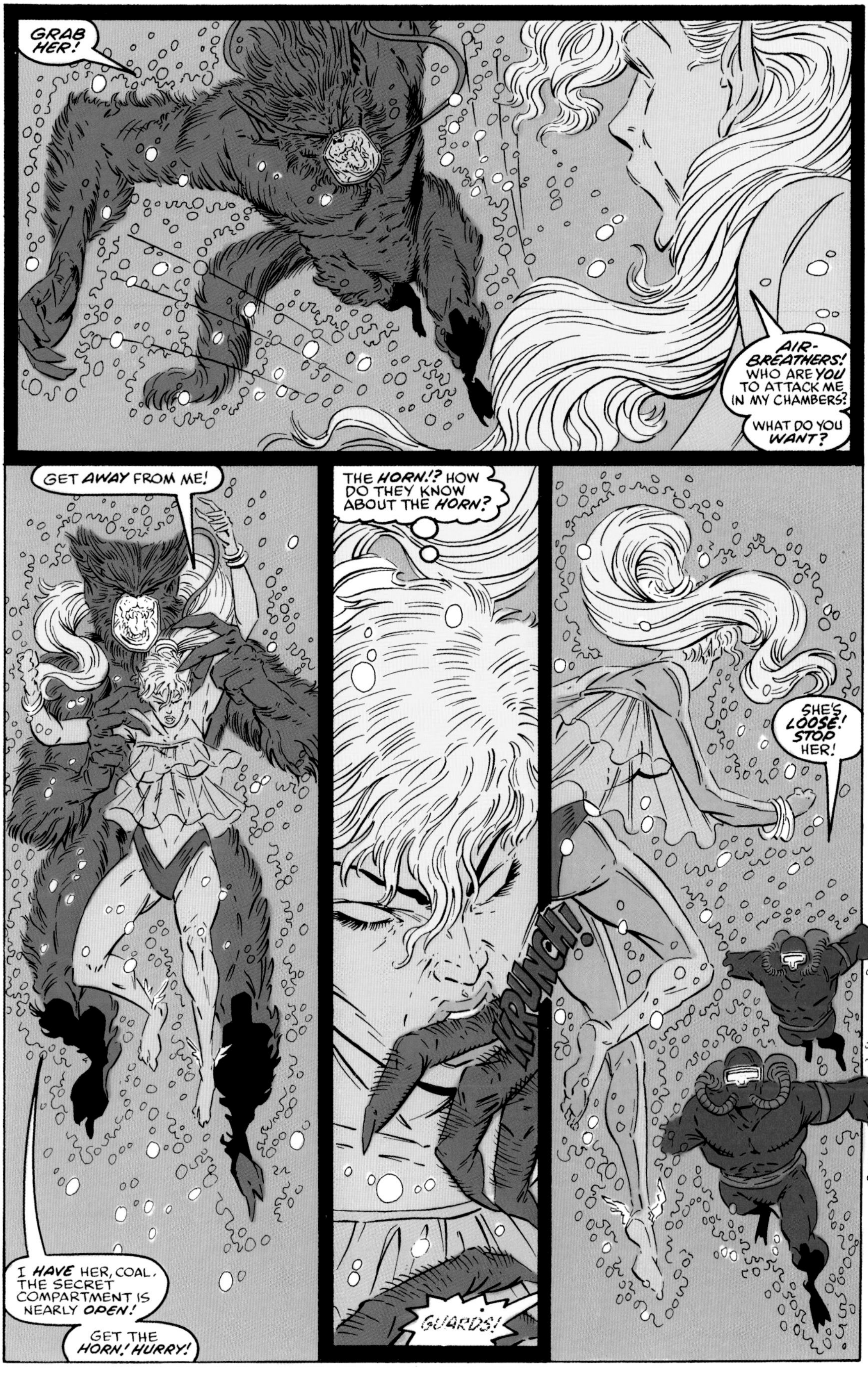
GRAB HER!
AIR-BREATHERS! WHO ARE YOU TO ATTACK ME IN MY CHAMBERS?
WHAT DO YOU WANT?
GET AWAY FROM ME!
I HAVE HER, COAL. THE SECRET COMPARTMENT IS NEARLY OPEN!
GET THE HORN! HURRY!
THE HORN!? HOW DO THEY KNOW ABOUT THE HORN?
KRUNCH!
GUARDS!
SHE'S LOOSE! STOP HER!

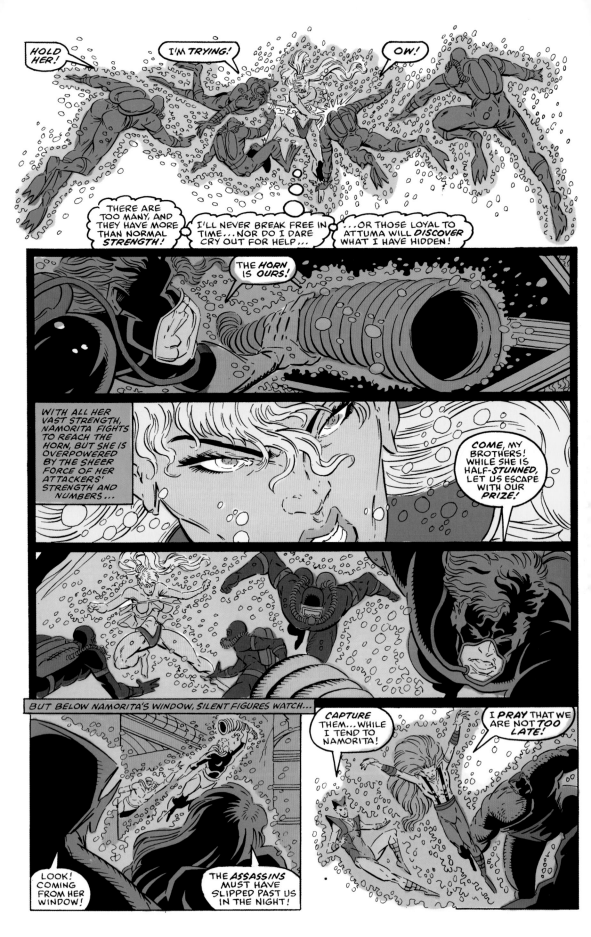

HOLD HER!

I'M TRYING!

OW!

THERE ARE TOO MANY, AND THEY HAVE MORE THAN NORMAL *STRENGTH!*

I'LL NEVER BREAK FREE IN TIME...NOR DO I DARE CRY OUT FOR HELP...

...OR THOSE LOYAL TO ATTUMA WILL *DISCOVER* WHAT I HAVE HIDDEN!

THE *HORN* IS OURS!

WITH ALL HER VAST STRENGTH, NAMORITA FIGHTS TO REACH THE HORN, BUT SHE IS OVERPOWERED BY THE SHEER FORCE OF HER ATTACKERS' STRENGTH AND NUMBERS...

COME, MY BROTHERS! WHILE SHE IS HALF-*STUNNED*, LET US ESCAPE WITH OUR *PRIZE!*

BUT BELOW NAMORITA'S WINDOW, SILENT FIGURES WATCH...

CAPTURE THEM...WHILE I TEND TO NAMORITA!

I *PRAY* THAT WE ARE NOT *TOO* LATE!

LOOK! COMING FROM HER WINDOW!

THE *ASSASSINS* MUST HAVE SLIPPED PAST US IN THE NIGHT!

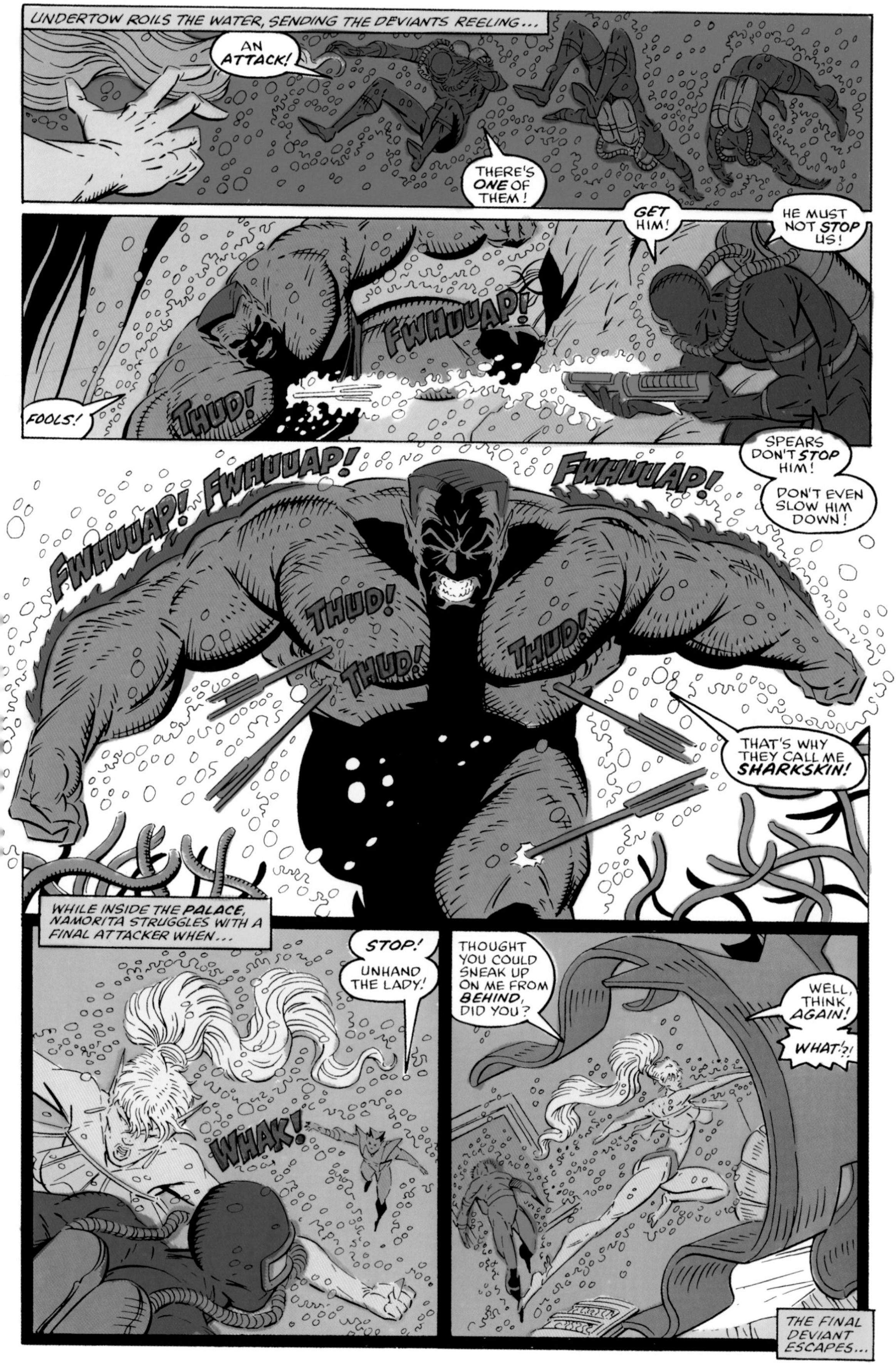

UNDERTOW ROILS THE WATER, SENDING THE DEVIANTS REELING...
AN ATTACK!
THERE'S ONE OF THEM!
GET HIM!
HE MUST NOT STOP US!
FWHUUAP!
THUD!
FOOLS!
SPEARS DON'T STOP HIM!
DON'T EVEN SLOW HIM DOWN!
FWHUUAP! FWHUUAP! FWHUUAP!
THUD! THUD! THUD!
THAT'S WHY THEY CALL ME SHARKSKIN!
WHILE INSIDE THE PALACE, NAMORITA STRUGGLES WITH A FINAL ATTACKER WHEN...
STOP!
UNHAND THE LADY!
WHAK!
THOUGHT YOU COULD SNEAK UP ON ME FROM BEHIND, DID YOU?
WELL, THINK AGAIN!
WHAT!?!
THE FINAL DEVIANT ESCAPES...

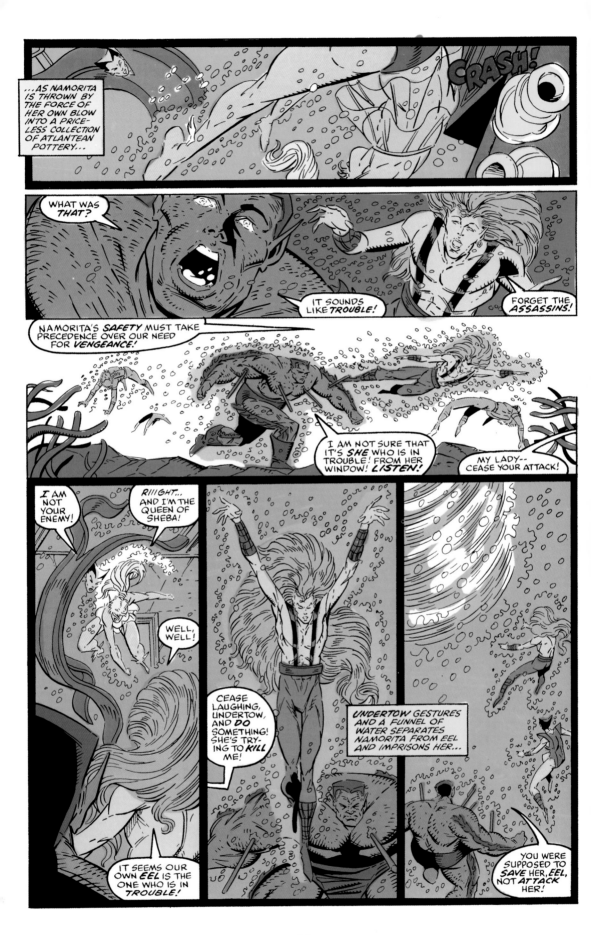

...AS NAMORITA IS THROWN BY THE FORCE OF HER OWN BLOW INTO A PRICELESS COLLECTION OF ATLANTEAN POTTERY...

CRASH!

WHAT WAS *THAT?*

IT SOUNDS LIKE *TROUBLE!*

FORGET THE *ASSASSINS!*

NAMORITA'S *SAFETY* MUST TAKE PRECEDENCE OVER OUR NEED FOR *VENGEANCE!*

I AM NOT SURE THAT IT'S *SHE* WHO IS IN TROUBLE! FROM HER WINDOW! *LISTEN!*

MY LADY-- CEASE YOUR ATTACK!

I AM NOT YOUR ENEMY!

RIIIGHT... AND I'M THE QUEEN OF SHEBA!

WELL, WELL!

IT SEEMS OUR OWN *EEL* IS THE ONE WHO IS IN *TROUBLE!*

CEASE LAUGHING, UNDERTOW, AND *DO* SOMETHING! SHE'S TRYING TO *KILL* ME!

UNDERTOW GESTURES AND A FUNNEL OF WATER SEPARATES NAMORITA FROM EEL AND IMPRISONS HER...

YOU WERE SUPPOSED TO *SAVE* HER, *EEL,* NOT *ATTACK* HER!

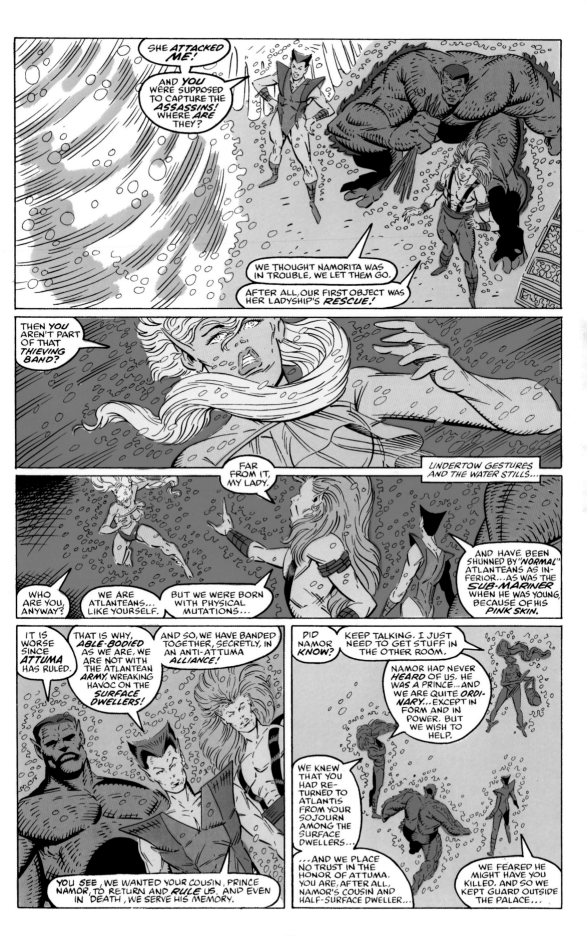

SHE *ATTACKED* ME!

AND *YOU* WERE SUPPOSED TO CAPTURE THE *ASSASSINS!* WHERE *ARE* THEY?

WE THOUGHT NAMORITA WAS IN TROUBLE, WE LET THEM GO.

AFTER ALL, OUR FIRST OBJECT WAS HER LADYSHIP'S *RESCUE!*

THEN *YOU* AREN'T PART OF THAT *THIEVING BAND?*

FAR FROM IT, MY LADY.

UNDERTOW GESTURES AND THE WATER STILLS...

AND HAVE BEEN SHUNNED BY "*NORMAL*" ATLANTEANS AS INFERIOR... AS WAS THE *SUB-MARINER* WHEN HE WAS YOUNG, BECAUSE OF HIS *PINK SKIN.*

WHO ARE YOU, ANYWAY?

WE ARE ATLANTEANS... LIKE YOURSELF.

BUT WE WERE BORN WITH PHYSICAL MUTATIONS...

IT IS WORSE SINCE *ATTUMA* HAS RULED.

THAT IS WHY, *ABLE-BODIED* AS WE ARE, WE ARE NOT WITH THE ATLANTEAN *ARMY,* WREAKING HAVOC ON THE *SURFACE DWELLERS!*

AND SO, WE HAVE BANDED TOGETHER, SECRETLY, IN AN ANTI-ATTUMA *ALLIANCE!*

YOU SEE, WE WANTED YOUR COUSIN, PRINCE NAMOR, TO RETURN AND *RULE* US. AND EVEN IN DEATH, WE SERVE HIS MEMORY.

DID NAMOR *KNOW?*

KEEP TALKING, I JUST NEED TO GET STUFF IN THE OTHER ROOM.

NAMOR HAD NEVER *HEARD* OF US. HE WAS A PRINCE... AND WE ARE QUITE *ORDINARY*... EXCEPT IN FORM AND IN POWER. BUT WE WISH TO HELP.

WE KNEW THAT YOU HAD RETURNED TO ATLANTIS FROM YOUR SOJOURN AMONG THE SURFACE DWELLERS...

...AND WE PLACE NO TRUST IN THE HONOR OF ATTUMA. YOU ARE, AFTER ALL, NAMOR'S COUSIN AND HALF-SURFACE DWELLER...

WE FEARED HE MIGHT HAVE YOU KILLED, AND SO WE KEPT GUARD OUTSIDE THE PALACE...

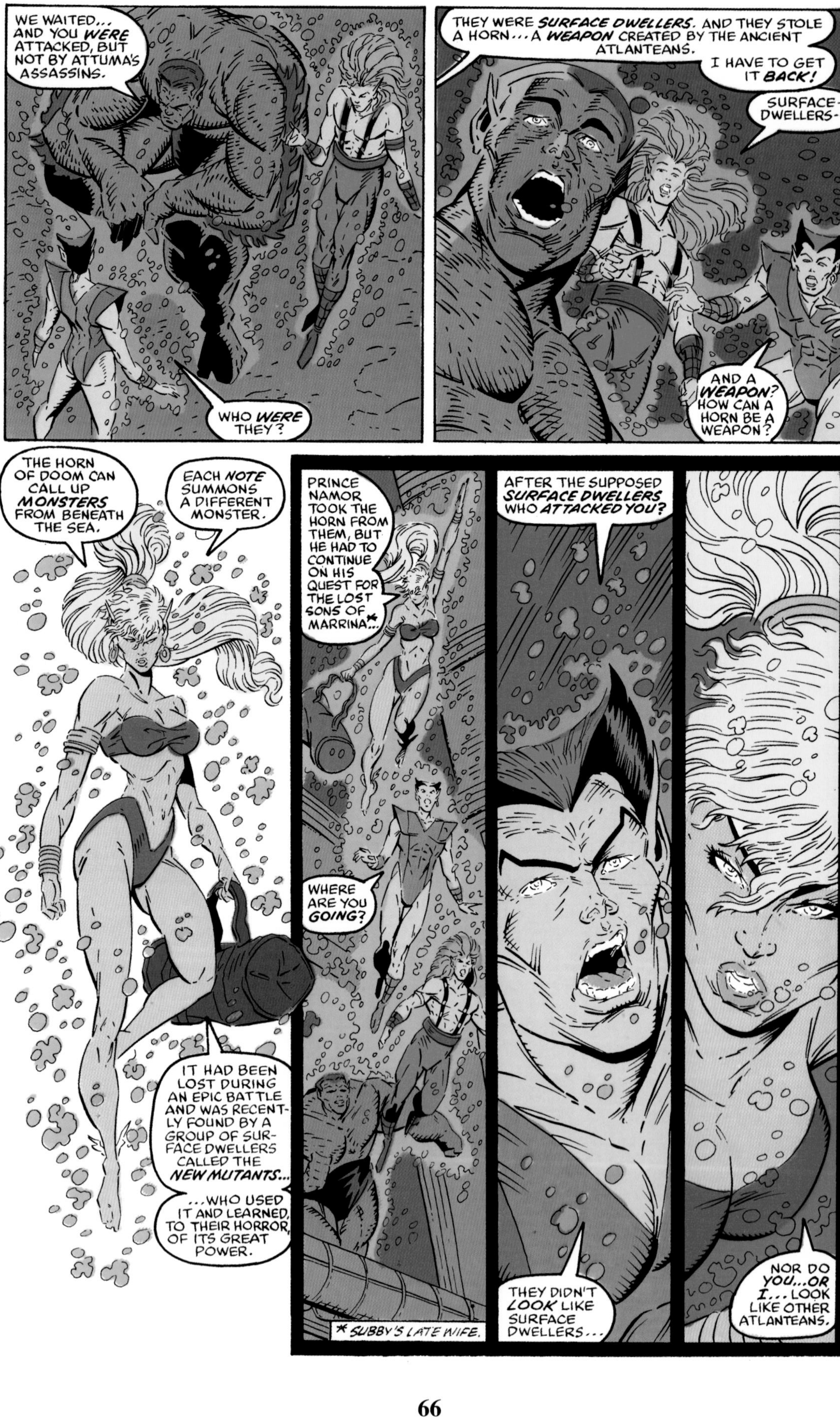
WE WAITED... AND YOU WERE ATTACKED, BUT NOT BY ATTUMA'S ASSASSINS.
WHO WERE THEY?
THEY WERE SURFACE DWELLERS. AND THEY STOLE A HORN... A WEAPON CREATED BY THE ANCIENT ATLANTEANS.
I HAVE TO GET IT BACK!
SURFACE-DWELLERS--?
AND A WEAPON? HOW CAN A HORN BE A WEAPON?
THE HORN OF DOOM CAN CALL UP MONSTERS FROM BENEATH THE SEA.
EACH NOTE SUMMONS A DIFFERENT MONSTER.
IT HAD BEEN LOST DURING AN EPIC BATTLE AND WAS RECENTLY FOUND BY A GROUP OF SURFACE DWELLERS CALLED THE NEW MUTANTS...
...WHO USED IT AND LEARNED, TO THEIR HORROR, OF ITS GREAT POWER.
PRINCE NAMOR TOOK THE HORN FROM THEM, BUT HE HAD TO CONTINUE ON HIS QUEST FOR THE LOST SONS OF MARRINA*...
WHERE ARE YOU GOING?
* SUBBY'S LATE WIFE.
AFTER THE SUPPOSED SURFACE DWELLERS WHO ATTACKED YOU?
THEY DIDN'T LOOK LIKE SURFACE DWELLERS...
NOR DO YOU...OR I... LOOK LIKE OTHER ATLANTEANS.

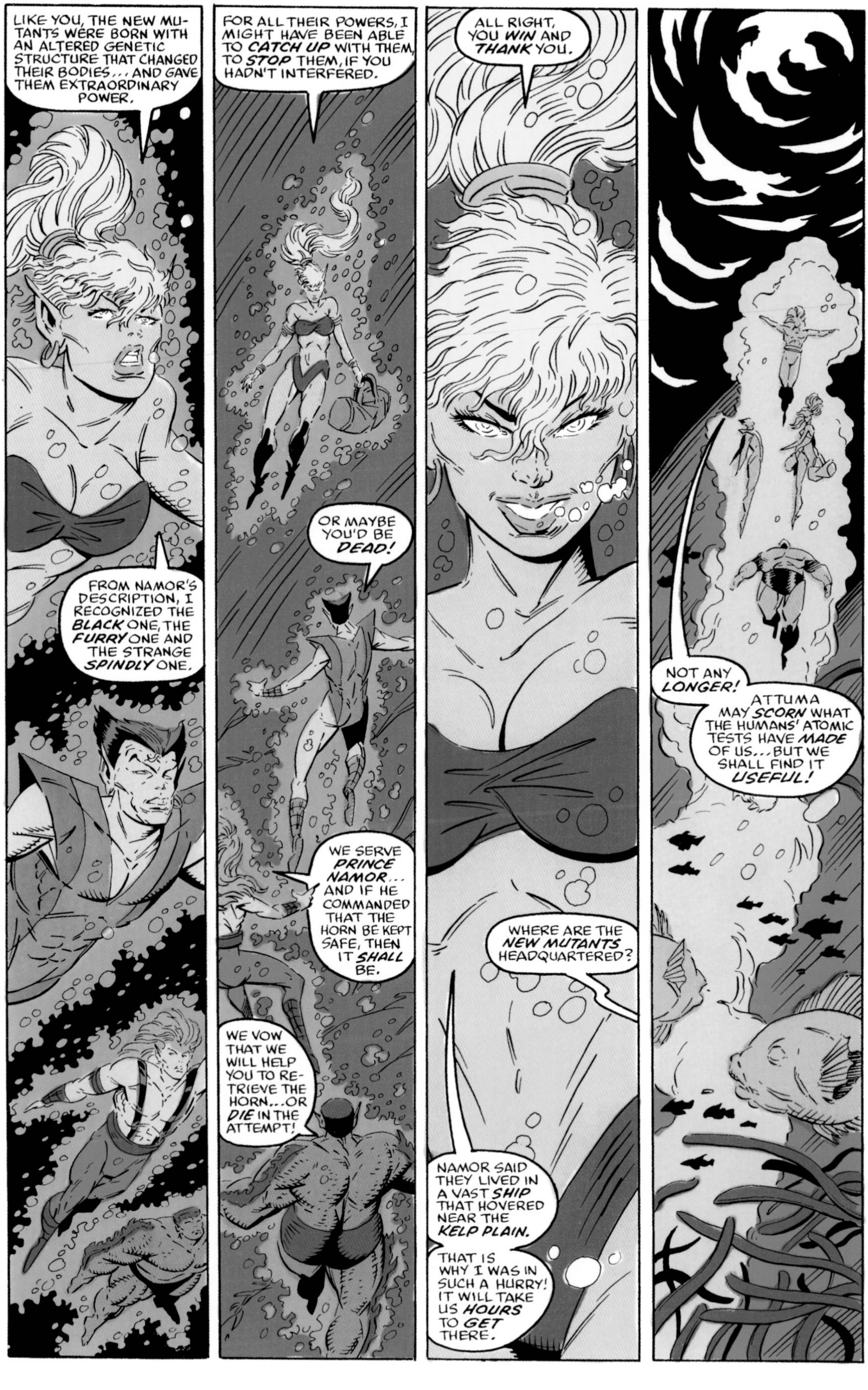
LIKE YOU, THE NEW MUTANTS WERE BORN WITH AN ALTERED GENETIC STRUCTURE THAT CHANGED THEIR BODIES... AND GAVE THEM EXTRAORDINARY POWER.
FROM NAMOR'S DESCRIPTION, I RECOGNIZED THE BLACK ONE, THE FURRY ONE AND THE STRANGE SPINDLY ONE.
FOR ALL THEIR POWERS, I MIGHT HAVE BEEN ABLE TO CATCH UP WITH THEM, TO STOP THEM, IF YOU HADN'T INTERFERED.
OR MAYBE YOU'D BE DEAD!
WE SERVE PRINCE NAMOR... AND IF HE COMMANDED THAT THE HORN BE KEPT SAFE, THEN IT SHALL BE.
WE VOW THAT WE WILL HELP YOU TO RETRIEVE THE HORN...OR DIE IN THE ATTEMPT!
ALL RIGHT, YOU WIN AND THANK YOU.
WHERE ARE THE NEW MUTANTS HEADQUARTERED?
NAMOR SAID THEY LIVED IN A VAST SHIP THAT HOVERED NEAR THE KELP PLAIN.
THAT IS WHY I WAS IN SUCH A HURRY! IT WILL TAKE US HOURS TO GET THERE.
NOT ANY LONGER!
ATTUMA MAY SCORN WHAT THE HUMANS' ATOMIC TESTS HAVE MADE OF US... BUT WE SHALL FIND IT USEFUL!

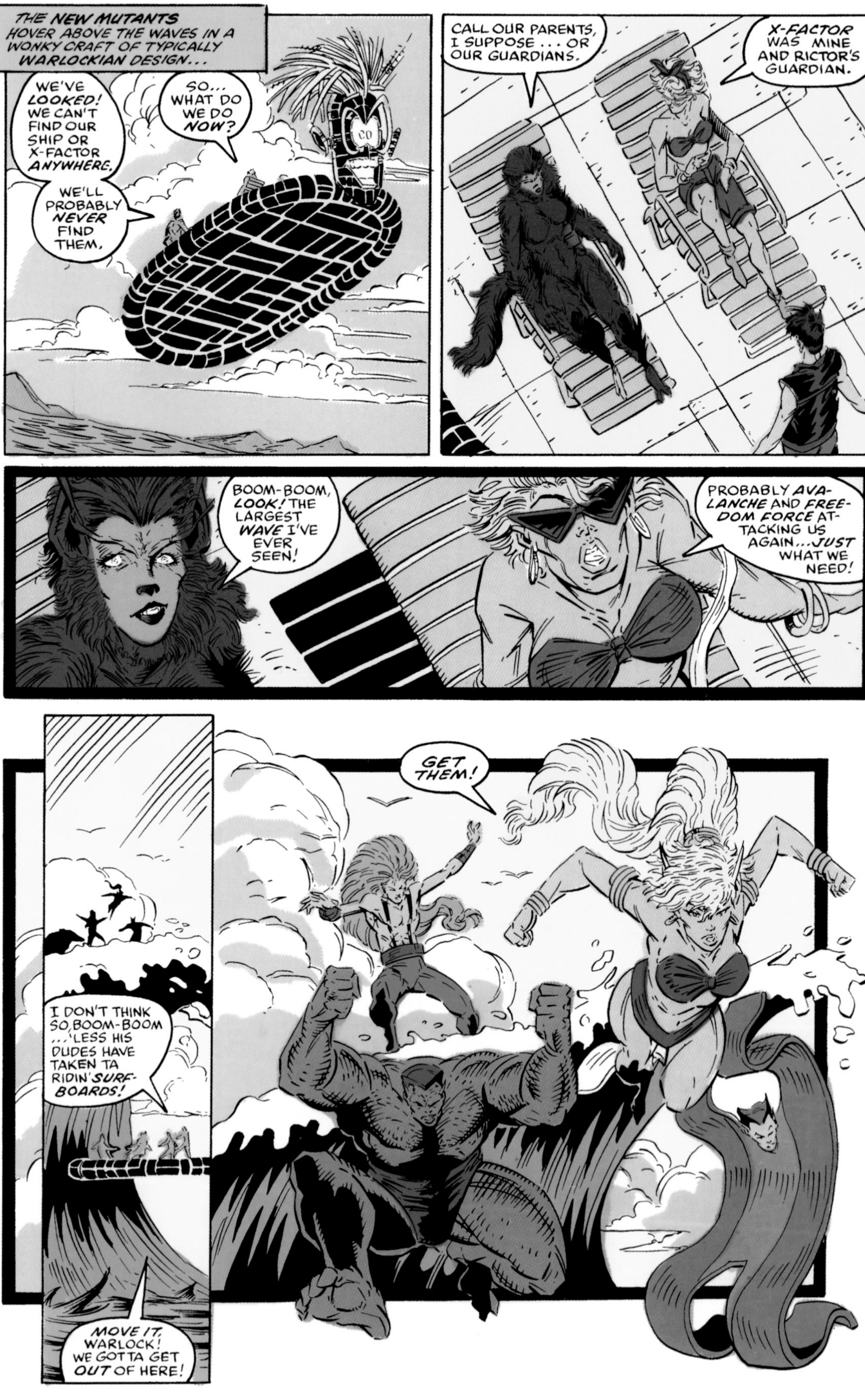
THE NEW MUTANTS HOVER ABOVE THE WAVES IN A WONKY CRAFT OF TYPICALLY WARLOCKIAN DESIGN...
WE'VE LOOKED! WE CAN'T FIND OUR SHIP OR X-FACTOR ANYWHERE.
SO... WHAT DO WE DO NOW?
WE'LL PROBABLY NEVER FIND THEM.
CALL OUR PARENTS, I SUPPOSE . . . OR OUR GUARDIANS.
X-FACTOR WAS MINE AND RICTOR'S GUARDIAN.
BOOM-BOOM, LOOK! THE LARGEST WAVE I'VE EVER SEEN!
PROBABLY AVALANCHE AND FREEDOM FORCE ATTACKING US AGAIN... JUST WHAT WE NEED!
GET THEM!
I DON'T THINK SO, BOOM-BOOM ...'LESS HIS DUDES HAVE TAKEN TA RIDIN' SURF-BOARDS!
MOVE IT, WARLOCK! WE GOTTA GET OUT OF HERE!

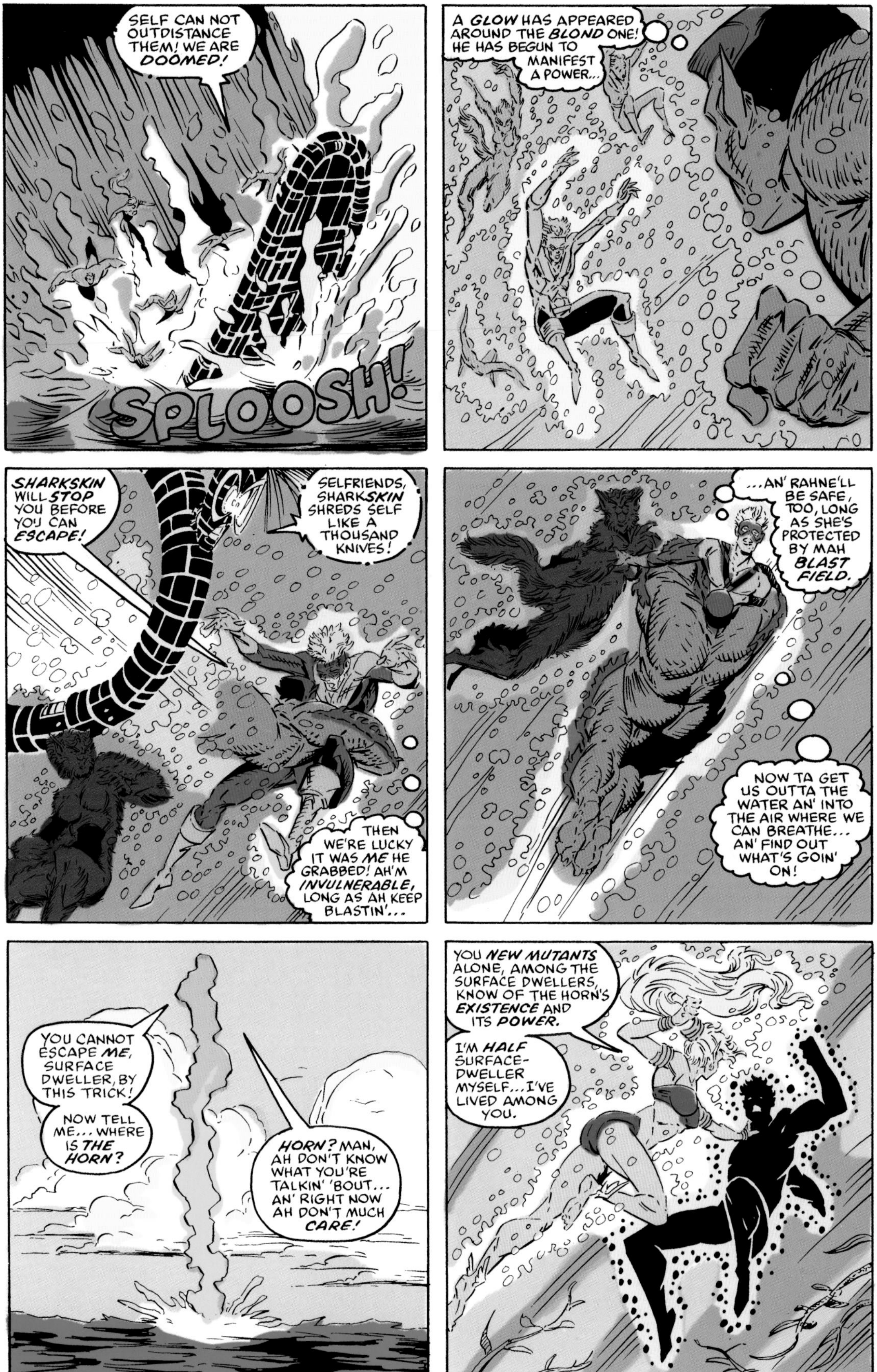
SELF CAN NOT OUTDISTANCE THEM! WE ARE DOOMED!
SPLOOSH!
A GLOW HAS APPEARED AROUND THE BLOND ONE! HE HAS BEGUN TO MANIFEST A POWER...
SHARKSKIN WILL STOP YOU BEFORE YOU CAN ESCAPE!
SELFRIENDS, SHARKSKIN SHREDS SELF LIKE A THOUSAND KNIVES!
THEN WE'RE LUCKY IT WAS ME HE GRABBED! AH'M INVULNERABLE, LONG AS AH KEEP BLASTIN'...
...AN' RAHNE'LL BE SAFE, TOO, LONG AS SHE'S PROTECTED BY MAH BLAST FIELD.
NOW TA GET US OUTTA THE WATER AN' INTO THE AIR WHERE WE CAN BREATHE... AN' FIND OUT WHAT'S GOIN' ON!
YOU CANNOT ESCAPE ME, SURFACE DWELLER, BY THIS TRICK!
NOW TELL ME... WHERE IS THE HORN?
HORN? MAN, AH DON'T KNOW WHAT YOU'RE TALKIN' 'BOUT... AN' RIGHT NOW AH DON'T MUCH CARE!
YOU NEW MUTANTS ALONE, AMONG THE SURFACE DWELLERS, KNOW OF THE HORN'S EXISTENCE AND ITS POWER.
I'M HALF SURFACE-DWELLER MYSELF... I'VE LIVED AMONG YOU.

I KNOW YOU AREN'T *ALL* EVIL, LIKE *ATTUMA* SAYS, BUT YOU DO HAVE A KIND OF *WEAPONS MADNESS...*

...AND COLLECT WEAPONS AS AN ATLANTEAN CHILD COLLECTS *SHELLS.*

BUT IN *THIS* CASE YOU MUST *RELENT! SURRENDER* THE *HORN...* AND WE'LL LET YOU *LIVE!*

WHO'S *ATTUMA?!* CAN IT BE THE *SUB-MARINER'S* HORN THAT SHE'S *BABBLING* ABOUT?

SHE'S *STRONG* ...AND DARN GOOD *LOOKING!*

BUT IF SHE THINKS THAT *SUNSPOT* IS *LESS* STRONG ...OR WILLING TO *BOW* BEFORE SUCH THREATS...

...SHE IS FAR MORE *FOOLISH* THAN SHE LOOKS!

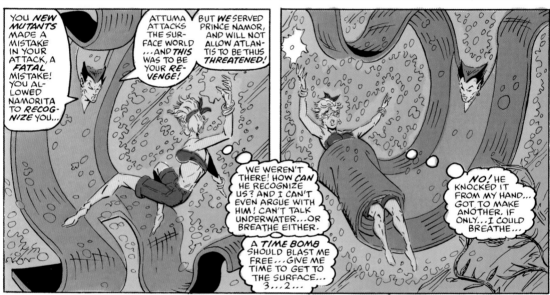

YOU *NEW MUTANTS* MADE A MISTAKE IN YOUR ATTACK, A *FATAL* MISTAKE! YOU AL- LOWED NAMORITA TO *RECOG- NIZE* YOU...

ATTUMA ATTACKS THE SUR- FACE WORLD ...AND *THIS* WAS TO BE YOUR *RE- VENGE!*

BUT *WE* SERVED PRINCE NAMOR, AND WILL NOT ALLOW ATLAN- TIS TO BE THUS *THREATENED!*

WE WEREN'T THERE! HOW *CAN* HE RECOGNIZE US? AND I CAN'T EVEN ARGUE WITH HIM! CAN'T TALK UNDERWATER...OR BREATHE EITHER.

A *TIME BOMB* SHOULD BLAST ME *FREE*...GIVE ME TIME TO GET TO THE SURFACE... 3...2...

NO! HE KNOCKED IT FROM MY HAND... GOT TO MAKE ANOTHER. IF ONLY...I COULD *BREATHE...*

SELF*FRIEND*RICTOR, SELF WILL SAVE YOU!

NEARLY OUT OF AIR. SWALLOWED SOME WATER TRYING TO YELL TO BOOM- BOOM. *SHE'S* IN WORSE TROUBLE THAN I AM!

70

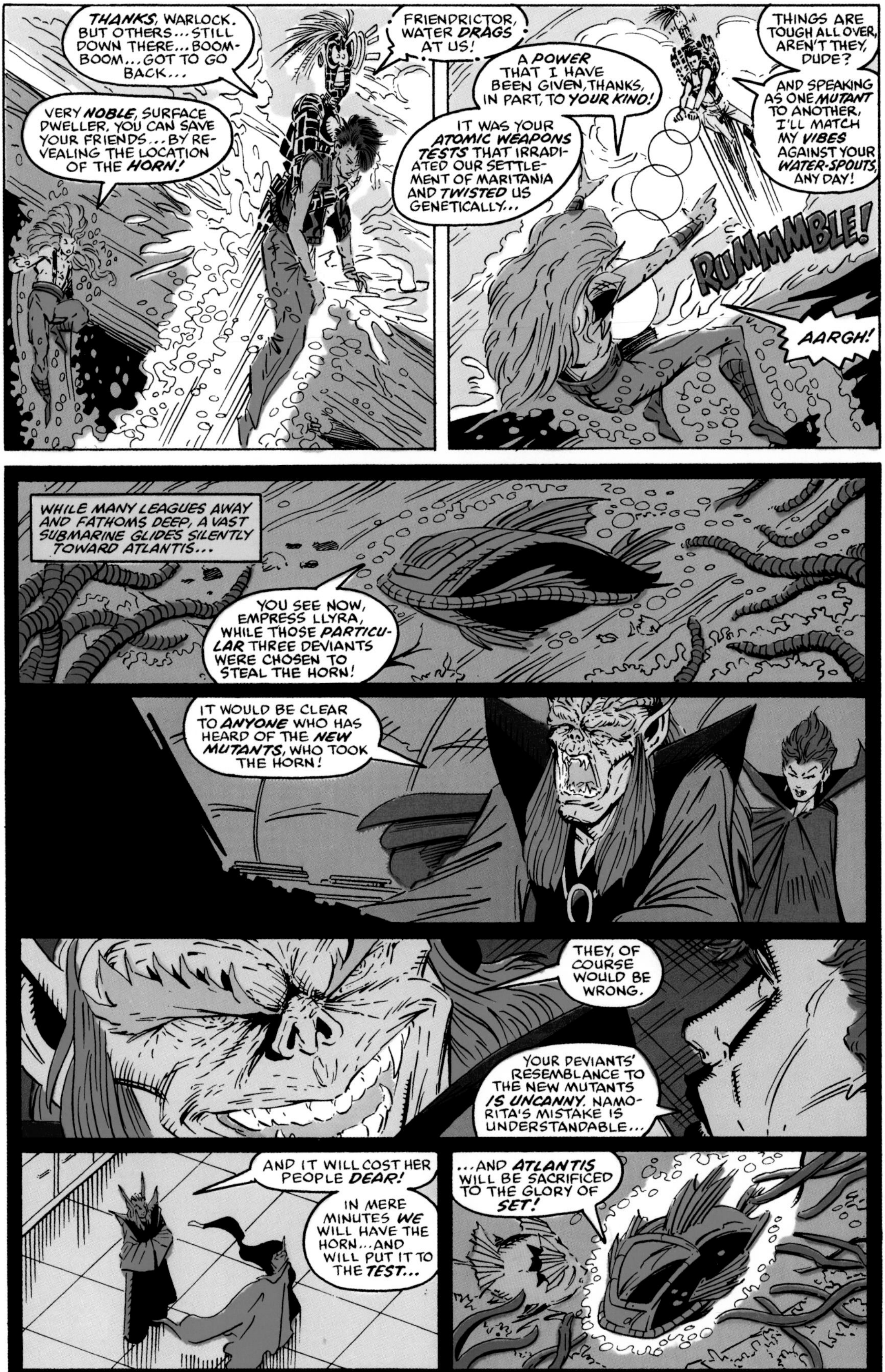
THANKS, WARLOCK. BUT OTHERS... STILL DOWN THERE... BOOM-BOOM... GOT TO GO BACK...
FRIENDRICTOR, WATER DRAGS AT US!
VERY NOBLE, SURFACE DWELLER. YOU CAN SAVE YOUR FRIENDS... BY REVEALING THE LOCATION OF THE HORN!
A POWER THAT I HAVE BEEN GIVEN, THANKS, IN PART, TO YOUR KIND!
IT WAS YOUR ATOMIC WEAPONS TESTS THAT IRRADIATED OUR SETTLEMENT OF MARITANIA AND TWISTED US GENETICALLY...
THINGS ARE TOUGH ALL OVER, AREN'T THEY, DUDE?
AND SPEAKING AS ONE MUTANT TO ANOTHER, I'LL MATCH MY VIBES AGAINST YOUR WATER-SPOUTS ANY DAY!
RUMMMBLE!
AARGH!
WHILE MANY LEAGUES AWAY AND FATHOMS DEEP, A VAST SUBMARINE GLIDES SILENTLY TOWARD ATLANTIS...
YOU SEE NOW, EMPRESS LLYRA, WHILE THOSE PARTICULAR THREE DEVIANTS WERE CHOSEN TO STEAL THE HORN!
IT WOULD BE CLEAR TO ANYONE WHO HAS HEARD OF THE NEW MUTANTS, WHO TOOK THE HORN!
THEY, OF COURSE WOULD BE WRONG.
YOUR DEVIANTS' RESEMBLANCE TO THE NEW MUTANTS IS UNCANNY. NAMORITA'S MISTAKE IS UNDERSTANDABLE...
AND IT WILL COST HER PEOPLE DEAR!
IN MERE MINUTES WE WILL HAVE THE HORN... AND WILL PUT IT TO THE TEST...
...AND ATLANTIS WILL BE SACRIFICED TO THE GLORY OF SET!

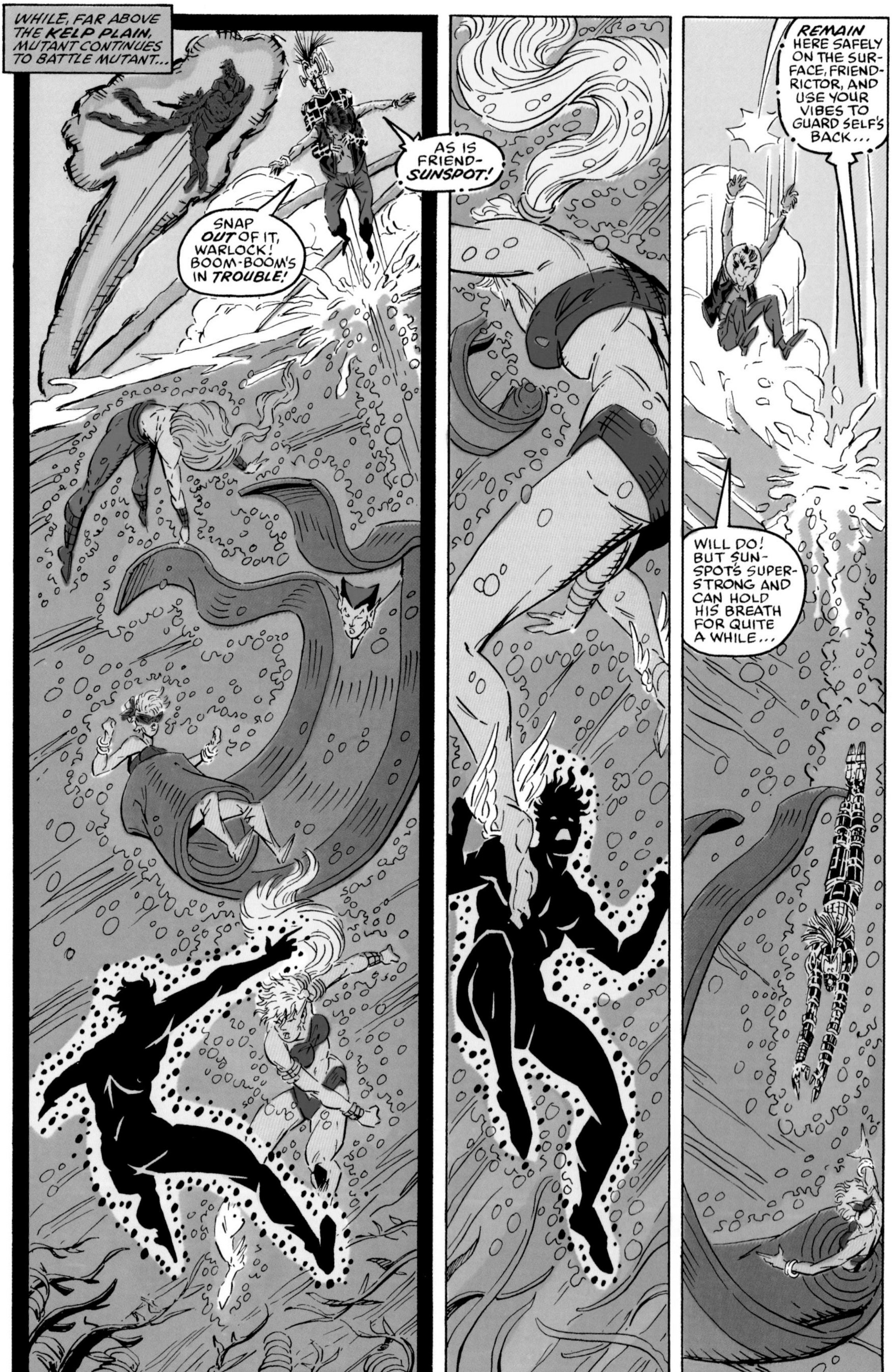
WHILE, FAR ABOVE THE KELP PLAIN, MUTANT CONTINUES TO BATTLE MUTANT...
AS IS FRIEND-SUNSPOT!
SNAP OUT OF IT, WARLOCK! BOOM-BOOM'S IN TROUBLE!
REMAIN HERE SAFELY ON THE SURFACE, FRIEND-RICTOR, AND USE YOUR VIBES TO GUARD SELF'S BACK...
WILL DO! BUT SUNSPOT'S SUPER-STRONG AND CAN HOLD HIS BREATH FOR QUITE A WHILE...

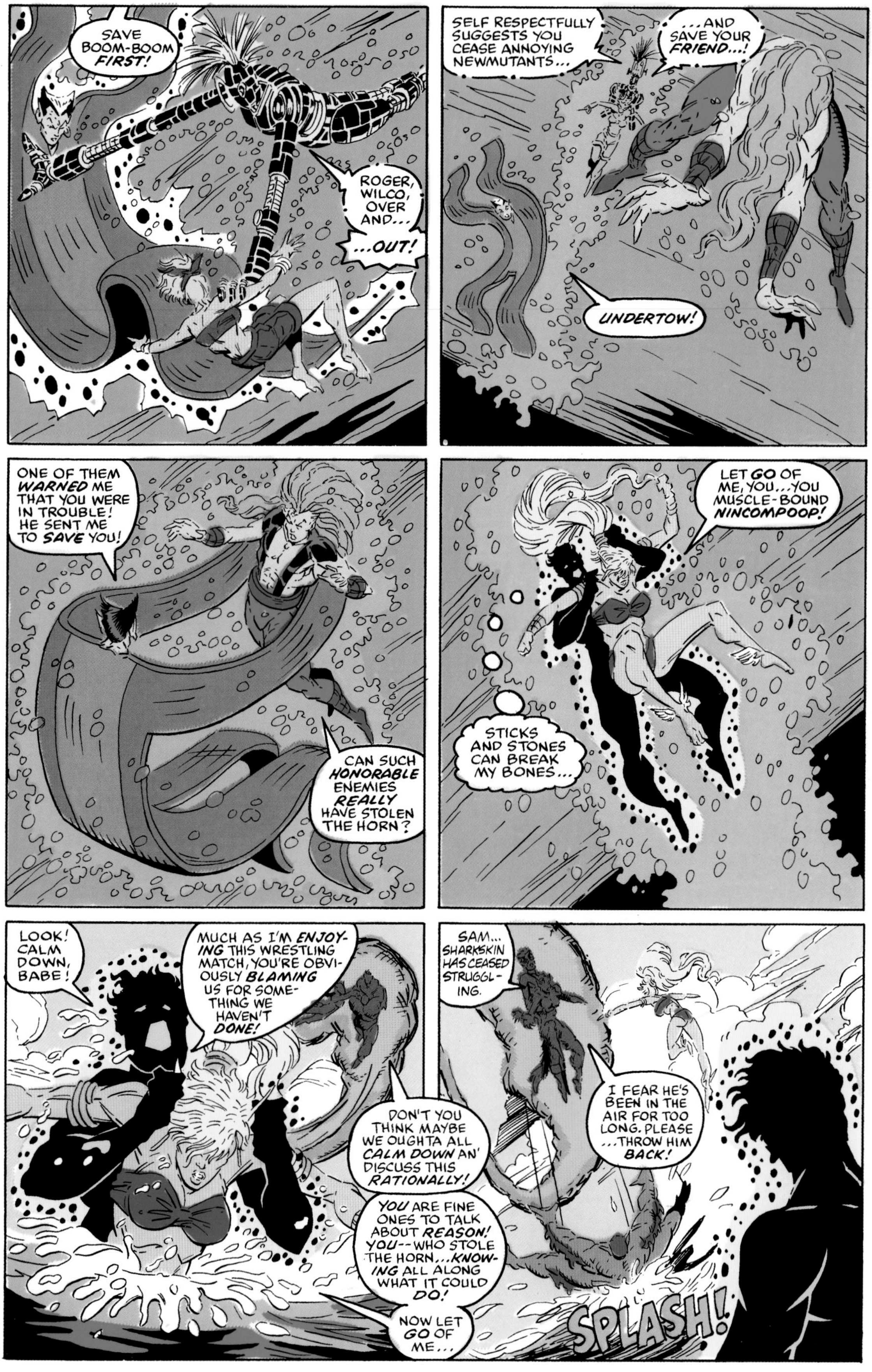
SAVE BOOM-BOOM FIRST!
ROGER, WILCO, OVER AND...
...OUT!
SELF RESPECTFULLY SUGGESTS YOU CEASE ANNOYING NEWMUTANTS...
...AND SAVE YOUR FRIEND...!
UNDERTOW!
ONE OF THEM WARNED ME THAT YOU WERE IN TROUBLE! HE SENT ME TO SAVE YOU!
CAN SUCH HONORABLE ENEMIES REALLY HAVE STOLEN THE HORN?
LET GO OF ME, YOU...YOU MUSCLE-BOUND NINCOMPOOP!
STICKS AND STONES CAN BREAK MY BONES...
LOOK! CALM DOWN, BABE!
MUCH AS I'M ENJOYING THIS WRESTLING MATCH, YOU'RE OBVIOUSLY BLAMING US FOR SOMETHING WE HAVEN'T DONE!
DON'T YOU THINK MAYBE WE OUGHTA ALL CALM DOWN AN' DISCUSS THIS RATIONALLY!
YOU ARE FINE ONES TO TALK ABOUT REASON! YOU--WHO STOLE THE HORN...KNOWING ALL ALONG WHAT IT COULD DO!
NOW LET GO OF ME...
SAM... SHARKSKIN HAS CEASED STRUGGLING.
I FEAR HE'S BEEN IN THE AIR FOR TOO LONG. PLEASE...THROW HIM BACK!
SPLASH!

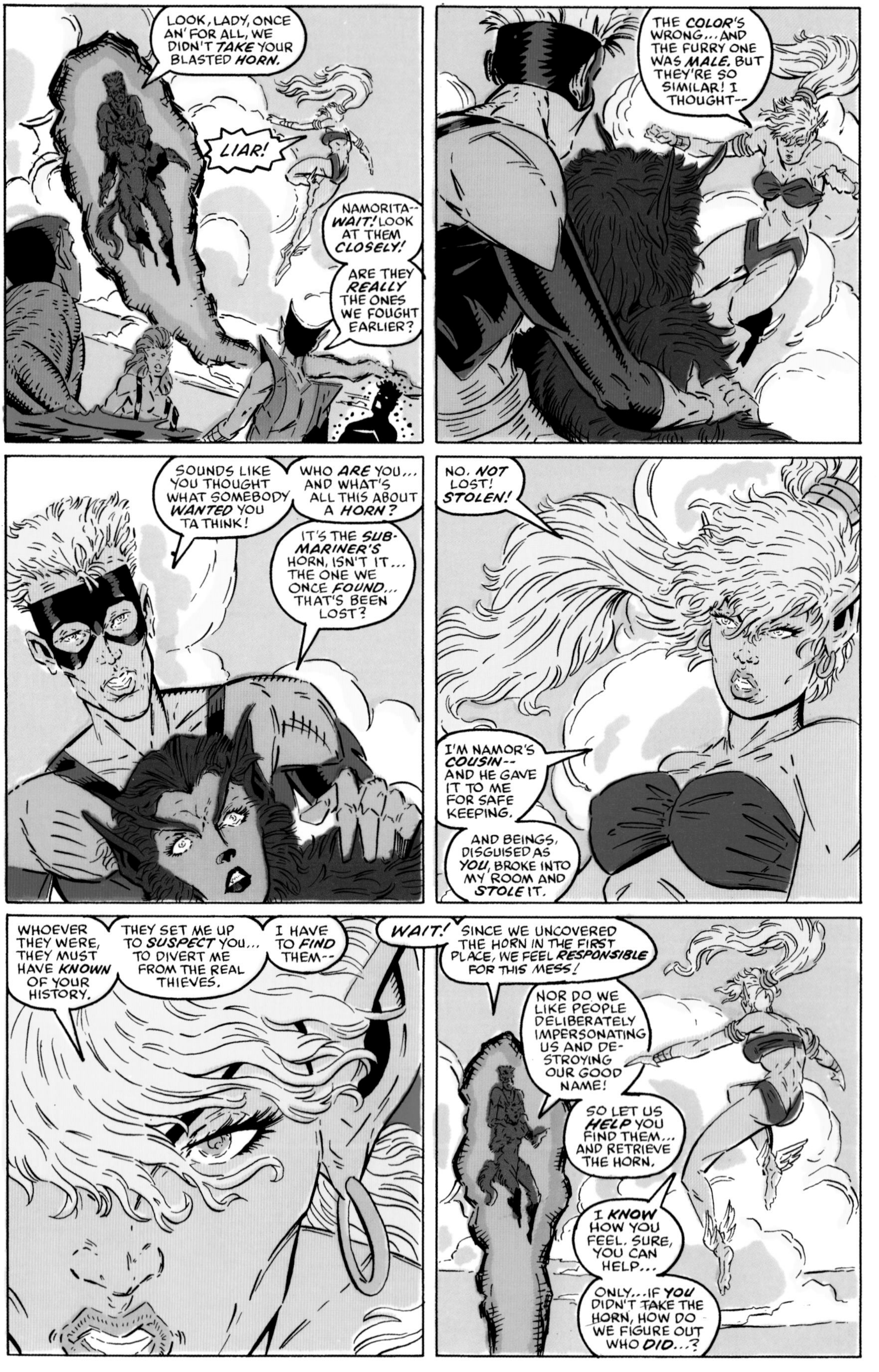

LOOK, LADY, ONCE AN' FOR ALL, WE DIDN'T TAKE YOUR BLASTED HORN.
LIAR!
NAMORITA-- WAIT! LOOK AT THEM CLOSELY!
ARE THEY REALLY THE ONES WE FOUGHT EARLIER?
THE COLOR'S WRONG... AND THE FURRY ONE WAS MALE. BUT THEY'RE SO SIMILAR! I THOUGHT--
SOUNDS LIKE YOU THOUGHT WHAT SOMEBODY WANTED YOU TA THINK!
WHO ARE YOU... AND WHAT'S ALL THIS ABOUT A HORN?
IT'S THE SUB-MARINER'S HORN, ISN'T IT... THE ONE WE ONCE FOUND... THAT'S BEEN LOST?
NO. NOT LOST! STOLEN!
I'M NAMOR'S COUSIN-- AND HE GAVE IT TO ME FOR SAFE KEEPING.
AND BEINGS, DISGUISED AS YOU, BROKE INTO MY ROOM AND STOLE IT.
WHOEVER THEY WERE, THEY MUST HAVE KNOWN OF YOUR HISTORY.
THEY SET ME UP TO SUSPECT YOU... TO DIVERT ME FROM THE REAL THIEVES.
I HAVE TO FIND THEM--
WAIT!
SINCE WE UNCOVERED THE HORN IN THE FIRST PLACE, WE FEEL RESPONSIBLE FOR THIS MESS!
NOR DO WE LIKE PEOPLE DELIBERATELY IMPERSONATING US AND DE-STROYING OUR GOOD NAME!
SO LET US HELP YOU FIND THEM... AND RETRIEVE THE HORN.
I KNOW HOW YOU FEEL. SURE, YOU CAN HELP...
ONLY... IF YOU DIDN'T TAKE THE HORN, HOW DO WE FIGURE OUT WHO DID...?

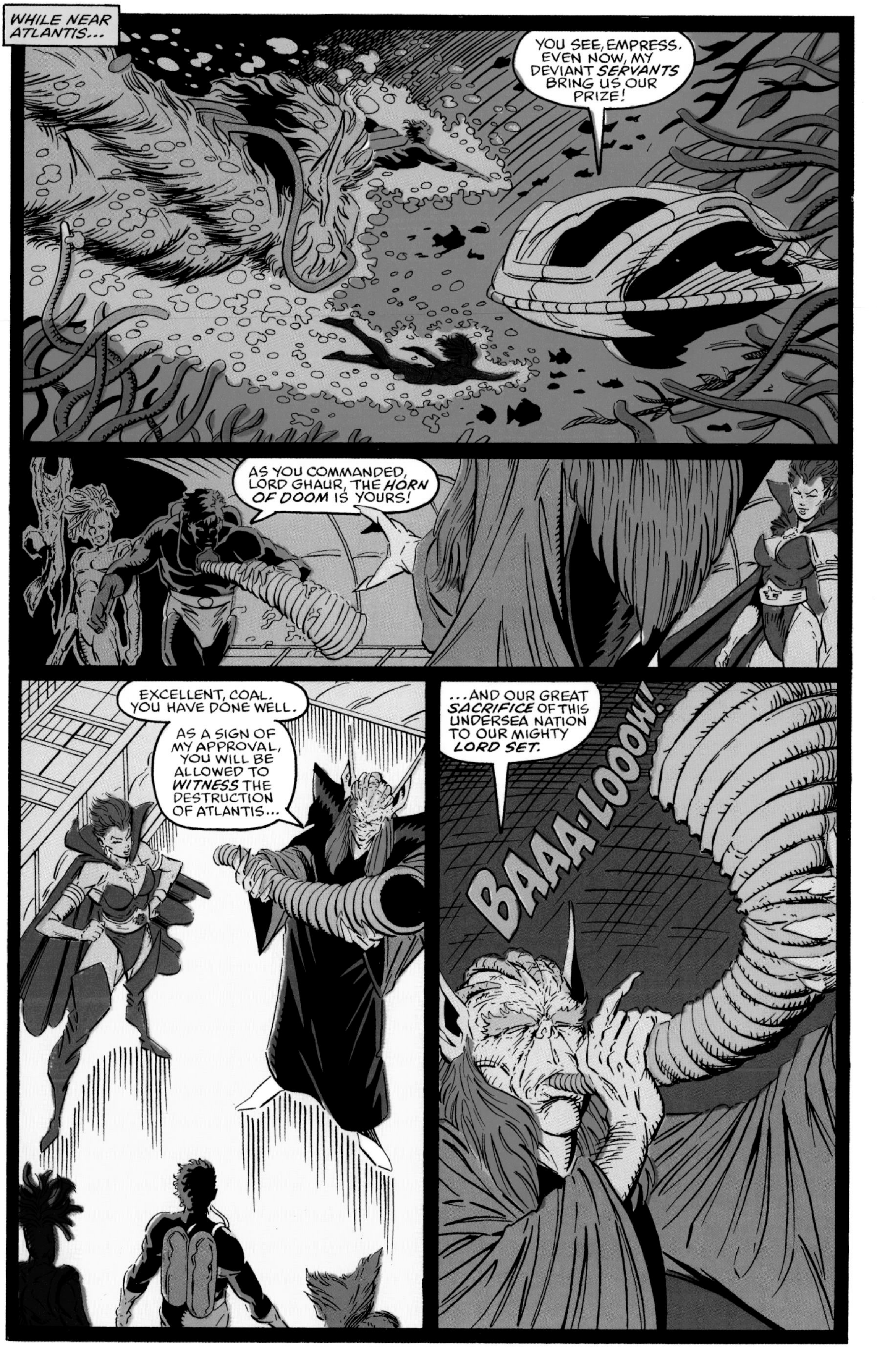
WHILE NEAR ATLANTIS...
YOU SEE, EMPRESS. EVEN NOW, MY DEVIANT SERVANTS BRING US OUR PRIZE!
AS YOU COMMANDED, LORD GHAUR, THE HORN OF DOOM IS YOURS!
EXCELLENT, COAL. YOU HAVE DONE WELL.
AS A SIGN OF MY APPROVAL, YOU WILL BE ALLOWED TO WITNESS THE DESTRUCTION OF ATLANTIS...
...AND OUR GREAT SACRIFICE OF THIS UNDERSEA NATION TO OUR MIGHTY LORD SET.
BAAA-LOOOW!

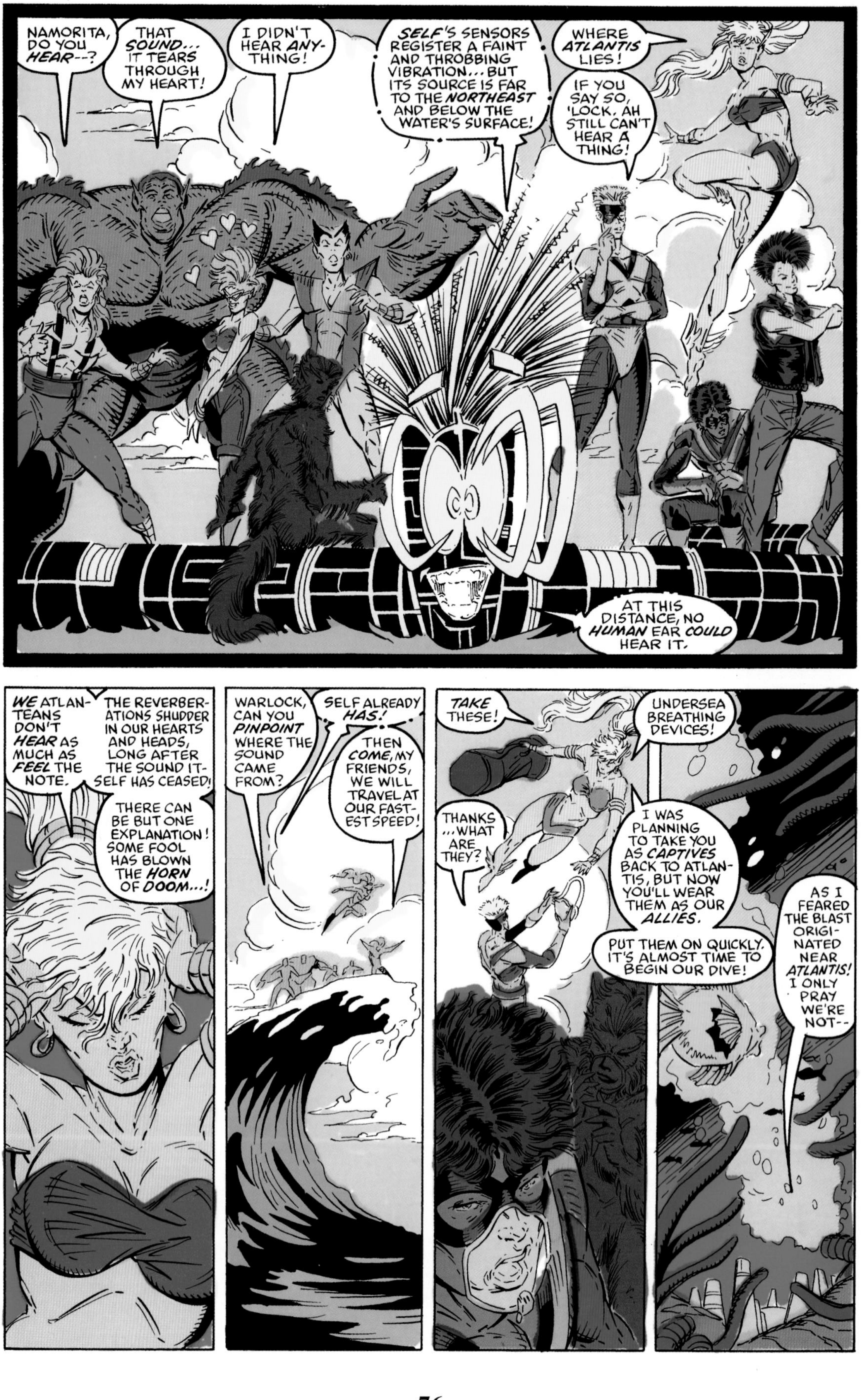
NAMORITA, DO YOU HEAR--?
THAT SOUND... IT TEARS THROUGH MY HEART!
I DIDN'T HEAR ANYTHING!
SELF'S SENSORS REGISTER A FAINT AND THROBBING VIBRATION... BUT ITS SOURCE IS FAR TO THE NORTHEAST AND BELOW THE WATER'S SURFACE!
WHERE ATLANTIS LIES!
IF YOU SAY SO, 'LOCK, AH STILL CAN'T HEAR A THING!
AT THIS DISTANCE, NO HUMAN EAR COULD HEAR IT.
WE ATLANTEANS DON'T HEAR AS MUCH AS FEEL THE NOTE.
THE REVERBERATIONS SHUDDER IN OUR HEARTS AND HEADS, LONG AFTER THE SOUND ITSELF HAS CEASED!
THERE CAN BE BUT ONE EXPLANATION! SOME FOOL HAS BLOWN THE HORN OF DOOM...!
WARLOCK, CAN YOU PINPOINT WHERE THE SOUND CAME FROM?
SELF ALREADY HAS!
THEN COME, MY FRIENDS, WE WILL TRAVEL AT OUR FASTEST SPEED!
TAKE THESE!
UNDERSEA BREATHING DEVICES!
THANKS ...WHAT ARE THEY?
I WAS PLANNING TO TAKE YOU AS CAPTIVES BACK TO ATLANTIS, BUT NOW YOU'LL WEAR THEM AS OUR ALLIES.
PUT THEM ON QUICKLY. IT'S ALMOST TIME TO BEGIN OUR DIVE!
AS I FEARED THE BLAST ORIGINATED NEAR ATLANTIS! I ONLY PRAY WE'RE NOT--

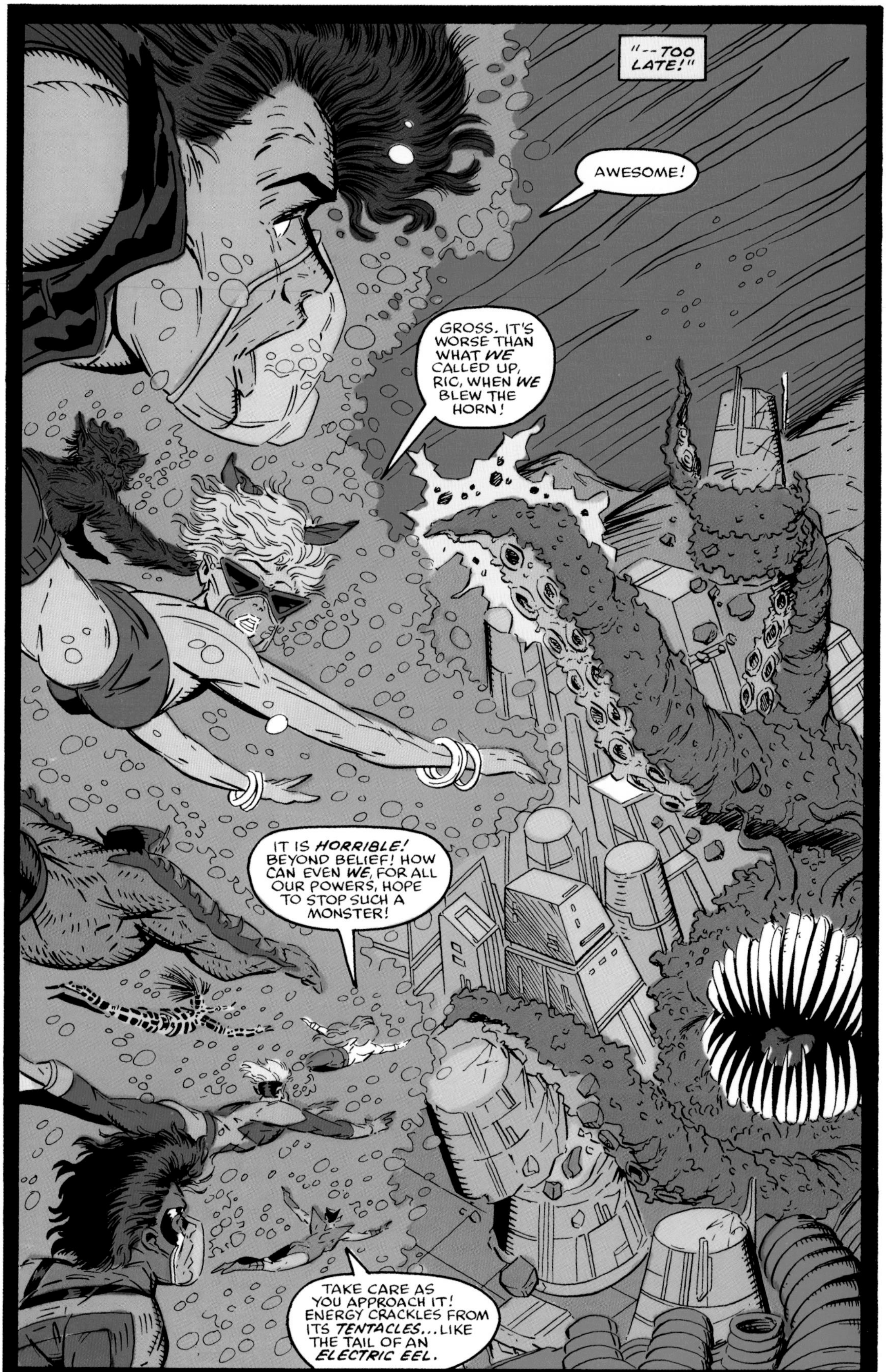
"--TOO LATE!"
AWESOME!
GROSS. IT'S WORSE THAN WHAT *WE* CALLED UP, RIC, WHEN *WE* BLEW THE HORN!
IT IS *HORRIBLE!* BEYOND BELIEF! HOW CAN EVEN *WE*, FOR ALL OUR POWERS, HOPE TO STOP SUCH A MONSTER!
TAKE CARE AS YOU APPROACH IT! ENERGY CRACKLES FROM ITS *TENTACLES*... LIKE THE TAIL OF AN *ELECTRIC EEL*.

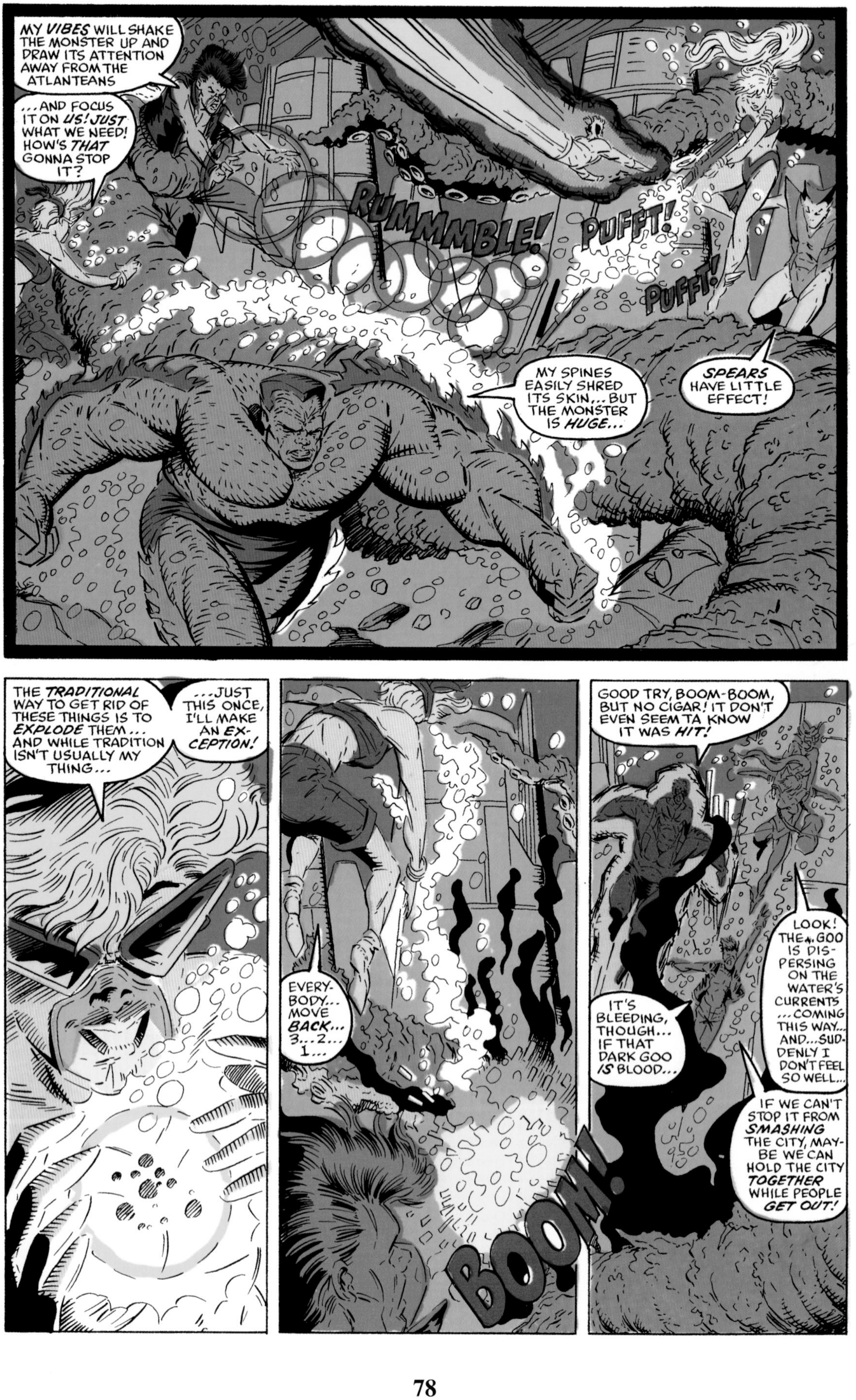
MY VIBES WILL SHAKE THE MONSTER UP AND DRAW ITS ATTENTION AWAY FROM THE ATLANTEANS
...AND FOCUS IT ON US! JUST WHAT WE NEED! HOW'S THAT GONNA STOP IT?
RUMMMBLE!
PUFFT!
PUFFT!
MY SPINES EASILY SHRED ITS SKIN... BUT THE MONSTER IS HUGE...
SPEARS HAVE LITTLE EFFECT!
THE TRADITIONAL WAY TO GET RID OF THESE THINGS IS TO EXPLODE THEM... AND WHILE TRADITION ISN'T USUALLY MY THING...
...JUST THIS ONCE, I'LL MAKE AN EXCEPTION!
EVERYBODY... MOVE BACK... 3...2... 1...
BOOM!
GOOD TRY, BOOM-BOOM, BUT NO CIGAR! IT DON'T EVEN SEEM TA KNOW IT WAS HIT!
IT'S BLEEDING, THOUGH... IF THAT DARK GOO IS BLOOD...
LOOK! THE GOO IS DISPERSING ON THE WATER'S CURRENTS ...COMING THIS WAY... AND...SUDDENLY I DON'T FEEL SO WELL...
IF WE CAN'T STOP IT FROM SMASHING THE CITY, MAYBE WE CAN HOLD THE CITY TOGETHER WHILE PEOPLE GET OUT!

NO! NAMORITA HAS RETURNED... AND WITH THE NEW MUTANTS AS HER ALLIES!

YOUR SHIP IS ARMED, IS IT NOT, MY LORD? LET US DRAW CLOSER AND FIRE UPON THEM...

...AND DESTROY THEM BE-FORE THEY CAN DISRUPT OUR GREAT PLAN!

HELP ME HOLD IT UP. WE'VE GOT TO KEEP IT BRACED LONG ENOUGH FOR THE PEOPLE INSIDE TO ESCAPE!

INSIDE THEY'LL BE CRUSHED...

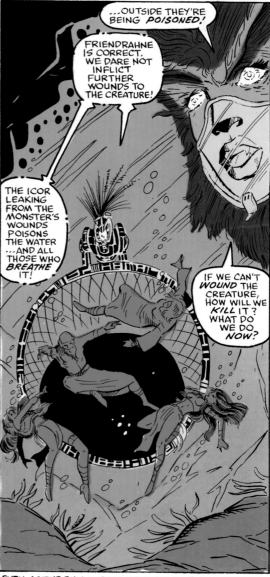

...OUTSIDE THEY'RE BEING POISONED!

FRIENDRAHNE IS CORRECT. WE DARE NOT INFLICT FURTHER WOUNDS TO THE CREATURE!

THE ICOR LEAKING FROM THE MONSTER'S WOUNDS POISONS THE WATER ...AND ALL THOSE WHO BREATHE IT!

IF WE CAN'T WOUND THE CREATURE, HOW WILL WE KILL IT? WHAT DO WE DO NOW?

EVEN AS THE FULL IMPACT OF THEIR DILEMMA STRIKES THE NEW MUTANTS, GHAUR'S SHIP DRAWS CLOSE.

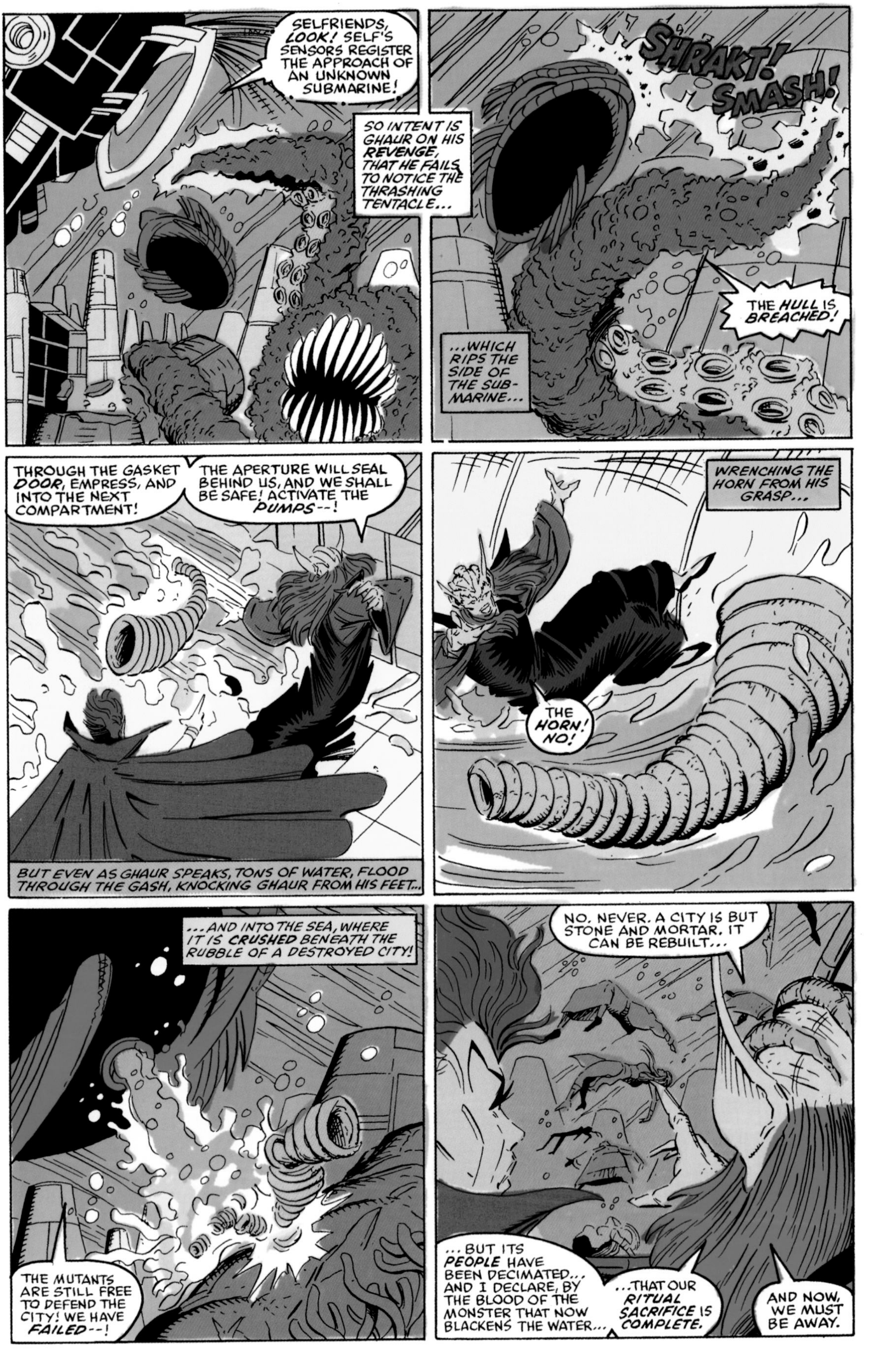
SELFRIENDS, LOOK! SELF'S SENSORS REGISTER THE APPROACH OF AN UNKNOWN SUBMARINE!
SO INTENT IS GHAUR ON HIS REVENGE, THAT HE FAILS TO NOTICE THE THRASHING TENTACLE...
SHRAKT! SMASH!
...WHICH RIPS THE SIDE OF THE SUB-MARINE...
THE HULL IS BREACHED!
THROUGH THE GASKET DOOR, EMPRESS, AND INTO THE NEXT COMPARTMENT!
THE APERTURE WILL SEAL BEHIND US, AND WE SHALL BE SAFE! ACTIVATE THE PUMPS--!
BUT EVEN AS GHAUR SPEAKS, TONS OF WATER, FLOOD THROUGH THE GASH, KNOCKING GHAUR FROM HIS FEET...
WRENCHING THE HORN FROM HIS GRASP...
THE HORN! NO!
...AND INTO THE SEA, WHERE IT IS CRUSHED BENEATH THE RUBBLE OF A DESTROYED CITY!
THE MUTANTS ARE STILL FREE TO DEFEND THE CITY! WE HAVE FAILED--!
NO. NEVER. A CITY IS BUT STONE AND MORTAR. IT CAN BE REBUILT...
...BUT ITS PEOPLE HAVE BEEN DECIMATED... AND I DECLARE, BY THE BLOOD OF THE MONSTER THAT NOW BLACKENS THE WATER...
...THAT OUR RITUAL SACRIFICE IS COMPLETE.
AND NOW, WE MUST BE AWAY.

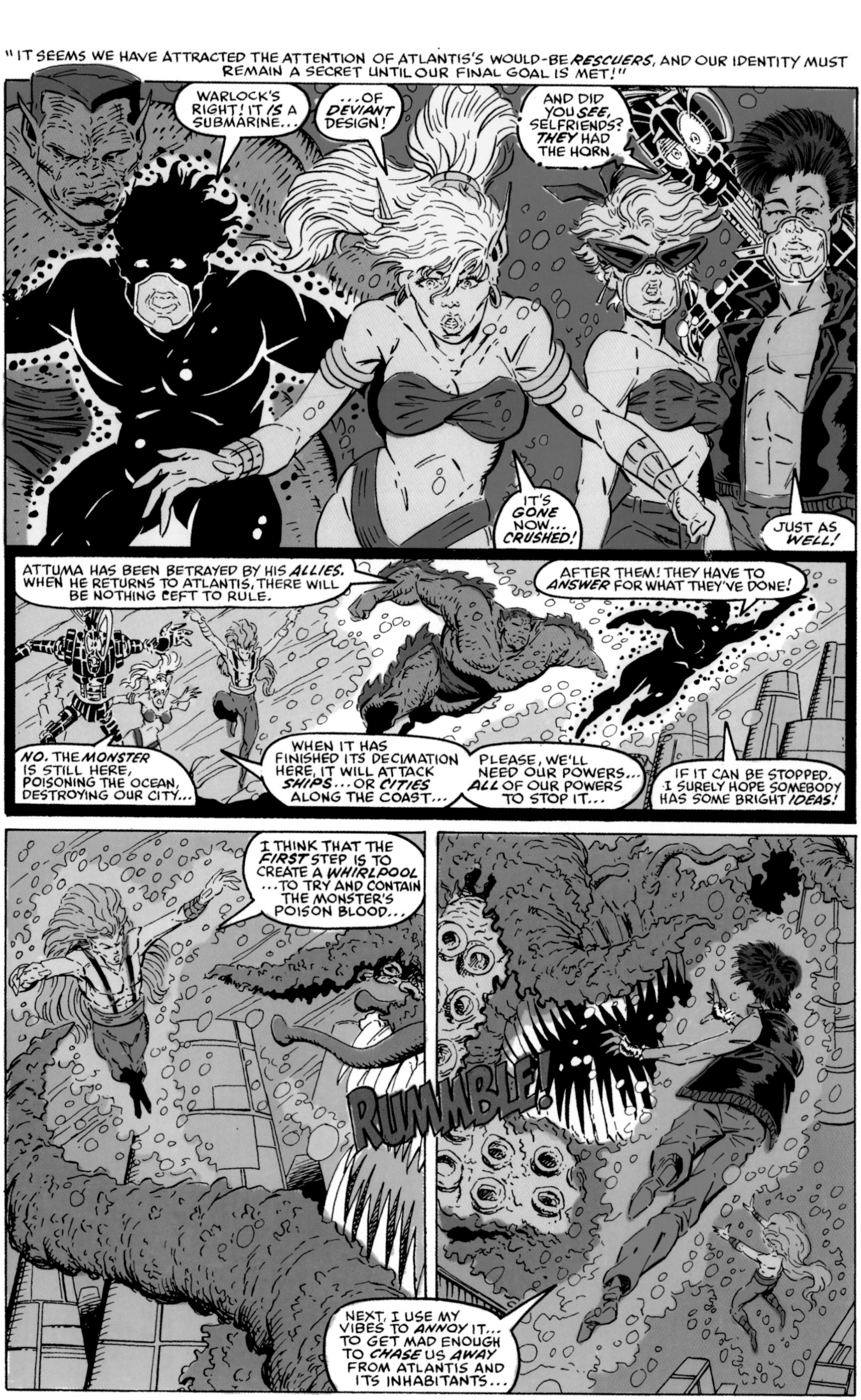
"IT SEEMS WE HAVE ATTRACTED THE ATTENTION OF ATLANTIS'S WOULD-BE RESCUERS, AND OUR IDENTITY MUST REMAIN A SECRET UNTIL OUR FINAL GOAL IS MET!"
WARLOCK'S RIGHT! IT IS A SUBMARINE...
...OF DEVIANT DESIGN!
AND DID YOU SEE, SELFRIENDS? THEY HAD THE HORN.
IT'S GONE NOW... CRUSHED!
JUST AS WELL!
ATTUMA HAS BEEN BETRAYED BY HIS ALLIES. WHEN HE RETURNS TO ATLANTIS, THERE WILL BE NOTHING LEFT TO RULE.
AFTER THEM! THEY HAVE TO ANSWER FOR WHAT THEY'VE DONE!
NO. THE MONSTER IS STILL HERE, POISONING THE OCEAN, DESTROYING OUR CITY...
WHEN IT HAS FINISHED ITS DECIMATION HERE, IT WILL ATTACK SHIPS... OR CITIES ALONG THE COAST...
PLEASE, WE'LL NEED OUR POWERS... ALL OF OUR POWERS TO STOP IT...
IF IT CAN BE STOPPED. I SURELY HOPE SOMEBODY HAS SOME BRIGHT IDEAS!
I THINK THAT THE FIRST STEP IS TO CREATE A WHIRLPOOL ...TO TRY AND CONTAIN THE MONSTER'S POISON BLOOD...
RUMMBLE!
NEXT, I USE MY VIBES TO ANNOY IT... TO GET MAD ENOUGH TO CHASE US AWAY FROM ATLANTIS AND ITS INHABITANTS...

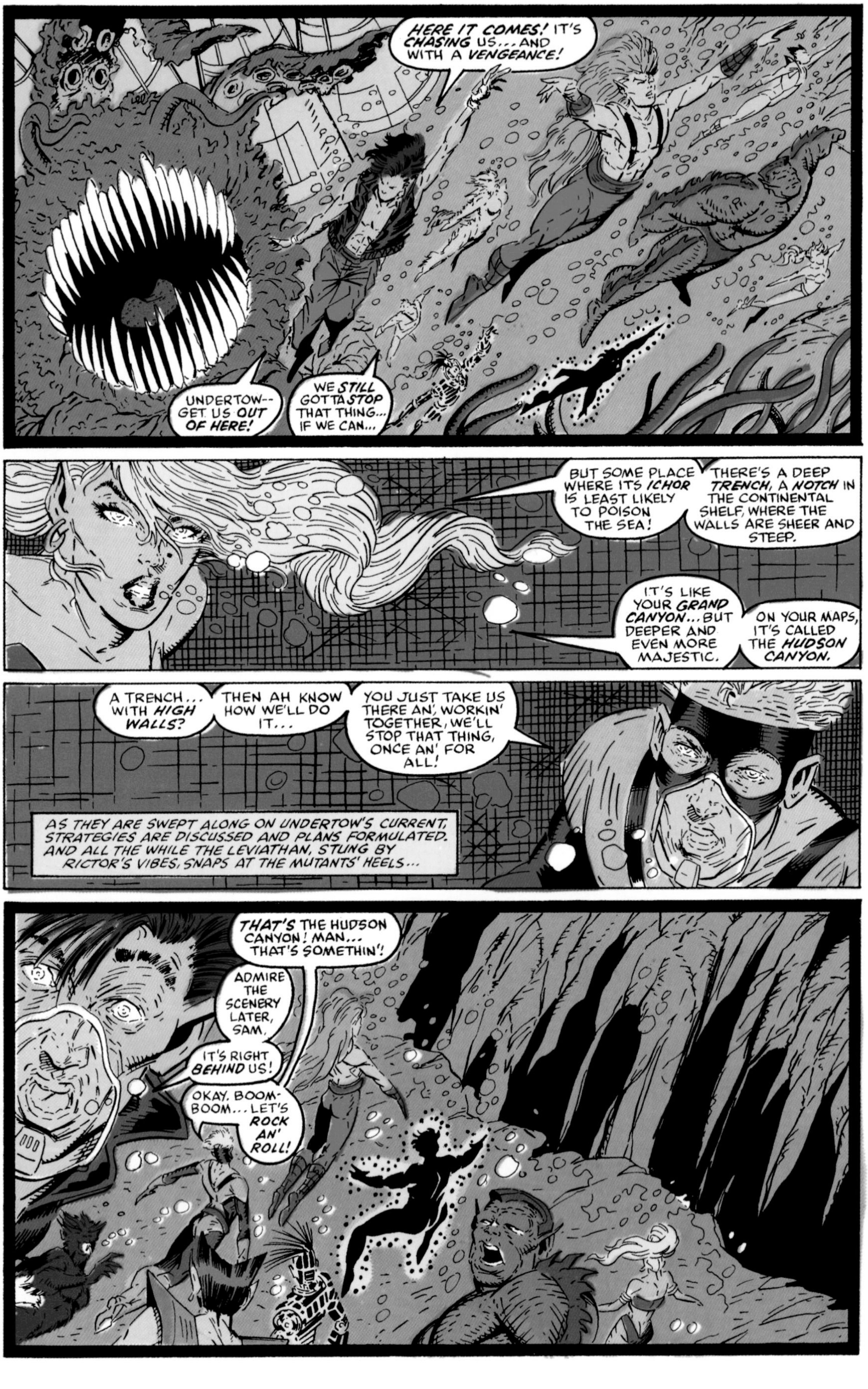
HERE IT COMES! IT'S CHASING US... AND WITH A VENGEANCE!
UNDERTOW-- GET US OUT OF HERE!
WE STILL GOTTA STOP THAT THING... IF WE CAN...
BUT SOME PLACE WHERE ITS ICHOR IS LEAST LIKELY TO POISON THE SEA!
THERE'S A DEEP TRENCH, A NOTCH IN THE CONTINENTAL SHELF, WHERE THE WALLS ARE SHEER AND STEEP.
IT'S LIKE YOUR GRAND CANYON... BUT DEEPER AND EVEN MORE MAJESTIC.
ON YOUR MAPS, IT'S CALLED THE HUDSON CANYON.
A TRENCH... WITH HIGH WALLS?
THEN AH KNOW HOW WE'LL DO IT...
YOU JUST TAKE US THERE AN', WORKIN' TOGETHER, WE'LL STOP THAT THING, ONCE AN' FOR ALL!
AS THEY ARE SWEPT ALONG ON UNDERTOW'S CURRENT, STRATEGIES ARE DISCUSSED AND PLANS FORMULATED. AND ALL THE WHILE THE LEVIATHAN, STUNG BY RICTOR'S VIBES, SNAPS AT THE MUTANTS' HEELS...
THAT'S THE HUDSON CANYON! MAN... THAT'S SOMETHIN'!
ADMIRE THE SCENERY LATER, SAM.
IT'S RIGHT BEHIND US!
OKAY, BOOM-BOOM... LET'S ROCK AN' ROLL!

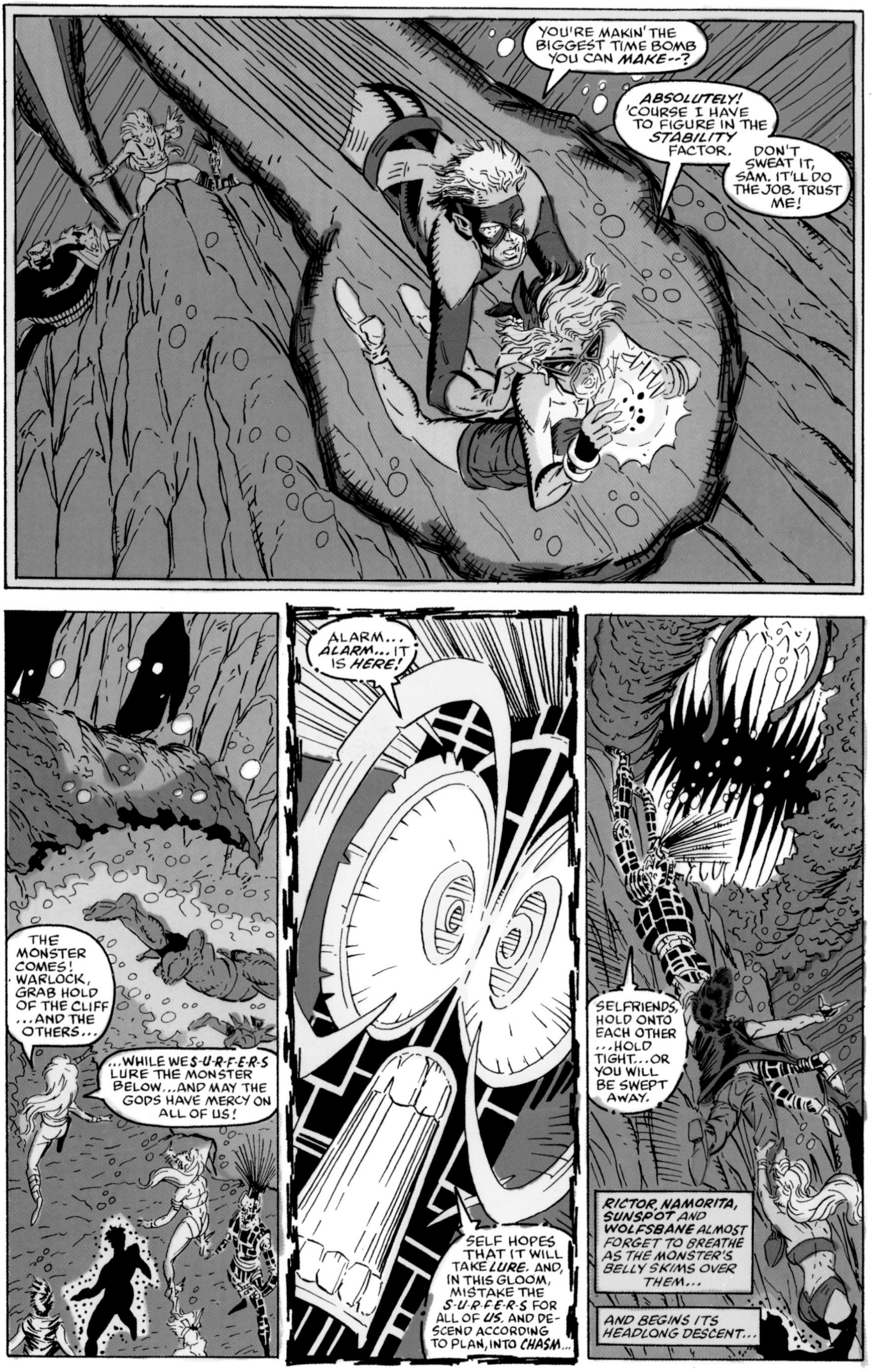

YOU'RE MAKIN' THE BIGGEST TIME BOMB YOU CAN MAKE--?
ABSOLUTELY! 'COURSE I HAVE TO FIGURE IN THE STABILITY FACTOR.
DON'T SWEAT IT, SAM. IT'LL DO THE JOB. TRUST ME!
THE MONSTER COMES! WARLOCK, GRAB HOLD OF THE CLIFF ...AND THE OTHERS...
...WHILE WE S-U-R-F-E-R-S LURE THE MONSTER BELOW...AND MAY THE GODS HAVE MERCY ON ALL OF US!
ALARM... ALARM... IT IS HERE!
SELF HOPES THAT IT WILL TAKE LURE. AND, IN THIS GLOOM, MISTAKE THE S-U-R-F-E-R-S FOR ALL OF US, AND DESCEND ACCORDING TO PLAN, INTO CHASM...
SELFRIENDS, HOLD ONTO EACH OTHER ...HOLD TIGHT...OR YOU WILL BE SWEPT AWAY.
RICTOR, NAMORITA, SUNSPOT AND WOLFSBANE ALMOST FORGET TO BREATHE AS THE MONSTER'S BELLY SKIMS OVER THEM...
AND BEGINS ITS HEADLONG DESCENT...

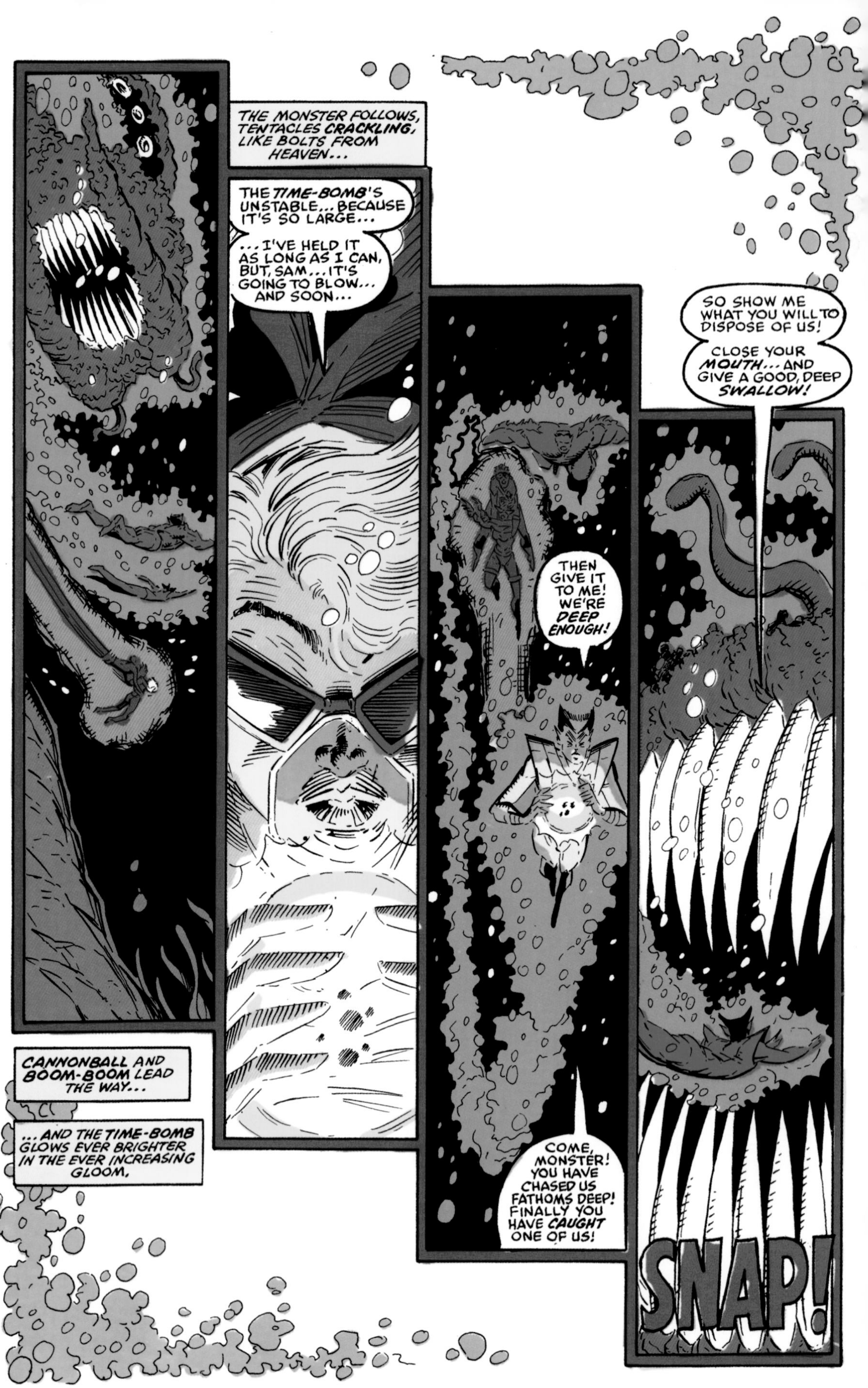
THE MONSTER FOLLOWS, TENTACLES CRACKLING, LIKE BOLTS FROM HEAVEN...
CANNONBALL AND BOOM-BOOM LEAD THE WAY...
...AND THE TIME-BOMB GLOWS EVER BRIGHTER IN THE EVER INCREASING GLOOM.
THE TIME-BOMB'S UNSTABLE... BECAUSE IT'S SO LARGE...
...I'VE HELD IT AS LONG AS I CAN, BUT, SAM...IT'S GOING TO BLOW... AND SOON...
THEN GIVE IT TO ME! WE'RE DEEP ENOUGH!
COME, MONSTER! YOU HAVE CHASED US FATHOMS DEEP! FINALLY YOU HAVE CAUGHT ONE OF US!
SO SHOW ME WHAT YOU WILL TO DISPOSE OF US!
CLOSE YOUR MOUTH... AND GIVE A GOOD, DEEP SWALLOW!
SNAP!

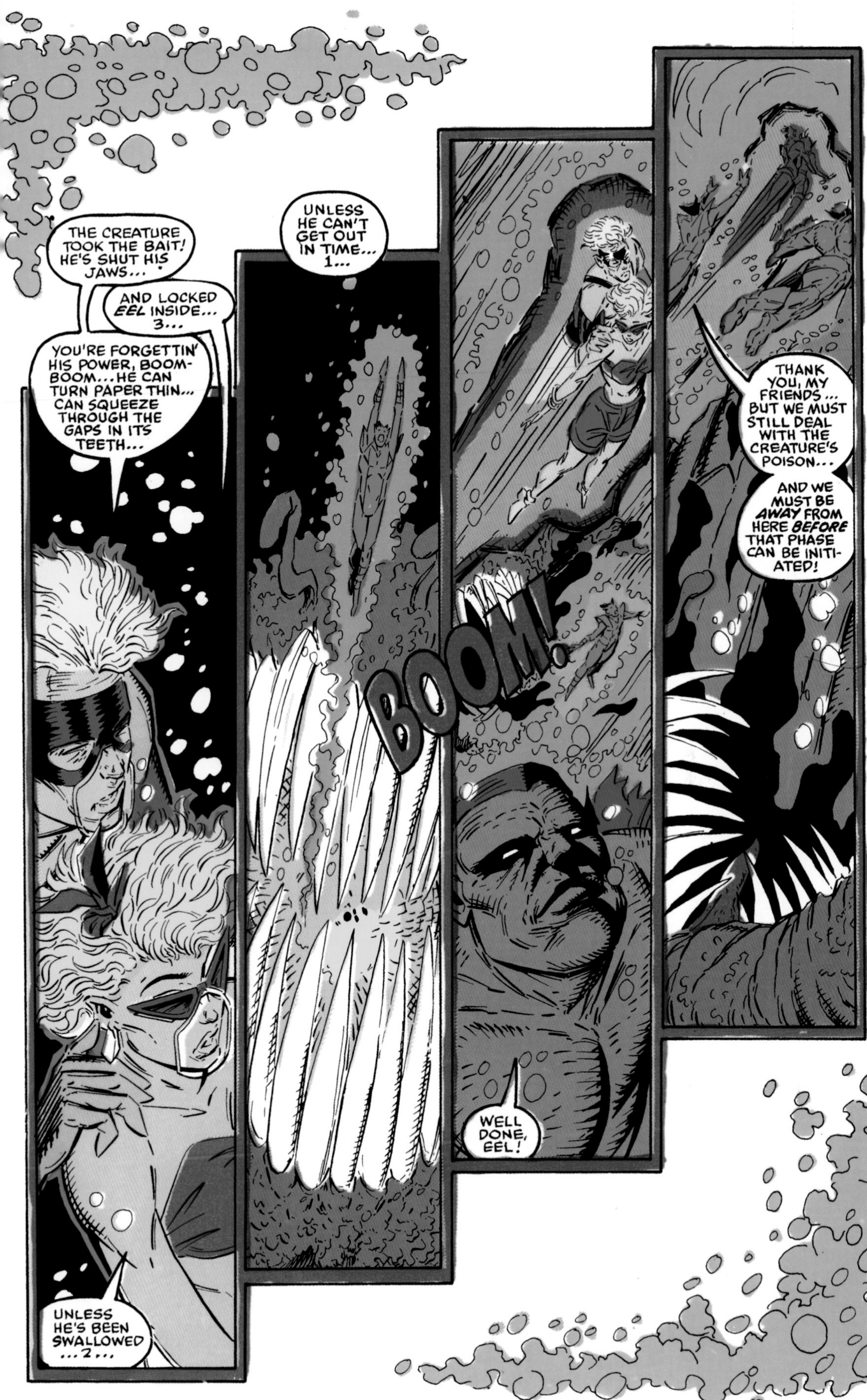
THE CREATURE TOOK THE BAIT! HE'S SHUT HIS JAWS...
AND LOCKED EEL INSIDE... 3...
YOU'RE FORGETTIN' HIS POWER, BOOM-BOOM... HE CAN TURN PAPER THIN... CAN SQUEEZE THROUGH THE GAPS IN ITS TEETH...
UNLESS HE'S BEEN SWALLOWED ...2...
UNLESS HE CAN'T GET OUT IN TIME... 1...
BOOM!
WELL DONE, EEL!
THANK YOU, MY FRIENDS... BUT WE MUST STILL DEAL WITH THE CREATURE'S POISON...
AND WE MUST BE AWAY FROM HERE BEFORE THAT PHASE CAN BE INITIATED!

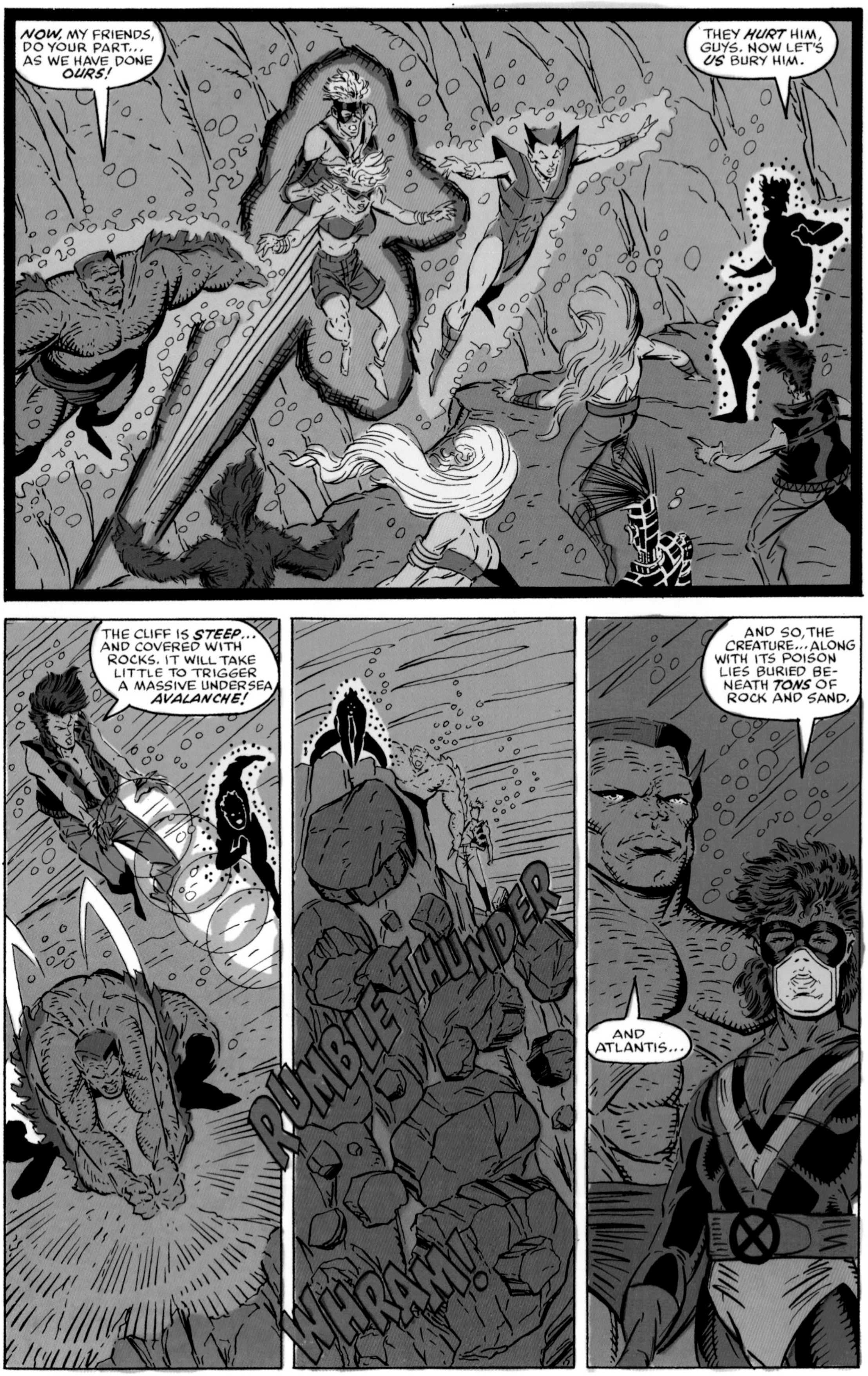
NOW, MY FRIENDS, DO YOUR PART... AS WE HAVE DONE OURS!
THEY HURT HIM, GUYS. NOW LET'S US BURY HIM.
THE CLIFF IS STEEP... AND COVERED WITH ROCKS. IT WILL TAKE LITTLE TO TRIGGER A MASSIVE UNDERSEA AVALANCHE!
RUMBLE THUNDER
WHRAM!
AND SO, THE CREATURE... ALONG WITH ITS POISON LIES BURIED BENEATH TONS OF ROCK AND SAND.
AND ATLANTIS...

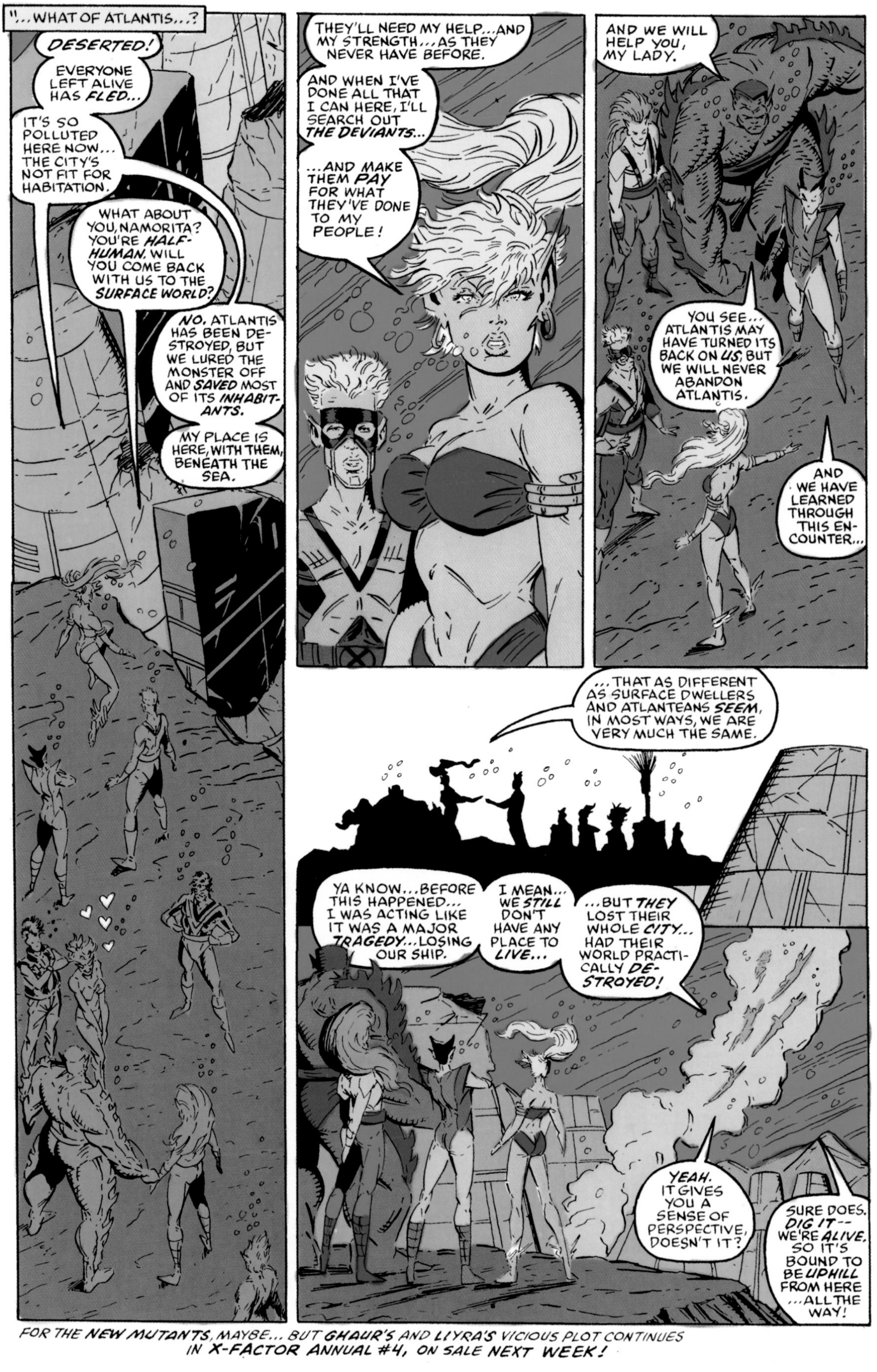
"...WHAT OF ATLANTIS...?
DESERTED!
EVERYONE LEFT ALIVE HAS FLED...
IT'S SO POLLUTED HERE NOW... THE CITY'S NOT FIT FOR HABITATION.
WHAT ABOUT YOU, NAMORITA? YOU'RE HALF-HUMAN. WILL YOU COME BACK WITH US TO THE SURFACE WORLD?
NO. ATLANTIS HAS BEEN DESTROYED, BUT WE LURED THE MONSTER OFF AND SAVED MOST OF ITS INHABITANTS.
MY PLACE IS HERE, WITH THEM, BENEATH THE SEA.
THEY'LL NEED MY HELP...AND MY STRENGTH... AS THEY NEVER HAVE BEFORE.
AND WHEN I'VE DONE ALL THAT I CAN HERE, I'LL SEARCH OUT THE DEVIANTS...
...AND MAKE THEM PAY FOR WHAT THEY'VE DONE TO MY PEOPLE!
AND WE WILL HELP YOU, MY LADY.
YOU SEE... ATLANTIS MAY HAVE TURNED ITS BACK ON US, BUT WE WILL NEVER ABANDON ATLANTIS.
AND WE HAVE LEARNED THROUGH THIS ENCOUNTER...
...THAT AS DIFFERENT AS SURFACE DWELLERS AND ATLANTEANS SEEM, IN MOST WAYS, WE ARE VERY MUCH THE SAME.
YA KNOW...BEFORE THIS HAPPENED... I WAS ACTING LIKE IT WAS A MAJOR TRAGEDY...LOSING OUR SHIP.
I MEAN... WE STILL DON'T HAVE ANY PLACE TO LIVE...
...BUT THEY LOST THEIR WHOLE CITY... HAD THEIR WORLD PRACTICALLY DESTROYED!
YEAH. IT GIVES YOU A SENSE OF PERSPECTIVE, DOESN'T IT?
SURE DOES. DIG IT-- WE'RE ALIVE. SO IT'S BOUND TO BE UPHILL FROM HERE ...ALL THE WAY!
FOR THE NEW MUTANTS, MAYBE... BUT GHAUR'S AND LLYRA'S VICIOUS PLOT CONTINUES IN X-FACTOR ANNUAL #4, ON SALE NEXT WEEK!

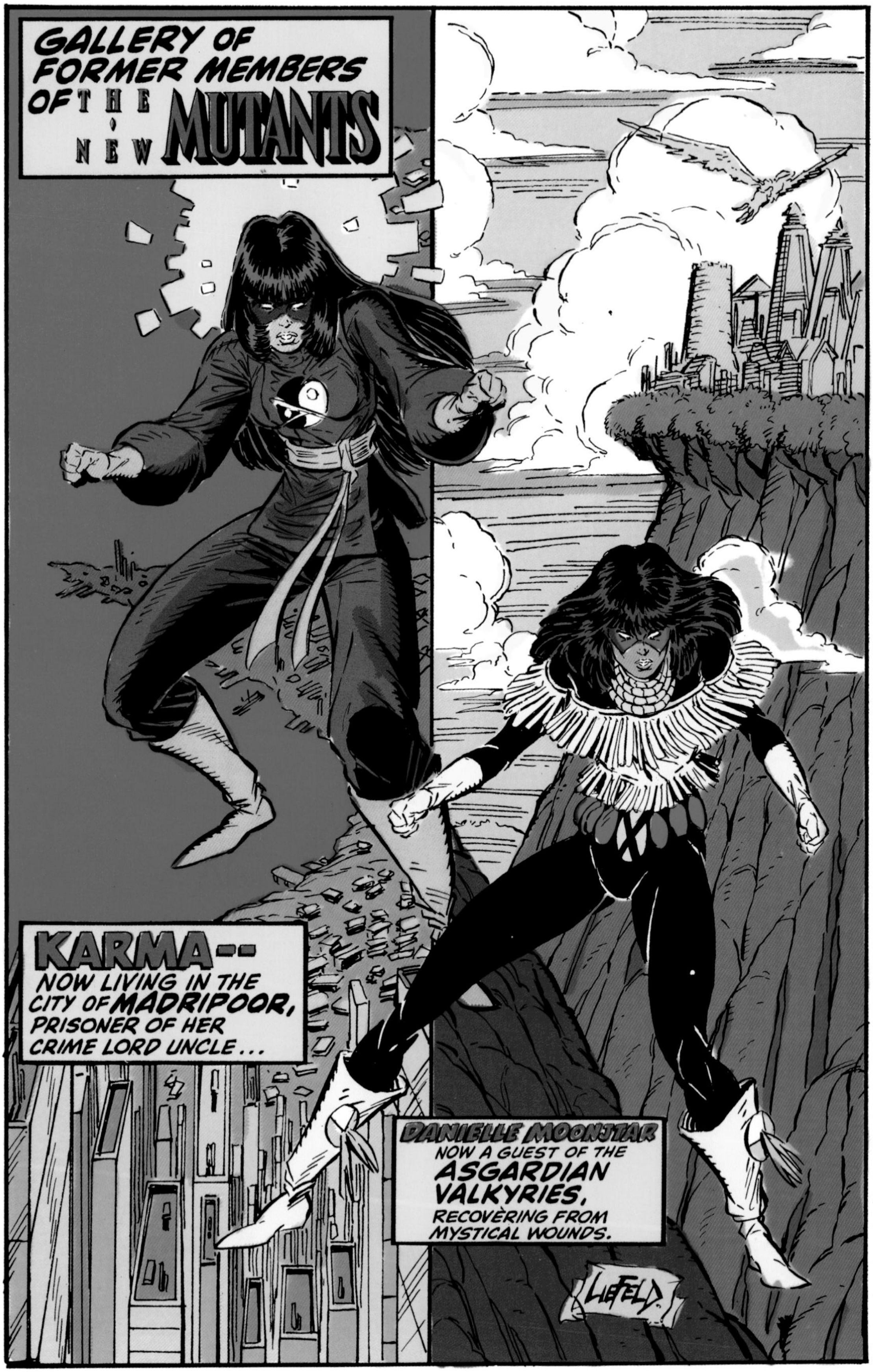
GALLERY OF FORMER MEMBERS OF THE NEW MUTANTS
KARMA-- NOW LIVING IN THE CITY OF MADRIPOOR, PRISONER OF HER CRIME LORD UNCLE...
DANIELLE MOONSTAR NOW A GUEST OF THE ASGARDIAN VALKYRIES, RECOVERING FROM MYSTICAL WOUNDS.
LIEFELD.

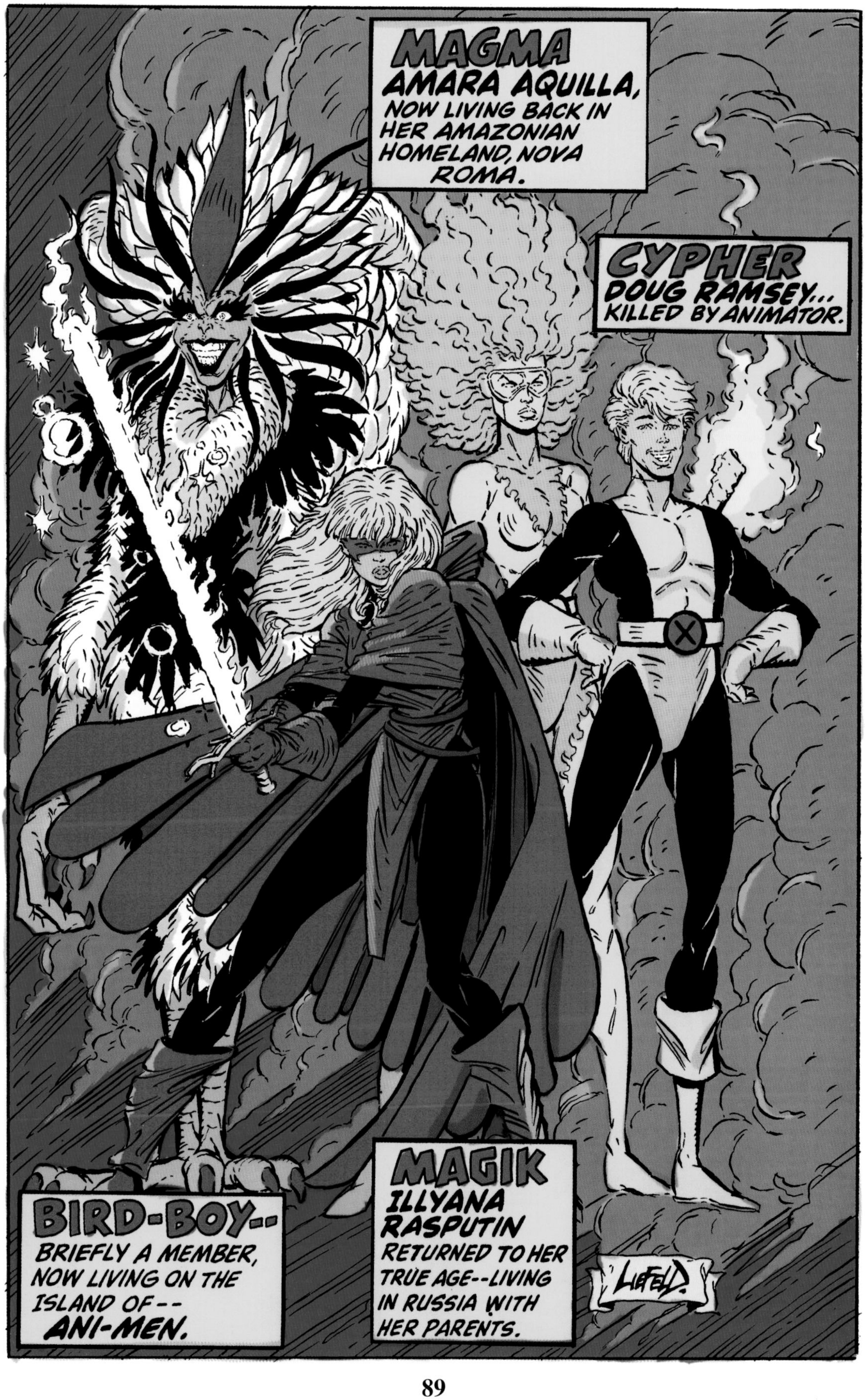
MAGMA
AMARA AQUILLA,
NOW LIVING BACK IN
HER AMAZONIAN
HOMELAND, NOVA
ROMA.
CYPHER
DOUG RAMSEY...
KILLED BY ANIMATOR.
BIRD-BOY--
BRIEFLY A MEMBER,
NOW LIVING ON THE
ISLAND OF --
ANI-MEN.
MAGIK
ILLYANA
RASPUTIN
RETURNED TO HER
TRUE AGE--LIVING
IN RUSSIA WITH
HER PARENTS.
LIEFELD.

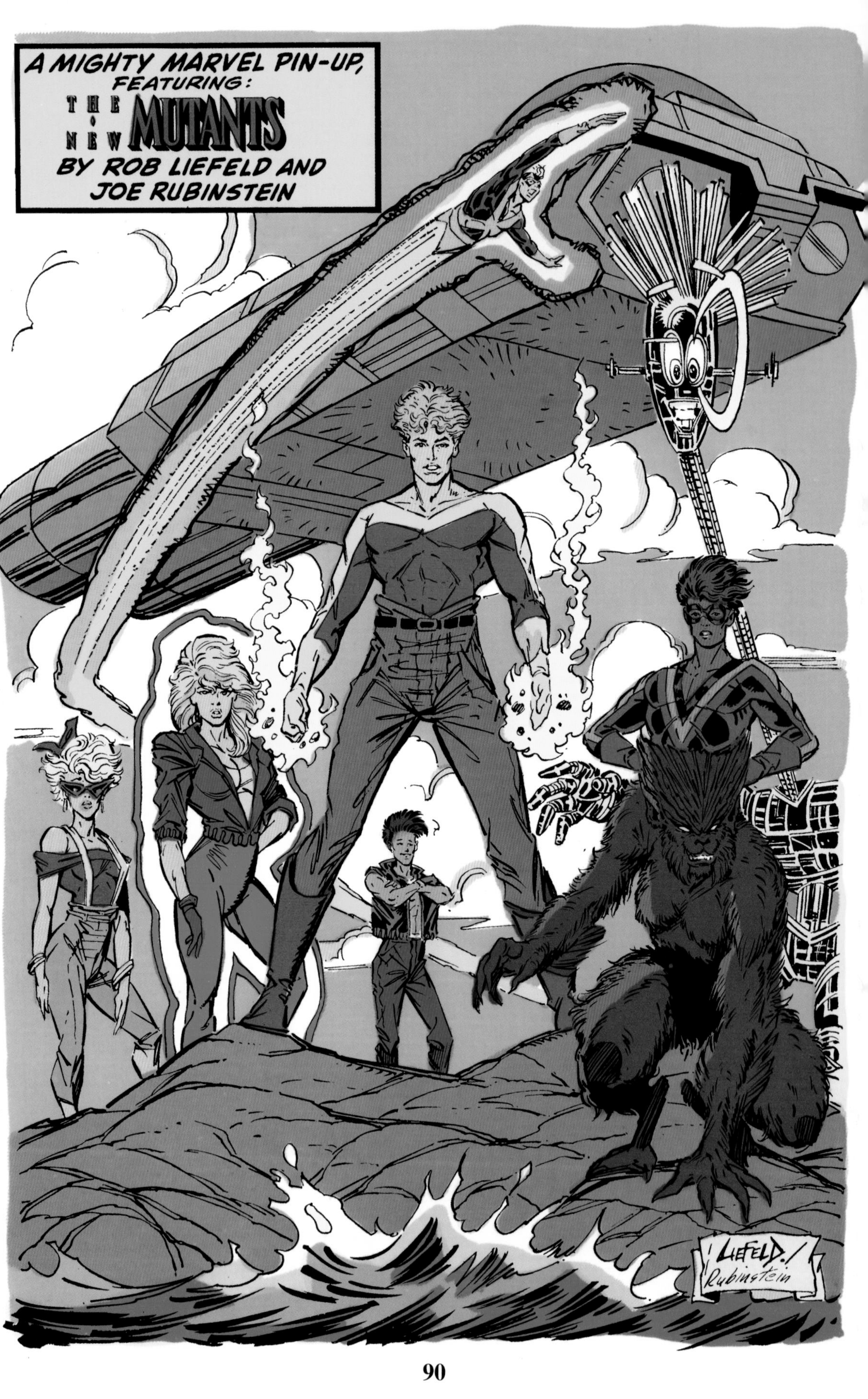
A MIGHTY MARVEL PIN-UP,
FEATURING:
THE NEW MUTANTS
BY ROB LIEFELD AND
JOE RUBINSTEIN
LIEFELD./
Rubinstein

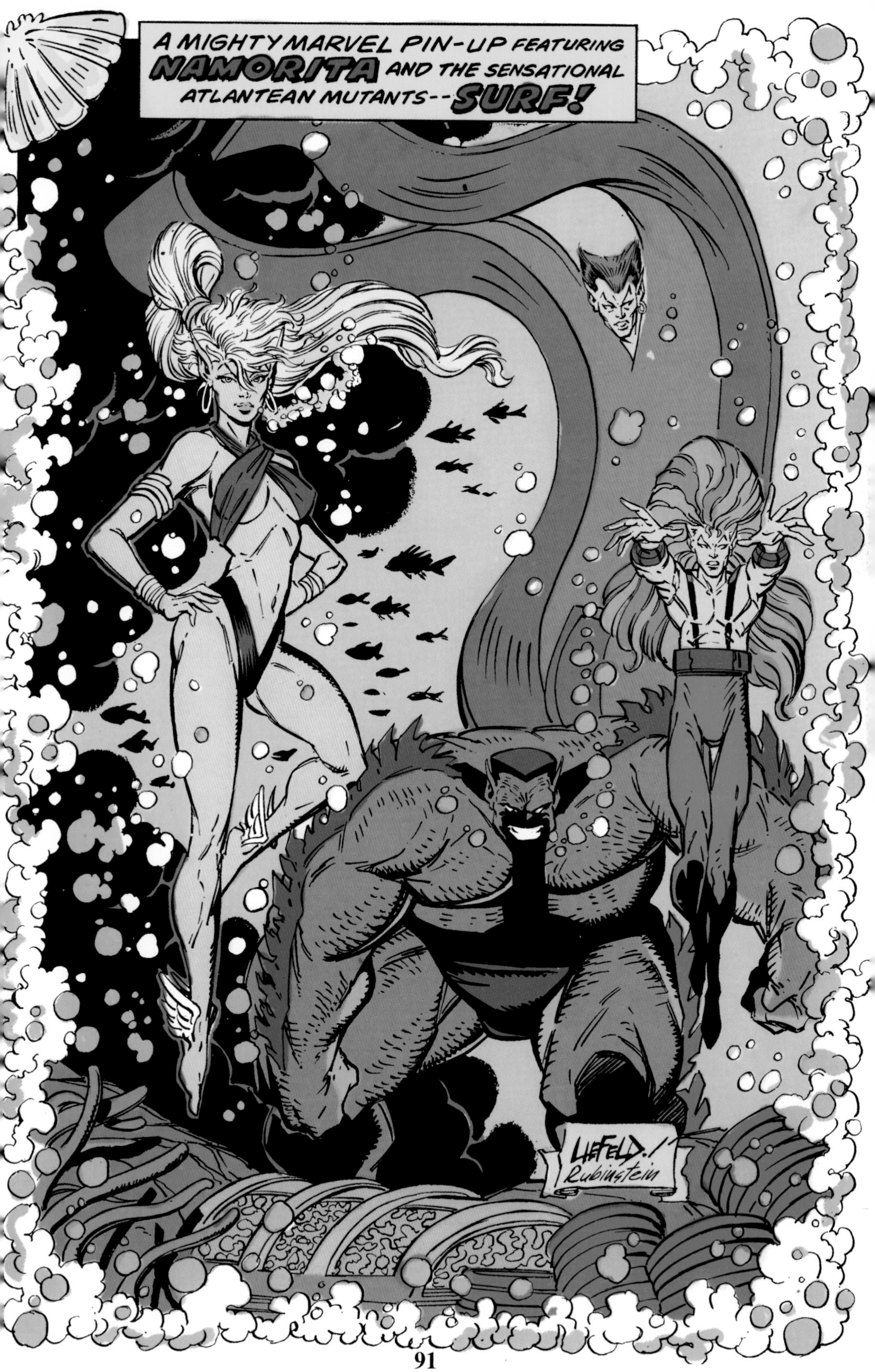
A MIGHTY MARVEL PIN-UP FEATURING NAMORITA AND THE SENSATIONAL ATLANTEAN MUTANTS--SURF!
LIEFELD.!
Rubinstein

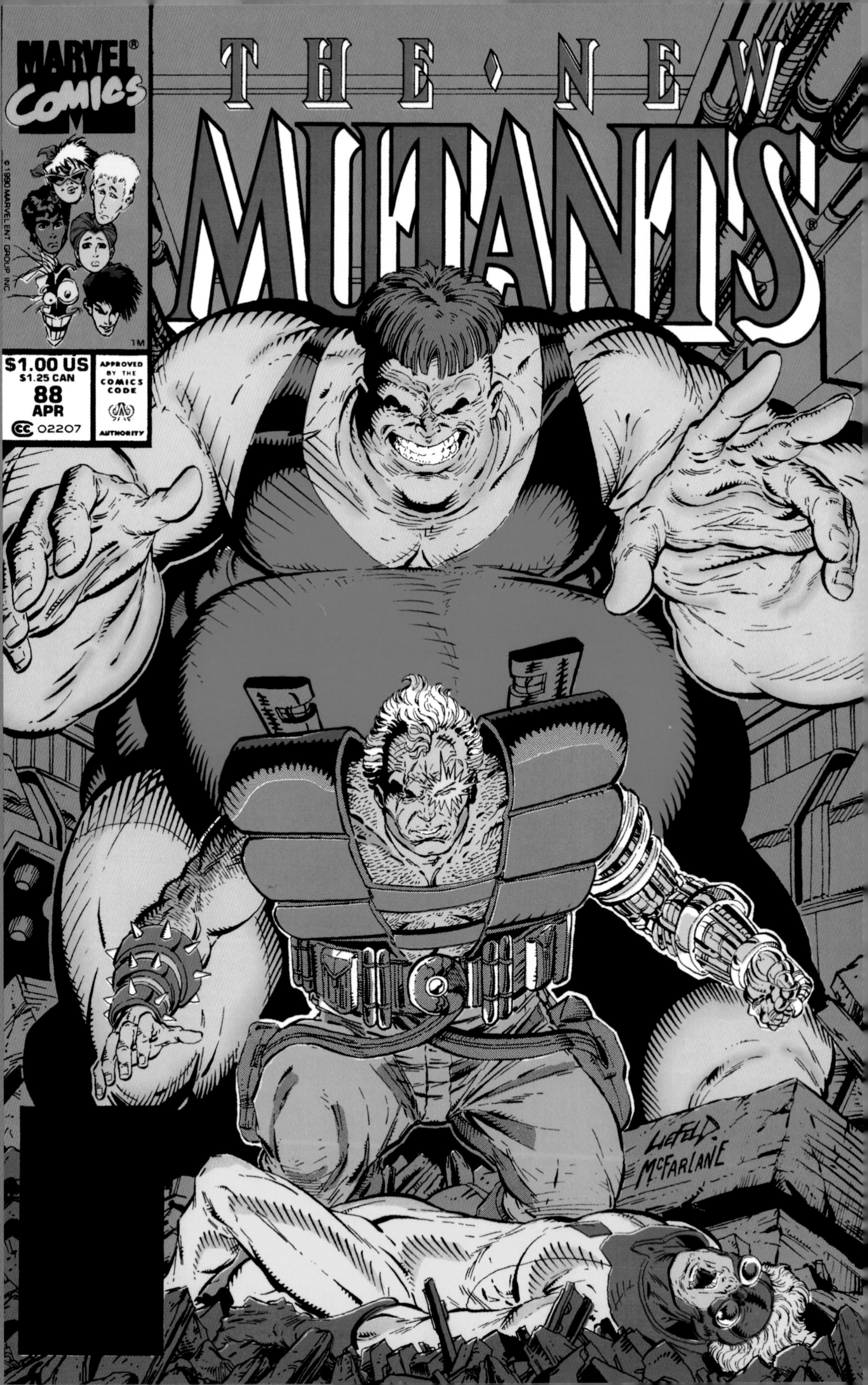
MARVEL® COMICS
THE NEW MUTANTS®
© 1990 MARVEL ENT. GROUP, INC.
TM
$1.00 US
$1.25 CAN
88
APR
CC 02207
APPROVED BY THE COMICS CODE AUTHORITY
LIEFELD
McFARLANE

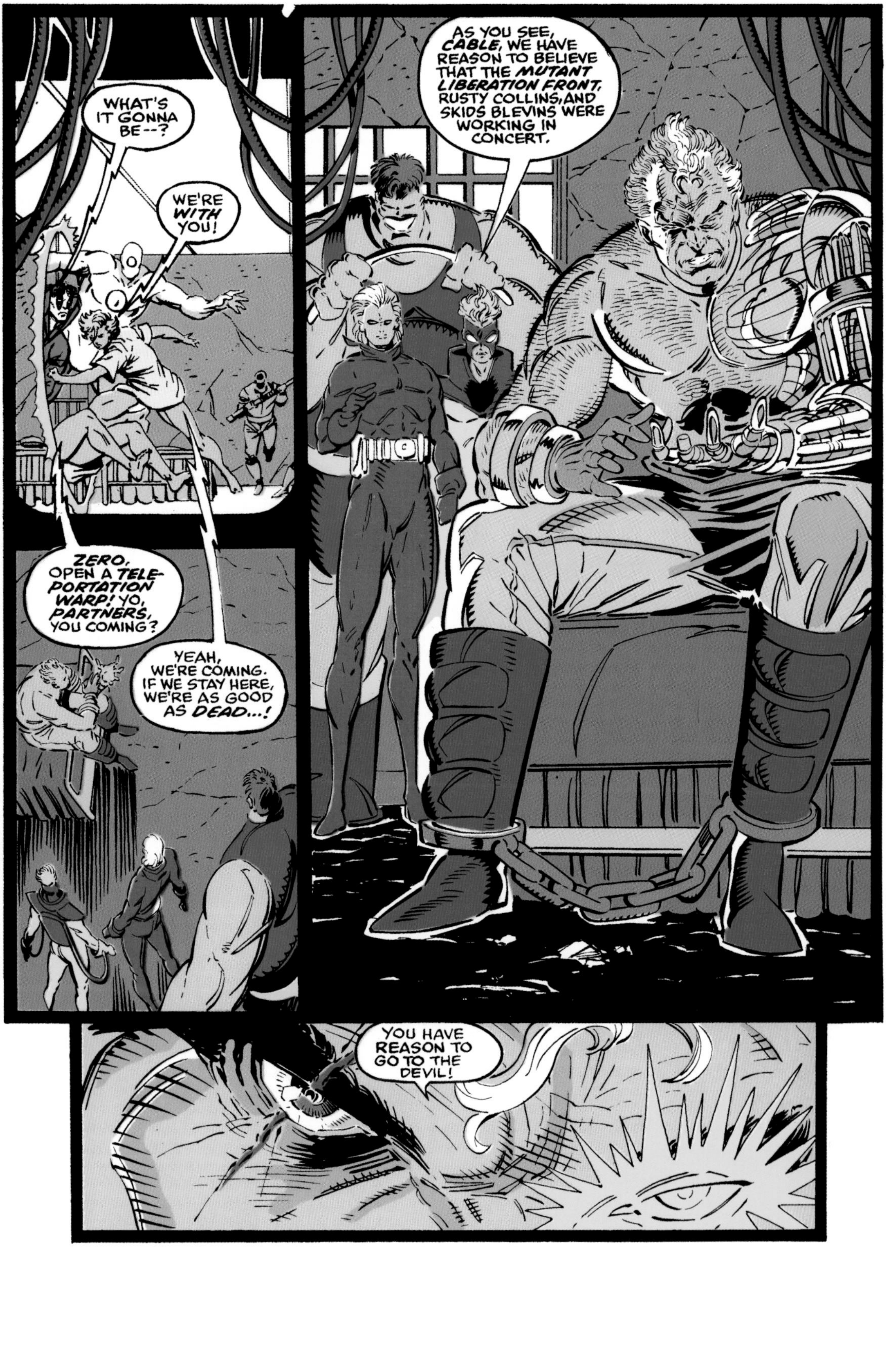
WHAT'S IT GONNA BE--?
WE'RE WITH YOU!
ZERO, OPEN A TELEPORTATION WARP! YO, PARTNERS, YOU COMING?
YEAH, WE'RE COMING. IF WE STAY HERE, WE'RE AS GOOD AS DEAD...!
AS YOU SEE, CABLE, WE HAVE REASON TO BELIEVE THAT THE MUTANT LIBERATION FRONT, RUSTY COLLINS, AND SKIDS BLEVINS WERE WORKING IN CONCERT.
YOU HAVE REASON TO GO TO THE DEVIL!

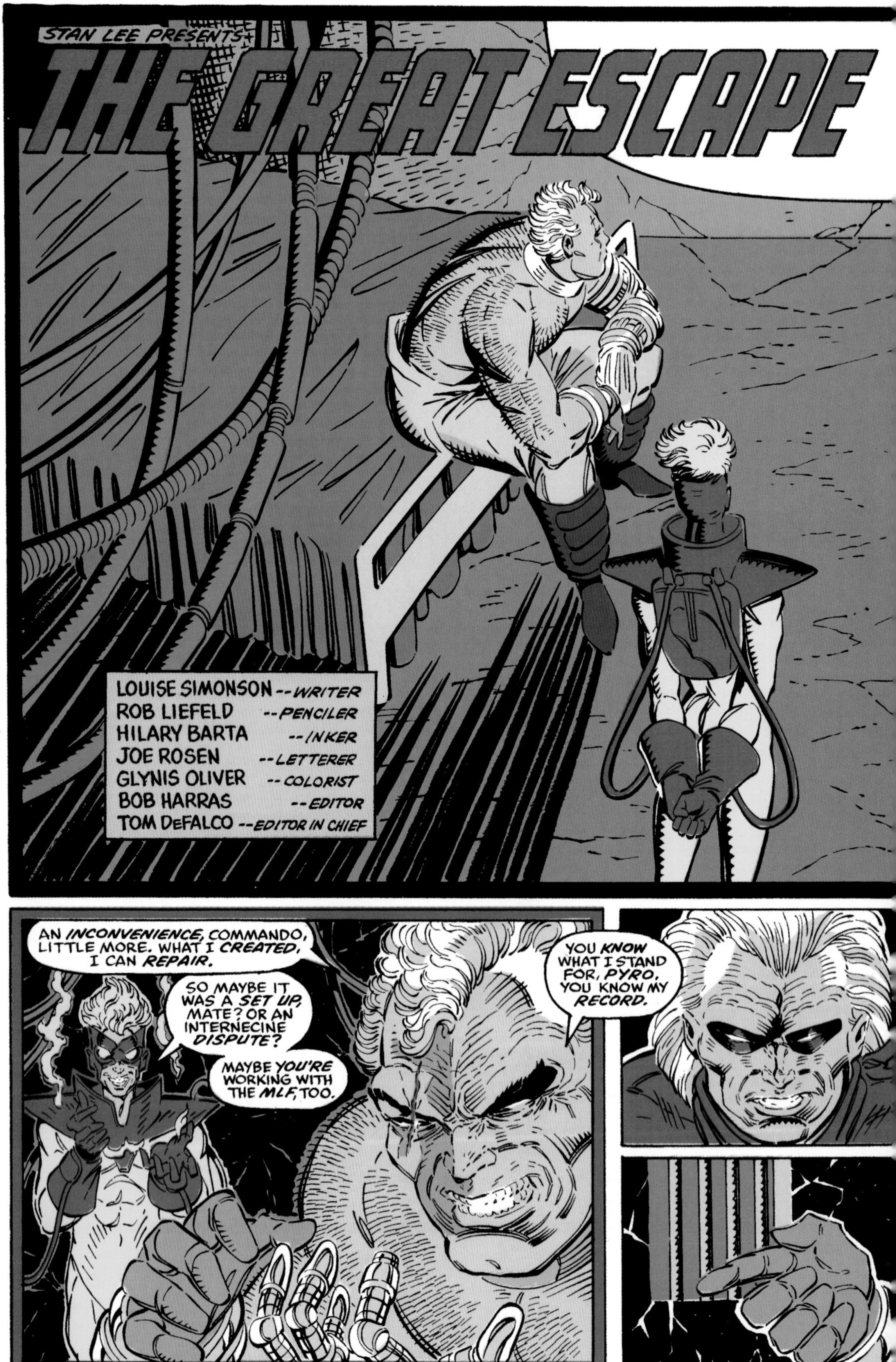
STAN LEE PRESENTS:
THE GREAT ESCAPE
LOUISE SIMONSON --WRITER
ROB LIEFELD --PENCILER
HILARY BARTA --INKER
JOE ROSEN --LETTERER
GLYNIS OLIVER --COLORIST
BOB HARRAS --EDITOR
TOM DeFALCO --EDITOR IN CHIEF
AN INCONVENIENCE, COMMANDO, LITTLE MORE. WHAT I CREATED, I CAN REPAIR.
SO MAYBE IT WAS A SET UP, MATE? OR AN INTERNECINE DISPUTE?
MAYBE YOU'RE WORKING WITH THE MLF, TOO.
YOU KNOW WHAT I STAND FOR, PYRO. YOU KNOW MY RECORD.

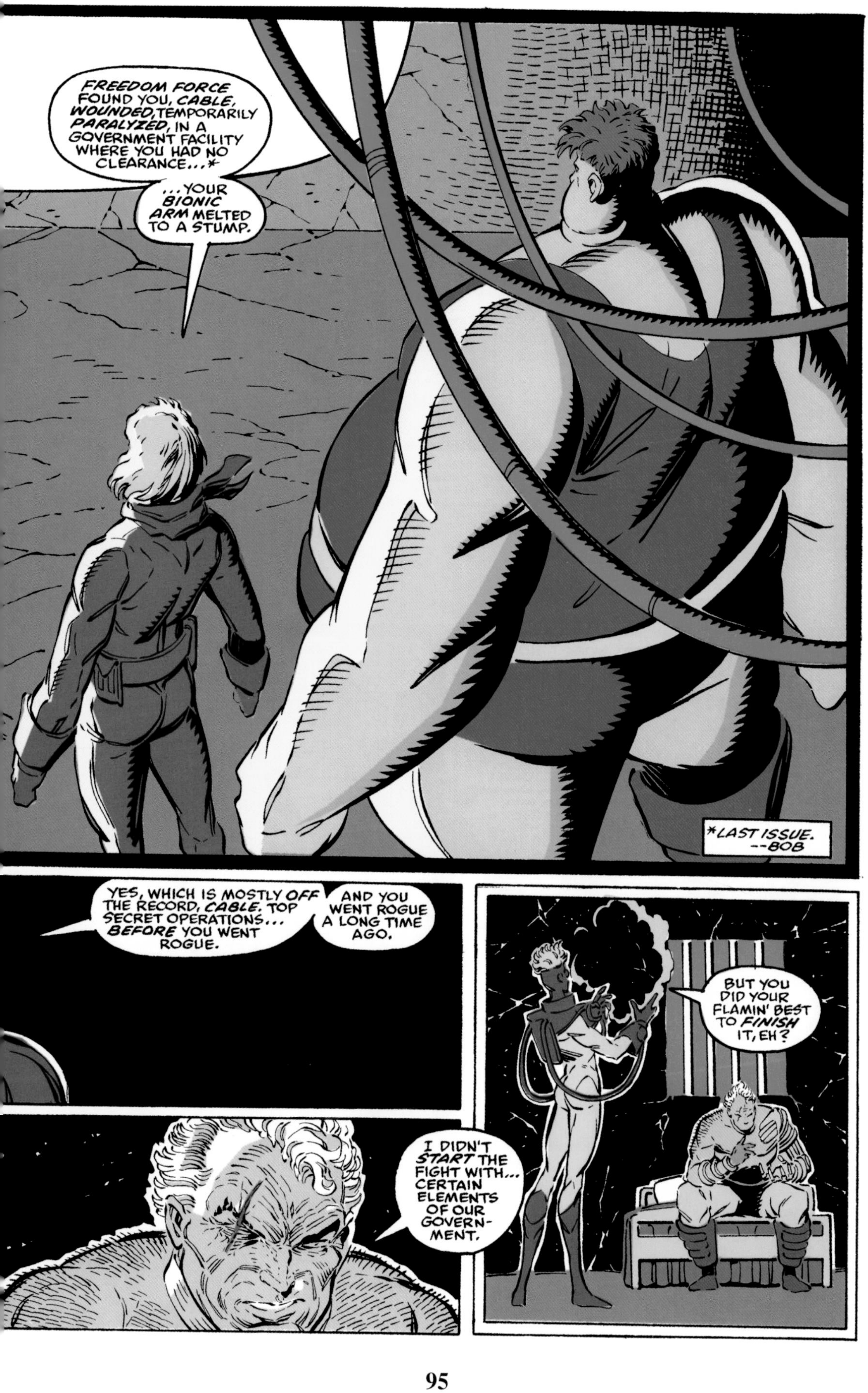
FREEDOM FORCE FOUND YOU, CABLE, WOUNDED, TEMPORARILY PARALYZED, IN A GOVERNMENT FACILITY WHERE YOU HAD NO CLEARANCE...*
...YOUR BIONIC ARM MELTED TO A STUMP.
*LAST ISSUE. --BOB
YES, WHICH IS MOSTLY OFF THE RECORD, CABLE. TOP SECRET OPERATIONS... BEFORE YOU WENT ROGUE.
AND YOU WENT ROGUE A LONG TIME AGO.
BUT YOU DID YOUR FLAMIN' BEST TO FINISH IT, EH?
I DIDN'T START THE FIGHT WITH... CERTAIN ELEMENTS OF OUR GOVERNMENT.

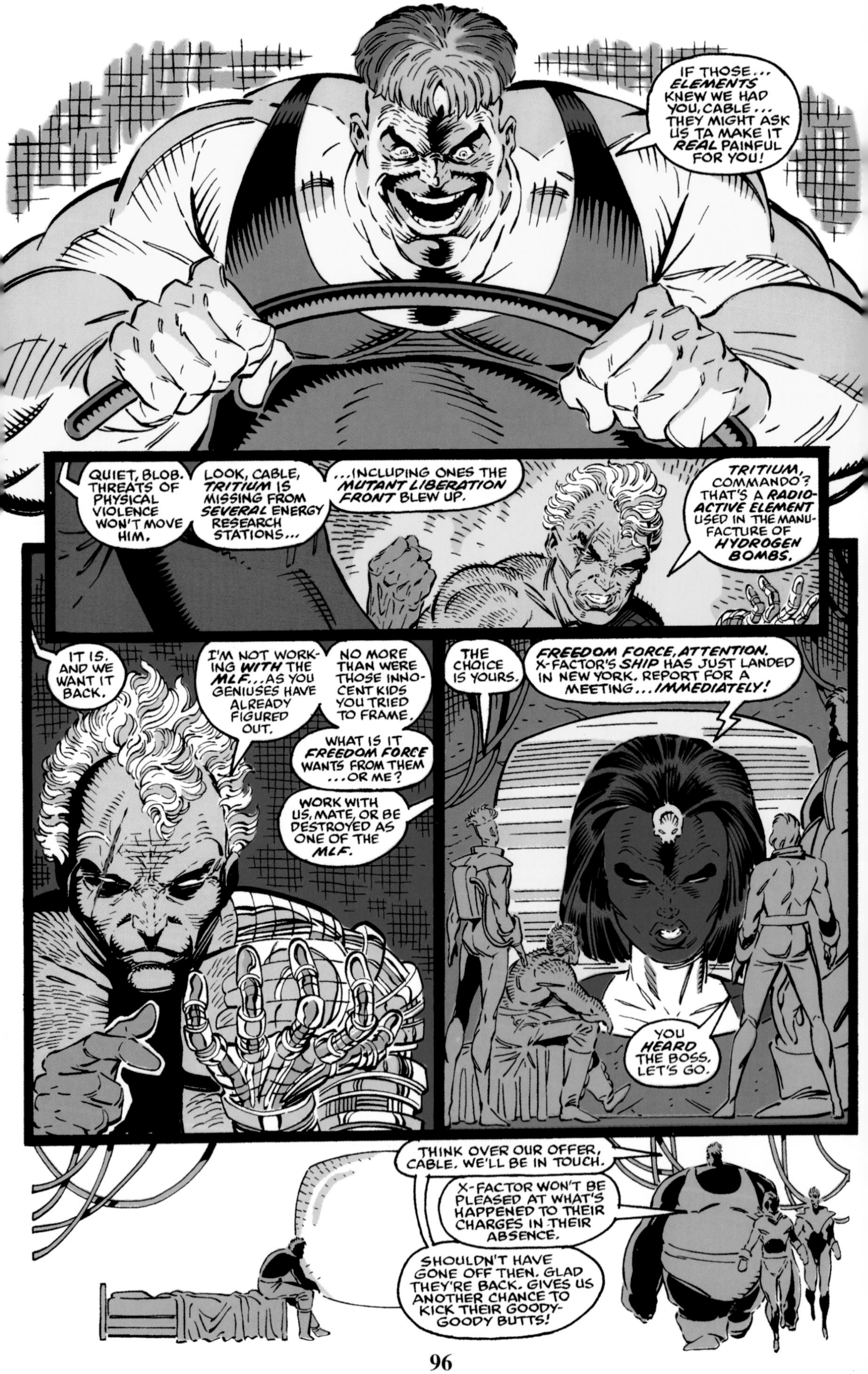
IF THOSE... ELEMENTS KNEW WE HAD YOU, CABLE... THEY MIGHT ASK US TA MAKE IT REAL PAINFUL FOR YOU!
QUIET, BLOB. THREATS OF PHYSICAL VIOLENCE WON'T MOVE HIM.
LOOK, CABLE, TRITIUM IS MISSING FROM SEVERAL ENERGY RESEARCH STATIONS...
...INCLUDING ONES THE MUTANT LIBERATION FRONT BLEW UP.
TRITIUM, COMMANDO? THAT'S A RADIO-ACTIVE ELEMENT USED IN THE MANUFACTURE OF HYDROGEN BOMBS.
IT IS. AND WE WANT IT BACK.
I'M NOT WORKING WITH THE MLF... AS YOU GENIUSES HAVE ALREADY FIGURED OUT.
NO MORE THAN WERE THOSE INNOCENT KIDS YOU TRIED TO FRAME.
WHAT IS IT FREEDOM FORCE WANTS FROM THEM ...OR ME?
WORK WITH US, MATE, OR BE DESTROYED AS ONE OF THE MLF.
THE CHOICE IS YOURS.
FREEDOM FORCE, ATTENTION. X-FACTOR'S SHIP HAS JUST LANDED IN NEW YORK. REPORT FOR A MEETING... IMMEDIATELY!
YOU HEARD THE BOSS. LET'S GO.
THINK OVER OUR OFFER, CABLE. WE'LL BE IN TOUCH.
X-FACTOR WON'T BE PLEASED AT WHAT'S HAPPENED TO THEIR CHARGES IN THEIR ABSENCE.
SHOULDN'T HAVE GONE OFF THEN. GLAD THEY'RE BACK. GIVES US ANOTHER CHANCE TO KICK THEIR GOODY-GOODY BUTTS!

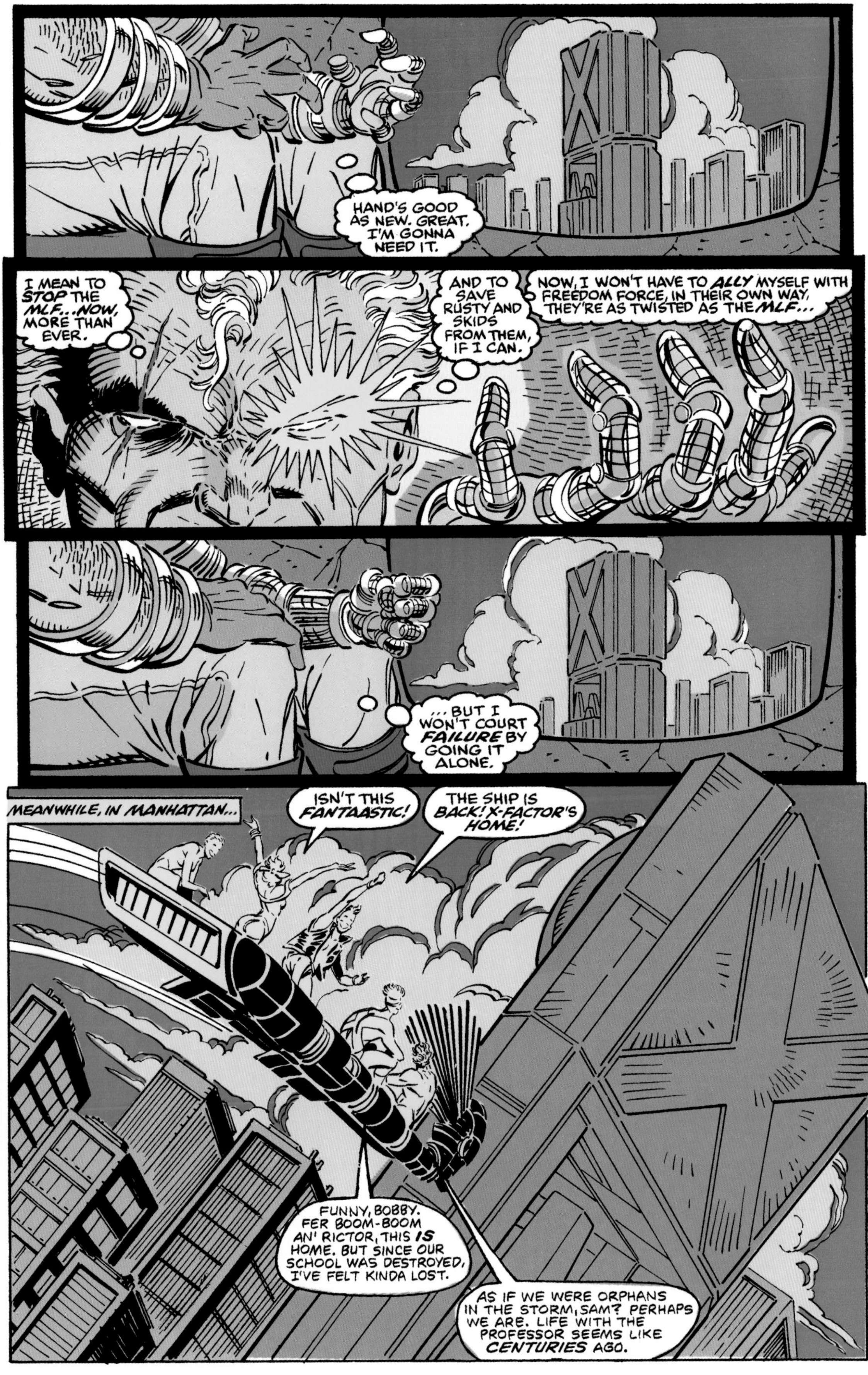

HAND'S GOOD AS NEW. GREAT, I'M GONNA NEED IT.
I MEAN TO STOP THE MLF...NOW, MORE THAN EVER.
AND TO SAVE RUSTY AND SKIDS FROM THEM, IF I CAN.
NOW, I WON'T HAVE TO ALLY MYSELF WITH FREEDOM FORCE. IN THEIR OWN WAY, THEY'RE AS TWISTED AS THE MLF...
...BUT I WON'T COURT FAILURE BY GOING IT ALONE.
MEANWHILE, IN MANHATTAN...
ISN'T THIS FANTAASTIC!
THE SHIP IS BACK! X-FACTOR'S HOME!
FUNNY, BOBBY. FER BOOM-BOOM AN' RICTOR, THIS IS HOME. BUT SINCE OUR SCHOOL WAS DESTROYED, I'VE FELT KINDA LOST.
AS IF WE WERE ORPHANS IN THE STORM, SAM? PERHAPS WE ARE. LIFE WITH THE PROFESSOR SEEMS LIKE CENTURIES AGO.

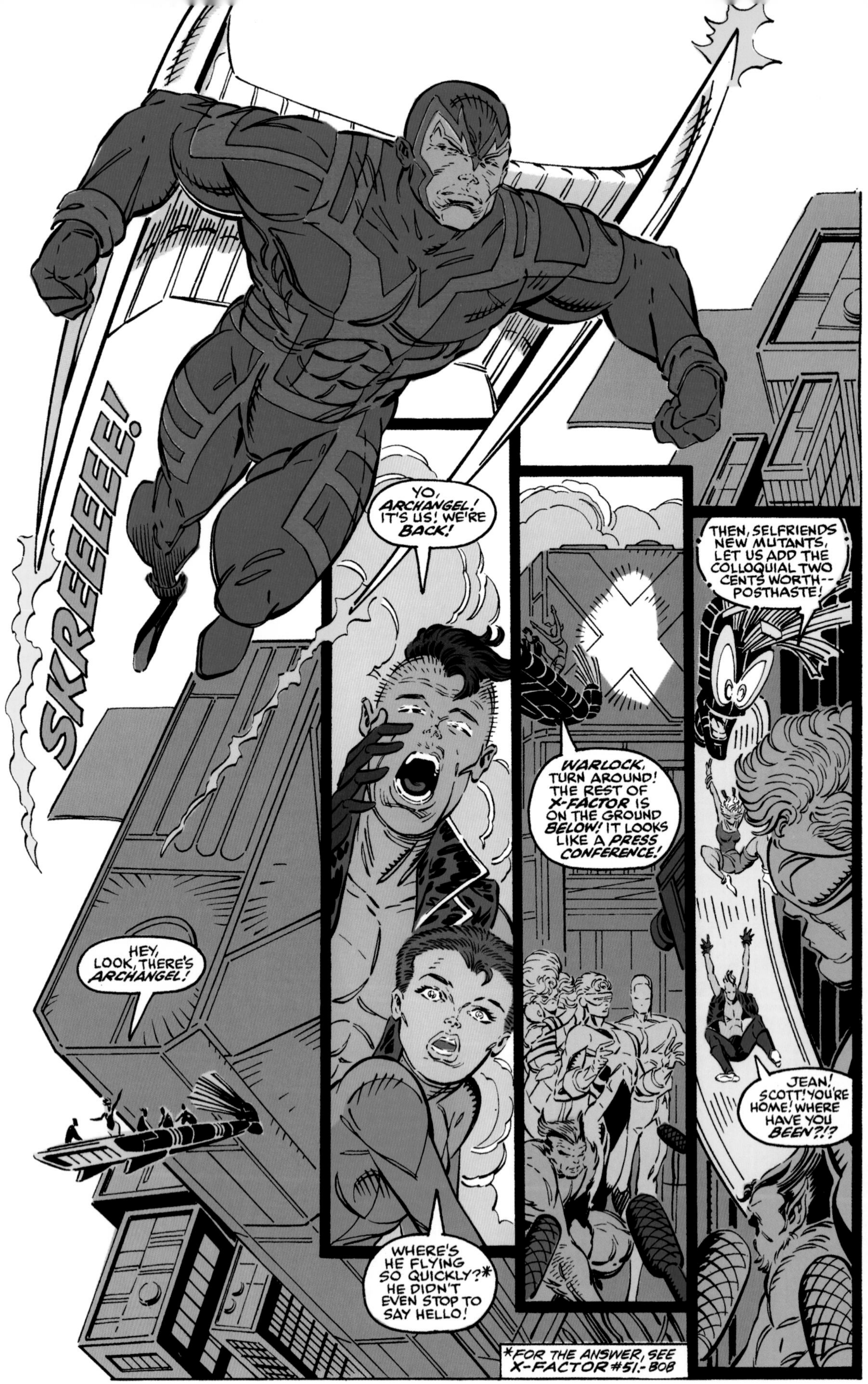
SKREEEEE!
YO, ARCHANGEL! IT'S US! WE'RE BACK!
HEY, LOOK, THERE'S ARCHANGEL!
WHERE'S HE FLYING SO QUICKLY?* HE DIDN'T EVEN STOP TO SAY HELLO!
WARLOCK, TURN AROUND! THE REST OF X-FACTOR IS ON THE GROUND BELOW! IT LOOKS LIKE A PRESS CONFERENCE!
THEN, SELFRIENDS NEW MUTANTS, LET US ADD THE COLLOQUIAL TWO CENTS WORTH--POSTHASTE!
JEAN! SCOTT! YOU'RE HOME! WHERE HAVE YOU BEEN?!?
*FOR THE ANSWER, SEE X-FACTOR #51.-BOB

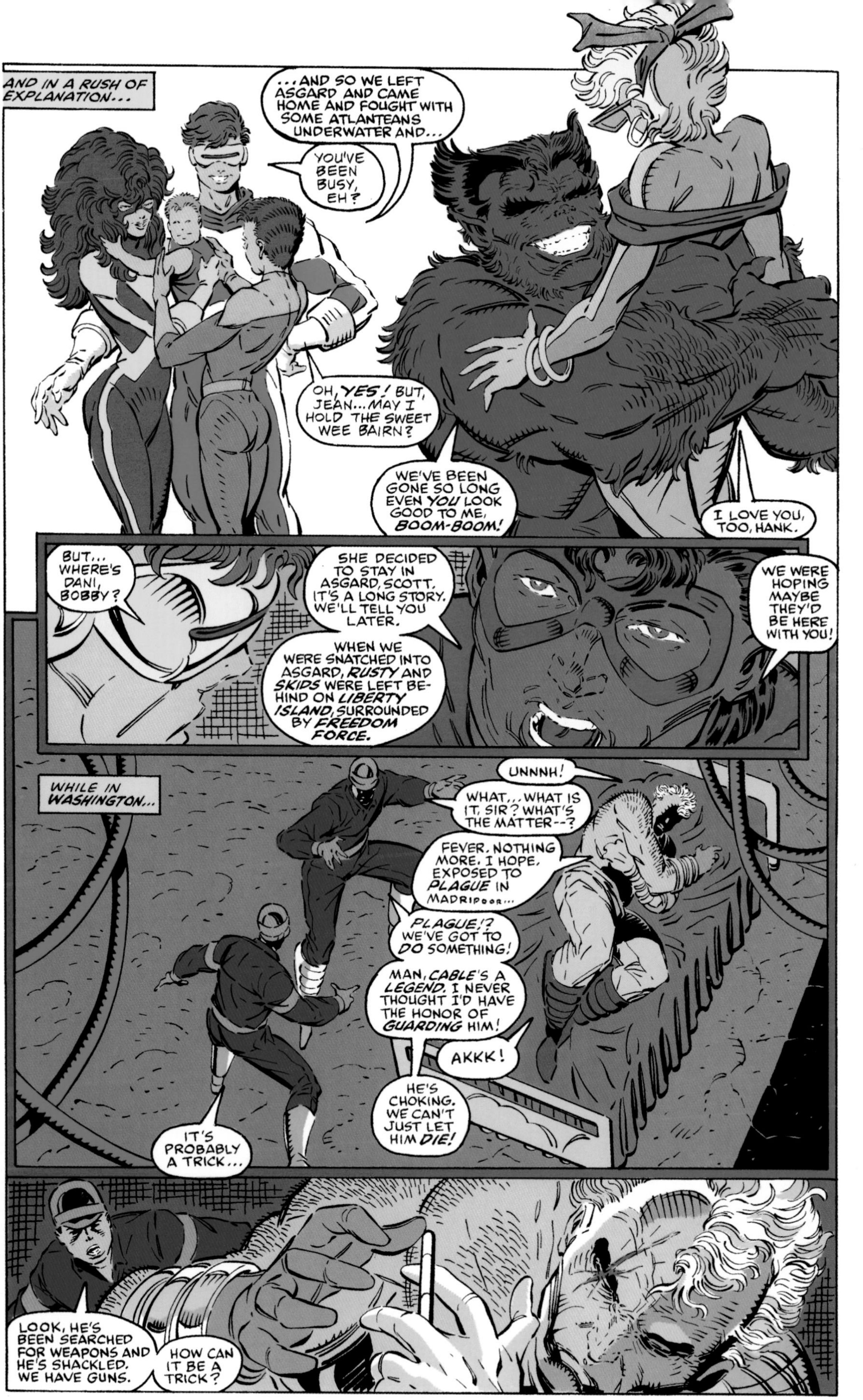

AND IN A RUSH OF EXPLANATION...
...AND SO WE LEFT ASGARD AND CAME HOME AND FOUGHT WITH SOME ATLANTEANS UNDERWATER AND...
YOU'VE BEEN BUSY, EH?
OH, YES! BUT, JEAN... MAY I HOLD THE SWEET WEE BAIRN?
WE'VE BEEN GONE SO LONG EVEN YOU LOOK GOOD TO ME, BOOM-BOOM!
I LOVE YOU, TOO, HANK.
BUT... WHERE'S DANI, BOBBY?
SHE DECIDED TO STAY IN ASGARD, SCOTT. IT'S A LONG STORY. WE'LL TELL YOU LATER.
WHEN WE WERE SNATCHED INTO ASGARD, RUSTY AND SKIDS WERE LEFT BEHIND ON LIBERTY ISLAND, SURROUNDED BY FREEDOM FORCE.
WE WERE HOPING MAYBE THEY'D BE HERE WITH YOU!
WHILE IN WASHINGTON...
UNNNH!
WHAT... WHAT IS IT, SIR? WHAT'S THE MATTER--?
FEVER. NOTHING MORE. I HOPE. EXPOSED TO PLAGUE IN MADRIPOOR...
PLAGUE!? WE'VE GOT TO DO SOMETHING!
MAN, CABLE'S A LEGEND. I NEVER THOUGHT I'D HAVE THE HONOR OF GUARDING HIM!
AKKK!
HE'S CHOKING. WE CAN'T JUST LET HIM DIE!
IT'S PROBABLY A TRICK...
LOOK, HE'S BEEN SEARCHED FOR WEAPONS AND HE'S SHACKLED. WE HAVE GUNS.
HOW CAN IT BE A TRICK?

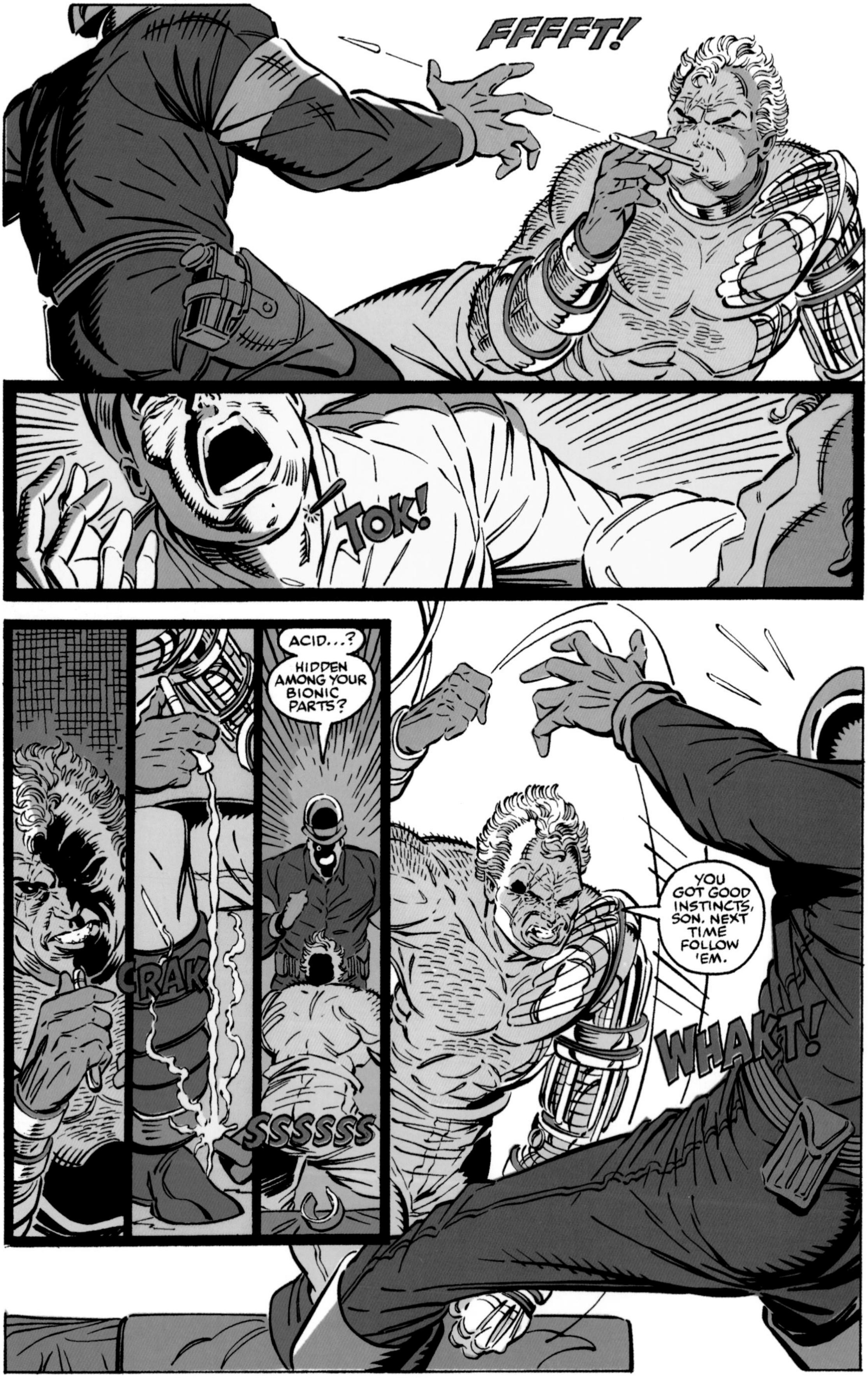
FFFFT!
TOK!
CRAK
ACID...? HIDDEN AMONG YOUR BIONIC PARTS?
SSSSSS
YOU GOT GOOD INSTINCTS, SON. NEXT TIME FOLLOW 'EM.
WHAKT!

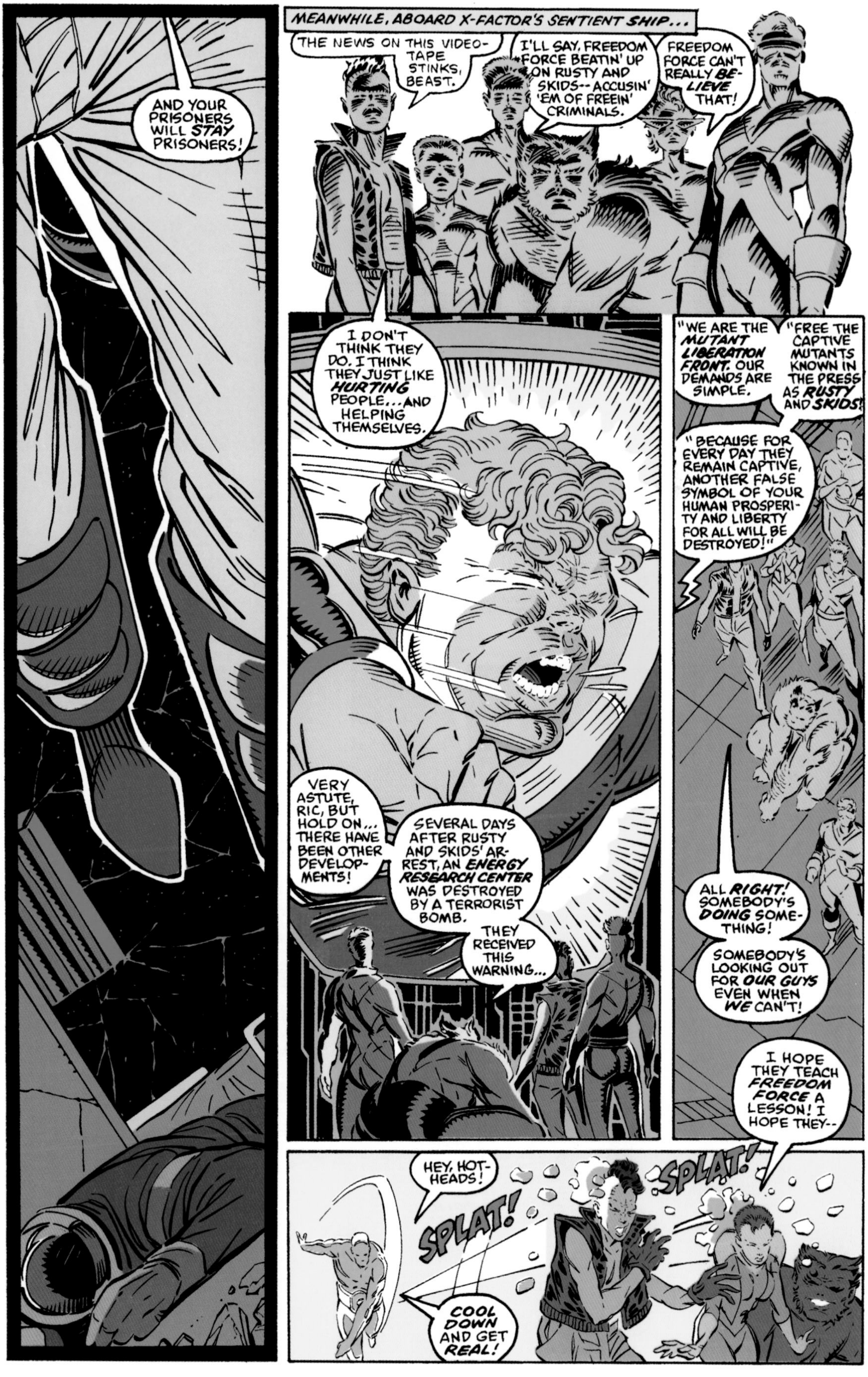
AND YOUR PRISONERS WILL STAY PRISONERS!
MEANWHILE, ABOARD X-FACTOR'S SENTIENT SHIP...
THE NEWS ON THIS VIDEO-TAPE STINKS, BEAST.
I'LL SAY. FREEDOM FORCE BEATIN' UP ON RUSTY AND SKIDS-- ACCUSIN' 'EM OF FREEIN' CRIMINALS.
FREEDOM FORCE CAN'T REALLY BE-LIEVE THAT!
I DON'T THINK THEY DO. I THINK THEY JUST LIKE HURTING PEOPLE... AND HELPING THEMSELVES.
VERY ASTUTE, RIC, BUT HOLD ON... THERE HAVE BEEN OTHER DEVELOP-MENTS!
SEVERAL DAYS AFTER RUSTY AND SKIDS' AR-REST, AN ENERGY RESEARCH CENTER WAS DESTROYED BY A TERRORIST BOMB.
THEY RECEIVED THIS WARNING...
"WE ARE THE MUTANT LIBERATION FRONT. OUR DEMANDS ARE SIMPLE.
"FREE THE CAPTIVE MUTANTS KNOWN IN THE PRESS AS RUSTY AND SKIDS!
"BECAUSE FOR EVERY DAY THEY REMAIN CAPTIVE, ANOTHER FALSE SYMBOL OF YOUR HUMAN PROSPERI-TY AND LIBERTY FOR ALL WILL BE DESTROYED!"
ALL RIGHT! SOMEBODY'S DOING SOME-THING!
SOMEBODY'S LOOKING OUT FOR OUR GUYS EVEN WHEN WE CAN'T!
I HOPE THEY TEACH FREEDOM FORCE A LESSON! I HOPE THEY--
HEY, HOT-HEADS!
SPLAT!
SPLAT!
COOL DOWN AND GET REAL!

THINK ABOUT WHAT YOU'RE SAYING. THE MLF ARE TERRORISTS, GUYS. THEY HAVE NO RIGHT TO DESTROY PROPERTY AND LIVES...

...EVEN IF WE MIGHT AGREE WITH THEIR GOALS... AT LEAST IN THIS ONE CASE.

WE KNOW THAT, BOBBY... BUT IT ISN'T RIGHT, HOW CAN WE LET FREEDOM FORCE GET AWAY WITH WHAT THEY'VE DONE?

WE CAN'T... AND WE WON'T. FREEDOM FORCE WAS NEVER LONG ON BRAINS, RAHNE.

THEY MAY NOT HAVE THOUGHT THROUGH THE RAMIFICATIONS OF THEIR ACTIONS. BUT THEY'RE GOING TO FIND OUT.

I'M SORRY, SIR. FREEDOM FORCE IS IN A MEETING AND CANNOT BE DISTURBED. MAY I TAKE A MESSAGE?

TELL THEM CYCLOPS OF X-FACTOR CALLED.

FREEDOM FORCE HAS ARRESTED TWO OF OUR WARDS IN AN ILLEGAL AND BRUTAL MANNER...

...ON WHAT WE BELIEVE TO BE TRUMPED UP CHARGES.

TELL THEM WE WANT THEM BACK SAFE AND SOUND, OR WE GO TO THE LAW... AND THE PRESS!

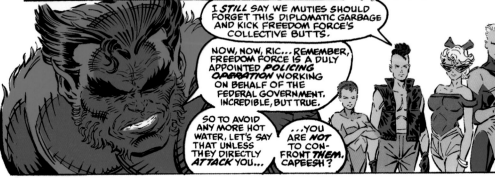

I STILL SAY WE MUTIES SHOULD FORGET THIS DIPLOMATIC GARBAGE AND KICK FREEDOM FORCE'S COLLECTIVE BUTTS.

NOW, NOW, RIC... REMEMBER, FREEDOM FORCE IS A DULY APPOINTED POLICING OPERATION WORKING ON BEHALF OF THE FEDERAL GOVERNMENT. INCREDIBLE, BUT TRUE.

SO TO AVOID ANY MORE HOT WATER, LET'S SAY THAT UNLESS THEY DIRECTLY ATTACK YOU...

...YOU ARE NOT TO CONFRONT THEM, CAPEESH?

YES, SIR. WE UNDERSTAND, BUT WE DON'T MUCH LIKE IT.

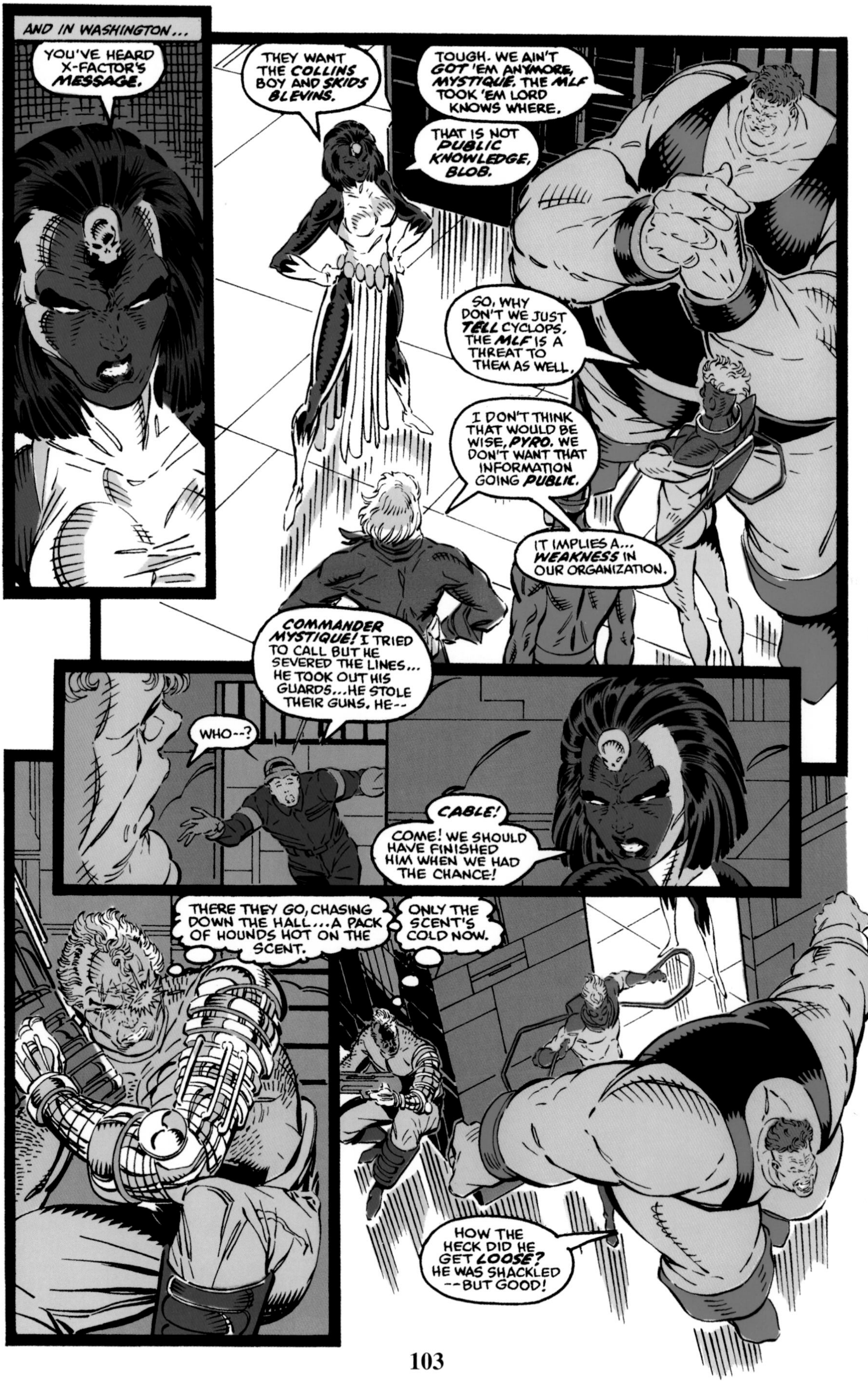
AND IN WASHINGTON...
YOU'VE HEARD X-FACTOR'S MESSAGE.
THEY WANT THE COLLINS BOY AND SKIDS BLEVINS.
TOUGH. WE AIN'T GOT 'EM ANYMORE, MYSTIQUE. THE MLF TOOK 'EM LORD KNOWS WHERE.
THAT IS NOT PUBLIC KNOWLEDGE, BLOB.
SO, WHY DON'T WE JUST TELL CYCLOPS, THE MLF IS A THREAT TO THEM AS WELL.
I DON'T THINK THAT WOULD BE WISE, PYRO. WE DON'T WANT THAT INFORMATION GOING PUBLIC.
IT IMPLIES A... WEAKNESS IN OUR ORGANIZATION.
COMMANDER MYSTIQUE! I TRIED TO CALL BUT HE SEVERED THE LINES... HE TOOK OUT HIS GUARDS... HE STOLE THEIR GUNS. HE--
WHO--?
CABLE!
COME! WE SHOULD HAVE FINISHED HIM WHEN WE HAD THE CHANCE!
THERE THEY GO, CHASING DOWN THE HALL... A PACK OF HOUNDS HOT ON THE SCENT.
ONLY THE SCENT'S COLD NOW.
HOW THE HECK DID HE GET LOOSE? HE WAS SHACKLED --BUT GOOD!

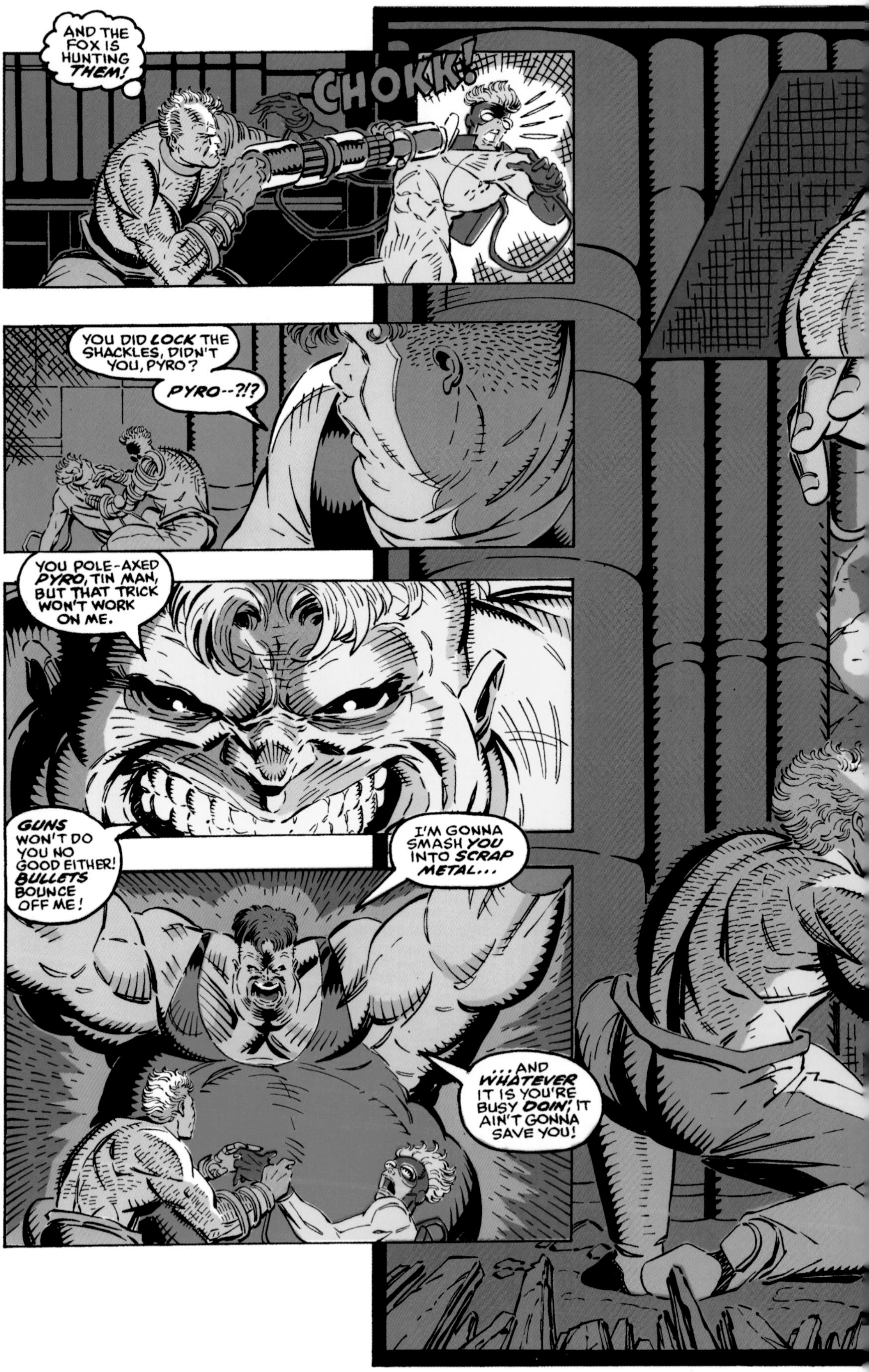

AND THE FOX IS HUNTING THEM!
CHOKK!
YOU DID LOCK THE SHACKLES, DIDN'T YOU, PYRO?
PYRO--?!?
YOU POLE-AXED PYRO, TIN MAN, BUT THAT TRICK WON'T WORK ON ME.
GUNS WON'T DO YOU NO GOOD EITHER! BULLETS BOUNCE OFF ME!
I'M GONNA SMASH YOU INTO SCRAP METAL...
...AND WHATEVER IT IS YOU'RE BUSY DOIN', IT AIN'T GONNA SAVE YOU!

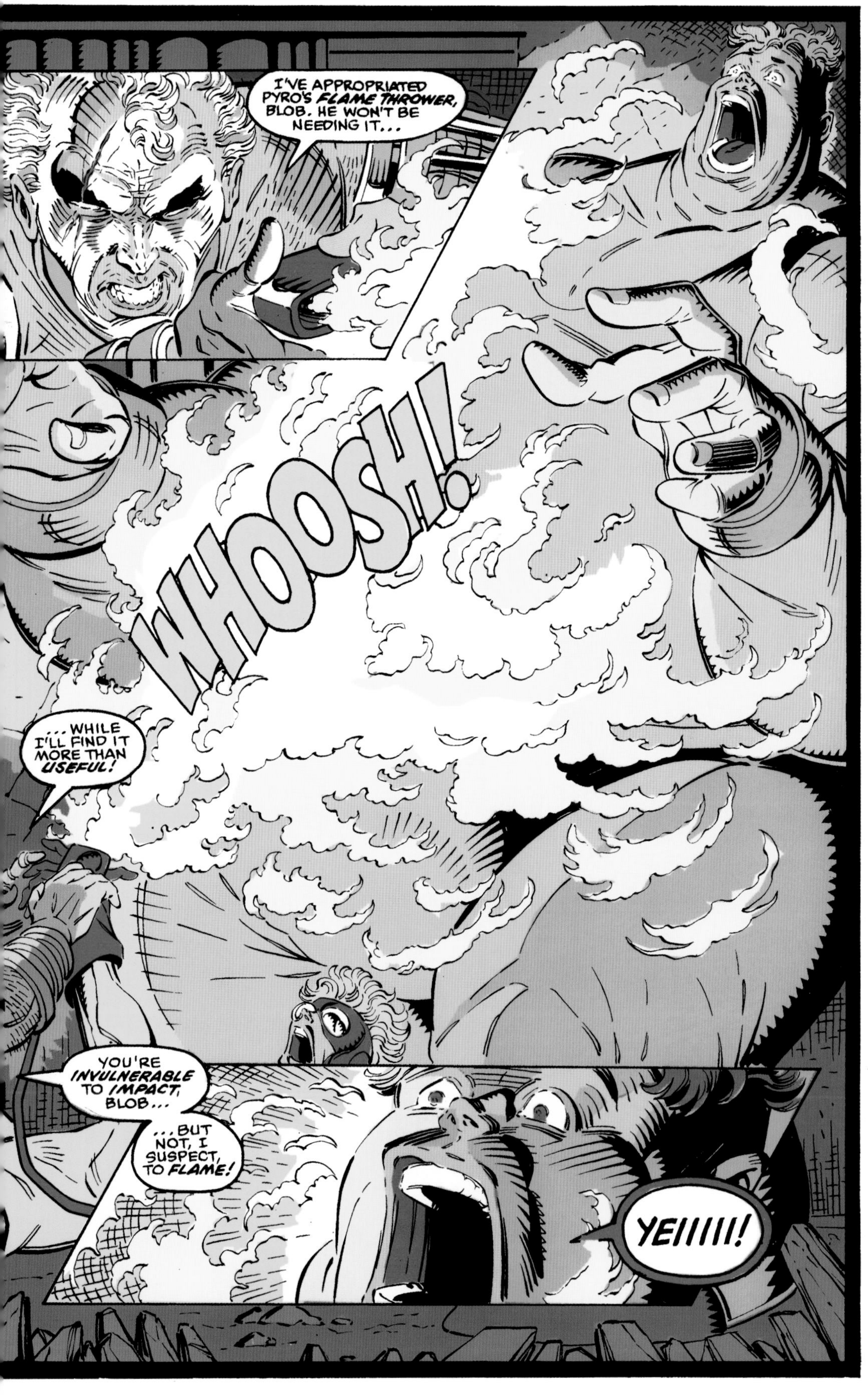

I'VE APPROPRIATED PYRO'S FLAME THROWER, BLOB. HE WON'T BE NEEDING IT...
WHOOSH!!
...WHILE I'LL FIND IT MORE THAN USEFUL!
YOU'RE INVULNERABLE TO IMPACT, BLOB...
...BUT NOT, I SUSPECT, TO FLAME!
YEIIIII!

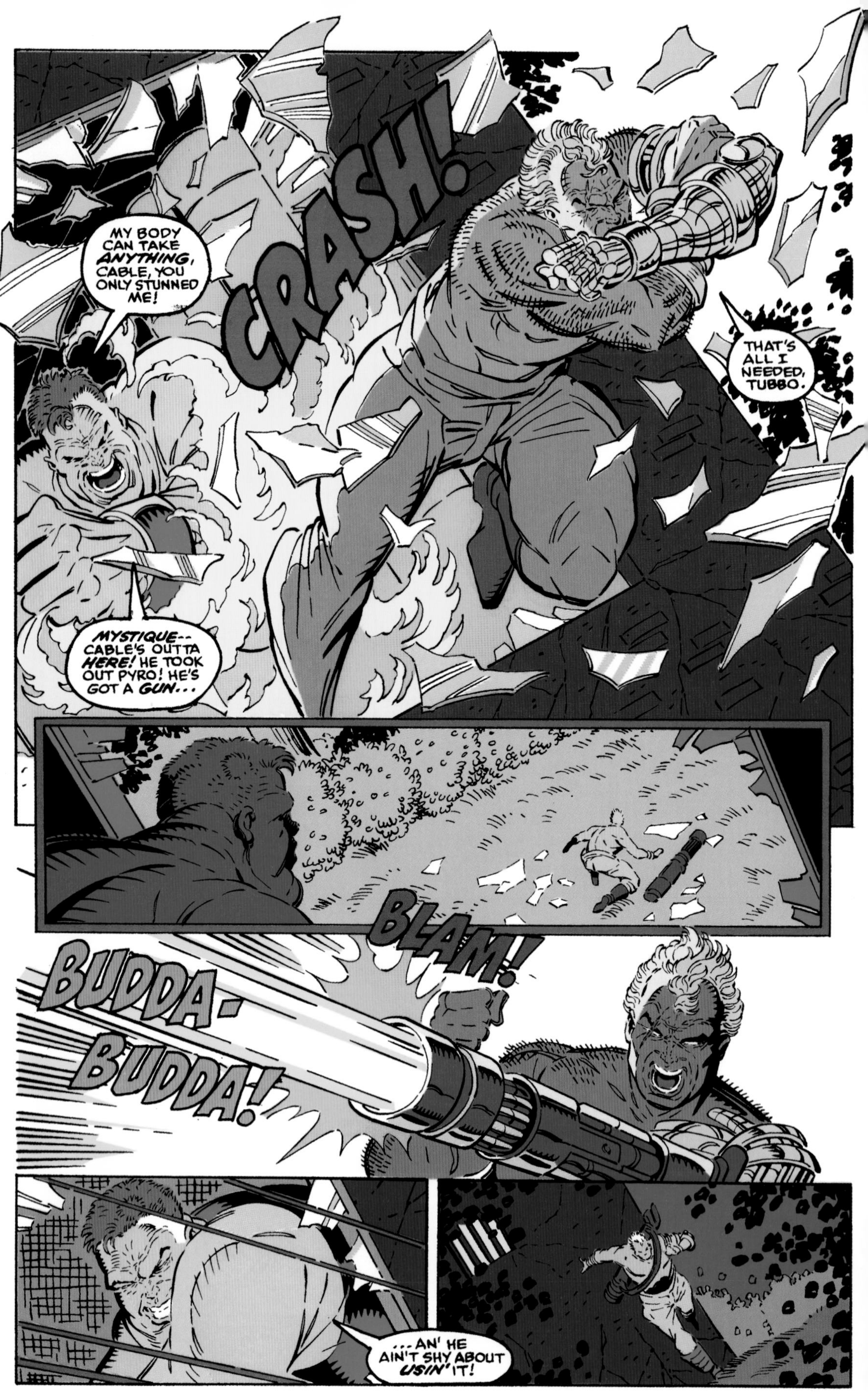
MY BODY CAN TAKE *ANYTHING*, CABLE, YOU ONLY STUNNED ME!
CRASH!
THAT'S ALL I NEEDED, TUBBO.
MYSTIQUE-- CABLE'S OUTTA *HERE!* HE TOOK OUT PYRO! HE'S GOT A *GUN*...
BLAM!
BUDDA-BUDDA!
...AN' HE AIN'T SHY ABOUT *USIN'* IT!

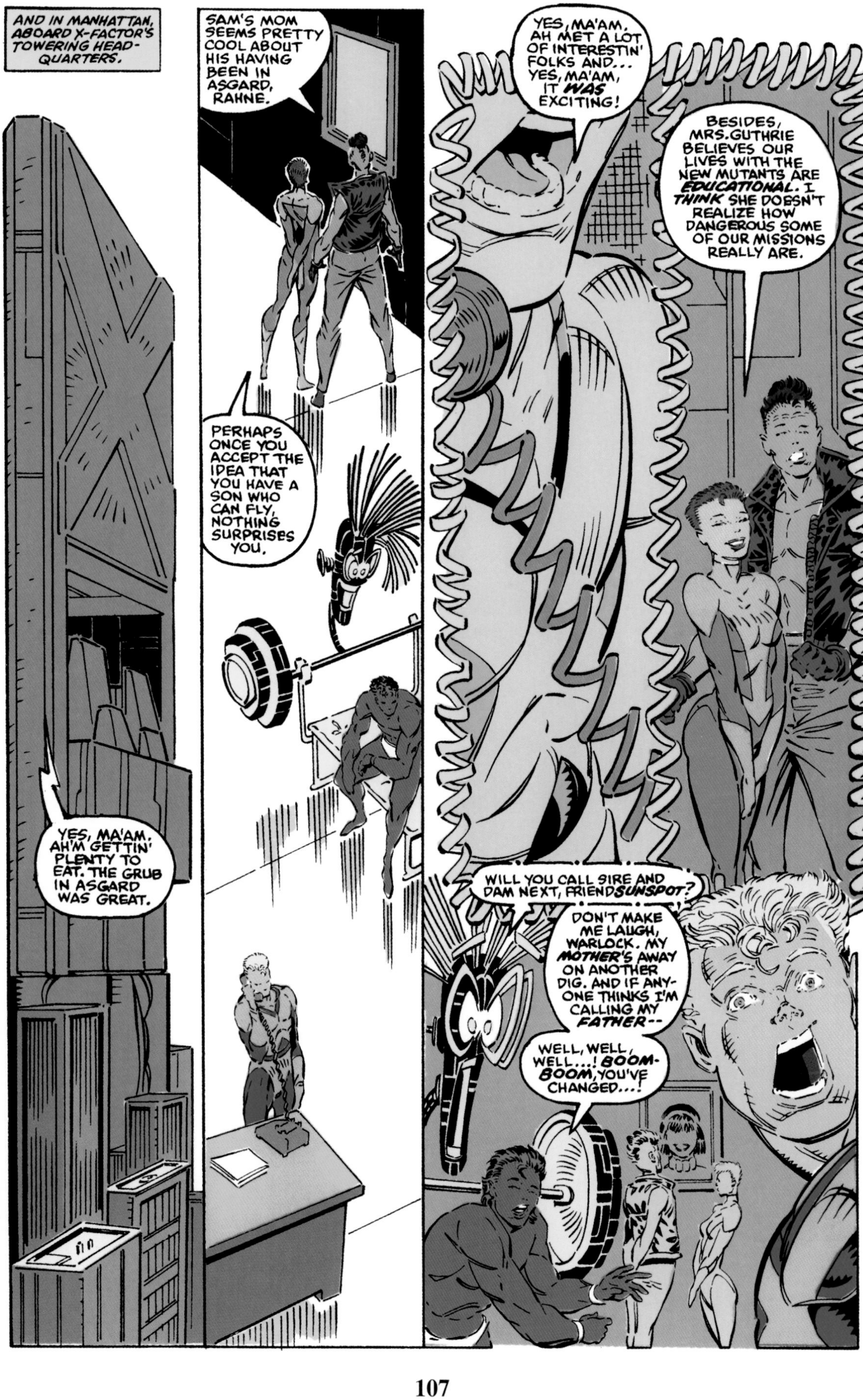
AND IN MANHATTAN, ABOARD X-FACTOR'S TOWERING HEAD-QUARTERS.
YES, MA'AM. AH'M GETTIN' PLENTY TO EAT. THE GRUB IN ASGARD WAS GREAT.
SAM'S MOM SEEMS PRETTY COOL ABOUT HIS HAVING BEEN IN ASGARD, RAHNE.
PERHAPS ONCE YOU ACCEPT THE IDEA THAT YOU HAVE A SON WHO CAN FLY, NOTHING SURPRISES YOU.
YES, MA'AM, AH MET A LOT OF INTERESTIN' FOLKS AND... YES, MA'AM, IT WAS EXCITING!
BESIDES, MRS. GUTHRIE BELIEVES OUR LIVES WITH THE NEW MUTANTS ARE EDUCATIONAL. I THINK SHE DOESN'T REALIZE HOW DANGEROUS SOME OF OUR MISSIONS REALLY ARE.
WILL YOU CALL SIRE AND DAM NEXT, FRIEND SUNSPOT?
DON'T MAKE ME LAUGH, WARLOCK. MY MOTHER'S AWAY ON ANOTHER DIG. AND IF ANY-ONE THINKS I'M CALLING MY FATHER--
WELL, WELL, WELL...! BOOM-BOOM, YOU'VE CHANGED...!

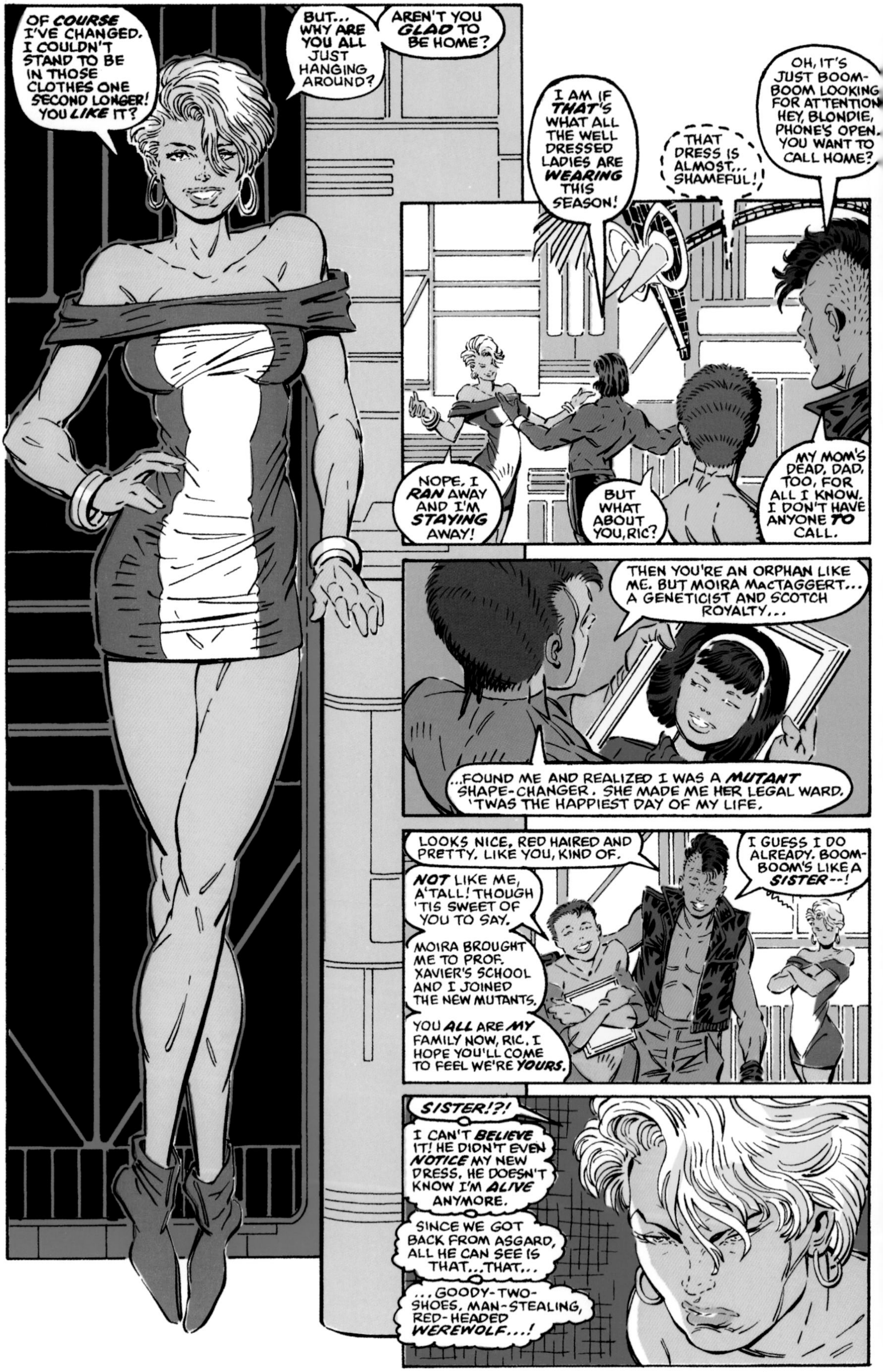
OF COURSE I'VE CHANGED. I COULDN'T STAND TO BE IN THOSE CLOTHES ONE SECOND LONGER! YOU LIKE IT?
BUT... WHY ARE YOU ALL JUST HANGING AROUND?
AREN'T YOU GLAD TO BE HOME?
I AM IF THAT'S WHAT ALL THE WELL DRESSED LADIES ARE WEARING THIS SEASON!
THAT DRESS IS ALMOST... SHAMEFUL!
OH, IT'S JUST BOOM-BOOM LOOKING FOR ATTENTION. HEY, BLONDIE, PHONE'S OPEN. YOU WANT TO CALL HOME?
NOPE, I RAN AWAY AND I'M STAYING AWAY!
BUT WHAT ABOUT YOU, RIC?
MY MOM'S DEAD, DAD, TOO, FOR ALL I KNOW. I DON'T HAVE ANYONE TO CALL.
THEN YOU'RE AN ORPHAN LIKE ME. BUT MOIRA MACTAGGERT... A GENETICIST AND SCOTCH ROYALTY...
...FOUND ME AND REALIZED I WAS A MUTANT SHAPE-CHANGER. SHE MADE ME HER LEGAL WARD. 'TWAS THE HAPPIEST DAY OF MY LIFE.
LOOKS NICE, RED HAIRED AND PRETTY. LIKE YOU, KIND OF.
NOT LIKE ME, A'TALL! THOUGH 'TIS SWEET OF YOU TO SAY.
MOIRA BROUGHT ME TO PROF. XAVIER'S SCHOOL AND I JOINED THE NEW MUTANTS.
YOU ALL ARE MY FAMILY NOW, RIC. I HOPE YOU'LL COME TO FEEL WE'RE YOURS.
I GUESS I DO ALREADY. BOOM-BOOM'S LIKE A SISTER--!
SISTER!?!
I CAN'T BELIEVE IT! HE DIDN'T EVEN NOTICE MY NEW DRESS. HE DOESN'T KNOW I'M ALIVE ANYMORE.
SINCE WE GOT BACK FROM ASGARD, ALL HE CAN SEE IS THAT...THAT...
...GOODY-TWO-SHOES, MAN-STEALING, RED-HEADED WEREWOLF...!

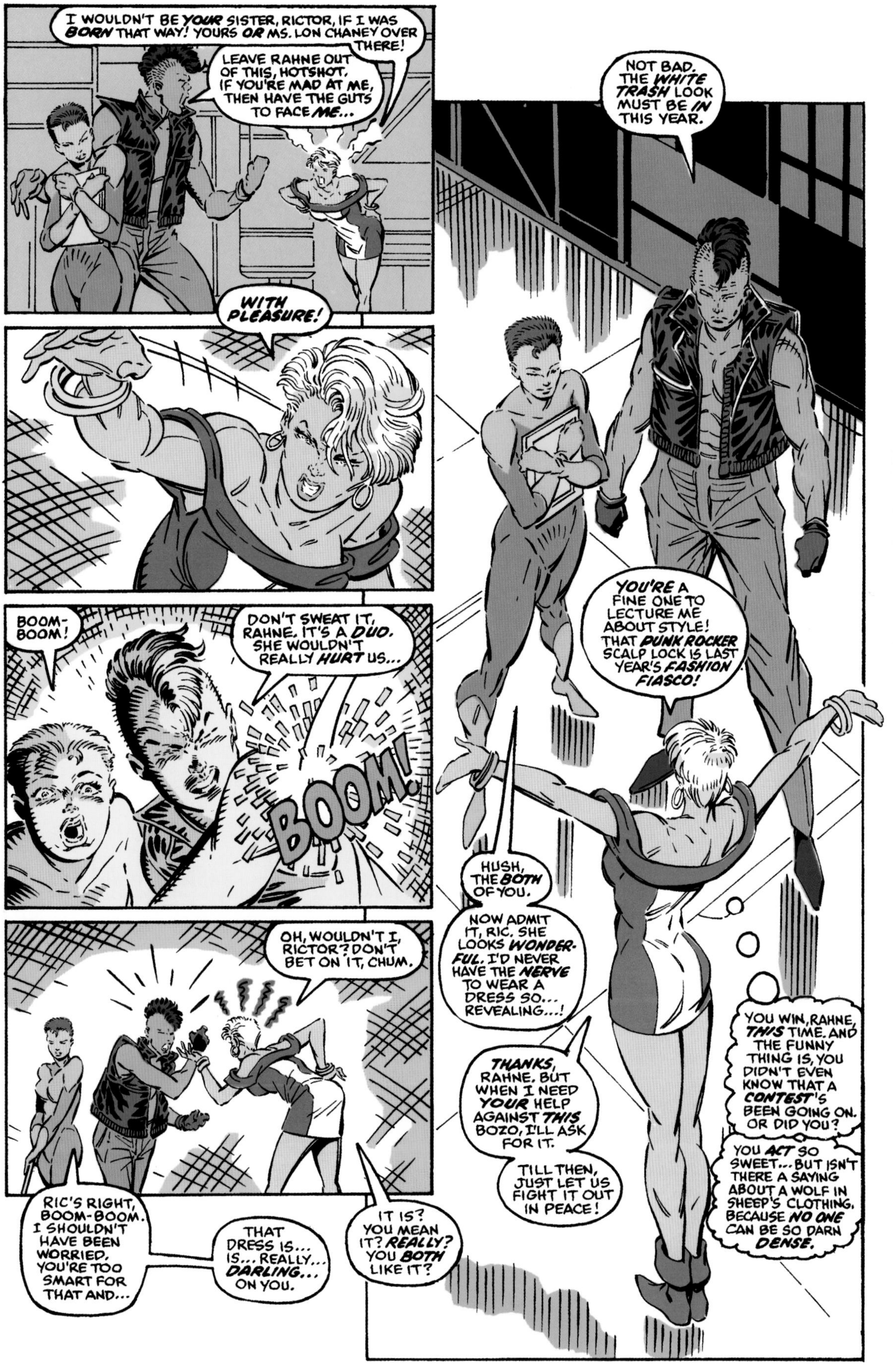
I WOULDN'T BE *YOUR* SISTER, RICTOR, IF I WAS *BORN* THAT WAY! YOURS *OR* MS. LON CHANEY OVER THERE!
LEAVE RAHNE OUT OF THIS, HOTSHOT. IF YOU'RE MAD AT ME, THEN HAVE THE GUTS TO FACE *ME*...
WITH PLEASURE!
BOOM-BOOM!
DON'T SWEAT IT, RAHNE. IT'S A *DUD*. SHE WOULDN'T REALLY *HURT* US...
BOOM!
OH, WOULDN'T I, RICTOR? DON'T BET ON IT, CHUM.
RIC'S RIGHT, BOOM-BOOM. I SHOULDN'T HAVE BEEN WORRIED. YOU'RE TOO SMART FOR THAT AND...
THAT DRESS IS... IS... REALLY... *DARLING*... ON YOU.
IT IS? YOU MEAN IT? *REALLY*? YOU *BOTH* LIKE IT?
NOT BAD. THE *WHITE TRASH* LOOK MUST BE *IN* THIS YEAR.
YOU'RE A FINE ONE TO LECTURE ME ABOUT STYLE! THAT *PUNK ROCKER* SCALP LOCK IS LAST YEAR'S *FASHION FIASCO!*
HUSH, THE *BOTH* OF YOU.
NOW ADMIT IT, RIC. SHE LOOKS *WONDERFUL*. I'D NEVER HAVE THE *NERVE* TO WEAR A DRESS SO... REVEALING...!
THANKS, RAHNE. BUT WHEN I NEED *YOUR* HELP AGAINST *THIS* BOZO, I'LL ASK FOR IT.
TILL THEN, JUST LET US FIGHT IT OUT IN PEACE!
YOU WIN, RAHNE. *THIS* TIME. AND THE FUNNY THING IS, YOU DIDN'T EVEN KNOW THAT A *CONTEST*'S BEEN GOING ON. OR DID YOU?
YOU *ACT* SO SWEET... BUT ISN'T THERE A SAYING ABOUT A WOLF IN SHEEP'S CLOTHING. BECAUSE *NO ONE* CAN BE SO DARN *DENSE*.

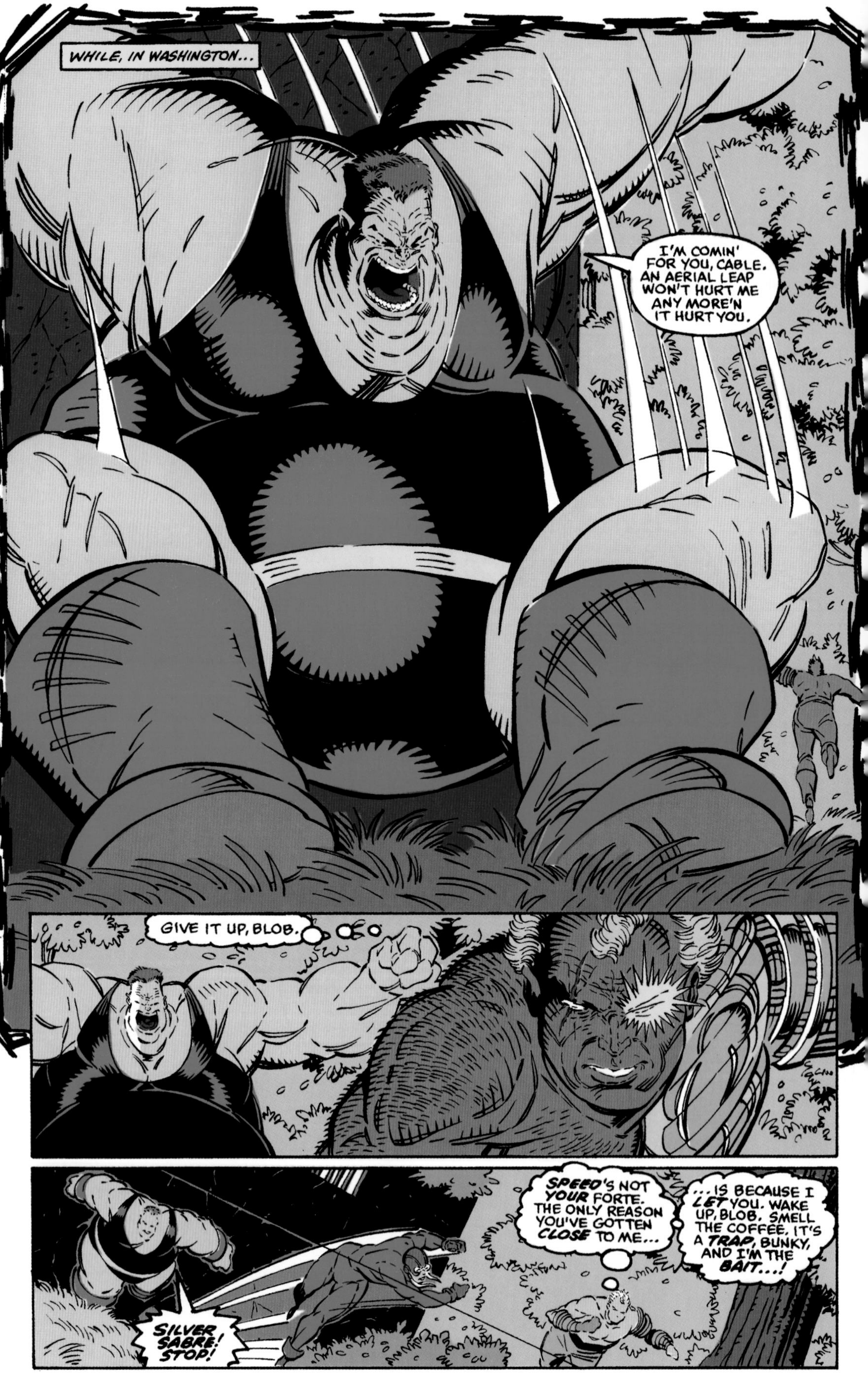
WHILE, IN WASHINGTON...
I'M COMIN' FOR YOU, CABLE. AN AERIAL LEAP WON'T HURT ME ANY MORE'N IT HURT YOU.
GIVE IT UP, BLOB.
SPEED'S NOT YOUR FORTE. THE ONLY REASON YOU'VE GOTTEN CLOSE TO ME...
...IS BECAUSE I LET YOU. WAKE UP, BLOB. SMELL THE COFFEE. IT'S A TRAP, BUNKY, AND I'M THE BAIT...!
SILVER SABRE! STOP!

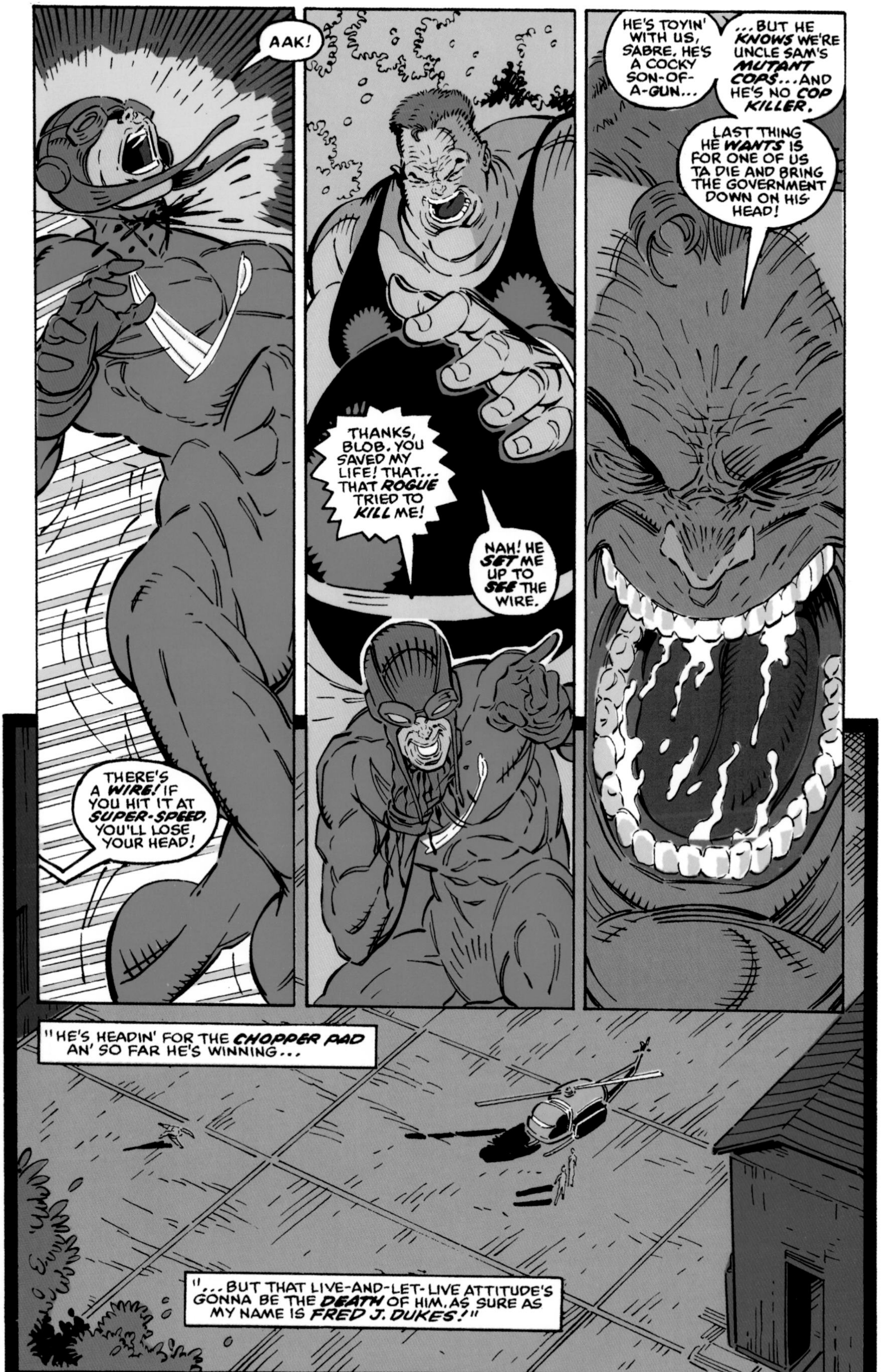
AAK!
THERE'S A WIRE! IF YOU HIT IT AT SUPER-SPEED, YOU'LL LOSE YOUR HEAD!
THANKS, BLOB. YOU SAVED MY LIFE! THAT... THAT ROGUE TRIED TO KILL ME!
NAH! HE SET ME UP TO SEE THE WIRE.
HE'S TOYIN' WITH US, SABRE. HE'S A COCKY SON-OF-A-GUN...
...BUT HE KNOWS WE'RE UNCLE SAM'S MUTANT COPS... AND HE'S NO COP KILLER.
LAST THING HE WANTS IS FOR ONE OF US TA DIE AND BRING THE GOVERNMENT DOWN ON HIS HEAD!
"HE'S HEADIN' FOR THE CHOPPER PAD AN' SO FAR HE'S WINNING...
"...BUT THAT LIVE-AND-LET-LIVE ATTITUDE'S GONNA BE THE DEATH OF HIM, AS SURE AS MY NAME IS FRED J. DUKES!"

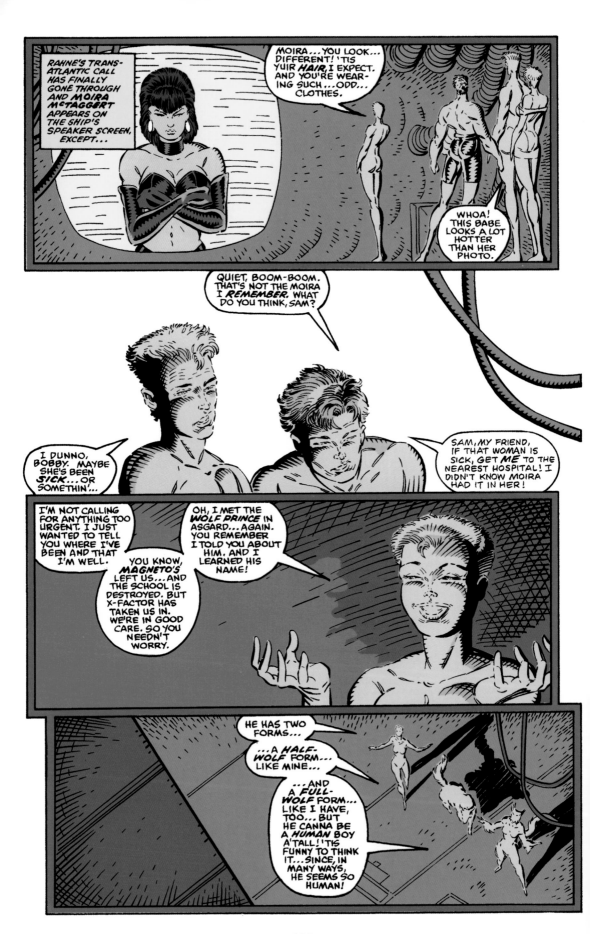

RAHNE'S TRANS-ATLANTIC CALL HAS FINALLY GONE THROUGH AND *MOIRA McTAGGERT* APPEARS ON THE SHIP'S SPEAKER SCREEN, EXCEPT...

MOIRA...YOU LOOK... *DIFFERENT!* 'TIS YUIR *HAIR*, I EXPECT. AND YOU'RE WEARING SUCH...*ODD*... CLOTHES.

WHOA! THIS BABE LOOKS A LOT *HOTTER* THAN HER PHOTO.

QUIET, BOOM-BOOM. THAT'S NOT THE MOIRA I *REMEMBER.* WHAT DO YOU THINK, *SAM?*

I *DUNNO,* BOBBY. MAYBE SHE'S BEEN *SICK...* OR SOMETHIN'...

SAM, MY FRIEND, IF THAT WOMAN IS SICK, GET *ME* TO THE NEAREST HOSPITAL! I DIDN'T KNOW MOIRA HAD IT IN HER!

I'M NOT CALLING FOR ANYTHING TOO URGENT. I JUST WANTED TO TELL YOU WHERE I'VE BEEN AND THAT I'M WELL.

YOU KNOW, *MAGNETO'S* LEFT US... AND THE SCHOOL IS DESTROYED. BUT *X-FACTOR* HAS TAKEN US IN. WE'RE IN GOOD CARE. SO YOU NEEDN'T WORRY.

OH, I MET THE *WOLF PRINCE* IN ASGARD... AGAIN. YOU REMEMBER I TOLD YOU ABOUT HIM. AND I LEARNED HIS NAME!

HE HAS TWO FORMS...

...A *HALF-WOLF* FORM... LIKE MINE...

...AND A *FULL-WOLF* FORM... LIKE I HAVE, TOO...BUT HE CANNA BE A *HUMAN* BOY A'TALL! 'TIS FUNNY TO THINK IT... SINCE, IN MANY WAYS, HE SEEMS SO *HUMAN!*

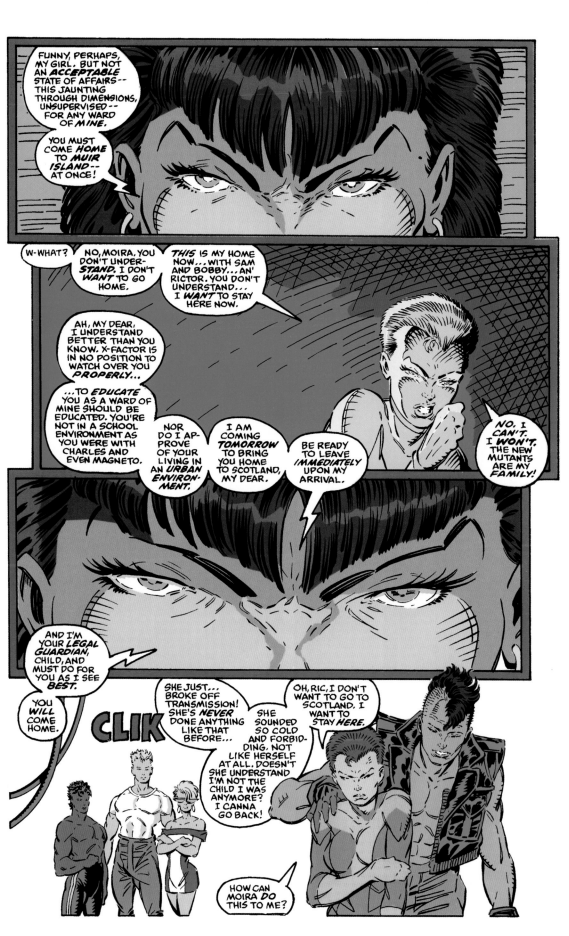

FUNNY, PERHAPS, MY GIRL. BUT NOT AN *ACCEPTABLE* STATE OF AFFAIRS-- THIS JAUNTING THROUGH DIMENSIONS, UNSUPERVISED-- FOR ANY WARD OF *MINE.*

YOU MUST COME *HOME* TO *MUIR ISLAND*-- AT ONCE!

W-WHAT?

NO, MOIRA, YOU DON'T UNDER- *STAND.* I DON'T *WANT* TO GO HOME.

THIS IS MY HOME NOW...WITH SAM AND BOBBY...AN' RICTOR. YOU DON'T UNDERSTAND... I *WANT* TO STAY HERE NOW.

AH, MY DEAR, I UNDERSTAND BETTER THAN YOU KNOW. X-FACTOR IS IN NO POSITION TO WATCH OVER YOU *PROPERLY...*

...TO *EDUCATE* YOU AS A WARD OF MINE SHOULD BE EDUCATED. YOU'RE NOT IN A SCHOOL ENVIRONMENT AS YOU WERE WITH CHARLES AND EVEN MAGNETO.

NOR DO I AP- PROVE OF YOUR LIVING IN AN *URBAN ENVIRON- MENT.*

I AM COMING *TOMORROW* TO BRING YOU HOME TO SCOTLAND, MY DEAR.

BE READY TO LEAVE *IMMEDIATELY* UPON MY ARRIVAL.

NO. I *CAN'T.* I *WON'T.* THE NEW MUTANTS ARE MY *FAMILY!*

AND I'M YOUR *LEGAL GUARDIAN,* CHILD, AND MUST DO FOR YOU AS I SEE *BEST.*

YOU *WILL* COME HOME.

CLIK

SHE JUST... BROKE OFF TRANSMISSION! SHE'S *NEVER* DONE ANYTHING LIKE THAT BEFORE...

SHE SOUNDED SO COLD AND FORBID- DING, NOT LIKE HERSELF AT ALL. DOESN'T SHE UNDERSTAND I'M NOT THE CHILD I WAS ANYMORE? I CANNA GO BACK!

OH, RIC, I DON'T WANT TO GO TO SCOTLAND, I WANT TO STAY *HERE.*

HOW CAN MOIRA *DO* THIS TO ME?

113

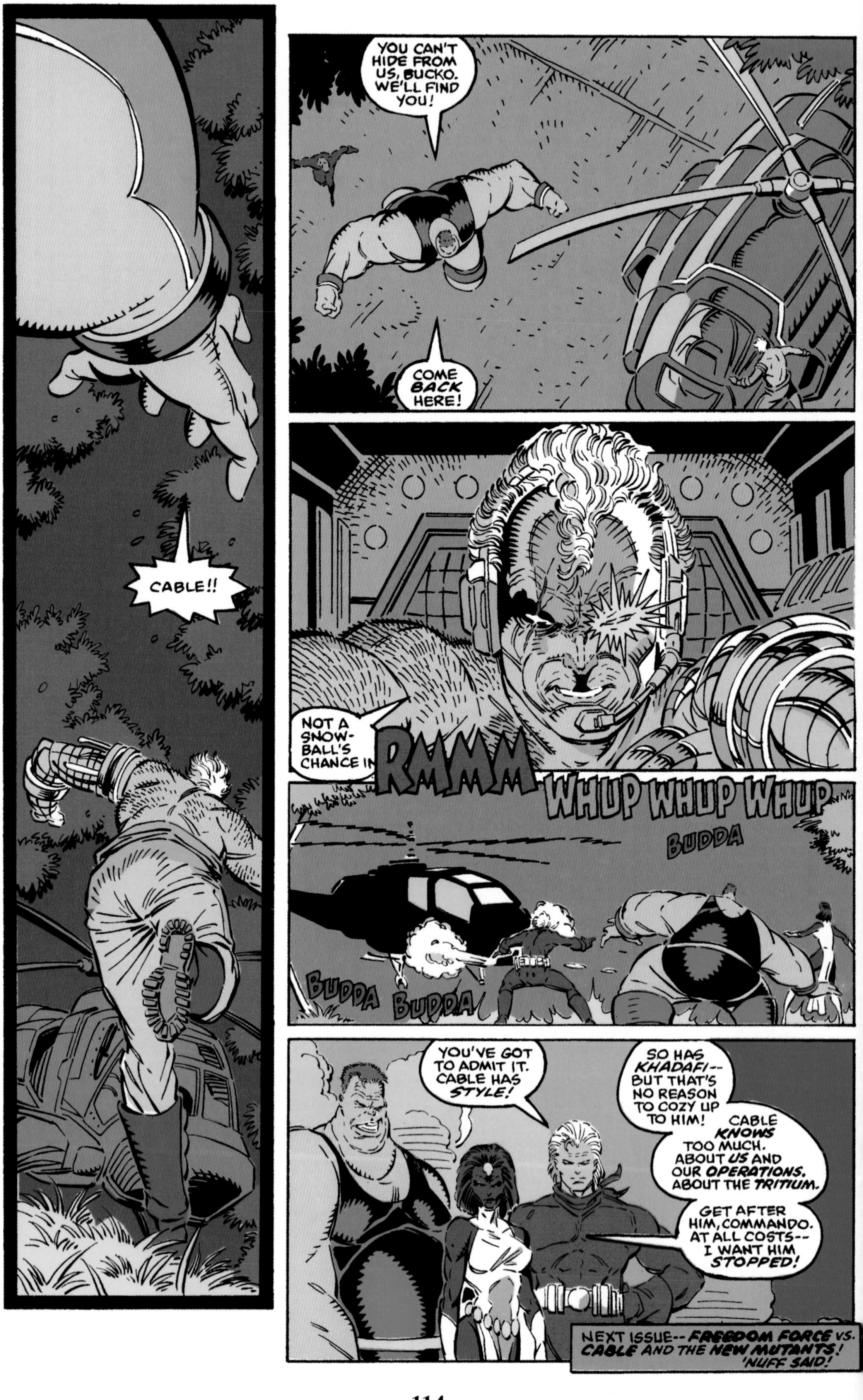
CABLE!!
YOU CAN'T HIDE FROM US, BUCKO. WE'LL FIND YOU!
COME BACK HERE!
NOT A SNOW-BALL'S CHANCE IN
RMMM
WHUP WHUP WHUP
BUDDA
BUDDA BUDDA
YOU'VE GOT TO ADMIT IT. CABLE HAS STYLE!
SO HAS KHADAFI-- BUT THAT'S NO REASON TO COZY UP TO HIM!
CABLE KNOWS TOO MUCH. ABOUT US AND OUR OPERATIONS. ABOUT THE TRITIUM.
GET AFTER HIM, COMMANDO. AT ALL COSTS-- I WANT HIM STOPPED!
NEXT ISSUE-- FREEDOM FORCE VS. CABLE AND THE NEW MUTANTS! 'NUFF SAID!

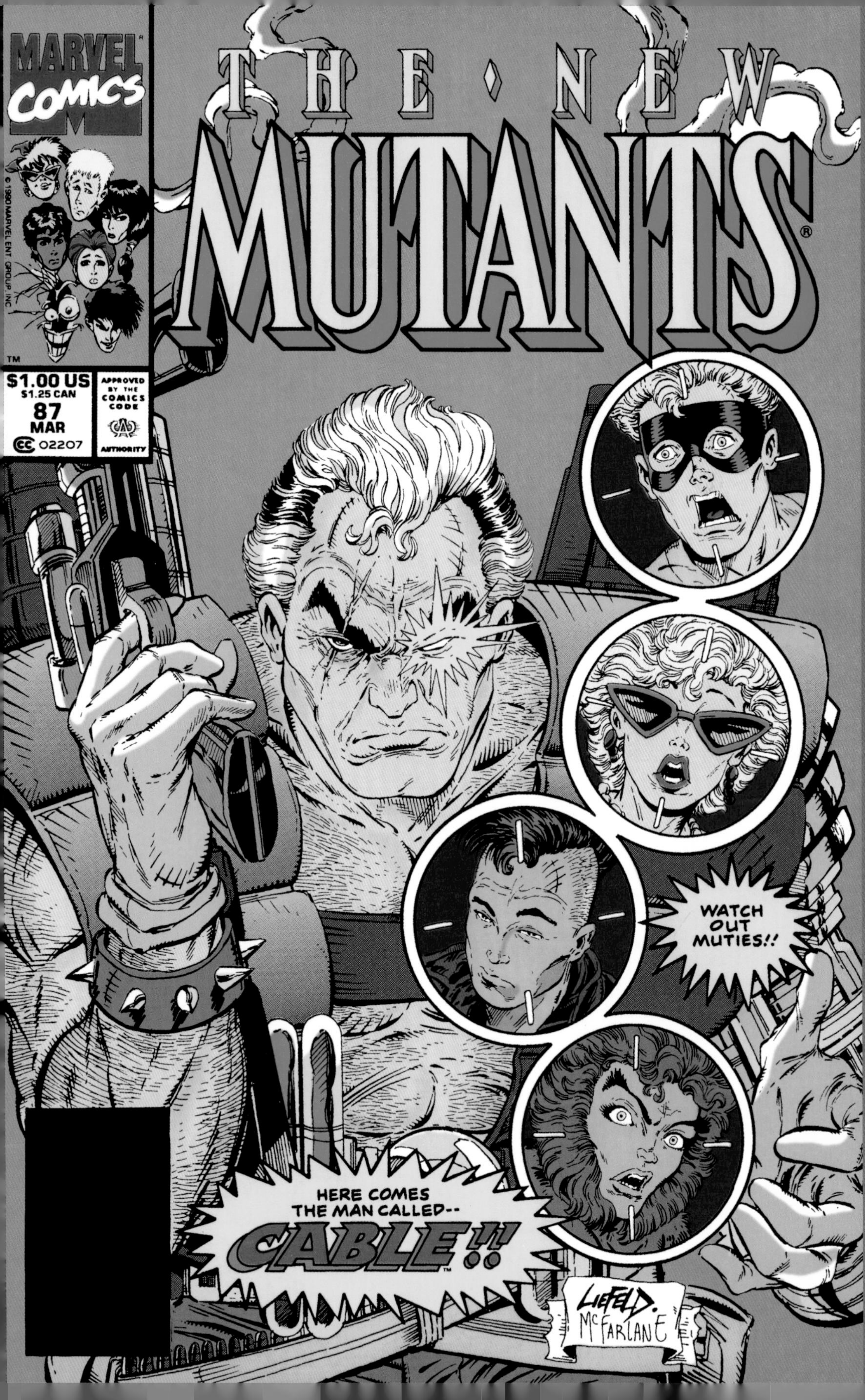
MARVEL COMICS
© 1990 MARVEL ENT. GROUP, INC.
THE NEW MUTANTS
$1.00 US
$1.25 CAN
87
MAR
02207
APPROVED BY THE COMICS CODE AUTHORITY
WATCH OUT MUTIES!!
HERE COMES THE MAN CALLED--
CABLE!!
LIEFELD.
McFARLANE

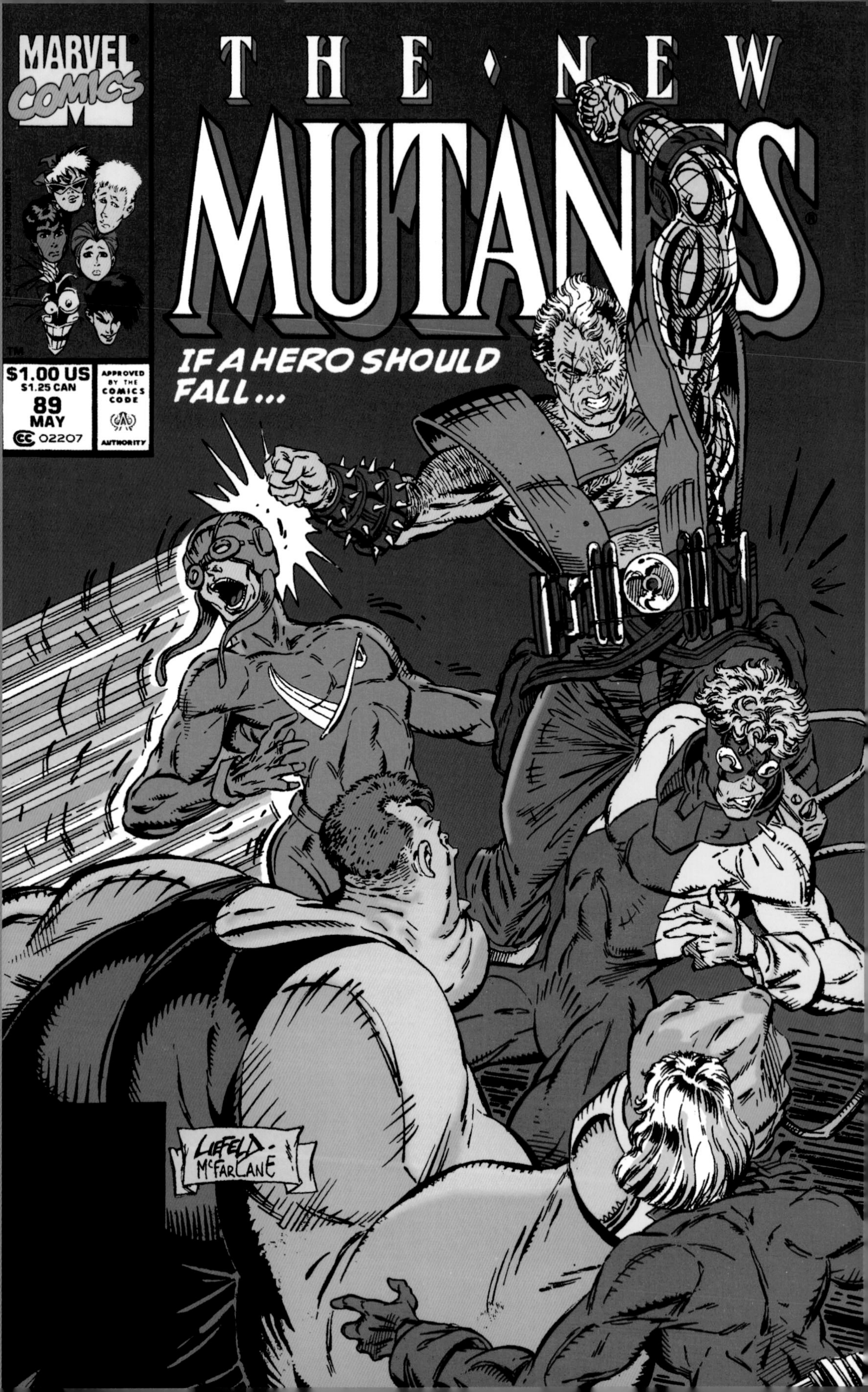
MARVEL COMICS
THE NEW
MUTANTS
IF A HERO SHOULD FALL...
$1.00 US
$1.25 CAN
89
MAY
02207
APPROVED BY THE COMICS CODE AUTHORITY
LIEFELD McFARLANE

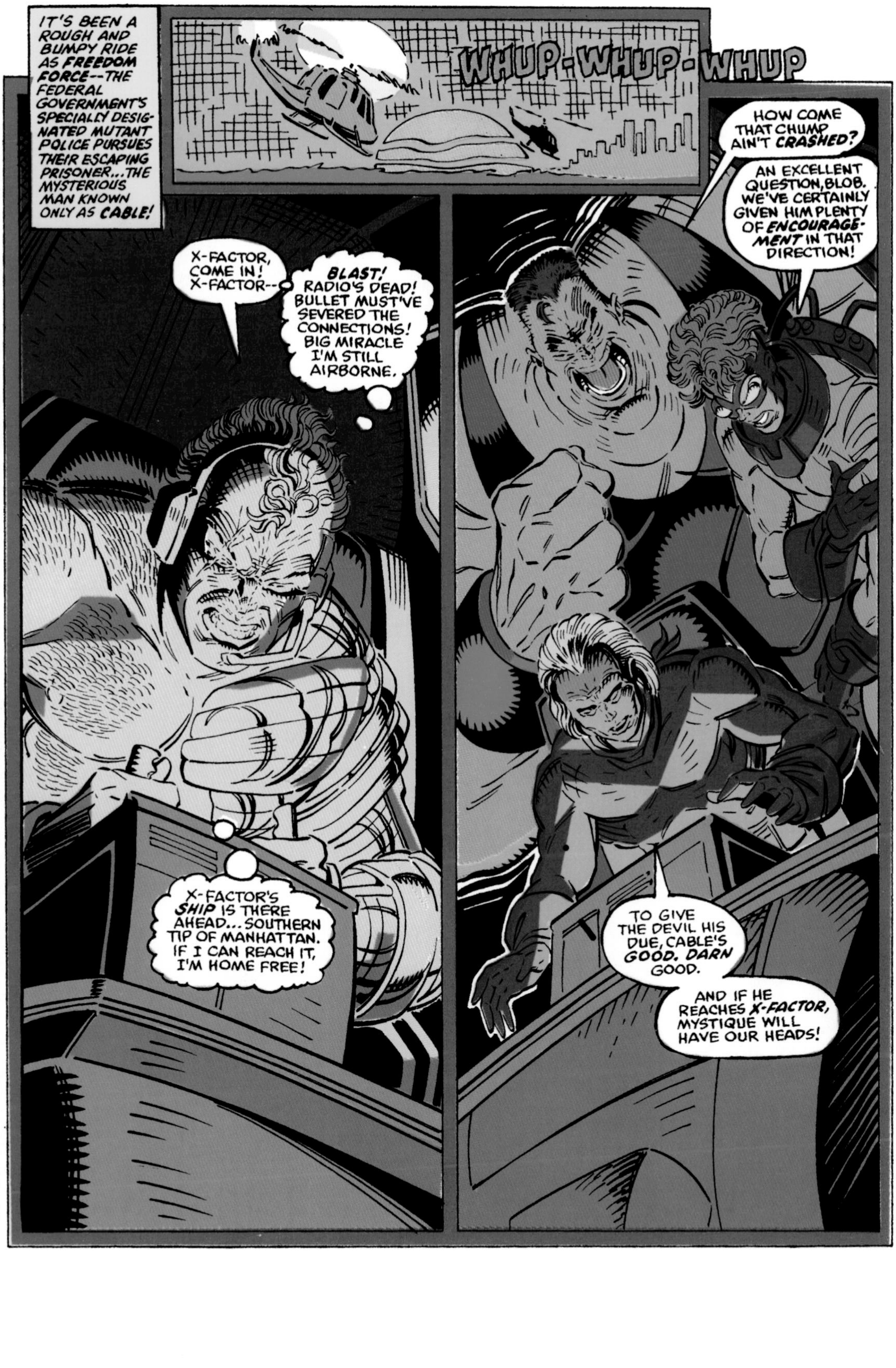

IT'S BEEN A ROUGH AND BUMPY RIDE AS FREEDOM FORCE--THE FEDERAL GOVERNMENT'S SPECIALLY DESIGNATED MUTANT POLICE PURSUES THEIR ESCAPING PRISONER...THE MYSTERIOUS MAN KNOWN ONLY AS CABLE!
WHUP-WHUP-WHUP
X-FACTOR, COME IN! X-FACTOR--
BLAST! RADIO'S DEAD! BULLET MUST'VE SEVERED THE CONNECTIONS! BIG MIRACLE I'M STILL AIRBORNE.
X-FACTOR'S SHIP IS THERE AHEAD... SOUTHERN TIP OF MANHATTAN. IF I CAN REACH IT, I'M HOME FREE!
HOW COME THAT CHUMP AIN'T CRASHED?
AN EXCELLENT QUESTION, BLOB. WE'VE CERTAINLY GIVEN HIM PLENTY OF ENCOURAGEMENT IN THAT DIRECTION!
TO GIVE THE DEVIL HIS DUE, CABLE'S GOOD. DARN GOOD.
AND IF HE REACHES X-FACTOR, MYSTIQUE WILL HAVE OUR HEADS!

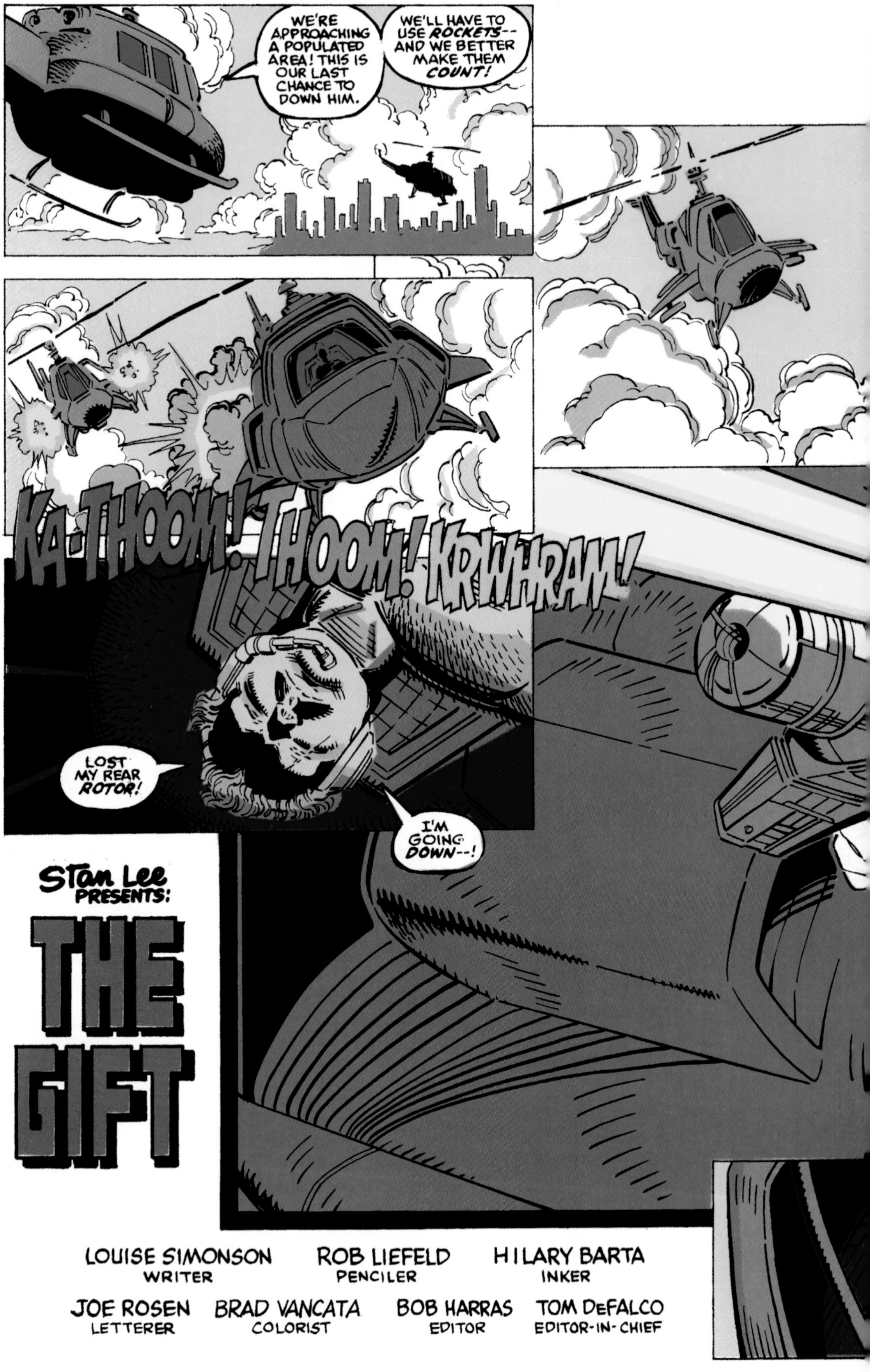
WE'RE APPROACHING A POPULATED AREA! THIS IS OUR LAST CHANCE TO DOWN HIM.
WE'LL HAVE TO USE ROCKETS-- AND WE BETTER MAKE THEM COUNT!
KA-THOOM! THOOM! KRWHRAM!
LOST MY REAR ROTOR!
I'M GOING DOWN--!
STAN LEE PRESENTS:
THE GIFT
LOUISE SIMONSON WRITER
ROB LIEFELD PENCILER
HILARY BARTA INKER
JOE ROSEN LETTERER
BRAD VANCATA COLORIST
BOB HARRAS EDITOR
TOM DeFALCO EDITOR-IN-CHIEF

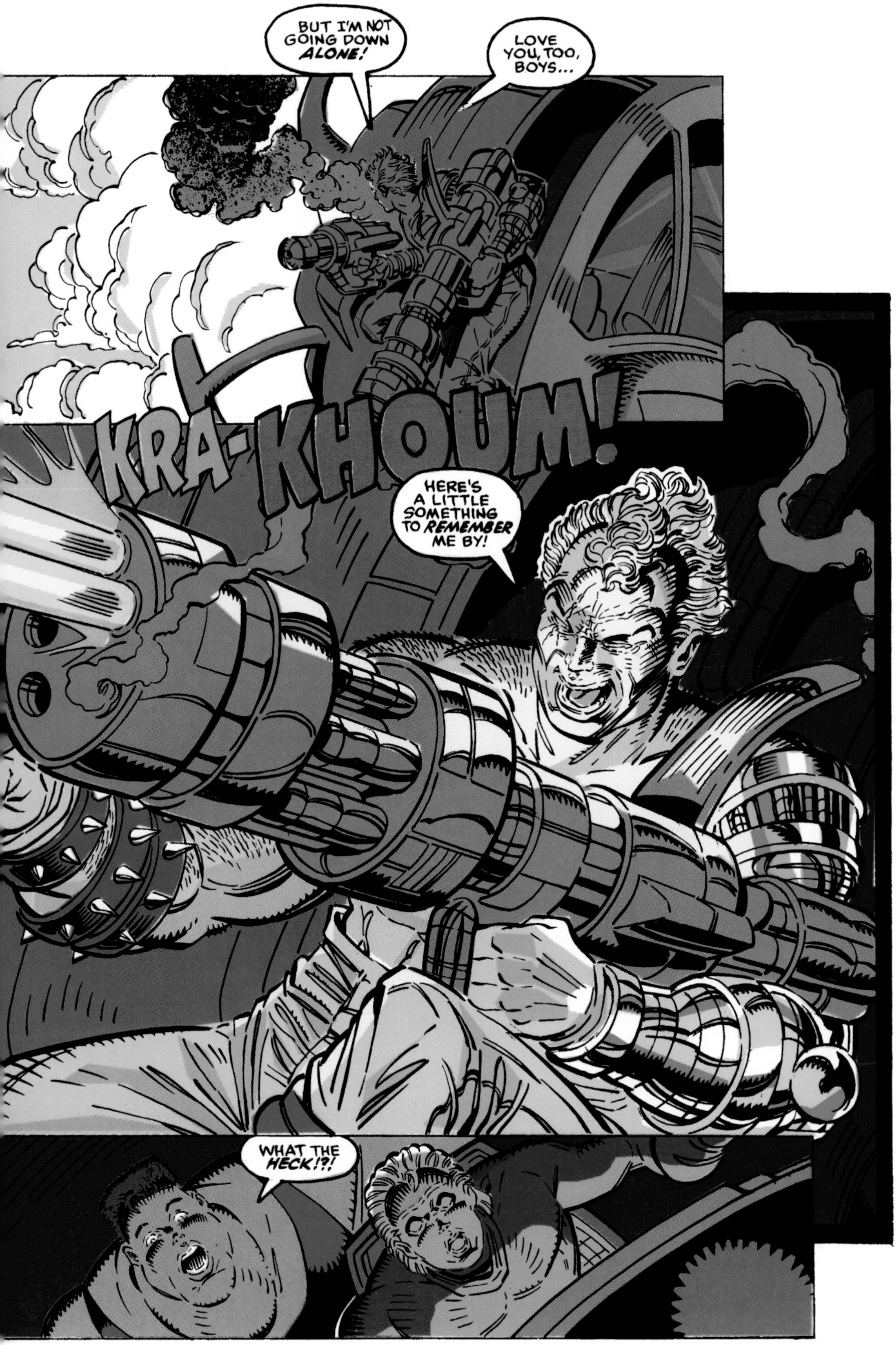

BUT I'M NOT GOING DOWN *ALONE!*
LOVE YOU, TOO, BOYS...
KRA-KHOUM!
HERE'S A LITTLE SOMETHING TO *REMEMBER* ME BY!
WHAT THE *HECK!?!*

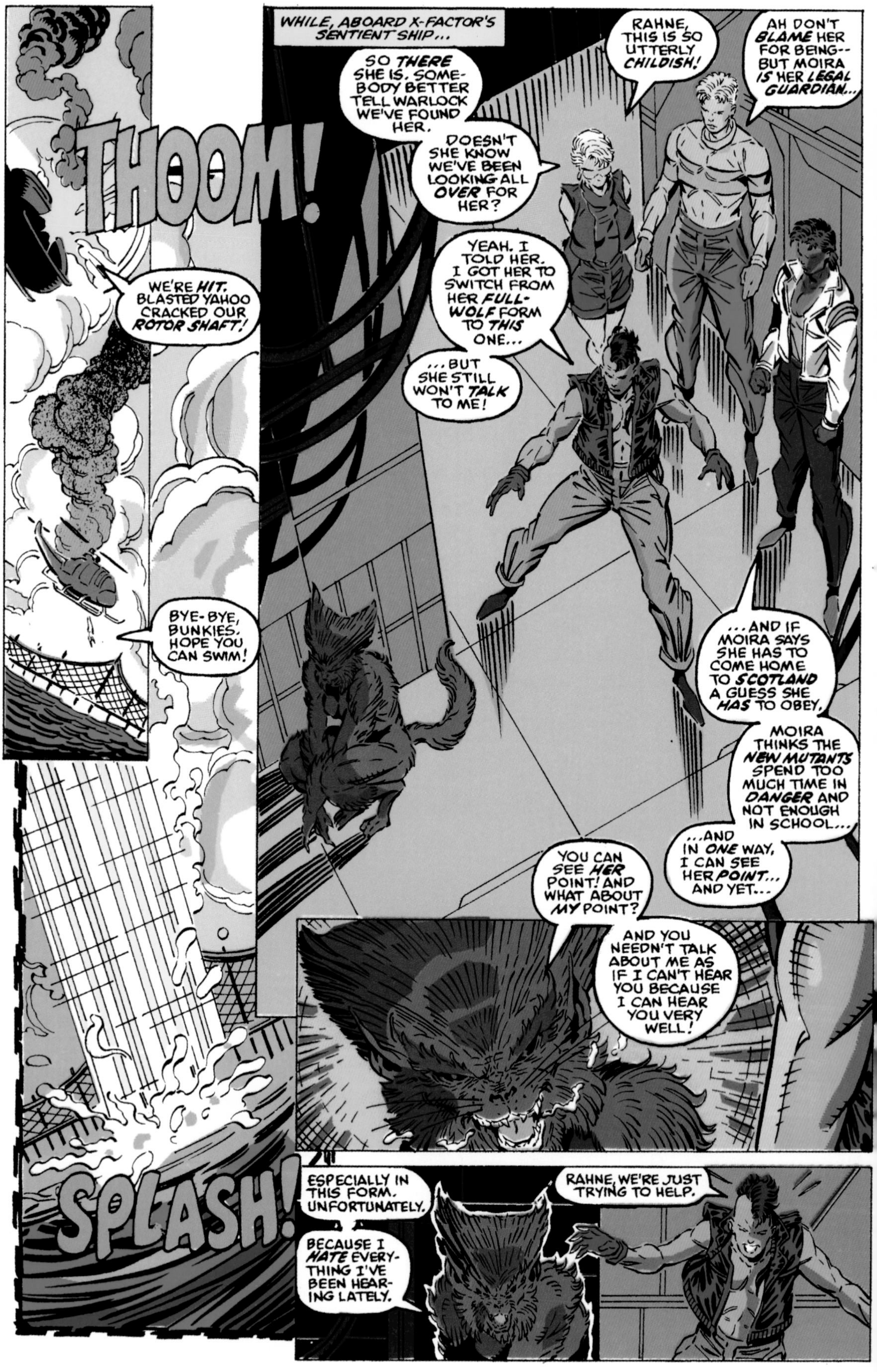
THOOM!
WE'RE HIT. BLASTED YAHOO CRACKED OUR ROTOR SHAFT!
BYE-BYE, BUNKIES. HOPE YOU CAN SWIM!
SPLASH!
WHILE, ABOARD X-FACTOR'S SENTIENT SHIP...
SO THERE SHE IS. SOMEBODY BETTER TELL WARLOCK WE'VE FOUND HER.
DOESN'T SHE KNOW WE'VE BEEN LOOKING ALL OVER FOR HER?
RAHNE, THIS IS SO UTTERLY CHILDISH!
AH DON'T BLAME HER FOR BEING-- BUT MOIRA IS HER LEGAL GUARDIAN...
YEAH. I TOLD HER. I GOT HER TO SWITCH FROM HER FULL-WOLF FORM TO THIS ONE...
...BUT SHE STILL WON'T TALK TO ME!
...AND IF MOIRA SAYS SHE HAS TO COME HOME TO SCOTLAND A GUESS SHE HAS TO OBEY.
MOIRA THINKS THE NEW MUTANTS SPEND TOO MUCH TIME IN DANGER AND NOT ENOUGH IN SCHOOL...
...AND IN ONE WAY, I CAN SEE HER POINT... AND YET...
YOU CAN SEE HER POINT! AND WHAT ABOUT MY POINT?
AND YOU NEEDN'T TALK ABOUT ME AS IF I CAN'T HEAR YOU BECAUSE I CAN HEAR YOU VERY WELL!
ESPECIALLY IN THIS FORM, UNFORTUNATELY.
BECAUSE I HATE EVERYTHING I'VE BEEN HEARING LATELY.
RAHNE, WE'RE JUST TRYING TO HELP.

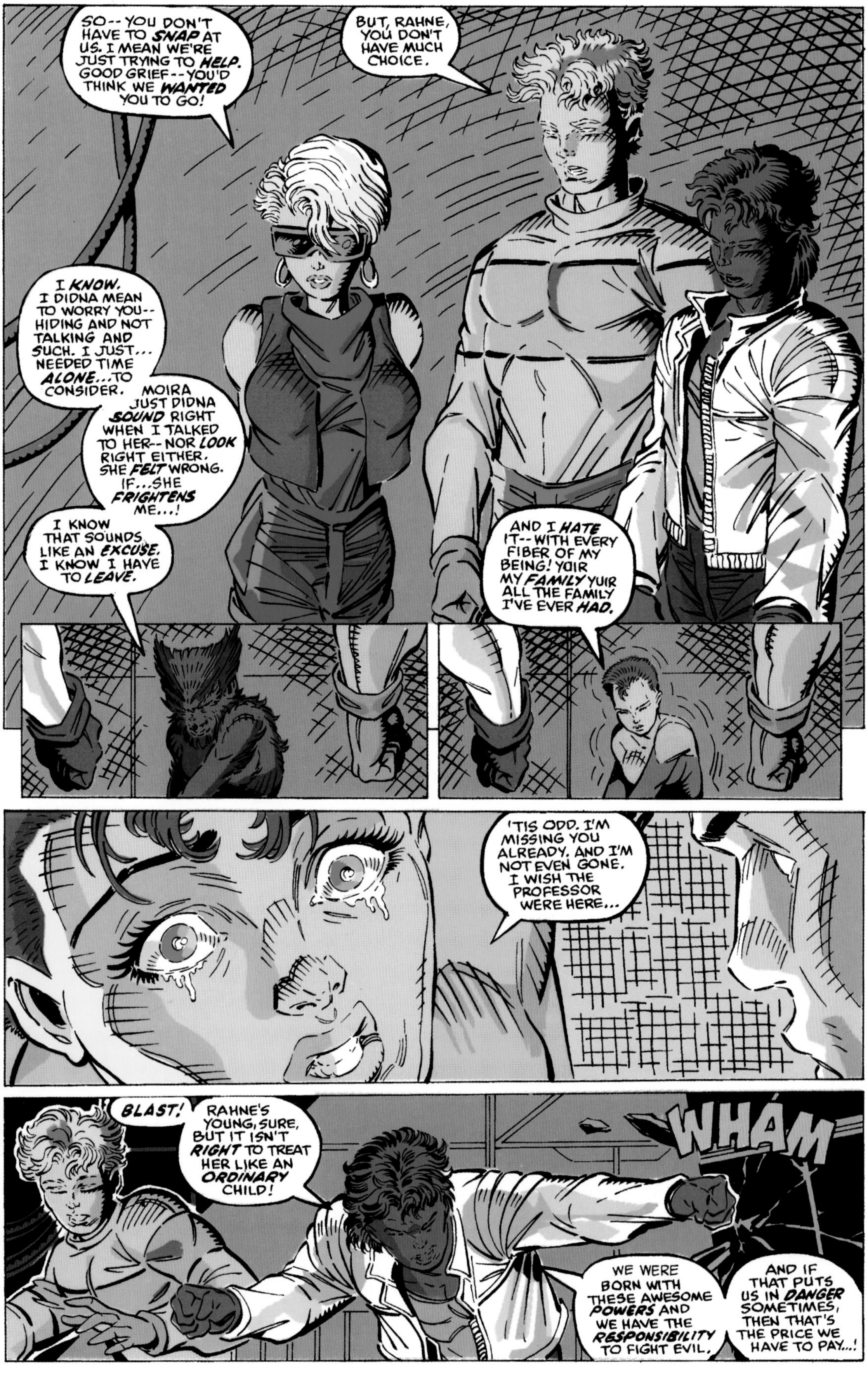

SO--YOU DON'T HAVE TO SNAP AT US. I MEAN WE'RE JUST TRYING TO HELP. GOOD GRIEF--YOU'D THINK WE WANTED YOU TO GO!
BUT, RAHNE, YOU DON'T HAVE MUCH CHOICE.
I KNOW. I DIDNA MEAN TO WORRY YOU--HIDING AND NOT TALKING AND SUCH. I JUST... NEEDED TIME ALONE...TO CONSIDER.
MOIRA JUST DIDNA SOUND RIGHT WHEN I TALKED TO HER--NOR LOOK RIGHT EITHER. SHE FELT WRONG. IF...SHE FRIGHTENS ME...!
I KNOW THAT SOUNDS LIKE AN EXCUSE. I KNOW I HAVE TO LEAVE.
AND I HATE IT--WITH EVERY FIBER OF MY BEING! YOIR MY FAMILY YUIR ALL THE FAMILY I'VE EVER HAD.
'TIS ODD. I'M MISSING YOU ALREADY. AND I'M NOT EVEN GONE. I WISH THE PROFESSOR WERE HERE...
BLAST!
RAHNE'S YOUNG, SURE, BUT IT ISN'T RIGHT TO TREAT HER LIKE AN ORDINARY CHILD!
WHAM
WE WERE BORN WITH THESE AWESOME POWERS AND WE HAVE THE RESPONSIBILITY TO FIGHT EVIL,
AND IF THAT PUTS US IN DANGER SOMETIMES, THEN THAT'S THE PRICE WE HAVE TO PAY...!

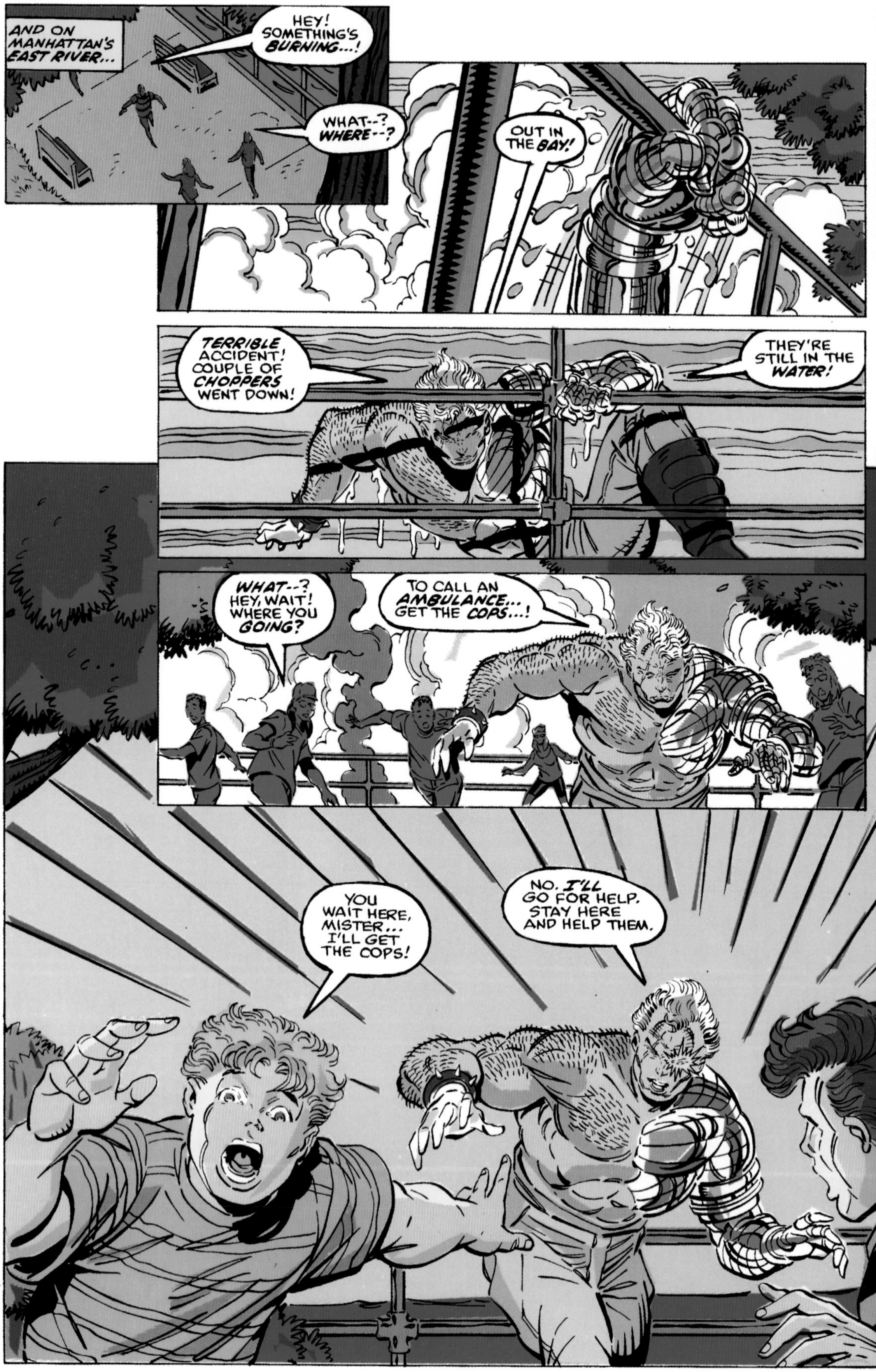

AND ON MANHATTAN'S EAST RIVER...
HEY! SOMETHING'S BURNING...!
WHAT--? WHERE--?
OUT IN THE BAY!
TERRIBLE ACCIDENT! COUPLE OF CHOPPERS WENT DOWN!
THEY'RE STILL IN THE WATER!
WHAT--? HEY, WAIT! WHERE YOU GOING?
TO CALL AN AMBULANCE... GET THE COPS...!
YOU WAIT HERE, MISTER... I'LL GET THE COPS!
NO. I'LL GO FOR HELP. STAY HERE AND HELP THEM.

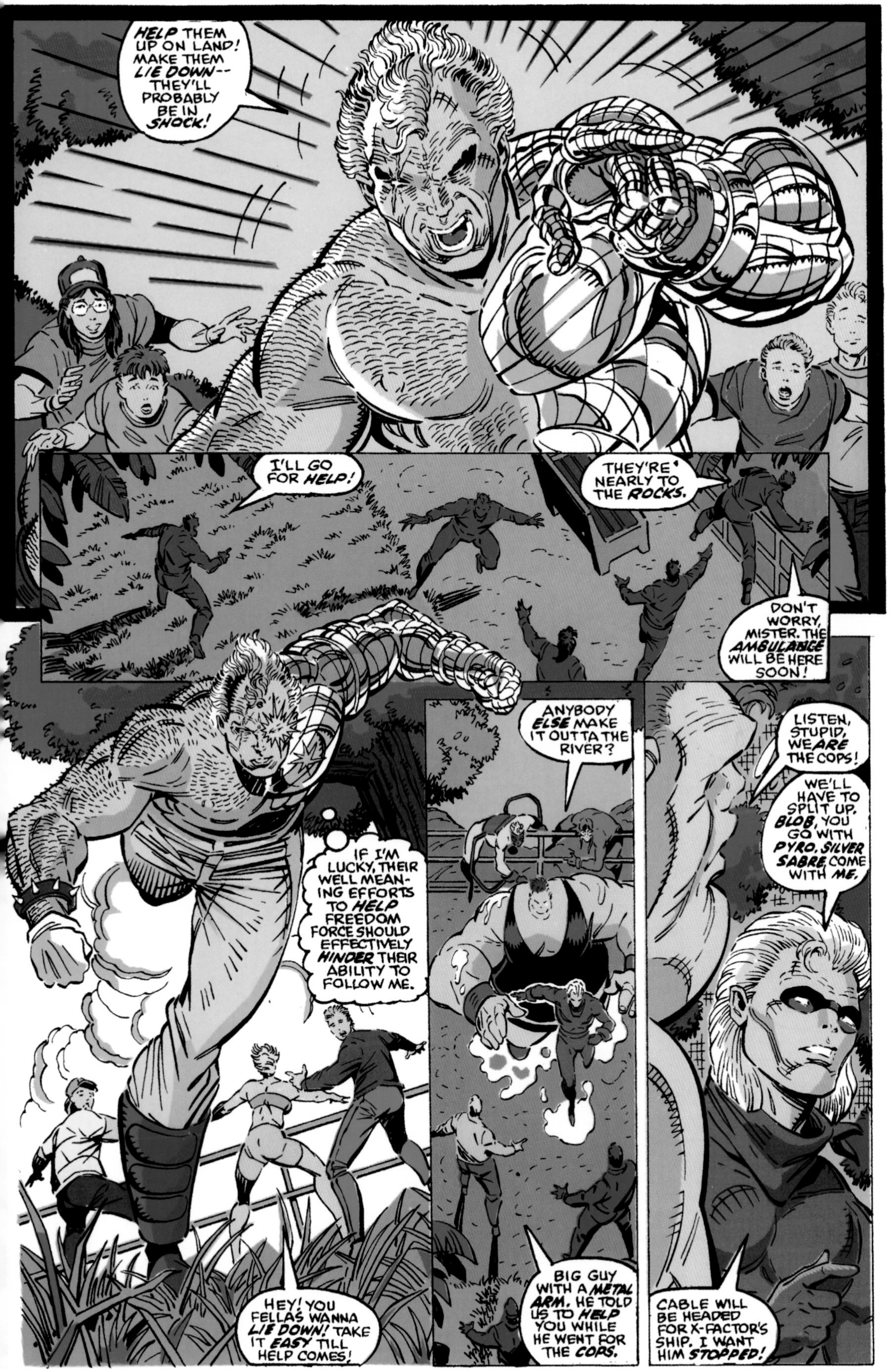
HELP THEM UP ON LAND! MAKE THEM LIE DOWN-- THEY'LL PROBABLY BE IN SHOCK!
I'LL GO FOR HELP!
THEY'RE NEARLY TO THE ROCKS.
DON'T WORRY, MISTER. THE AMBULANCE WILL BE HERE SOON!
IF I'M LUCKY, THEIR WELL MEANING EFFORTS TO HELP FREEDOM FORCE SHOULD EFFECTIVELY HINDER THEIR ABILITY TO FOLLOW ME.
HEY! YOU FELLAS WANNA LIE DOWN! TAKE IT EASY TILL HELP COMES!
ANYBODY ELSE MAKE IT OUTTA THE RIVER?
BIG GUY WITH A METAL ARM. HE TOLD US TO HELP YOU WHILE HE WENT FOR THE COPS.
LISTEN, STUPID, WE ARE THE COPS!
WE'LL HAVE TO SPLIT UP. BLOB, YOU GO WITH PYRO. SILVER SABRE, COME WITH ME.
CABLE WILL BE HEADED FOR X-FACTOR'S SHIP. I WANT HIM STOPPED!

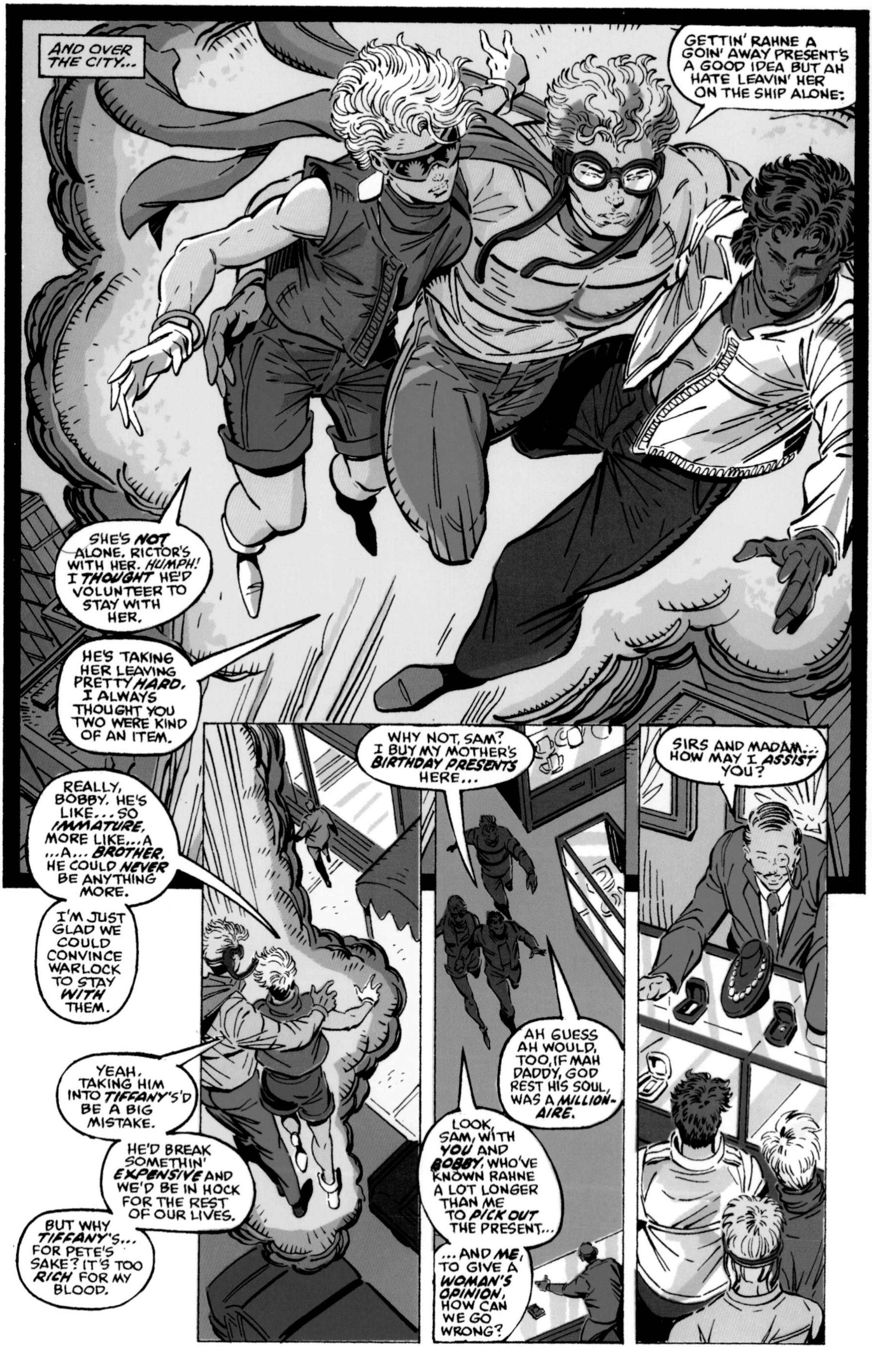
AND OVER THE CITY...
GETTIN' RAHNE A GOIN' AWAY PRESENT'S A GOOD IDEA BUT AH HATE LEAVIN' HER ON THE SHIP ALONE.
SHE'S NOT ALONE. RICTOR'S WITH HER. HUMPH! I THOUGHT HE'D VOLUNTEER TO STAY WITH HER.
HE'S TAKING HER LEAVING PRETTY HARD. I ALWAYS THOUGHT YOU TWO WERE KIND OF AN ITEM.
REALLY, BOBBY. HE'S LIKE... SO IMMATURE. MORE LIKE... A ...A... BROTHER. HE COULD NEVER BE ANYTHING MORE.
I'M JUST GLAD WE COULD CONVINCE WARLOCK TO STAY WITH THEM.
YEAH. TAKING HIM INTO TIFFANY'S'D BE A BIG MISTAKE.
HE'D BREAK SOMETHIN' EXPENSIVE AND WE'D BE IN HOCK FOR THE REST OF OUR LIVES.
BUT WHY TIFFANY'S... FOR PETE'S SAKE? IT'S TOO RICH FOR MY BLOOD.
WHY NOT, SAM? I BUY MY MOTHER'S BIRTHDAY PRESENTS HERE...
AH GUESS AH WOULD, TOO, IF MAH DADDY, GOD REST HIS SOUL, WAS A MILLIONAIRE.
LOOK, SAM, WITH YOU AND BOBBY, WHO'VE KNOWN RAHNE A LOT LONGER THAN ME TO PICK OUT THE PRESENT...
...AND ME, TO GIVE A WOMAN'S OPINION, HOW CAN WE GO WRONG?
SIRS AND MADAM... HOW MAY I ASSIST YOU?

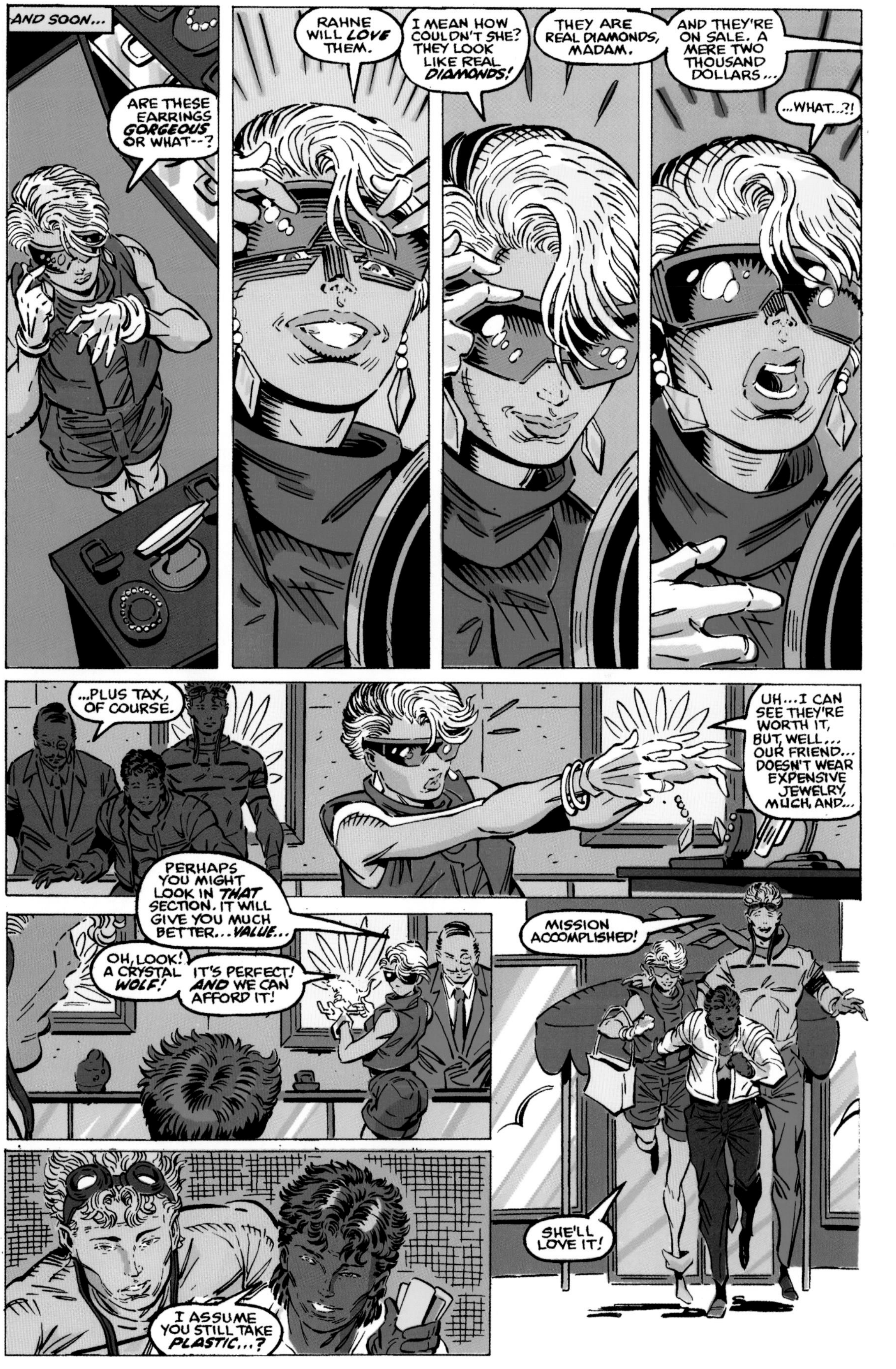
AND SOON...
ARE THESE EARRINGS GORGEOUS OR WHAT--?
RAHNE WILL LOVE THEM.
I MEAN HOW COULDN'T SHE? THEY LOOK LIKE REAL DIAMONDS!
THEY ARE REAL DIAMONDS, MADAM.
AND THEY'RE ON SALE. A MERE TWO THOUSAND DOLLARS...
...WHAT..?!
...PLUS TAX, OF COURSE.
UH...I CAN SEE THEY'RE WORTH IT, BUT, WELL... OUR FRIEND... DOESN'T WEAR EXPENSIVE JEWELRY, MUCH, AND...
PERHAPS YOU MIGHT LOOK IN THAT SECTION. IT WILL GIVE YOU MUCH BETTER... VALUE...
OH, LOOK! A CRYSTAL WOLF!
IT'S PERFECT! AND WE CAN AFFORD IT!
I ASSUME YOU STILL TAKE PLASTIC...?
MISSION ACCOMPLISHED!
SHE'LL LOVE IT!

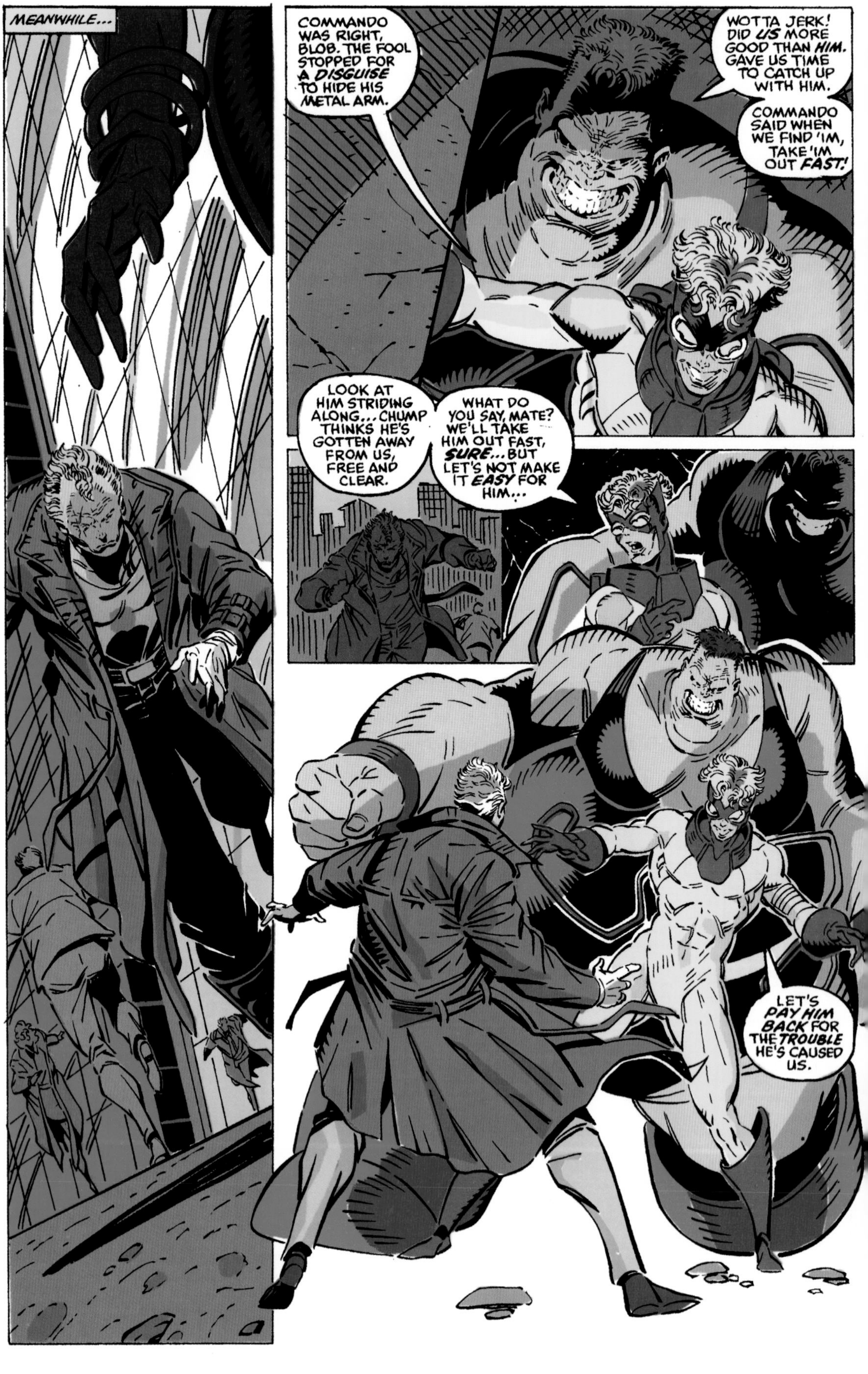
MEANWHILE...
COMMANDO WAS RIGHT, BLOB. THE FOOL STOPPED FOR A DISGUISE TO HIDE HIS METAL ARM.
WOTTA JERK! DID US MORE GOOD THAN HIM. GAVE US TIME TO CATCH UP WITH HIM.
COMMANDO SAID WHEN WE FIND 'IM, TAKE 'IM OUT FAST!
LOOK AT HIM STRIDING ALONG... CHUMP THINKS HE'S GOTTEN AWAY FROM US, FREE AND CLEAR.
WHAT DO YOU SAY, MATE? WE'LL TAKE HIM OUT FAST, SURE... BUT LET'S NOT MAKE IT EASY FOR HIM...
LET'S PAY HIM BACK FOR THE TROUBLE HE'S CAUSED US.

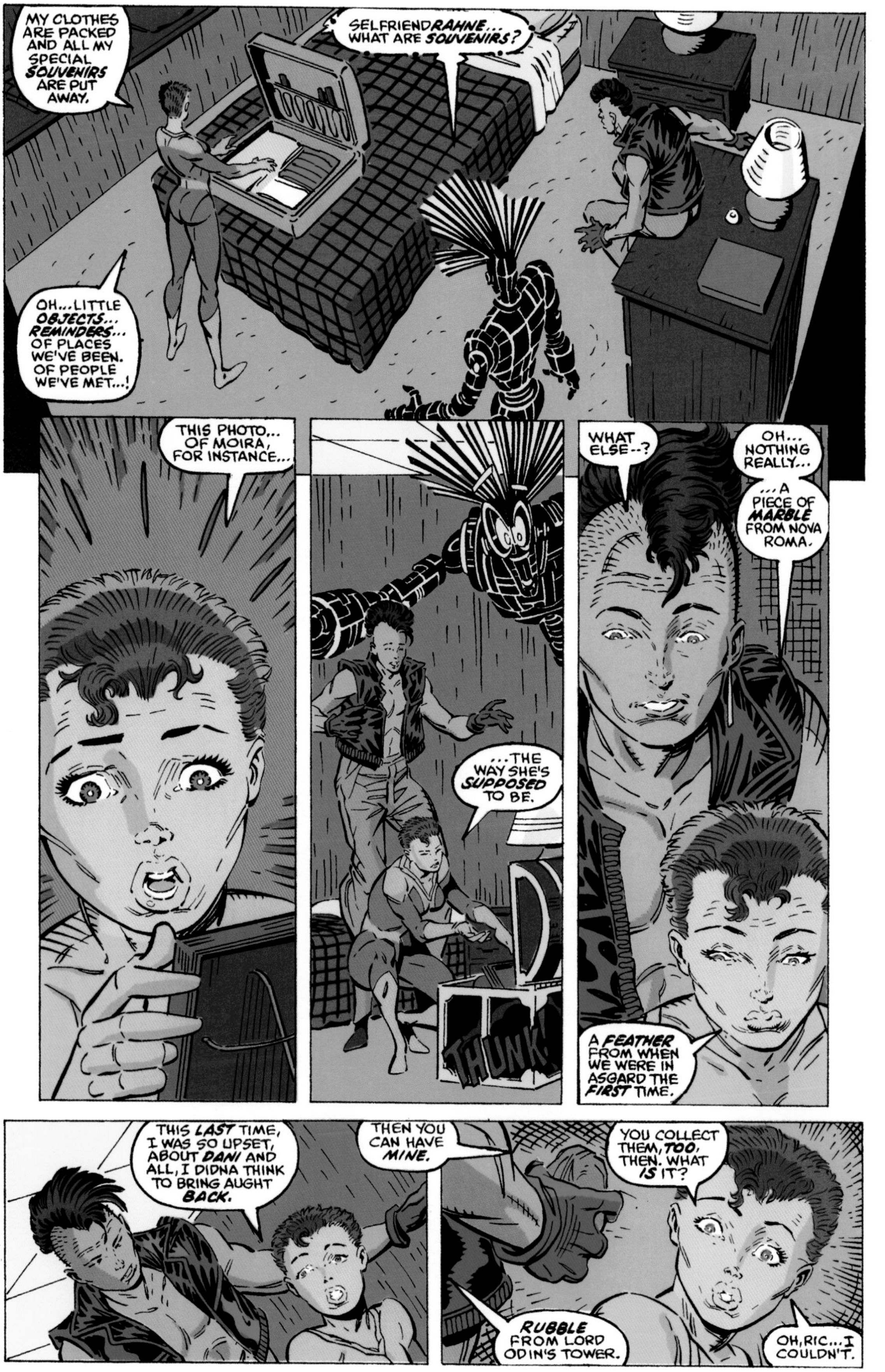
MY CLOTHES ARE PACKED AND ALL MY SPECIAL SOUVENIRS ARE PUT AWAY.
SELFRIEND RAHNE... WHAT ARE SOUVENIRS?
OH...LITTLE OBJECTS... REMINDERS... OF PLACES WE'VE BEEN. OF PEOPLE WE'VE MET...!
THIS PHOTO... OF MOIRA, FOR INSTANCE...
...THE WAY SHE'S SUPPOSED TO BE.
THUNK
WHAT ELSE--?
OH... NOTHING REALLY...
...A PIECE OF MARBLE FROM NOVA ROMA.
A FEATHER FROM WHEN WE WERE IN ASGARD THE FIRST TIME.
THIS LAST TIME, I WAS SO UPSET, ABOUT DANI AND ALL, I DIDNA THINK TO BRING AUGHT BACK.
THEN YOU CAN HAVE MINE.
YOU COLLECT THEM, TOO, THEN. WHAT IS IT?
RUBBLE FROM LORD ODIN'S TOWER.
OH, RIC... I COULDN'T.

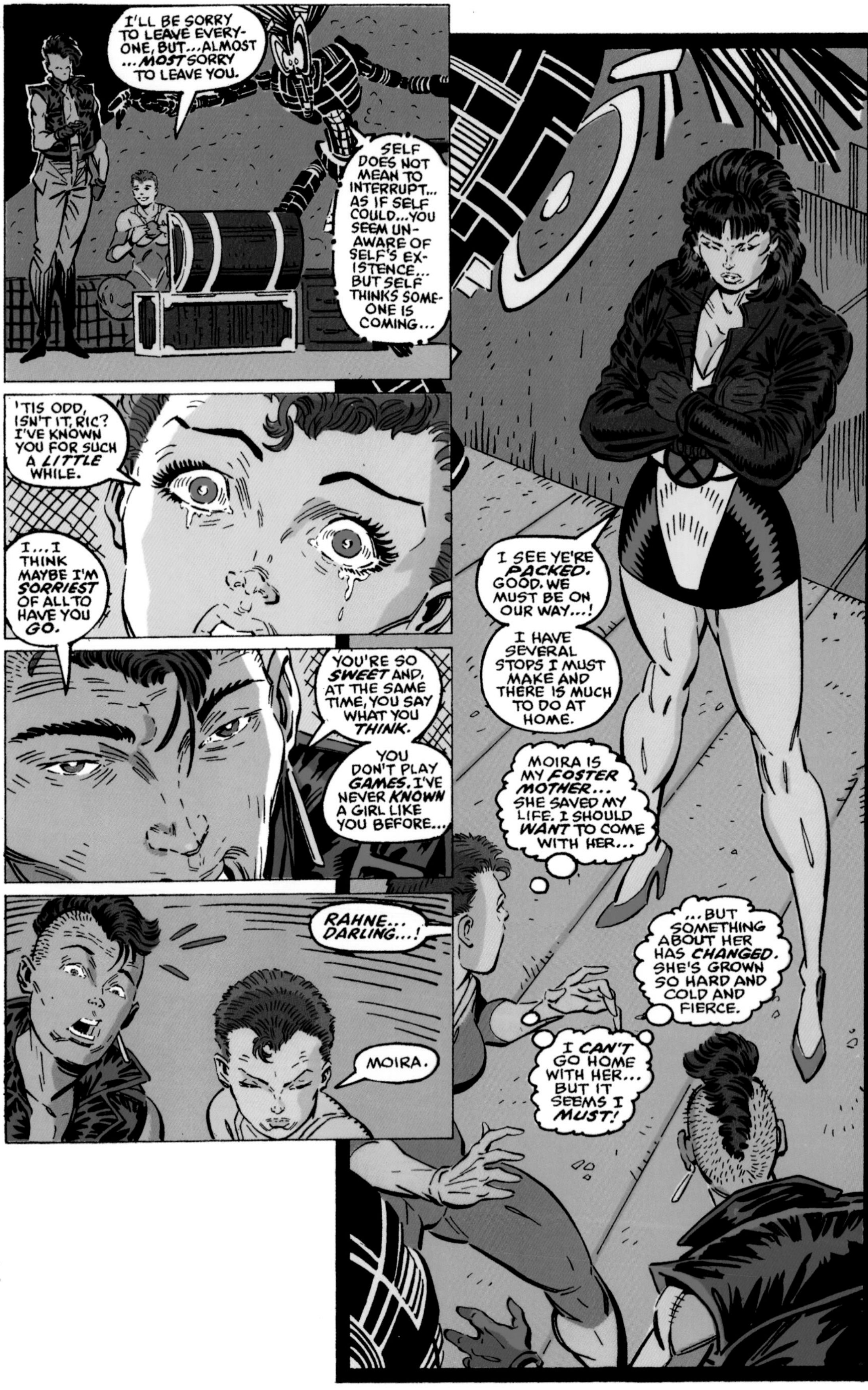

I'LL BE SORRY TO LEAVE EVERYONE, BUT...ALMOST ...MOST SORRY TO LEAVE YOU.
SELF DOES NOT MEAN TO INTERRUPT... AS IF SELF COULD...YOU SEEM UNAWARE OF SELF'S EXISTENCE... BUT SELF THINKS SOMEONE IS COMING...
'TIS ODD, ISN'T IT, RIC? I'VE KNOWN YOU FOR SUCH A LITTLE WHILE.
I...I THINK MAYBE I'M SORRIEST OF ALL TO HAVE YOU GO.
YOU'RE SO SWEET AND, AT THE SAME TIME, YOU SAY WHAT YOU THINK.
YOU DON'T PLAY GAMES. I'VE NEVER KNOWN A GIRL LIKE YOU BEFORE...
RAHNE... DARLING...!
MOIRA.
I SEE YE'RE PACKED. GOOD. WE MUST BE ON OUR WAY...!
I HAVE SEVERAL STOPS I MUST MAKE AND THERE IS MUCH TO DO AT HOME.
MOIRA IS MY FOSTER MOTHER... SHE SAVED MY LIFE. I SHOULD WANT TO COME WITH HER...
...BUT SOMETHING ABOUT HER HAS CHANGED. SHE'S GROWN SO HARD AND COLD AND FIERCE.
I CAN'T GO HOME WITH HER... BUT IT SEEMS I MUST!

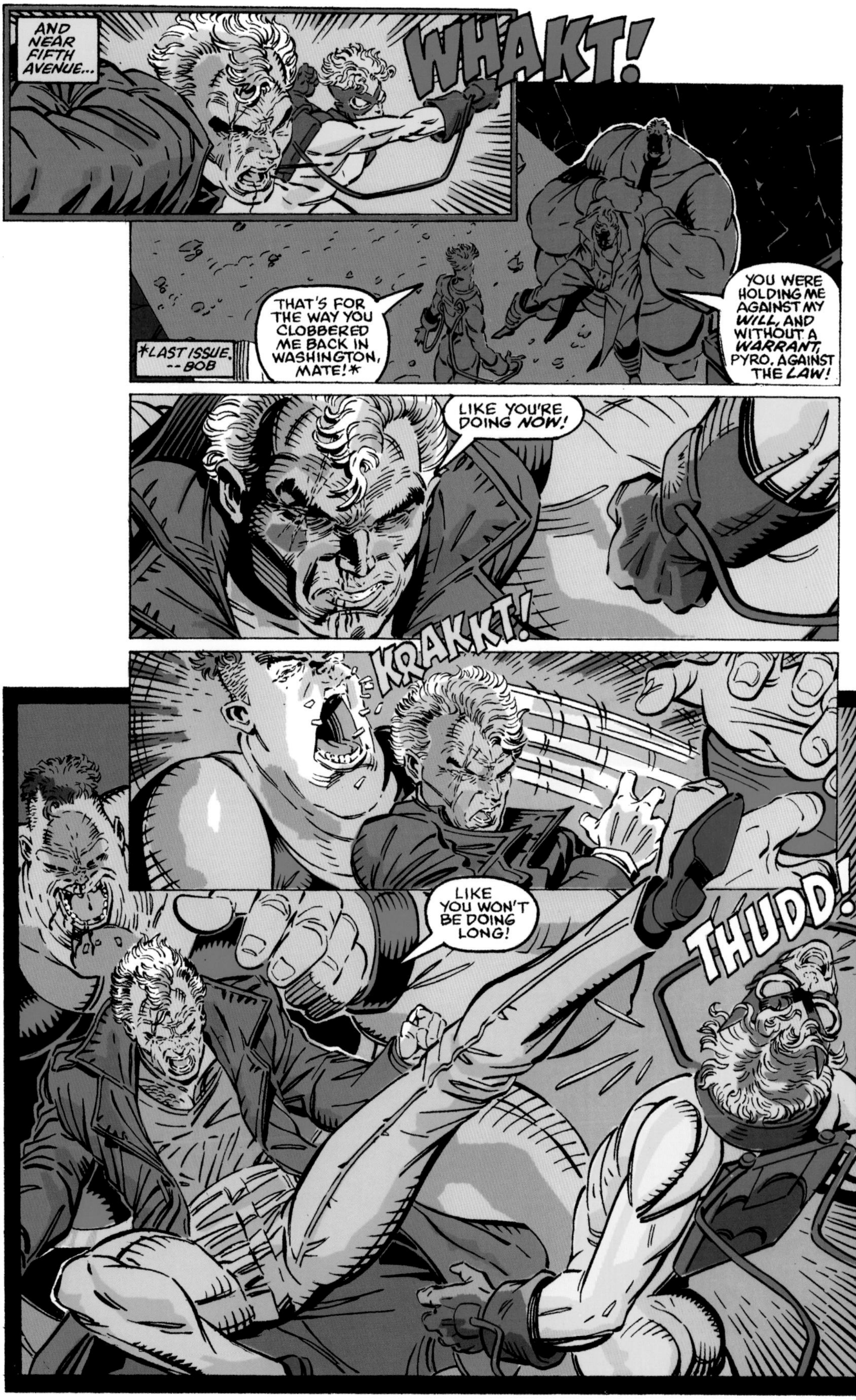
AND NEAR FIFTH AVENUE...
WHAKT!
THAT'S FOR THE WAY YOU CLOBBERED ME BACK IN WASHINGTON, MATE! *
*LAST ISSUE. --BOB
YOU WERE HOLDING ME AGAINST MY WILL, AND WITHOUT A WARRANT, PYRO. AGAINST THE LAW!
LIKE YOU'RE DOING NOW!
KRAKKT!
LIKE YOU WON'T BE DOING LONG!
THUDD!

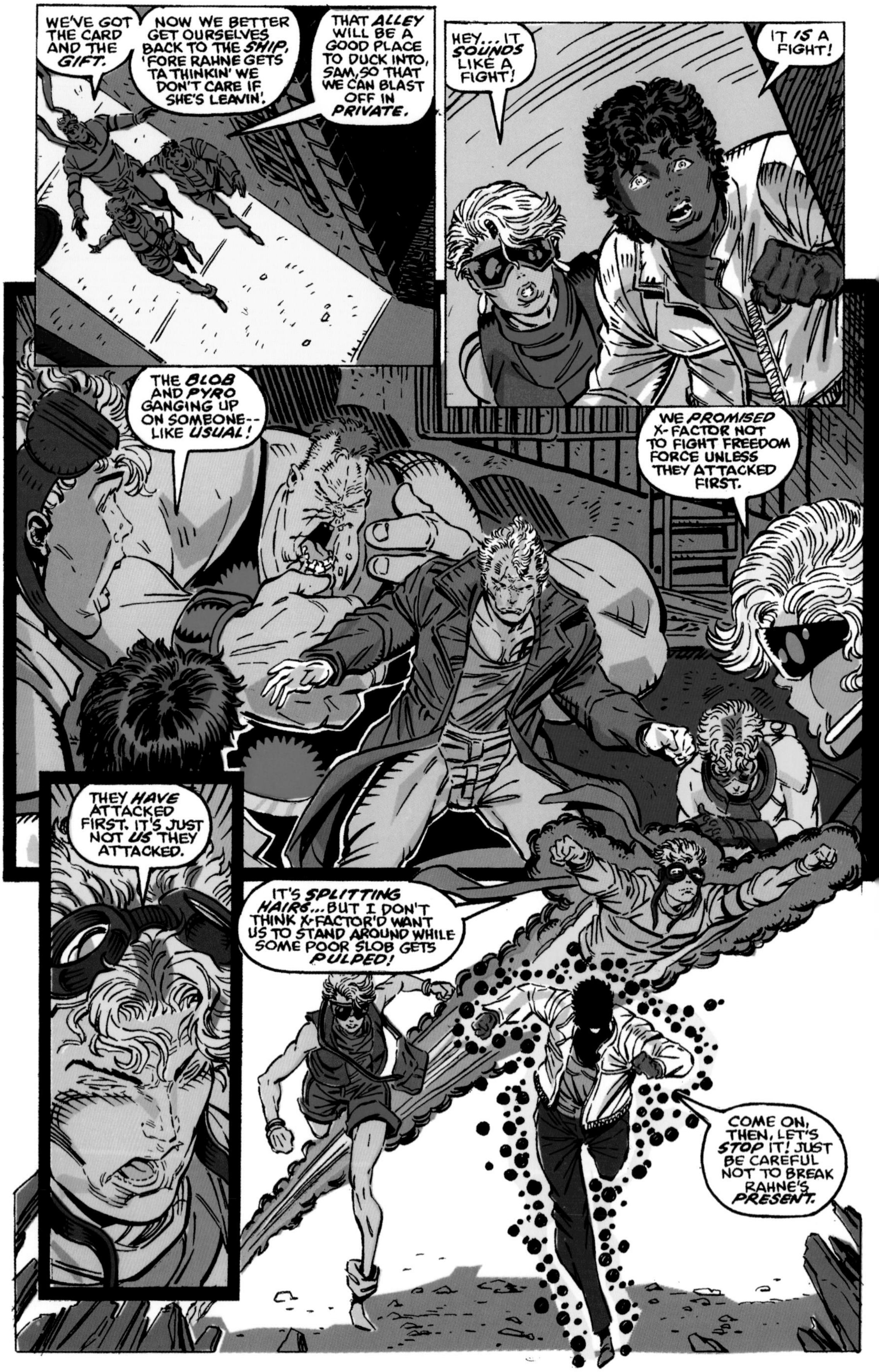
WE'VE GOT THE CARD AND THE GIFT.
NOW WE BETTER GET OURSELVES BACK TO THE SHIP, 'FORE RAHNE GETS TA THINKIN' WE DON'T CARE IF SHE'S LEAVIN'.
THAT ALLEY WILL BE A GOOD PLACE TO DUCK INTO, SAM, SO THAT WE CAN BLAST OFF IN PRIVATE.
HEY... IT SOUNDS LIKE A FIGHT!
IT IS A FIGHT!
THE BLOB AND PYRO GANGING UP ON SOMEONE-- LIKE USUAL!
WE PROMISED X-FACTOR NOT TO FIGHT FREEDOM FORCE UNLESS THEY ATTACKED FIRST.
THEY HAVE ATTACKED FIRST. IT'S JUST NOT US THEY ATTACKED.
IT'S SPLITTING HAIRS... BUT I DON'T THINK X-FACTOR'D WANT US TO STAND AROUND WHILE SOME POOR SLOB GETS PULPED!
COME ON, THEN, LET'S STOP IT! JUST BE CAREFUL NOT TO BREAK RAHNE'S PRESENT.

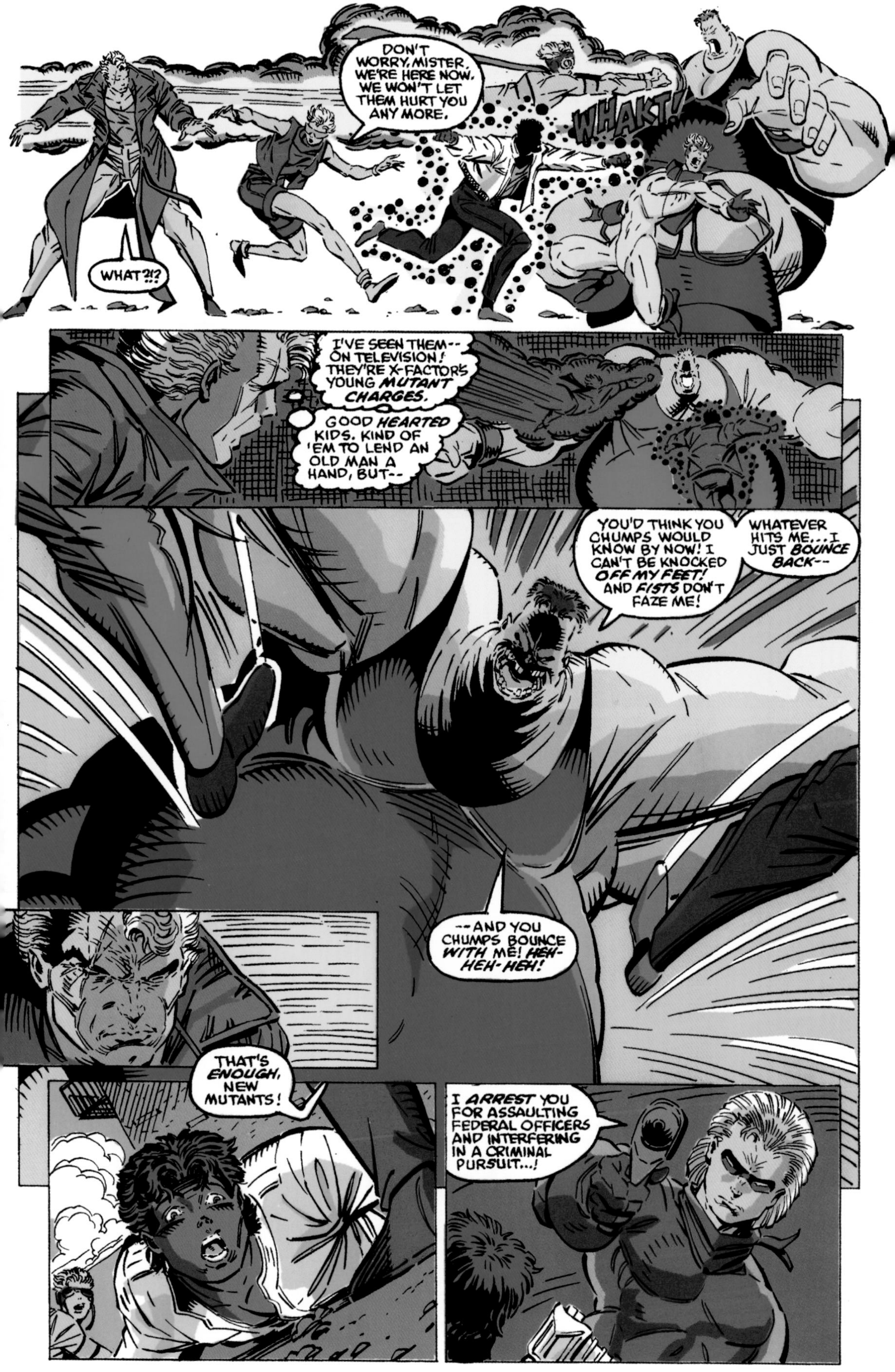
DON'T WORRY, MISTER. WE'RE HERE NOW. WE WON'T LET THEM HURT YOU ANY MORE.
WHAKT!
WHAT?!?
I'VE SEEN THEM-- ON TELEVISION! THEY'RE X-FACTOR'S YOUNG MUTANT CHARGES.
GOOD HEARTED KIDS. KIND OF 'EM TO LEND AN OLD MAN A HAND, BUT--
YOU'D THINK YOU CHUMPS WOULD KNOW BY NOW! I CAN'T BE KNOCKED OFF MY FEET! AND FISTS DON'T FAZE ME!
WHATEVER HITS ME... I JUST BOUNCE BACK--
--AND YOU CHUMPS BOUNCE WITH ME! HEH-HEH-HEH!
THAT'S ENOUGH, NEW MUTANTS!
I ARREST YOU FOR ASSAULTING FEDERAL OFFICERS AND INTERFERING IN A CRIMINAL PURSUIT...!

AND INSIDE THE SHIP...

X-FACTOR AND THE NEW MUTANTS ARE GONE, MOIRA, CAN'T WE WAIT TILL THEY GET BACK?

I'M IN A HURRY, RAHNE. YOU MAY CALL THEM FROM SCOTLAND TO SAY GOOD-BYE...!

BUT...

NO! YOU CAN'T GO! YOU CAN'T TAKE HER!

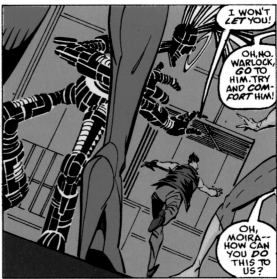

I WON'T LET YOU!

OH, HO. WARLOCK, GO TO HIM. TRY AND COMFORT HIM!

OH, MOIRA-- HOW CAN YOU DO THIS TO US?

SELFFRIENDRICTOR, YOU ARE UPSET! FRIENDRAHNE SAID I MUST CALM YOU AND--

DON'T SWEAT IT, WARLOCK. I HATED TO WORRY RAHNE, BUT THE FREAK-OUT WAS NECESSARY... FOR THE BENEFIT OF THAT LEATHER BOUND WITCH.

FRIENDRICTOR, SELF DOES NOT UNDERSTAND...!

I HAVE A PLAN, WARLOCK, ONE THAT WILL KEEP RAHNE HERE... NOT FOREVER, MAYBE... BUT AT LEAST UNTIL THE OTHERS... AND I HOPE, X-FACTOR ...RETURN.

THERE'S THE ELEVATOR. COME ON!

I AGREE WITH RAHNE. MOIRA'S NOT RIGHT. I WANT THE OTHERS... THE ONES WHO KNOW HER TO GET A LOOK AT HER.

SHIP, TAKE US TO THE HELIPAD-- AT ONCE!

AND CLOSE THE DOOR BEFORE MOIRA REACHES US. I'M BEGINNING TO THINK THERE'S SOMETHING SERIOUSLY WRONG WITH HER.

132

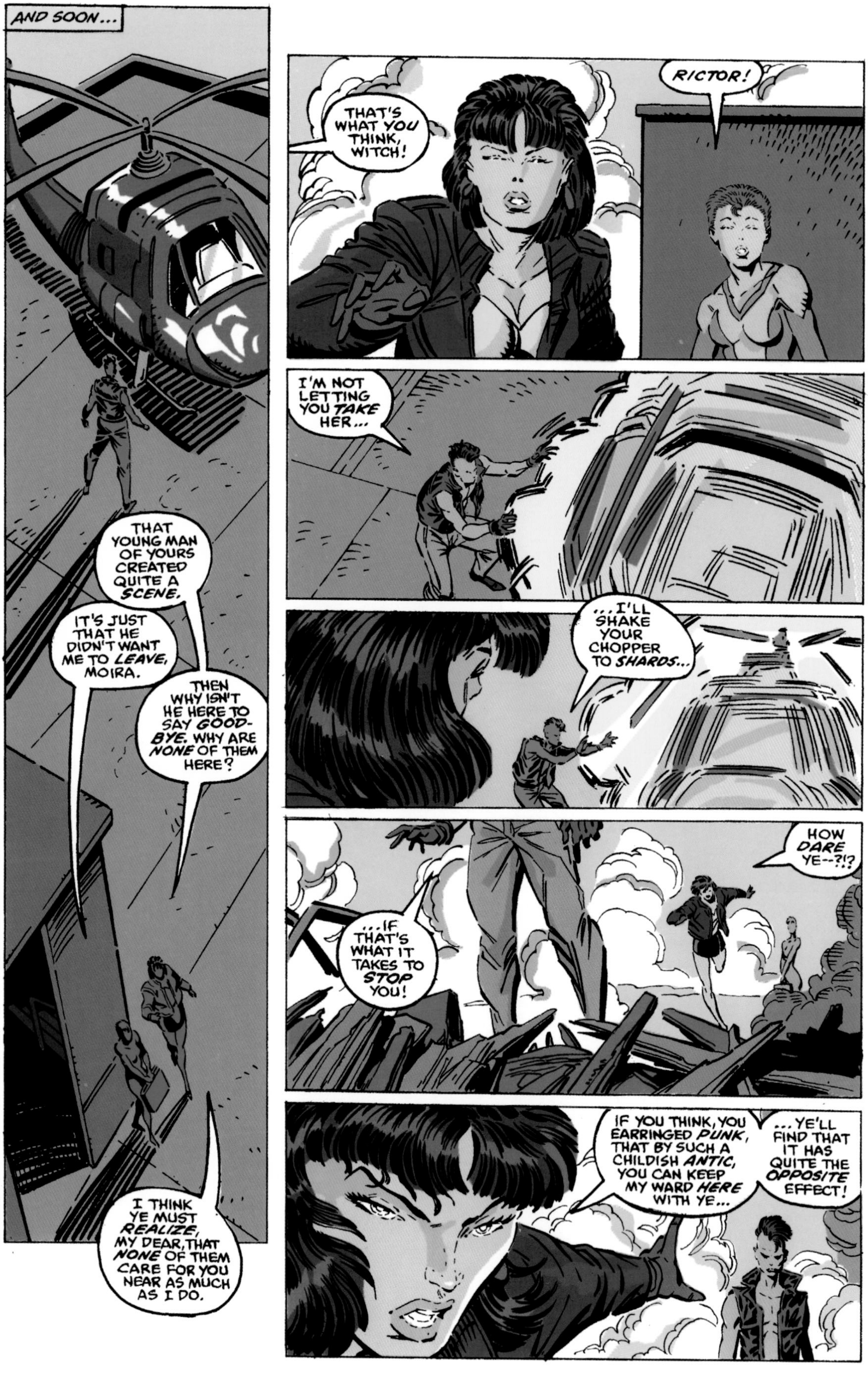
AND SOON...
THAT YOUNG MAN OF YOURS CREATED QUITE A SCENE.
IT'S JUST THAT HE DIDN'T WANT ME TO LEAVE, MOIRA.
THEN WHY ISN'T HE HERE TO SAY GOOD-BYE. WHY ARE NONE OF THEM HERE?
I THINK YE MUST REALIZE, MY DEAR, THAT NONE OF THEM CARE FOR YOU NEAR AS MUCH AS I DO.
THAT'S WHAT YOU THINK, WITCH!
RICTOR!
I'M NOT LETTING YOU TAKE HER...
...I'LL SHAKE YOUR CHOPPER TO SHARDS...
...IF THAT'S WHAT IT TAKES TO STOP YOU!
HOW DARE YE--?!?
IF YOU THINK, YOU EARRINGED PUNK, THAT BY SUCH A CHILDISH ANTIC, YOU CAN KEEP MY WARD HERE WITH YE...
...YE'LL FIND THAT IT HAS QUITE THE OPPOSITE EFFECT!

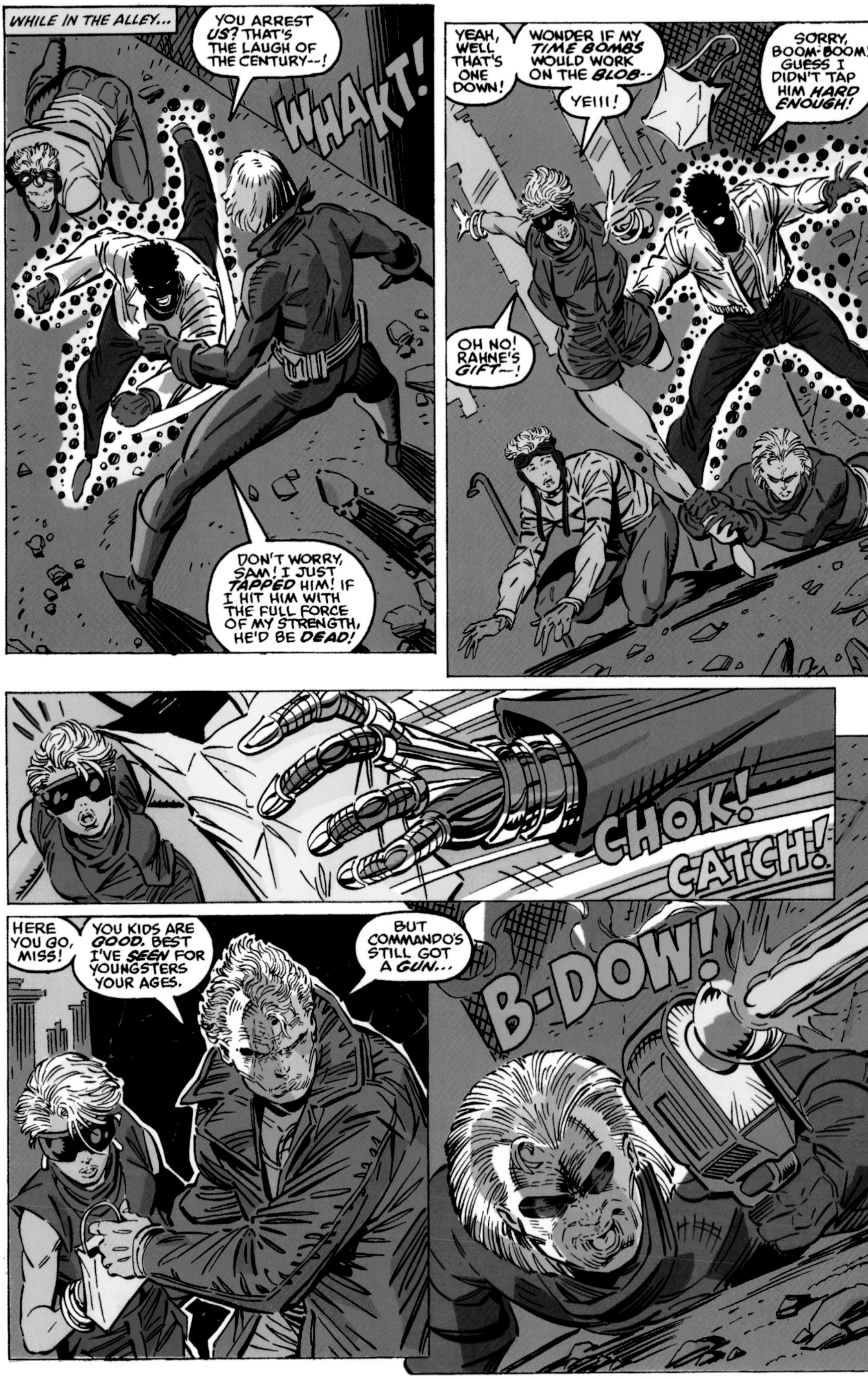

WHILE IN THE ALLEY...
YOU ARREST US? THAT'S THE LAUGH OF THE CENTURY--!
WHAKT!
DON'T WORRY, SAM! I JUST TAPPED HIM! IF I HIT HIM WITH THE FULL FORCE OF MY STRENGTH, HE'D BE DEAD!
YEAH, WELL THAT'S ONE DOWN!
WONDER IF MY TIME BOMBS WOULD WORK ON THE BLOB--
YEIII!
SORRY, BOOM-BOOM! GUESS I DIDN'T TAP HIM HARD ENOUGH!
OH NO! RAHNE'S GIFT--!
CHOK!
CATCH!
HERE YOU GO, MISS!
YOU KIDS ARE GOOD. BEST I'VE SEEN FOR YOUNGSTERS YOUR AGES.
BUT COMMANDO'S STILL GOT A GUN...
B-DOW!

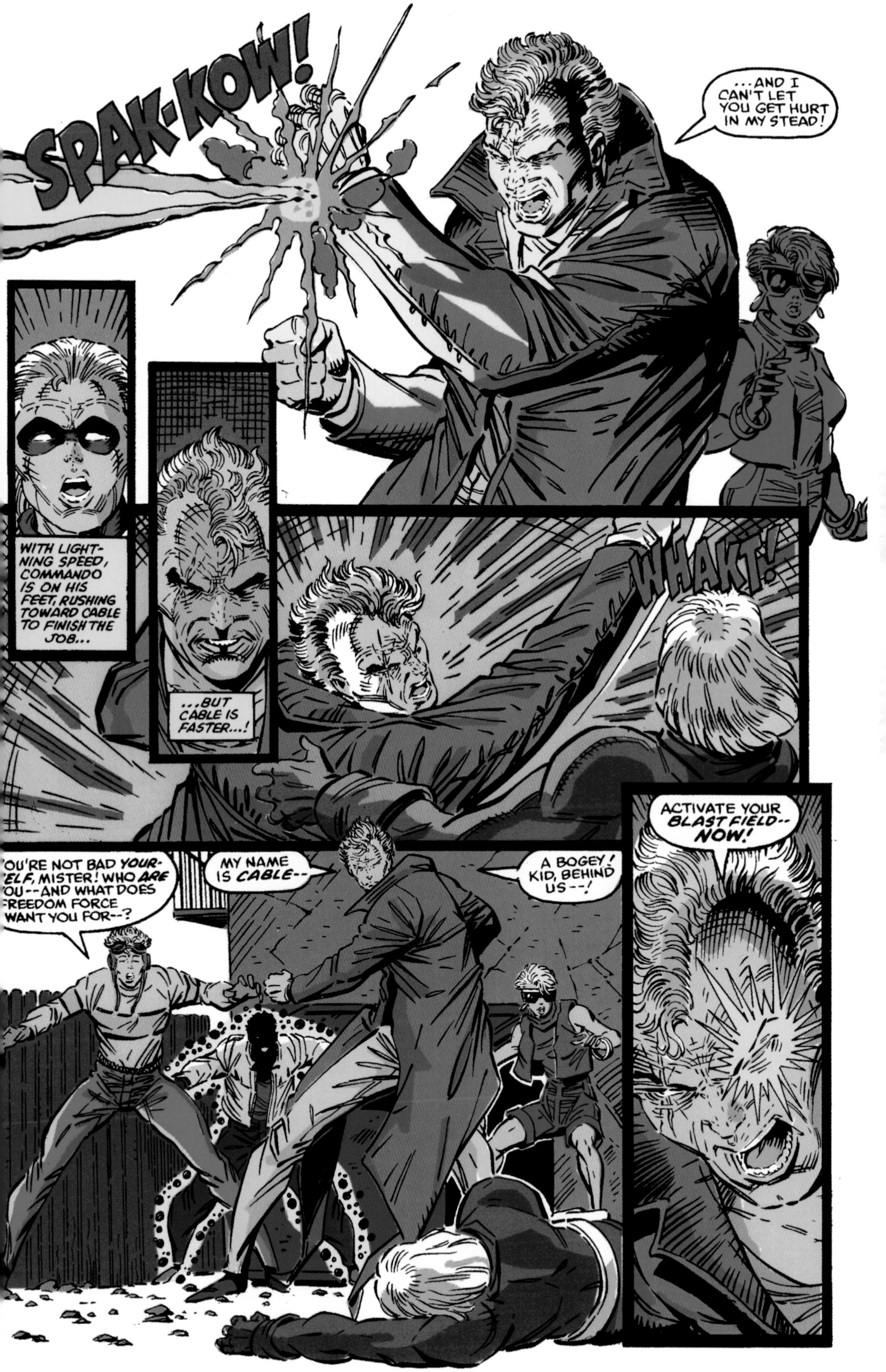
SPAK-KOW!
...AND I CAN'T LET YOU GET HURT IN MY STEAD!
WITH LIGHTNING SPEED, COMMANDO IS ON HIS FEET, RUSHING TOWARD CABLE TO FINISH THE JOB...
...BUT CABLE IS FASTER...!
WHAKT!
ACTIVATE YOUR BLAST FIELD-- NOW!
OU'RE NOT BAD YOUR-ELF, MISTER! WHO ARE OU--AND WHAT DOES FREEDOM FORCE WANT YOU FOR--?
MY NAME IS CABLE--
A BOGEY! KID, BEHIND US--!

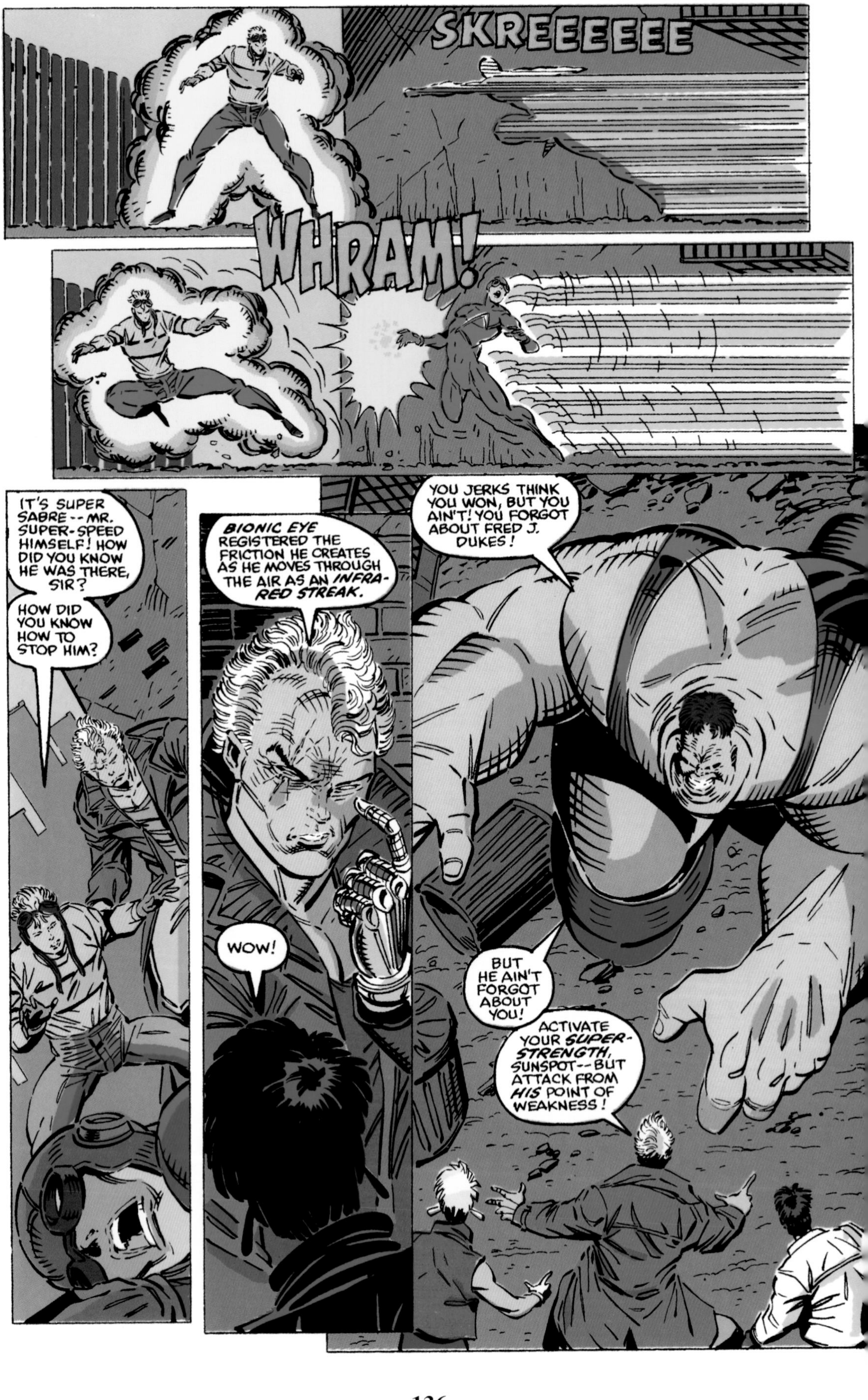
SKREEEEEEE
WHRAM!
IT'S SUPER SABRE--MR. SUPER-SPEED HIMSELF! HOW DID YOU KNOW HE WAS THERE, SIR?
HOW DID YOU KNOW HOW TO STOP HIM?
BIONIC EYE REGISTERED THE FRICTION HE CREATES AS HE MOVES THROUGH THE AIR AS AN INFRA-RED STREAK.
WOW!
YOU JERKS THINK YOU WON, BUT YOU AIN'T! YOU FORGOT ABOUT FRED J. DUKES!
BUT HE AIN'T FORGOT ABOUT YOU!
ACTIVATE YOUR SUPER-STRENGTH, SUNSPOT--BUT ATTACK FROM HIS POINT OF WEAKNESS!

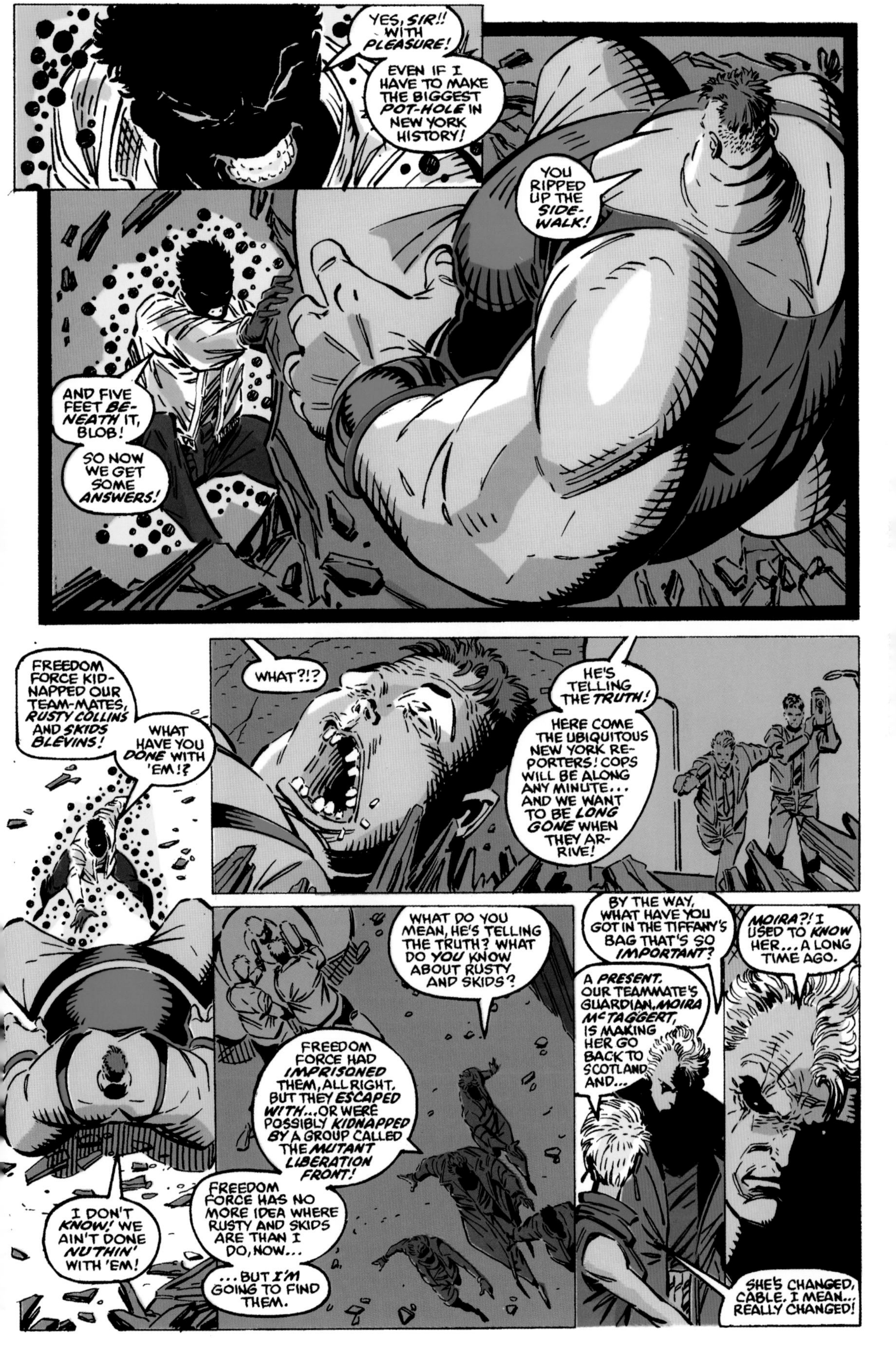
YES, SIR!! WITH PLEASURE!
EVEN IF I HAVE TO MAKE THE BIGGEST POT-HOLE IN NEW YORK HISTORY!
YOU RIPPED UP THE SIDE-WALK!
AND FIVE FEET BE-NEATH IT, BLOB!
SO NOW WE GET SOME ANSWERS!
FREEDOM FORCE KID-NAPPED OUR TEAM-MATES, RUSTY COLLINS AND SKIDS BLEVINS!
WHAT HAVE YOU DONE WITH 'EM!?
WHAT?!?
HE'S TELLING THE TRUTH!
HERE COME THE UBIQUITOUS NEW YORK RE-PORTERS! COPS WILL BE ALONG ANY MINUTE... AND WE WANT TO BE LONG GONE WHEN THEY AR-RIVE!
I DON'T KNOW! WE AIN'T DONE NUTHIN' WITH 'EM!
WHAT DO YOU MEAN, HE'S TELLING THE TRUTH? WHAT DO YOU KNOW ABOUT RUSTY AND SKIDS?
FREEDOM FORCE HAD IMPRISONED THEM, ALL RIGHT, BUT THEY ESCAPED WITH... OR WERE POSSIBLY KIDNAPPED BY A GROUP CALLED THE MUTANT LIBERATION FRONT!
FREEDOM FORCE HAS NO MORE IDEA WHERE RUSTY AND SKIDS ARE THAN I DO, NOW...
...BUT I'M GOING TO FIND THEM.
BY THE WAY, WHAT HAVE YOU GOT IN THE TIFFANY'S BAG THAT'S SO IMPORTANT?
A PRESENT. OUR TEAMMATE'S GUARDIAN, MOIRA McTAGGERT, IS MAKING HER GO BACK TO SCOTLAND AND...
MOIRA?! I USED TO KNOW HER... A LONG TIME AGO.
SHE'S CHANGED, CABLE. I MEAN... REALLY CHANGED!

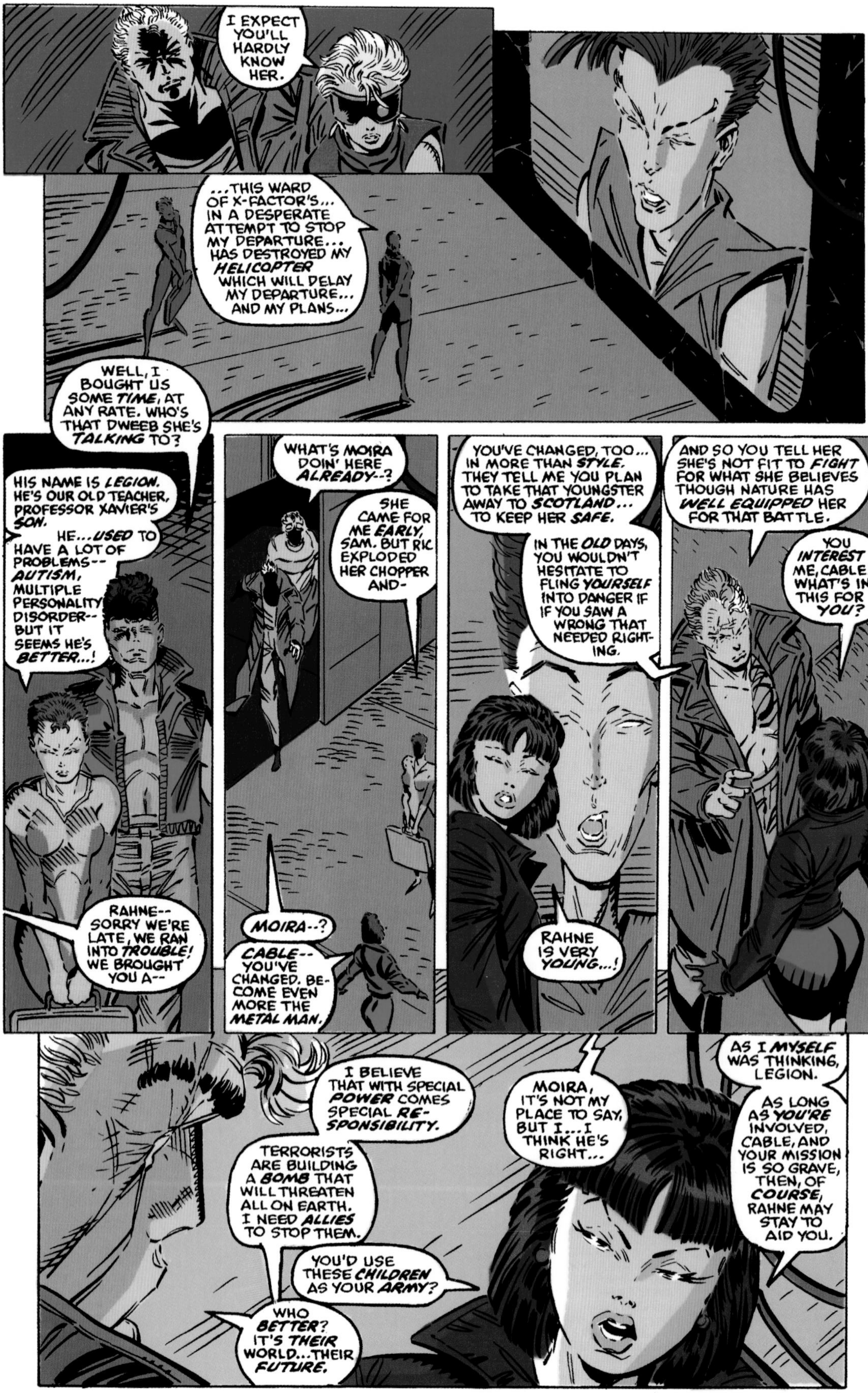
I EXPECT YOU'LL HARDLY KNOW HER.
...THIS WARD OF X-FACTOR'S... IN A DESPERATE ATTEMPT TO STOP MY DEPARTURE... HAS DESTROYED MY HELICOPTER WHICH WILL DELAY MY DEPARTURE... AND MY PLANS...
WELL, I BOUGHT US SOME TIME, AT ANY RATE. WHO'S THAT DWEEB SHE'S TALKING TO?
HIS NAME IS LEGION. HE'S OUR OLD TEACHER, PROFESSOR XAVIER'S SON.
HE...USED TO HAVE A LOT OF PROBLEMS-- AUTISM, MULTIPLE PERSONALITY DISORDER-- BUT IT SEEMS HE'S BETTER...!
RAHNE-- SORRY WE'RE LATE, WE RAN INTO TROUBLE! WE BROUGHT YOU A--
WHAT'S MOIRA DOIN' HERE ALREADY--?
SHE CAME FOR ME EARLY, SAM. BUT RIC EXPLODED HER CHOPPER AND-
MOIRA--?
CABLE-- YOU'VE CHANGED. BECOME EVEN MORE THE METAL MAN.
YOU'VE CHANGED, TOO... IN MORE THAN STYLE. THEY TELL ME YOU PLAN TO TAKE THAT YOUNGSTER AWAY TO SCOTLAND... TO KEEP HER SAFE.
IN THE OLD DAYS, YOU WOULDN'T HESITATE TO FLING YOURSELF INTO DANGER IF YOU SAW A WRONG THAT NEEDED RIGHTING.
RAHNE IS VERY YOUNG...!
AND SO YOU TELL HER SHE'S NOT FIT TO FIGHT FOR WHAT SHE BELIEVES THOUGH NATURE HAS WELL EQUIPPED HER FOR THAT BATTLE.
YOU INTEREST ME, CABLE. WHAT'S IN THIS FOR YOU?
I BELIEVE THAT WITH SPECIAL POWER COMES SPECIAL RESPONSIBILITY.
TERRORISTS ARE BUILDING A BOMB THAT WILL THREATEN ALL ON EARTH. I NEED ALLIES TO STOP THEM.
YOU'D USE THESE CHILDREN AS YOUR ARMY?
WHO BETTER? IT'S THEIR WORLD...THEIR FUTURE.
MOIRA, IT'S NOT MY PLACE TO SAY, BUT I...I THINK HE'S RIGHT...
AS I MYSELF WAS THINKING, LEGION.
AS LONG AS YOU'RE INVOLVED, CABLE, AND YOUR MISSION IS SO GRAVE, THEN, OF COURSE, RAHNE MAY STAY TO AID YOU.

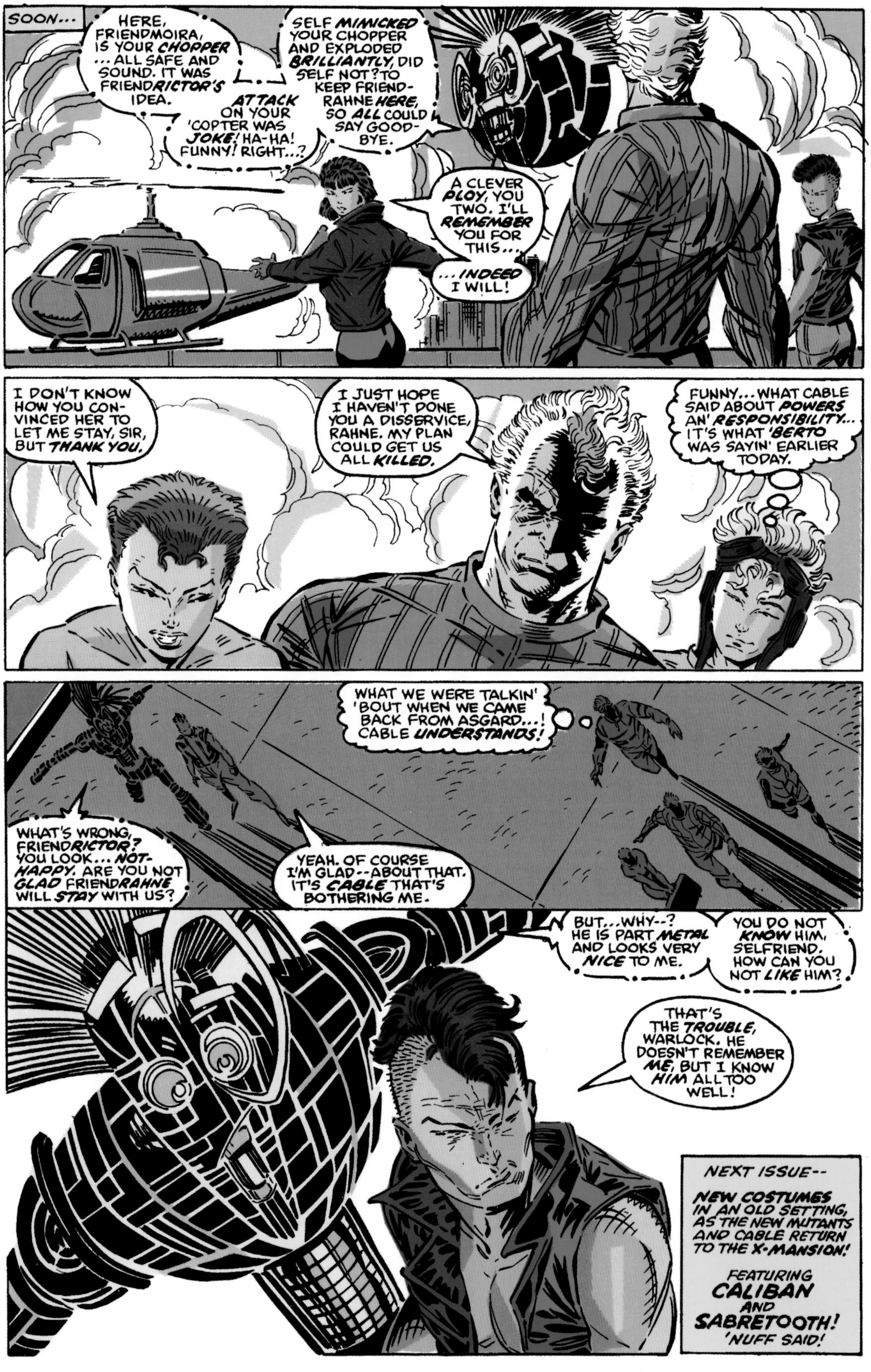
SOON...
HERE, FRIENDMOIRA, IS YOUR CHOPPER ...ALL SAFE AND SOUND. IT WAS FRIENDRICTOR'S IDEA.
ATTACK ON YOUR 'COPTER WAS JOKE! HA-HA! FUNNY! RIGHT...?
SELF MIMICKED YOUR CHOPPER AND EXPLODED BRILLIANTLY, DID SELF NOT? TO KEEP FRIEND-RAHNE HERE, SO ALL COULD SAY GOOD-BYE.
A CLEVER PLOY, YOU TWO. I'LL REMEMBER YOU FOR THIS....
...INDEED I WILL!
I DON'T KNOW HOW YOU CONVINCED HER TO LET ME STAY, SIR, BUT THANK YOU.
I JUST HOPE I HAVEN'T DONE YOU A DISSERVICE, RAHNE. MY PLAN COULD GET US ALL KILLED.
FUNNY... WHAT CABLE SAID ABOUT POWERS AN' RESPONSIBILITY... IT'S WHAT 'BERTO WAS SAYIN' EARLIER TODAY.
WHAT WE WERE TALKIN' 'BOUT WHEN WE CAME BACK FROM ASGARD...! CABLE UNDERSTANDS!
WHAT'S WRONG, FRIENDRICTOR? YOU LOOK... NOT-HAPPY. ARE YOU NOT GLAD FRIENDRAHNE WILL STAY WITH US?
YEAH. OF COURSE I'M GLAD--ABOUT THAT. IT'S CABLE THAT'S BOTHERING ME.
BUT...WHY--? HE IS PART METAL AND LOOKS VERY NICE TO ME.
YOU DO NOT KNOW HIM, SELFRIEND. HOW CAN YOU NOT LIKE HIM?
THAT'S THE TROUBLE, WARLOCK. HE DOESN'T REMEMBER ME, BUT I KNOW HIM ALL TOO WELL!
NEXT ISSUE-- NEW COSTUMES IN AN OLD SETTING, AS THE NEW MUTANTS AND CABLE RETURN TO THE X-MANSION!
FEATURING CALIBAN AND SABRETOOTH! 'NUFF SAID!

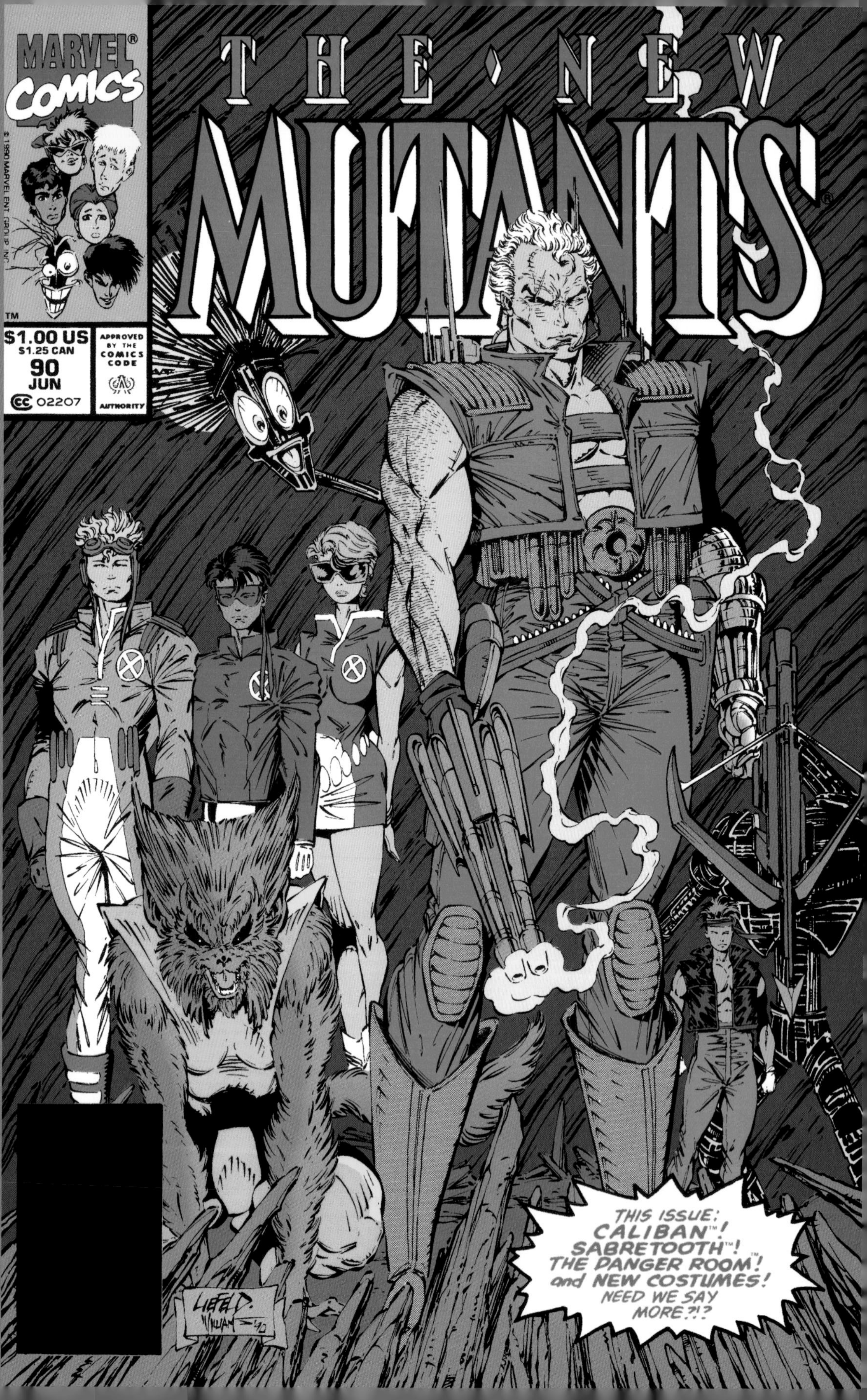
MARVEL® COMICS
THE NEW MUTANTS®
© 1990 MARVEL ENT. GROUP, INC.
TM
$1.00 US
$1.25 CAN
90
JUN
CC 02207
APPROVED BY THE COMICS CODE AUTHORITY
THIS ISSUE: CALIBAN™! SABRETOOTH™! THE DANGER ROOM™! and NEW COSTUMES! NEED WE SAY MORE?!?
LIEFELD.

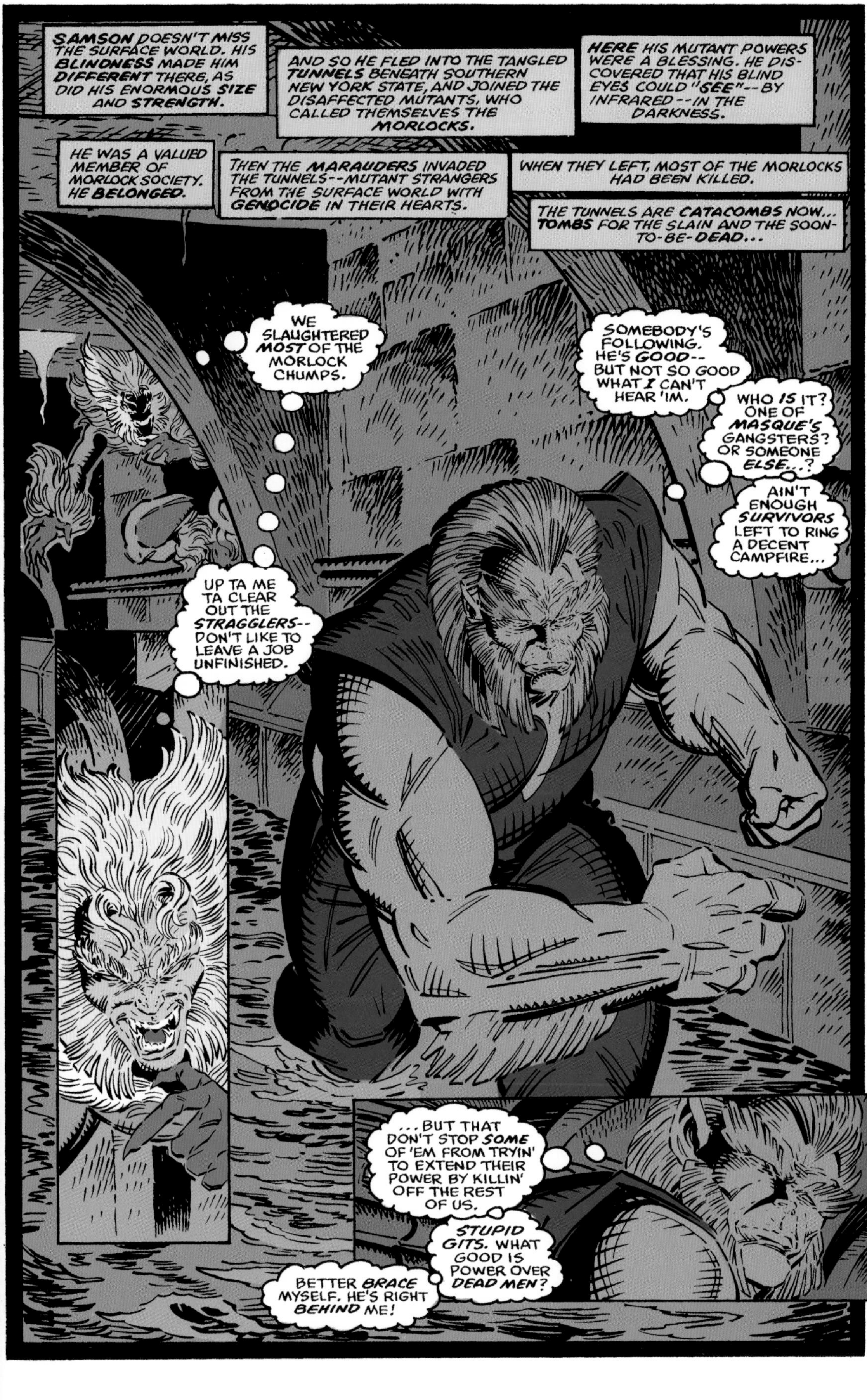
SAMSON DOESN'T MISS THE SURFACE WORLD. HIS BLINDNESS MADE HIM DIFFERENT THERE, AS DID HIS ENORMOUS SIZE AND STRENGTH.
AND SO HE FLED INTO THE TANGLED TUNNELS BENEATH SOUTHERN NEW YORK STATE, AND JOINED THE DISAFFECTED MUTANTS, WHO CALLED THEMSELVES THE MORLOCKS.
HERE HIS MUTANT POWERS WERE A BLESSING. HE DISCOVERED THAT HIS BLIND EYES COULD "SEE"--BY INFRARED--IN THE DARKNESS.
HE WAS A VALUED MEMBER OF MORLOCK SOCIETY. HE BELONGED.
THEN THE MARAUDERS INVADED THE TUNNELS--MUTANT STRANGERS FROM THE SURFACE WORLD WITH GENOCIDE IN THEIR HEARTS.
WHEN THEY LEFT, MOST OF THE MORLOCKS HAD BEEN KILLED.
THE TUNNELS ARE CATACOMBS NOW... TOMBS FOR THE SLAIN AND THE SOON-TO-BE-DEAD...
WE SLAUGHTERED MOST OF THE MORLOCK CHUMPS.
UP TA ME TA CLEAR OUT THE STRAGGLERS--DON'T LIKE TO LEAVE A JOB UNFINISHED.
SOMEBODY'S FOLLOWING. HE'S GOOD--BUT NOT SO GOOD WHAT I CAN'T HEAR 'IM.
WHO IS IT? ONE OF MASQUE'S GANGSTERS? OR SOMEONE ELSE...?
AIN'T ENOUGH SURVIVORS LEFT TO RING A DECENT CAMPFIRE...
...BUT THAT DON'T STOP SOME OF 'EM FROM TRYIN' TO EXTEND THEIR POWER BY KILLIN' OFF THE REST OF US.
STUPID GITS. WHAT GOOD IS POWER OVER DEAD MEN?
BETTER BRACE MYSELF. HE'S RIGHT BEHIND ME!

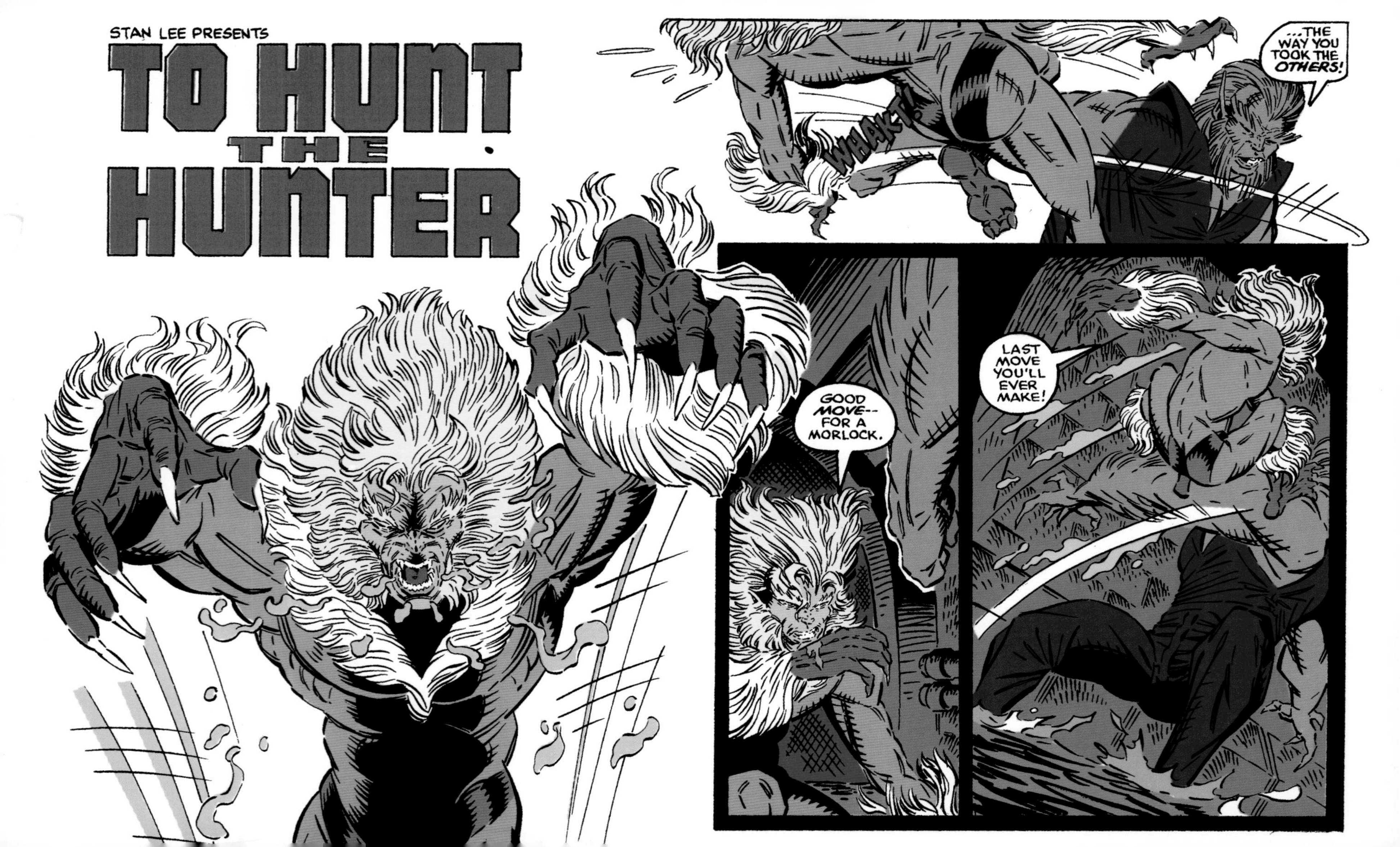
STAN LEE PRESENTS
TO HUNT THE HUNTER
WHAKT!
...THE WAY YOU TOOK THE OTHERS!
GOOD MOVE-- FOR A MORLOCK.
LAST MOVE YOU'LL EVER MAKE!

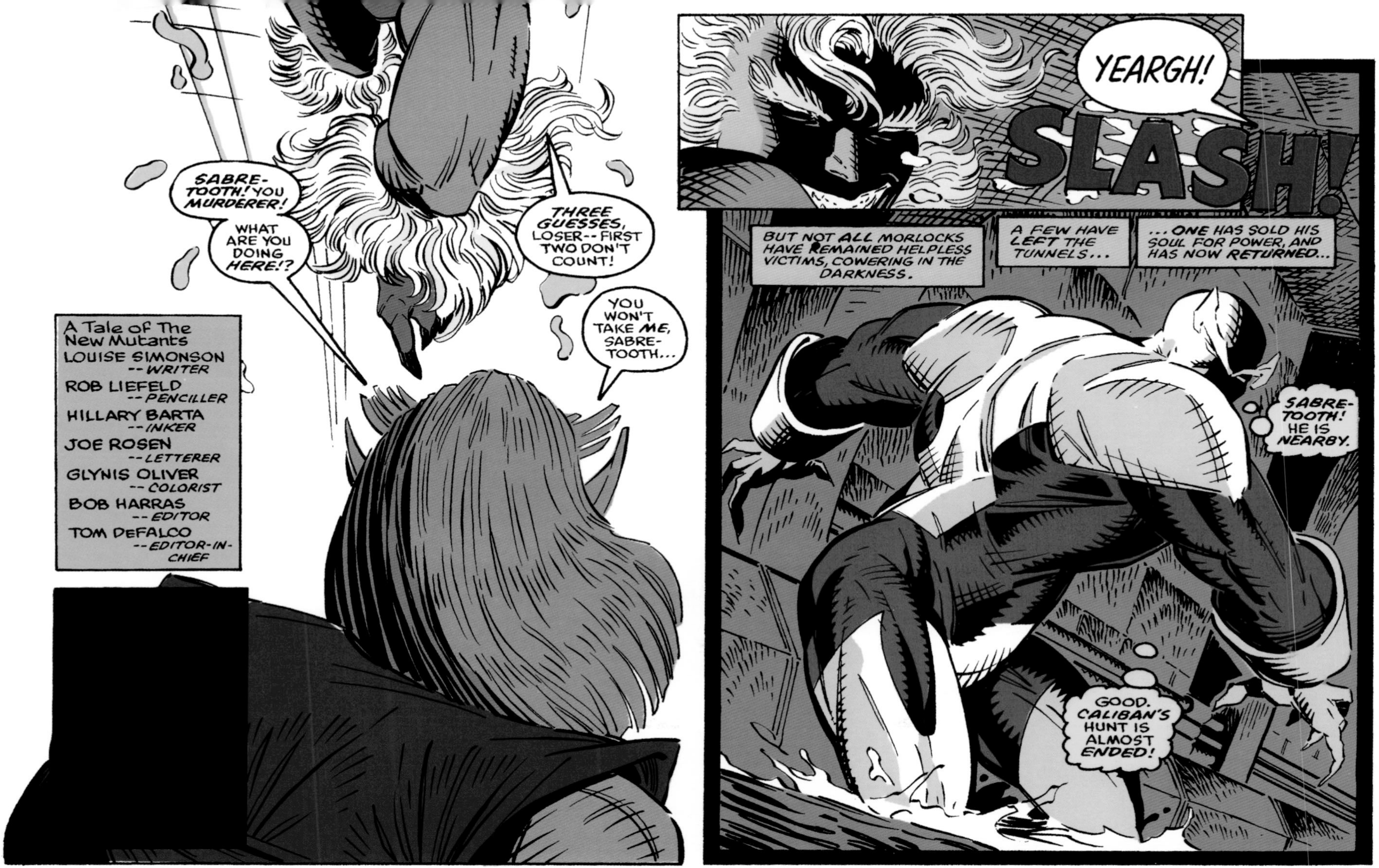
SABRE-TOOTH! YOU MURDERER!
WHAT ARE YOU DOING HERE!?
THREE GUESSES, LOSER-- FIRST TWO DON'T COUNT!
YOU WON'T TAKE ME, SABRE-TOOTH...
A Tale of The New Mutants
LOUISE SIMONSON --WRITER
ROB LIEFELD --PENCILLER
HILLARY BARTA --INKER
JOE ROSEN --LETTERER
GLYNIS OLIVER --COLORIST
BOB HARRAS --EDITOR
TOM DeFALCO --EDITOR-IN-CHIEF
YEARGH!
SLASH!
BUT NOT ALL MORLOCKS HAVE REMAINED HELPLESS VICTIMS, COWERING IN THE DARKNESS.
A FEW HAVE LEFT THE TUNNELS...
...ONE HAS SOLD HIS SOUL FOR POWER, AND HAS NOW RETURNED...
SABRE-TOOTH! HE IS NEARBY.
GOOD. CALIBAN'S HUNT IS ALMOST ENDED!

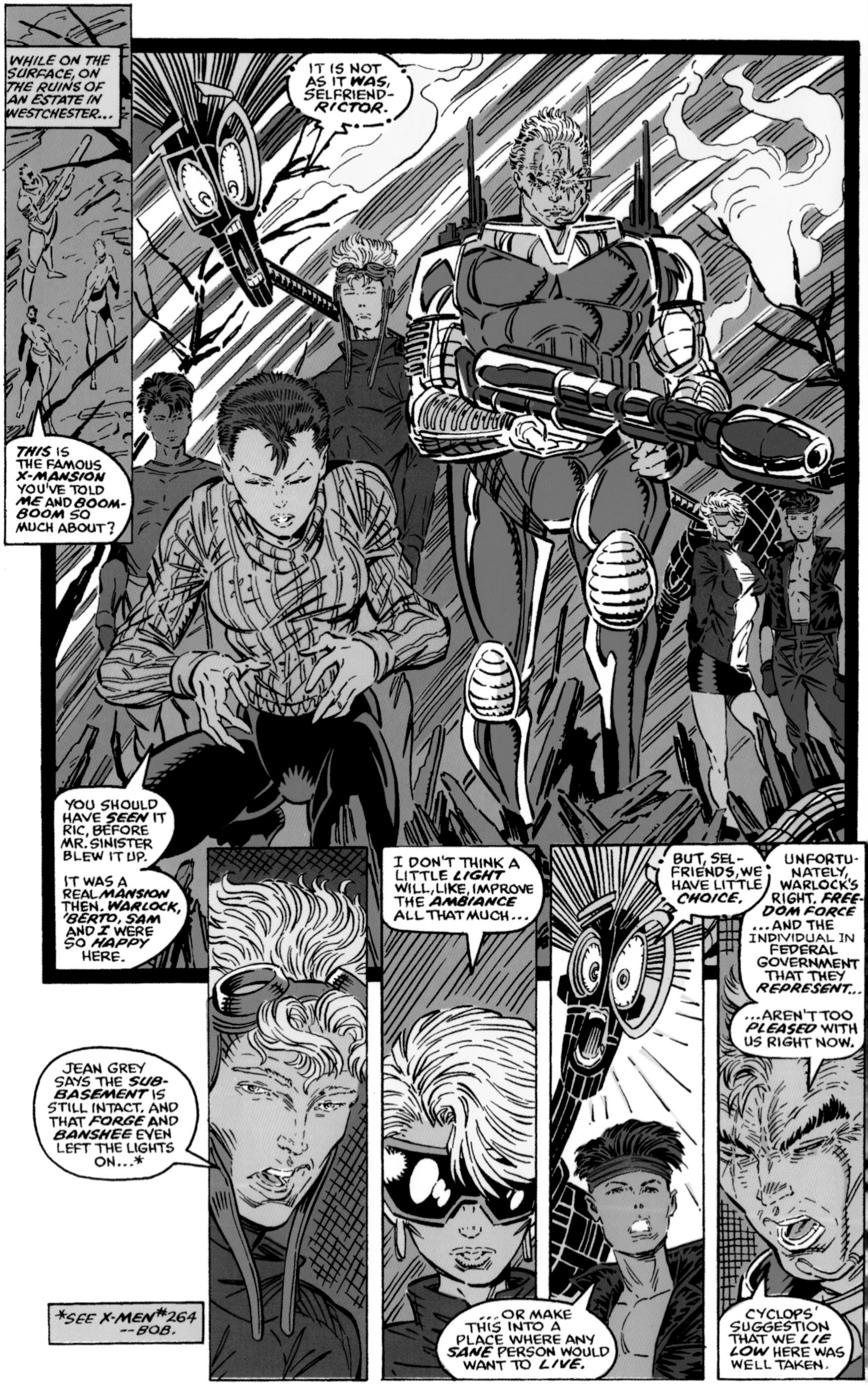

WHILE ON THE SURFACE, ON THE RUINS OF AN ESTATE IN WESTCHESTER...
IT IS NOT AS IT WAS, SELFRIEND-RICTOR.
THIS IS THE FAMOUS X-MANSION YOU'VE TOLD ME AND BOOM-BOOM SO MUCH ABOUT?
YOU SHOULD HAVE SEEN IT RIC, BEFORE MR. SINISTER BLEW IT UP.
IT WAS A REAL MANSION THEN. WARLOCK, 'BERTO, SAM AND I WERE SO HAPPY HERE.
JEAN GREY SAYS THE SUB-BASEMENT IS STILL INTACT, AND THAT FORGE AND BANSHEE EVEN LEFT THE LIGHTS ON...*
I DON'T THINK A LITTLE LIGHT WILL, LIKE, IMPROVE THE AMBIANCE ALL THAT MUCH...
...OR MAKE THIS INTO A PLACE WHERE ANY SANE PERSON WOULD WANT TO LIVE.
BUT, SEL-FRIENDS, WE HAVE LITTLE CHOICE.
UNFORTU-NATELY, WARLOCK'S RIGHT. FREE-DOM FORCE ...AND THE INDIVIDUAL IN FEDERAL GOVERNMENT THAT THEY REPRESENT...
...AREN'T TOO PLEASED WITH US RIGHT NOW.
CYCLOPS' SUGGESTION THAT WE LIE LOW HERE WAS WELL TAKEN.
*SEE X-MEN #264 --BOB.

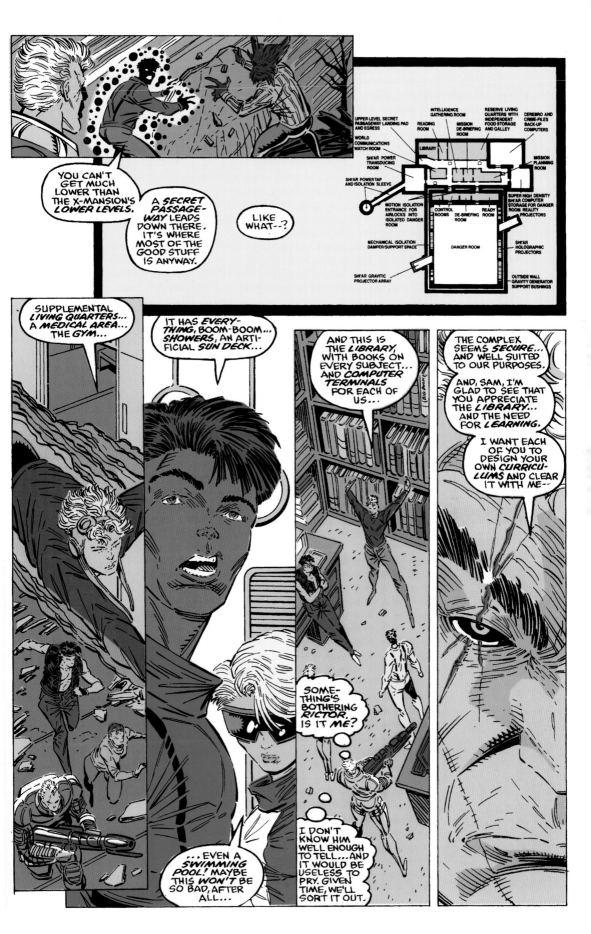

YOU CAN'T GET MUCH LOWER THAN THE X-MANSION'S *LOWER LEVELS.*

A *SECRET PASSAGE-WAY* LEADS DOWN THERE. IT'S WHERE MOST OF THE GOOD STUFF IS ANYWAY.

LIKE *WHAT--?*

UPPER LEVEL SECRET PASSAGEWAY LANDING PAD AND EGRESS

WORLD COMMUNICATIONS WATCH ROOM

INTELLIGENCE GATHERING ROOM

READING ROOM

MISSION DE-BRIEFING ROOM

RESERVE LIVING QUARTERS WITH INDEPENDENT FOOD STORAGE AND GALLEY

CEREBRO AND CRIME-FILES BACK-UP COMPUTERS

LIBRARY

MISSION PLANNING ROOM

SHI'AR POWER TRANSDUCING ROOM

SHI'AR POWER TAP AND ISOLATION SLEEVE

MOTION ISOLATION ENTRANCE FOR AIRLOCKS INTO ISOLATED DANGER ROOM

CONTROL ROOMS

DE-BRIEFING ROOM

READY ROOM

SUPER HIGH DENSITY SHI'AR COMPUTER STORAGE FOR DANGER ROOM REALITY PROJECTORS

MECHANICAL ISOLATION DAMPER/SUPPORT SPACE

DANGER ROOM

SHI'AR HOLOGRAPHIC PROJECTORS

SHI'AR GRAVITIC PROJECTOR ARRAY

OUTSIDE WALL GRAVITY GENERATOR SUPPORT BUSHINGS

SUPPLEMENTAL *LIVING QUARTERS...* A *MEDICAL AREA...* THE *GYM...*

IT HAS *EVERY-THING,* BOOM-BOOM... *SHOWERS,* AN ARTI-FICIAL *SUN DECK...*

AND THIS IS THE *LIBRARY,* WITH BOOKS ON *EVERY SUBJECT...* AND *COMPUTER TERMINALS* FOR EACH OF US...

THE COMPLEX SEEMS *SECURE...* AND WELL SUITED TO OUR PURPOSES.

AND, SAM, I'M GLAD TO SEE THAT YOU *APPRECIATE* THE *LIBRARY...* AND THE NEED FOR *LEARNING.*

I WANT EACH OF YOU TO DESIGN YOUR OWN *CURRICU-LUMS* AND CLEAR IT WITH ME--

SOME-THING'S BOTHERING *RICTOR.* IS IT *ME?*

I DON'T KNOW HIM WELL ENOUGH TO TELL... AND IT WOULD BE USELESS TO PRY. GIVEN TIME, WE'LL SORT IT OUT.

...EVEN A *SWIMMING POOL!* MAYBE THIS *WON'T* BE SO BAD, AFTER ALL...

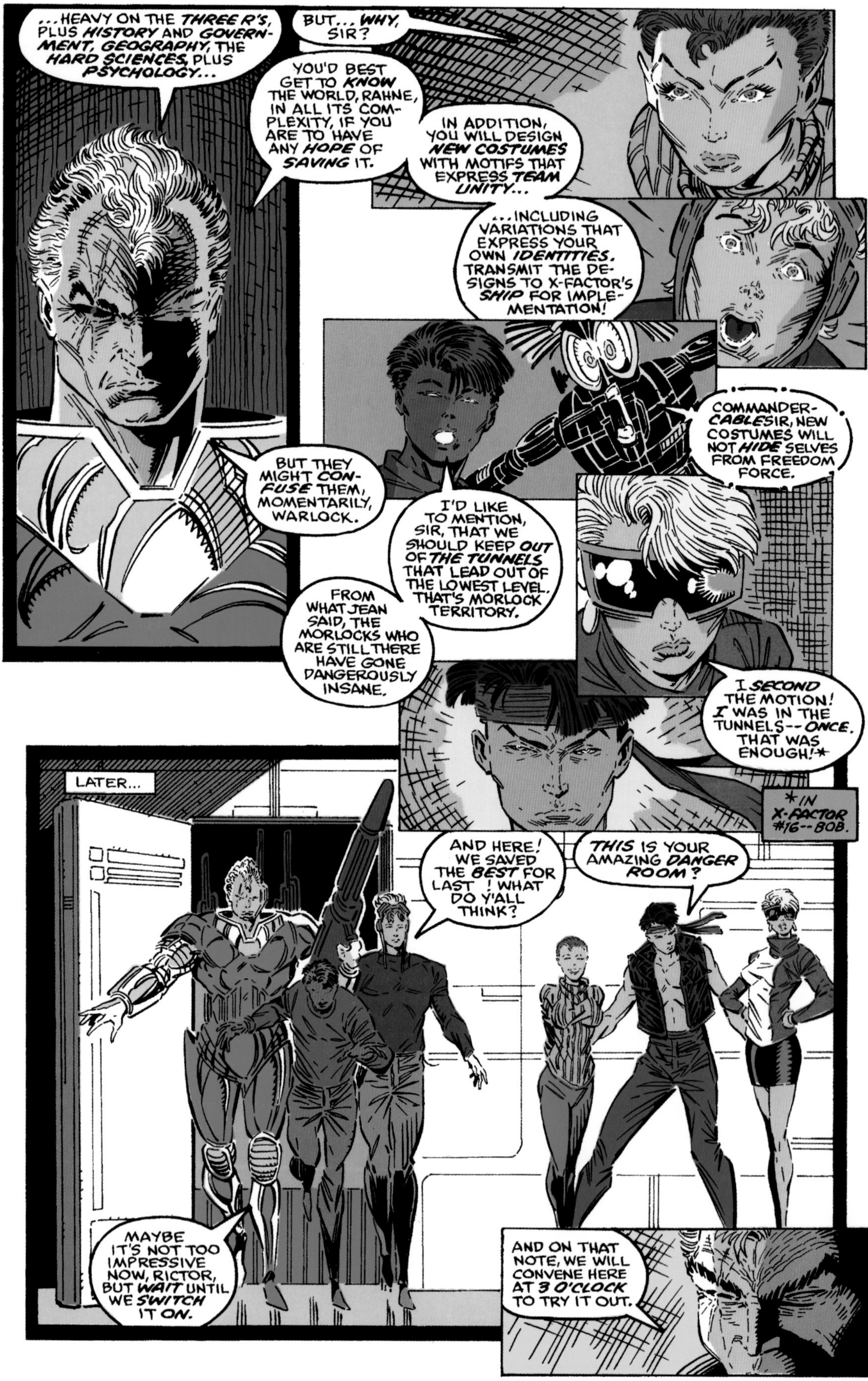
...HEAVY ON THE THREE R'S, PLUS HISTORY AND GOVERNMENT, GEOGRAPHY, THE HARD SCIENCES, PLUS PSYCHOLOGY...
BUT... WHY, SIR?
YOU'D BEST GET TO KNOW THE WORLD, RAHNE, IN ALL ITS COMPLEXITY, IF YOU ARE TO HAVE ANY HOPE OF SAVING IT.
IN ADDITION, YOU WILL DESIGN NEW COSTUMES WITH MOTIFS THAT EXPRESS TEAM UNITY...
...INCLUDING VARIATIONS THAT EXPRESS YOUR OWN IDENTITIES. TRANSMIT THE DESIGNS TO X-FACTOR'S SHIP FOR IMPLEMENTATION!
COMMANDER-CABLESIR, NEW COSTUMES WILL NOT HIDE SELVES FROM FREEDOM FORCE.
BUT THEY MIGHT CONFUSE THEM, MOMENTARILY, WARLOCK.
I'D LIKE TO MENTION, SIR, THAT WE SHOULD KEEP OUT OF THE TUNNELS THAT LEAD OUT OF THE LOWEST LEVEL. THAT'S MORLOCK TERRITORY.
FROM WHAT JEAN SAID, THE MORLOCKS WHO ARE STILL THERE HAVE GONE DANGEROUSLY INSANE.
I SECOND THE MOTION! I WAS IN THE TUNNELS--ONCE. THAT WAS ENOUGH!*
*IN X-FACTOR #16--BOB.
LATER...
AND HERE! WE SAVED THE BEST FOR LAST ! WHAT DO Y'ALL THINK?
THIS IS YOUR AMAZING DANGER ROOM?
MAYBE IT'S NOT TOO IMPRESSIVE NOW, RICTOR, BUT WAIT UNTIL WE SWITCH IT ON.
AND ON THAT NOTE, WE WILL CONVENE HERE AT 3 O'CLOCK TO TRY IT OUT.

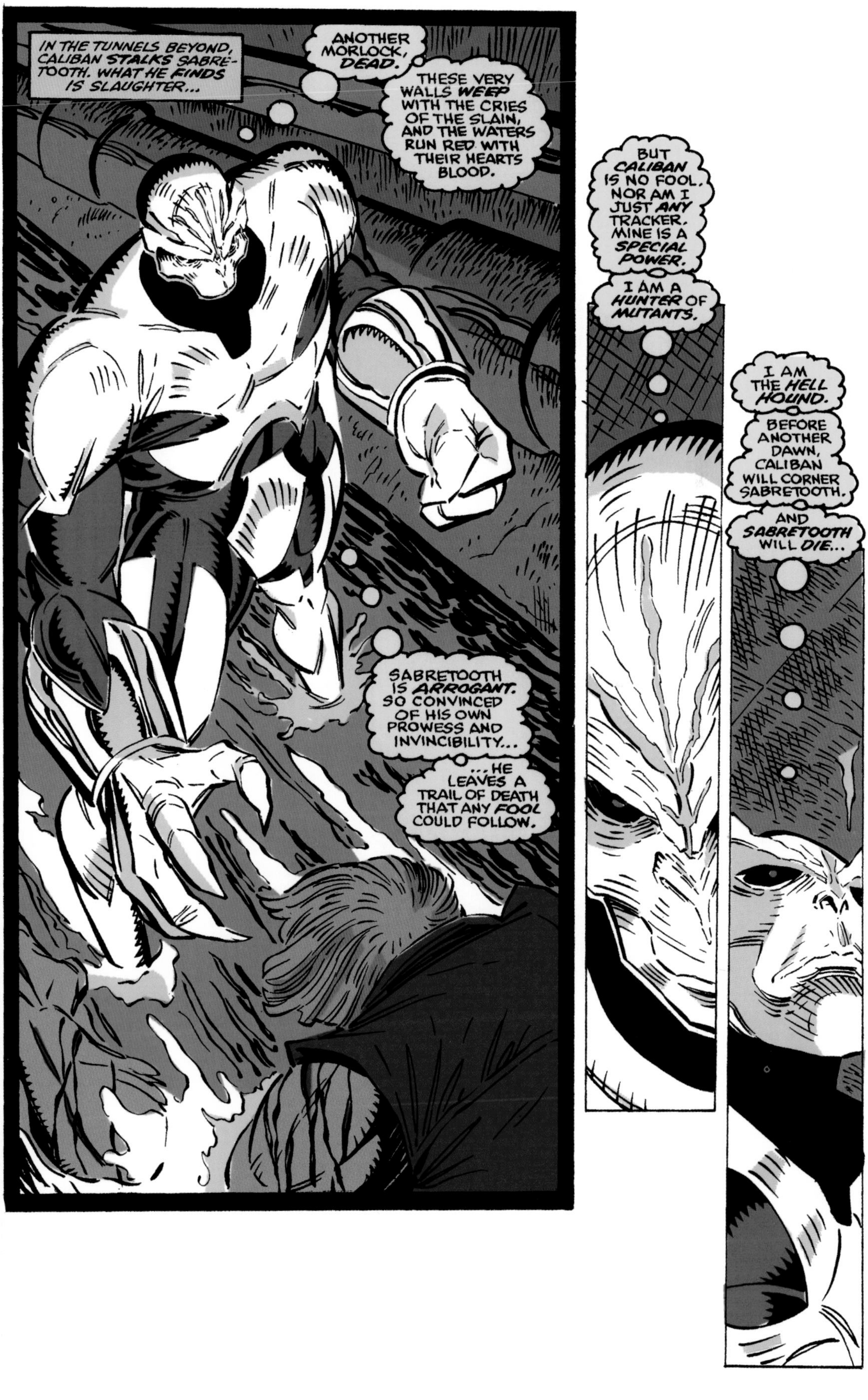
IN THE TUNNELS BEYOND, CALIBAN STALKS SABRETOOTH. WHAT HE FINDS IS SLAUGHTER...
ANOTHER MORLOCK, DEAD.
THESE VERY WALLS WEEP WITH THE CRIES OF THE SLAIN, AND THE WATERS RUN RED WITH THEIR HEARTS BLOOD.
SABRETOOTH IS ARROGANT. SO CONVINCED OF HIS OWN PROWESS AND INVINCIBILITY...
...HE LEAVES A TRAIL OF DEATH THAT ANY FOOL COULD FOLLOW.
BUT CALIBAN IS NO FOOL. NOR AM I JUST ANY TRACKER. MINE IS A SPECIAL POWER.
I AM A HUNTER OF MUTANTS.
I AM THE HELL HOUND.
BEFORE ANOTHER DAWN, CALIBAN WILL CORNER SABRETOOTH.
AND SABRETOOTH WILL DIE...

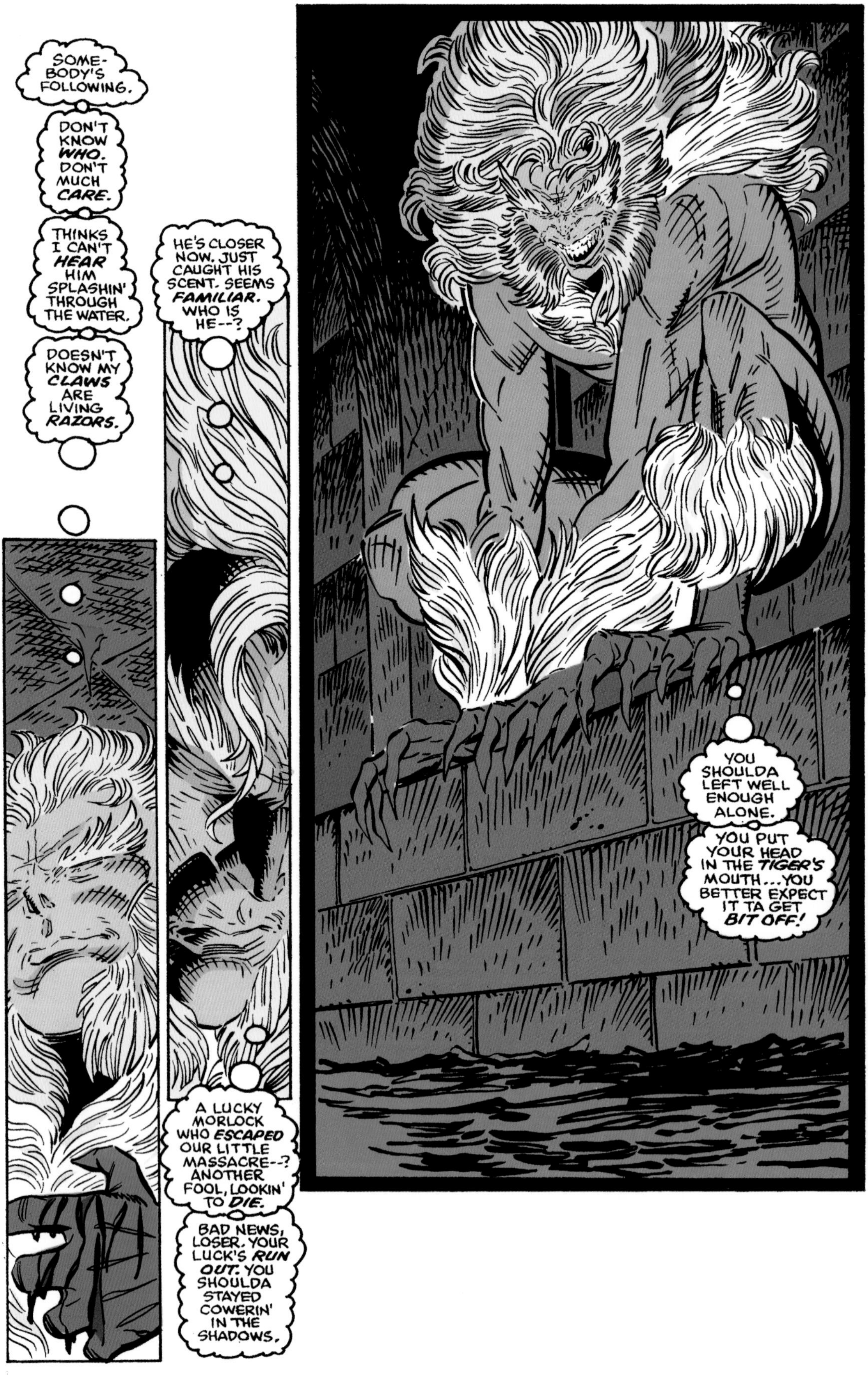
SOME-BODY'S FOLLOWING.
DON'T KNOW WHO. DON'T MUCH CARE.
THINKS I CAN'T HEAR HIM SPLASHIN' THROUGH THE WATER.
DOESN'T KNOW MY CLAWS ARE LIVING RAZORS.
HE'S CLOSER NOW. JUST CAUGHT HIS SCENT. SEEMS FAMILIAR. WHO IS HE--?
A LUCKY MORLOCK WHO ESCAPED OUR LITTLE MASSACRE--? ANOTHER FOOL, LOOKIN' TO DIE.
BAD NEWS, LOSER. YOUR LUCK'S RUN OUT. YOU SHOULDA STAYED COWERIN' IN THE SHADOWS.
YOU SHOULDA LEFT WELL ENOUGH ALONE.
YOU PUT YOUR HEAD IN THE TIGER'S MOUTH...YOU BETTER EXPECT IT TA GET BIT OFF!

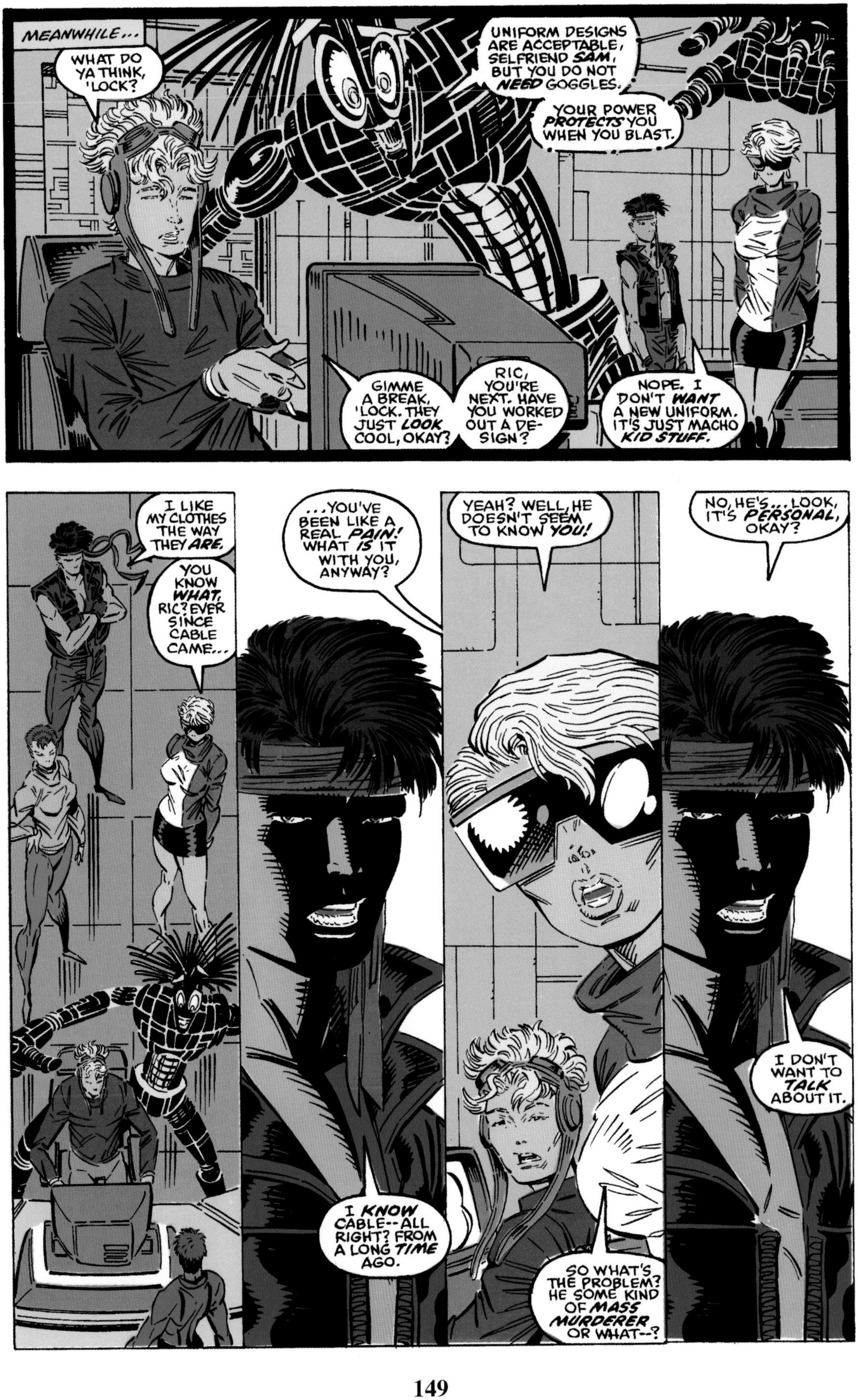
MEANWHILE...
WHAT DO YA THINK, 'LOCK?
UNIFORM DESIGNS ARE ACCEPTABLE, SELFRIEND SAM, BUT YOU DO NOT NEED GOGGLES.
YOUR POWER PROTECTS YOU WHEN YOU BLAST.
GIMME A BREAK, 'LOCK. THEY JUST LOOK COOL, OKAY?
RIC, YOU'RE NEXT. HAVE YOU WORKED OUT A DE-SIGN?
NOPE. I DON'T WANT A NEW UNIFORM. IT'S JUST MACHO KID STUFF.
I LIKE MY CLOTHES THE WAY THEY ARE.
YOU KNOW WHAT, RIC? EVER SINCE CABLE CAME...
...YOU'VE BEEN LIKE A REAL PAIN! WHAT IS IT WITH YOU, ANYWAY?
I KNOW CABLE--ALL RIGHT? FROM A LONG TIME AGO.
YEAH? WELL, HE DOESN'T SEEM TO KNOW YOU!
SO WHAT'S THE PROBLEM? HE SOME KIND OF MASS MURDERER OR WHAT--?
NO, HE'S...LOOK, IT'S PERSONAL, OKAY?
I DON'T WANT TO TALK ABOUT IT.

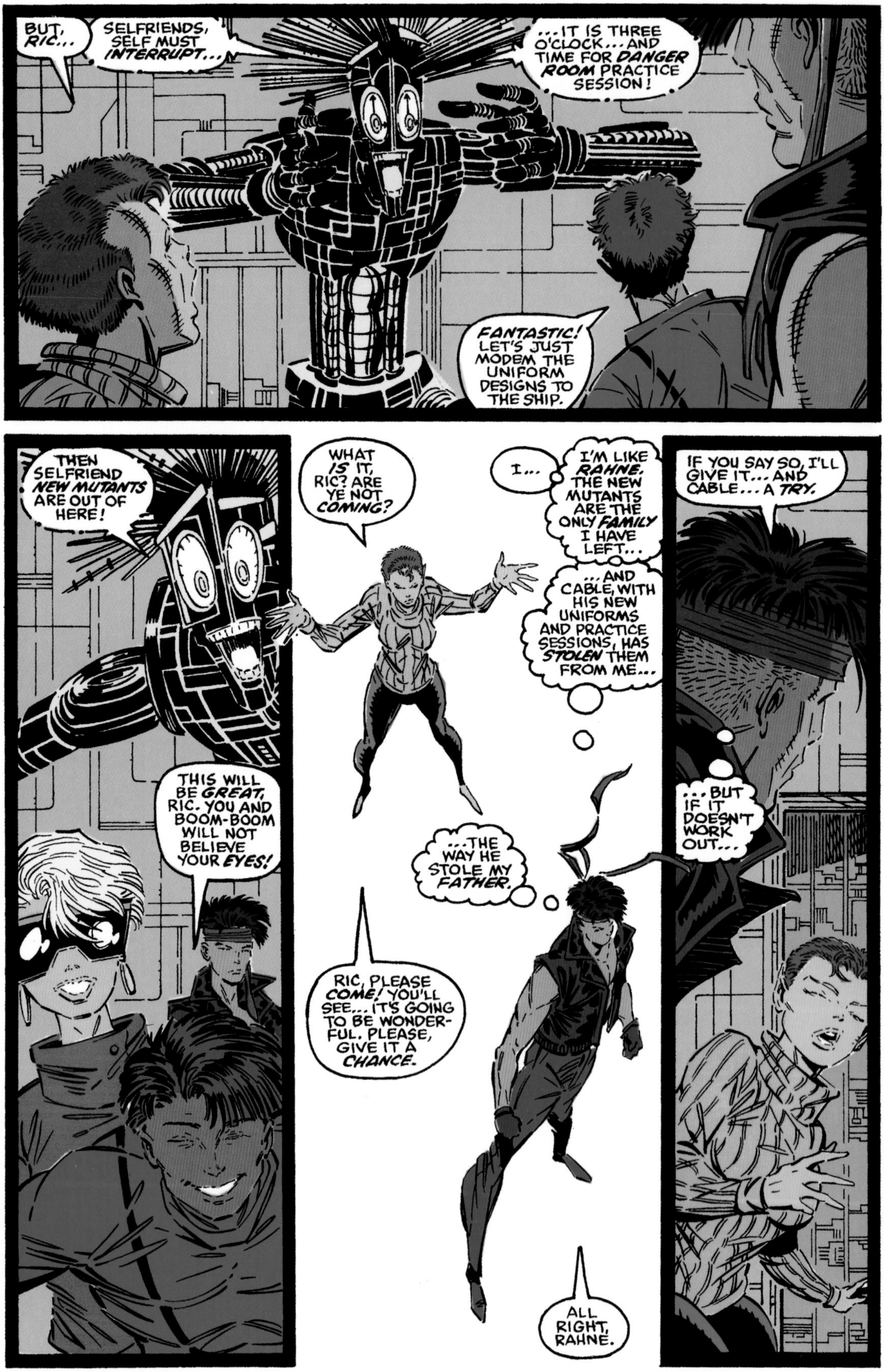
BUT, RIC...
SELFRIENDS, SELF MUST INTERRUPT...
...IT IS THREE O'CLOCK... AND TIME FOR DANGER ROOM PRACTICE SESSION!
FANTASTIC! LET'S JUST MODEM THE UNIFORM DESIGNS TO THE SHIP.
THEN SELFRIEND NEW MUTANTS ARE OUT OF HERE!
WHAT IS IT, RIC? ARE YE NOT COMING?
I...
I'M LIKE RAHNE. THE NEW MUTANTS ARE THE ONLY FAMILY I HAVE LEFT...
...AND CABLE, WITH HIS NEW UNIFORMS AND PRACTICE SESSIONS, HAS STOLEN THEM FROM ME...
IF YOU SAY SO, I'LL GIVE IT... AND CABLE... A TRY.
...BUT IF IT DOESN'T WORK OUT...
THIS WILL BE GREAT, RIC. YOU AND BOOM-BOOM WILL NOT BELIEVE YOUR EYES!
...THE WAY HE STOLE MY FATHER.
RIC, PLEASE COME! YOU'LL SEE... IT'S GOING TO BE WONDERFUL. PLEASE, GIVE IT A CHANCE.
ALL RIGHT, RAHNE.

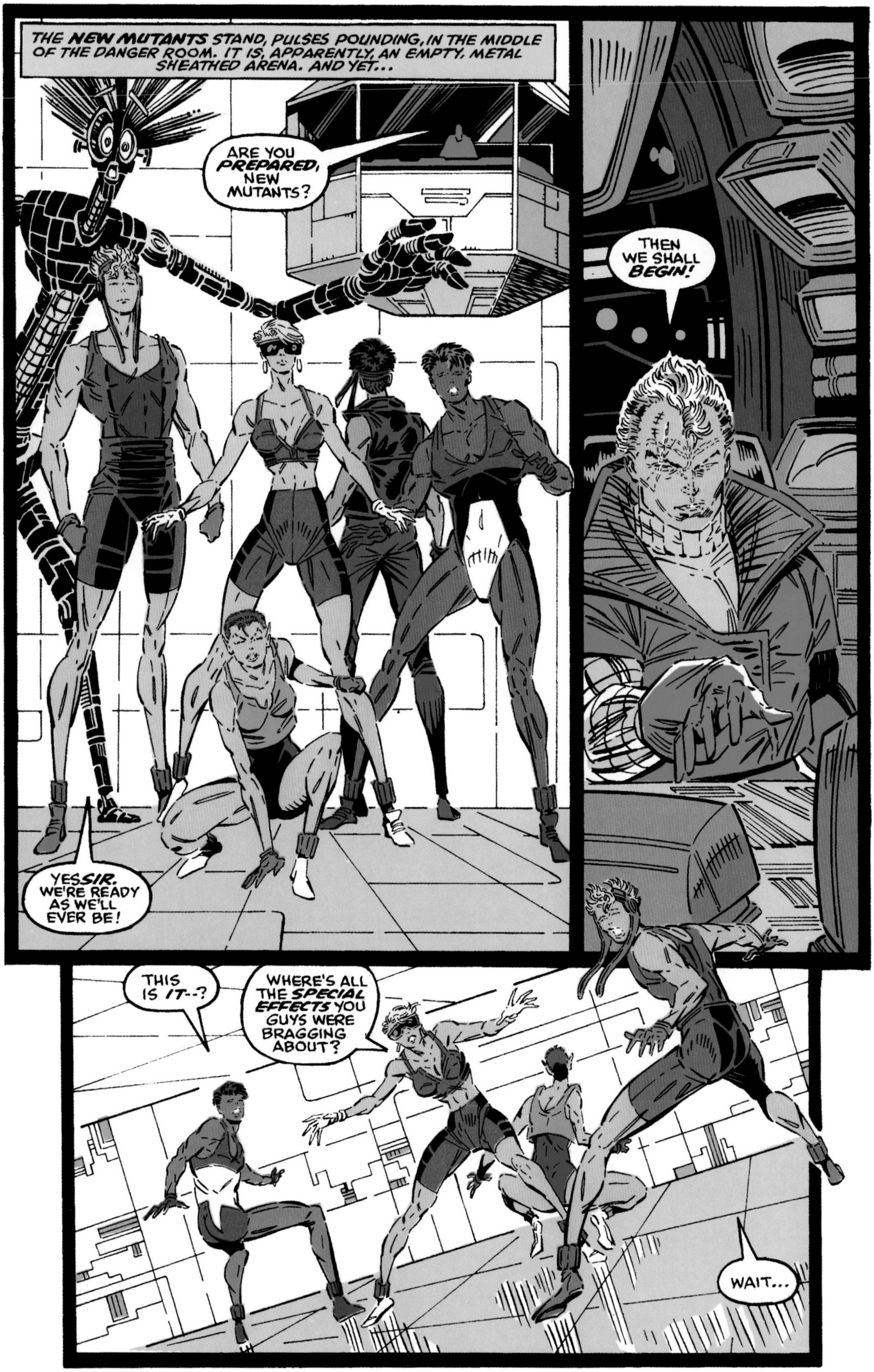
THE NEW MUTANTS STAND, PULSES POUNDING, IN THE MIDDLE OF THE DANGER ROOM. IT IS, APPARENTLY, AN EMPTY, METAL SHEATHED ARENA. AND YET...
ARE YOU PREPARED, NEW MUTANTS?
YESSIR. WE'RE READY AS WE'LL EVER BE!
THEN WE SHALL BEGIN!
THIS IS IT--?
WHERE'S ALL THE SPECIAL EFFECTS YOU GUYS WERE BRAGGING ABOUT?
WAIT...

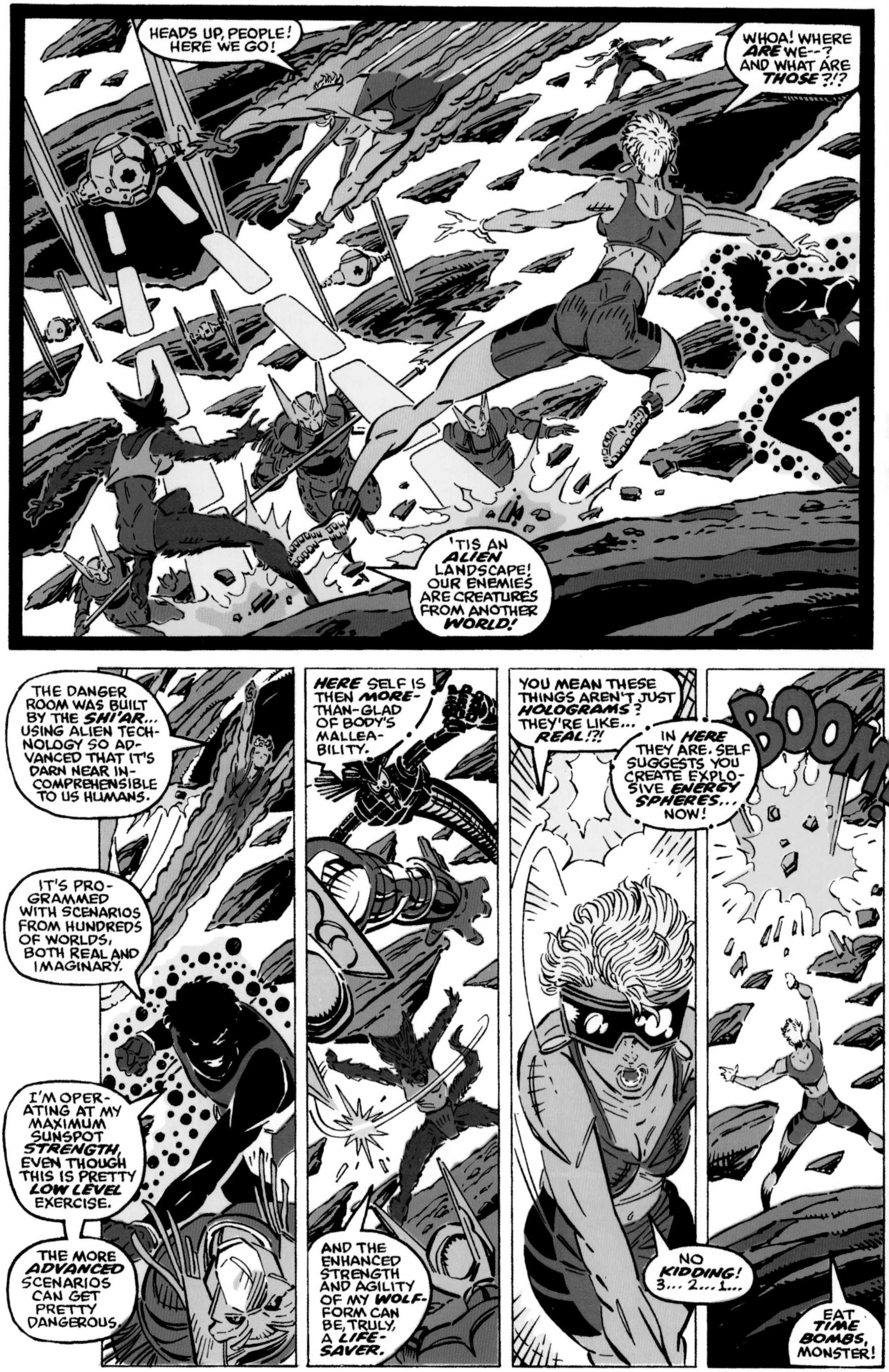

HEADS UP, PEOPLE! HERE WE GO!
WHOA! WHERE ARE WE--? AND WHAT ARE THOSE?!?
'TIS AN ALIEN LANDSCAPE! OUR ENEMIES ARE CREATURES FROM ANOTHER WORLD!
THE DANGER ROOM WAS BUILT BY THE SHI'AR... USING ALIEN TECHNOLOGY SO ADVANCED THAT IT'S DARN NEAR INCOMPREHENSIBLE TO US HUMANS.
IT'S PROGRAMMED WITH SCENARIOS FROM HUNDREDS OF WORLDS, BOTH REAL AND IMAGINARY.
I'M OPERATING AT MY MAXIMUM SUNSPOT STRENGTH, EVEN THOUGH THIS IS PRETTY LOW LEVEL EXERCISE.
THE MORE ADVANCED SCENARIOS CAN GET PRETTY DANGEROUS.
HERE SELF IS THEN MORE-THAN-GLAD OF BODY'S MALLEABILITY.
AND THE ENHANCED STRENGTH AND AGILITY OF MY WOLF-FORM CAN BE, TRULY, A LIFE-SAVER.
YOU MEAN THESE THINGS AREN'T JUST HOLOGRAMS? THEY'RE LIKE... REAL!?!
IN HERE THEY ARE. SELF SUGGESTS YOU CREATE EXPLOSIVE ENERGY SPHERES... NOW!
NO KIDDING! 3... 2... 1...
BOOM!
EAT TIME BOMBS, MONSTER!

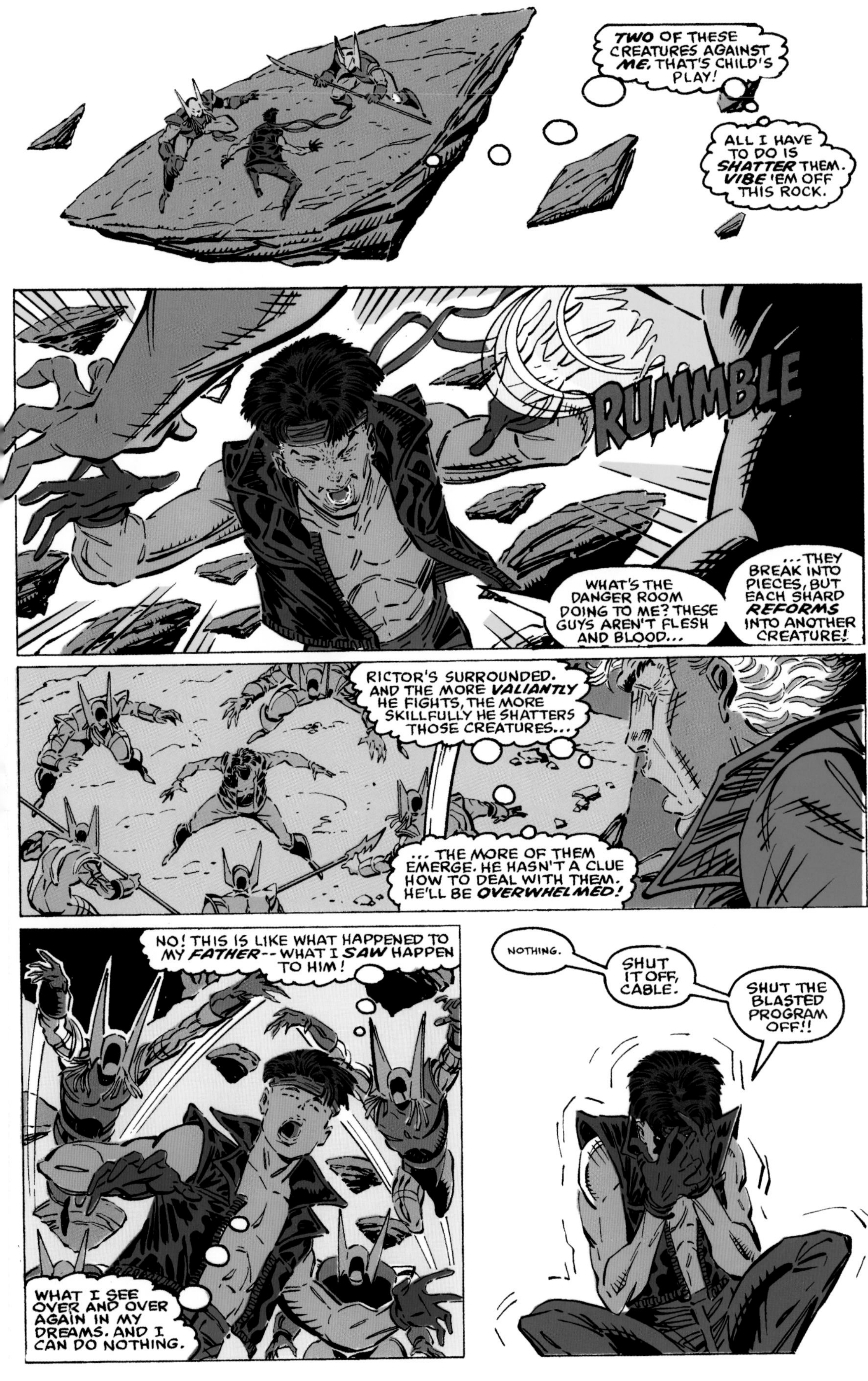
TWO OF THESE CREATURES AGAINST ME, THAT'S CHILD'S PLAY!
ALL I HAVE TO DO IS SHATTER THEM. VIBE 'EM OFF THIS ROCK.
RUMMBLE
WHAT'S THE DANGER ROOM DOING TO ME? THESE GUYS AREN'T FLESH AND BLOOD...
...THEY BREAK INTO PIECES, BUT EACH SHARD REFORMS INTO ANOTHER CREATURE!
RICTOR'S SURROUNDED. AND THE MORE VALIANTLY HE FIGHTS, THE MORE SKILLFULLY HE SHATTERS THOSE CREATURES...
...THE MORE OF THEM EMERGE. HE HASN'T A CLUE HOW TO DEAL WITH THEM. HE'LL BE OVERWHELMED!
NO! THIS IS LIKE WHAT HAPPENED TO MY FATHER--WHAT I SAW HAPPEN TO HIM!
WHAT I SEE OVER AND OVER AGAIN IN MY DREAMS. AND I CAN DO NOTHING.
NOTHING.
SHUT IT OFF, CABLE.
SHUT THE BLASTED PROGRAM OFF!!

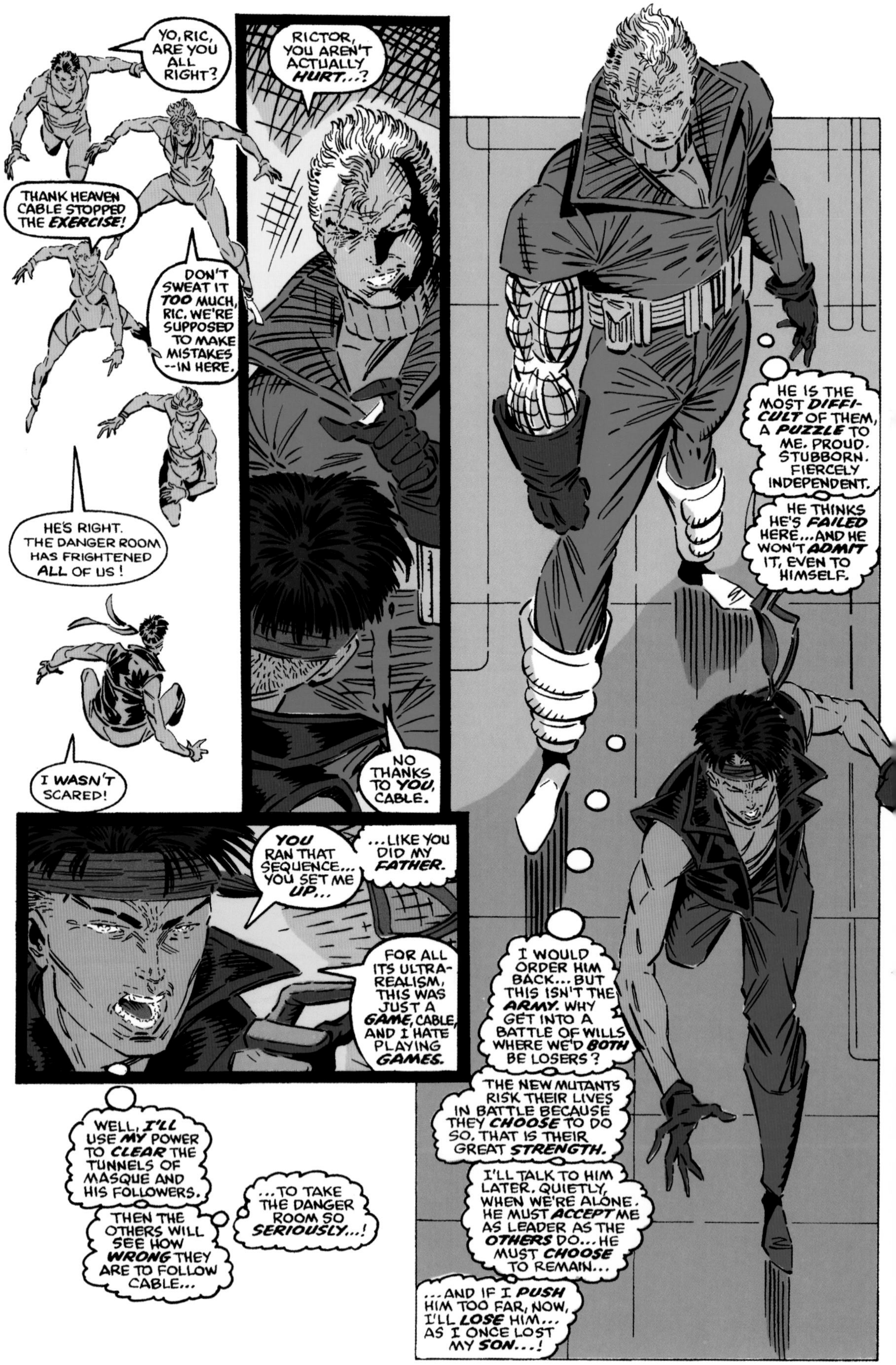

YO, RIC, ARE YOU ALL RIGHT?
THANK HEAVEN CABLE STOPPED THE EXERCISE!
DON'T SWEAT IT TOO MUCH, RIC. WE'RE SUPPOSED TO MAKE MISTAKES --IN HERE.
HE'S RIGHT. THE DANGER ROOM HAS FRIGHTENED ALL OF US!
I WASN'T SCARED!
RICTOR, YOU AREN'T ACTUALLY HURT...?
NO THANKS TO YOU, CABLE.
HE IS THE MOST DIFFICULT OF THEM, A PUZZLE TO ME. PROUD. STUBBORN. FIERCELY INDEPENDENT.
HE THINKS HE'S FAILED HERE...AND HE WON'T ADMIT IT, EVEN TO HIMSELF.
YOU RAN THAT SEQUENCE... YOU SET ME UP...
...LIKE YOU DID MY FATHER.
FOR ALL ITS ULTRA-REALISM, THIS WAS JUST A GAME, CABLE, AND I HATE PLAYING GAMES.
I WOULD ORDER HIM BACK... BUT THIS ISN'T THE ARMY. WHY GET INTO A BATTLE OF WILLS WHERE WE'D BOTH BE LOSERS?
THE NEW MUTANTS RISK THEIR LIVES IN BATTLE BECAUSE THEY CHOOSE TO DO SO. THAT IS THEIR GREAT STRENGTH.
I'LL TALK TO HIM LATER. QUIETLY, WHEN WE'RE ALONE. HE MUST ACCEPT ME AS LEADER AS THE OTHERS DO... HE MUST CHOOSE TO REMAIN...
...AND IF I PUSH HIM TOO FAR, NOW, I'LL LOSE HIM... AS I ONCE LOST MY SON...!
WELL, I'LL USE MY POWER TO CLEAR THE TUNNELS OF MASQUE AND HIS FOLLOWERS.
THEN THE OTHERS WILL SEE HOW WRONG THEY ARE TO FOLLOW CABLE...
...TO TAKE THE DANGER ROOM SO SERIOUSLY...!

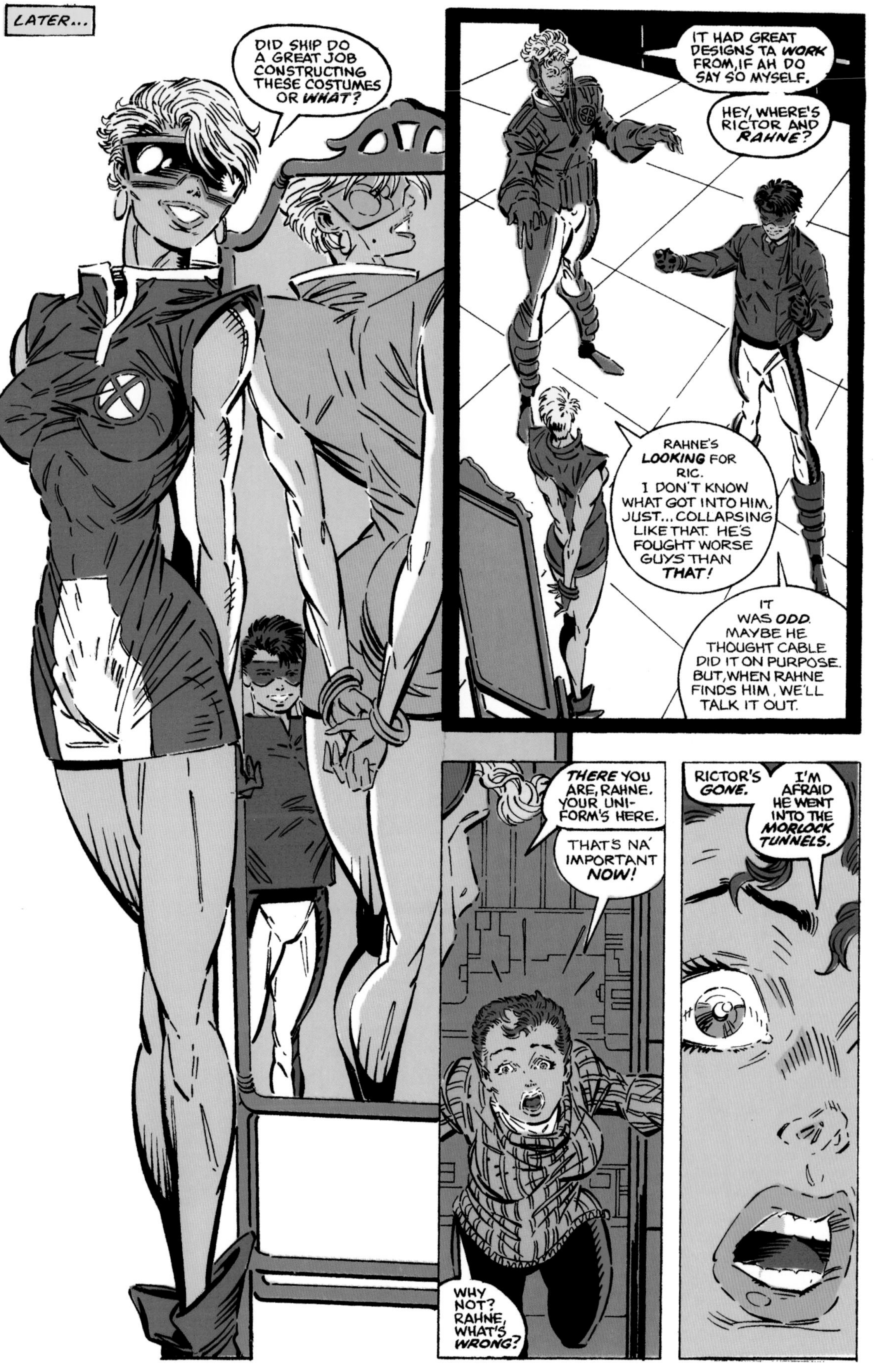
LATER...
DID SHIP DO A GREAT JOB CONSTRUCTING THESE COSTUMES OR WHAT?
IT HAD GREAT DESIGNS TA WORK FROM, IF AH DO SAY SO MYSELF.
HEY, WHERE'S RICTOR AND RAHNE?
RAHNE'S LOOKING FOR RIC. I DON'T KNOW WHAT GOT INTO HIM, JUST... COLLAPSING LIKE THAT. HE'S FOUGHT WORSE GUYS THAN THAT!
IT WAS ODD. MAYBE HE THOUGHT CABLE DID IT ON PURPOSE. BUT, WHEN RAHNE FINDS HIM, WE'LL TALK IT OUT.
THERE YOU ARE, RAHNE. YOUR UNI-FORM'S HERE.
THAT'S NA' IMPORTANT NOW!
WHY NOT? RAHNE, WHAT'S WRONG?
RICTOR'S GONE.
I'M AFRAID HE WENT INTO THE MORLOCK TUNNELS.

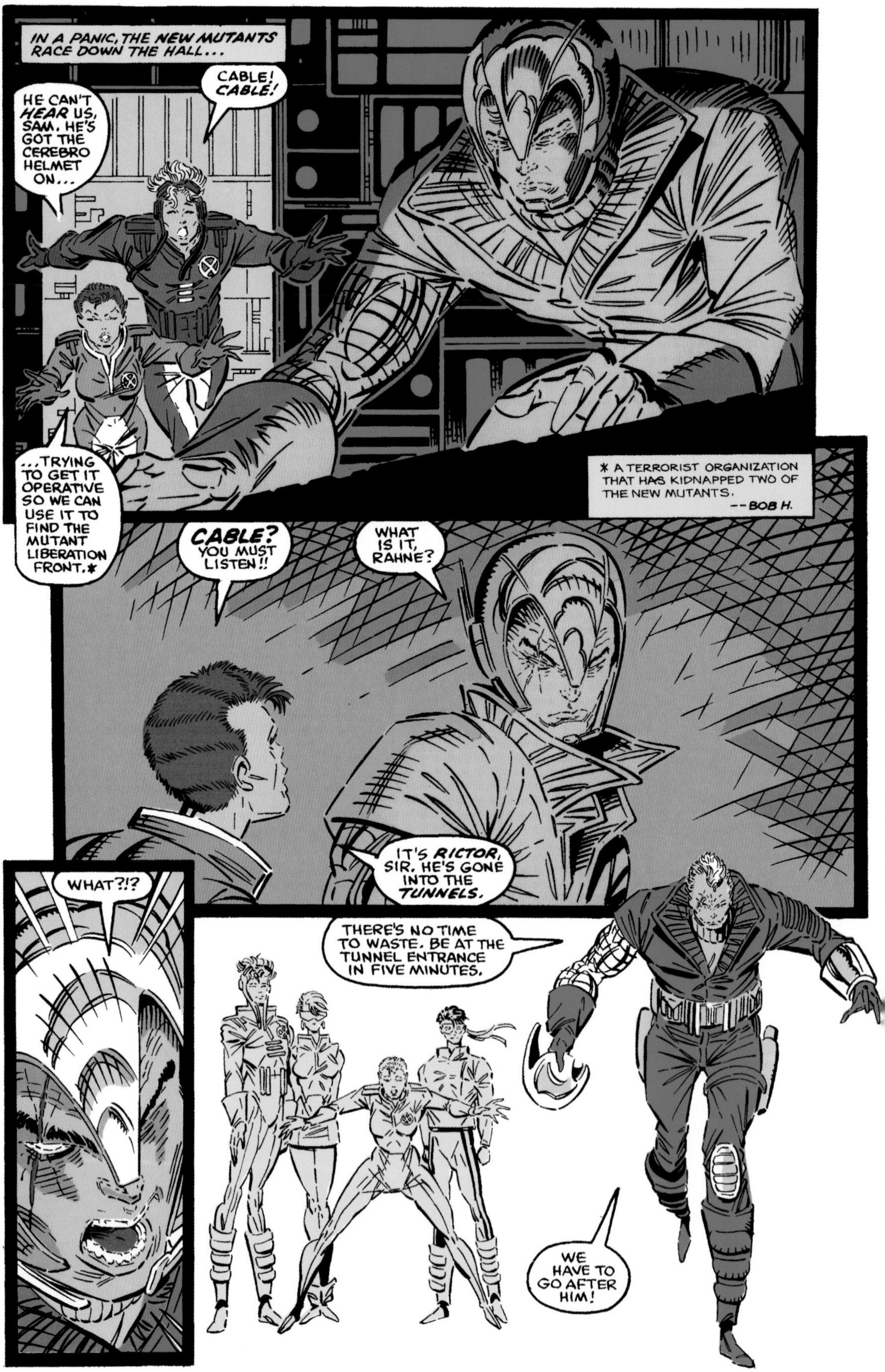
IN A PANIC, THE NEW MUTANTS RACE DOWN THE HALL...
CABLE! CABLE!
HE CAN'T HEAR US, SAM. HE'S GOT THE CEREBRO HELMET ON...
...TRYING TO GET IT OPERATIVE SO WE CAN USE IT TO FIND THE MUTANT LIBERATION FRONT.*
* A TERRORIST ORGANIZATION THAT HAS KIDNAPPED TWO OF THE NEW MUTANTS. --BOB H.
CABLE? YOU MUST LISTEN!!
WHAT IS IT, RAHNE?
IT'S RICTOR, SIR. HE'S GONE INTO THE TUNNELS.
WHAT?!?
THERE'S NO TIME TO WASTE. BE AT THE TUNNEL ENTRANCE IN FIVE MINUTES.
WE HAVE TO GO AFTER HIM!

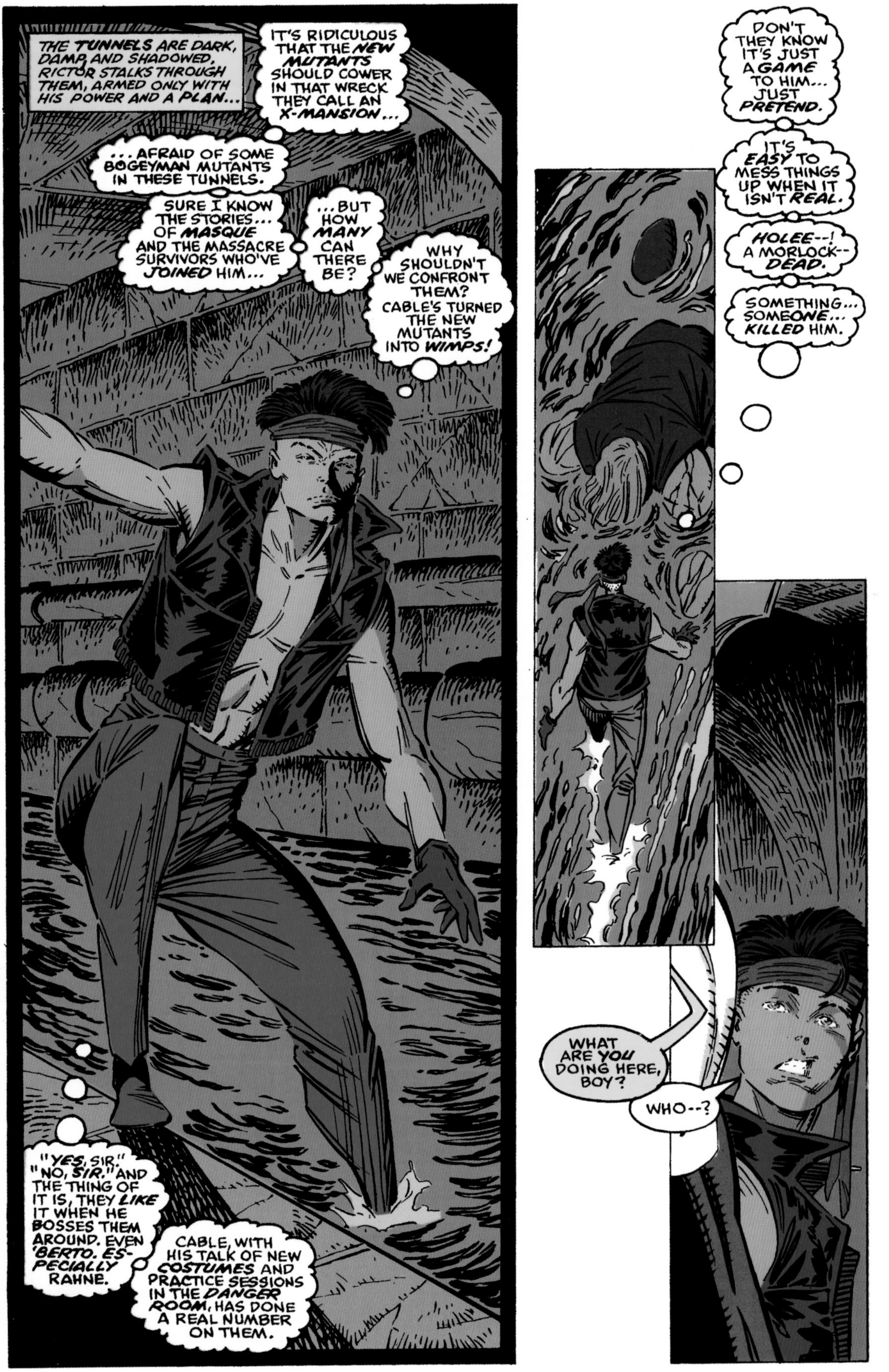
THE TUNNELS ARE DARK, DAMP, AND SHADOWED. RICTOR STALKS THROUGH THEM, ARMED ONLY WITH HIS POWER AND A PLAN...
IT'S RIDICULOUS THAT THE NEW MUTANTS SHOULD COWER IN THAT WRECK THEY CALL AN X-MANSION...
...AFRAID OF SOME BOGEYMAN MUTANTS IN THESE TUNNELS.
SURE I KNOW THE STORIES... OF MASQUE AND THE MASSACRE SURVIVORS WHO'VE JOINED HIM...
...BUT HOW MANY CAN THERE BE?
WHY SHOULDN'T WE CONFRONT THEM? CABLE'S TURNED THE NEW MUTANTS INTO WIMPS!
"YES, SIR." "NO, SIR." AND THE THING OF IT IS, THEY LIKE IT WHEN HE BOSSES THEM AROUND. EVEN 'BERTO. ESPECIALLY RAHNE.
CABLE, WITH HIS TALK OF NEW COSTUMES AND PRACTICE SESSIONS IN THE DANGER ROOM, HAS DONE A REAL NUMBER ON THEM.
DON'T THEY KNOW IT'S JUST A GAME TO HIM... JUST PRETEND.
IT'S EASY TO MESS THINGS UP WHEN IT ISN'T REAL.
HOLEE--! A MORLOCK-- DEAD.
SOMETHING... SOMEONE... KILLED HIM.
WHAT ARE YOU DOING HERE, BOY?
WHO--?

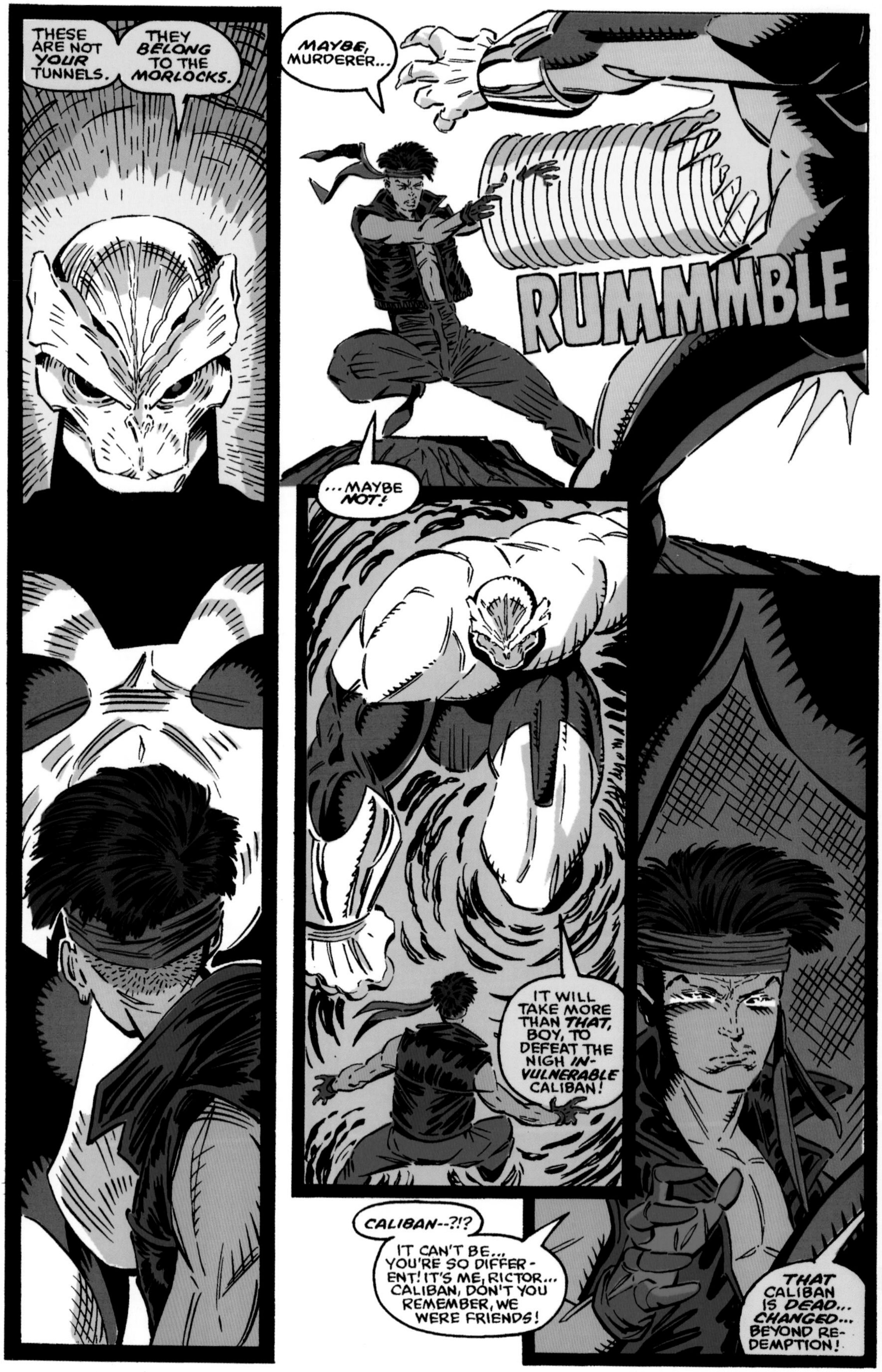
THESE ARE NOT YOUR TUNNELS.
THEY BELONG TO THE MORLOCKS.
MAYBE, MURDERER...
RUMMMBLE
...MAYBE NOT!
IT WILL TAKE MORE THAN THAT, BOY, TO DEFEAT THE NIGH IN-VULNERABLE CALIBAN!
CALIBAN--?!?
IT CAN'T BE... YOU'RE SO DIFFER-ENT! IT'S ME, RICTOR... CALIBAN, DON'T YOU REMEMBER, WE WERE FRIENDS!
THAT CALIBAN IS DEAD... CHANGED... BEYOND RE-DEMPTION!

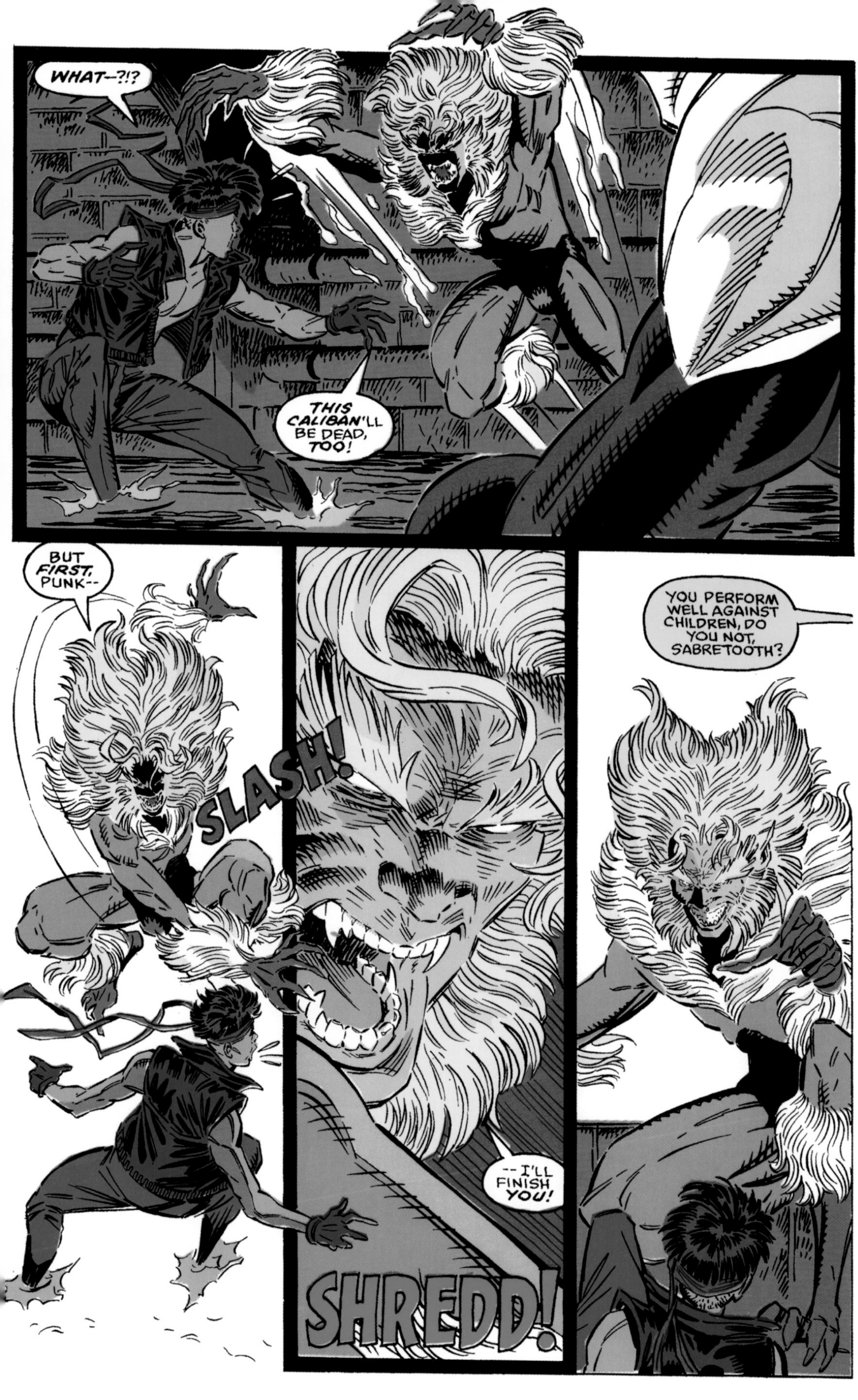
WHAT--?!?
THIS CALIBAN'LL BE DEAD, TOO!
BUT FIRST, PUNK--
SLASH!
--I'LL FINISH YOU!
SHREDD!
YOU PERFORM WELL AGAINST CHILDREN, DO YOU NOT, SABRETOOTH?

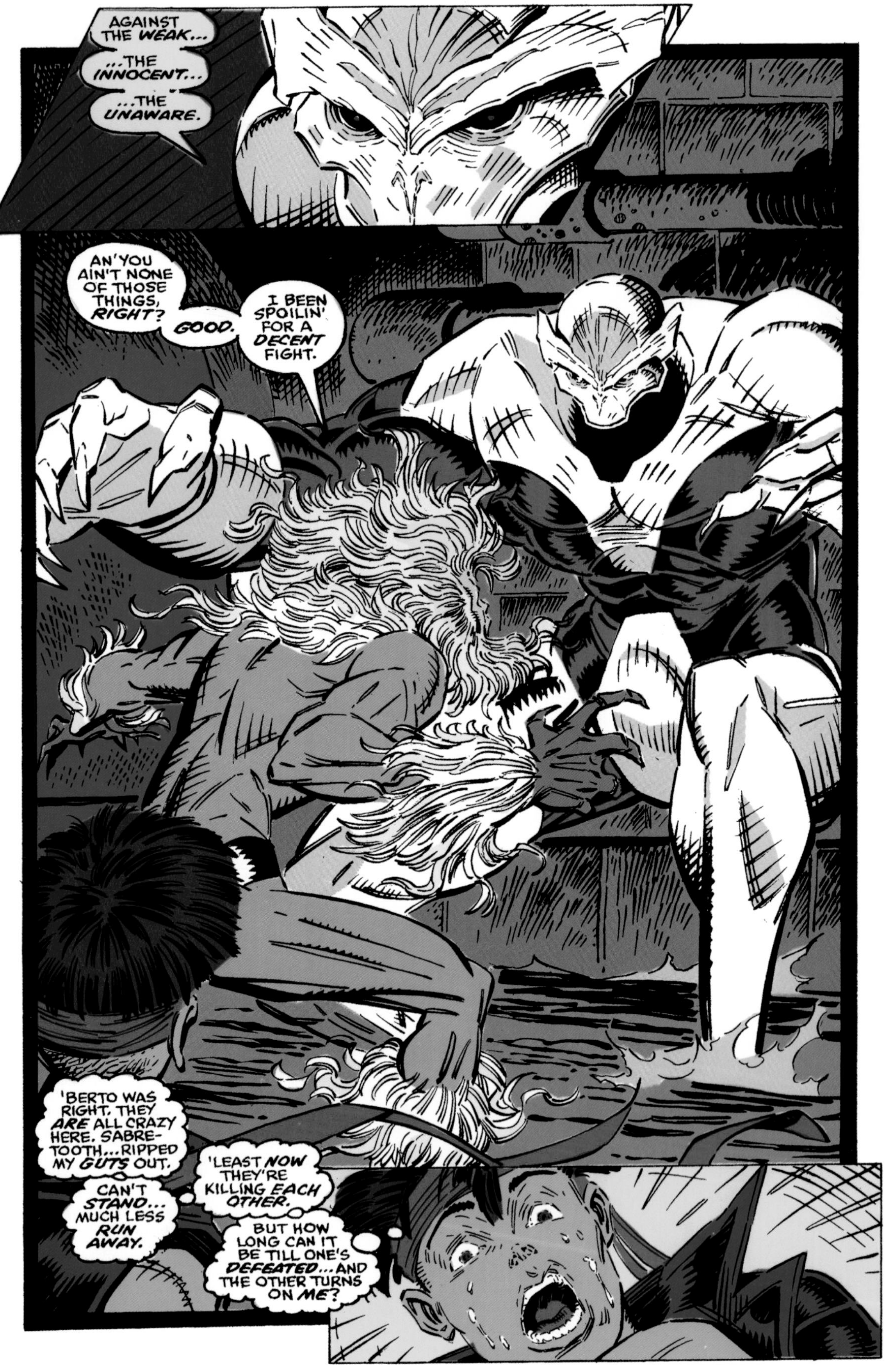
AGAINST THE WEAK...
...THE INNOCENT...
...THE UNAWARE.
AN' YOU AIN'T NONE OF THOSE THINGS, RIGHT? GOOD.
I BEEN SPOILIN' FOR A DECENT FIGHT.
'BERTO WAS RIGHT. THEY ARE ALL CRAZY HERE. SABRETOOTH...RIPPED MY GUTS OUT.
CAN'T STAND... MUCH LESS RUN AWAY.
'LEAST NOW THEY'RE KILLING EACH OTHER.
BUT HOW LONG CAN IT BE TILL ONE'S DEFEATED... AND THE OTHER TURNS ON ME?

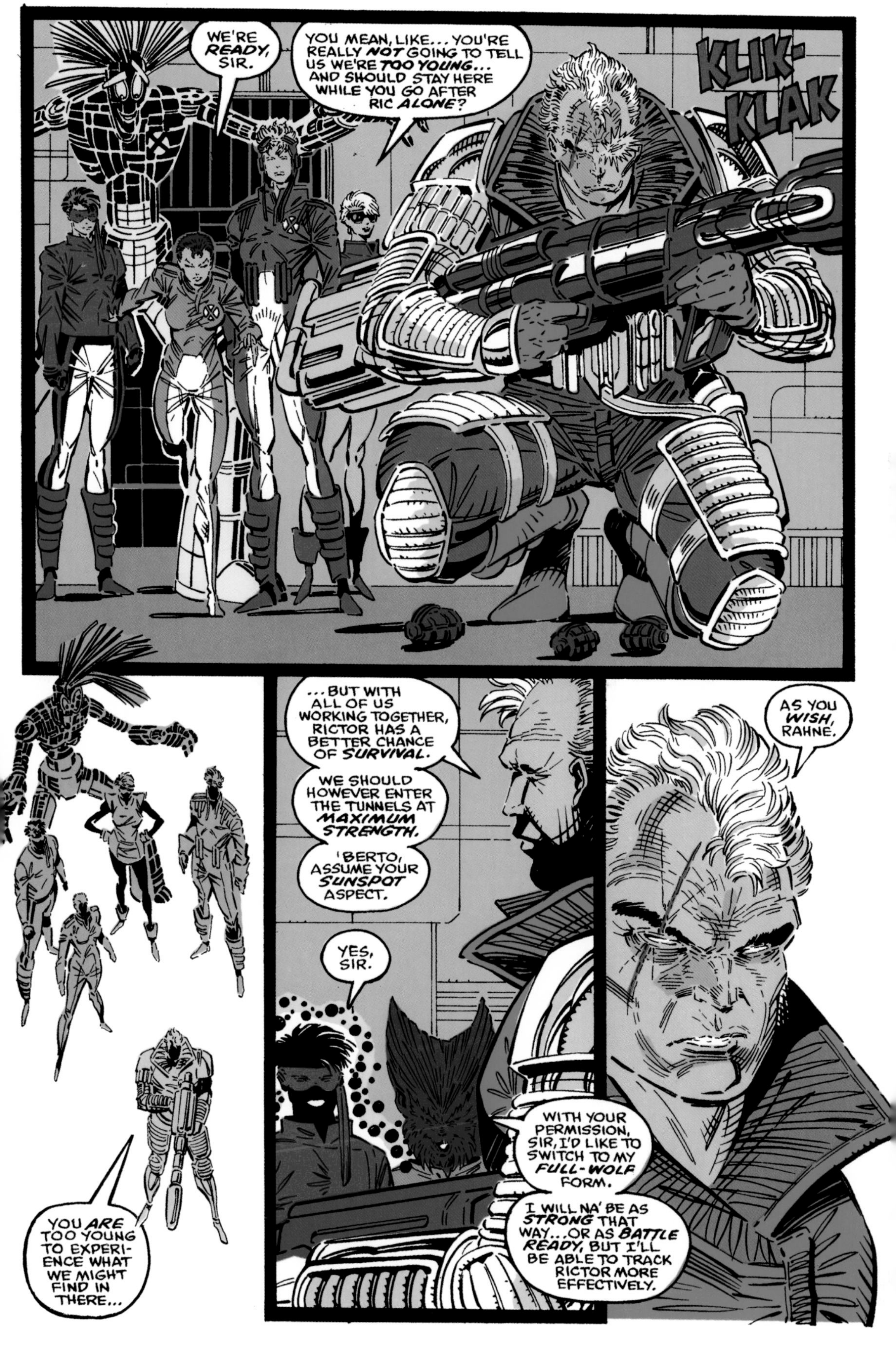

WE'RE READY, SIR.
YOU MEAN, LIKE... YOU'RE REALLY NOT GOING TO TELL US WE'RE TOO YOUNG... AND SHOULD STAY HERE WHILE YOU GO AFTER RIC ALONE?
KLIK-KLAK
YOU ARE TOO YOUNG TO EXPERIENCE WHAT WE MIGHT FIND IN THERE...
...BUT WITH ALL OF US WORKING TOGETHER, RICTOR HAS A BETTER CHANCE OF SURVIVAL.
WE SHOULD HOWEVER ENTER THE TUNNELS AT MAXIMUM STRENGTH.
'BERTO, ASSUME YOUR SUNSPOT ASPECT.
YES, SIR.
WITH YOUR PERMISSION, SIR, I'D LIKE TO SWITCH TO MY FULL-WOLF FORM.
I WILL NA' BE AS STRONG THAT WAY... OR AS BATTLE READY, BUT I'LL BE ABLE TO TRACK RICTOR MORE EFFECTIVELY.
AS YOU WISH, RAHNE.

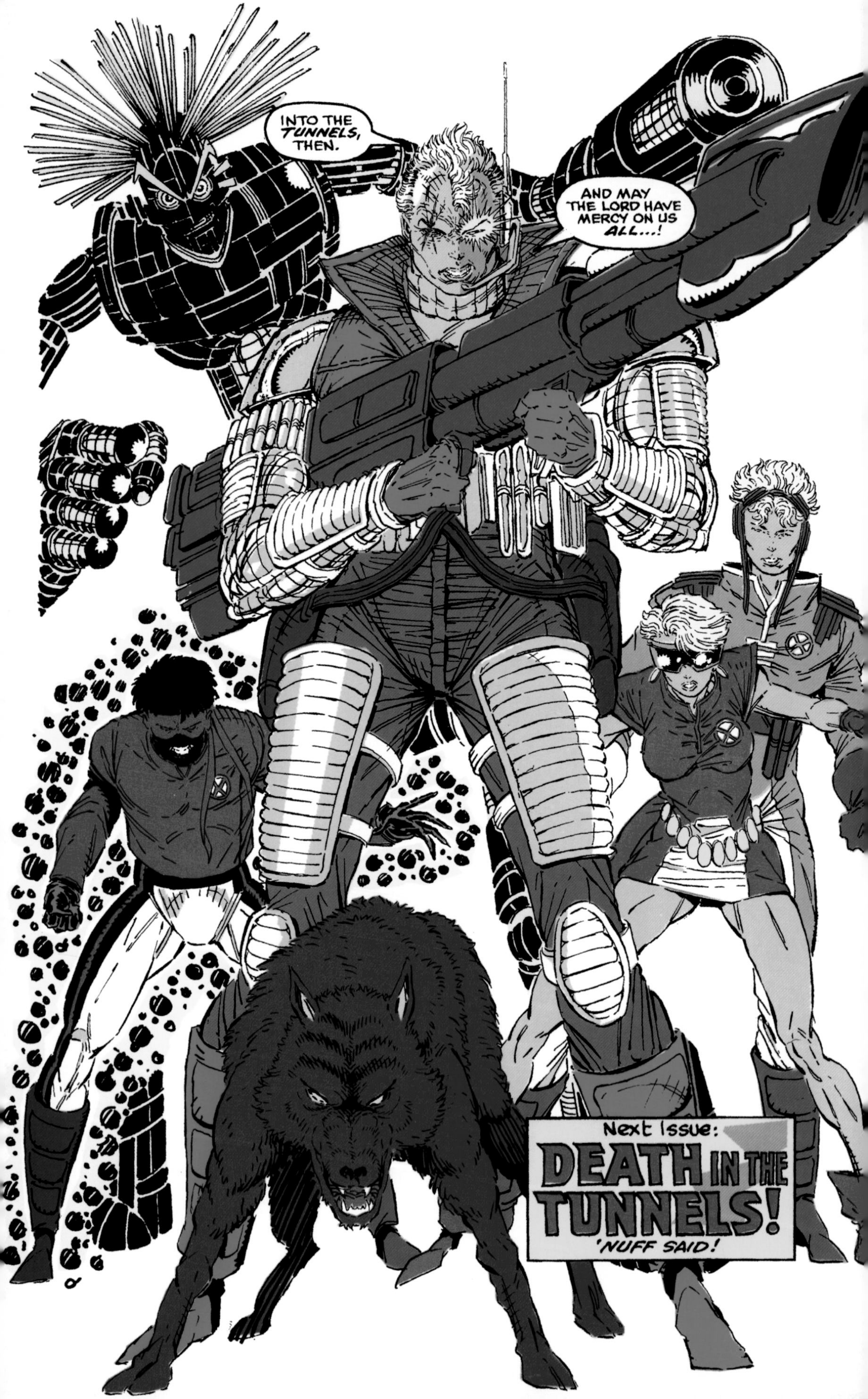

INTO THE TUNNELS, THEN.
AND MAY THE LORD HAVE MERCY ON US ALL...!
Next Issue:
DEATH IN THE TUNNELS!
'NUFF SAID!

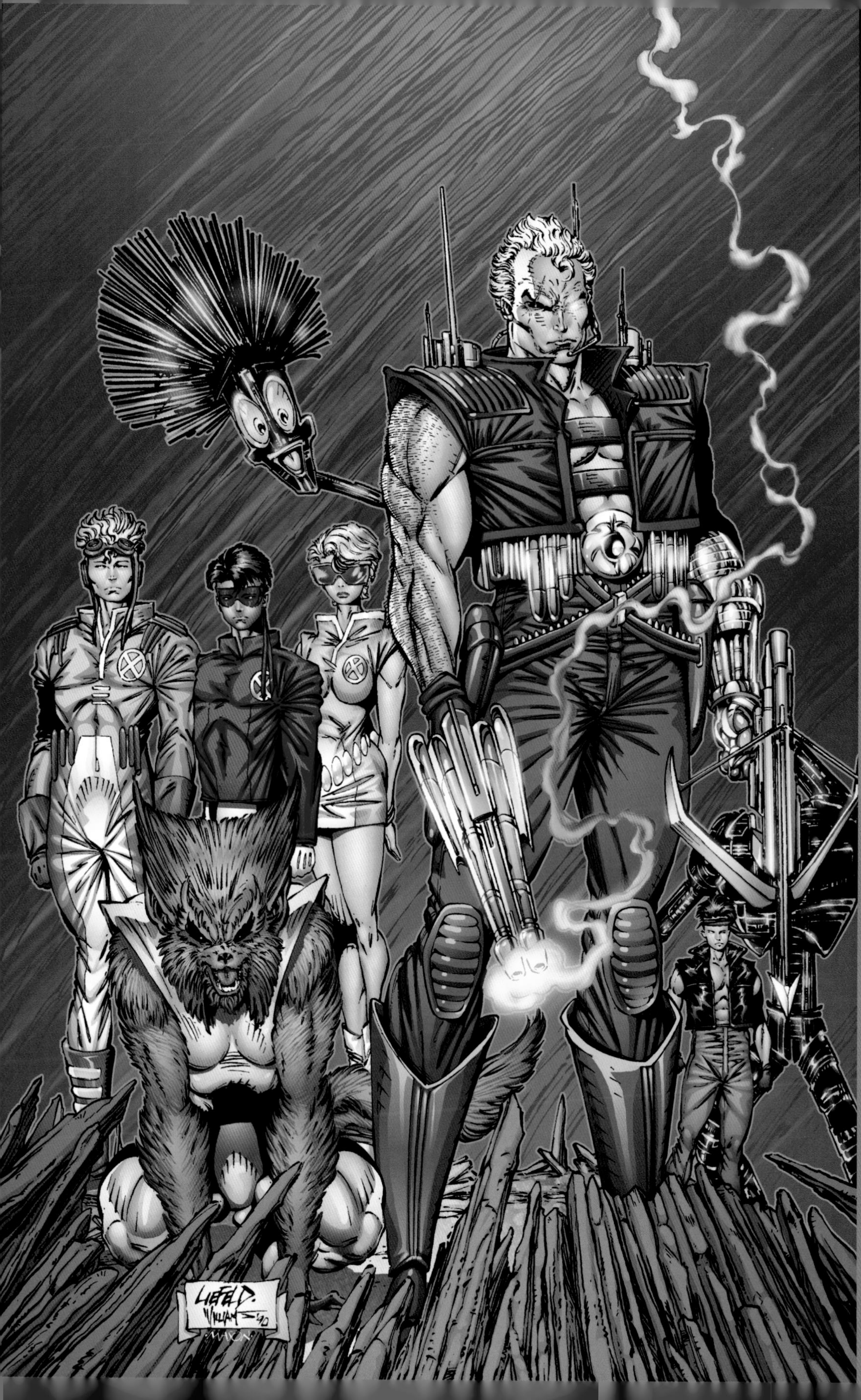
LIEFELD

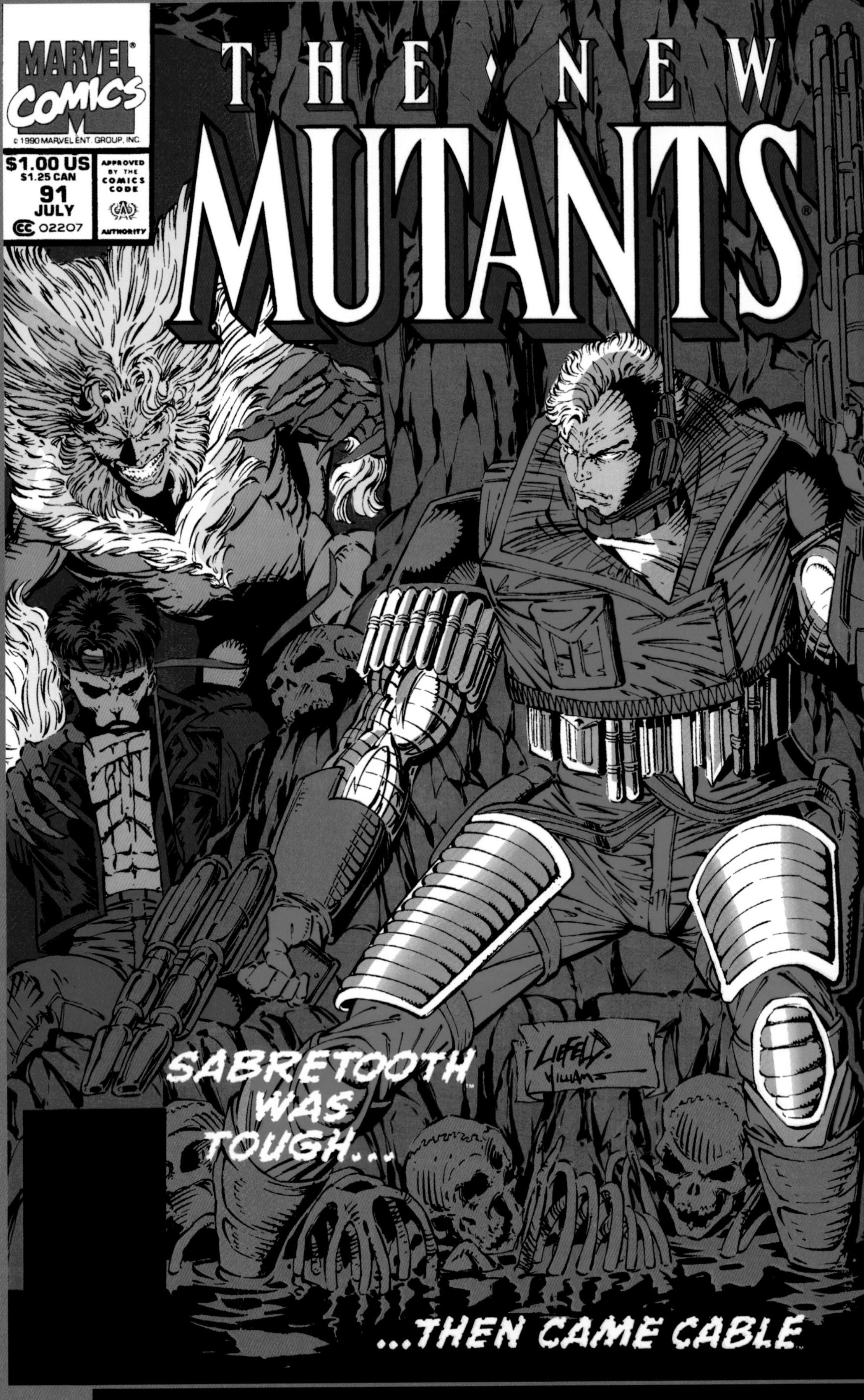
MARVEL COMICS
© 1990 MARVEL ENT. GROUP, INC.
$1.00 US
$1.25 CAN
91
JULY
02207
APPROVED BY THE COMICS CODE AUTHORITY
THE NEW MUTANTS
SABRETOOTH WAS TOUGH...
...THEN CAME CABLE

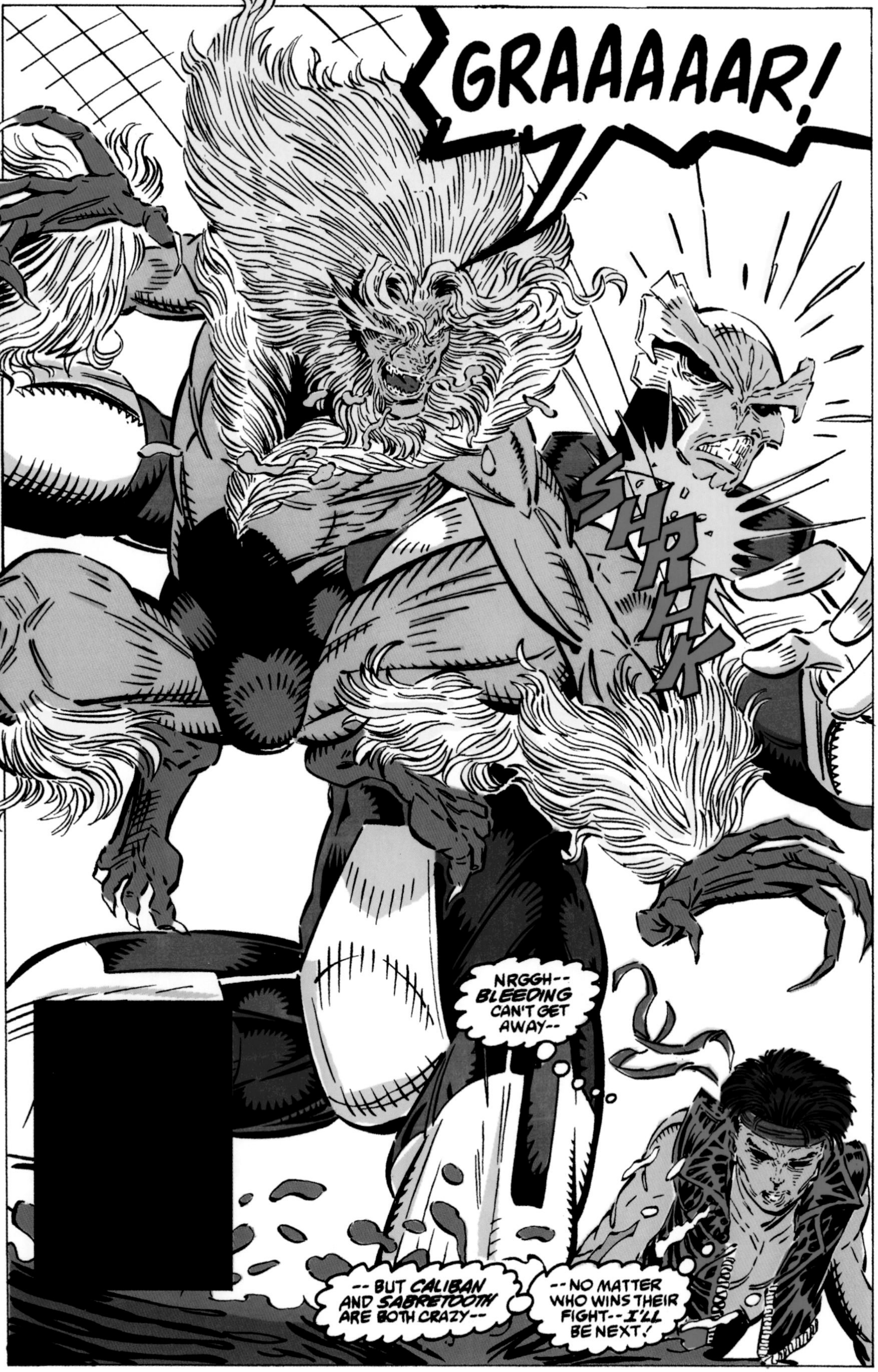
GRAAAAAR!
SHRAK
NRGGH-- BLEEDING CAN'T GET AWAY--
[redacted]
-- BUT CALIBAN AND SABRETOOTH ARE BOTH CRAZY--
-- NO MATTER WHO WINS THEIR FIGHT-- I'LL BE NEXT!

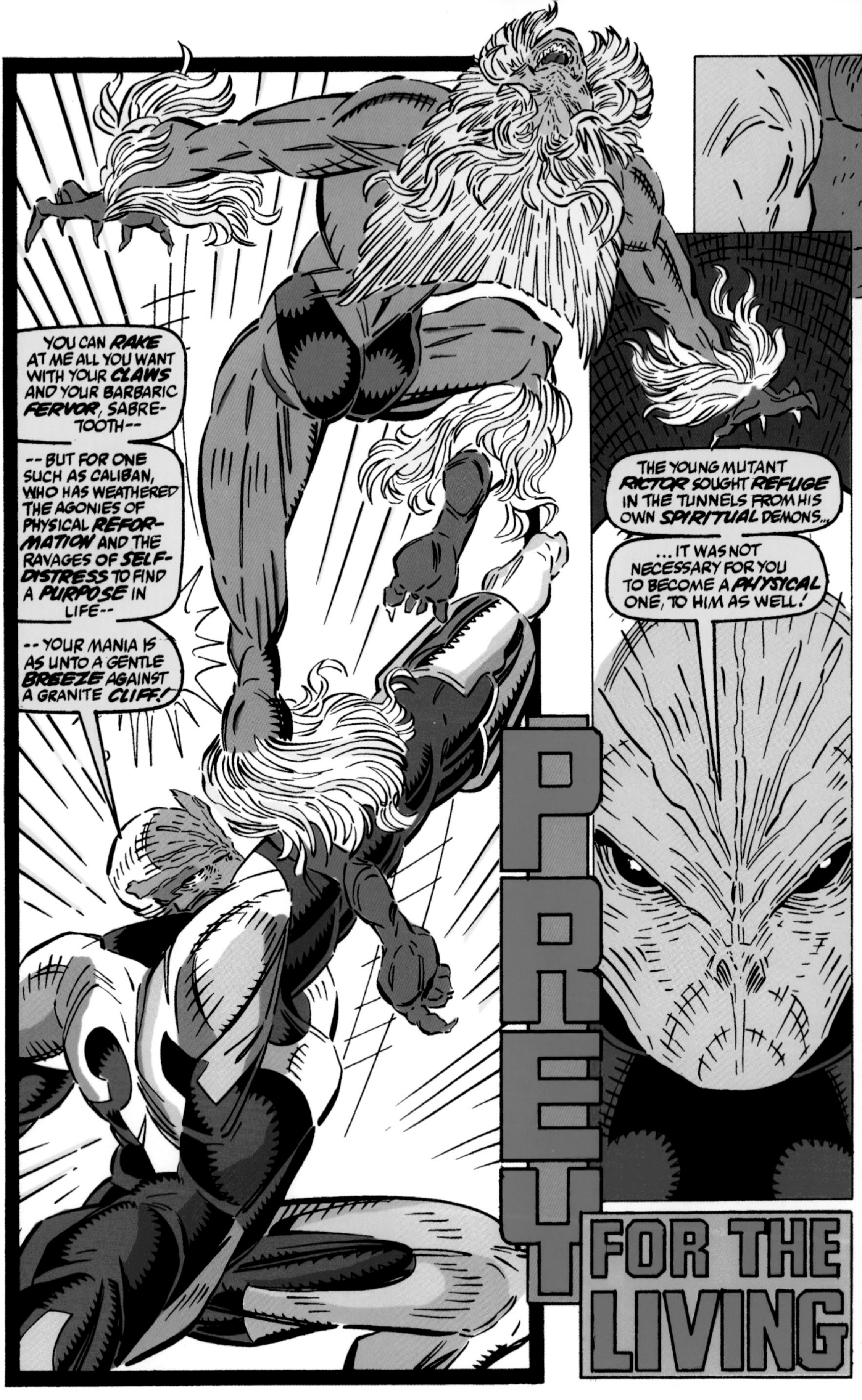
YOU CAN RAKE AT ME ALL YOU WANT WITH YOUR CLAWS AND YOUR BARBARIC FERVOR, SABRETOOTH--
--BUT FOR ONE SUCH AS CALIBAN, WHO HAS WEATHERED THE AGONIES OF PHYSICAL REFORMATION AND THE RAVAGES OF SELF-DISTRESS TO FIND A PURPOSE IN LIFE--
--YOUR MANIA IS AS UNTO A GENTLE BREEZE AGAINST A GRANITE CLIFF!
THE YOUNG MUTANT RICTOR SOUGHT REFUGE IN THE TUNNELS FROM HIS OWN SPIRITUAL DEMONS...
...IT WAS NOT NECESSARY FOR YOU TO BECOME A PHYSICAL ONE, TO HIM AS WELL!
PREY FOR THE LIVING

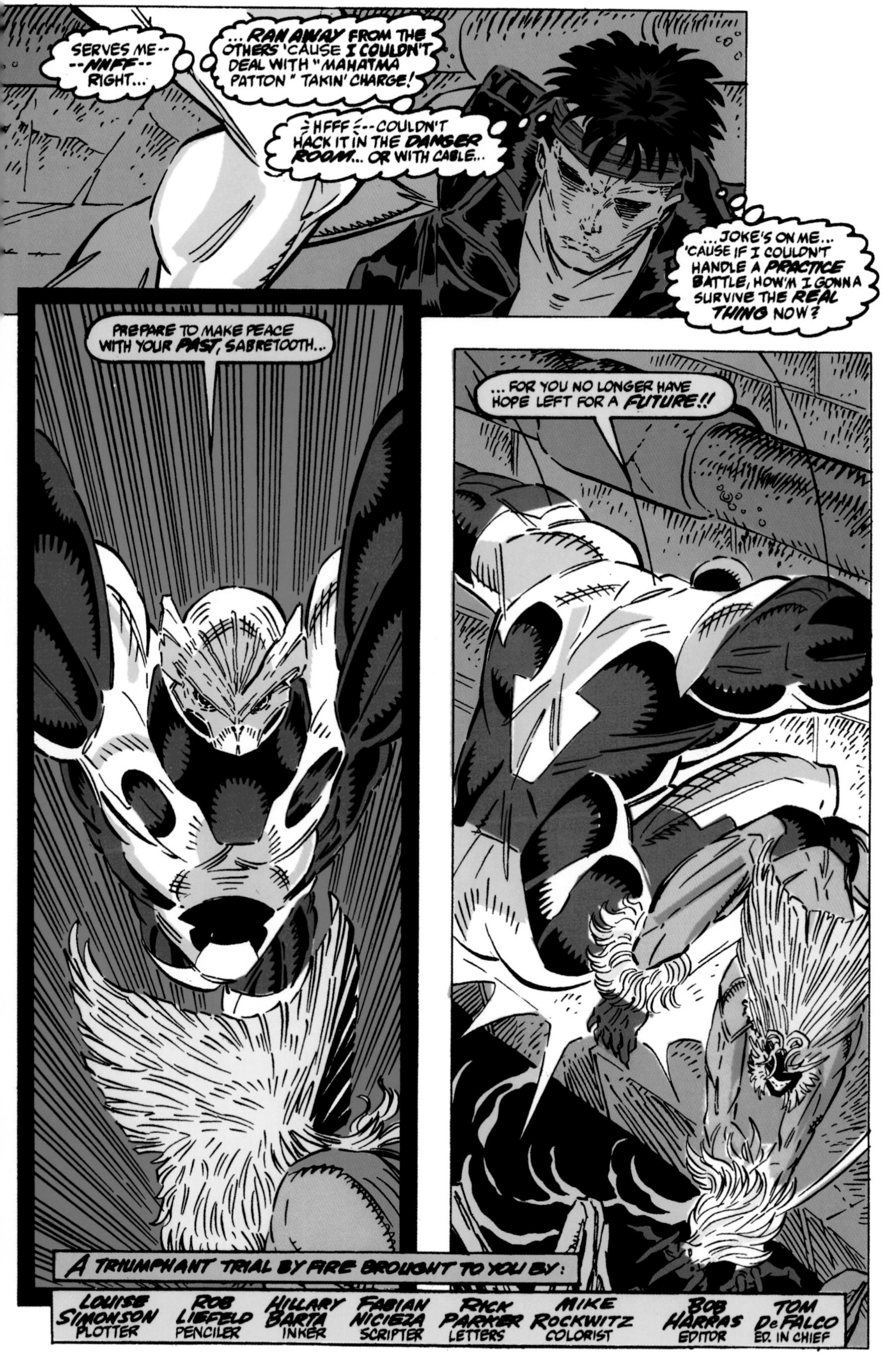
SERVES ME-- --NNFF-- RIGHT...
...RAN AWAY FROM THE OTHERS 'CAUSE I COULDN'T DEAL WITH "MAHATMA PATTON" TAKIN' CHARGE!
HFFF--COULDN'T HACK IT IN THE DANGER ROOM... OR WITH CABLE...
...JOKE'S ON ME... 'CAUSE IF I COULDN'T HANDLE A PRACTICE BATTLE, HOW'M I GONNA SURVIVE THE REAL THING NOW?
PREPARE TO MAKE PEACE WITH YOUR PAST, SABRETOOTH...
...FOR YOU NO LONGER HAVE HOPE LEFT FOR A FUTURE!!
A TRIUMPHANT TRIAL BY FIRE BROUGHT TO YOU BY:
LOUISE SIMONSON PLOTTER
ROB LIEFELD PENCILER
HILLARY BARTA INKER
FABIAN NICIEZA SCRIPTER
RICK PARKER LETTERS
MIKE ROCKWITZ COLORIST
BOB HARRAS EDITOR
TOM DeFALCO ED. IN CHIEF

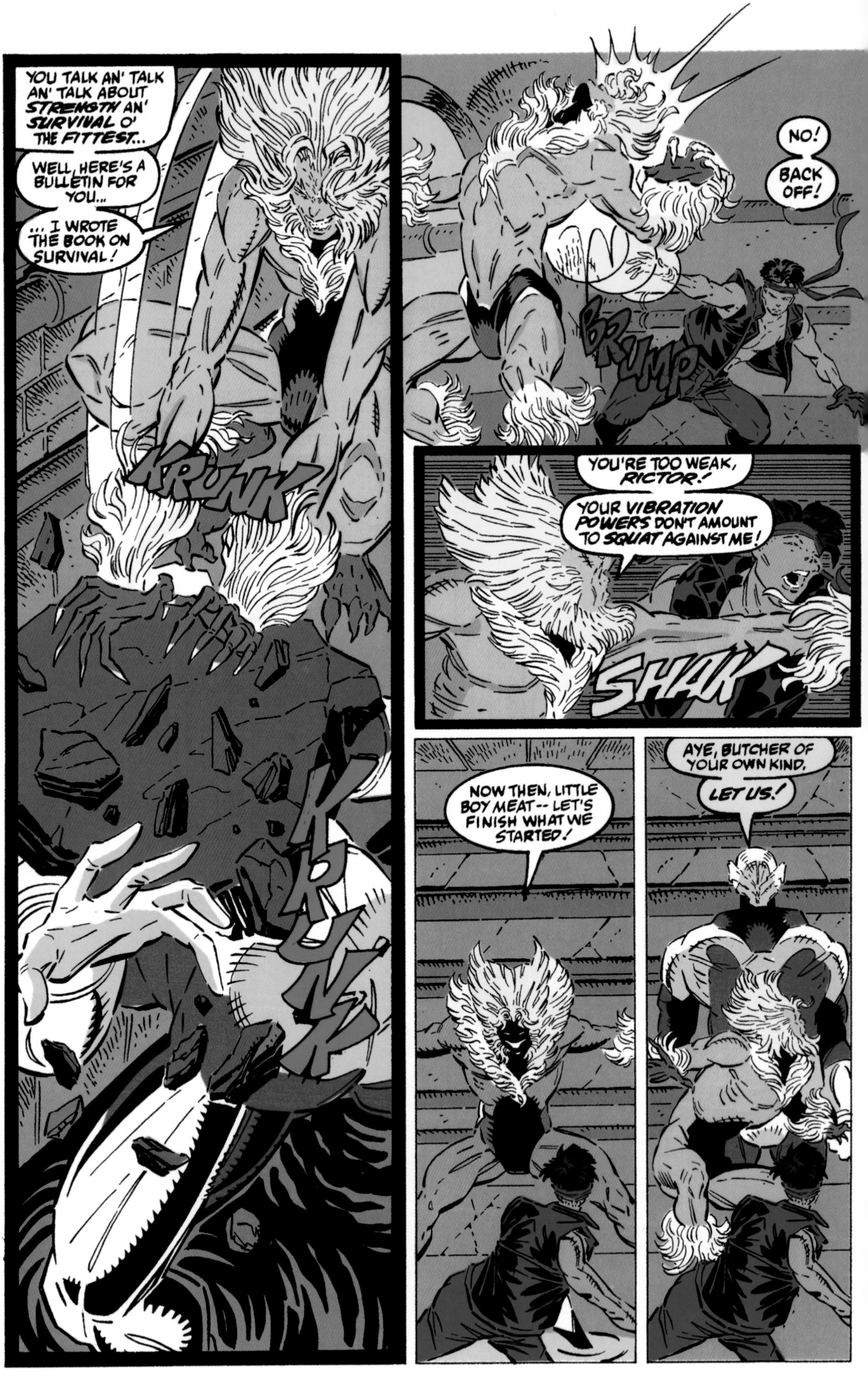
YOU TALK AN' TALK AN' TALK ABOUT STRENGTH AN' SURVIVAL O' THE FITTEST...
WELL, HERE'S A BULLETIN FOR YOU...
... I WROTE THE BOOK ON SURVIVAL!
KRUNK
KRUNK
NO!
BACK OFF!
BRUMP
YOU'RE TOO WEAK, RICTOR!
YOUR VIBRATION POWERS DON'T AMOUNT TO SQUAT AGAINST ME!
SHAK
NOW THEN, LITTLE BOY MEAT-- LET'S FINISH WHAT WE STARTED!
AYE, BUTCHER OF YOUR OWN KIND.
LET US!

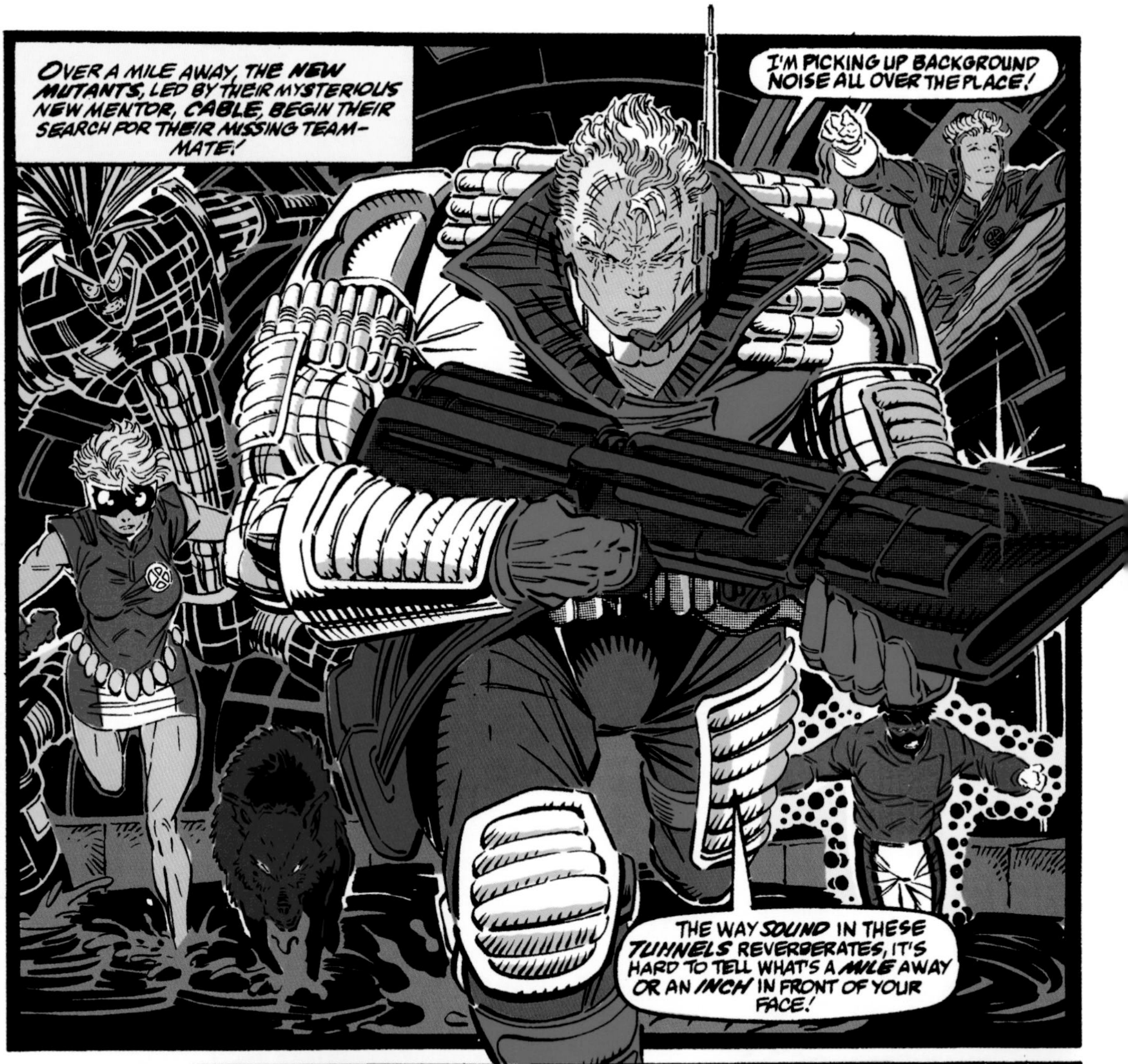
OVER A MILE AWAY, THE NEW MUTANTS, LED BY THEIR MYSTERIOUS NEW MENTOR, CABLE, BEGIN THEIR SEARCH FOR THEIR MISSING TEAM-MATE!
I'M PICKING UP BACKGROUND NOISE ALL OVER THE PLACE!
THE WAY SOUND IN THESE TUNNELS REVERBERATES, IT'S HARD TO TELL WHAT'S A MILE AWAY OR AN INCH IN FRONT OF YOUR FACE!
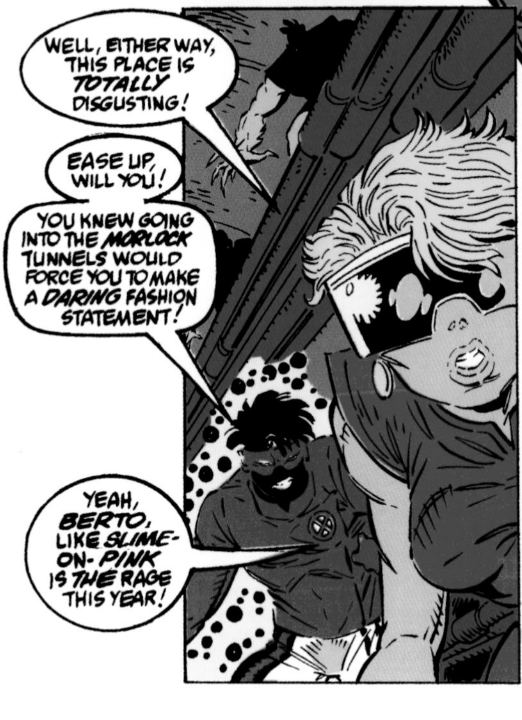
WELL, EITHER WAY, THIS PLACE IS TOTALLY DISGUSTING!
EASE UP, WILL YOU!
YOU KNEW GOING INTO THE MORLOCK TUNNELS WOULD FORCE YOU TO MAKE A DARING FASHION STATEMENT!
YEAH, BERTO, LIKE SLIME-ON-PINK IS THE RAGE THIS YEAR!
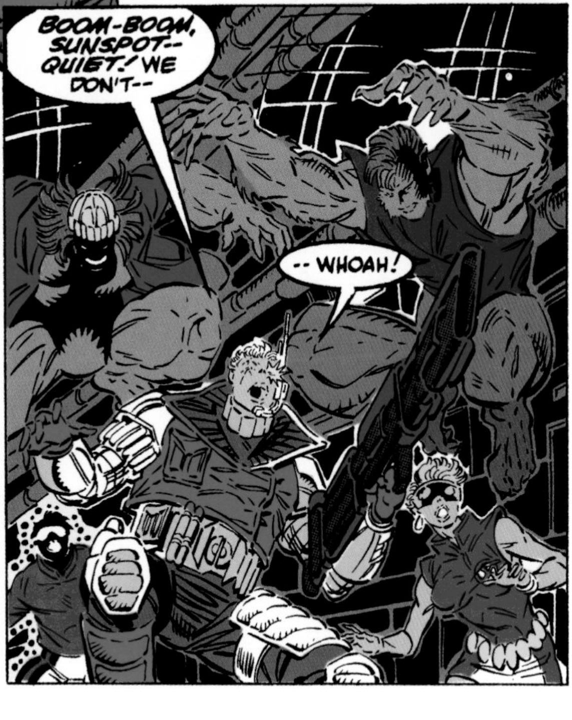
BOOM-BOOM, SUNSPOT-- QUIET! WE DON'T--
-- WHOAH!

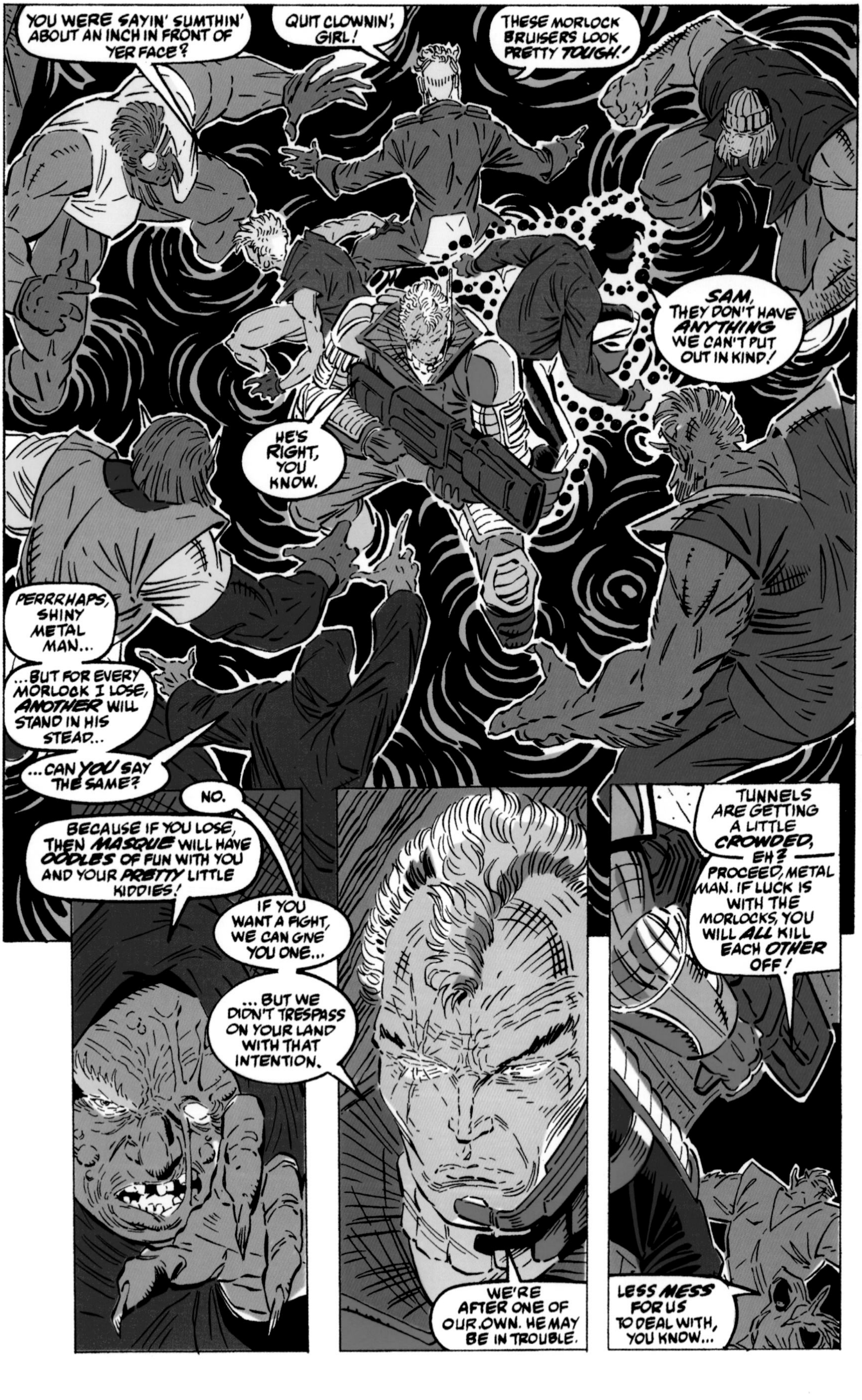

YOU WERE SAYIN' SUMTHIN' ABOUT AN INCH IN FRONT OF YER FACE?
QUIT CLOWNIN', GIRL!
THESE MORLOCK BRUISERS LOOK PRETTY TOUGH!
SAM, THEY DON'T HAVE ANYTHING WE CAN'T PUT OUT IN KIND!
HE'S RIGHT, YOU KNOW.
PERRRHAPS, SHINY METAL MAN...
...BUT FOR EVERY MORLOCK I LOSE, ANOTHER WILL STAND IN HIS STEAD...
...CAN YOU SAY THE SAME?
NO.
BECAUSE IF YOU LOSE, THEN MASQUE WILL HAVE OODLES OF FUN WITH YOU AND YOUR PRETTY LITTLE KIDDIES!
IF YOU WANT A FIGHT, WE CAN GIVE YOU ONE...
... BUT WE DIDN'T TRESPASS ON YOUR LAND WITH THAT INTENTION.
WE'RE AFTER ONE OF OUR OWN. HE MAY BE IN TROUBLE.
TUNNELS ARE GETTING A LITTLE CROWDED, EH?
PROCEED, METAL MAN. IF LUCK IS WITH THE MORLOCKS, YOU WILL ALL KILL EACH OTHER OFF!
LESS MESS FOR US TO DEAL WITH, YOU KNOW...

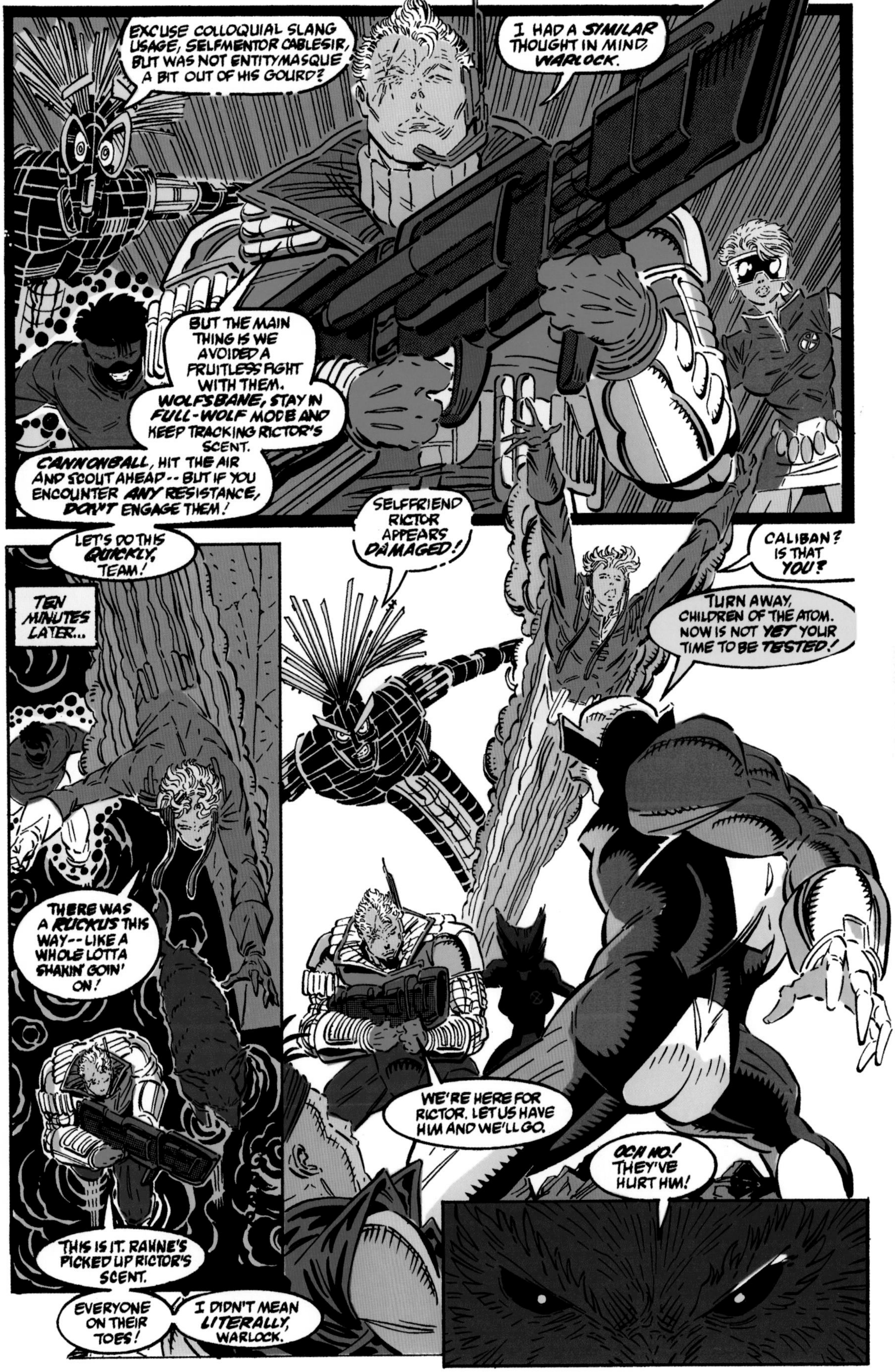
EXCUSE COLLOQUIAL SLANG USAGE, SELFMENTOR CABLESIR, BUT WAS NOT ENTITYMASQUE A BIT OUT OF HIS GOURD?
I HAD A SIMILAR THOUGHT IN MIND, WARLOCK.
BUT THE MAIN THING IS WE AVOIDED A FRUITLESS FIGHT WITH THEM.
WOLFSBANE, STAY IN FULL-WOLF MODE AND KEEP TRACKING RICTOR'S SCENT.
CANNONBALL, HIT THE AIR AND SCOUT AHEAD-- BUT IF YOU ENCOUNTER ANY RESISTANCE, DON'T ENGAGE THEM!
LET'S DO THIS QUICKLY, TEAM!
TEN MINUTES LATER...
THERE WAS A RUCKUS THIS WAY--LIKE A WHOLE LOTTA SHAKIN' GOIN' ON!
THIS IS IT. RAHNE'S PICKED UP RICTOR'S SCENT.
EVERYONE ON THEIR TOES!
I DIDN'T MEAN LITERALLY, WARLOCK.
SELFFRIEND RICTOR APPEARS DAMAGED!
CALIBAN? IS THAT YOU?
TURN AWAY, CHILDREN OF THE ATOM. NOW IS NOT YET YOUR TIME TO BE TESTED!
WE'RE HERE FOR RICTOR. LET US HAVE HIM AND WE'LL GO.
OCH NO! THEY'VE HURT HIM!

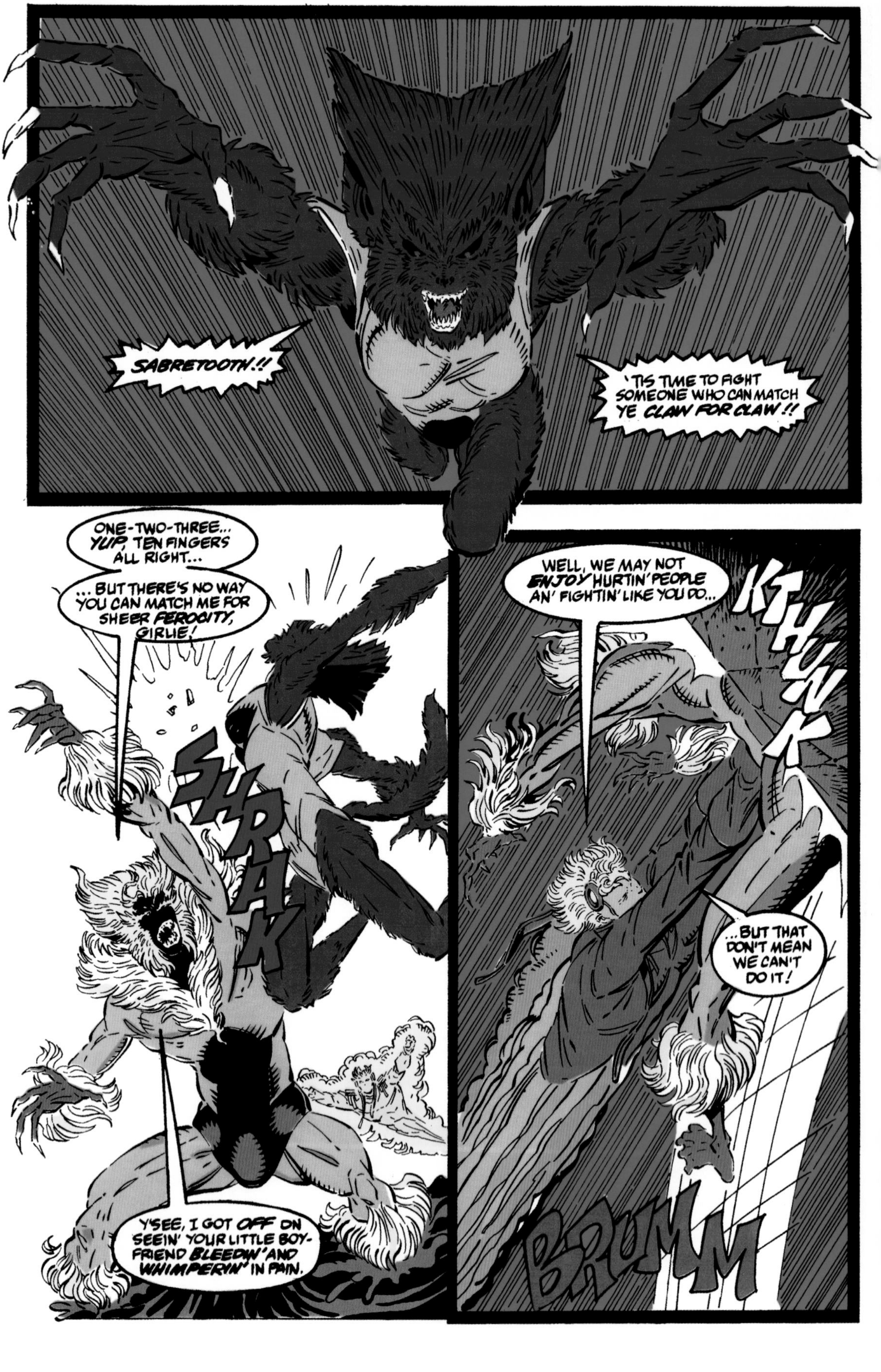
SABRETOOTH!!
'TIS TIME TO FIGHT SOMEONE WHO CAN MATCH YE CLAW FOR CLAW!!
ONE-TWO-THREE... YUP, TEN FINGERS ALL RIGHT...
...BUT THERE'S NO WAY YOU CAN MATCH ME FOR SHEER FEROCITY, GIRLIE!
SHRAK
Y'SEE, I GOT OFF ON SEEIN' YOUR LITTLE BOY-FRIEND BLEEDIN' AND WHIMPERIN' IN PAIN.
WELL, WE MAY NOT ENJOY HURTIN' PEOPLE AN' FIGHTIN' LIKE YOU DO...
KTHUNK
...BUT THAT DON'T MEAN WE CAN'T DO IT!
BRUMM

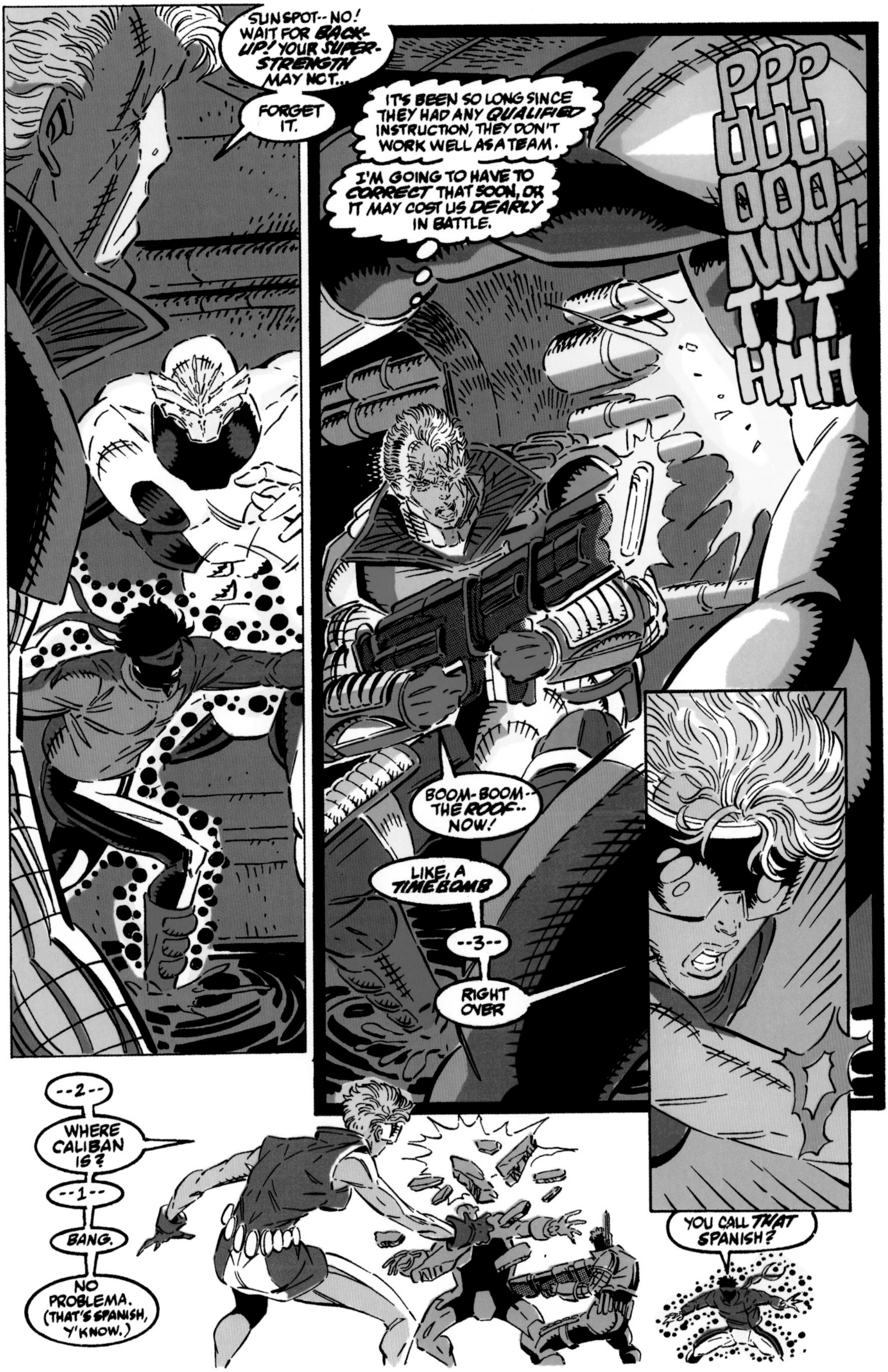
SUNSPOT--NO! WAIT FOR BACK-UP! YOUR SUPER-STRENGTH MAY NOT...
FORGET IT.
IT'S BEEN SO LONG SINCE THEY HAD ANY QUALIFIED INSTRUCTION, THEY DON'T WORK WELL AS A TEAM.
I'M GOING TO HAVE TO CORRECT THAT SOON, OR IT MAY COST US DEARLY IN BATTLE.
PPPOOOOOONNNTTTHHH
BOOM-BOOM--THE ROOF.. NOW!
LIKE, A TIMEBOMB
--3--
RIGHT OVER
--2--
WHERE CALIBAN IS?
--1--
BANG.
NO PROBLEMA. (THAT'S SPANISH, Y'KNOW.)
YOU CALL THAT SPANISH?

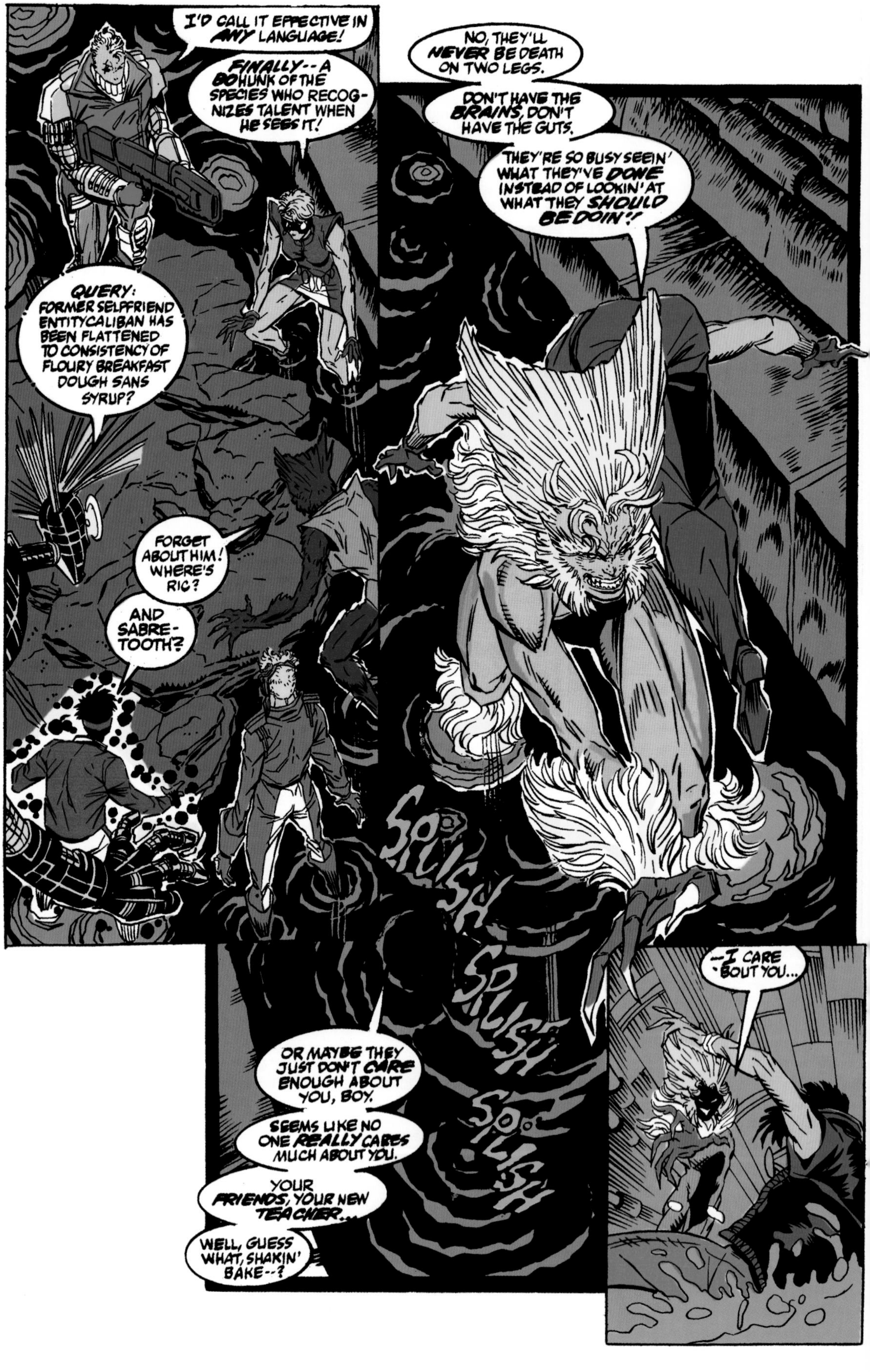
I'D CALL IT EFFECTIVE IN ANY LANGUAGE!
FINALLY--A BOHUNK OF THE SPECIES WHO RECOGNIZES TALENT WHEN HE SEES IT!
QUERY: FORMER SELFFRIEND ENTITYCALIBAN HAS BEEN FLATTENED TO CONSISTENCY OF FLOURY BREAKFAST DOUGH SANS SYRUP?
FORGET ABOUT HIM! WHERE'S RIC?
AND SABRE-TOOTH?
NO, THEY'LL NEVER BE DEATH ON TWO LEGS.
DON'T HAVE THE BRAINS, DON'T HAVE THE GUTS.
THEY'RE SO BUSY SEEIN' WHAT THEY'VE DONE INSTEAD OF LOOKIN' AT WHAT THEY SHOULD BE DOIN'!
SPLISH SPLISH SPLISH SPLISH
OR MAYBE THEY JUST DON'T CARE ENOUGH ABOUT YOU, BOY.
SEEMS LIKE NO ONE REALLY CARES MUCH ABOUT YOU.
YOUR FRIENDS, YOUR NEW TEACHER...
WELL, GUESS WHAT, SHAKIN' BAKE--?
--I CARE 'BOUT YOU...

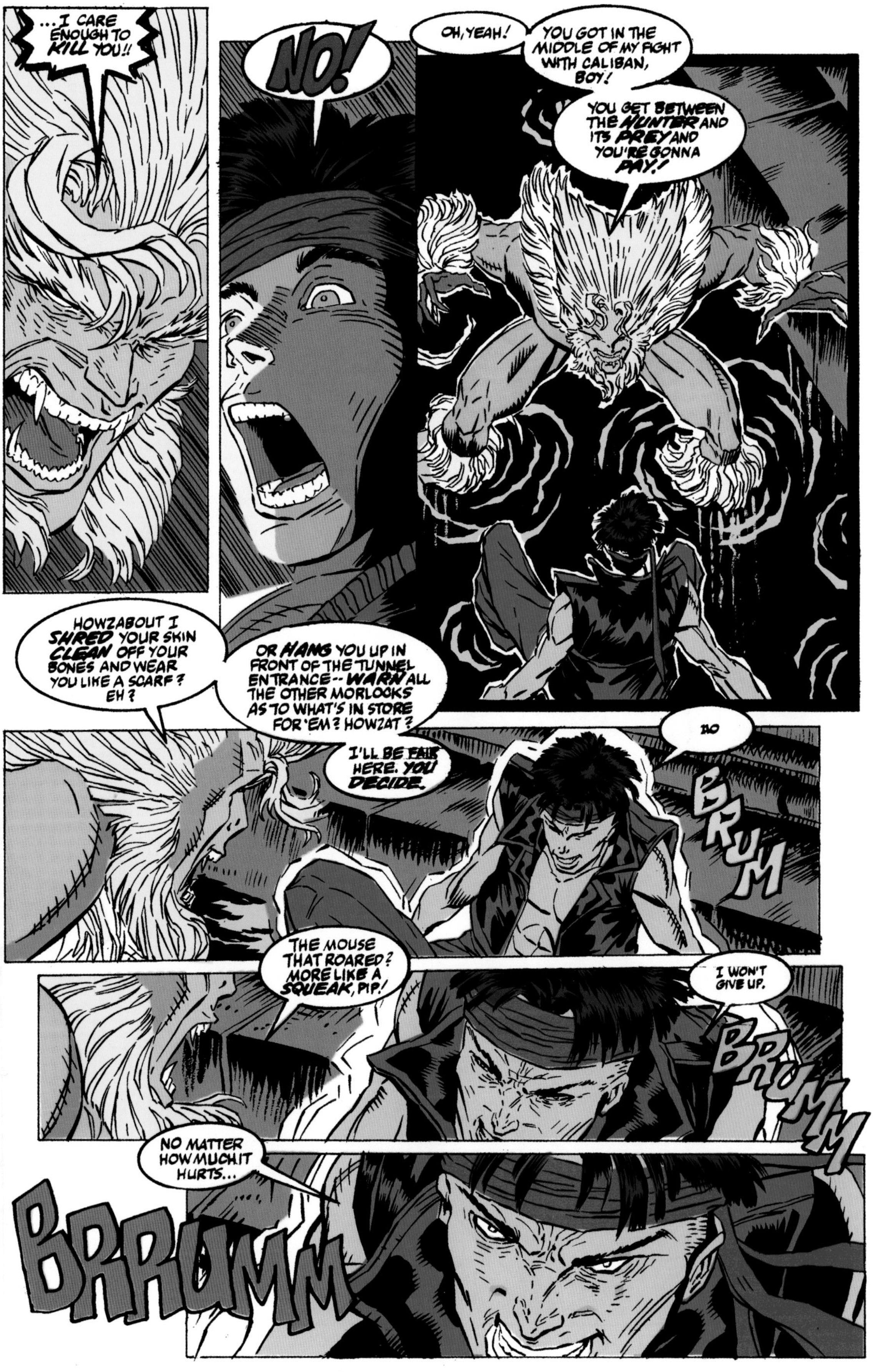
...I CARE ENOUGH TO KILL YOU!!
NO!
OH, YEAH!
YOU GOT IN THE MIDDLE OF MY FIGHT WITH CALIBAN, BOY!
YOU GET BETWEEN THE HUNTER AND ITS PREY AND YOU'RE GONNA PAY!
HOWZABOUT I SHRED YOUR SKIN CLEAN OFF YOUR BONES AND WEAR YOU LIKE A SCARF? EH?
OR HANG YOU UP IN FRONT OF THE TUNNEL ENTRANCE-- WARN ALL THE OTHER MORLOCKS AS TO WHAT'S IN STORE FOR 'EM? HOWZAT?
I'LL BE FAIR HERE. YOU DECIDE.
NO
BRUM
THE MOUSE THAT ROARED? MORE LIKE A SQUEAK, PIP!
I WON'T GIVE UP.
BRUMM
NO MATTER HOW MUCH IT HURTS...
BRRUMM

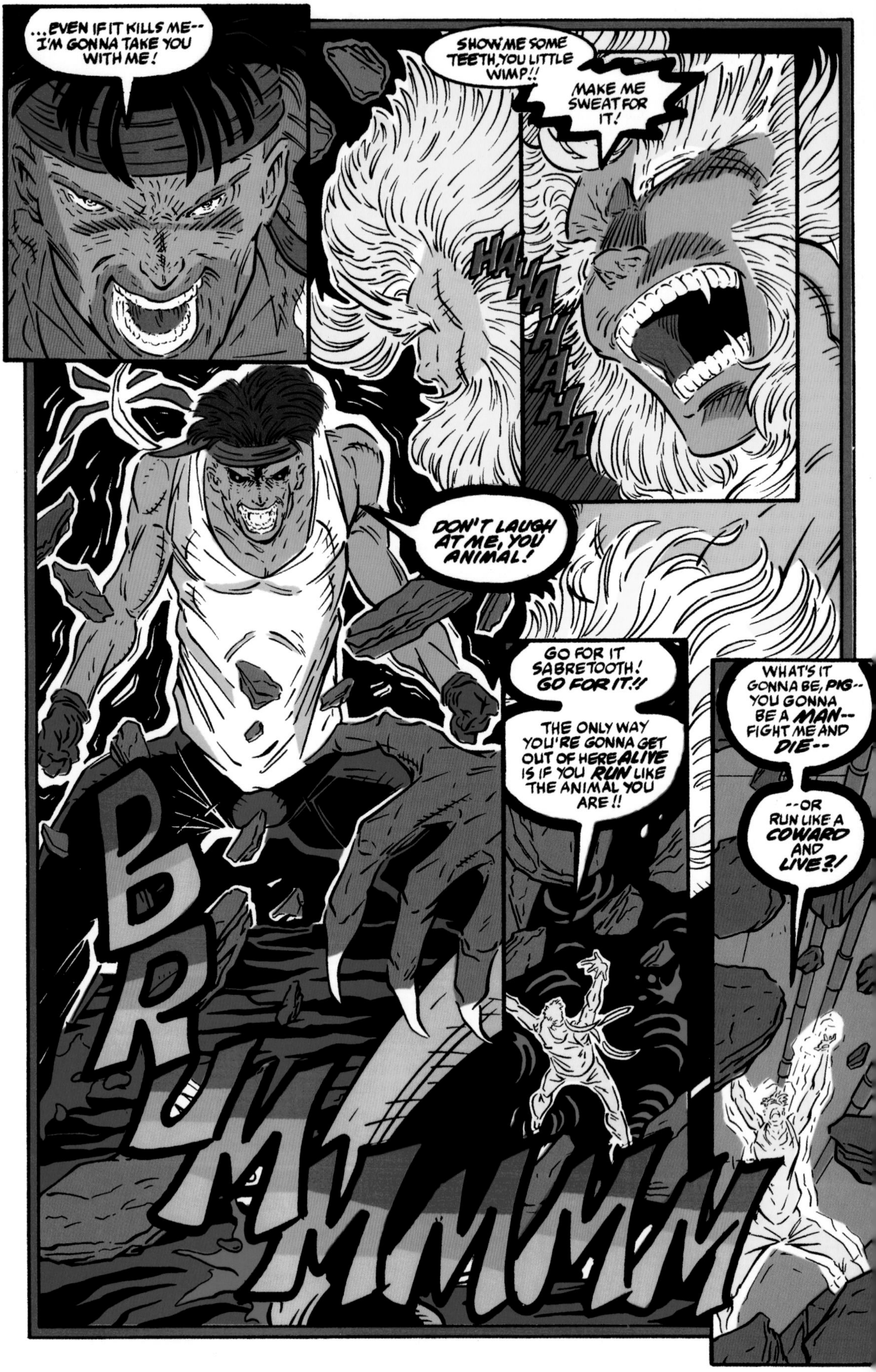
...EVEN IF IT KILLS ME-- I'M GONNA TAKE YOU WITH ME!
SHOW ME SOME TEETH, YOU LITTLE WIMP!!
MAKE ME SWEAT FOR IT!
HAHAHAHAHAHA
DON'T LAUGH AT ME, YOU ANIMAL!
GO FOR IT SABRETOOTH! GO FOR IT!!
THE ONLY WAY YOU'RE GONNA GET OUT OF HERE ALIVE IS IF YOU RUN LIKE THE ANIMAL YOU ARE!!
WHAT'S IT GONNA BE, PIG-- YOU GONNA BE A MAN-- FIGHT ME AND DIE--
--OR RUN LIKE A COWARD AND LIVE?!
DRUMMMMMMM

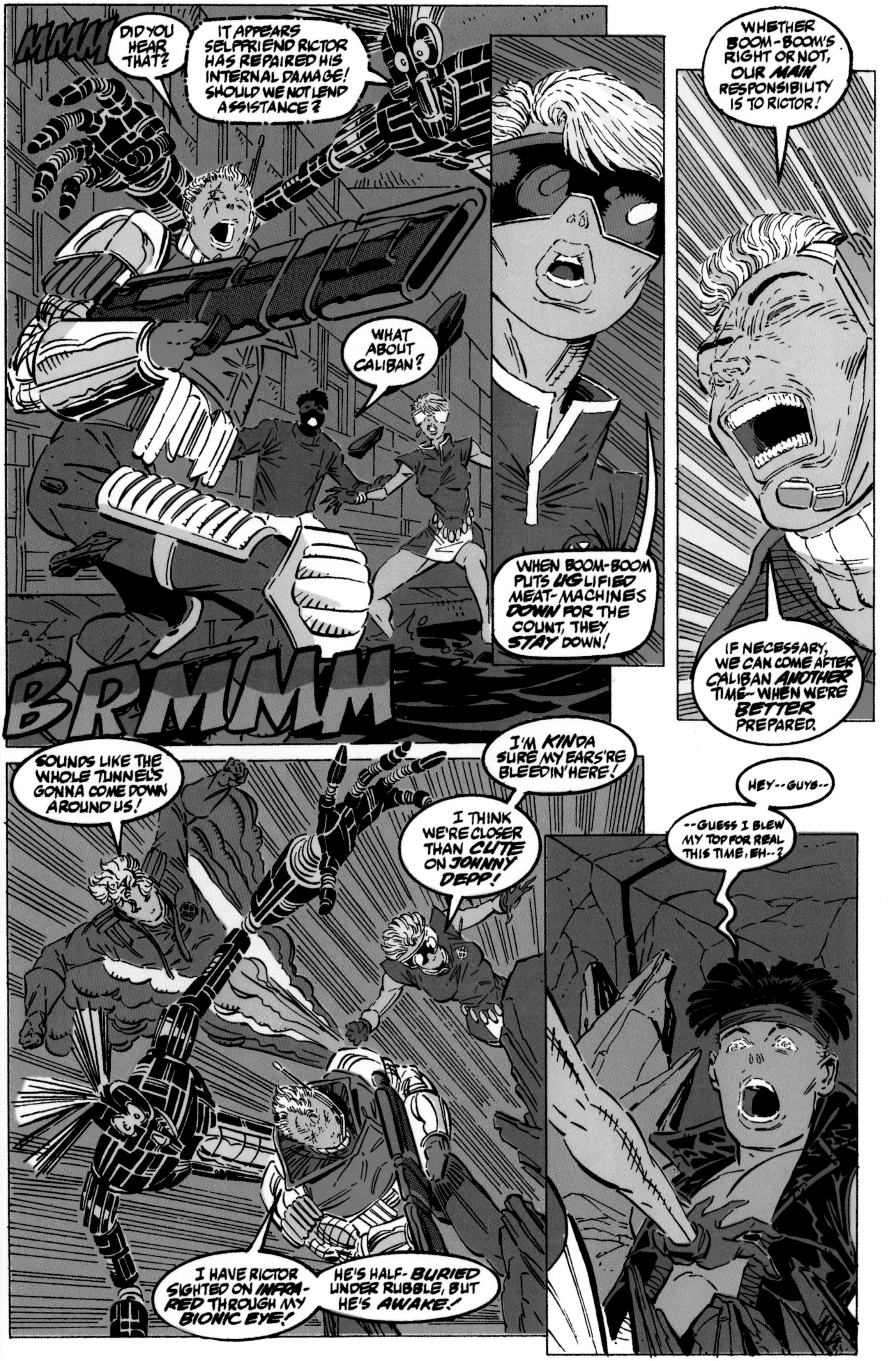
MMM
DID YOU HEAR THAT?
IT APPEARS SELFFRIEND RICTOR HAS REPAIRED HIS INTERNAL DAMAGE! SHOULD WE NOT LEND ASSISTANCE?
WHAT ABOUT CALIBAN?
BRMMM
WHEN BOOM-BOOM PUTS UGLIFIED MEAT-MACHINES DOWN FOR THE COUNT, THEY STAY DOWN!
WHETHER BOOM-BOOM'S RIGHT OR NOT, OUR MAIN RESPONSIBILITY IS TO RICTOR!
IF NECESSARY, WE CAN COME AFTER CALIBAN ANOTHER TIME-- WHEN WE'RE BETTER PREPARED.
SOUNDS LIKE THE WHOLE TUNNEL'S GONNA COME DOWN AROUND US!
I'M KINDA SURE MY EARS'RE BLEEDIN' HERE!
I THINK WE'RE CLOSER THAN CUTE ON JOHNNY DEPP!
I HAVE RICTOR SIGHTED ON INFRA-RED THROUGH MY BIONIC EYE!
HE'S HALF-BURIED UNDER RUBBLE, BUT HE'S AWAKE!
HEY--GUYS--
--GUESS I BLEW MY TOP FOR REAL THIS TIME, EH--?

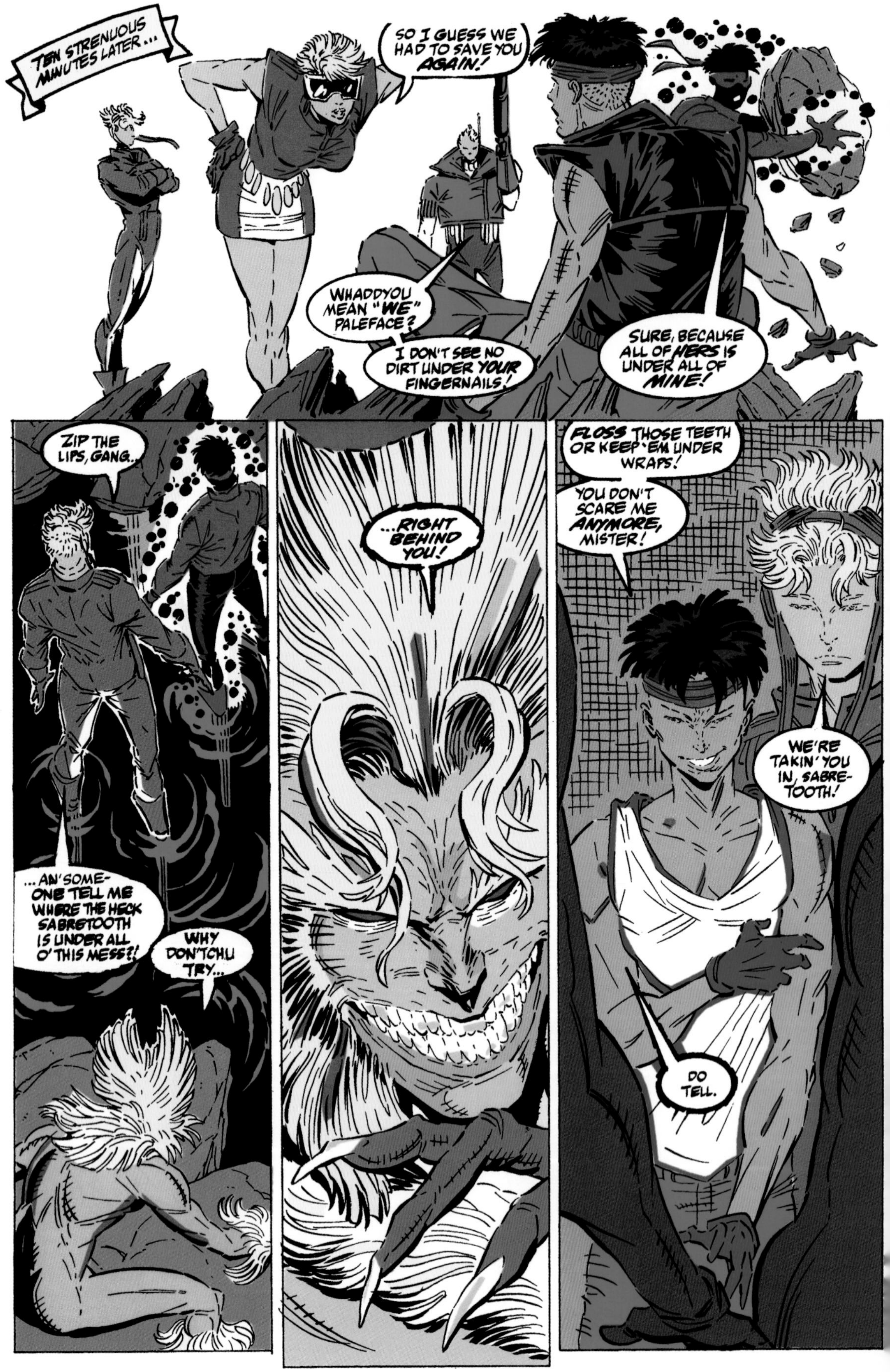
TEN STRENUOUS MINUTES LATER...
SO I GUESS WE HAD TO SAVE YOU AGAIN!
WHADDYOU MEAN "WE" PALEFACE?
I DON'T SEE NO DIRT UNDER YOUR FINGERNAILS!
SURE, BECAUSE ALL OF HERS IS UNDER ALL OF MINE!
ZIP THE LIPS, GANG..
...AN' SOME-ONE TELL ME WHERE THE HECK SABRETOOTH IS UNDER ALL O' THIS MESS?!
WHY DON'TCHU TRY...
...RIGHT BEHIND YOU!
FLOSS THOSE TEETH OR KEEP 'EM UNDER WRAPS!
YOU DON'T SCARE ME ANYMORE, MISTER!
WE'RE TAKIN' YOU IN, SABRE-TOOTH!
DO TELL.

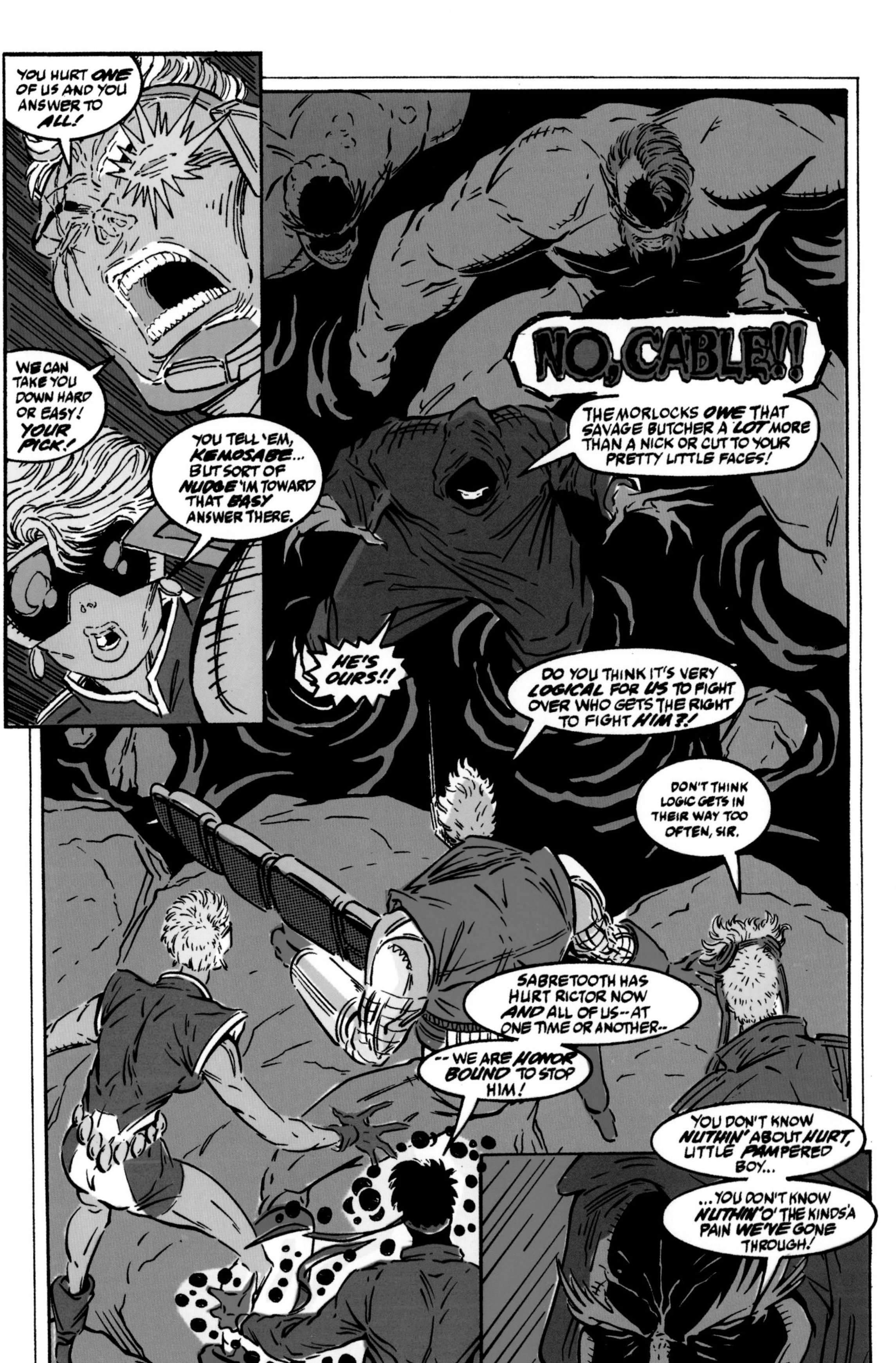
YOU HURT ONE OF US AND YOU ANSWER TO ALL!
WE CAN TAKE YOU DOWN HARD OR EASY! YOUR PICK!
YOU TELL 'EM, KEMOSABE... BUT SORT OF NUDGE 'IM TOWARD THAT EASY ANSWER THERE.
NO, CABLE!!
THE MORLOCKS OWE THAT SAVAGE BUTCHER A LOT MORE THAN A NICK OR CUT TO YOUR PRETTY LITTLE FACES!
HE'S OURS!!
DO YOU THINK IT'S VERY LOGICAL FOR US TO FIGHT OVER WHO GETS THE RIGHT TO FIGHT HIM?!
DON'T THINK LOGIC GETS IN THEIR WAY TOO OFTEN, SIR.
SABRETOOTH HAS HURT RICTOR NOW AND ALL OF US--AT ONE TIME OR ANOTHER--
--WE ARE HONOR BOUND TO STOP HIM!
YOU DON'T KNOW NUTHIN' ABOUT HURT, LITTLE PAMPERED BOY...
...YOU DON'T KNOW NUTHIN' 'O' THE KINDS'A PAIN WE'VE GONE THROUGH!

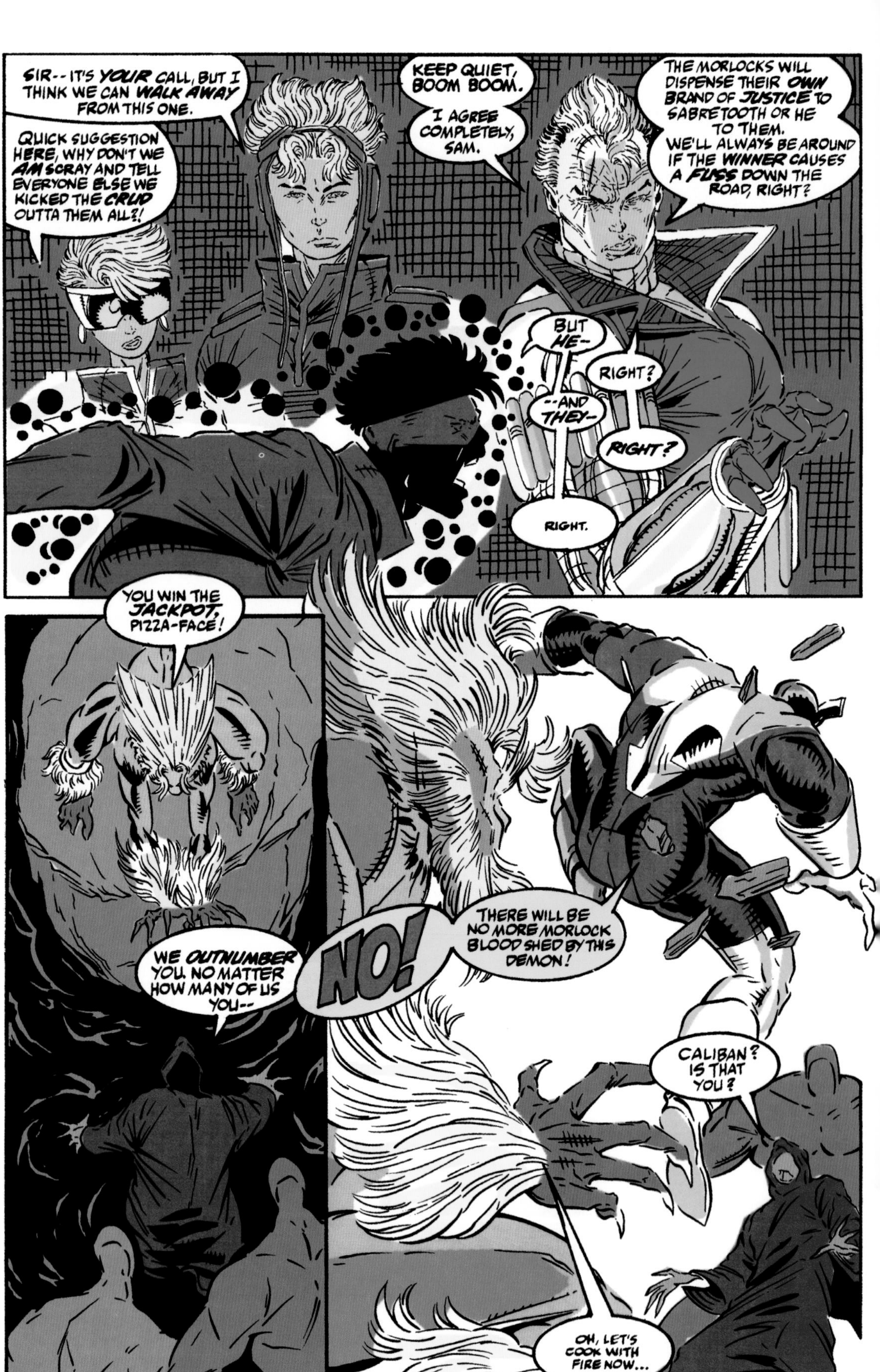
SIR-- IT'S YOUR CALL, BUT I THINK WE CAN WALK AWAY FROM THIS ONE.
QUICK SUGGESTION HERE, WHY DON'T WE AM SCRAY AND TELL EVERYONE ELSE WE KICKED THE CRUD OUTTA THEM ALL?!
KEEP QUIET, BOOM BOOM.
I AGREE COMPLETELY, SAM.
THE MORLOCKS WILL DISPENSE THEIR OWN BRAND OF JUSTICE TO SABRETOOTH OR HE TO THEM. WE'LL ALWAYS BE AROUND IF THE WINNER CAUSES A FUSS DOWN THE ROAD, RIGHT?
BUT HE--
--AND THEY--
RIGHT?
RIGHT?
RIGHT.
YOU WIN THE JACKPOT, PIZZA-FACE!
WE OUTNUMBER YOU. NO MATTER HOW MANY OF US YOU--
NO!
THERE WILL BE NO MORE MORLOCK BLOOD SHED BY THIS DEMON!
CALIBAN? IS THAT YOU?
OH, LET'S COOK WITH FIRE NOW...

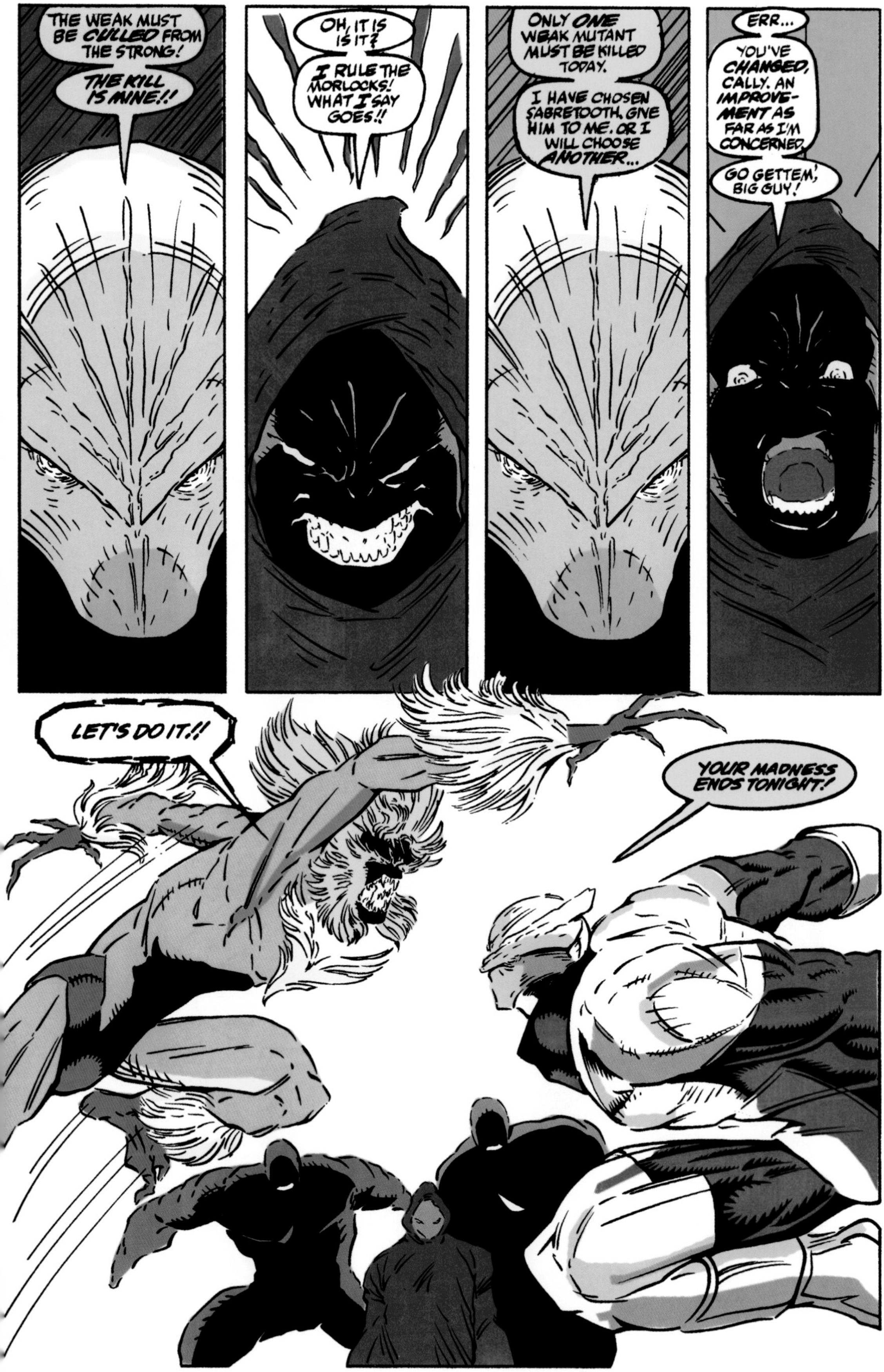
THE WEAK MUST BE CULLED FROM THE STRONG!
THE KILL IS MINE!!
OH, IT IS IS IT?
I RULE THE MORLOCKS! WHAT I SAY GOES!!
ONLY ONE WEAK MUTANT MUST BE KILLED TODAY.
I HAVE CHOSEN SABRETOOTH. GIVE HIM TO ME, OR I WILL CHOOSE ANOTHER...
ERR...
YOU'VE CHANGED, CALLY. AN IMPROVEMENT AS FAR AS I'M CONCERNED.
GO GETTEM', BIG GUY!
LET'S DO IT!!
YOUR MADNESS ENDS TONIGHT!

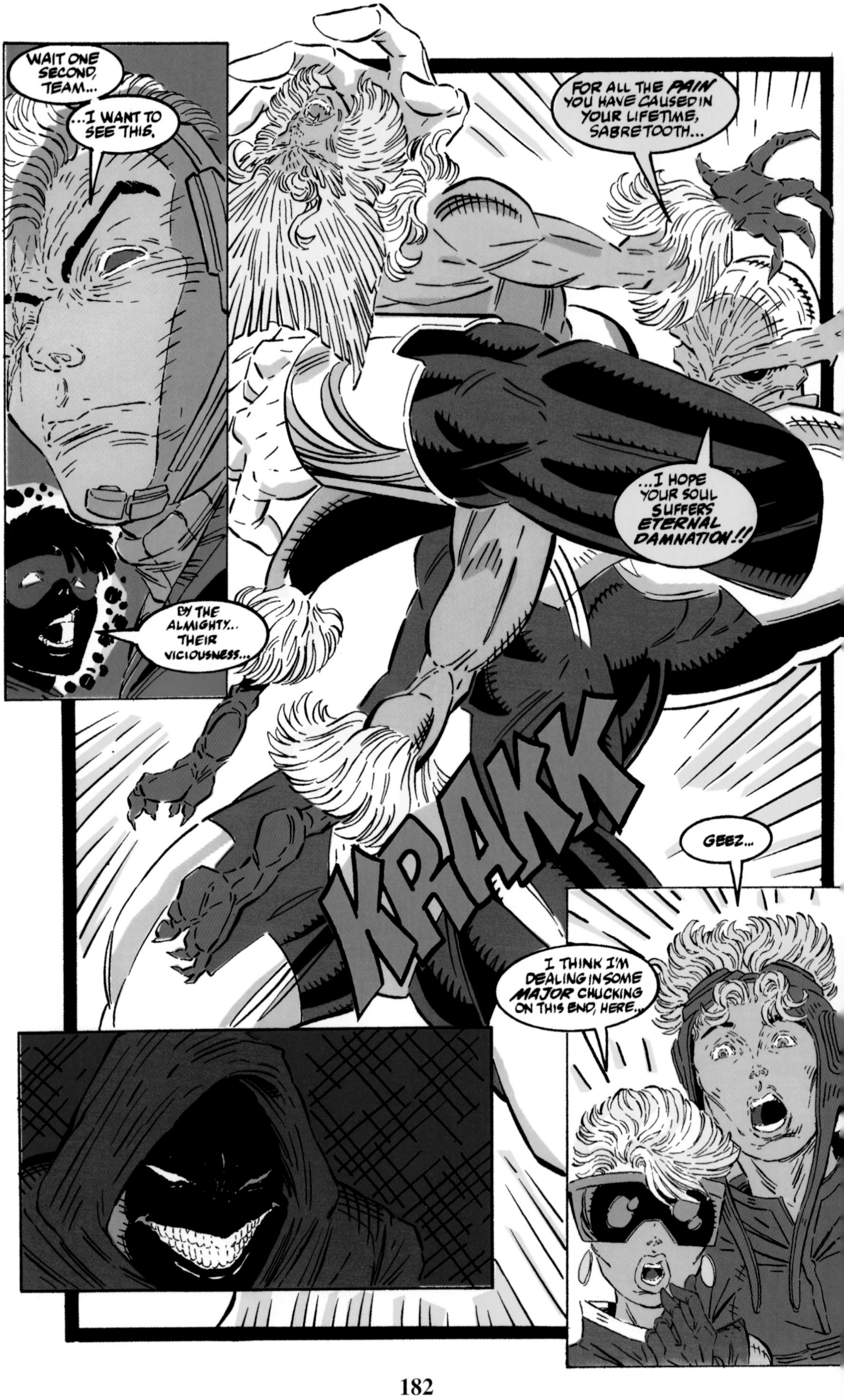
WAIT ONE SECOND, TEAM...
...I WANT TO SEE THIS.
FOR ALL THE PAIN YOU HAVE CAUSED IN YOUR LIFETIME, SABRETOOTH...
...I HOPE YOUR SOUL SUFFERS ETERNAL DAMNATION!!
BY THE ALMIGHTY... THEIR VICIOUSNESS...
KRAKK
GEEZ...
I THINK I'M DEALING IN SOME MAJOR CHUCKING ON THIS END, HERE...

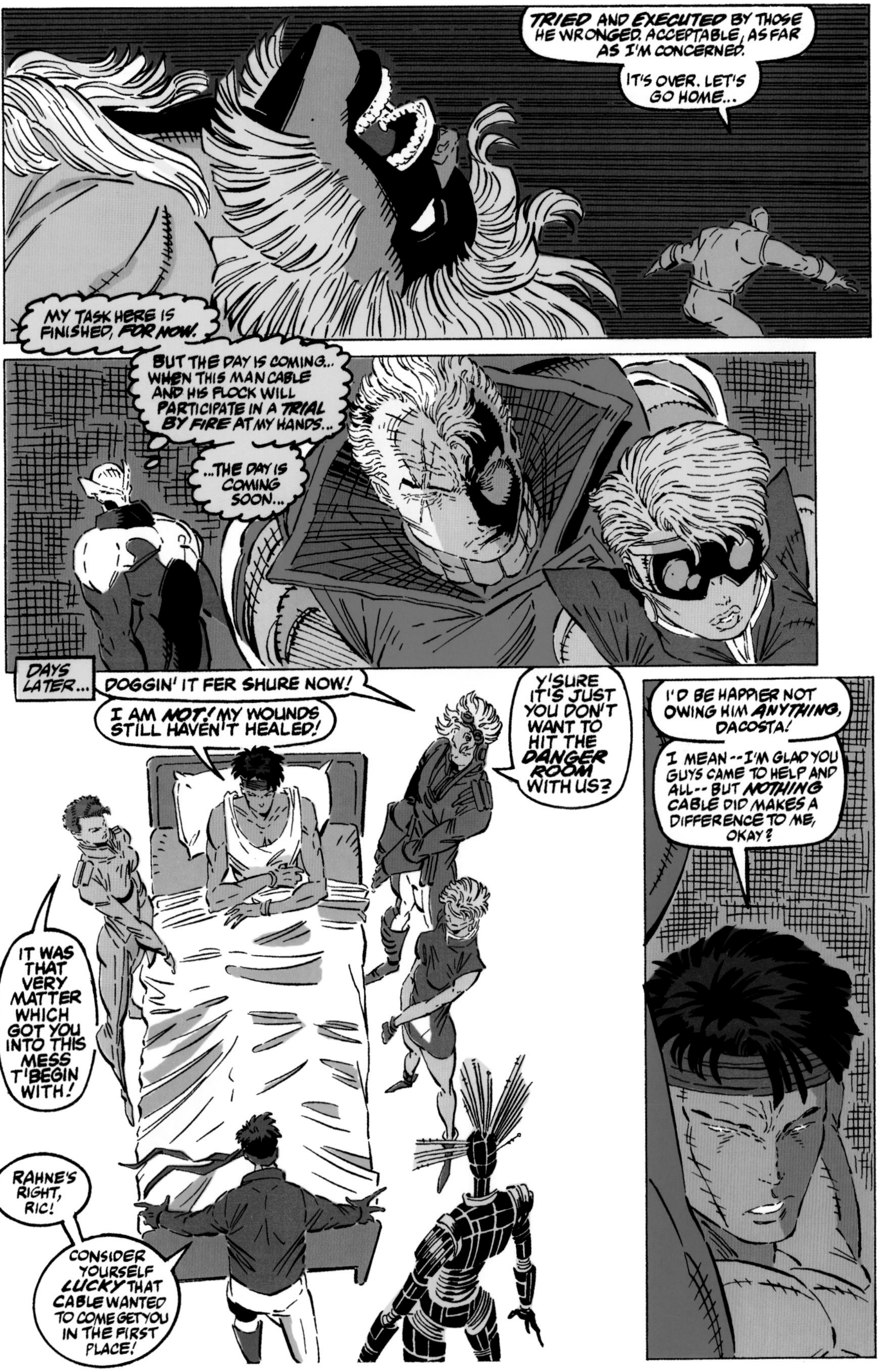

TRIED AND EXECUTED BY THOSE HE WRONGED. ACCEPTABLE, AS FAR AS I'M CONCERNED.
IT'S OVER. LET'S GO HOME...
MY TASK HERE IS FINISHED, FOR NOW.
BUT THE DAY IS COMING... WHEN THIS MAN CABLE AND HIS FLOCK WILL PARTICIPATE IN A TRIAL BY FIRE AT MY HANDS...
...THE DAY IS COMING SOON...
DAYS LATER...
DOGGIN' IT FER SHURE NOW!
I AM NOT! MY WOUNDS STILL HAVEN'T HEALED!
Y'SURE IT'S JUST YOU DON'T WANT TO HIT THE DANGER ROOM WITH US?
IT WAS THAT VERY MATTER WHICH GOT YOU INTO THIS MESS T'BEGIN WITH!
RAHNE'S RIGHT, RIC!
CONSIDER YOURSELF LUCKY THAT CABLE WANTED TO COME GET YOU IN THE FIRST PLACE!
I'D BE HAPPIER NOT OWING HIM ANYTHING, DACOSTA!
I MEAN--I'M GLAD YOU GUYS CAME TO HELP AND ALL--BUT NOTHING CABLE DID MAKES A DIFFERENCE TO ME, OKAY?

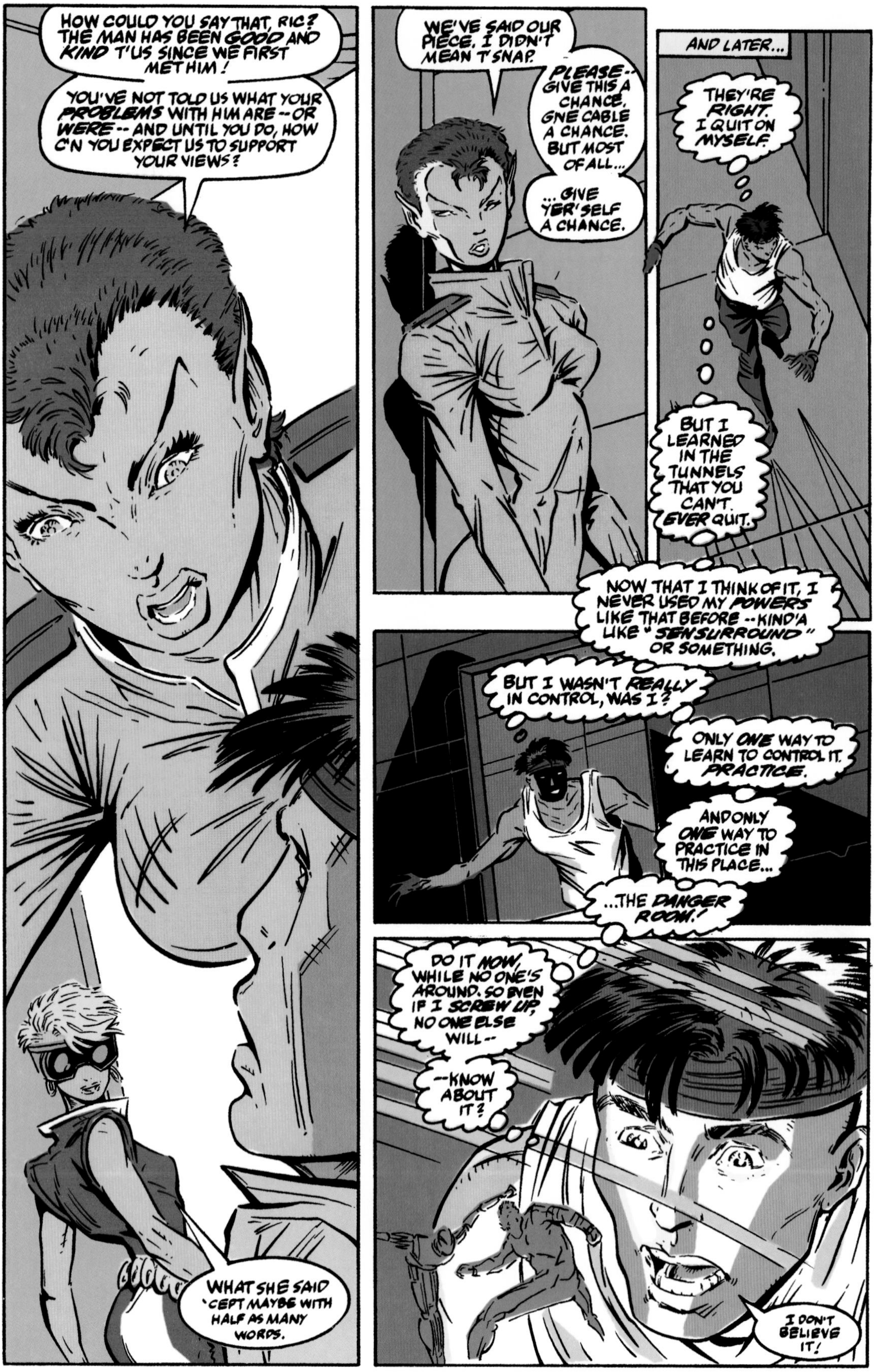
HOW COULD YOU SAY THAT, RIC? THE MAN HAS BEEN GOOD AND KIND T'US SINCE WE FIRST MET HIM!
YOU'VE NOT TOLD US WHAT YOUR PROBLEMS WITH HIM ARE -- OR WERE -- AND UNTIL YOU DO, HOW C'N YOU EXPECT US TO SUPPORT YOUR VIEWS?
WHAT SHE SAID 'CEPT MAYBE WITH HALF AS MANY WORDS.
WE'VE SAID OUR PIECE. I DIDN'T MEAN T'SNAP.
PLEASE -- GIVE THIS A CHANCE. GIVE CABLE A CHANCE. BUT MOST OF ALL...
...GIVE YER'SELF A CHANCE.
AND LATER...
THEY'RE RIGHT. I QUIT ON MYSELF.
BUT I LEARNED IN THE TUNNELS THAT YOU CAN'T EVER QUIT.
NOW THAT I THINK OF IT, I NEVER USED MY POWERS LIKE THAT BEFORE -- KIND'A LIKE "SENSURROUND" OR SOMETHING.
BUT I WASN'T REALLY IN CONTROL, WAS I?
ONLY ONE WAY TO LEARN TO CONTROL IT. PRACTICE.
AND ONLY ONE WAY TO PRACTICE IN THIS PLACE...
...THE DANGER ROOM!
DO IT NOW, WHILE NO ONE'S AROUND. SO EVEN IF I SCREW UP, NO ONE ELSE WILL --
--KNOW ABOUT IT?
I DON'T BELIEVE IT!

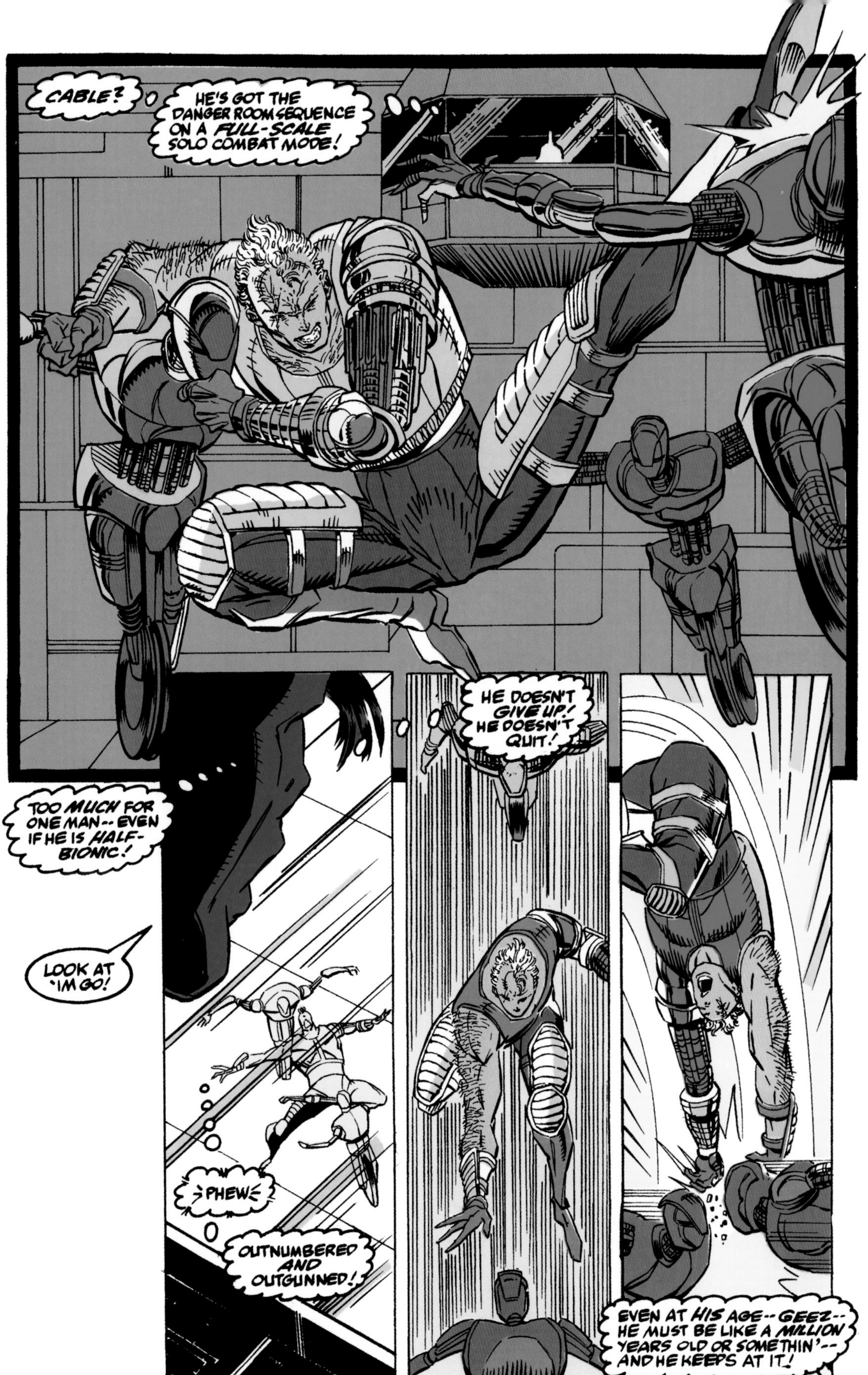

CABLE?
HE'S GOT THE DANGER ROOM SEQUENCE ON A FULL-SCALE SOLO COMBAT MODE!
TOO MUCH FOR ONE MAN-- EVEN IF HE IS HALF-BIONIC!
LOOK AT 'IM GO!
PHEW
OUTNUMBERED AND OUTGUNNED!
HE DOESN'T GIVE UP! HE DOESN'T QUIT!
EVEN AT HIS AGE-- GEEZ-- HE MUST BE LIKE A MILLION YEARS OLD OR SOMETHIN'-- AND HE KEEPS AT IT!

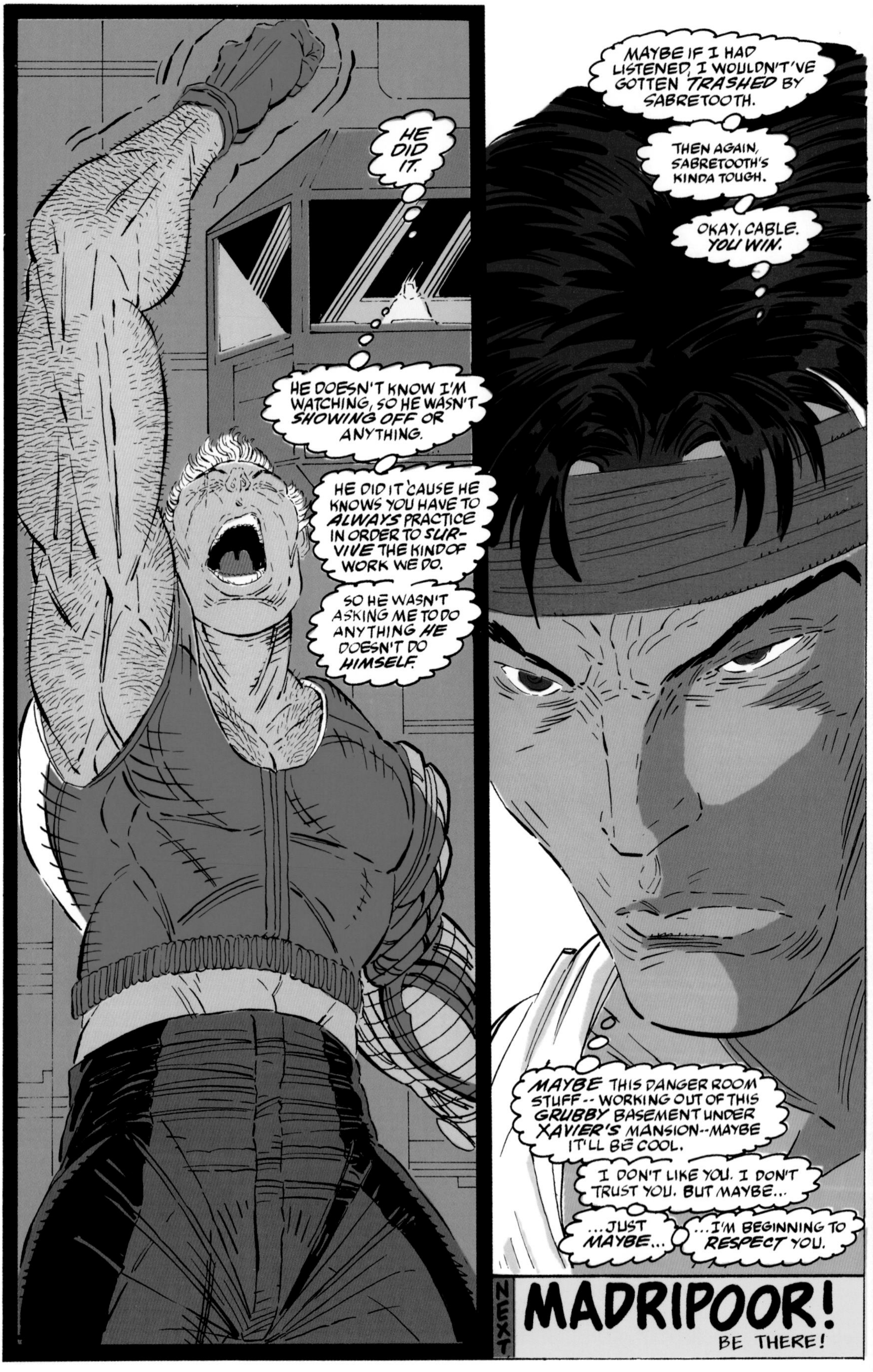
HE DID IT.
HE DOESN'T KNOW I'M WATCHING, SO HE WASN'T SHOWING OFF OR ANYTHING.
HE DID IT 'CAUSE HE KNOWS YOU HAVE TO ALWAYS PRACTICE IN ORDER TO SURVIVE THE KIND OF WORK WE DO.
SO HE WASN'T ASKING ME TO DO ANYTHING HE DOESN'T DO HIMSELF.
MAYBE IF I HAD LISTENED, I WOULDN'T'VE GOTTEN TRASHED BY SABRETOOTH.
THEN AGAIN, SABRETOOTH'S KINDA TOUGH.
OKAY, CABLE. YOU WIN.
MAYBE THIS DANGER ROOM STUFF-- WORKING OUT OF THIS GRUBBY BASEMENT UNDER XAVIER'S MANSION--MAYBE IT'LL BE COOL.
I DON'T LIKE YOU. I DON'T TRUST YOU. BUT MAYBE...
...JUST MAYBE...
...I'M BEGINNING TO RESPECT YOU.
NEXT
MADRIPOOR!
BE THERE!

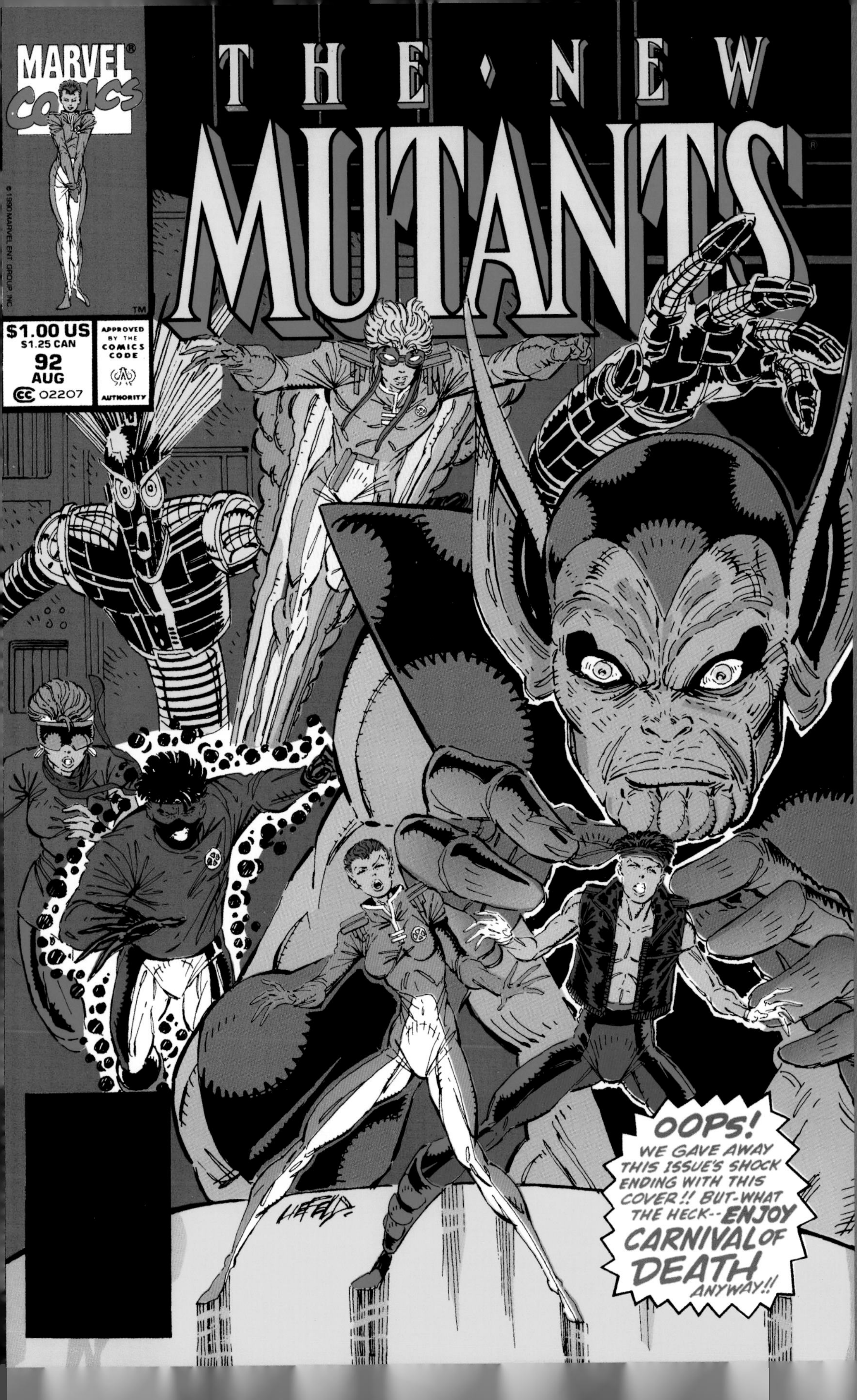
MARVEL COMICS
THE NEW MUTANTS
$1.00 US
$1.25 CAN
92
AUG
02207
APPROVED BY THE COMICS CODE AUTHORITY
© 1990 MARVEL ENT. GROUP, INC.
LIEFELD
OOPS!
WE GAVE AWAY THIS ISSUE'S SHOCK ENDING WITH THIS COVER!! BUT-WHAT THE HECK--ENJOY
CARNIVAL OF DEATH
ANYWAY!!

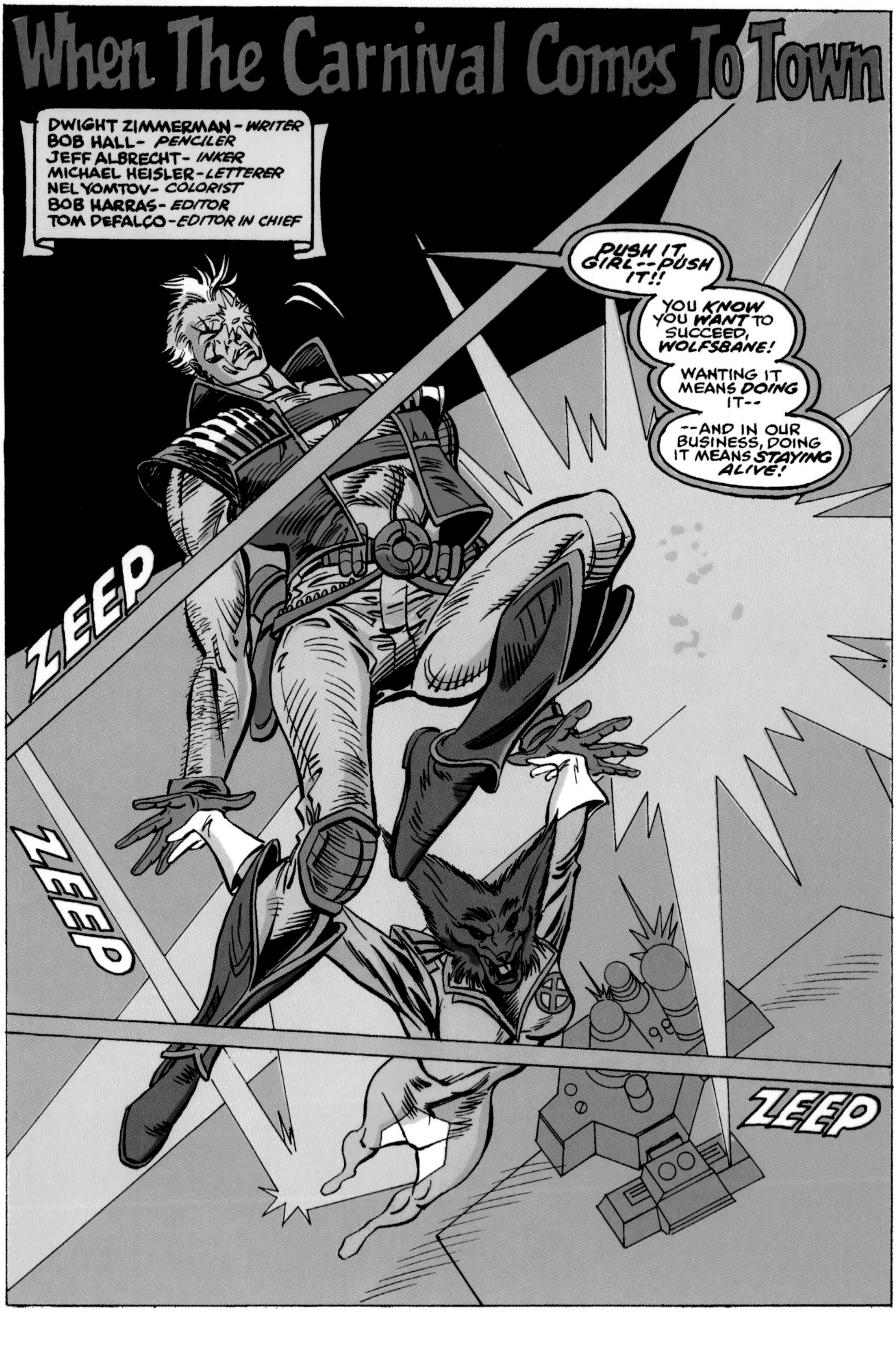

When The Carnival Comes To Town
DWIGHT ZIMMERMAN - WRITER
BOB HALL- PENCILER
JEFF ALBRECHT- INKER
MICHAEL HEISLER-LETTERER
NEL YOMTOV- COLORIST
BOB HARRAS- EDITOR
TOM DEFALCO-EDITOR IN CHIEF
PUSH IT, GIRL--PUSH IT!!
YOU KNOW YOU WANT TO SUCCEED, WOLFSBANE!
WANTING IT MEANS DOING IT--
--AND IN OUR BUSINESS, DOING IT MEANS STAYING ALIVE!
ZEEP
ZEEP
ZEEP

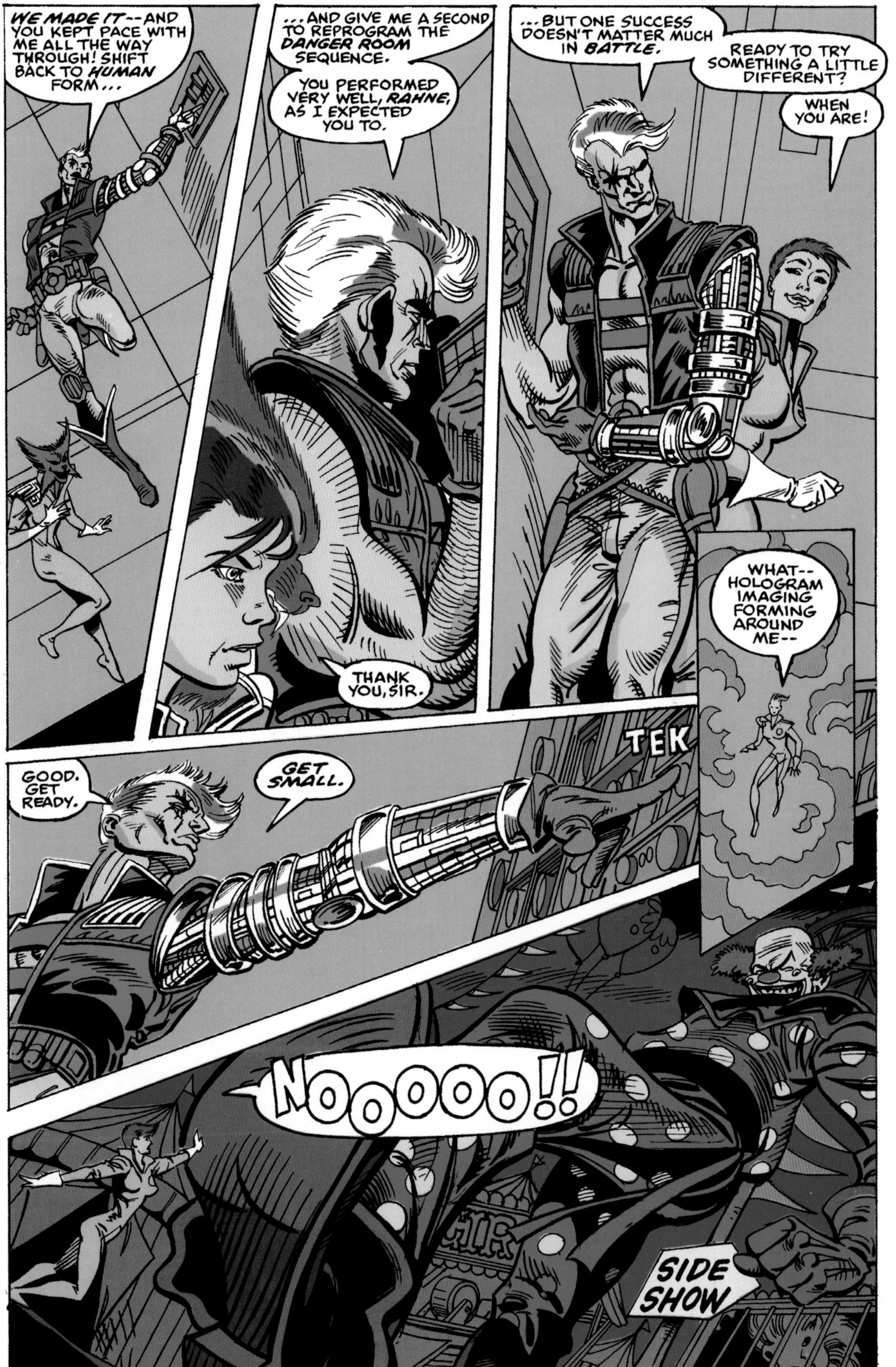
WE MADE IT--AND YOU KEPT PACE WITH ME ALL THE WAY THROUGH! SHIFT BACK TO HUMAN FORM...
...AND GIVE ME A SECOND TO REPROGRAM THE DANGER ROOM SEQUENCE.
YOU PERFORMED VERY WELL, RAHNE, AS I EXPECTED YOU TO.
THANK YOU, SIR.
...BUT ONE SUCCESS DOESN'T MATTER MUCH IN BATTLE.
READY TO TRY SOMETHING A LITTLE DIFFERENT?
WHEN YOU ARE!
GOOD. GET READY.
GET SMALL.
TEK
WHAT-- HOLOGRAM IMAGING FORMING AROUND ME--
NOOOOO!!
SIDE SHOW

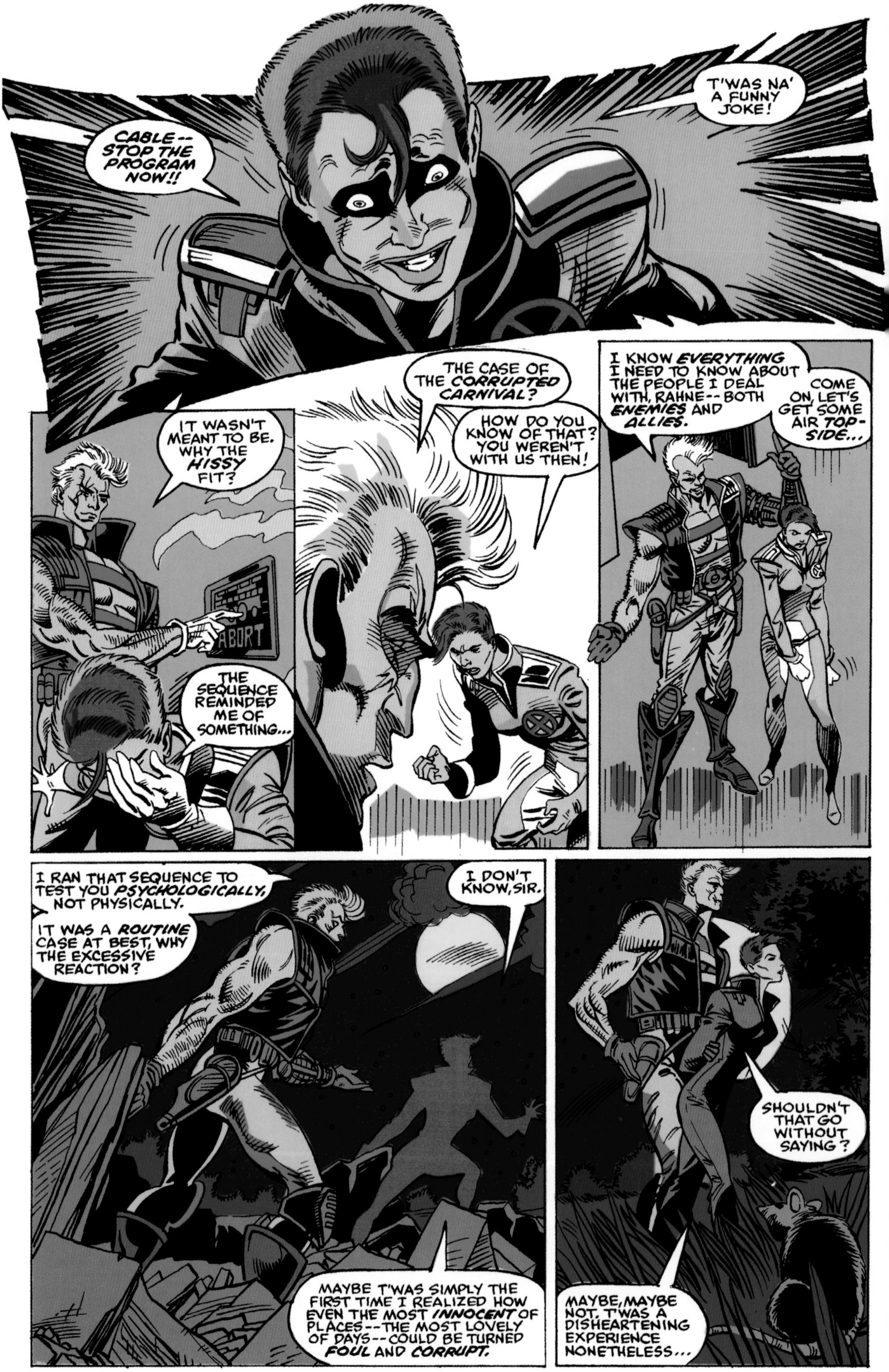
T'WAS NA' A FUNNY JOKE!
CABLE-- STOP THE PROGRAM NOW!!
IT WASN'T MEANT TO BE. WHY THE HISSY FIT?
ABORT
THE SEQUENCE REMINDED ME OF SOMETHING...
THE CASE OF THE CORRUPTED CARNIVAL?
HOW DO YOU KNOW OF THAT? YOU WEREN'T WITH US THEN!
I KNOW EVERYTHING I NEED TO KNOW ABOUT THE PEOPLE I DEAL WITH, RAHNE-- BOTH ENEMIES AND ALLIES.
COME ON, LET'S GET SOME AIR TOP-SIDE...
I RAN THAT SEQUENCE TO TEST YOU PSYCHOLOGICALLY, NOT PHYSICALLY.
IT WAS A ROUTINE CASE AT BEST, WHY THE EXCESSIVE REACTION?
I DON'T KNOW, SIR.
MAYBE T'WAS SIMPLY THE FIRST TIME I REALIZED HOW EVEN THE MOST INNOCENT OF PLACES--THE MOST LOVELY OF DAYS--COULD BE TURNED FOUL AND CORRUPT.
SHOULDN'T THAT GO WITHOUT SAYING?
MAYBE, MAYBE NOT. T'WAS A DISHEARTENING EXPERIENCE NONETHELESS...

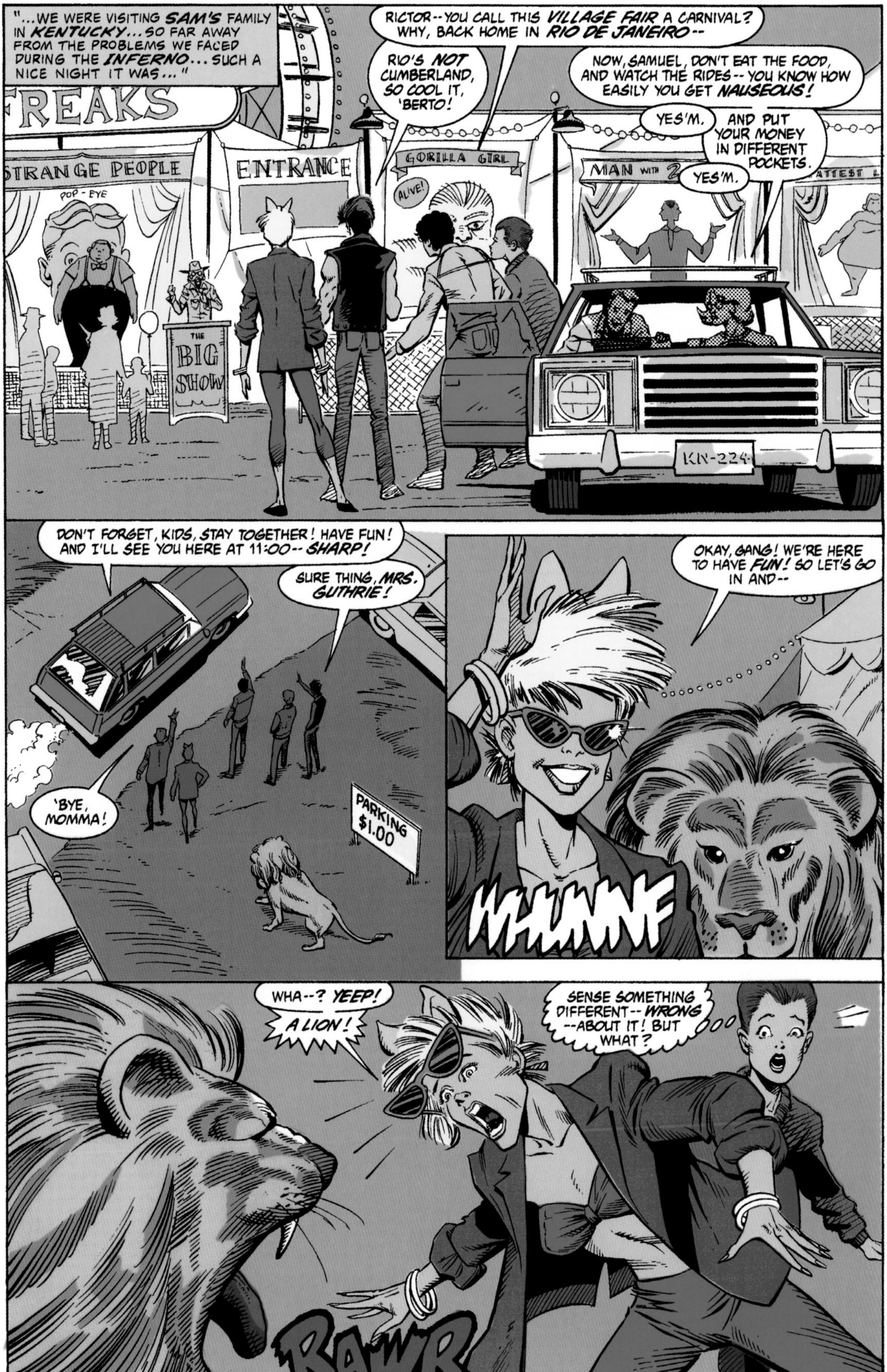
"...WE WERE VISITING SAM'S FAMILY IN KENTUCKY... SO FAR AWAY FROM THE PROBLEMS WE FACED DURING THE INFERNO... SUCH A NICE NIGHT IT WAS..."
FREAKS
STRANGE PEOPLE
ENTRANCE
RICTOR--YOU CALL THIS VILLAGE FAIR A CARNIVAL? WHY, BACK HOME IN RIO DE JANEIRO--
RIO'S NOT CUMBERLAND, SO COOL IT, 'BERTO!
NOW, SAMUEL, DON'T EAT THE FOOD, AND WATCH THE RIDES--YOU KNOW HOW EASILY YOU GET NAUSEOUS!
YES'M.
AND PUT YOUR MONEY IN DIFFERENT POCKETS.
YES'M.
GORILLA GIRL
ALIVE!
POP-EYE
THE BIG SHOW
MAN WITH 2
KN-224
DON'T FORGET, KIDS, STAY TOGETHER! HAVE FUN! AND I'LL SEE YOU HERE AT 11:00--SHARP!
SURE THING, MRS. GUTHRIE!
'BYE, MOMMA!
PARKING $1.00
OKAY, GANG! WE'RE HERE TO HAVE FUN! SO LET'S GO IN AND--
WHUNNF
WHA--? YEEP! A LION!
SENSE SOMETHING DIFFERENT--WRONG--ABOUT IT! BUT WHAT?
RAWR

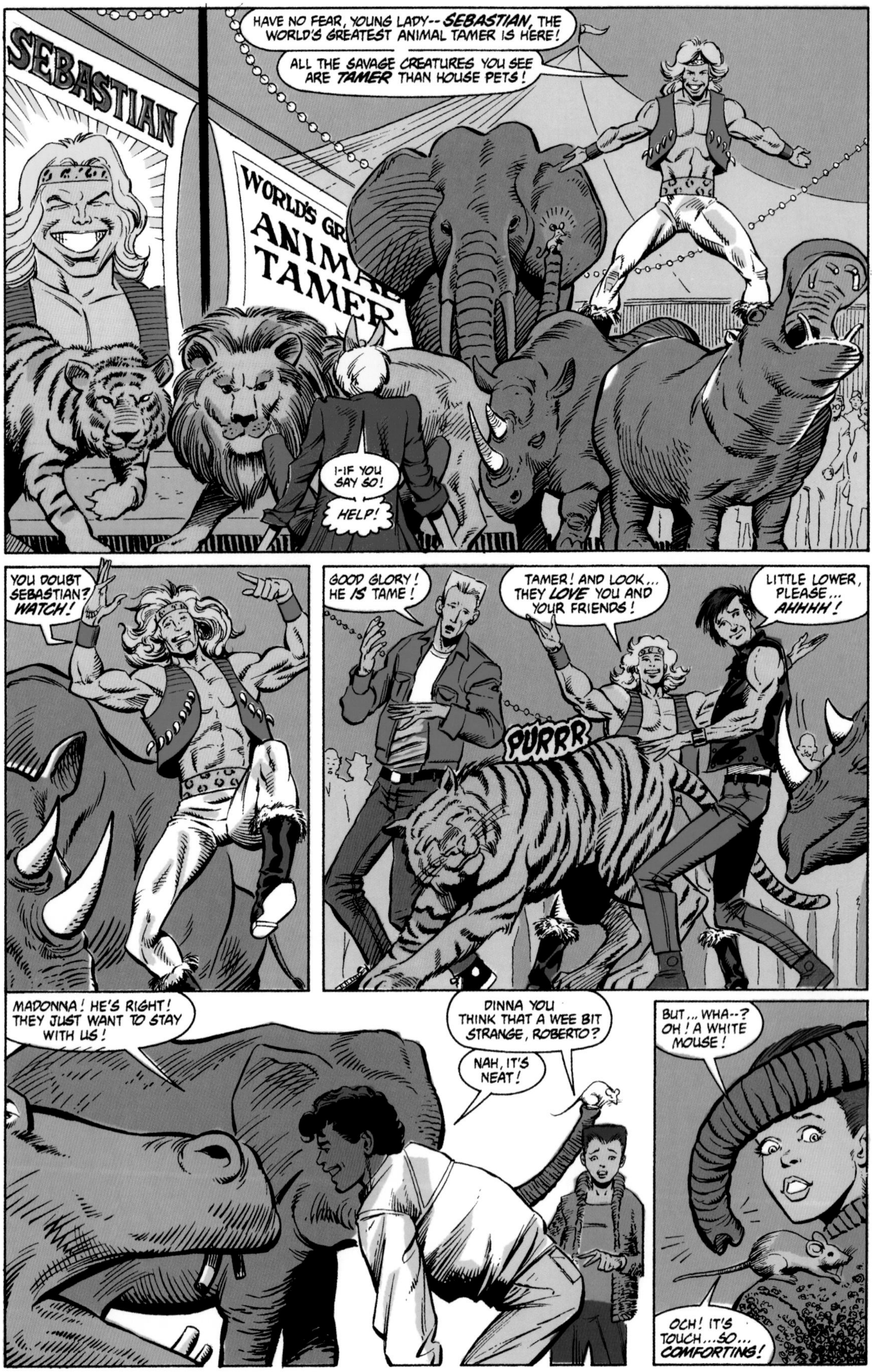
SEBASTIAN
WORLD'S GR
ANIMA
TAMER
HAVE NO FEAR, YOUNG LADY-- SEBASTIAN, THE WORLD'S GREATEST ANIMAL TAMER IS HERE!
ALL THE SAVAGE CREATURES YOU SEE ARE TAMER THAN HOUSE PETS!
I-IF YOU SAY SO!
HELP!
YOU DOUBT SEBASTIAN? WATCH!
GOOD GLORY! HE IS TAME!
TAMER! AND LOOK... THEY LOVE YOU AND YOUR FRIENDS!
LITTLE LOWER, PLEASE... AHHHH!
PURRR
MADONNA! HE'S RIGHT! THEY JUST WANT TO STAY WITH US!
DINNA YOU THINK THAT A WEE BIT STRANGE, ROBERTO?
NAH, IT'S NEAT!
BUT... WHA--? OH! A WHITE MOUSE!
OCH! IT'S TOUCH... SO... COMFORTING!

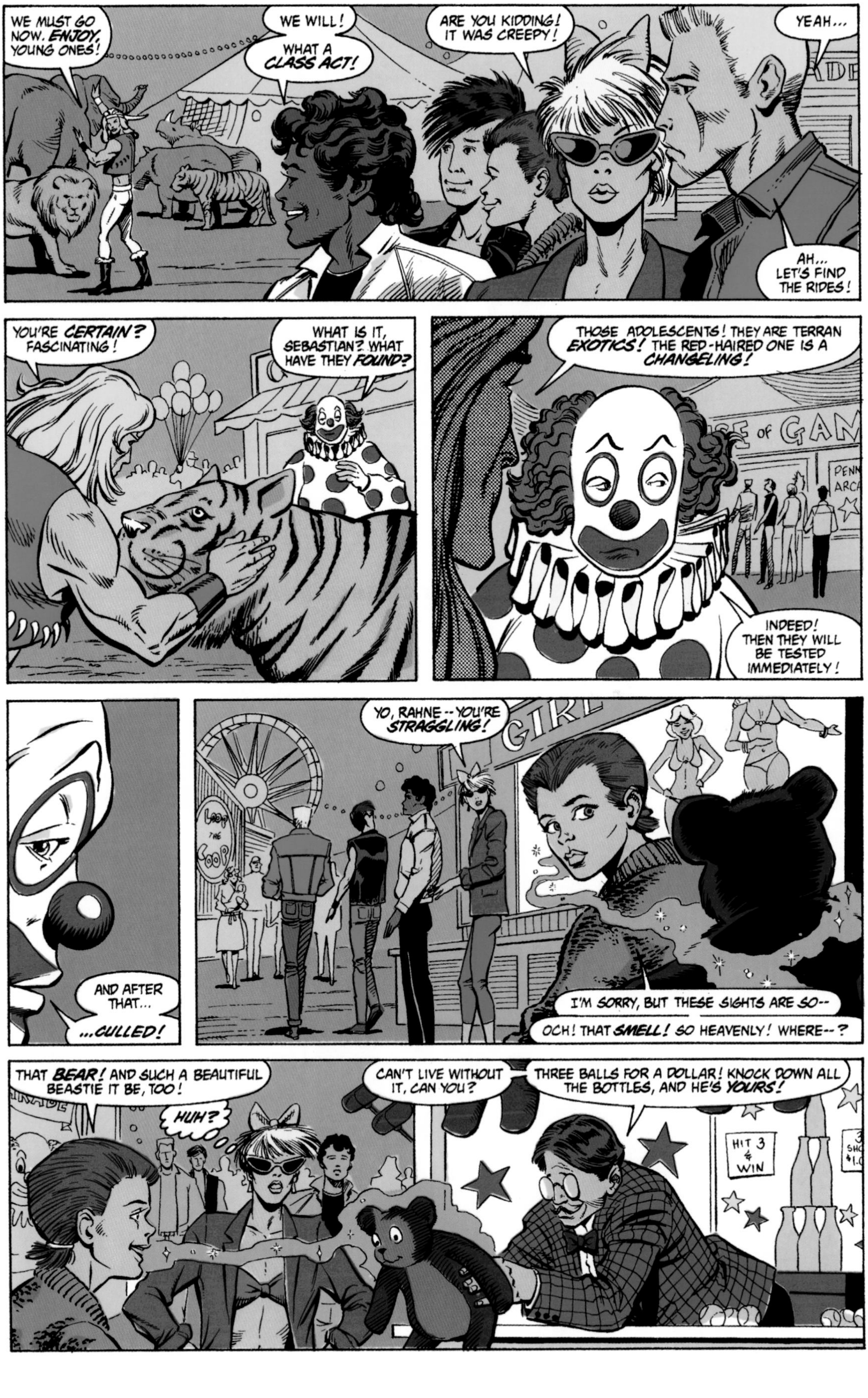
WE MUST GO NOW. ENJOY, YOUNG ONES!
WE WILL!
WHAT A CLASS ACT!
ARE YOU KIDDING! IT WAS CREEPY!
YEAH...
AH... LET'S FIND THE RIDES!
YOU'RE CERTAIN? FASCINATING!
WHAT IS IT, SEBASTIAN? WHAT HAVE THEY FOUND?
THOSE ADOLESCENTS! THEY ARE TERRAN EXOTICS! THE RED-HAIRED ONE IS A CHANGELING!
INDEED! THEN THEY WILL BE TESTED IMMEDIATELY!
AND AFTER THAT...
...CULLED!
YO, RAHNE -- YOU'RE STRAGGLING!
I'M SORRY, BUT THESE SIGHTS ARE SO--
OCH! THAT SMELL! SO HEAVENLY! WHERE--?
THAT BEAR! AND SUCH A BEAUTIFUL BEASTIE IT BE, TOO!
HUH?
CAN'T LIVE WITHOUT IT, CAN YOU?
THREE BALLS FOR A DOLLAR! KNOCK DOWN ALL THE BOTTLES, AND HE'S YOURS!
HIT 3 & WIN

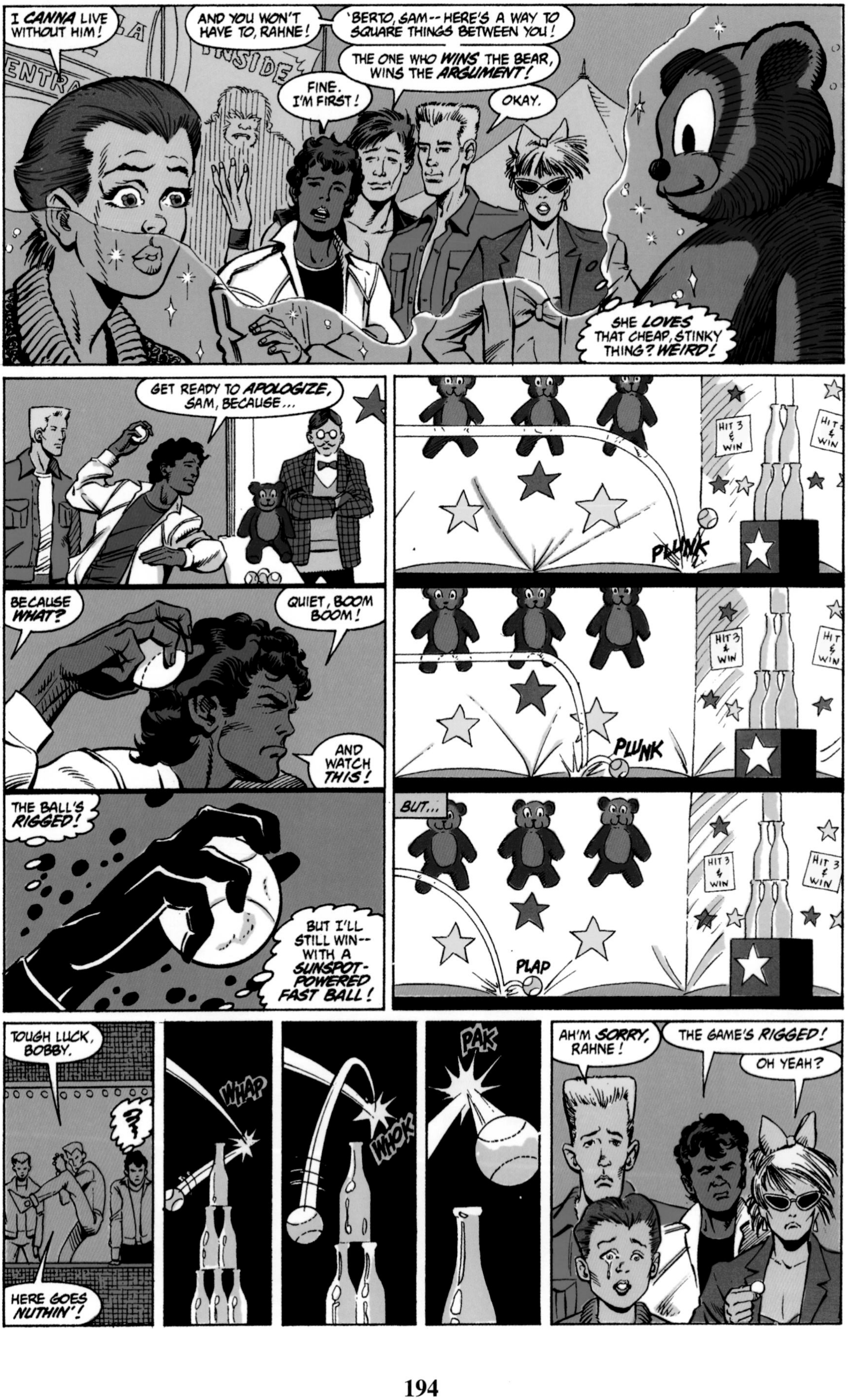

I CANNA LIVE WITHOUT HIM!
AND YOU WON'T HAVE TO, RAHNE!
'BERTO, SAM-- HERE'S A WAY TO SQUARE THINGS BETWEEN YOU!
THE ONE WHO WINS THE BEAR, WINS THE ARGUMENT!
FINE. I'M FIRST!
OKAY.
SHE LOVES THAT CHEAP, STINKY THING? WEIRD!
GET READY TO APOLOGIZE, SAM, BECAUSE...
BECAUSE WHAT?
QUIET, BOOM BOOM!
AND WATCH THIS!
THE BALL'S RIGGED!
BUT I'LL STILL WIN-- WITH A SUNSPOT-POWERED FAST BALL!
HIT 3 & WIN
PLUNK
PLUNK
BUT...
PLAP
TOUGH LUCK, BOBBY.
HERE GOES NUTHIN'!
WHAP
WHOK
PAK
AH'M SORRY, RAHNE!
THE GAME'S RIGGED!
OH YEAH?

GIMME THAT BALL!

IT'S YOUR DOLLAR, MISSY!

YEAH...

...AN' IT JUST BOUGHT ME A BEAR!

PROVIDED YOU DON'T SEE MY LI'L BOOM BOOM!

...3...

...2...

WHOK

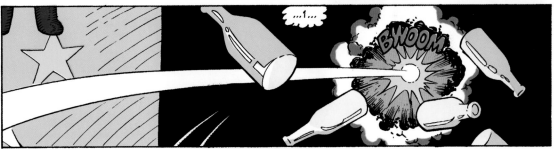

...1...

BWOOM

STEERIKE!

AND WE HAVE A WINNAH!

ENJOY YOUR PRIZE, LITTLE LADY!

OH, THANK' YOU, BOOM BOOM!

THOSE EXOTICS COULD BE DANGEROUS, HORIO. LOOK AT WHAT THE BLOND FEMALE DID TO THE ANALYSIS BALL!

SO? THAT MERELY SEALED THEIR FATE -- AND DOUBLED THEIR VALUE!

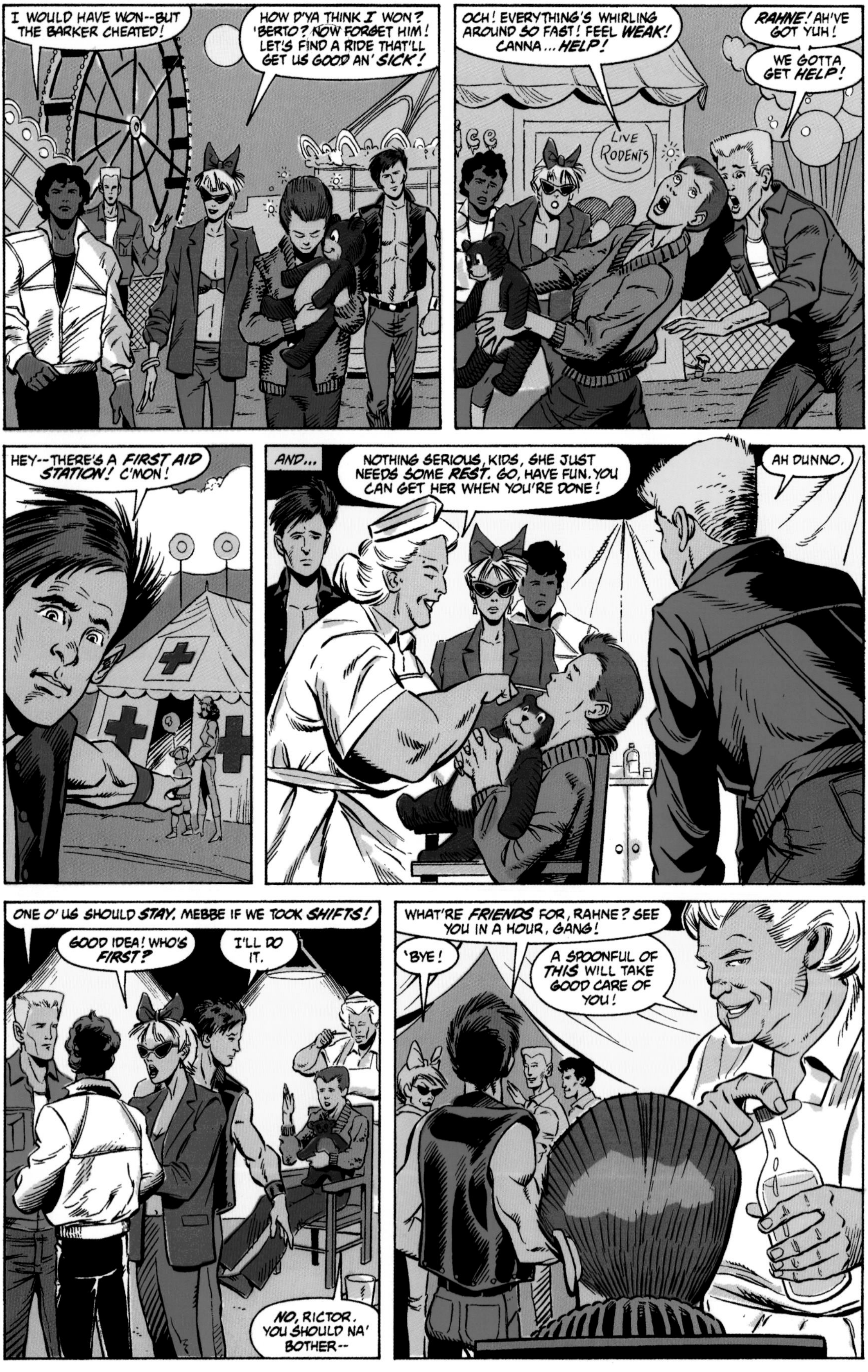
I WOULD HAVE WON--BUT THE BARKER CHEATED!
HOW D'YA THINK I WON? 'BERTO? NOW FORGET HIM! LET'S FIND A RIDE THAT'LL GET US GOOD AN' SICK!
OCH! EVERYTHING'S WHIRLING AROUND SO FAST! FEEL WEAK! CANNA... HELP!
RAHNE! AH'VE GOT YUH!
WE GOTTA GET HELP!
LIVE RODENTS
HEY--THERE'S A FIRST AID STATION! C'MON!
AND...
NOTHING SERIOUS, KIDS, SHE JUST NEEDS SOME REST. GO, HAVE FUN. YOU CAN GET HER WHEN YOU'RE DONE!
AH DUNNO.
ONE O' US SHOULD STAY. MEBBE IF WE TOOK SHIFTS!
GOOD IDEA! WHO'S FIRST?
I'LL DO IT.
NO, RICTOR. YOU SHOULD NA' BOTHER--
WHAT'RE FRIENDS FOR, RAHNE? SEE YOU IN A HOUR, GANG!
'BYE!
A SPOONFUL OF THIS WILL TAKE GOOD CARE OF YOU!

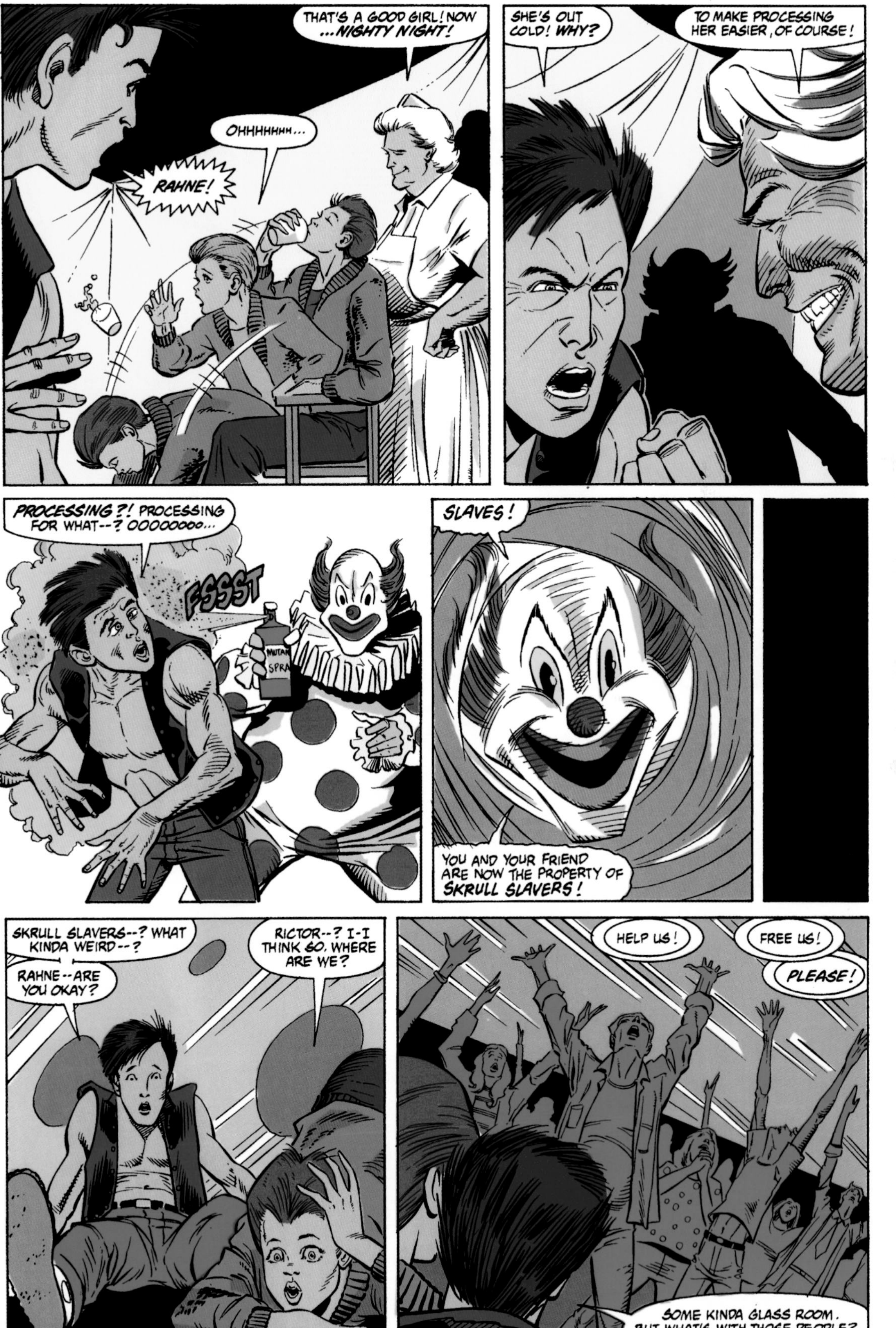
THAT'S A GOOD GIRL! NOW ...NIGHTY NIGHT!
OHHHHHHH...
RAHNE!
SHE'S OUT COLD! WHY?
TO MAKE PROCESSING HER EASIER, OF COURSE!
PROCESSING?! PROCESSING FOR WHAT--? OOOOOOOO...
FSSST
SLAVES!
YOU AND YOUR FRIEND ARE NOW THE PROPERTY OF SKRULL SLAVERS!
SKRULL SLAVERS--? WHAT KINDA WEIRD--?
RAHNE--ARE YOU OKAY?
RICTOR--? I-I THINK SO. WHERE ARE WE?
HELP US!
FREE US!
PLEASE!
SOME KINDA GLASS ROOM. BUT WHAT'S WITH THOSE PEOPLE? WHY'RE THEY--

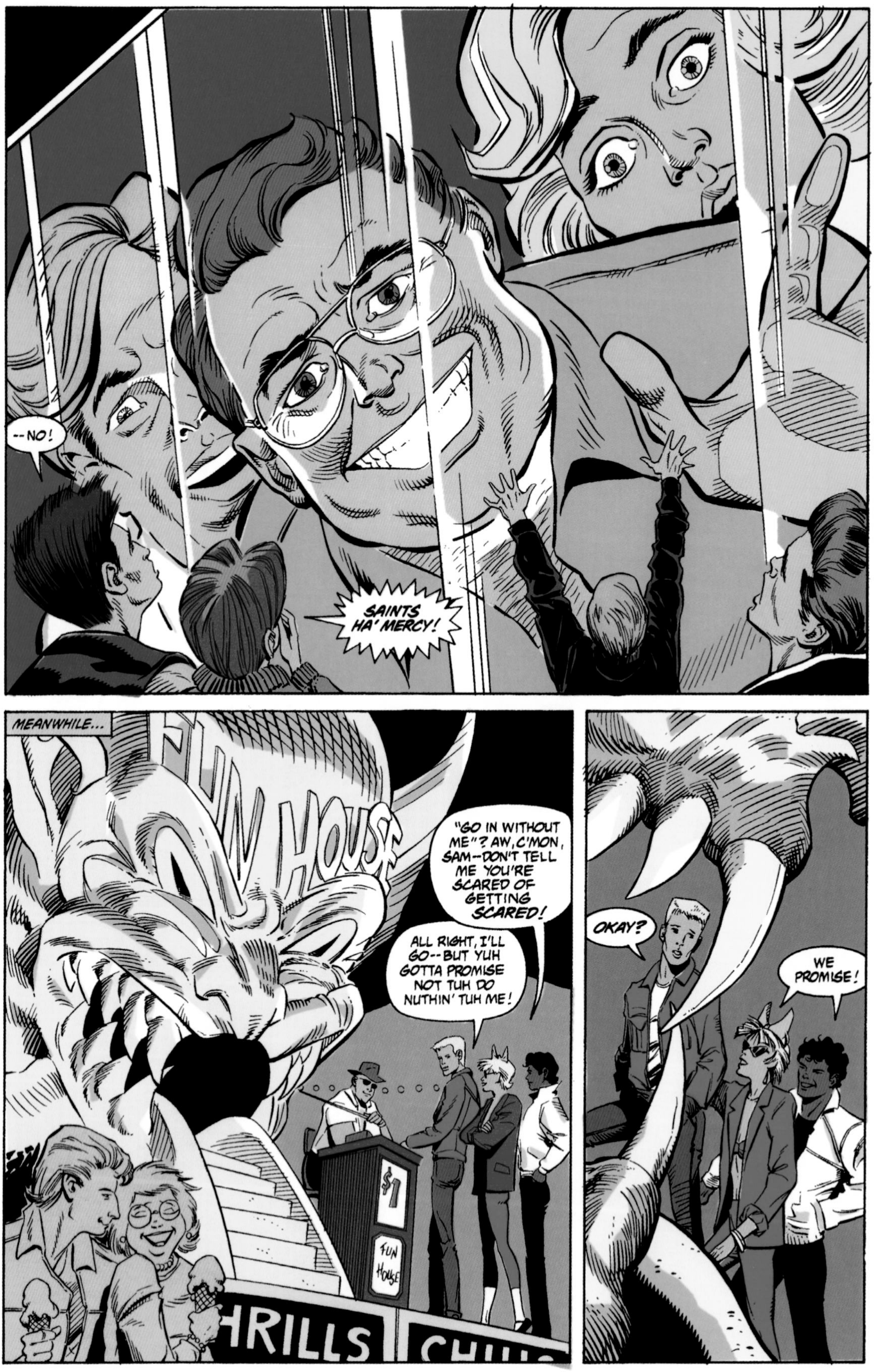
--NO!
SAINTS HA' MERCY!
MEANWHILE...
FUN HOUSE
"GO IN WITHOUT ME"? AW, C'MON, SAM--DON'T TELL ME YOU'RE SCARED OF GETTING SCARED!
ALL RIGHT, I'LL GO--BUT YUH GOTTA PROMISE NOT TUH DO NUTHIN' TUH ME!
$1
FUN HOUSE
HRILLS
OKAY?
WE PROMISE!

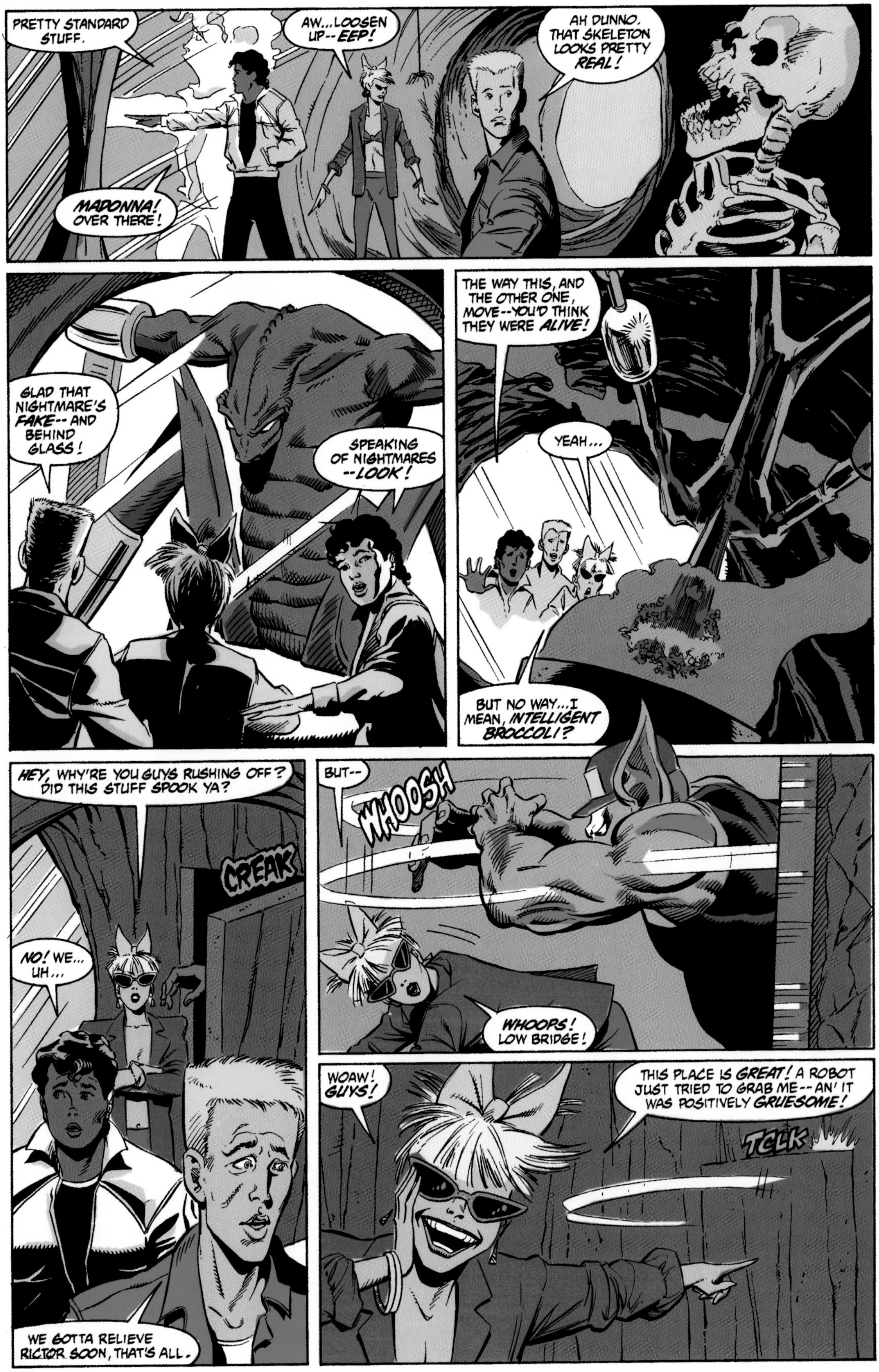
PRETTY STANDARD STUFF.
AW...LOOSEN UP--EEP!
AH DUNNO. THAT SKELETON LOOKS PRETTY REAL!
MADONNA! OVER THERE!
GLAD THAT NIGHTMARE'S FAKE-- AND BEHIND GLASS!
SPEAKING OF NIGHTMARES --LOOK!
THE WAY THIS, AND THE OTHER ONE, MOVE--YOU'D THINK THEY WERE ALIVE!
YEAH...
BUT NO WAY...I MEAN, INTELLIGENT BROCCOLI?
HEY, WHY'RE YOU GUYS RUSHING OFF? DID THIS STUFF SPOOK YA?
CREAK
NO! WE... UH...
WE GOTTA RELIEVE RICTOR SOON, THAT'S ALL.
BUT--
WHOOSH
WHOOPS! LOW BRIDGE!
WOAW! GUYS!
THIS PLACE IS GREAT! A ROBOT JUST TRIED TO GRAB ME--AN' IT WAS POSITIVELY GRUESOME!
TCLK

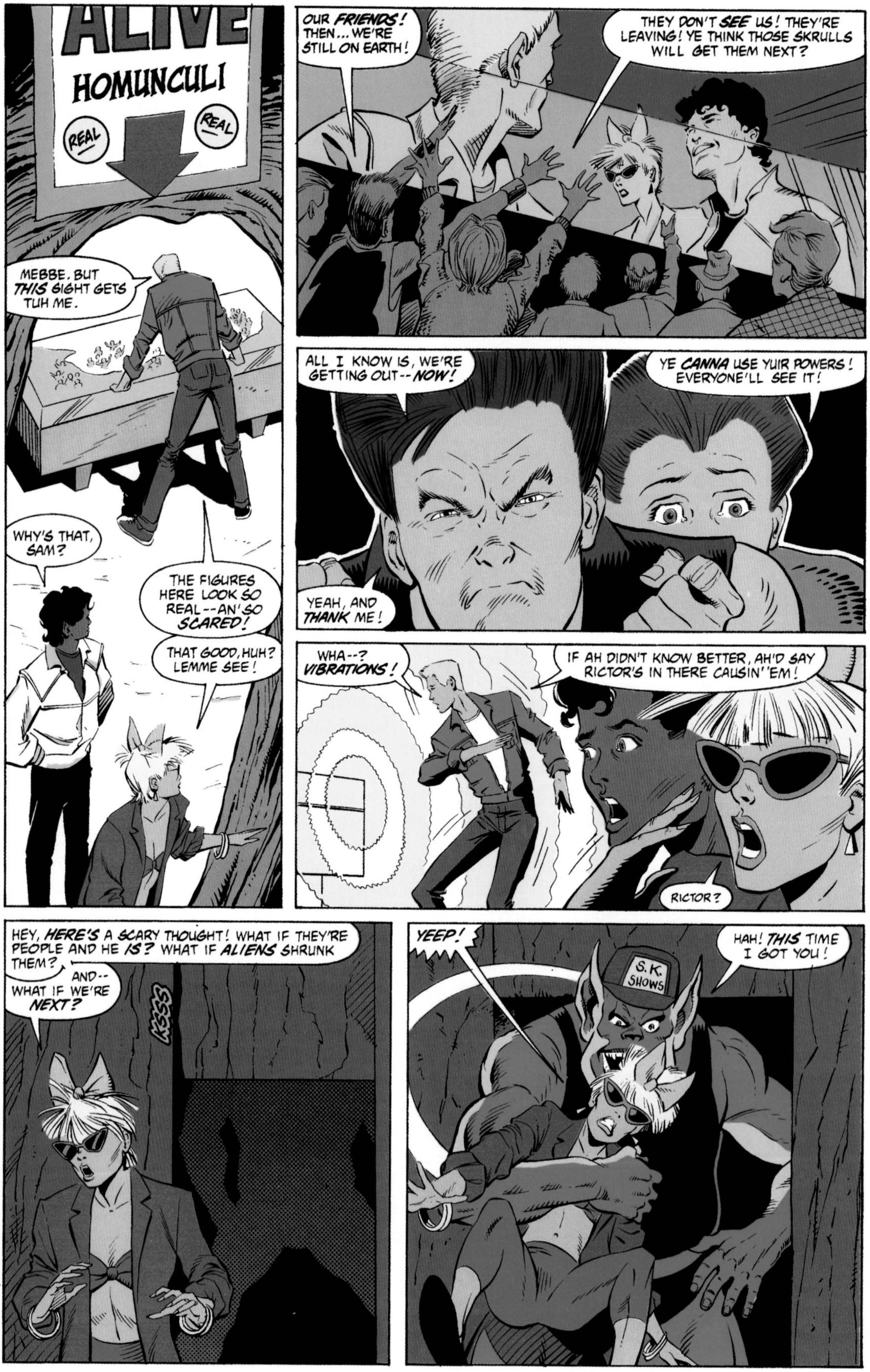
ALIVE
HOMUNCULI
REAL
REAL
MEBBE. BUT THIS SIGHT GETS TUH ME.
WHY'S THAT, SAM?
THE FIGURES HERE LOOK SO REAL--AN' SO SCARED!
THAT GOOD, HUH? LEMME SEE!
OUR FRIENDS! THEN... WE'RE STILL ON EARTH!
THEY DON'T SEE US! THEY'RE LEAVING! YE THINK THOSE SKRULLS WILL GET THEM NEXT?
ALL I KNOW IS, WE'RE GETTING OUT--NOW!
YE CANNA USE YUIR POWERS! EVERYONE'LL SEE IT!
YEAH, AND THANK ME!
WHA--? VIBRATIONS!
IF AH DIDN'T KNOW BETTER, AH'D SAY RICTOR'S IN THERE CAUSIN' 'EM!
RICTOR?
HEY, HERE'S A SCARY THOUGHT! WHAT IF THEY'RE PEOPLE AND HE IS? WHAT IF ALIENS SHRUNK THEM?
AND--WHAT IF WE'RE NEXT?
KSSS
YEEP!
HAH! THIS TIME I GOT YOU!
S.K. SHOWS

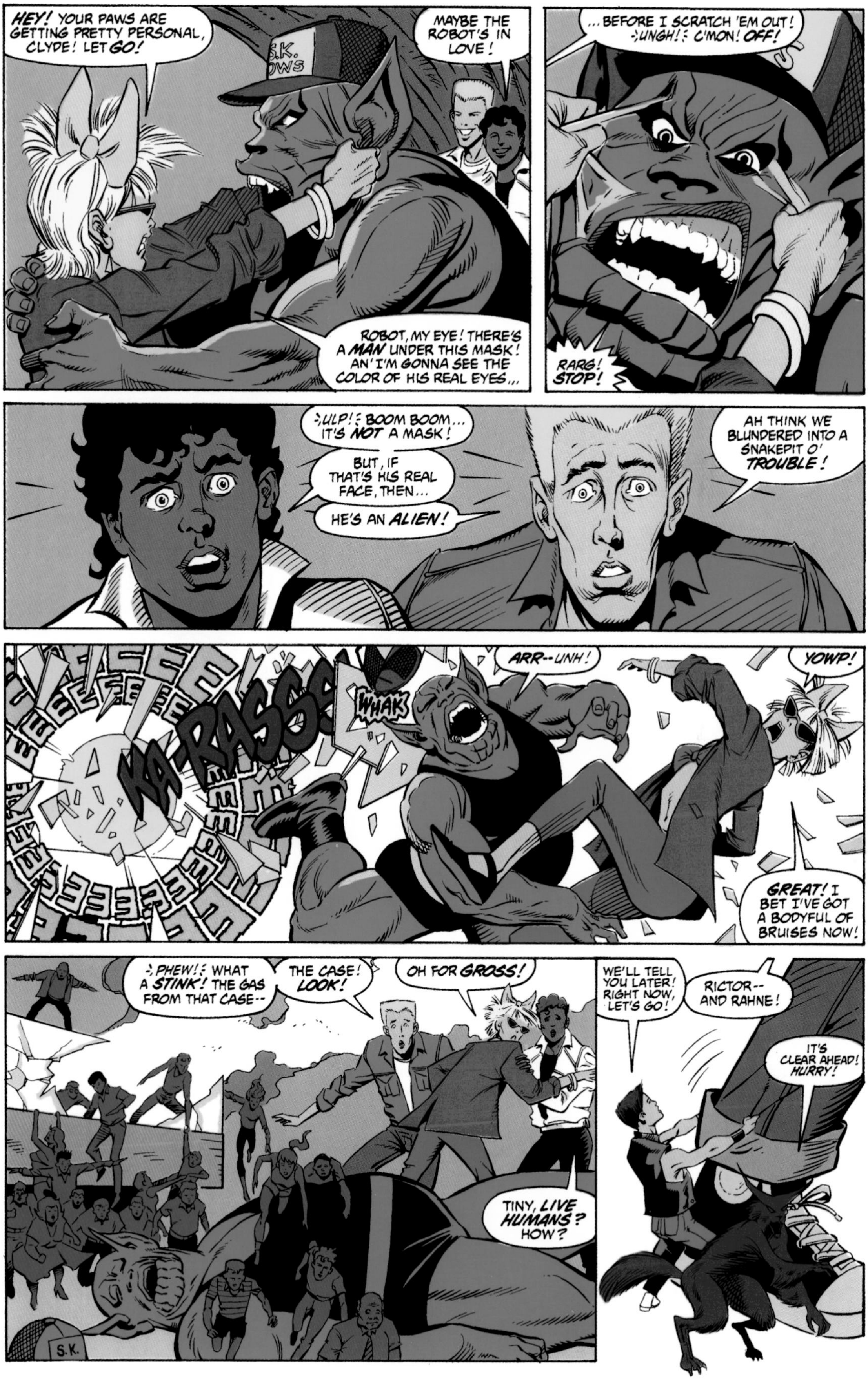
HEY! YOUR PAWS ARE GETTING PRETTY PERSONAL, CLYDE! LET GO!
MAYBE THE ROBOT'S IN LOVE!
ROBOT, MY EYE! THERE'S A MAN UNDER THIS MASK! AN' I'M GONNA SEE THE COLOR OF HIS REAL EYES...
...BEFORE I SCRATCH 'EM OUT! UNGH! C'MON! OFF!
RARG! STOP!
ULP! BOOM BOOM... IT'S NOT A MASK!
BUT, IF THAT'S HIS REAL FACE, THEN...
HE'S AN ALIEN!
AH THINK WE BLUNDERED INTO A SNAKEPIT O' TROUBLE!
KA-RASSS
WHAK
ARR--UNH!
YOWP!
GREAT! I BET I'VE GOT A BODYFUL OF BRUISES NOW!
PHEW! WHAT A STINK! THE GAS FROM THAT CASE--
THE CASE! LOOK!
OH FOR GROSS!
TINY, LIVE HUMANS? HOW?
WE'LL TELL YOU LATER! RIGHT NOW, LET'S GO!
RICTOR-- AND RAHNE!
IT'S CLEAR AHEAD! HURRY!

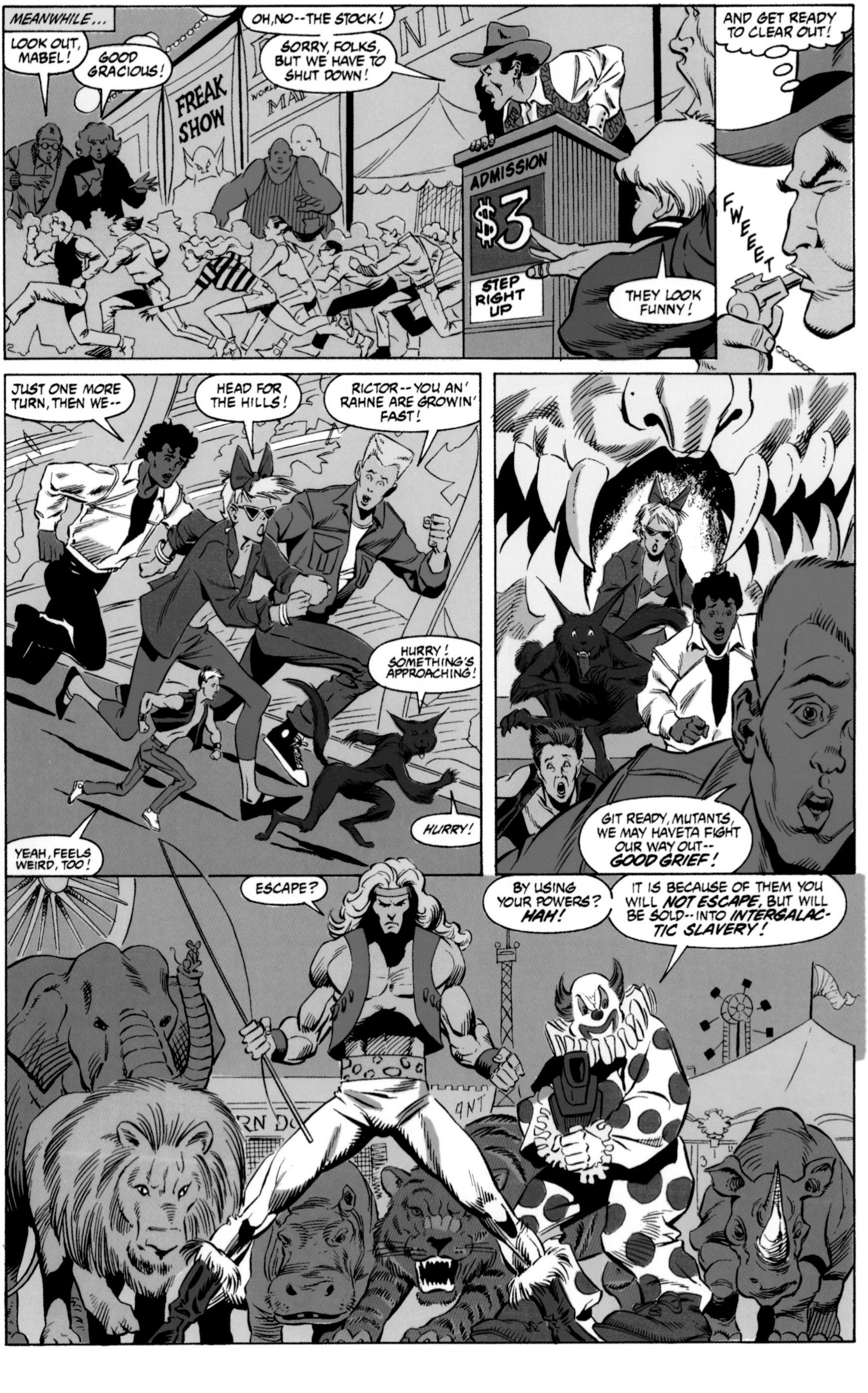
MEANWHILE...
LOOK OUT, MABEL!
GOOD GRACIOUS!
OH, NO--THE STOCK!
SORRY, FOLKS, BUT WE HAVE TO SHUT DOWN!
FREAK SHOW
ADMISSION
$3
STEP RIGHT UP
THEY LOOK FUNNY!
AND GET READY TO CLEAR OUT!
FWEEET
JUST ONE MORE TURN, THEN WE--
HEAD FOR THE HILLS!
RICTOR--YOU AN' RAHNE ARE GROWIN' FAST!
HURRY! SOMETHING'S APPROACHING!
HURRY!
YEAH, FEELS WEIRD, TOO!
GIT READY, MUTANTS, WE MAY HAVETA FIGHT OUR WAY OUT-- GOOD GRIEF!
ESCAPE?
BY USING YOUR POWERS? HAH!
IT IS BECAUSE OF THEM YOU WILL NOT ESCAPE, BUT WILL BE SOLD--INTO INTERGALACTIC SLAVERY!

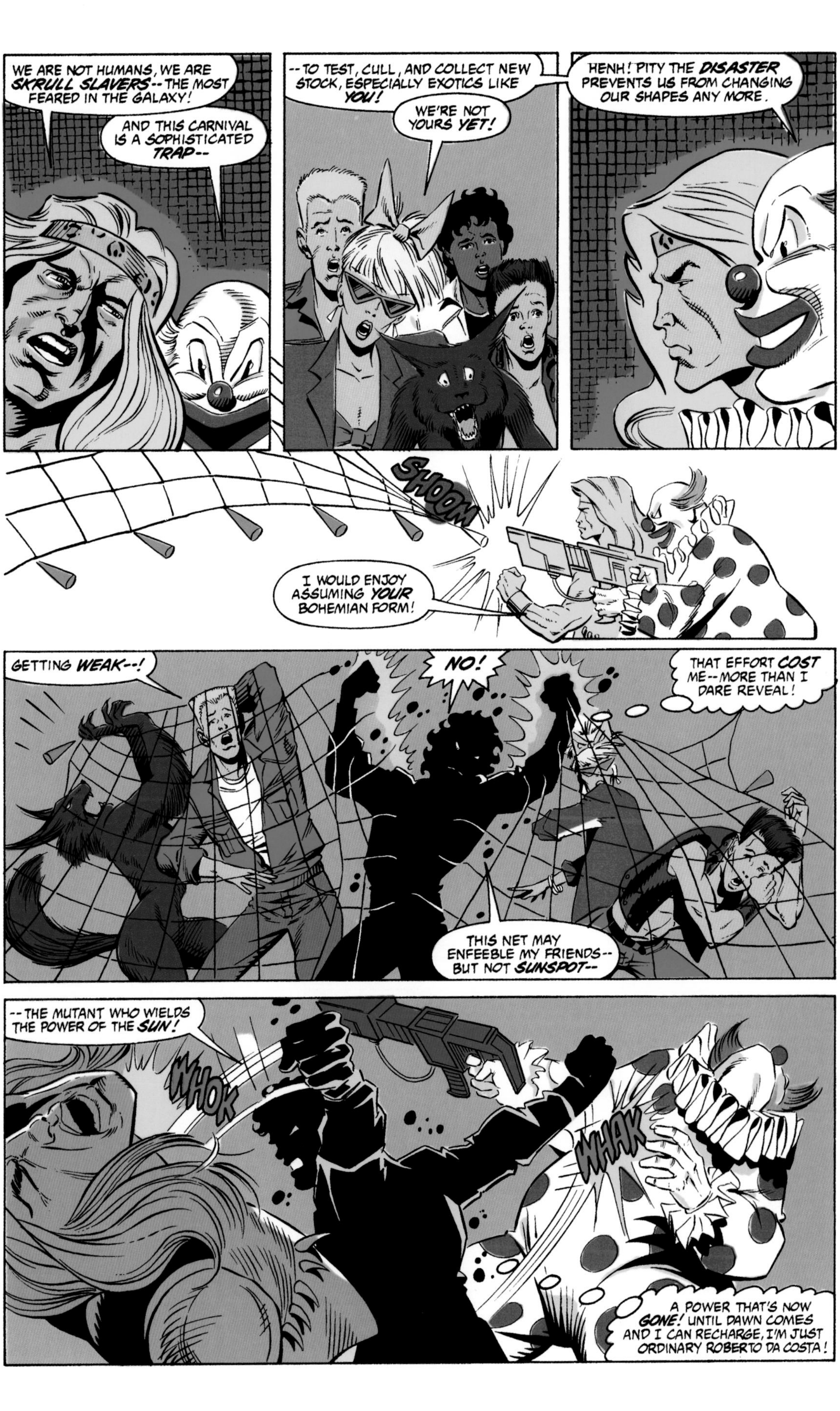
WE ARE NOT HUMANS, WE ARE SKRULL SLAVERS--THE MOST FEARED IN THE GALAXY!
AND THIS CARNIVAL IS A SOPHISTICATED TRAP--
--TO TEST, CULL, AND COLLECT NEW STOCK, ESPECIALLY EXOTICS LIKE YOU!
WE'RE NOT YOURS YET!
HENH! PITY THE DISASTER PREVENTS US FROM CHANGING OUR SHAPES ANY MORE.
SHOOOM
I WOULD ENJOY ASSUMING YOUR BOHEMIAN FORM!
GETTING WEAK--!
NO!
THAT EFFORT COST ME--MORE THAN I DARE REVEAL!
THIS NET MAY ENFEEBLE MY FRIENDS--BUT NOT SUNSPOT--
--THE MUTANT WHO WIELDS THE POWER OF THE SUN!
WHOK
WHAK
A POWER THAT'S NOW GONE! UNTIL DAWN COMES AND I CAN RECHARGE, I'M JUST ORDINARY ROBERTO DA COSTA!

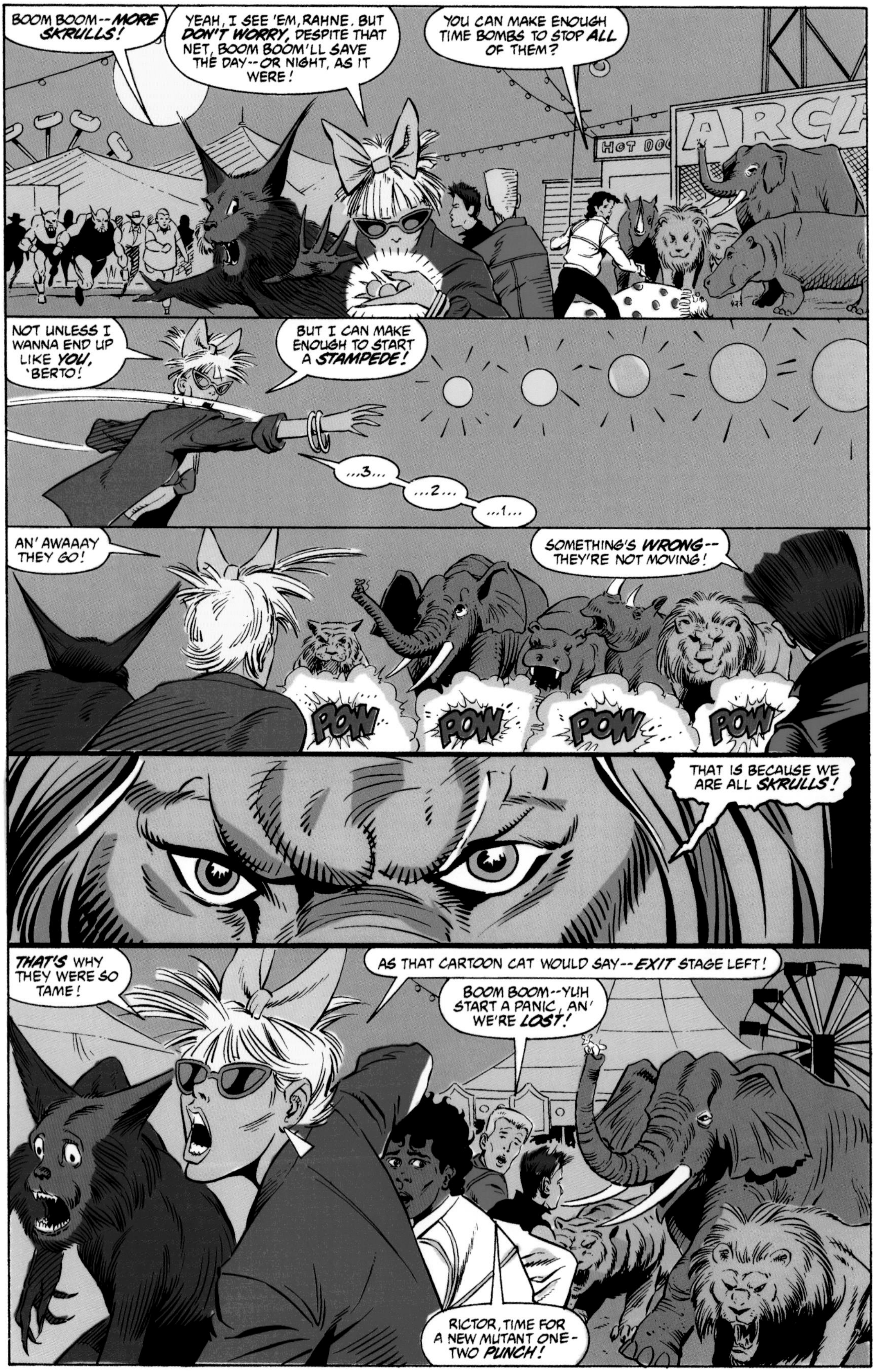
BOOM BOOM--MORE SKRULLS!
YEAH, I SEE 'EM, RAHNE. BUT DON'T WORRY, DESPITE THAT NET, BOOM BOOM'LL SAVE THE DAY--OR NIGHT, AS IT WERE!
YOU CAN MAKE ENOUGH TIME BOMBS TO STOP ALL OF THEM?
HOT DOG
ARCA
NOT UNLESS I WANNA END UP LIKE YOU, 'BERTO!
BUT I CAN MAKE ENOUGH TO START A STAMPEDE!
...3...
...2...
...1...
AN' AWAAAY THEY GO!
SOMETHING'S WRONG-- THEY'RE NOT MOVING!
POW
POW
POW
POW
THAT IS BECAUSE WE ARE ALL SKRULLS!
THAT'S WHY THEY WERE SO TAME!
AS THAT CARTOON CAT WOULD SAY--EXIT STAGE LEFT!
BOOM BOOM--YUH START A PANIC, AN' WE'RE LOST!
RICTOR, TIME FOR A NEW MUTANT ONE-TWO PUNCH!

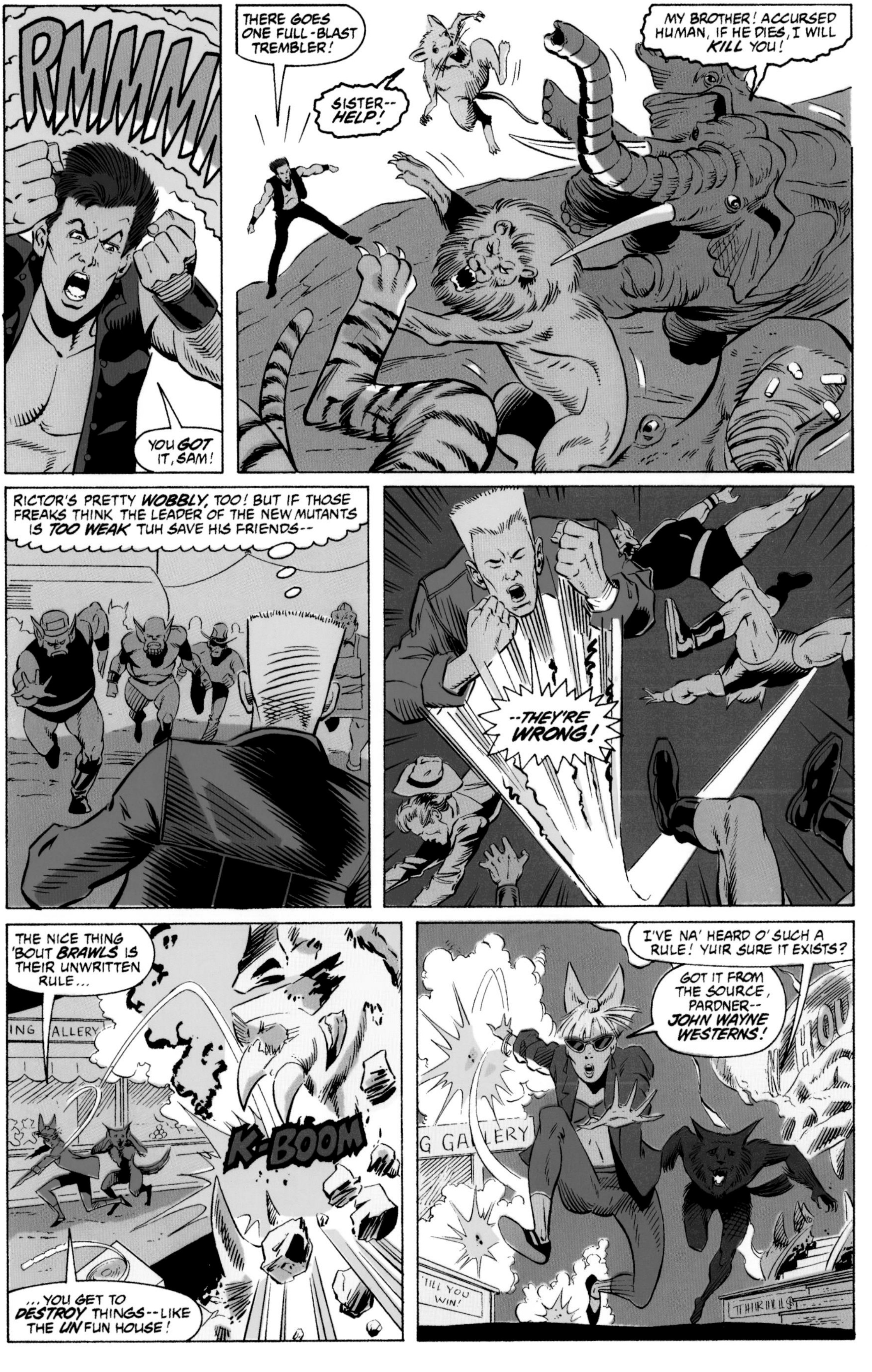
RMMMM
YOU GOT IT, SAM!
THERE GOES ONE FULL-BLAST TREMBLER!
SISTER-- HELP!
MY BROTHER! ACCURSED HUMAN, IF HE DIES, I WILL KILL YOU!
RICTOR'S PRETTY WOBBLY, TOO! BUT IF THOSE FREAKS THINK THE LEADER OF THE NEW MUTANTS IS TOO WEAK TUH SAVE HIS FRIENDS--
--THEY'RE WRONG!
THE NICE THING 'BOUT BRAWLS IS THEIR UNWRITTEN RULE...
ING GALLERY
K-BOOM
...YOU GET TO DESTROY THINGS--LIKE THE UNFUN HOUSE!
I'VE NA' HEARD O' SUCH A RULE! YUIR SURE IT EXISTS?
GOT IT FROM THE SOURCE, PARDNER-- JOHN WAYNE WESTERNS!
G GALLERY
TILL YOU WIN!
THRILLS

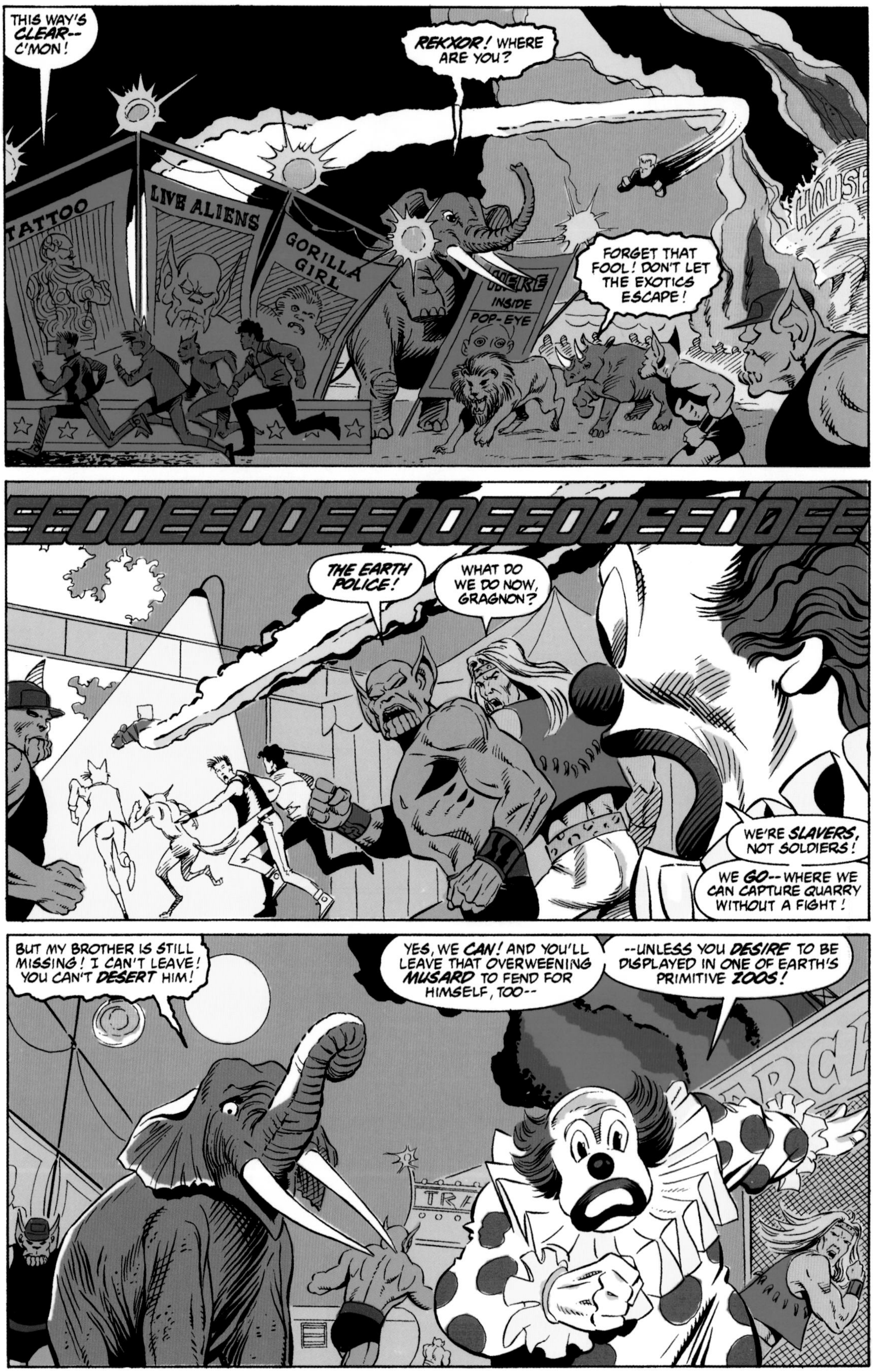
THIS WAY'S CLEAR-- C'MON!
REKXOR! WHERE ARE YOU?
TATTOO
LIVE ALIENS
GORILLA GIRL
INSIDE
POP-EYE
FORGET THAT FOOL! DON'T LET THE EXOTICS ESCAPE!
EEOOEEEOOEEEOOEEEOOEEEOOEE
THE EARTH POLICE!
WHAT DO WE DO NOW, GRAGNON?
WE'RE SLAVERS, NOT SOLDIERS!
WE GO-- WHERE WE CAN CAPTURE QUARRY WITHOUT A FIGHT!
BUT MY BROTHER IS STILL MISSING! I CAN'T LEAVE! YOU CAN'T DESERT HIM!
YES, WE CAN! AND YOU'LL LEAVE THAT OVERWEENING MUSARD TO FEND FOR HIMSELF, TOO--
--UNLESS YOU DESIRE TO BE DISPLAYED IN ONE OF EARTH'S PRIMITIVE ZOOS!

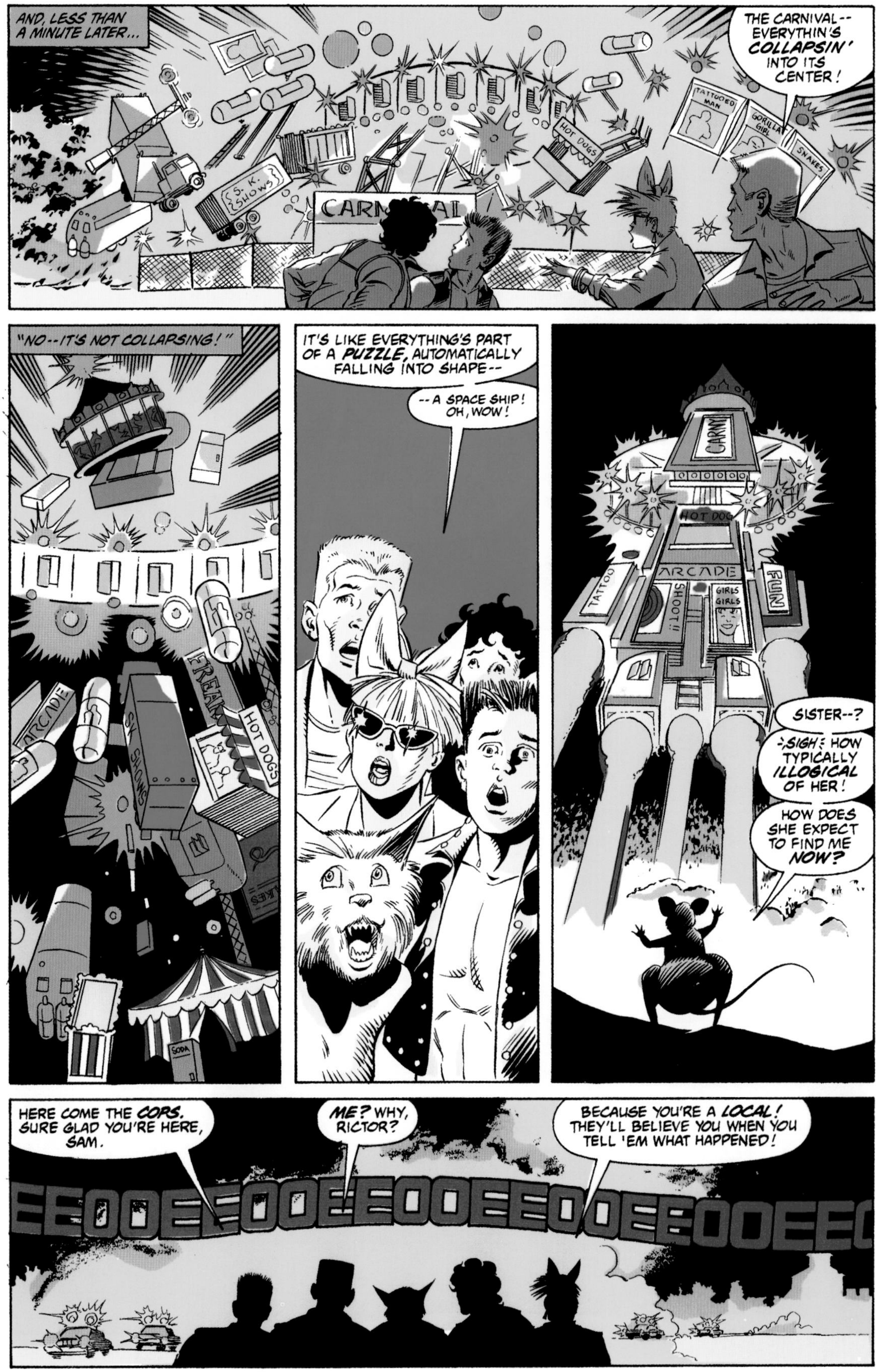
AND, LESS THAN A MINUTE LATER...
THE CARNIVAL-- EVERYTHIN'S COLLAPSIN' INTO ITS CENTER!
"NO--IT'S NOT COLLAPSING!"
IT'S LIKE EVERYTHING'S PART OF A PUZZLE, AUTOMATICALLY FALLING INTO SHAPE--
--A SPACE SHIP! OH, WOW!
SISTER--?
SIGH HOW TYPICALLY ILLOGICAL OF HER!
HOW DOES SHE EXPECT TO FIND ME NOW?
HERE COME THE COPS. SURE GLAD YOU'RE HERE, SAM.
ME? WHY, RICTOR?
BECAUSE YOU'RE A LOCAL! THEY'LL BELIEVE YOU WHEN YOU TELL 'EM WHAT HAPPENED!
EEOOEEOOEEOOEEOOEEOOEEO

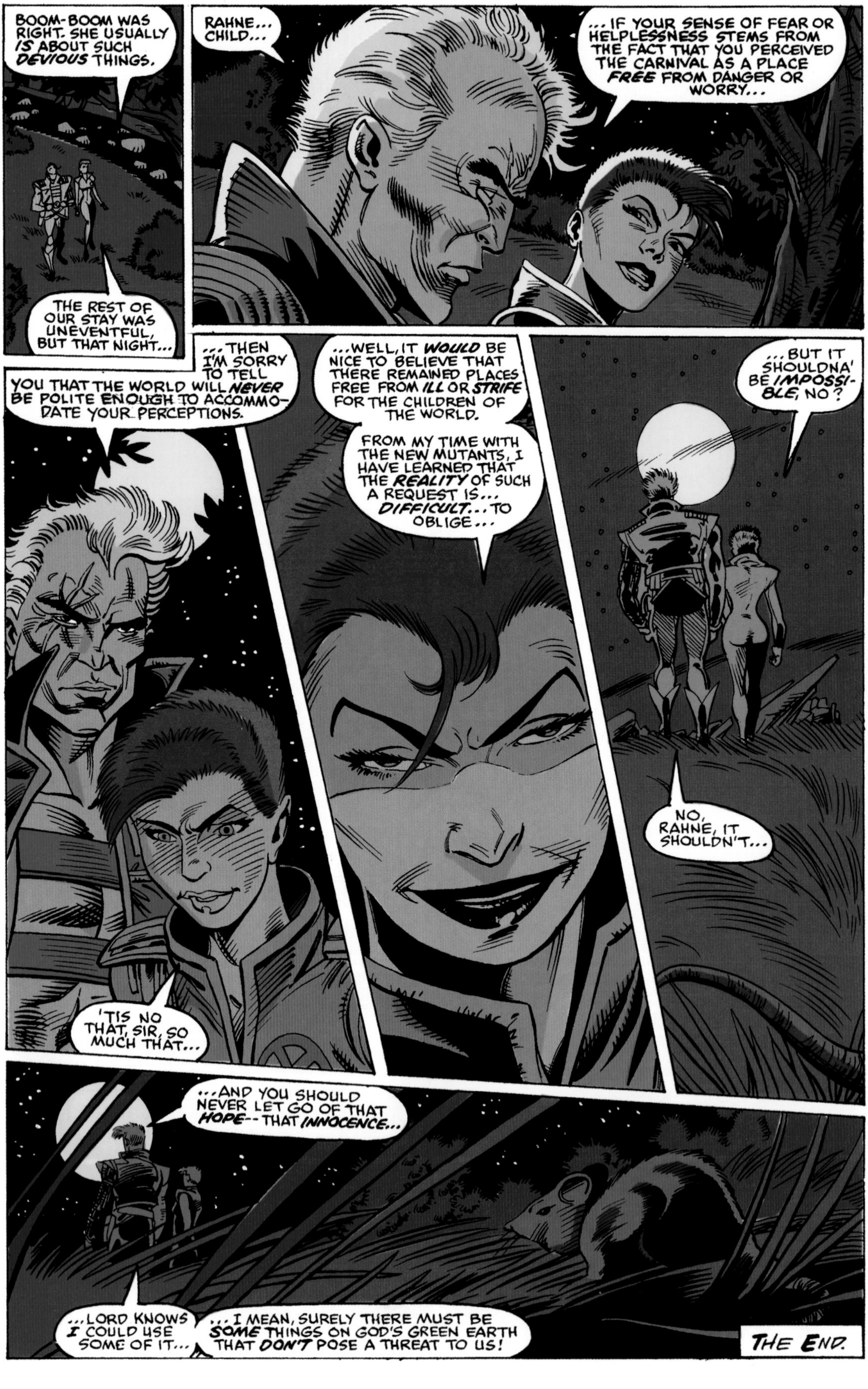
BOOM-BOOM WAS RIGHT. SHE USUALLY IS ABOUT SUCH DEVIOUS THINGS.
THE REST OF OUR STAY WAS UNEVENTFUL, BUT THAT NIGHT...
RAHNE... CHILD...
...IF YOUR SENSE OF FEAR OR HELPLESSNESS STEMS FROM THE FACT THAT YOU PERCEIVED THE CARNIVAL AS A PLACE FREE FROM DANGER OR WORRY...
...THEN I'M SORRY TO TELL YOU THAT THE WORLD WILL NEVER BE POLITE ENOUGH TO ACCOMMODATE YOUR PERCEPTIONS.
'TIS NO THAT, SIR, SO MUCH THAT...
...WELL, IT WOULD BE NICE TO BELIEVE THAT THERE REMAINED PLACES FREE FROM ILL OR STRIFE FOR THE CHILDREN OF THE WORLD.
FROM MY TIME WITH THE NEW MUTANTS, I HAVE LEARNED THAT THE REALITY OF SUCH A REQUEST IS... DIFFICULT... TO OBLIGE...
...BUT IT SHOULDNA' BE IMPOSSIBLE, NO?
NO, RAHNE, IT SHOULDN'T...
...AND YOU SHOULD NEVER LET GO OF THAT HOPE--THAT INNOCENCE...
...LORD KNOWS I COULD USE SOME OF IT...
...I MEAN, SURELY THERE MUST BE SOME THINGS ON GOD'S GREEN EARTH THAT DON'T POSE A THREAT TO US!
THE END.

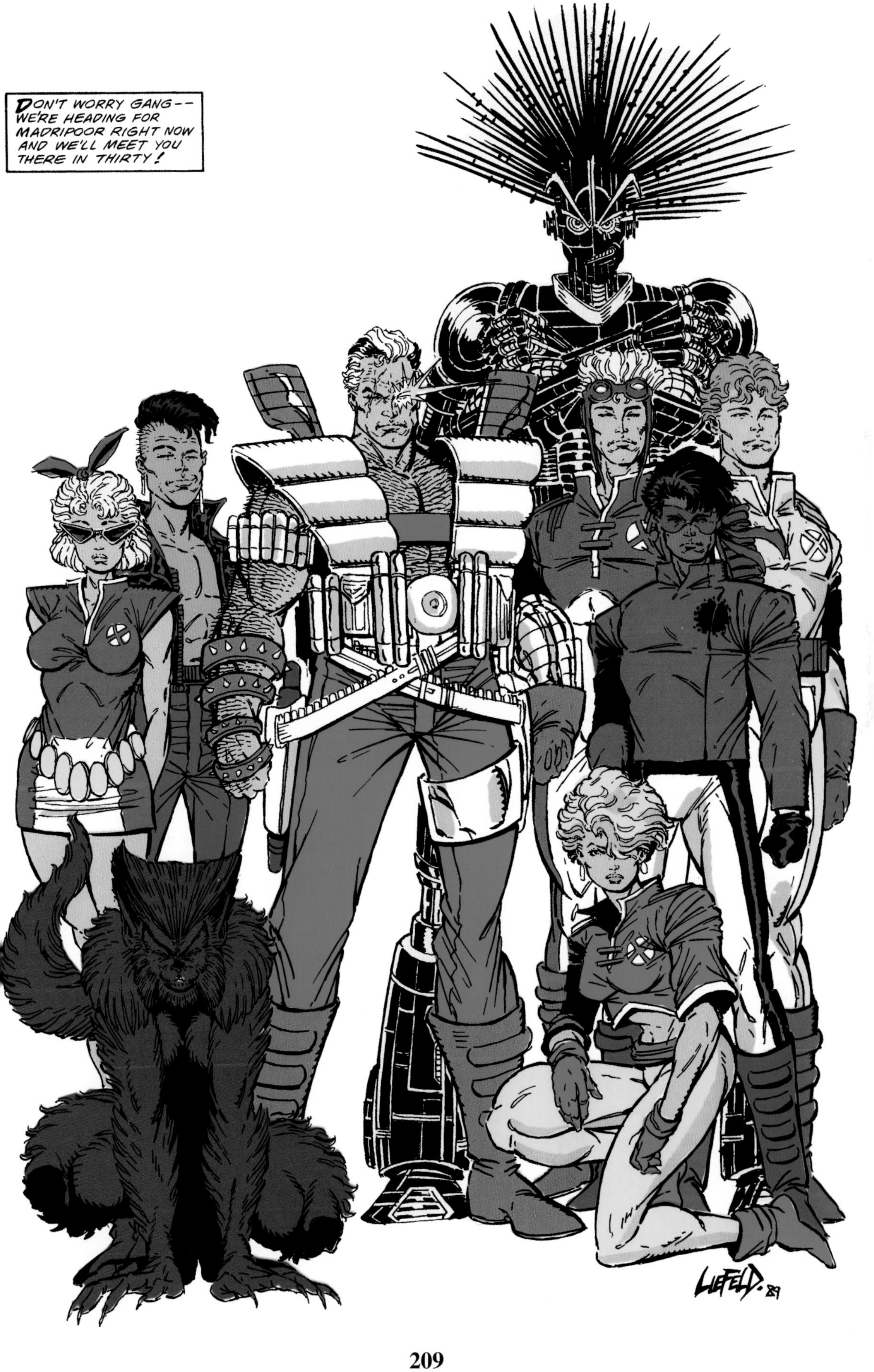
DON'T WORRY GANG-- WE'RE HEADING FOR MADRIPOOR RIGHT NOW AND WE'LL MEET YOU THERE IN THIRTY!
LIEFELD. 89

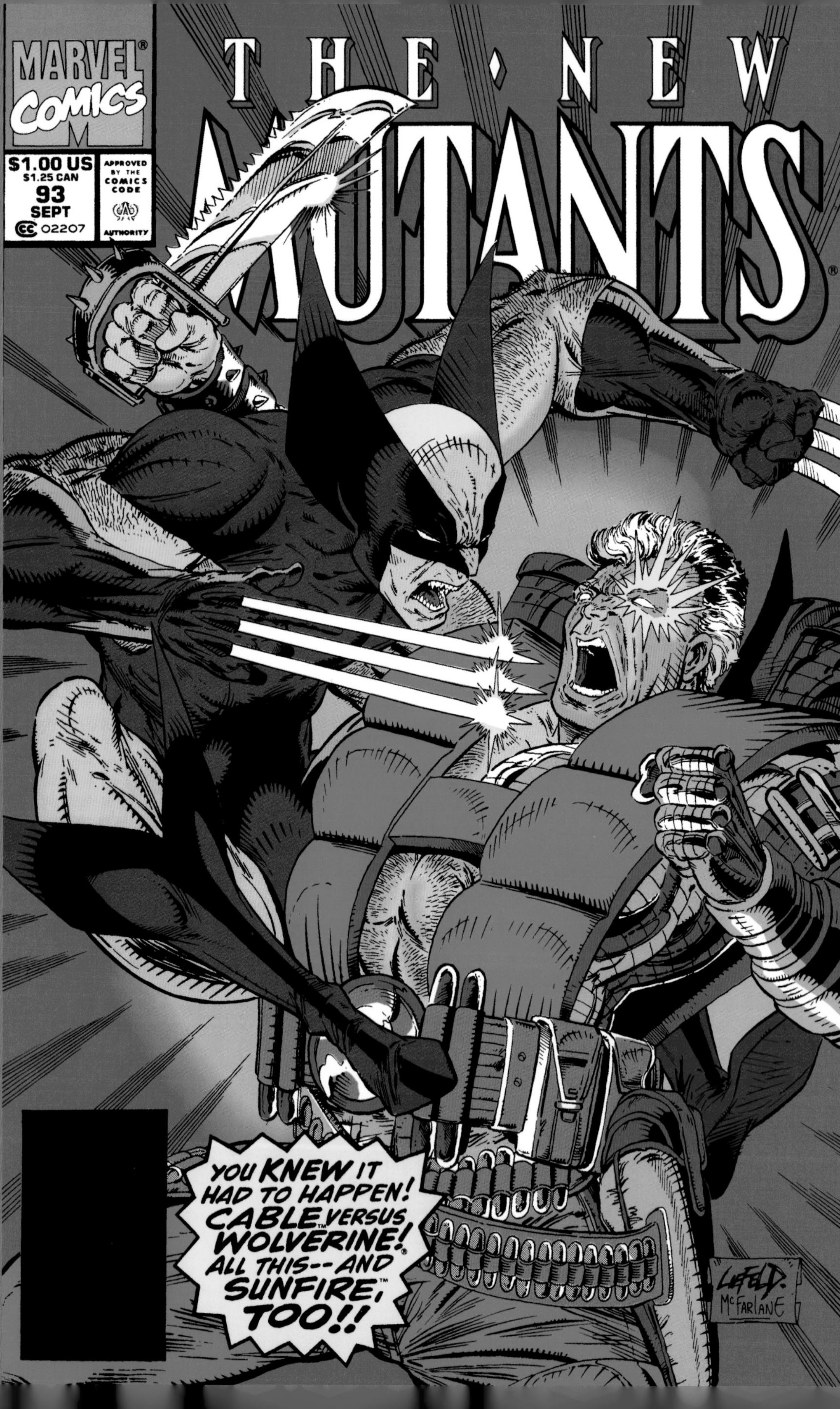
MARVEL COMICS
$1.00 US
$1.25 CAN
93
SEPT
02207
APPROVED BY THE COMICS CODE AUTHORITY
THE NEW MUTANTS
YOU KNEW IT HAD TO HAPPEN! CABLE VERSUS WOLVERINE! ALL THIS--AND SUNFIRE, TOO!!
LIEFELD.
McFARLANE

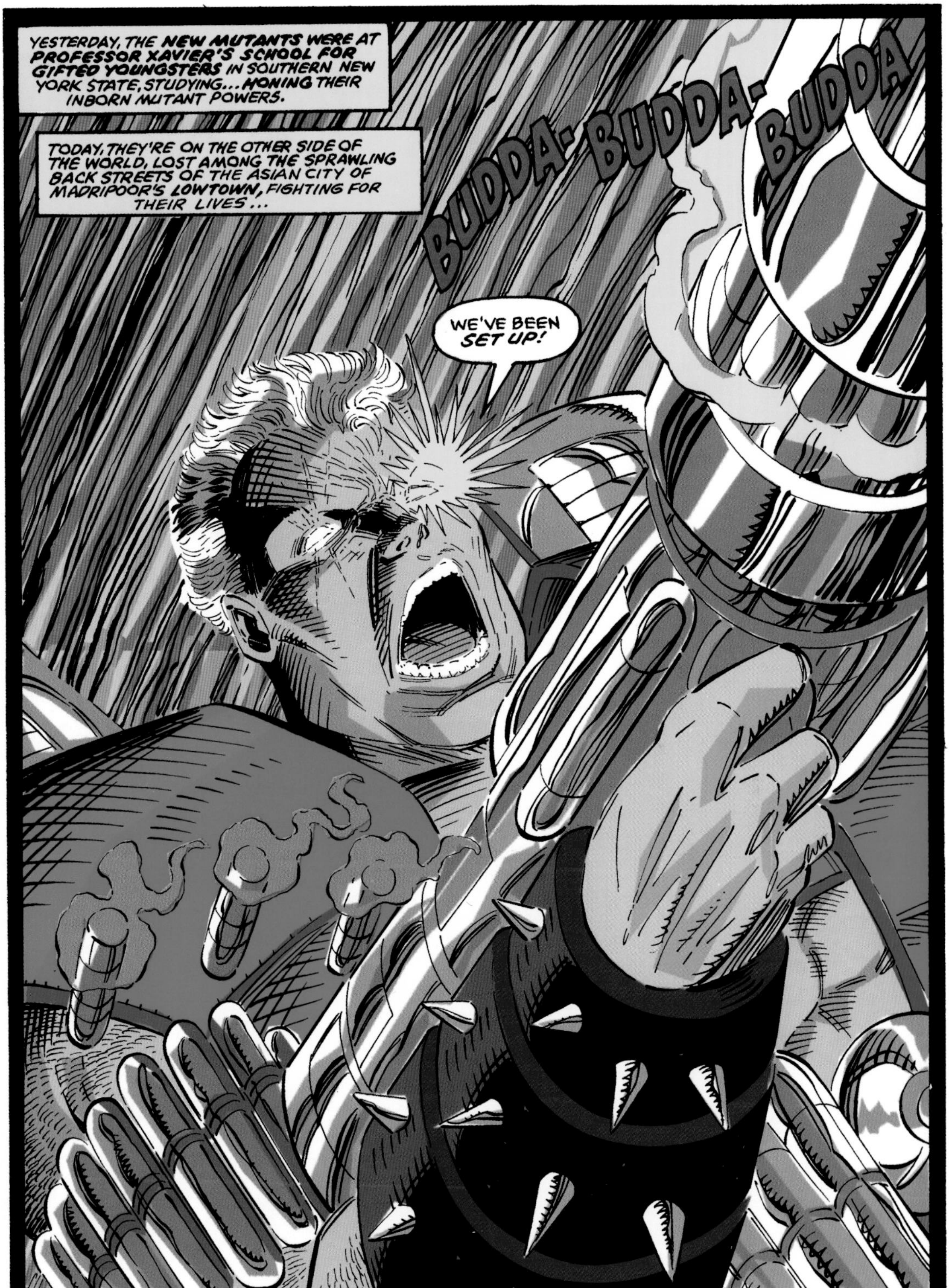
YESTERDAY, THE NEW MUTANTS WERE AT PROFESSOR XAVIER'S SCHOOL FOR GIFTED YOUNGSTERS IN SOUTHERN NEW YORK STATE, STUDYING... HONING THEIR INBORN MUTANT POWERS.
TODAY, THEY'RE ON THE OTHER SIDE OF THE WORLD, LOST AMONG THE SPRAWLING BACK STREETS OF THE ASIAN CITY OF MADRIPOOR'S LOWTOWN, FIGHTING FOR THEIR LIVES...
BUDDA-BUDDA-BUDDA-BUDDA
WE'VE BEEN SET UP!

LOUISE SIMONSON WRITER · ROB LIEFELD PENCILER · HILARY BARTA INKER · JOE ROSEN LETTERER · BRAD VANCATA COLORIST · BOB HARRAS EDITOR · TOM DeFALCO EDITOR-IN-CHIEF

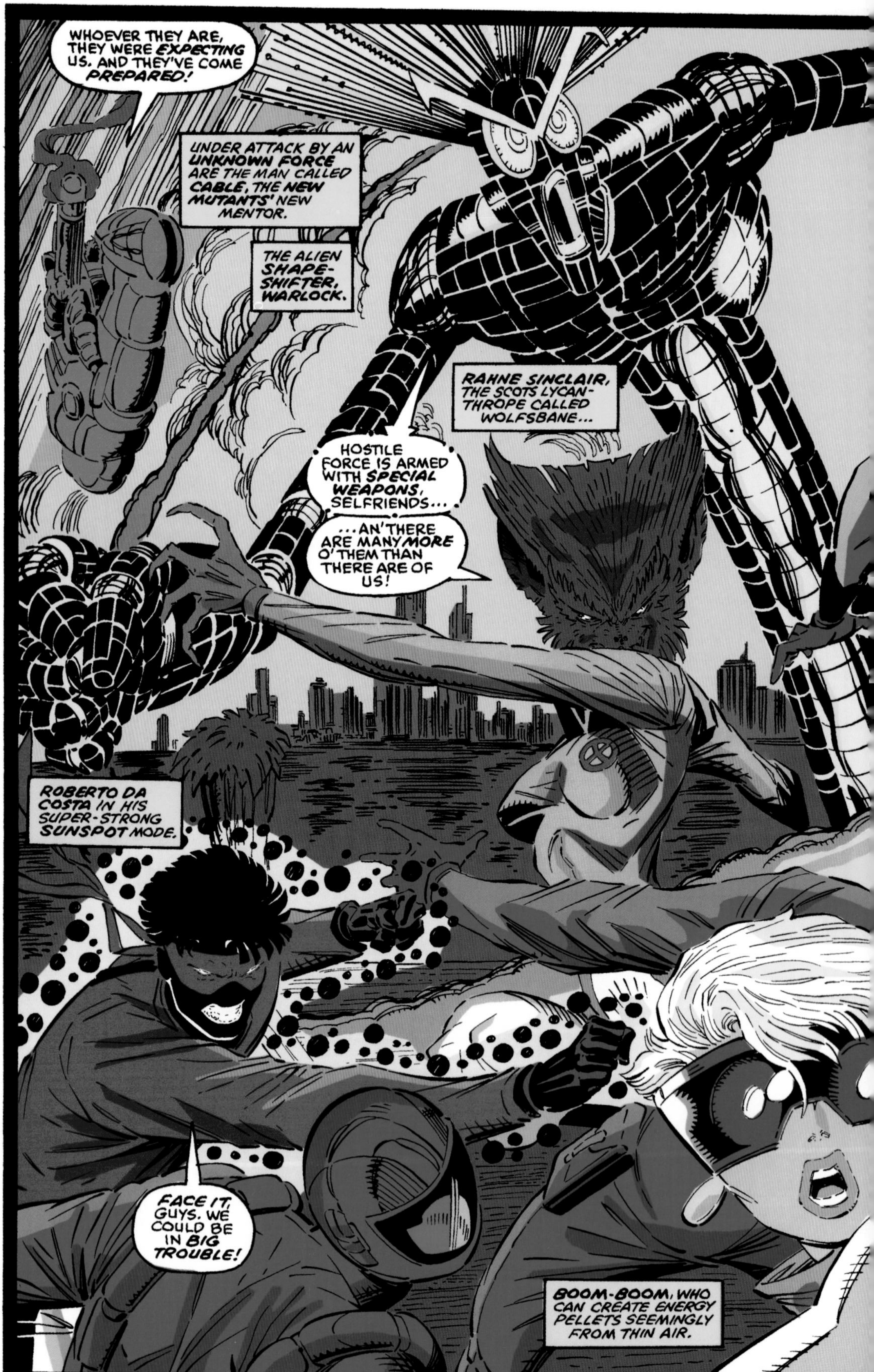
WHOEVER THEY ARE, THEY WERE EXPECTING US. AND THEY'VE COME PREPARED!
UNDER ATTACK BY AN UNKNOWN FORCE ARE THE MAN CALLED CABLE, THE NEW MUTANTS' NEW MENTOR.
THE ALIEN SHAPE-SHIFTER, WARLOCK.
RAHNE SINCLAIR, THE SCOTS LYCANTHROPE CALLED WOLFSBANE...
HOSTILE FORCE IS ARMED WITH SPECIAL WEAPONS, SELFRIENDS...
...AN' THERE ARE MANY MORE O' THEM THAN THERE ARE OF US!
ROBERTO DA COSTA IN HIS SUPER-STRONG SUNSPOT MODE.
FACE IT, GUYS. WE COULD BE IN BIG TROUBLE!
BOOM-BOOM, WHO CAN CREATE ENERGY PELLETS SEEMINGLY FROM THIN AIR.

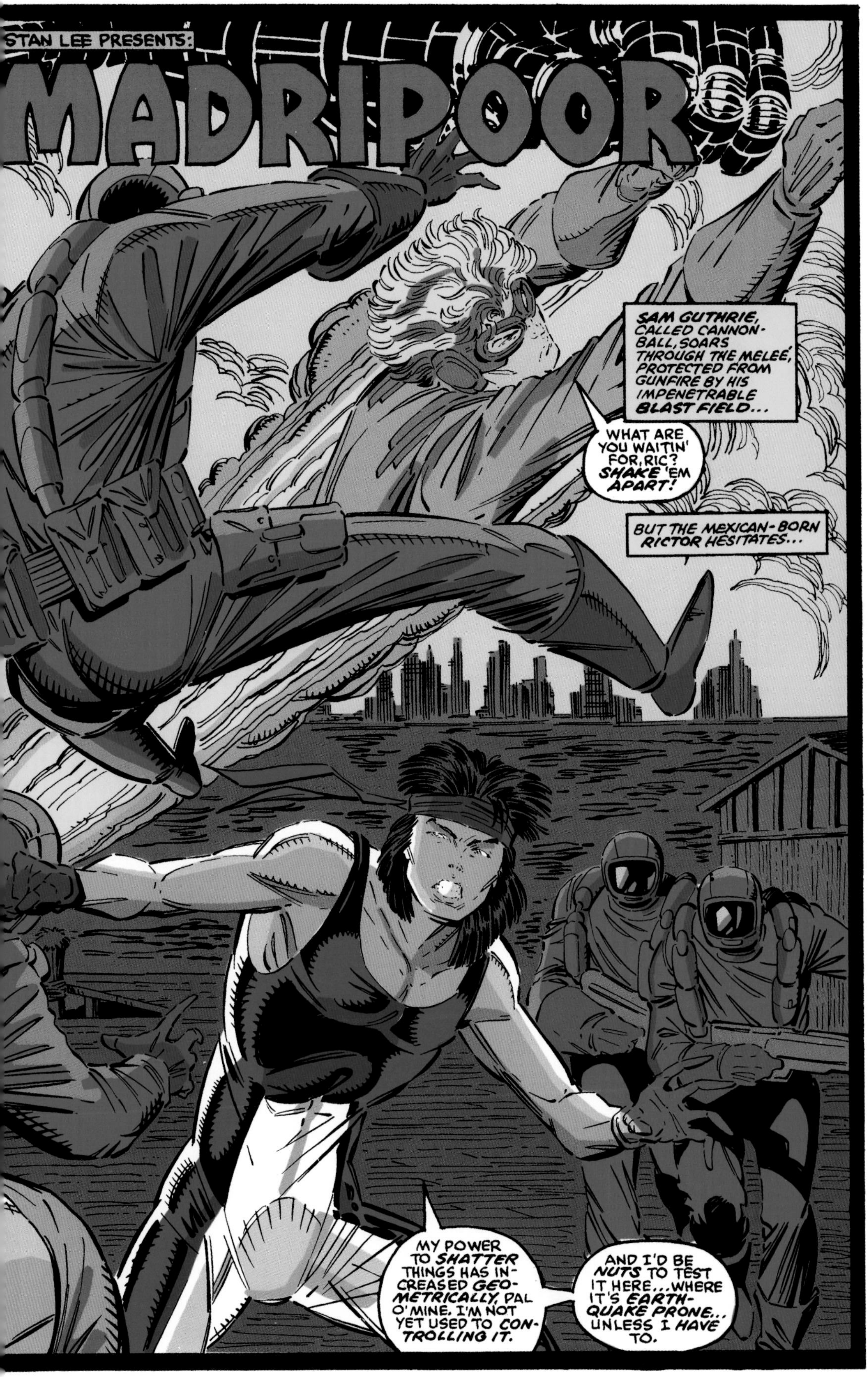
STAN LEE PRESENTS:
MADRIPOOR
SAM GUTHRIE, CALLED CANNON-BALL, SOARS THROUGH THE MELEÉ, PROTECTED FROM GUNFIRE BY HIS IMPENETRABLE BLAST FIELD...
WHAT ARE YOU WAITIN' FOR, RIC? SHAKE 'EM APART!
BUT THE MEXICAN-BORN RICTOR HESITATES...
MY POWER TO SHATTER THINGS HAS IN-CREASED GEO-METRICALLY, PAL O'MINE. I'M NOT YET USED TO CON-TROLLING IT.
AND I'D BE NUTS TO TEST IT HERE... WHERE IT'S EARTH-QUAKE PRONE... UNLESS I HAVE TO.

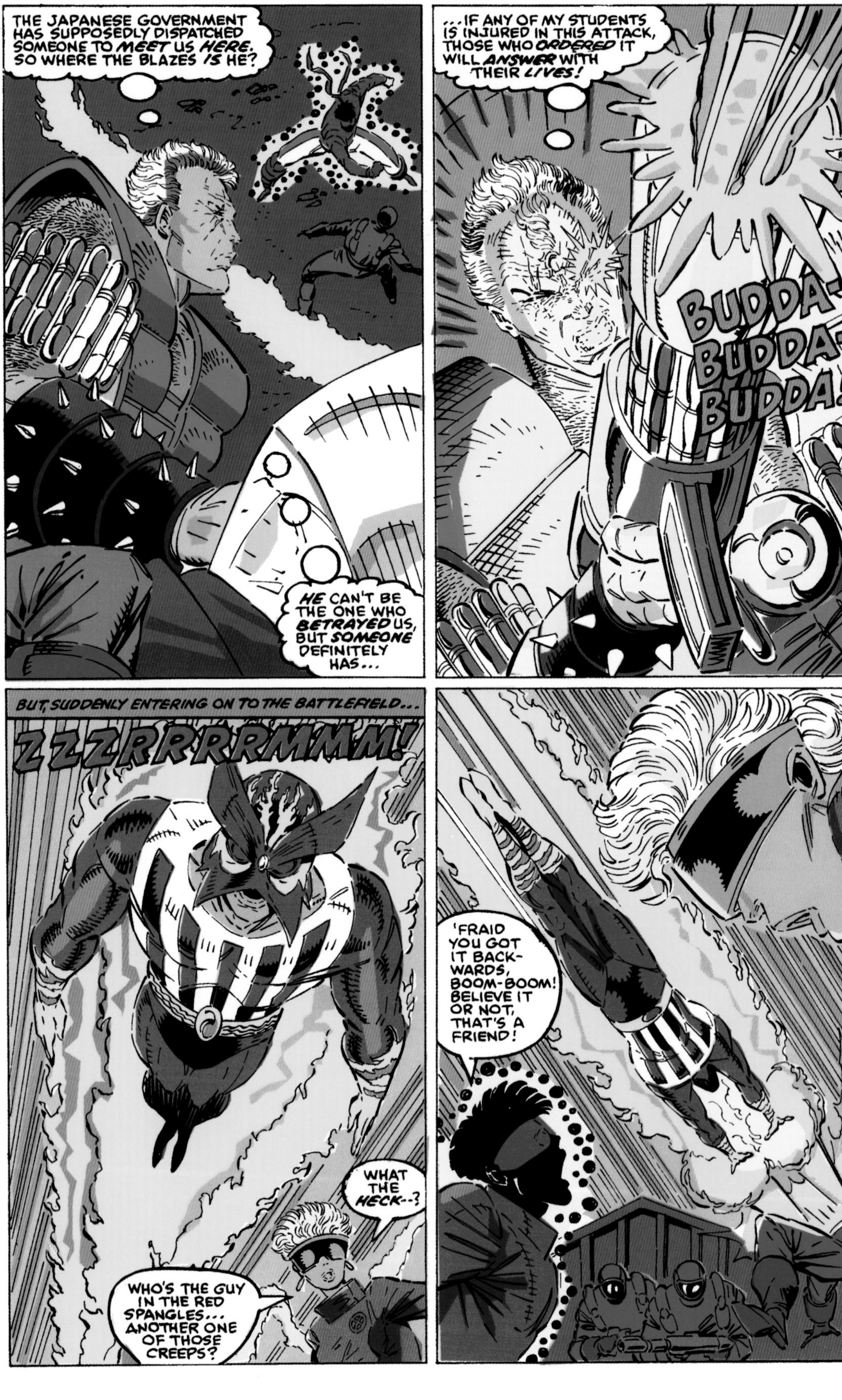
THE JAPANESE GOVERNMENT HAS SUPPOSEDLY DISPATCHED SOMEONE TO MEET US HERE. SO WHERE THE BLAZES IS HE?
HE CAN'T BE THE ONE WHO BETRAYED US, BUT SOMEONE DEFINITELY HAS...
...IF ANY OF MY STUDENTS IS INJURED IN THIS ATTACK, THOSE WHO ORDERED IT WILL ANSWER WITH THEIR LIVES!
BUDDA-BUDDA-BUDDA!
BUT, SUDDENLY ENTERING ON TO THE BATTLEFIELD...
ZZZRRRRRMMMM!
WHAT THE HECK--?
WHO'S THE GUY IN THE RED SPANGLES... ANOTHER ONE OF THOSE CREEPS?
'FRAID YOU GOT IT BACK-WARDS, BOOM-BOOM! BELIEVE IT OR NOT, THAT'S A FRIEND!

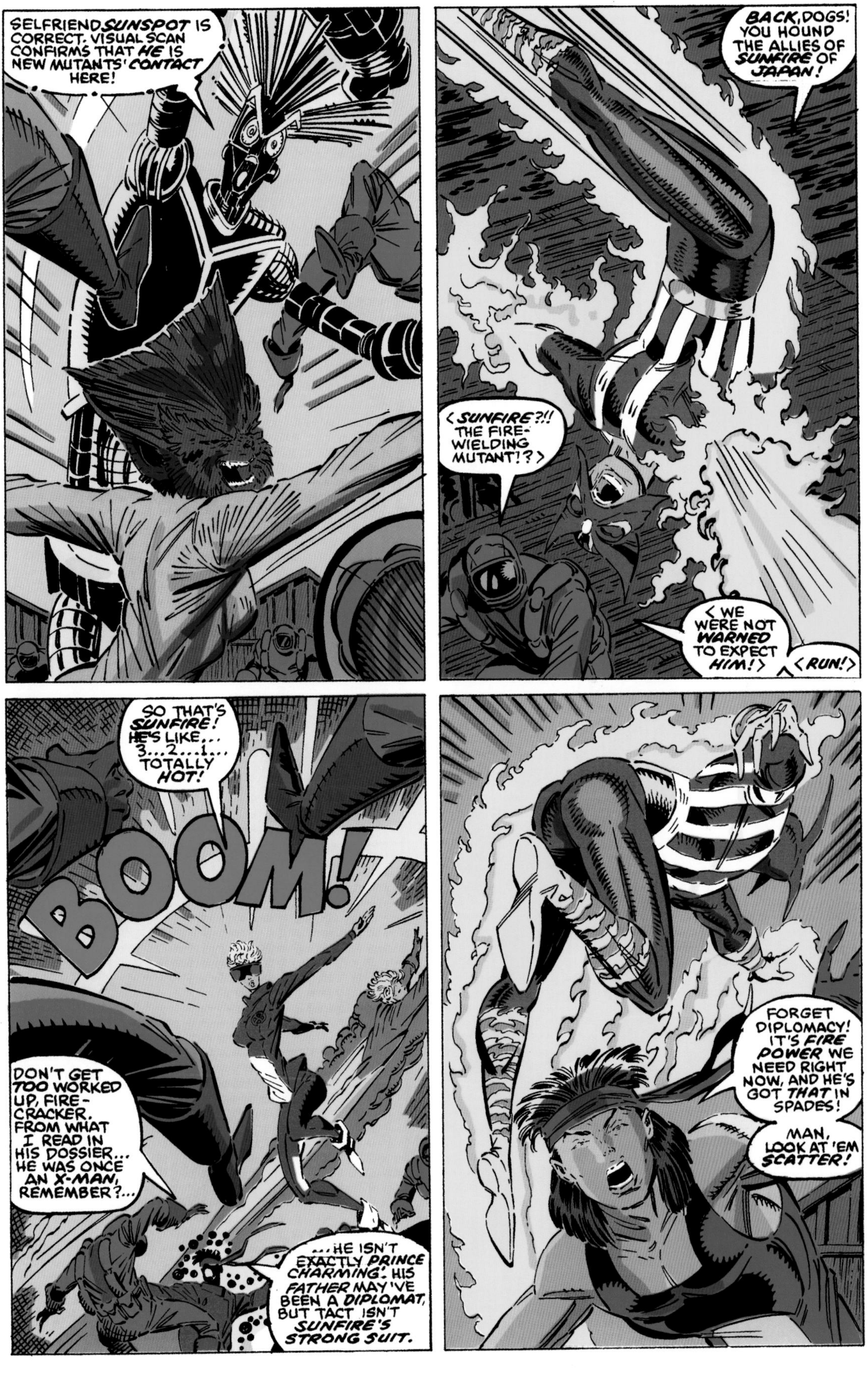
SELFRIEND SUNSPOT IS CORRECT. VISUAL SCAN CONFIRMS THAT HE IS NEW MUTANTS' CONTACT HERE!
BACK, DOGS! YOU HOUND THE ALLIES OF SUNFIRE OF JAPAN!
<SUNFIRE?!! THE FIRE-WIELDING MUTANT!?>
<WE WERE NOT WARNED TO EXPECT HIM!>
<RUN!>
SO THAT'S SUNFIRE! HE'S LIKE... 3...2...1... TOTALLY HOT!
BOOM!
DON'T GET TOO WORKED UP, FIRE-CRACKER. FROM WHAT I READ IN HIS DOSSIER... HE WAS ONCE AN X-MAN, REMEMBER?...
...HE ISN'T EXACTLY PRINCE CHARMING! HIS FATHER MAY'VE BEEN A DIPLOMAT, BUT TACT ISN'T SUNFIRE'S STRONG SUIT.
FORGET DIPLOMACY! IT'S FIRE POWER WE NEED RIGHT NOW, AND HE'S GOT THAT IN SPADES!
MAN, LOOK AT 'EM SCATTER!

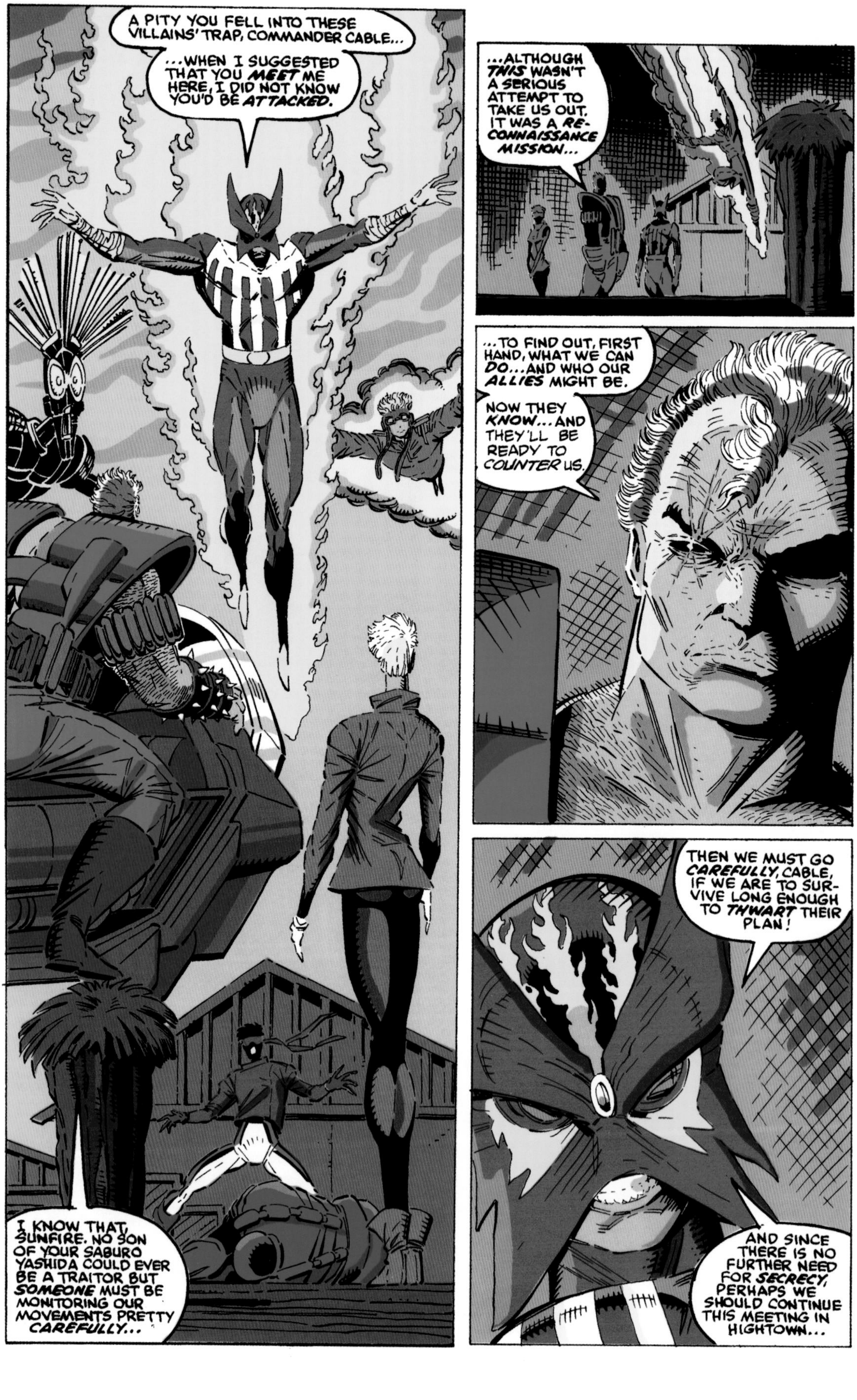

A PITY YOU FELL INTO THESE VILLAINS' TRAP, COMMANDER CABLE...
...WHEN I SUGGESTED THAT YOU MEET ME HERE, I DID NOT KNOW YOU'D BE ATTACKED.
I KNOW THAT, SUNFIRE. NO SON OF YOUR SABURO YASHIDA COULD EVER BE A TRAITOR BUT SOMEONE MUST BE MONITORING OUR MOVEMENTS PRETTY CAREFULLY...
...ALTHOUGH THIS WASN'T A SERIOUS ATTEMPT TO TAKE US OUT. IT WAS A RE-CONNAISSANCE MISSION...
...TO FIND OUT, FIRST HAND, WHAT WE CAN DO...AND WHO OUR ALLIES MIGHT BE.
NOW THEY KNOW...AND THEY'LL BE READY TO COUNTER US.
THEN WE MUST GO CAREFULLY, CABLE, IF WE ARE TO SUR-VIVE LONG ENOUGH TO THWART THEIR PLAN!
AND SINCE THERE IS NO FURTHER NEED FOR SECRECY, PERHAPS WE SHOULD CONTINUE THIS MEETING IN HIGHTOWN...

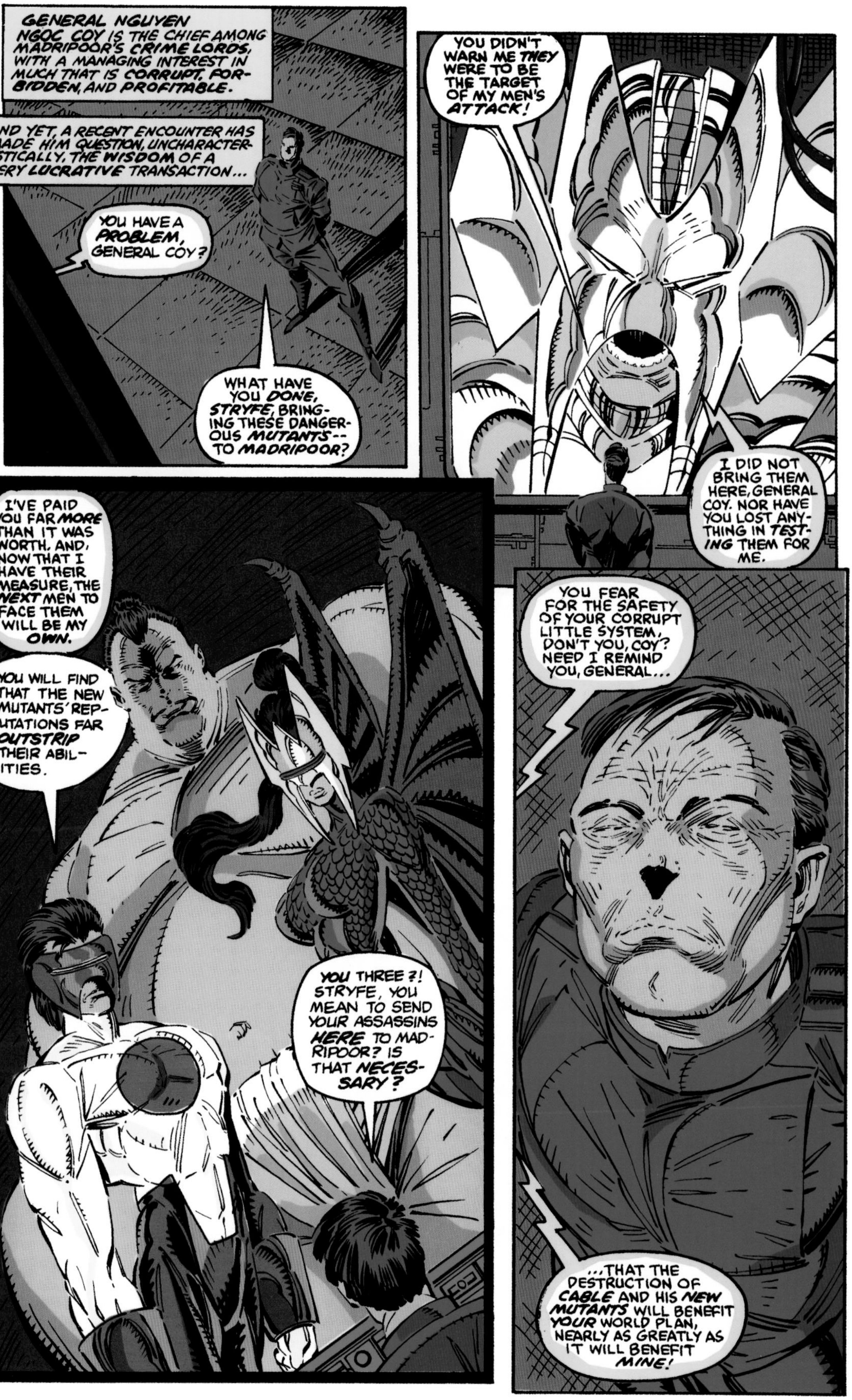
GENERAL NGUYEN NGOC COY IS THE CHIEF AMONG MADRIPOOR'S CRIME LORDS, WITH A MANAGING INTEREST IN MUCH THAT IS CORRUPT, FORBIDDEN, AND PROFITABLE.
AND YET, A RECENT ENCOUNTER HAS MADE HIM QUESTION, UNCHARACTERISTICALLY, THE WISDOM OF A VERY LUCRATIVE TRANSACTION...
YOU HAVE A PROBLEM, GENERAL COY?
WHAT HAVE YOU DONE, STRYFE, BRINGING THESE DANGEROUS MUTANTS-- TO MADRIPOOR?
YOU DIDN'T WARN ME THEY WERE TO BE THE TARGET OF MY MEN'S ATTACK!
I DID NOT BRING THEM HERE, GENERAL COY. NOR HAVE YOU LOST ANYTHING IN TESTING THEM FOR ME.
I'VE PAID YOU FAR MORE THAN IT WAS WORTH. AND, NOW THAT I HAVE THEIR MEASURE, THE NEXT MEN TO FACE THEM WILL BE MY OWN.
YOU WILL FIND THAT THE NEW MUTANTS' REPUTATIONS FAR OUTSTRIP THEIR ABILITIES.
YOU THREE?! STRYFE, YOU MEAN TO SEND YOUR ASSASSINS HERE TO MADRIPOOR? IS THAT NECESSARY?
YOU FEAR FOR THE SAFETY OF YOUR CORRUPT LITTLE SYSTEM, DON'T YOU, COY? NEED I REMIND YOU, GENERAL...
...THAT THE DESTRUCTION OF CABLE AND HIS NEW MUTANTS WILL BENEFIT YOUR WORLD PLAN, NEARLY AS GREATLY AS IT WILL BENEFIT MINE!

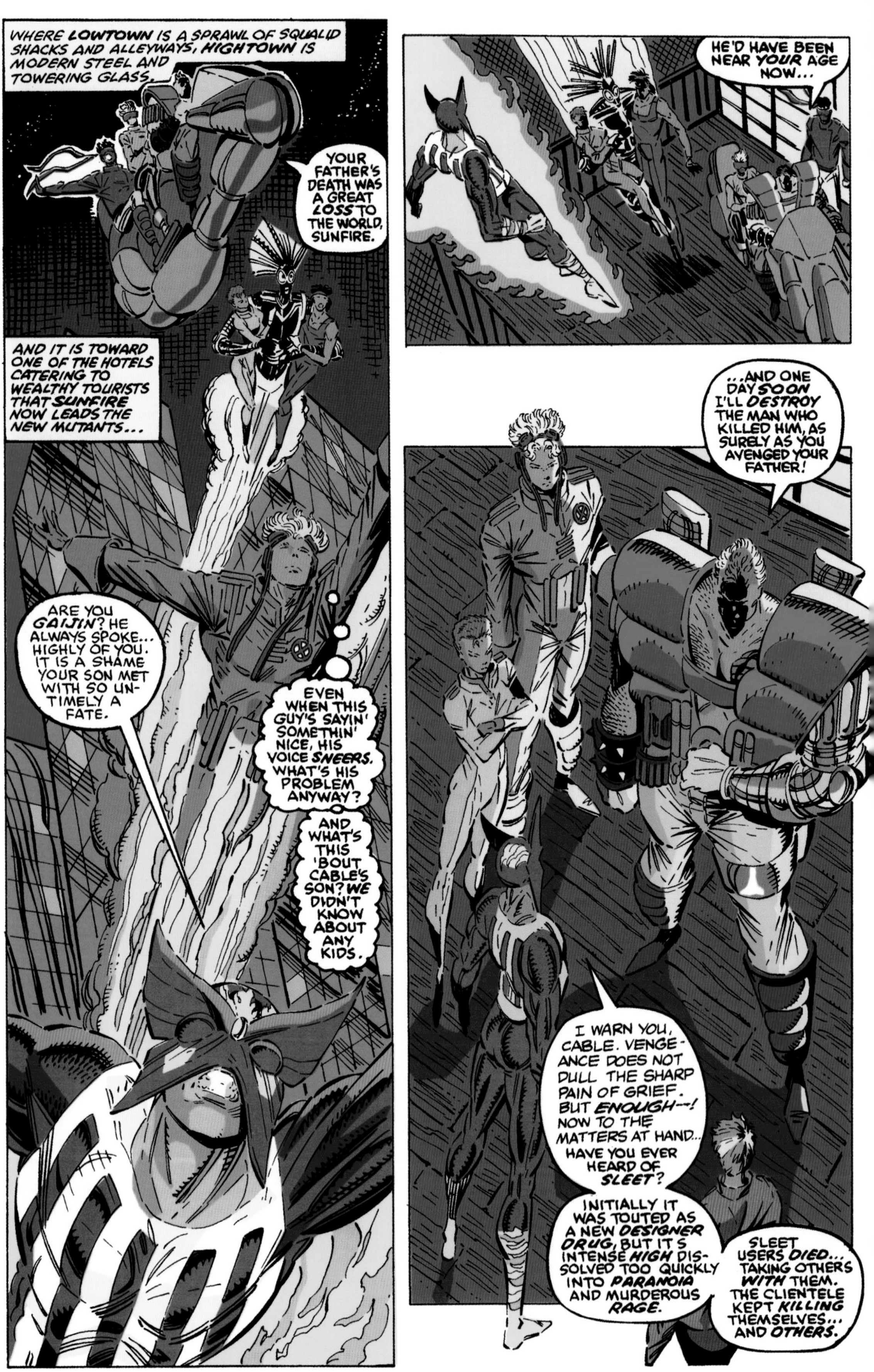
WHERE LOWTOWN IS A SPRAWL OF SQUALID SHACKS AND ALLEYWAYS, HIGHTOWN IS MODERN STEEL AND TOWERING GLASS.
YOUR FATHER'S DEATH WAS A GREAT LOSS TO THE WORLD, SUNFIRE.
AND IT IS TOWARD ONE OF THE HOTELS CATERING TO WEALTHY TOURISTS THAT SUNFIRE NOW LEADS THE NEW MUTANTS...
ARE YOU GAIJIN? HE ALWAYS SPOKE... HIGHLY OF YOU. IT IS A SHAME YOUR SON MET WITH SO UNTIMELY A FATE.
EVEN WHEN THIS GUY'S SAYIN' SOMETHIN' NICE, HIS VOICE SNEERS. WHAT'S HIS PROBLEM ANYWAY?
AND WHAT'S THIS 'BOUT CABLE'S SON? WE DIDN'T KNOW ABOUT ANY KIDS.
HE'D HAVE BEEN NEAR YOUR AGE NOW...
...AND ONE DAY SOON I'LL DESTROY THE MAN WHO KILLED HIM, AS SURELY AS YOU AVENGED YOUR FATHER!
I WARN YOU, CABLE. VENGEANCE DOES NOT DULL THE SHARP PAIN OF GRIEF. BUT ENOUGH--! NOW TO THE MATTERS AT HAND... HAVE YOU EVER HEARD OF SLEET?
INITIALLY IT WAS TOUTED AS A NEW DESIGNER DRUG, BUT ITS INTENSE HIGH DISSOLVED TOO QUICKLY INTO PARANOIA AND MURDEROUS RAGE.
SLEET USERS DIED... TAKING OTHERS WITH THEM. THE CLIENTELE KEPT KILLING THEMSELVES... AND OTHERS.

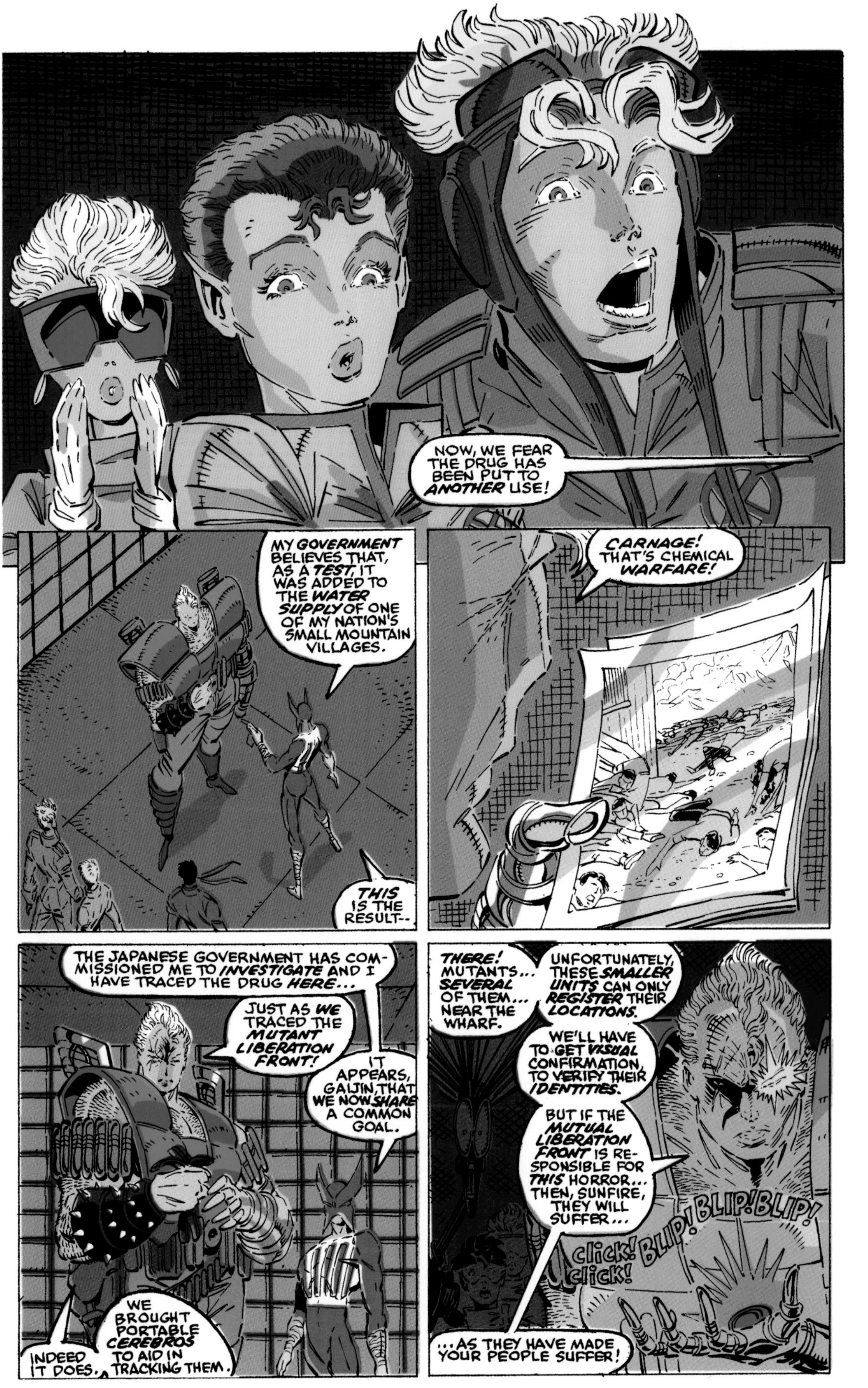
NOW, WE FEAR THE DRUG HAS BEEN PUT TO ANOTHER USE!
MY GOVERNMENT BELIEVES THAT, AS A TEST, IT WAS ADDED TO THE WATER SUPPLY OF ONE OF MY NATION'S SMALL MOUNTAIN VILLAGES.
THIS IS THE RESULT--
CARNAGE! THAT'S CHEMICAL WARFARE!
THE JAPANESE GOVERNMENT HAS COMMISSIONED ME TO INVESTIGATE AND I HAVE TRACED THE DRUG HERE...
JUST AS WE TRACED THE MUTANT LIBERATION FRONT!
IT APPEARS, GAIJIN, THAT WE NOW SHARE A COMMON GOAL.
INDEED IT DOES.
WE BROUGHT PORTABLE CEREBROS TO AID IN TRACKING THEM.
THERE! MUTANTS... SEVERAL OF THEM... NEAR THE WHARF.
UNFORTUNATELY, THESE SMALLER UNITS CAN ONLY REGISTER THEIR LOCATIONS.
WE'LL HAVE TO GET VISUAL CONFIRMATION, TO VERIFY THEIR IDENTITIES.
BUT IF THE MUTUAL LIBERATION FRONT IS RESPONSIBLE FOR THIS HORROR... THEN, SUNFIRE, THEY WILL SUFFER...
click! click! BLIP! BLIP! BLIP!
...AS THEY HAVE MADE YOUR PEOPLE SUFFER!

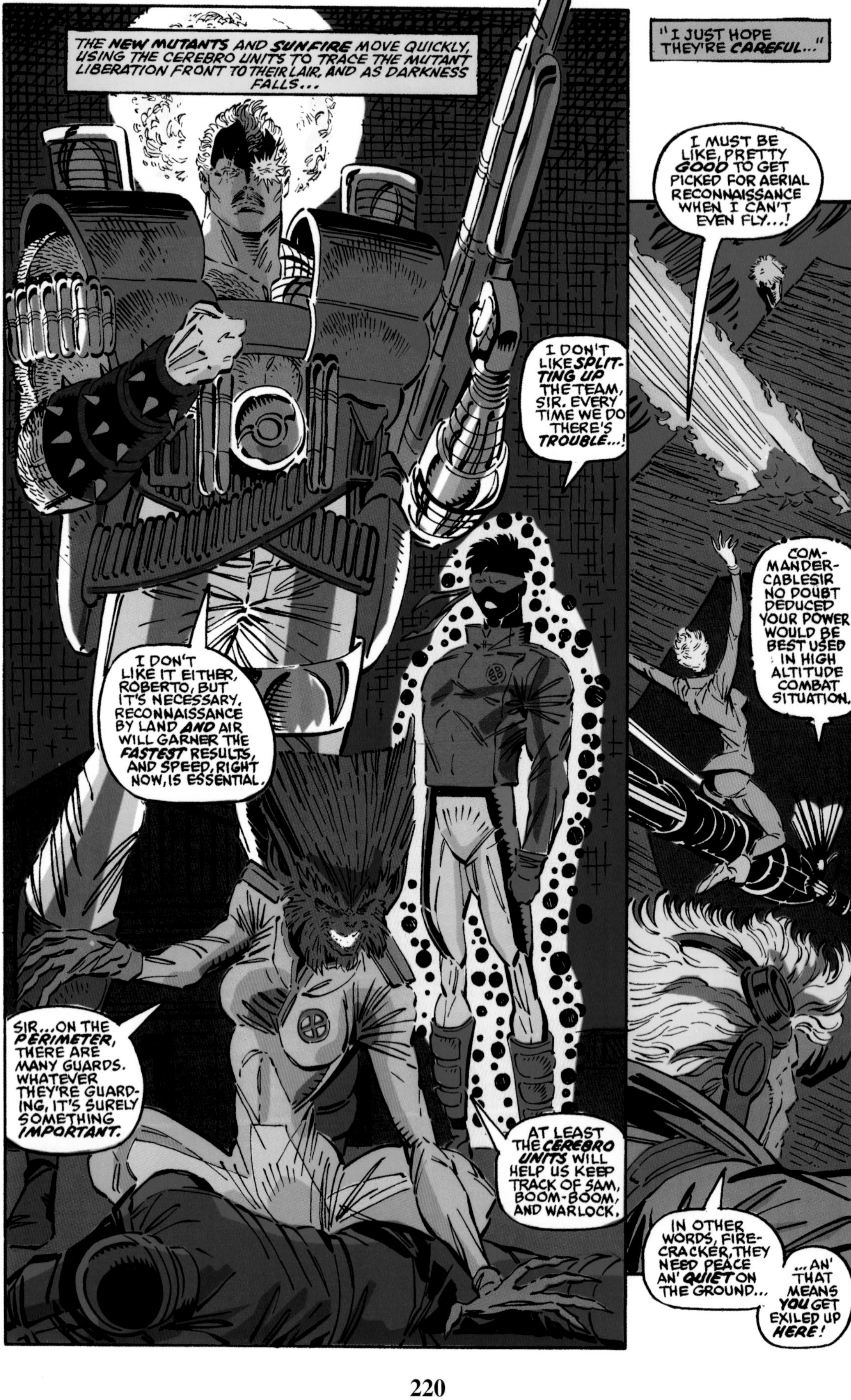
THE NEW MUTANTS AND SUNFIRE MOVE QUICKLY, USING THE CEREBRO UNITS TO TRACE THE MUTANT LIBERATION FRONT TO THEIR LAIR. AND AS DARKNESS FALLS...
I DON'T LIKE SPLITTING UP THE TEAM, SIR. EVERY TIME WE DO THERE'S TROUBLE...!
I DON'T LIKE IT EITHER, ROBERTO, BUT IT'S NECESSARY. RECONNAISSANCE BY LAND AND AIR WILL GARNER THE FASTEST RESULTS, AND SPEED, RIGHT NOW, IS ESSENTIAL.
SIR...ON THE PERIMETER, THERE ARE MANY GUARDS. WHATEVER THEY'RE GUARDING, IT'S SURELY SOMETHING IMPORTANT.
AT LEAST THE CEREBRO UNITS WILL HELP US KEEP TRACK OF SAM, BOOM-BOOM, AND WARLOCK.
"I JUST HOPE THEY'RE CAREFUL..."
I MUST BE LIKE, PRETTY GOOD TO GET PICKED FOR AERIAL RECONNAISSANCE WHEN I CAN'T EVEN FLY...!
COMMANDER-CABLESIR NO DOUBT DEDUCED YOUR POWER WOULD BE BEST USED IN HIGH ALTITUDE COMBAT SITUATION.
IN OTHER WORDS, FIRECRACKER, THEY NEED PEACE AN' QUIET ON THE GROUND...
...AN' THAT MEANS YOU GET EXILED UP HERE!

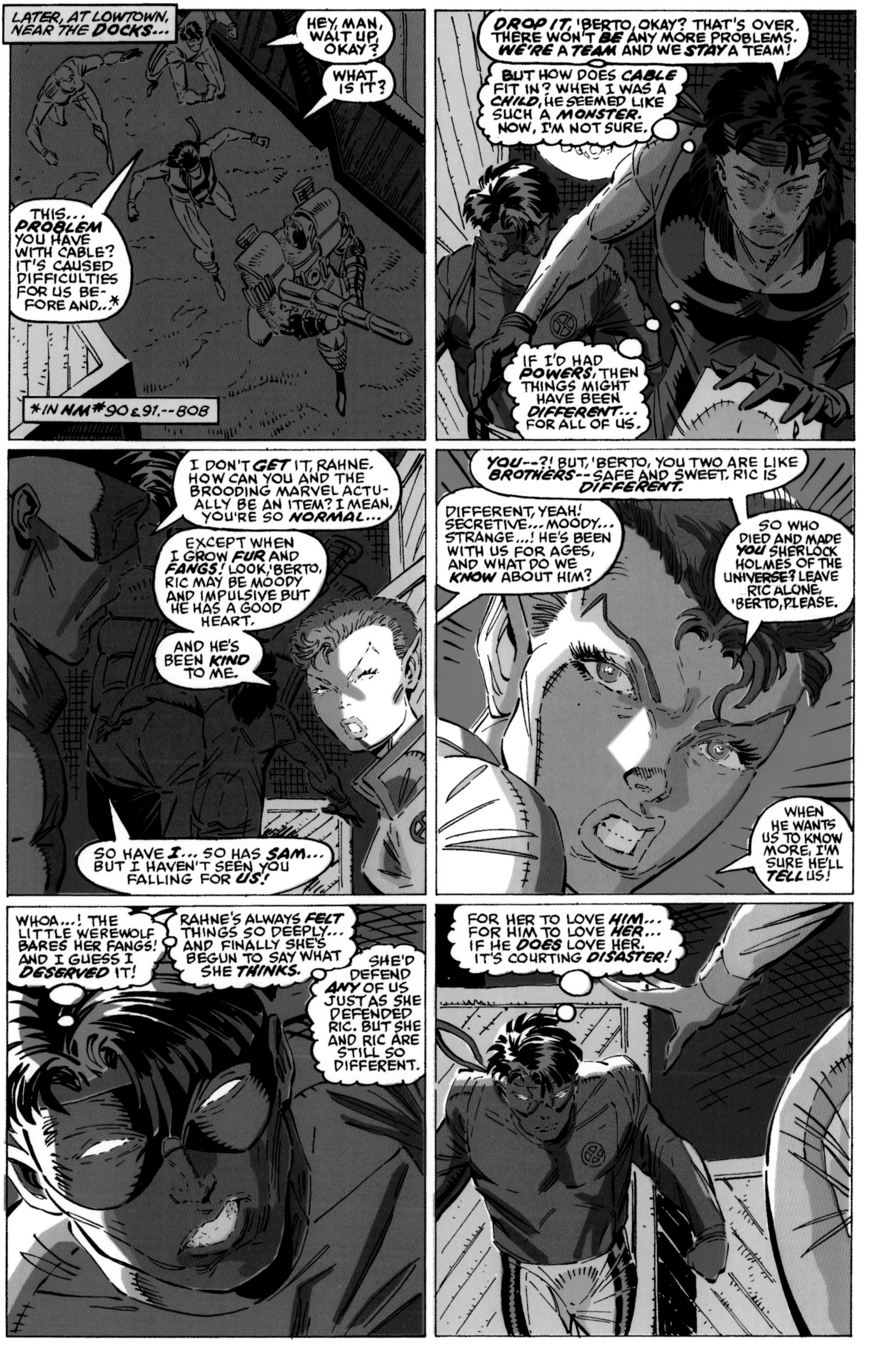
LATER, AT LOWTOWN, NEAR THE DOCKS...
HEY, MAN, WAIT UP, OKAY?
WHAT IS IT?
THIS... PROBLEM YOU HAVE WITH CABLE? IT'S CAUSED DIFFICULTIES FOR US BEFORE AND...*
*IN NM#90 & 91.--BOB
DROP IT, 'BERTO, OKAY? THAT'S OVER. THERE WON'T BE ANY MORE PROBLEMS. WE'RE A TEAM AND WE STAY A TEAM!
BUT HOW DOES CABLE FIT IN? WHEN I WAS A CHILD, HE SEEMED LIKE SUCH A MONSTER. NOW, I'M NOT SURE.
IF I'D HAD POWERS, THEN THINGS MIGHT HAVE BEEN DIFFERENT... FOR ALL OF US.
I DON'T GET IT, RAHNE. HOW CAN YOU AND THE BROODING MARVEL ACTUALLY BE AN ITEM? I MEAN, YOU'RE SO NORMAL...
EXCEPT WHEN I GROW FUR AND FANGS! LOOK, 'BERTO, RIC MAY BE MOODY AND IMPULSIVE BUT HE HAS A GOOD HEART.
AND HE'S BEEN KIND TO ME.
SO HAVE I... SO HAS SAM... BUT I HAVEN'T SEEN YOU FALLING FOR US!
YOU--?! BUT, 'BERTO, YOU TWO ARE LIKE BROTHERS--SAFE AND SWEET. RIC IS DIFFERENT.
DIFFERENT, YEAH! SECRETIVE... MOODY... STRANGE...! HE'S BEEN WITH US FOR AGES, AND WHAT DO WE KNOW ABOUT HIM?
SO WHO DIED AND MADE YOU SHERLOCK HOLMES OF THE UNIVERSE? LEAVE RIC ALONE, 'BERTO, PLEASE.
WHEN HE WANTS US TO KNOW MORE, I'M SURE HE'LL TELL US!
WHOA...! THE LITTLE WEREWOLF BARES HER FANGS! AND I GUESS I DESERVED IT!
RAHNE'S ALWAYS FELT THINGS SO DEEPLY... AND FINALLY SHE'S BEGUN TO SAY WHAT SHE THINKS.
SHE'D DEFEND ANY OF US JUST AS SHE DEFENDED RIC. BUT SHE AND RIC ARE STILL SO DIFFERENT.
FOR HER TO LOVE HIM... FOR HIM TO LOVE HER... IF HE DOES LOVE HER. IT'S COURTING DISASTER!

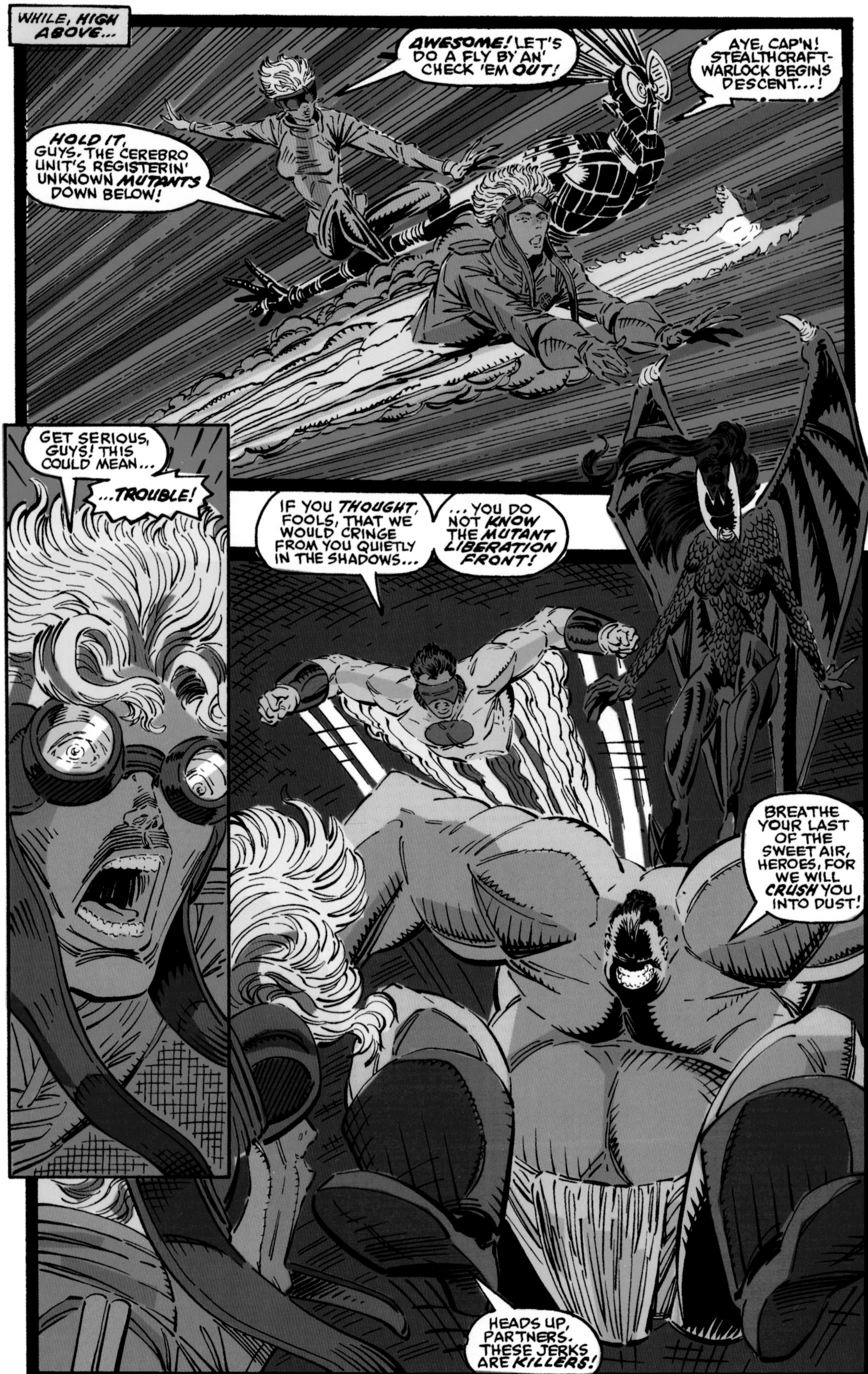
WHILE, HIGH ABOVE...
AWESOME! LET'S DO A FLY BY AN' CHECK 'EM OUT!
AYE, CAP'N! STEALTHCRAFT-WARLOCK BEGINS DESCENT...!
HOLD IT, GUYS. THE CEREBRO UNIT'S REGISTERIN' UNKNOWN MUTANTS DOWN BELOW!
GET SERIOUS, GUYS! THIS COULD MEAN...
...TROUBLE!
IF YOU THOUGHT, FOOLS, THAT WE WOULD CRINGE FROM YOU QUIETLY IN THE SHADOWS...
...YOU DO NOT KNOW THE MUTANT LIBERATION FRONT!
BREATHE YOUR LAST OF THE SWEET AIR, HEROES, FOR WE WILL CRUSH YOU INTO DUST!
HEADS UP, PARTNERS. THESE JERKS ARE KILLERS!

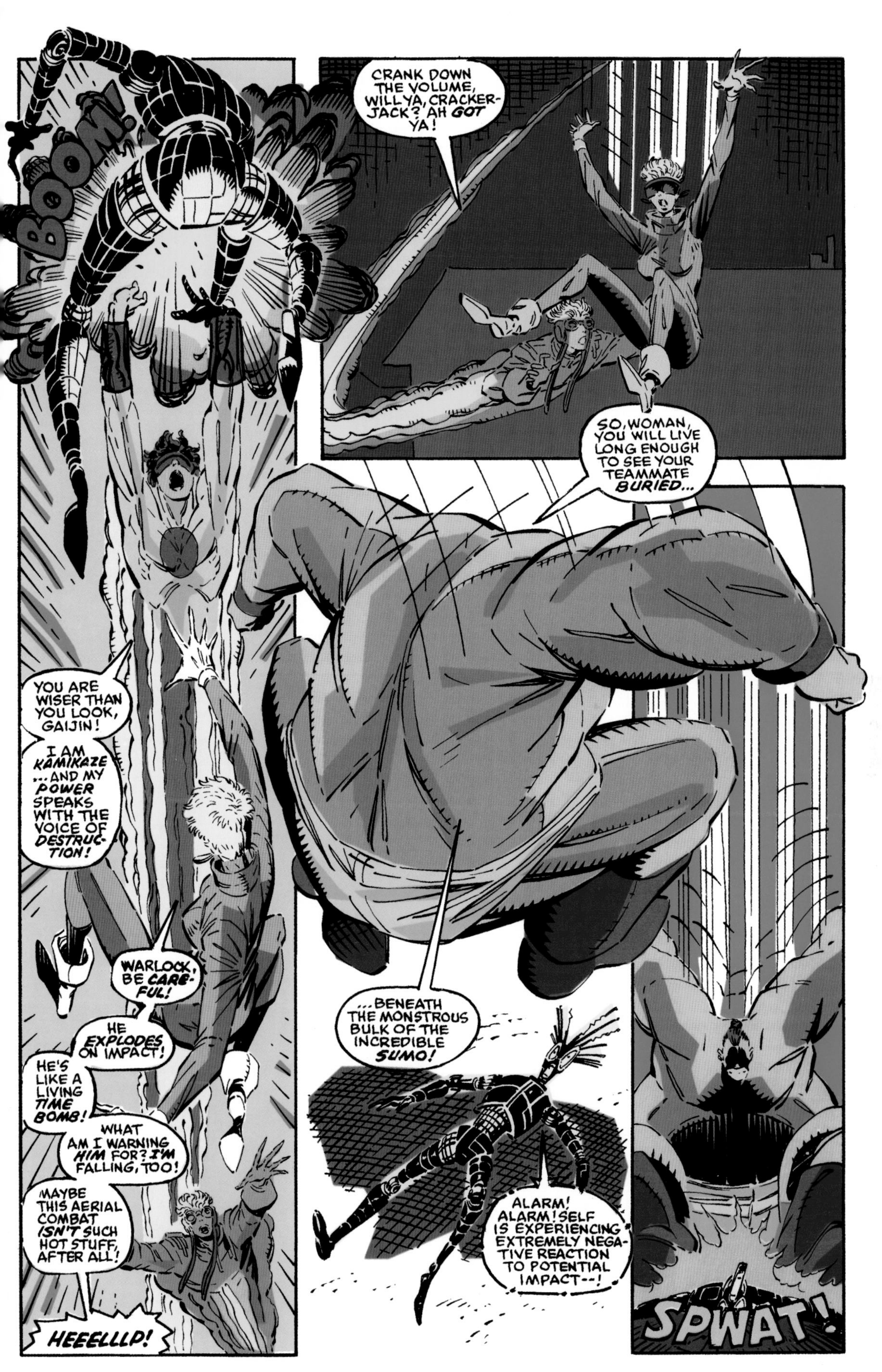

BOOOM!
CRANK DOWN THE VOLUME, WILLYA, CRACKER-JACK? AH GOT YA!
SO, WOMAN, YOU WILL LIVE LONG ENOUGH TO SEE YOUR TEAMMATE BURIED...
YOU ARE WISER THAN YOU LOOK, GAIJIN!
I AM KAMIKAZE ...AND MY POWER SPEAKS WITH THE VOICE OF DESTRUCTION!
WARLOCK! BE CAREFUL!
HE EXPLODES ON IMPACT!
HE'S LIKE A LIVING TIME BOMB!
WHAT AM I WARNING HIM FOR? I'M FALLING, TOO!
MAYBE THIS AERIAL COMBAT ISN'T SUCH HOT STUFF, AFTER ALL!
HEEELLLP!
...BENEATH THE MONSTROUS BULK OF THE INCREDIBLE SUMO!
ALARM! ALARM! SELF IS EXPERIENCING EXTREMELY NEGATIVE REACTION TO POTENTIAL IMPACT--!
SPWAT!

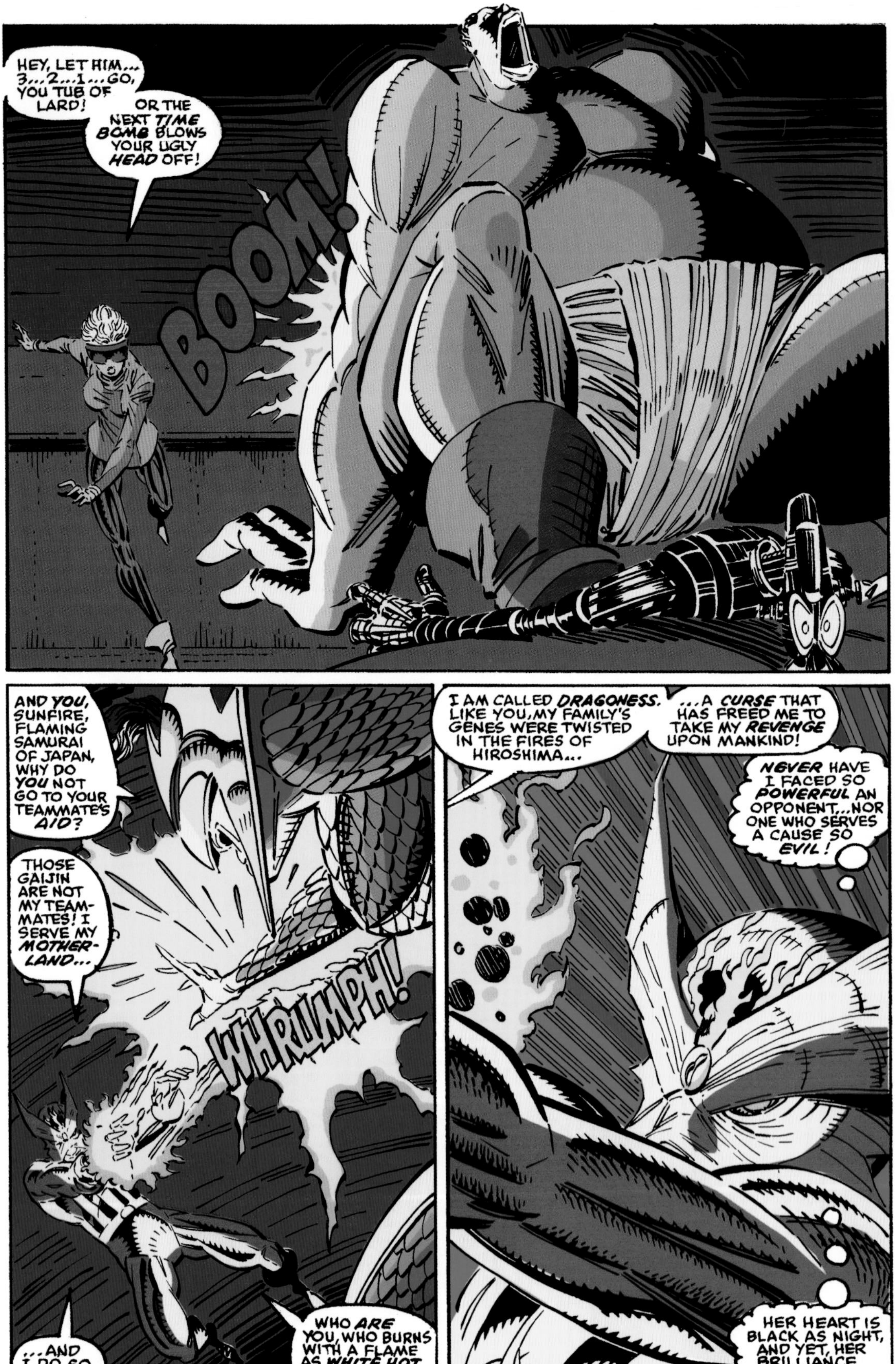
HEY, LET HIM... 3...2...1...GO, YOU TUB OF LARD!
OR THE NEXT TIME BOMB BLOWS YOUR UGLY HEAD OFF!
BOOM!
AND YOU, SUNFIRE, FLAMING SAMURAI OF JAPAN, WHY DO YOU NOT GO TO YOUR TEAMMATE'S AID?
THOSE GAIJIN ARE NOT MY TEAMMATES! I SERVE MY MOTHERLAND...
WHRUMPH!
...AND I DO SO ALONE!
WHO ARE YOU, WHO BURNS WITH A FLAME AS WHITE HOT AS MY OWN?
I AM CALLED DRAGONESS. LIKE YOU, MY FAMILY'S GENES WERE TWISTED IN THE FIRES OF HIROSHIMA...
...A CURSE THAT HAS FREED ME TO TAKE MY REVENGE UPON MANKIND!
NEVER HAVE I FACED SO POWERFUL AN OPPONENT...NOR ONE WHO SERVES A CAUSE SO EVIL!
HER HEART IS BLACK AS NIGHT, AND YET, HER BRILLIANCE DAZZLES ME.

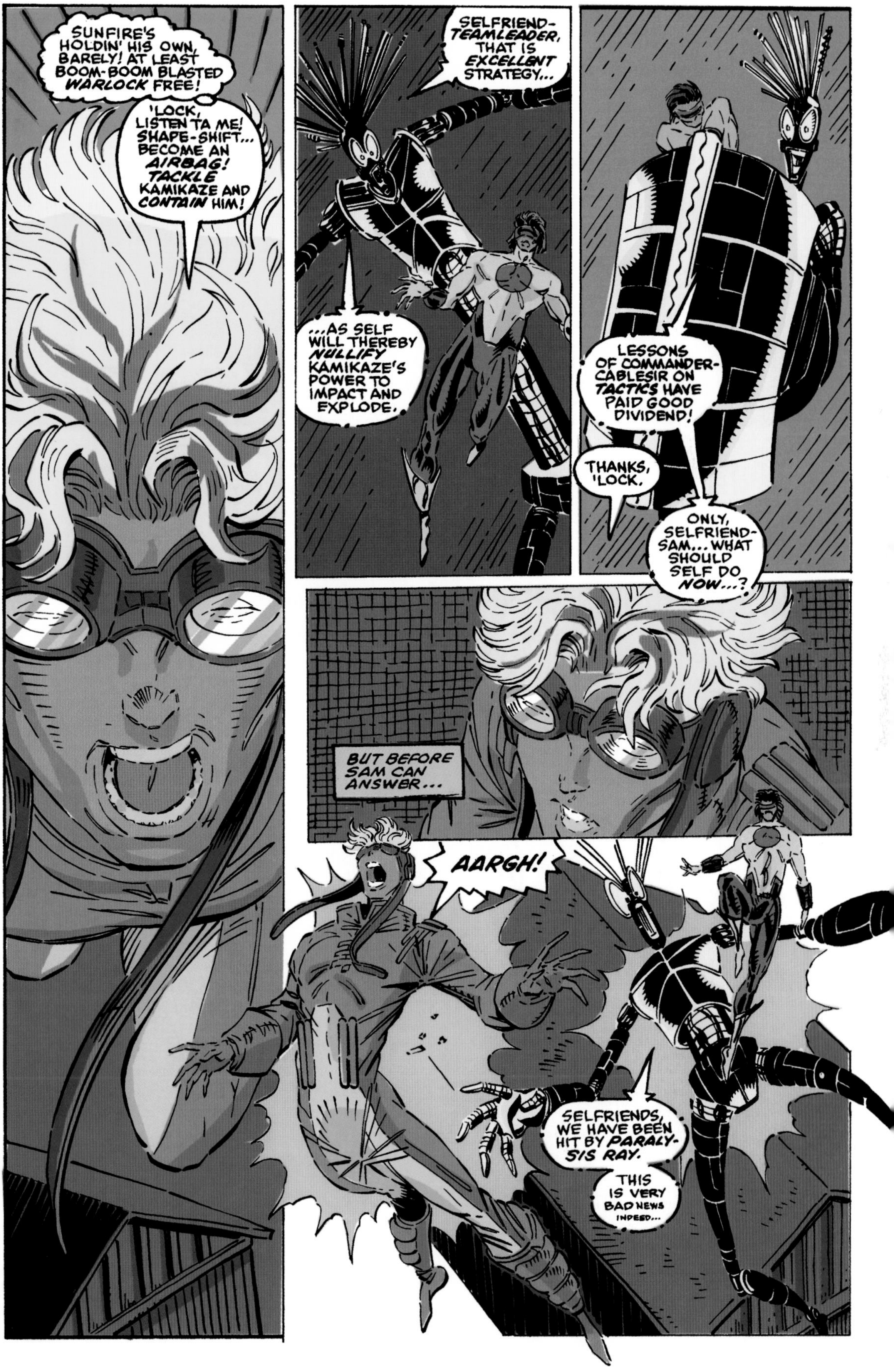
SUNFIRE'S HOLDIN' HIS OWN, BARELY! AT LEAST BOOM-BOOM BLASTED WARLOCK FREE!
'LOCK, LISTEN TA ME! SHAPE-SHIFT... BECOME AN AIRBAG! TACKLE KAMIKAZE AND CONTAIN HIM!
SELFRIEND-TEAMLEADER, THAT IS EXCELLENT STRATEGY...
...AS SELF WILL THEREBY NULLIFY KAMIKAZE'S POWER TO IMPACT AND EXPLODE.
LESSONS OF COMMANDER-CABLESIR ON TACTICS HAVE PAID GOOD DIVIDEND!
THANKS, 'LOCK.
ONLY, SELFRIEND-SAM... WHAT SHOULD SELF DO NOW...?
BUT BEFORE SAM CAN ANSWER...
AARGH!
SELFRIENDS, WE HAVE BEEN HIT BY PARALY-SIS RAY.
THIS IS VERY BAD NEWS INDEED...

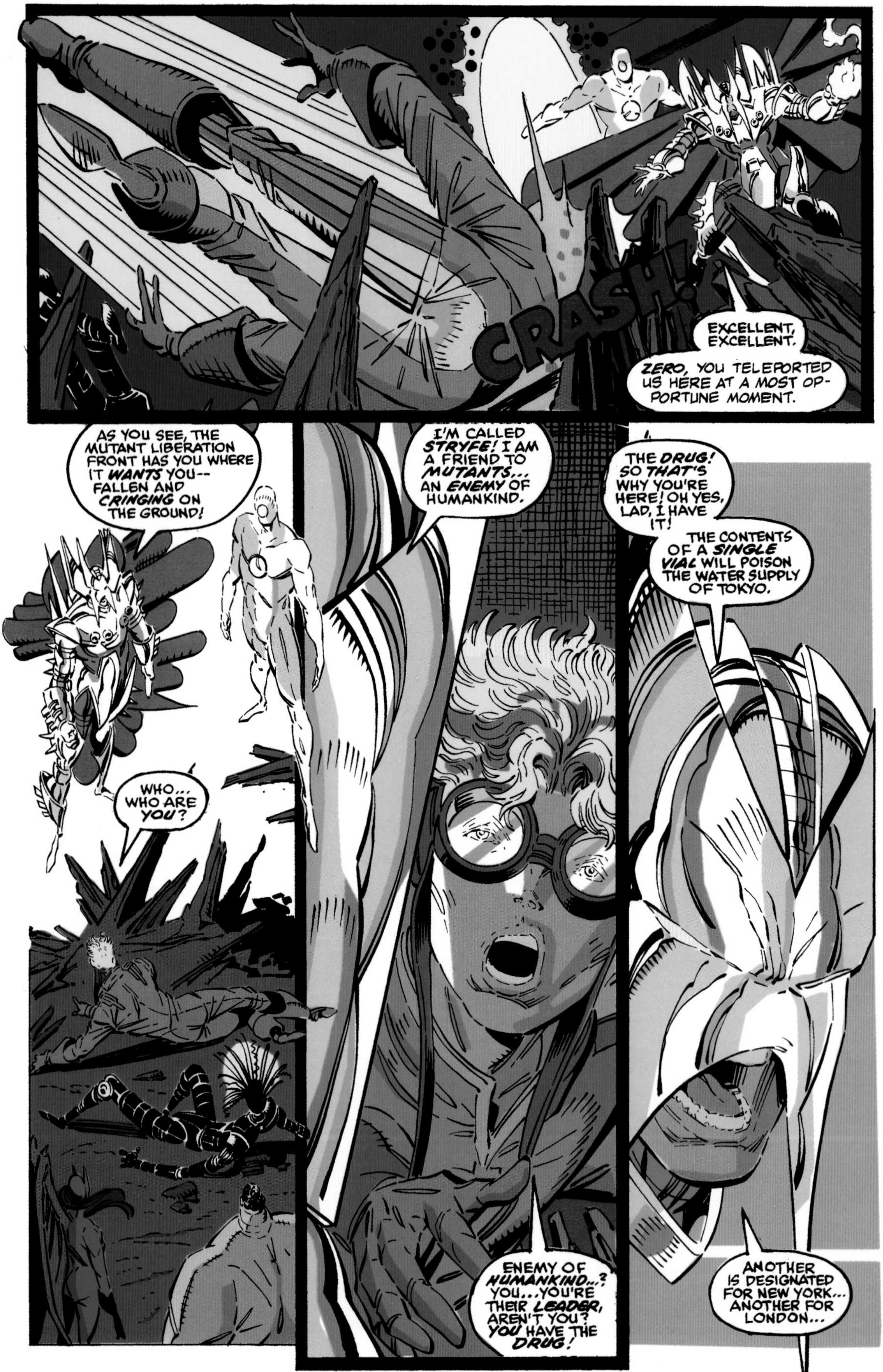
CRASH!
EXCELLENT, EXCELLENT.
ZERO, YOU TELEPORTED US HERE AT A MOST OP-PORTUNE MOMENT.
AS YOU SEE, THE MUTANT LIBERATION FRONT HAS YOU WHERE IT WANTS YOU-- FALLEN AND CRINGING ON THE GROUND!
WHO... WHO ARE YOU?
I'M CALLED STRYFE! I AM A FRIEND TO MUTANTS... AN ENEMY OF HUMANKIND.
ENEMY OF HUMANKIND...? YOU...YOU'RE THEIR LEADER, AREN'T YOU? YOU HAVE THE DRUG!
THE DRUG! SO THAT'S WHY YOU'RE HERE! OH YES, LAD, I HAVE IT!
THE CONTENTS OF A SINGLE VIAL WILL POISON THE WATER SUPPLY OF TOKYO.
ANOTHER IS DESIGNATED FOR NEW YORK... ANOTHER FOR LONDON...

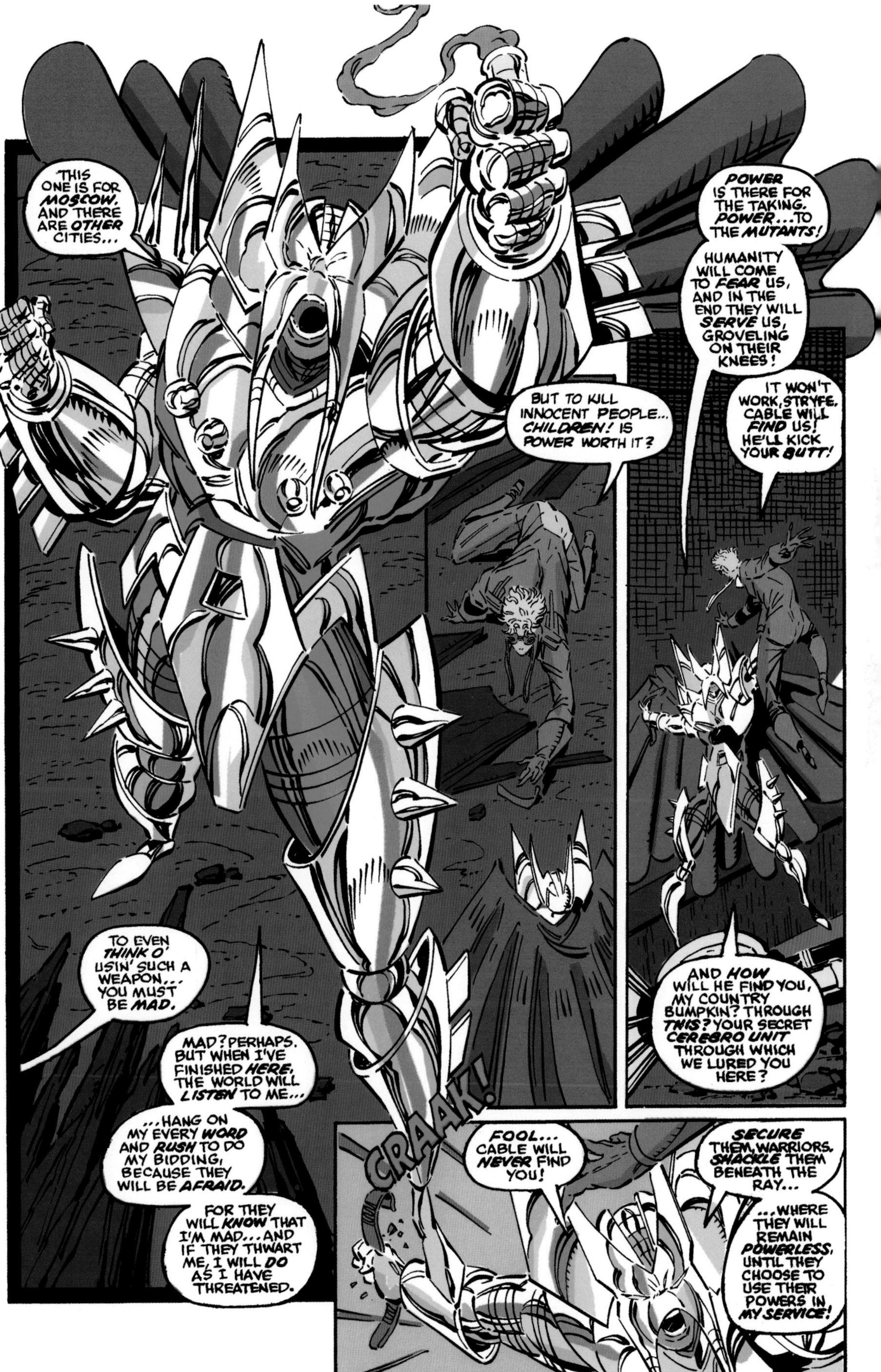

THIS ONE IS FOR MOSCOW. AND THERE ARE OTHER CITIES...
POWER IS THERE FOR THE TAKING. POWER...TO THE MUTANTS!
HUMANITY WILL COME TO FEAR US, AND IN THE END THEY WILL SERVE US, GROVELING ON THEIR KNEES!
BUT TO KILL INNOCENT PEOPLE... CHILDREN! IS POWER WORTH IT?
IT WON'T WORK, STRYFE. CABLE WILL FIND US! HE'LL KICK YOUR BUTT!
TO EVEN THINK O' USIN' SUCH A WEAPON... YOU MUST BE MAD.
MAD? PERHAPS. BUT WHEN I'VE FINISHED HERE, THE WORLD WILL LISTEN TO ME...
...HANG ON MY EVERY WORD AND RUSH TO DO MY BIDDING, BECAUSE THEY WILL BE AFRAID.
FOR THEY WILL KNOW THAT I'M MAD...AND IF THEY THWART ME, I WILL DO AS I HAVE THREATENED.
AND HOW WILL HE FIND YOU, MY COUNTRY BUMPKIN? THROUGH THIS? YOUR SECRET CEREBRO UNIT THROUGH WHICH WE LURED YOU HERE?
CRAAK!
FOOL... CABLE WILL NEVER FIND YOU!
SECURE THEM, WARRIORS. SHACKLE THEM BENEATH THE RAY...
...WHERE THEY WILL REMAIN POWERLESS, UNTIL THEY CHOOSE TO USE THEIR POWERS IN MY SERVICE!

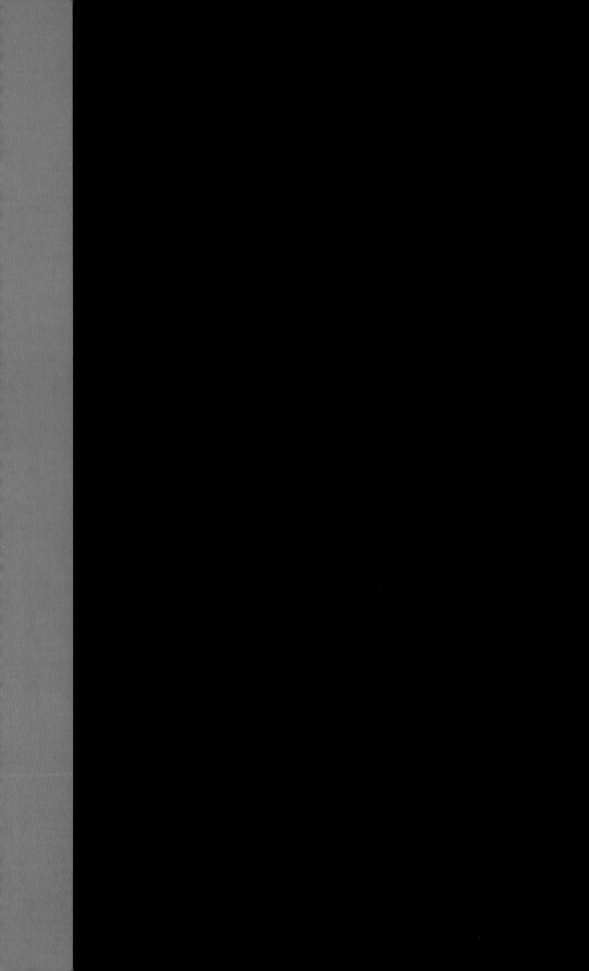

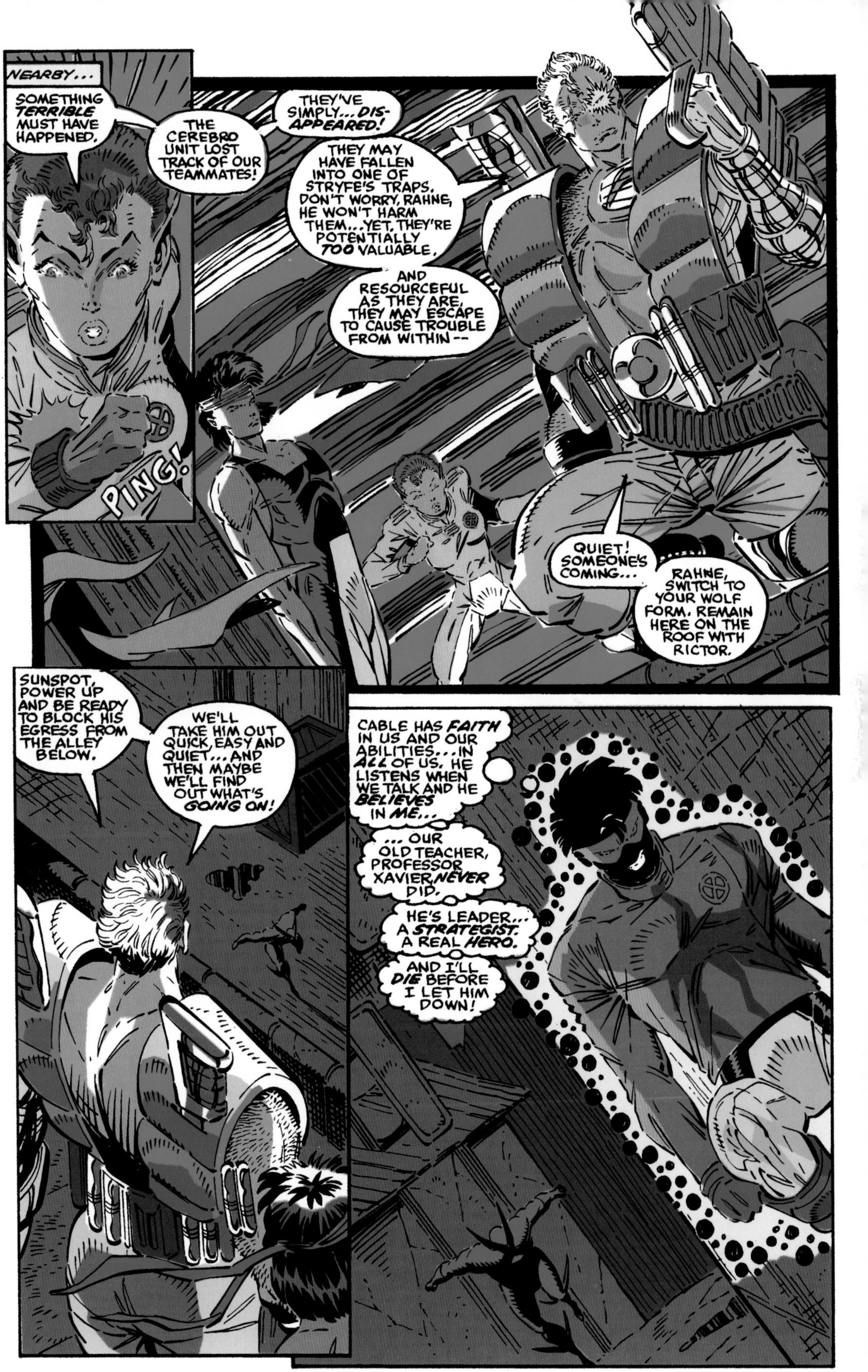
NEARBY...
SOMETHING TERRIBLE MUST HAVE HAPPENED.
THE CEREBRO UNIT LOST TRACK OF OUR TEAMMATES!
THEY'VE SIMPLY... DIS-APPEARED!
PING!
THEY MAY HAVE FALLEN INTO ONE OF STRYFE'S TRAPS. DON'T WORRY, RAHNE, HE WON'T HARM THEM... YET. THEY'RE POTENTIALLY TOO VALUABLE,
AND RESOURCEFUL AS THEY ARE, THEY MAY ESCAPE TO CAUSE TROUBLE FROM WITHIN --
QUIET! SOMEONE'S COMING...
RAHNE, SWITCH TO YOUR WOLF FORM. REMAIN HERE ON THE ROOF WITH RICTOR.
SUNSPOT, POWER UP AND BE READY TO BLOCK HIS EGRESS FROM THE ALLEY BELOW.
WE'LL TAKE HIM OUT QUICK, EASY AND QUIET... AND THEN MAYBE WE'LL FIND OUT WHAT'S GOING ON!
CABLE HAS FAITH IN US AND OUR ABILITIES... IN ALL OF US. HE LISTENS WHEN WE TALK AND HE BELIEVES IN ME...
... OUR OLD TEACHER, PROFESSOR XAVIER, NEVER DID.
HE'S LEADER... A STRATEGIST. A REAL HERO.
AND I'LL DIE BEFORE I LET HIM DOWN!

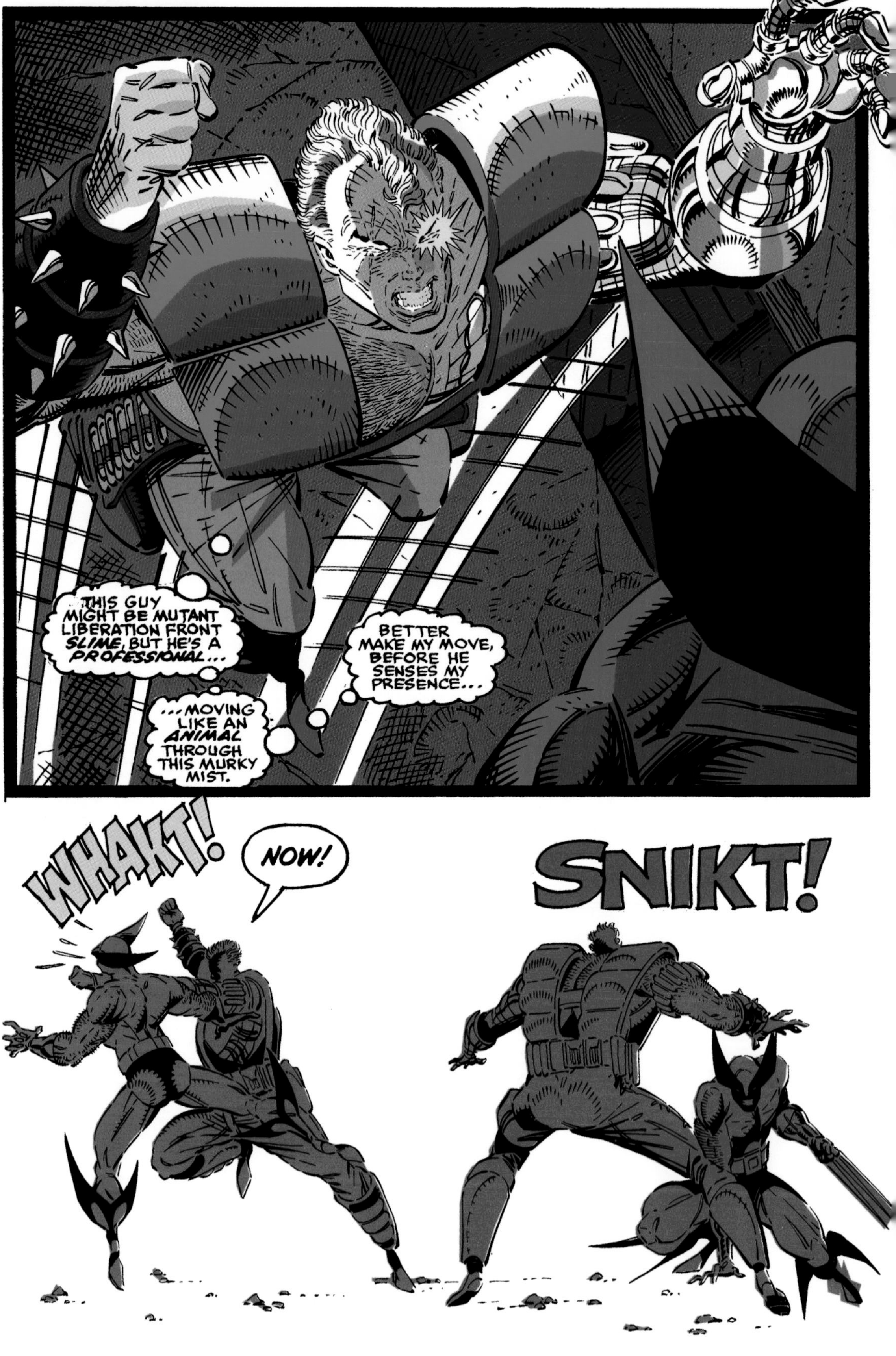
THIS GUY MIGHT BE MUTANT LIBERATION FRONT SLIME, BUT HE'S A PROFESSIONAL...
...MOVING LIKE AN ANIMAL THROUGH THIS MURKY MIST.
BETTER MAKE MY MOVE, BEFORE HE SENSES MY PRESENCE...
WHAKT!
NOW!
SNIKT!

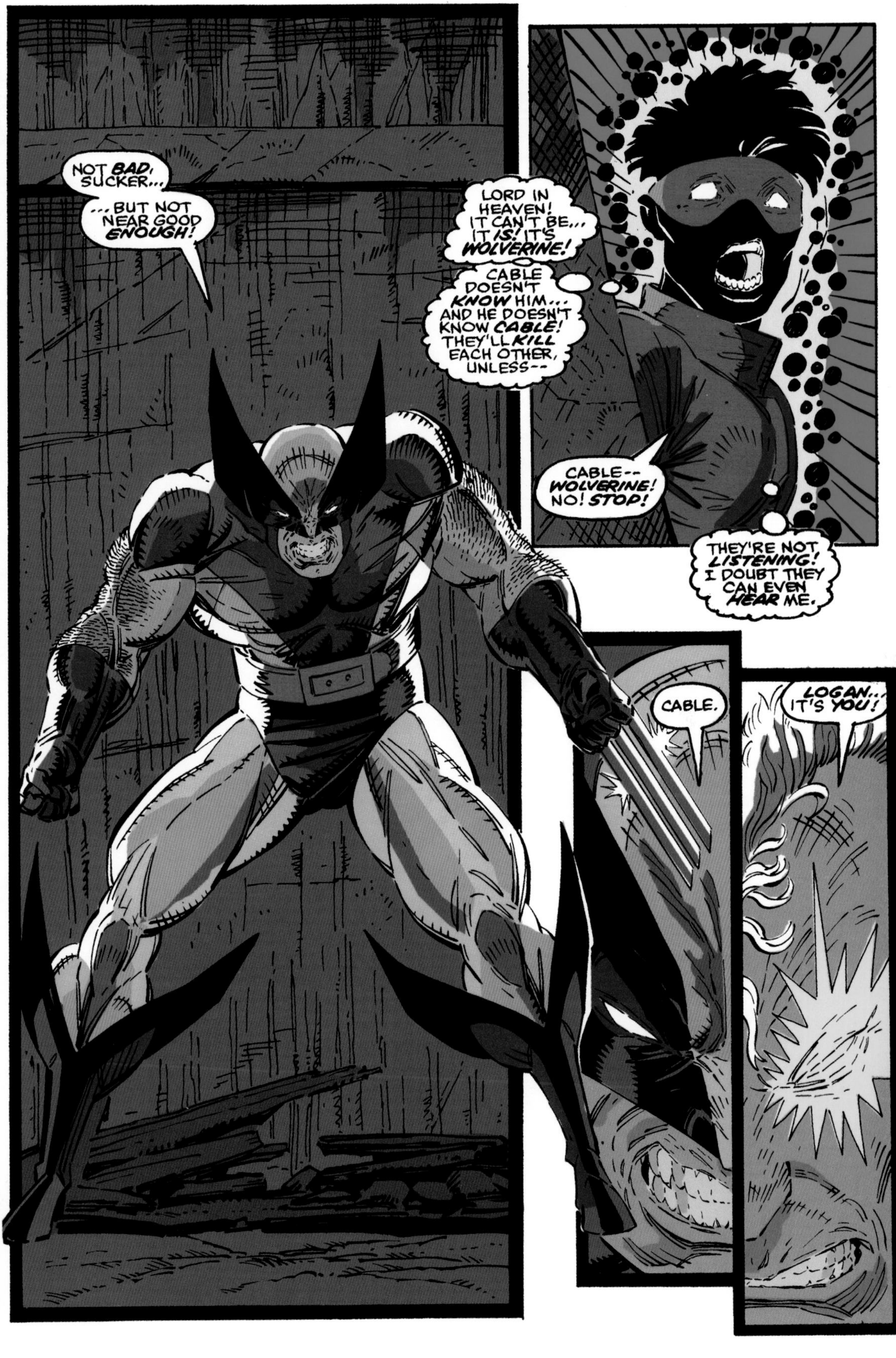
NOT BAD, SUCKER...
...BUT NOT NEAR GOOD ENOUGH!
LORD IN HEAVEN! IT CAN'T BE... IT IS! IT'S WOLVERINE!
CABLE DOESN'T KNOW HIM... AND HE DOESN'T KNOW CABLE! THEY'LL KILL EACH OTHER, UNLESS--
CABLE-- WOLVERINE! NO! STOP!
THEY'RE NOT LISTENING! I DOUBT THEY CAN EVEN HEAR ME.
CABLE.
LOGAN... IT'S YOU!

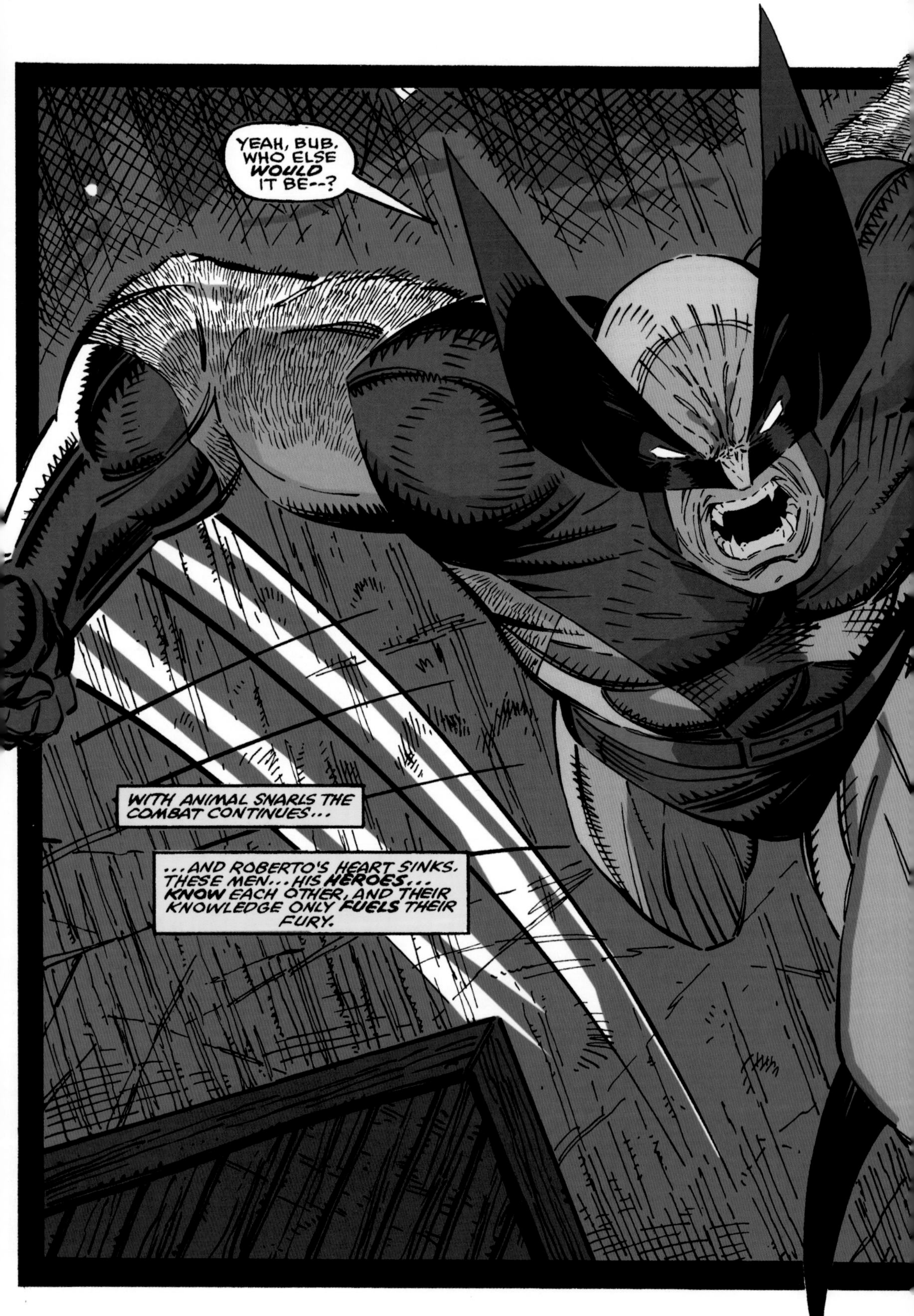
YEAH, BUB. WHO ELSE WOULD IT BE--?
WITH ANIMAL SNARLS THE COMBAT CONTINUES...
...AND ROBERTO'S HEART SINKS. THESE MEN...HIS HEROES... KNOW EACH OTHER, AND THEIR KNOWLEDGE ONLY FUELS THEIR FURY.

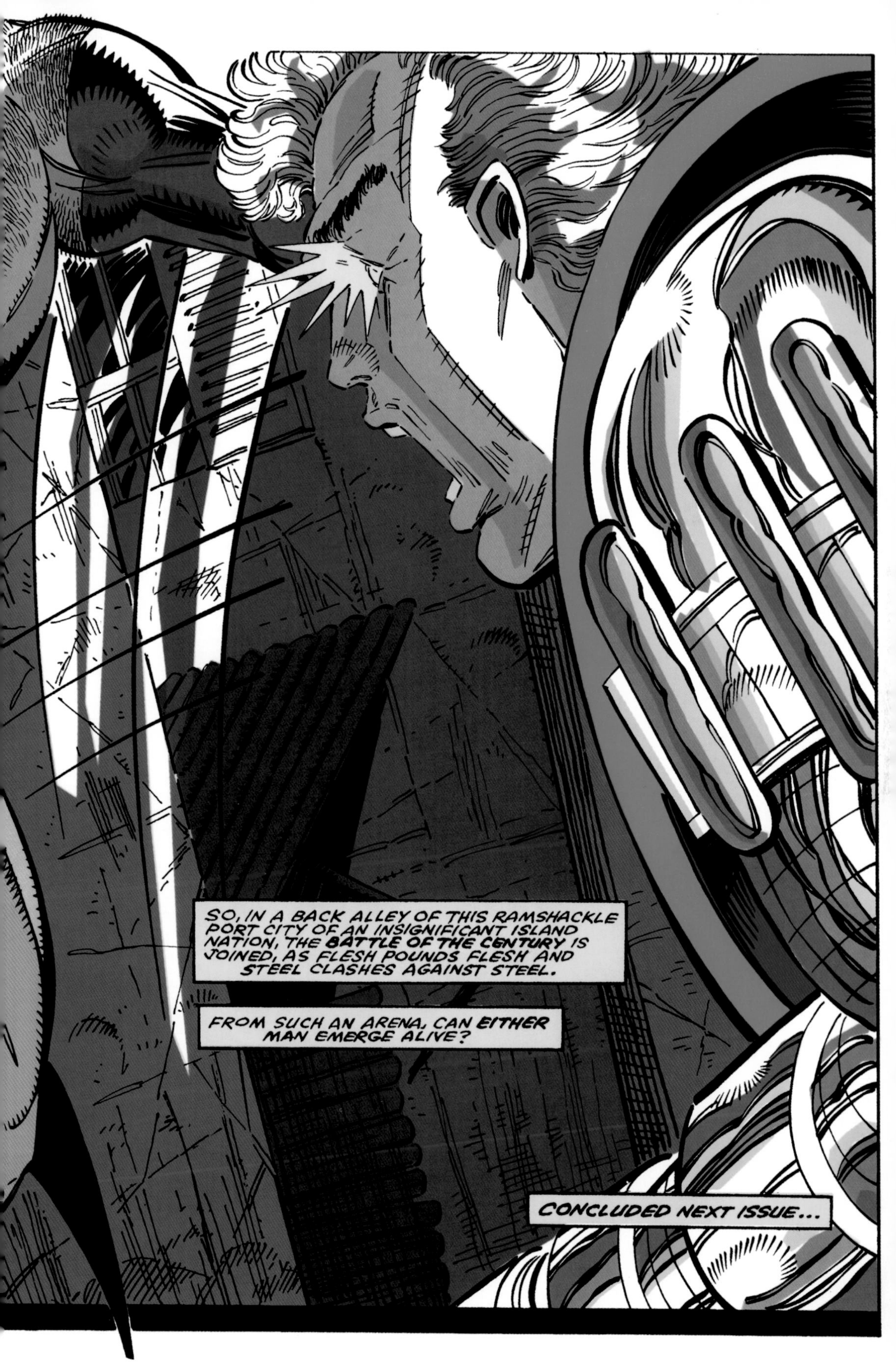
SO, IN A BACK ALLEY OF THIS RAMSHACKLE PORT CITY OF AN INSIGNIFICANT ISLAND NATION, THE BATTLE OF THE CENTURY IS JOINED, AS FLESH POUNDS FLESH AND STEEL CLASHES AGAINST STEEL.
FROM SUCH AN ARENA, CAN EITHER MAN EMERGE ALIVE?
CONCLUDED NEXT ISSUE...

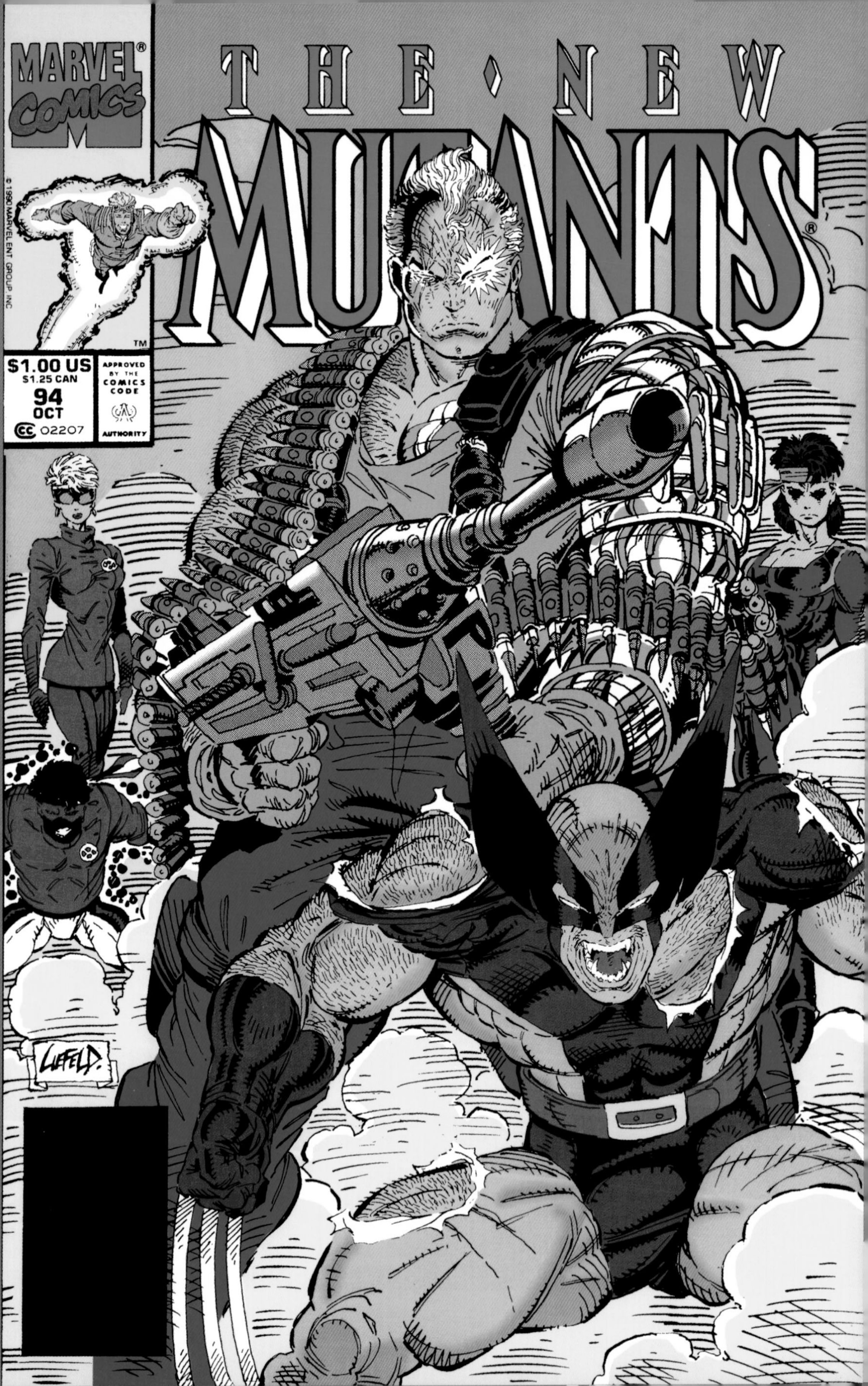

MARVEL® COMICS
THE NEW MUTANTS®
© 1990 MARVEL ENT GROUP INC
TM
$1.00 US
$1.25 CAN
94
OCT
CC 02207
APPROVED BY THE COMICS CODE AUTHORITY
LIEFELD

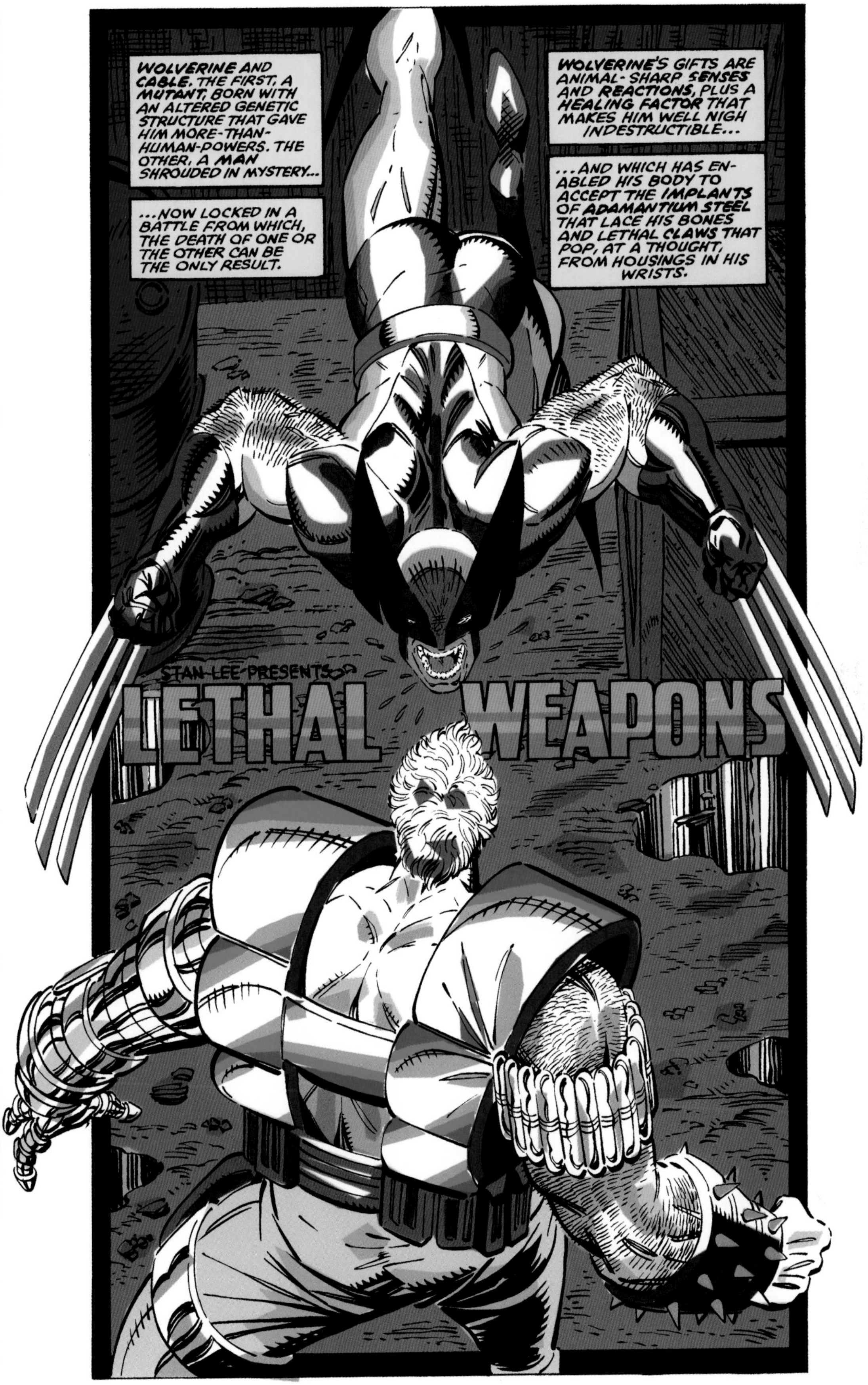
WOLVERINE AND CABLE. THE FIRST, A MUTANT, BORN WITH AN ALTERED GENETIC STRUCTURE THAT GAVE HIM MORE-THAN-HUMAN-POWERS. THE OTHER, A MAN SHROUDED IN MYSTERY...
...NOW LOCKED IN A BATTLE FROM WHICH, THE DEATH OF ONE OR THE OTHER CAN BE THE ONLY RESULT.
WOLVERINE'S GIFTS ARE ANIMAL-SHARP SENSES AND REACTIONS, PLUS A HEALING FACTOR THAT MAKES HIM WELL NIGH INDESTRUCTIBLE...
...AND WHICH HAS ENABLED HIS BODY TO ACCEPT THE IMPLANTS OF ADAMANTIUM STEEL THAT LACE HIS BONES AND LETHAL CLAWS THAT POP, AT A THOUGHT, FROM HOUSINGS IN HIS WRISTS.
STAN LEE PRESENTS
LETHAL WEAPONS

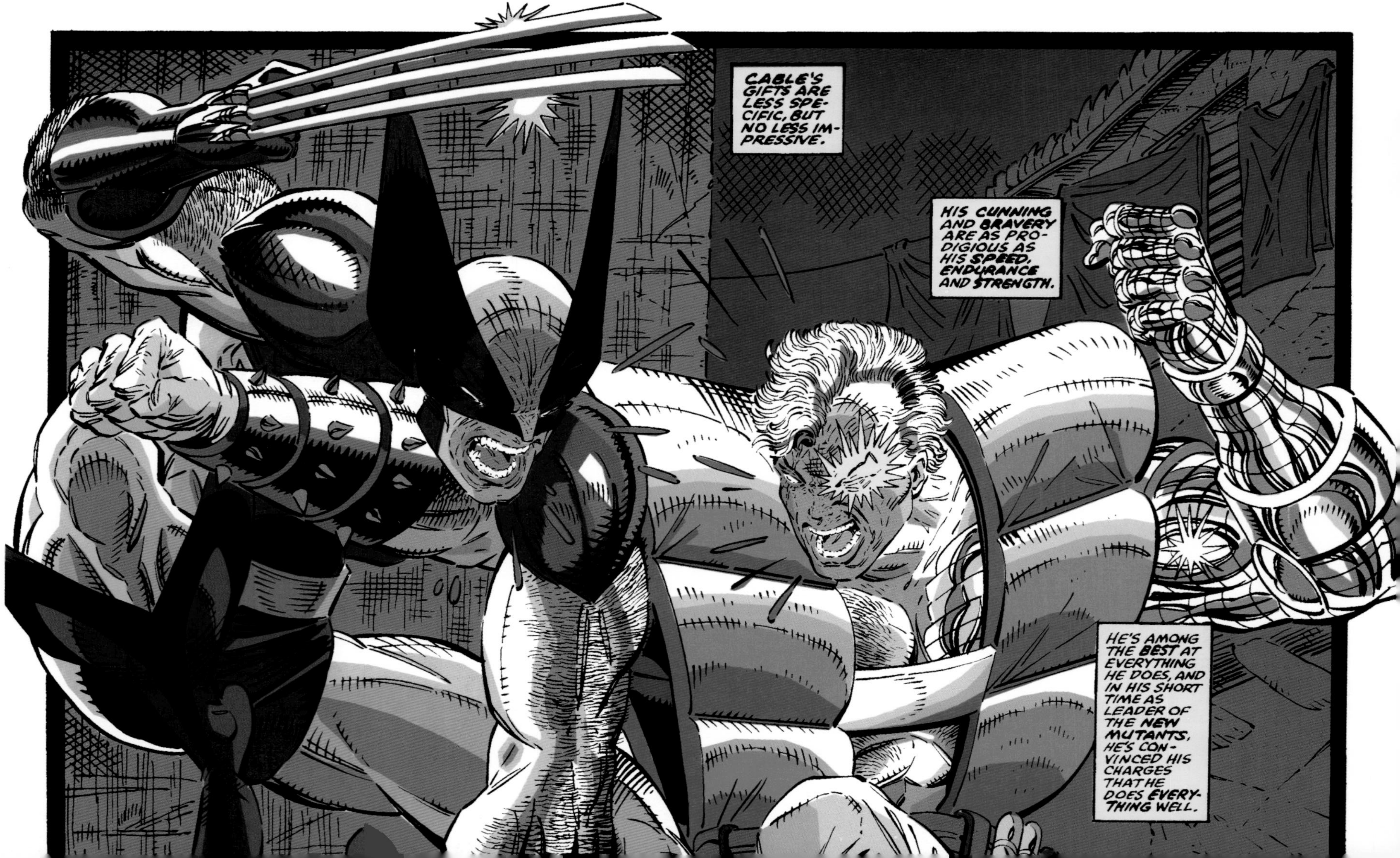
CABLE'S GIFTS ARE LESS SPE-CIFIC, BUT NO LESS IM-PRESSIVE.
HIS CUNNING AND BRAVERY ARE AS PRO-DIGIOUS AS HIS SPEED, ENDURANCE AND STRENGTH.
HE'S AMONG THE BEST AT EVERYTHING HE DOES, AND IN HIS SHORT TIME AS LEADER OF THE NEW MUTANTS, HE'S CON-VINCED HIS CHARGES THAT HE DOES EVERY-THING WELL.

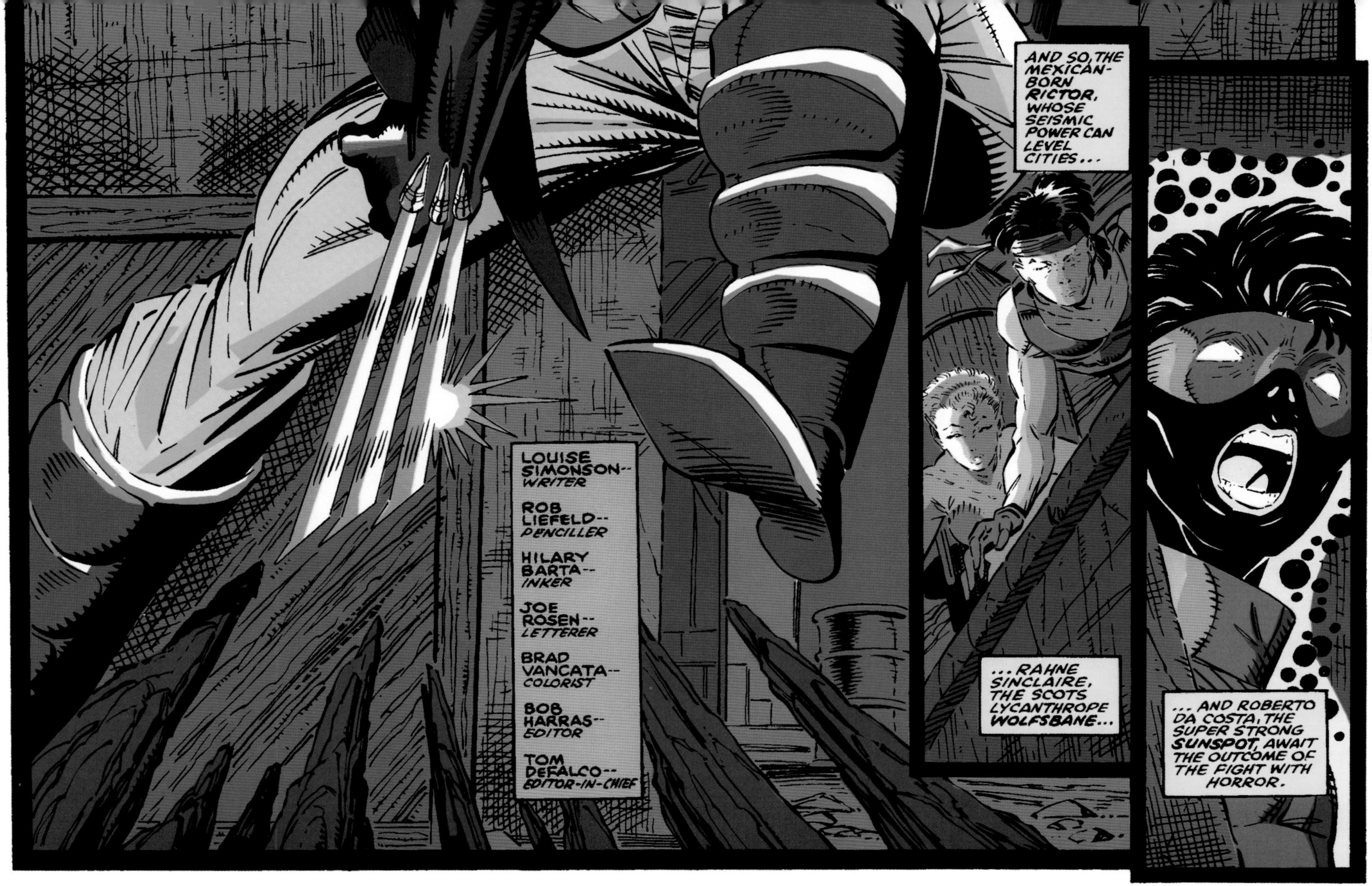
LOUISE SIMONSON--WRITER
ROB LIEFELD--PENCILLER
HILARY BARTA--INKER
JOE ROSEN--LETTERER
BRAD VANCATA--COLORIST
BOB HARRAS--EDITOR
TOM DeFALCO--EDITOR-IN-CHIEF
AND SO, THE MEXICAN-BORN RICTOR, WHOSE SEISMIC POWER CAN LEVEL CITIES...
...RAHNE SINCLAIRE, THE SCOTS LYCANTHROPE WOLFSBANE...
...AND ROBERTO DA COSTA, THE SUPER STRONG SUNSPOT, AWAIT THE OUTCOME OF THE FIGHT WITH HORROR.

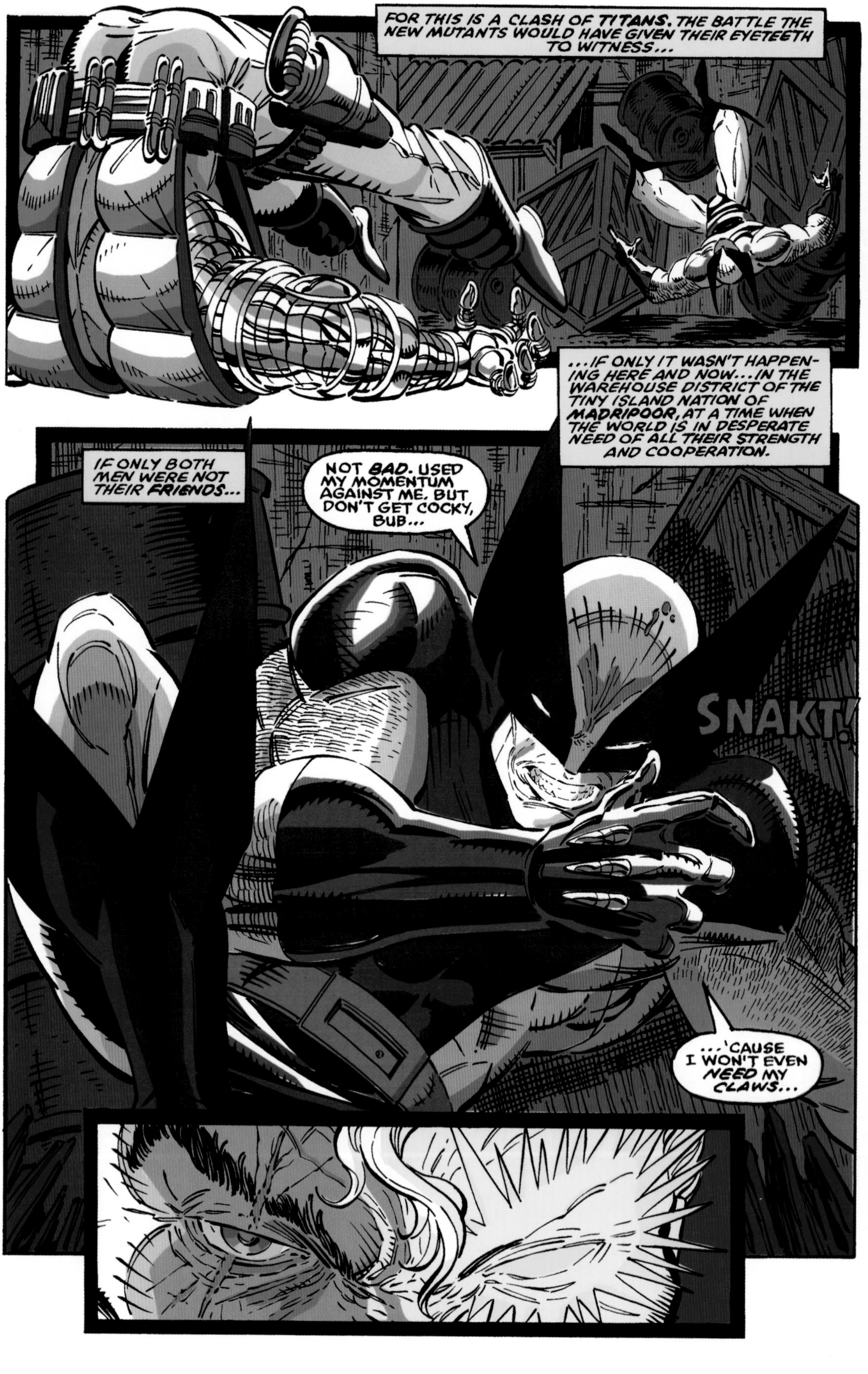
FOR THIS IS A CLASH OF TITANS. THE BATTLE THE NEW MUTANTS WOULD HAVE GIVEN THEIR EYETEETH TO WITNESS...
...IF ONLY IT WASN'T HAPPENING HERE AND NOW...IN THE WAREHOUSE DISTRICT OF THE TINY ISLAND NATION OF MADRIPOOR, AT A TIME WHEN THE WORLD IS IN DESPERATE NEED OF ALL THEIR STRENGTH AND COOPERATION.
IF ONLY BOTH MEN WERE NOT THEIR FRIENDS...
NOT BAD. USED MY MOMENTUM AGAINST ME. BUT DON'T GET COCKY, BUB...
SNAKT!
...'CAUSE I WON'T EVEN NEED MY CLAWS...

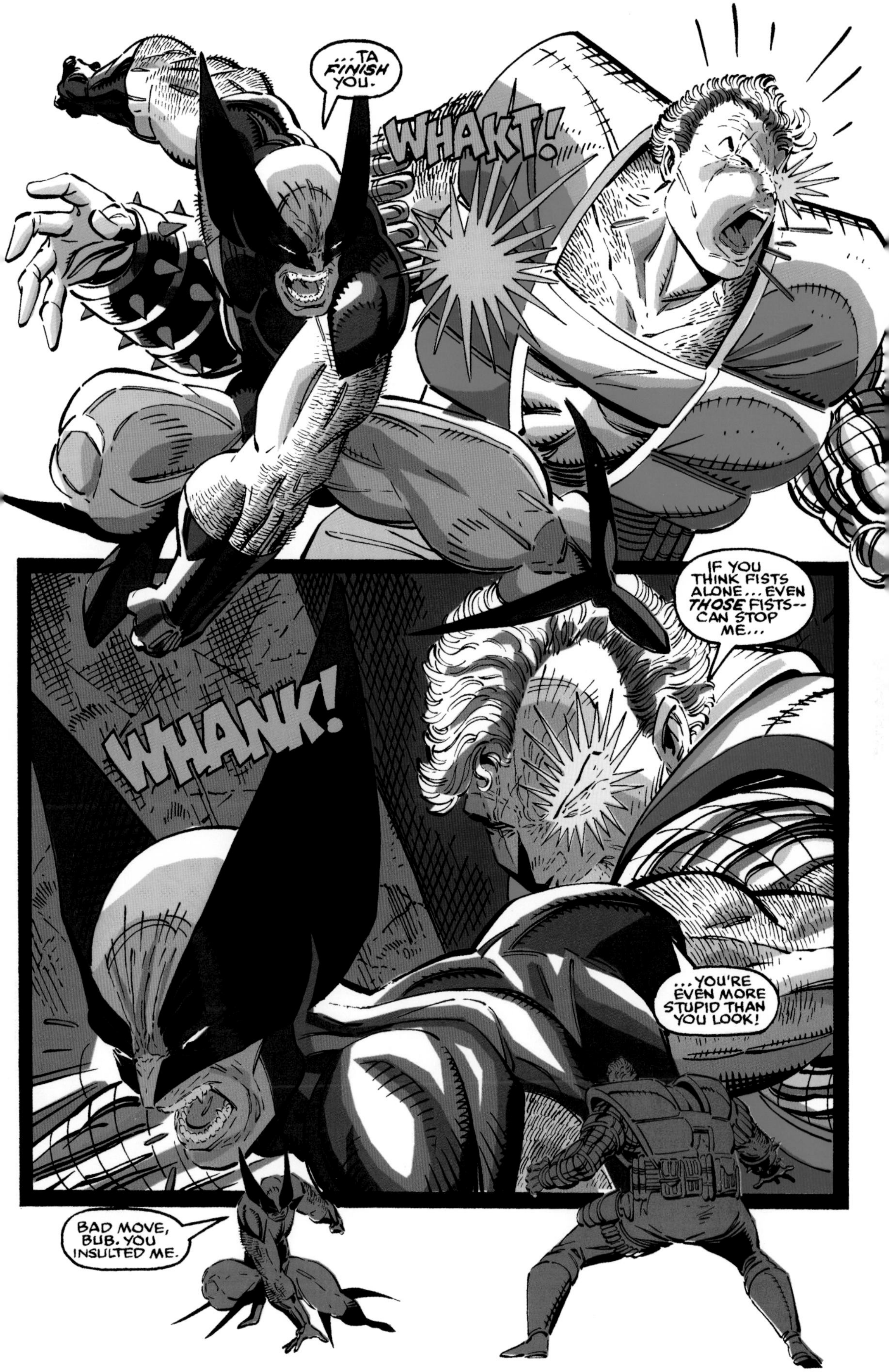
...TA FINISH YOU.
WHAKT!
IF YOU THINK FISTS ALONE... EVEN THOSE FISTS-- CAN STOP ME...
WHANK!
...YOU'RE EVEN MORE STUPID THAN YOU LOOK!
BAD MOVE, BUB. YOU INSULTED ME.

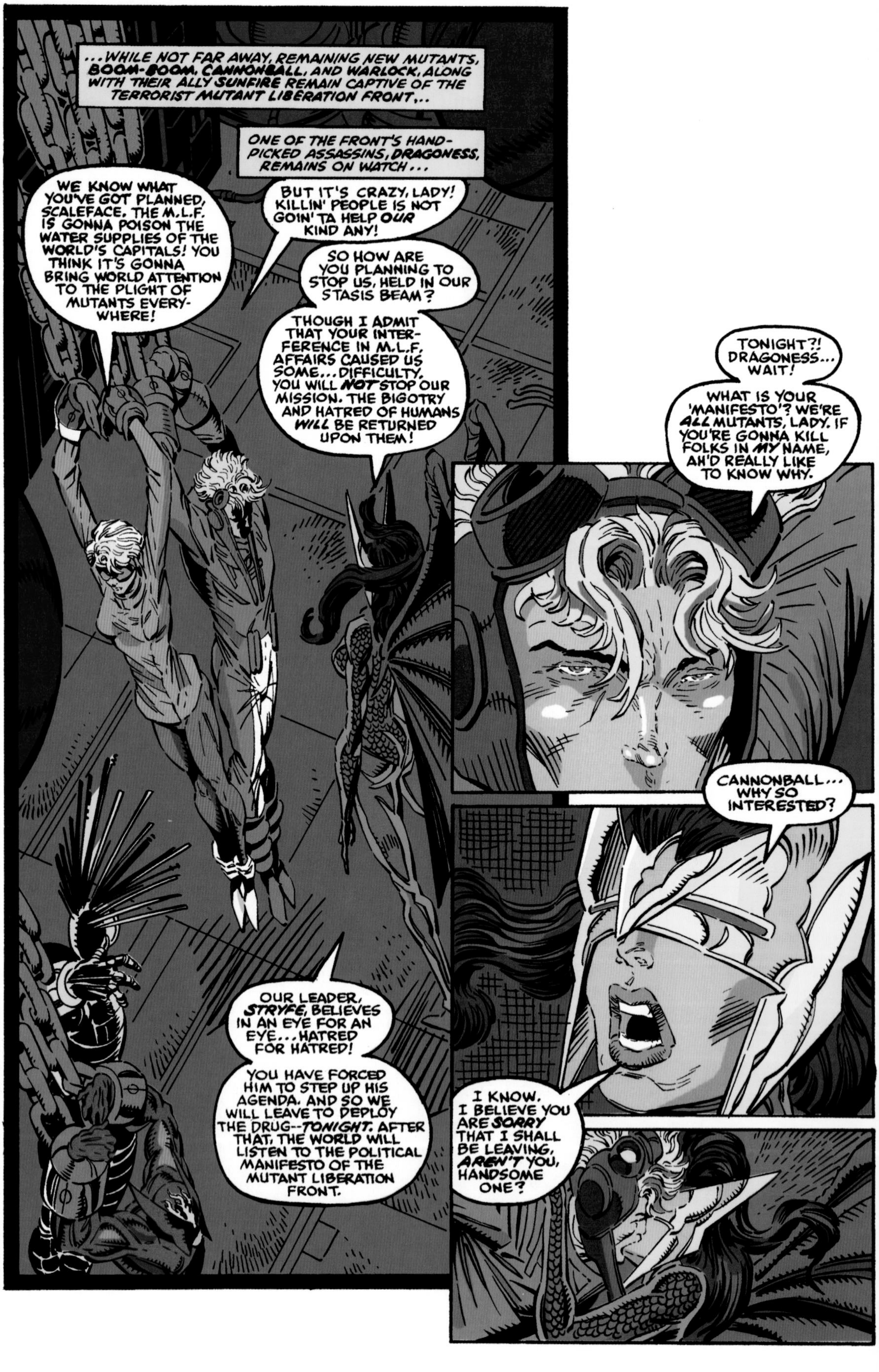
...WHILE NOT FAR AWAY, REMAINING NEW MUTANTS, BOOM-BOOM, CANNONBALL, AND WARLOCK, ALONG WITH THEIR ALLY SUNFIRE REMAIN CAPTIVE OF THE TERRORIST MUTANT LIBERATION FRONT...
ONE OF THE FRONT'S HAND-PICKED ASSASSINS, DRAGONESS, REMAINS ON WATCH...
WE KNOW WHAT YOU'VE GOT PLANNED, SCALEFACE. THE M.L.F. IS GONNA POISON THE WATER SUPPLIES OF THE WORLD'S CAPITALS! YOU THINK IT'S GONNA BRING WORLD ATTENTION TO THE PLIGHT OF MUTANTS EVERYWHERE!
BUT IT'S CRAZY, LADY! KILLIN' PEOPLE IS NOT GOIN' TA HELP OUR KIND ANY!
SO HOW ARE YOU PLANNING TO STOP US, HELD IN OUR STASIS BEAM?
THOUGH I ADMIT THAT YOUR INTERFERENCE IN M.L.F. AFFAIRS CAUSED US SOME... DIFFICULTY, YOU WILL NOT STOP OUR MISSION. THE BIGOTRY AND HATRED OF HUMANS WILL BE RETURNED UPON THEM!
OUR LEADER, STRYFE, BELIEVES IN AN EYE FOR AN EYE... HATRED FOR HATRED!
YOU HAVE FORCED HIM TO STEP UP HIS AGENDA. AND SO WE WILL LEAVE TO DEPLOY THE DRUG--TONIGHT. AFTER THAT, THE WORLD WILL LISTEN TO THE POLITICAL MANIFESTO OF THE MUTANT LIBERATION FRONT.
TONIGHT?! DRAGONESS... WAIT!
WHAT IS YOUR 'MANIFESTO'? WE'RE ALL MUTANTS, LADY. IF YOU'RE GONNA KILL FOLKS IN MY NAME, AH'D REALLY LIKE TO KNOW WHY.
CANNONBALL... WHY SO INTERESTED?
I KNOW. I BELIEVE YOU ARE SORRY THAT I SHALL BE LEAVING, AREN'T YOU, HANDSOME ONE?

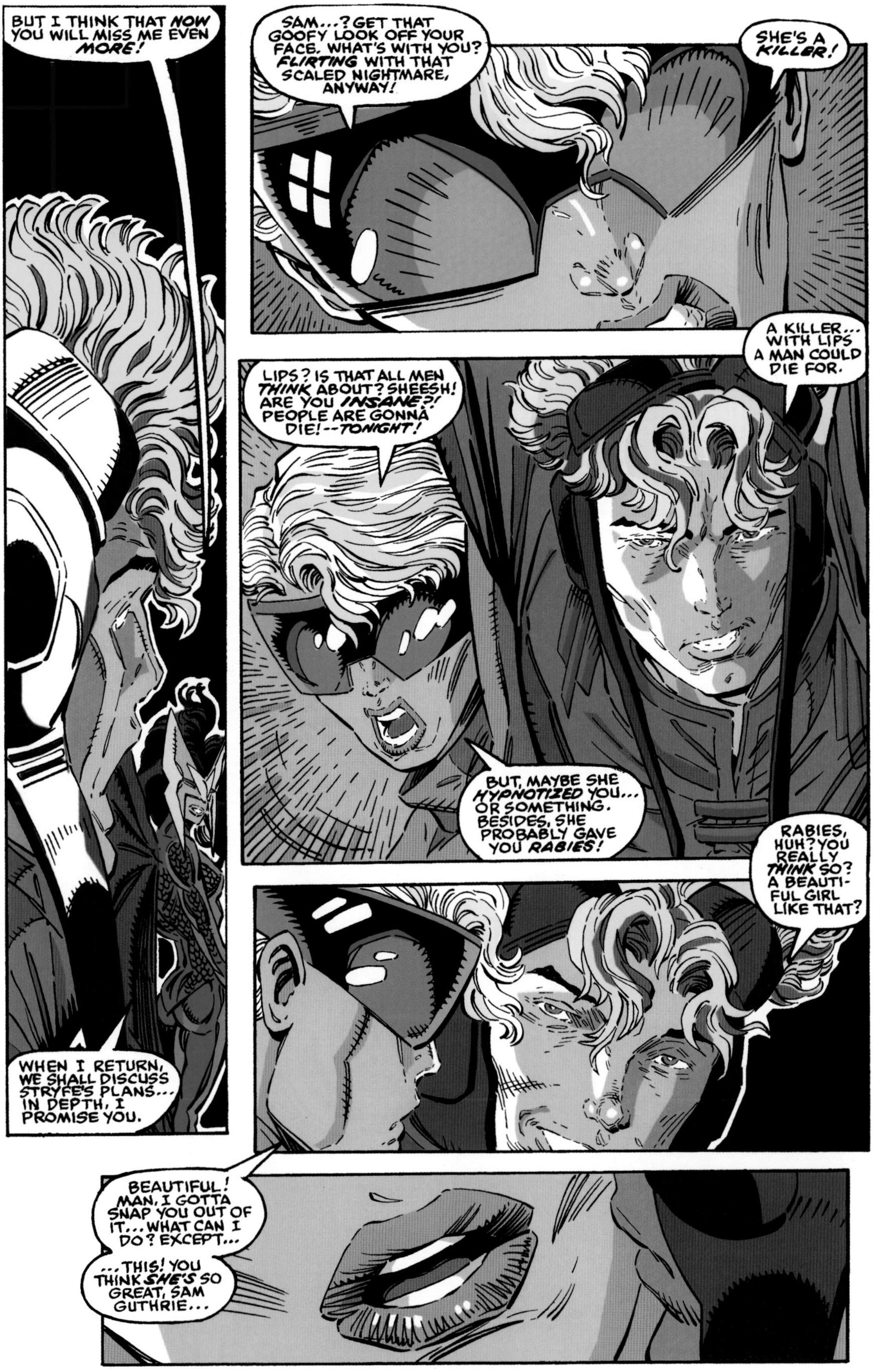
BUT I THINK THAT NOW YOU WILL MISS ME EVEN MORE!
WHEN I RETURN, WE SHALL DISCUSS STRYFE'S PLANS... IN DEPTH, I PROMISE YOU.
SAM...? GET THAT GOOFY LOOK OFF YOUR FACE. WHAT'S WITH YOU? FLIRTING WITH THAT SCALED NIGHTMARE, ANYWAY!
SHE'S A KILLER!
A KILLER... WITH LIPS A MAN COULD DIE FOR.
LIPS? IS THAT ALL MEN THINK ABOUT? SHEESH! ARE YOU INSANE?! PEOPLE ARE GONNA DIE!--TONIGHT!
BUT, MAYBE SHE HYPNOTIZED YOU... OR SOMETHING. BESIDES, SHE PROBABLY GAVE YOU RABIES!
RABIES, HUH? YOU REALLY THINK SO? A BEAUTIFUL GIRL LIKE THAT?
BEAUTIFUL! MAN, I GOTTA SNAP YOU OUT OF IT... WHAT CAN I DO? EXCEPT...
...THIS! YOU THINK SHE'S SO GREAT, SAM GUTHRIE...

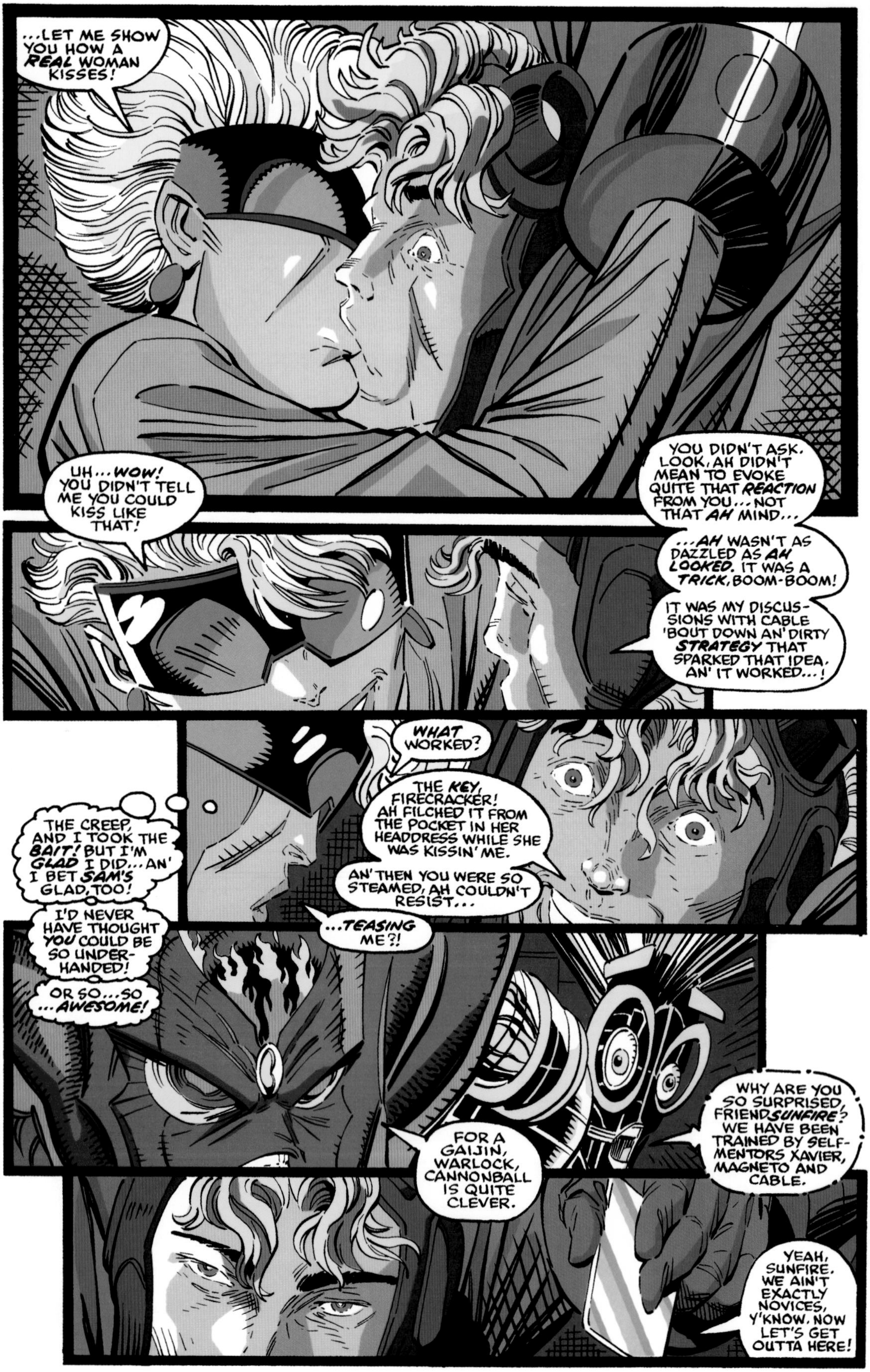
...LET ME SHOW YOU HOW A REAL WOMAN KISSES!
UH...WOW! YOU DIDN'T TELL ME YOU COULD KISS LIKE THAT!
YOU DIDN'T ASK. LOOK, AH DIDN'T MEAN TO EVOKE QUITE THAT REACTION FROM YOU...NOT THAT AH MIND...
...AH WASN'T AS DAZZLED AS AH LOOKED. IT WAS A TRICK, BOOM-BOOM!
IT WAS MY DISCUSSIONS WITH CABLE 'BOUT DOWN AN' DIRTY STRATEGY THAT SPARKED THAT IDEA. AN' IT WORKED...!
WHAT WORKED?
THE KEY, FIRECRACKER! AH FILCHED IT FROM THE POCKET IN HER HEADDRESS WHILE SHE WAS KISSIN' ME.
AN' THEN YOU WERE SO STEAMED, AH COULDN'T RESIST...
...TEASING ME?!
THE CREEP, AND I TOOK THE BAIT! BUT I'M GLAD I DID...AN' I BET SAM'S GLAD, TOO!
I'D NEVER HAVE THOUGHT YOU COULD BE SO UNDER-HANDED!
OR SO...SO ...AWESOME!
FOR A GAIJIN, WARLOCK, CANNONBALL IS QUITE CLEVER.
WHY ARE YOU SO SURPRISED, FRIEND SUNFIRE? WE HAVE BEEN TRAINED BY SELF-MENTORS XAVIER, MAGNETO AND CABLE.
YEAH, SUNFIRE. WE AIN'T EXACTLY NOVICES, Y'KNOW. NOW LET'S GET OUTTA HERE!

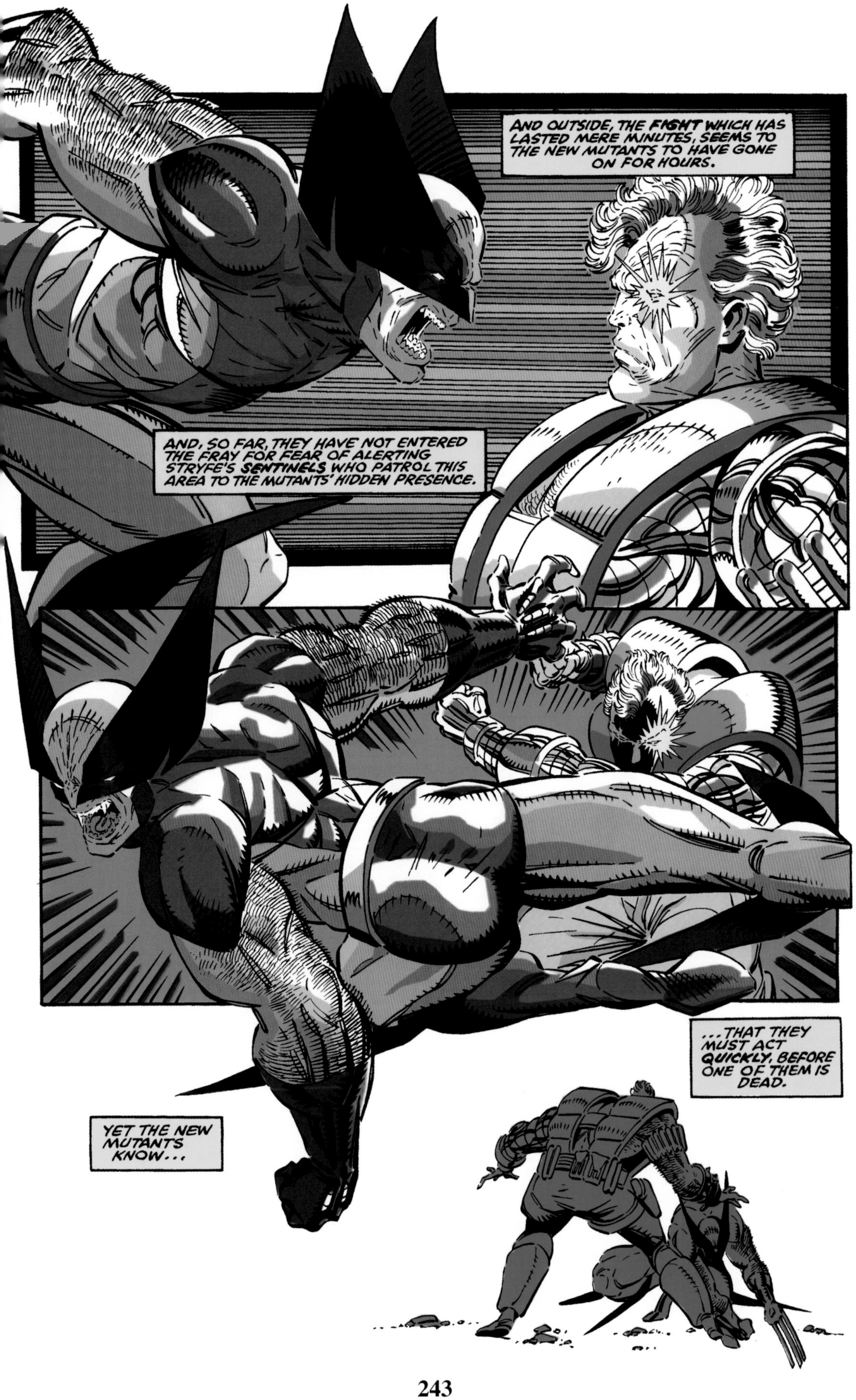
AND OUTSIDE, THE FIGHT WHICH HAS LASTED MERE MINUTES, SEEMS TO THE NEW MUTANTS TO HAVE GONE ON FOR HOURS.
AND, SO FAR, THEY HAVE NOT ENTERED THE FRAY FOR FEAR OF ALERTING STRYFE'S SENTINELS WHO PATROL THIS AREA TO THE MUTANTS' HIDDEN PRESENCE.
YET THE NEW MUTANTS KNOW...
...THAT THEY MUST ACT QUICKLY, BEFORE ONE OF THEM IS DEAD.

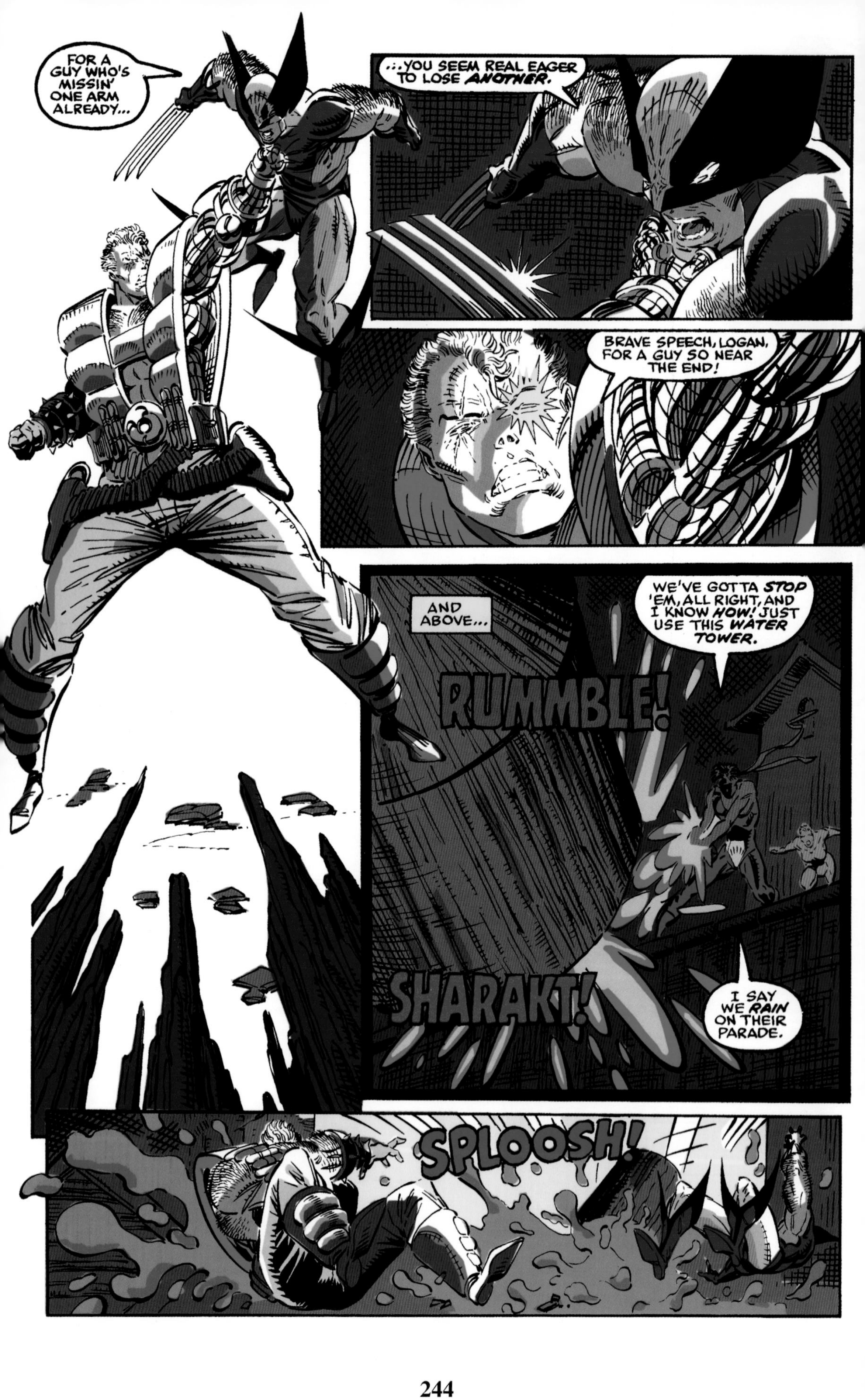
FOR A GUY WHO'S MISSIN' ONE ARM ALREADY...
...YOU SEEM REAL EAGER TO LOSE ANOTHER.
BRAVE SPEECH, LOGAN, FOR A GUY SO NEAR THE END!
AND ABOVE...
WE'VE GOTTA STOP 'EM, ALL RIGHT, AND I KNOW HOW! JUST USE THIS WATER TOWER.
RUMMBLE!
SHARAKT!
I SAY WE RAIN ON THEIR PARADE.
SPLOOSH!

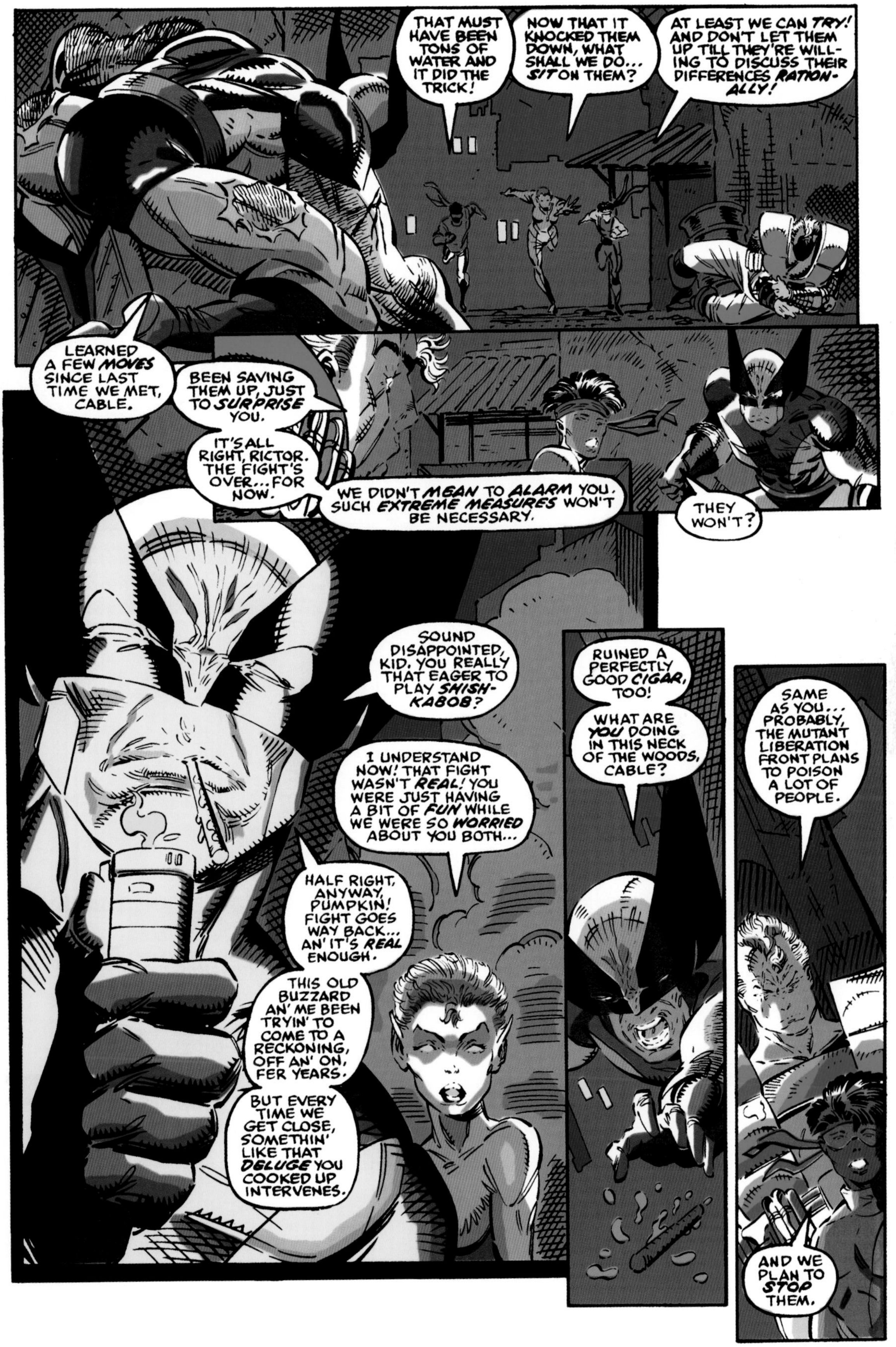
THAT MUST HAVE BEEN TONS OF WATER AND IT DID THE TRICK!
NOW THAT IT KNOCKED THEM DOWN, WHAT SHALL WE DO... SIT ON THEM?
AT LEAST WE CAN TRY! AND DON'T LET THEM UP TILL THEY'RE WILLING TO DISCUSS THEIR DIFFERENCES RATIONALLY!
LEARNED A FEW MOVES SINCE LAST TIME WE MET, CABLE.
BEEN SAVING THEM UP, JUST TO SURPRISE YOU.
IT'S ALL RIGHT, RICTOR. THE FIGHT'S OVER... FOR NOW.
WE DIDN'T MEAN TO ALARM YOU. SUCH EXTREME MEASURES WON'T BE NECESSARY.
THEY WON'T?
SOUND DISAPPOINTED, KID. YOU REALLY THAT EAGER TO PLAY SHISH-KABOB?
I UNDERSTAND NOW! THAT FIGHT WASN'T REAL! YOU WERE JUST HAVING A BIT OF FUN WHILE WE WERE SO WORRIED ABOUT YOU BOTH...
HALF RIGHT, ANYWAY, PUMPKIN! FIGHT GOES WAY BACK... AN' IT'S REAL ENOUGH.
THIS OLD BUZZARD AN' ME BEEN TRYIN' TO COME TO A RECKONING, OFF AN' ON, FER YEARS.
BUT EVERY TIME WE GET CLOSE, SOMETHIN' LIKE THAT DELUGE YOU COOKED UP INTERVENES.
RUINED A PERFECTLY GOOD CIGAR, TOO!
WHAT ARE YOU DOING IN THIS NECK OF THE WOODS, CABLE?
SAME AS YOU... PROBABLY. THE MUTANT LIBERATION FRONT PLANS TO POISON A LOT OF PEOPLE.
AND WE PLAN TO STOP THEM.

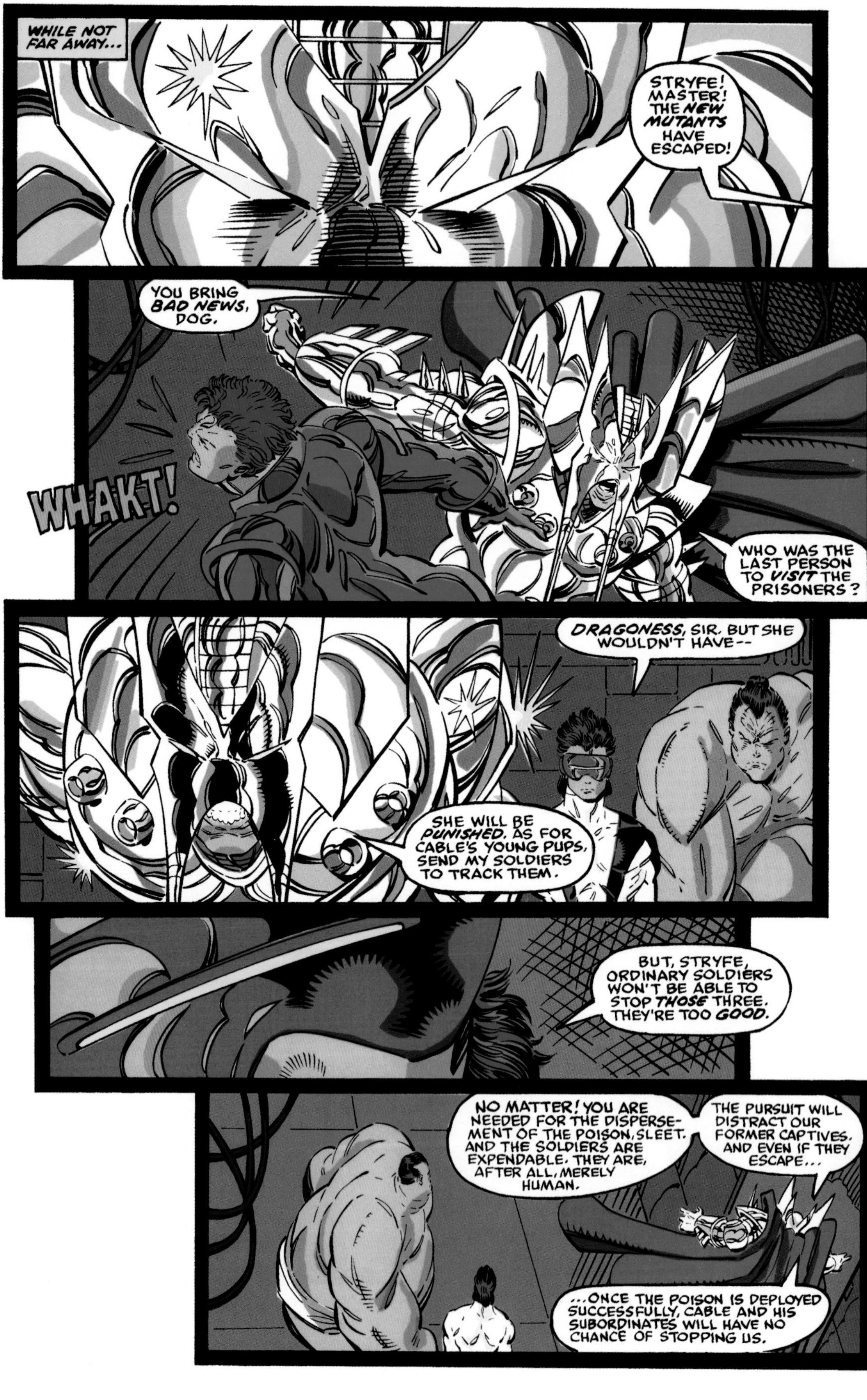
WHILE NOT FAR AWAY...
STRYFE! MASTER! THE NEW MUTANTS HAVE ESCAPED!
YOU BRING BAD NEWS, DOG.
WHAKT!
WHO WAS THE LAST PERSON TO VISIT THE PRISONERS?
DRAGONESS, SIR. BUT SHE WOULDN'T HAVE--
SHE WILL BE PUNISHED. AS FOR CABLE'S YOUNG PUPS, SEND MY SOLDIERS TO TRACK THEM.
BUT, STRYFE, ORDINARY SOLDIERS WON'T BE ABLE TO STOP THOSE THREE. THEY'RE TOO GOOD.
NO MATTER! YOU ARE NEEDED FOR THE DISPERSEMENT OF THE POISON, SLEET. AND THE SOLDIERS ARE EXPENDABLE. THEY ARE, AFTER ALL, MERELY HUMAN.
THE PURSUIT WILL DISTRACT OUR FORMER CAPTIVES. AND EVEN IF THEY ESCAPE...
...ONCE THE POISON IS DEPLOYED SUCCESSFULLY, CABLE AND HIS SUBORDINATES WILL HAVE NO CHANCE OF STOPPING US.

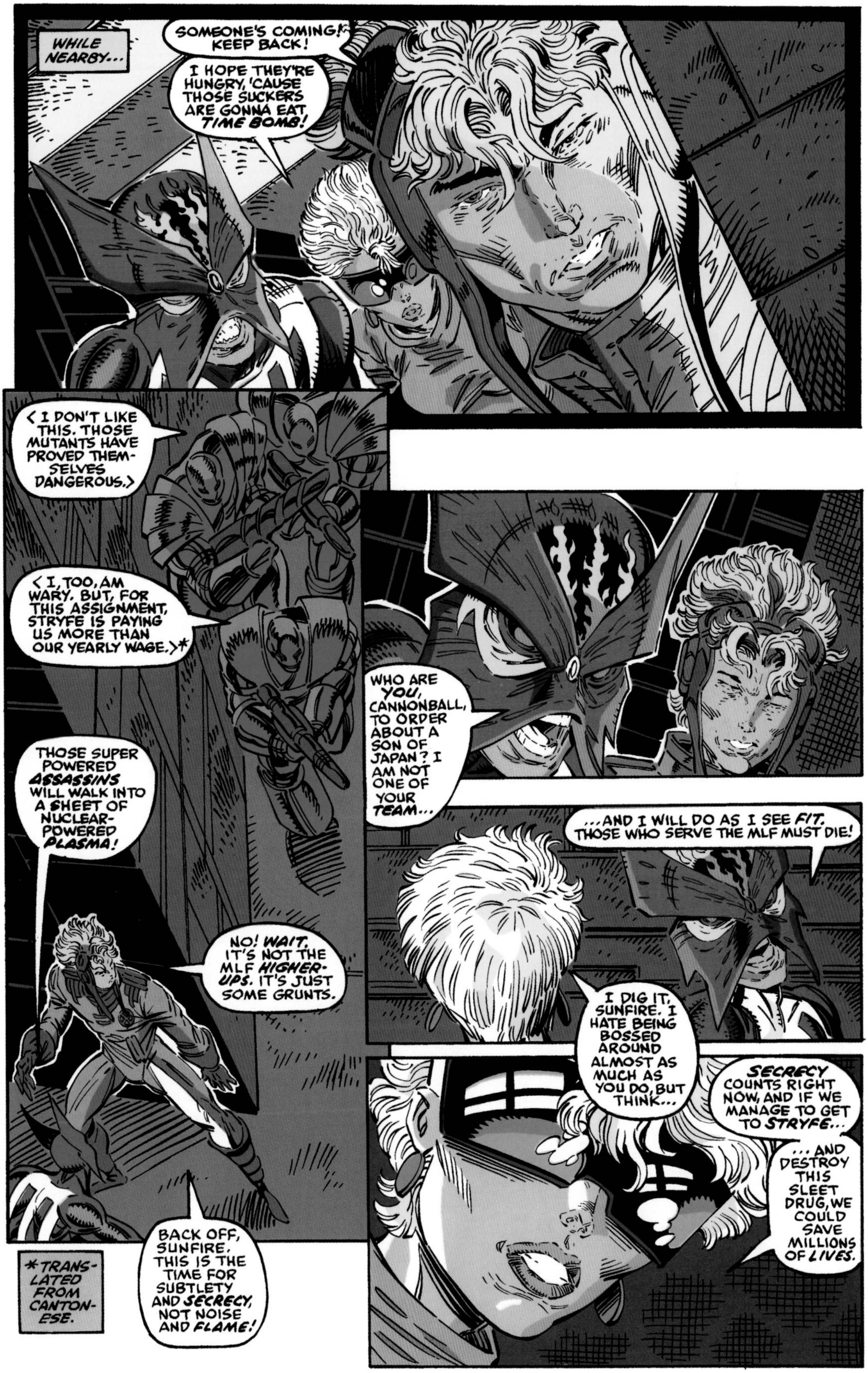
WHILE NEARBY...
SOMEONE'S COMING! KEEP BACK!
I HOPE THEY'RE HUNGRY, 'CAUSE THOSE SUCKERS ARE GONNA EAT TIME BOMB!
< I DON'T LIKE THIS. THOSE MUTANTS HAVE PROVED THEM-SELVES DANGEROUS.>
< I, TOO, AM WARY. BUT, FOR THIS ASSIGNMENT, STRYFE IS PAYING US MORE THAN OUR YEARLY WAGE.>*
THOSE SUPER POWERED ASSASSINS WILL WALK INTO A SHEET OF NUCLEAR-POWERED PLASMA!
NO! WAIT. IT'S NOT THE MLF HIGHER-UPS. IT'S JUST SOME GRUNTS.
BACK OFF, SUNFIRE. THIS IS THE TIME FOR SUBTLETY AND SECRECY, NOT NOISE AND FLAME!
*TRANS-LATED FROM CANTON-ESE.
WHO ARE YOU, CANNONBALL, TO ORDER ABOUT A SON OF JAPAN? I AM NOT ONE OF YOUR TEAM...
...AND I WILL DO AS I SEE FIT. THOSE WHO SERVE THE MLF MUST DIE!
I DIG IT, SUNFIRE. I HATE BEING BOSSED AROUND ALMOST AS MUCH AS YOU DO, BUT THINK...
SECRECY COUNTS RIGHT NOW, AND IF WE MANAGE TO GET TO STRYFE...
...AND DESTROY THIS SLEET DRUG, WE COULD SAVE MILLIONS OF LIVES.

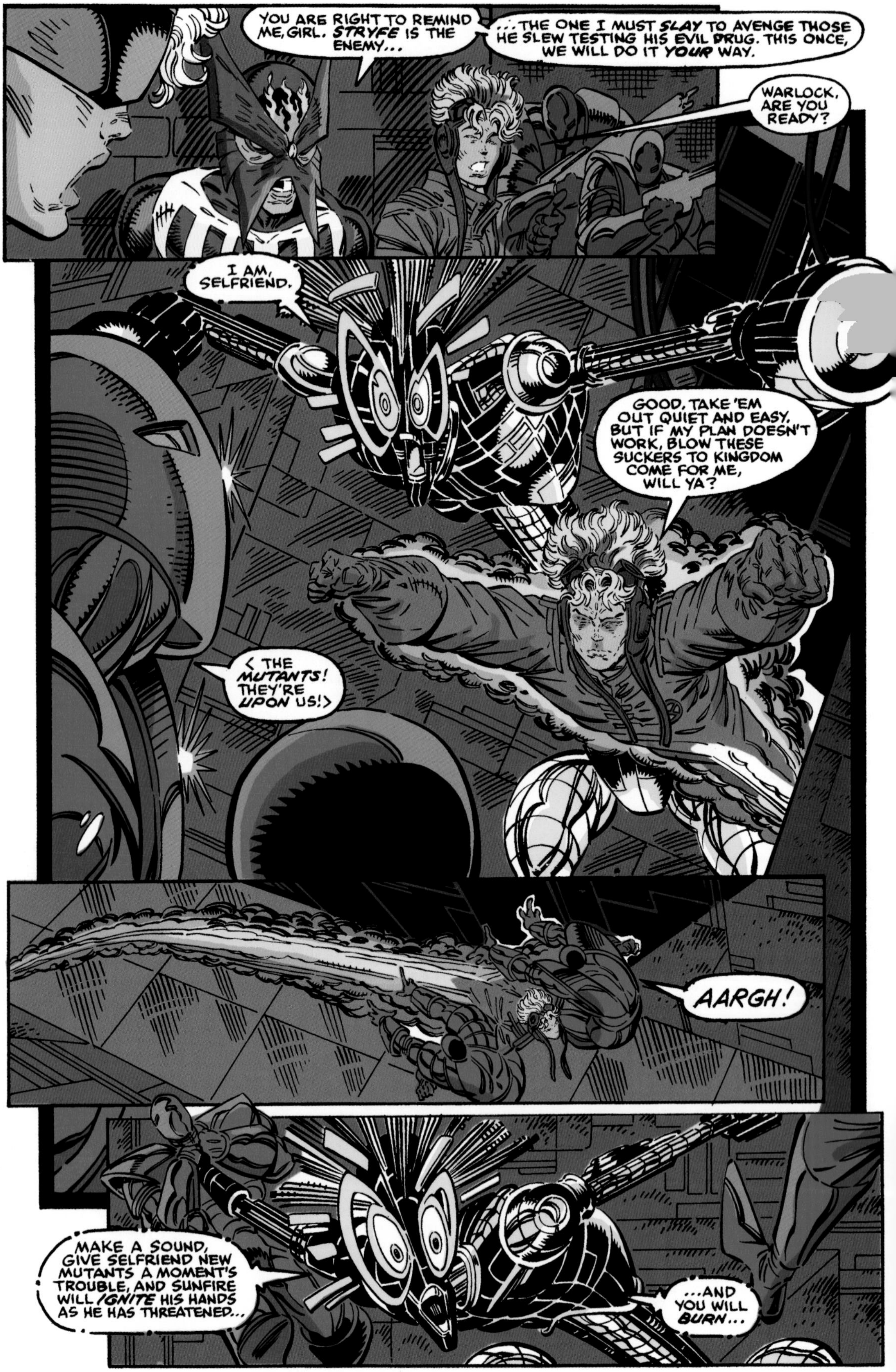
YOU ARE RIGHT TO REMIND ME, GIRL. STRYFE IS THE ENEMY...
...THE ONE I MUST SLAY TO AVENGE THOSE HE SLEW TESTING HIS EVIL DRUG. THIS ONCE, WE WILL DO IT YOUR WAY.
WARLOCK, ARE YOU READY?
I AM, SELFRIEND.
GOOD. TAKE 'EM OUT QUIET AND EASY. BUT IF MY PLAN DOESN'T WORK, BLOW THESE SUCKERS TO KINGDOM COME FOR ME, WILL YA?
< THE MUTANTS! THEY'RE UPON US!>
AARGH!
MAKE A SOUND, GIVE SELFRIEND NEW MUTANTS A MOMENT'S TROUBLE, AND SUNFIRE WILL IGNITE HIS HANDS AS HE HAS THREATENED...
...AND YOU WILL BURN...

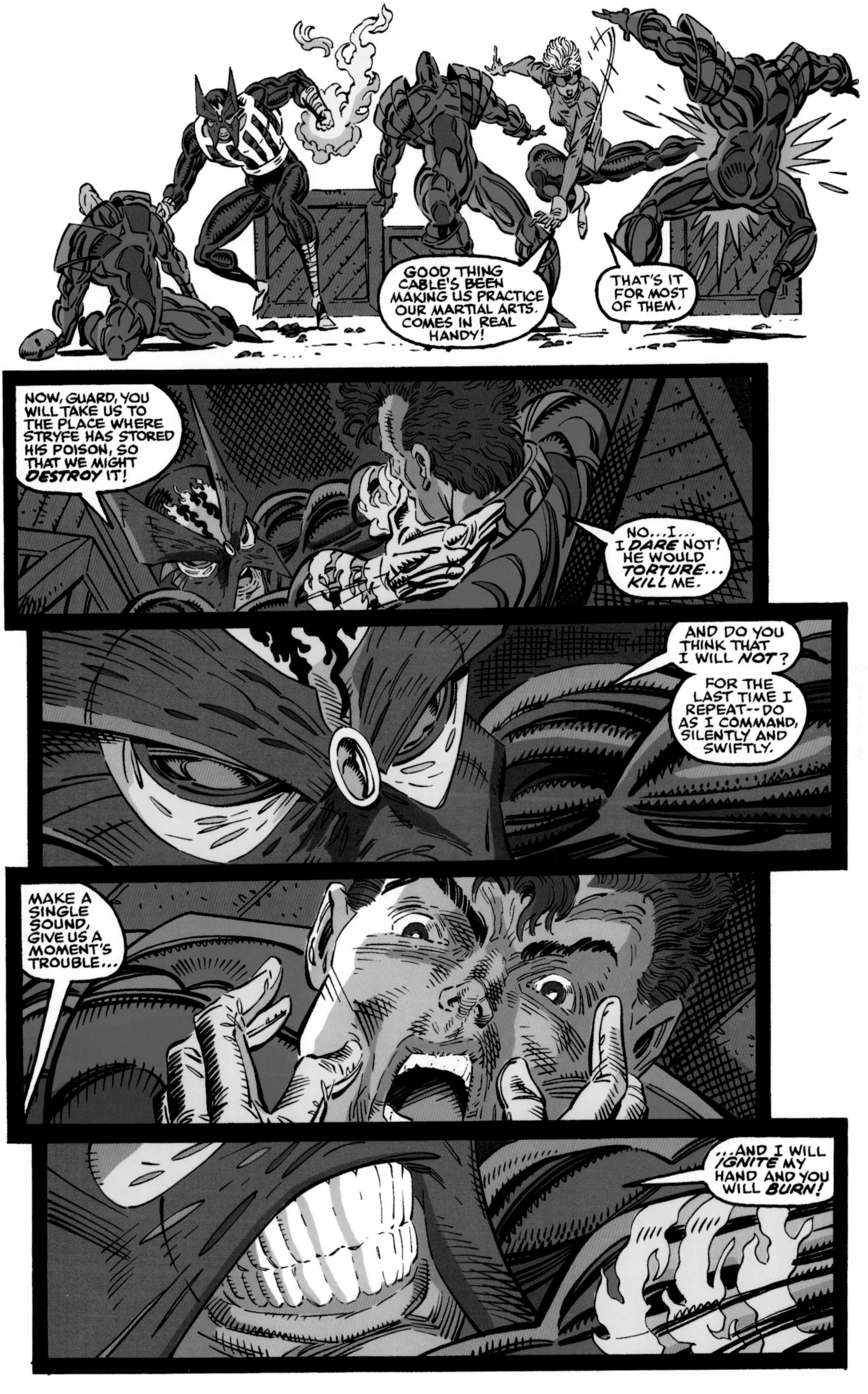
GOOD THING CABLE'S BEEN MAKING US PRACTICE OUR MARTIAL ARTS. COMES IN REAL HANDY!
THAT'S IT FOR MOST OF THEM.
NOW, GUARD, YOU WILL TAKE US TO THE PLACE WHERE STRYFE HAS STORED HIS POISON, SO THAT WE MIGHT DESTROY IT!
NO...I... I DARE NOT! HE WOULD TORTURE... KILL ME.
AND DO YOU THINK THAT I WILL NOT?
FOR THE LAST TIME I REPEAT--DO AS I COMMAND, SILENTLY AND SWIFTLY.
MAKE A SINGLE SOUND, GIVE US A MOMENT'S TROUBLE...
...AND I WILL IGNITE MY HAND AND YOU WILL BURN!

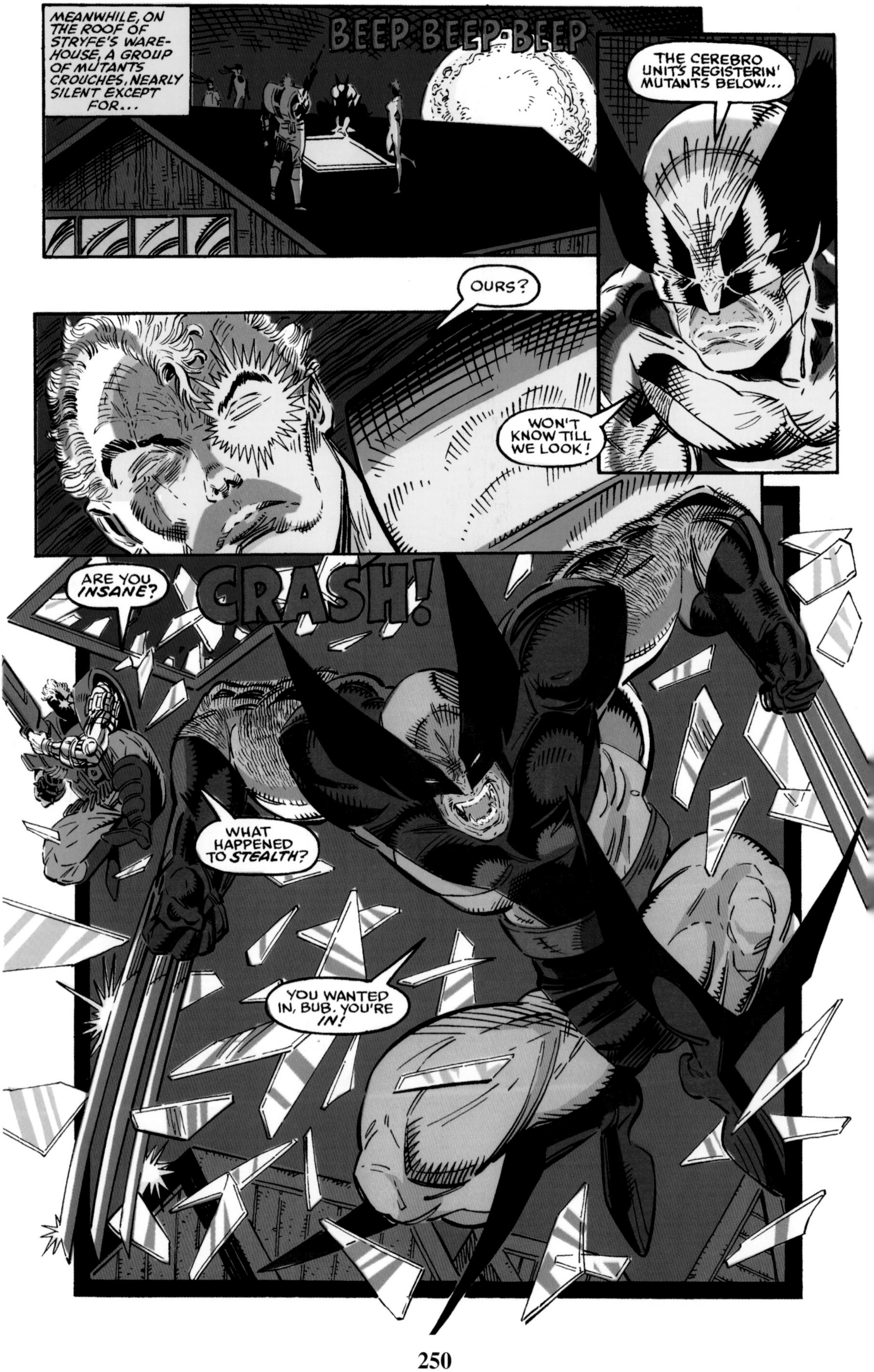
MEANWHILE, ON THE ROOF OF STRYFE'S WARE-HOUSE, A GROUP OF MUTANTS CROUCHES, NEARLY SILENT EXCEPT FOR...
BEEP BEEP BEEP
THE CEREBRO UNIT'S REGISTERIN' MUTANTS BELOW...
OURS?
WON'T KNOW TILL WE LOOK!
ARE YOU INSANE?
CRASH!
WHAT HAPPENED TO STEALTH?
YOU WANTED IN, BUB. YOU'RE IN!

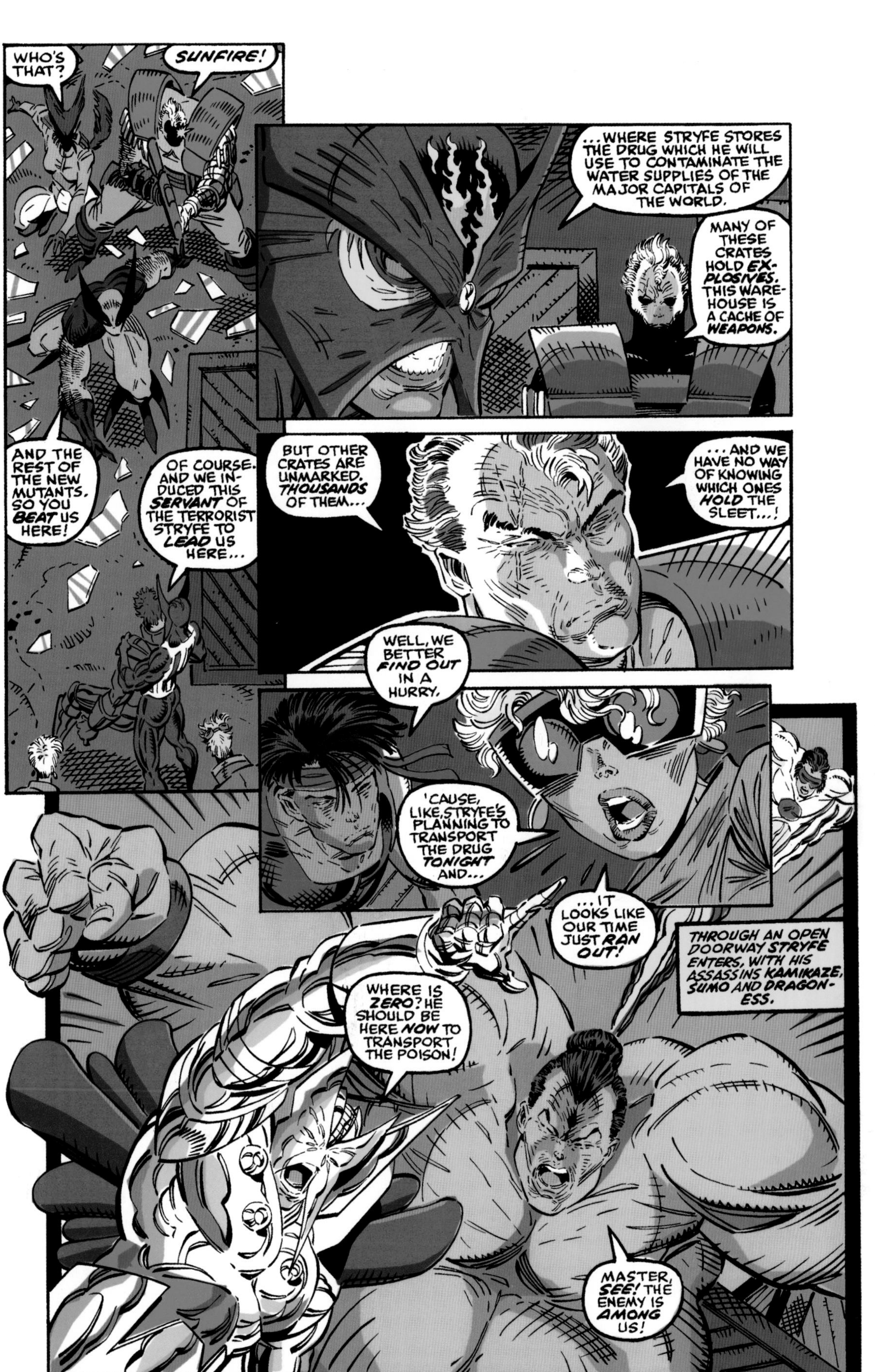

WHO'S THAT?
SUNFIRE!
...WHERE STRYFE STORES THE DRUG WHICH HE WILL USE TO CONTAMINATE THE WATER SUPPLIES OF THE MAJOR CAPITALS OF THE WORLD.
MANY OF THESE CRATES HOLD EXPLOSIVES. THIS WAREHOUSE IS A CACHE OF WEAPONS.
AND THE REST OF THE NEW MUTANTS. SO YOU BEAT US HERE!
OF COURSE. AND WE INDUCED THIS SERVANT OF THE TERRORIST STRYFE TO LEAD US HERE...
BUT OTHER CRATES ARE UNMARKED. THOUSANDS OF THEM...
...AND WE HAVE NO WAY OF KNOWING WHICH ONES HOLD THE SLEET...!
WELL, WE BETTER FIND OUT IN A HURRY.
'CAUSE, LIKE, STRYFE'S PLANNING TO TRANSPORT THE DRUG TONIGHT AND...
...IT LOOKS LIKE OUR TIME JUST RAN OUT!
THROUGH AN OPEN DOORWAY STRYFE ENTERS, WITH HIS ASSASSINS KAMIKAZE, SUMO AND DRAGONESS.
WHERE IS ZERO? HE SHOULD BE HERE NOW TO TRANSPORT THE POISON!
MASTER, SEE! THE ENEMY IS AMONG US!

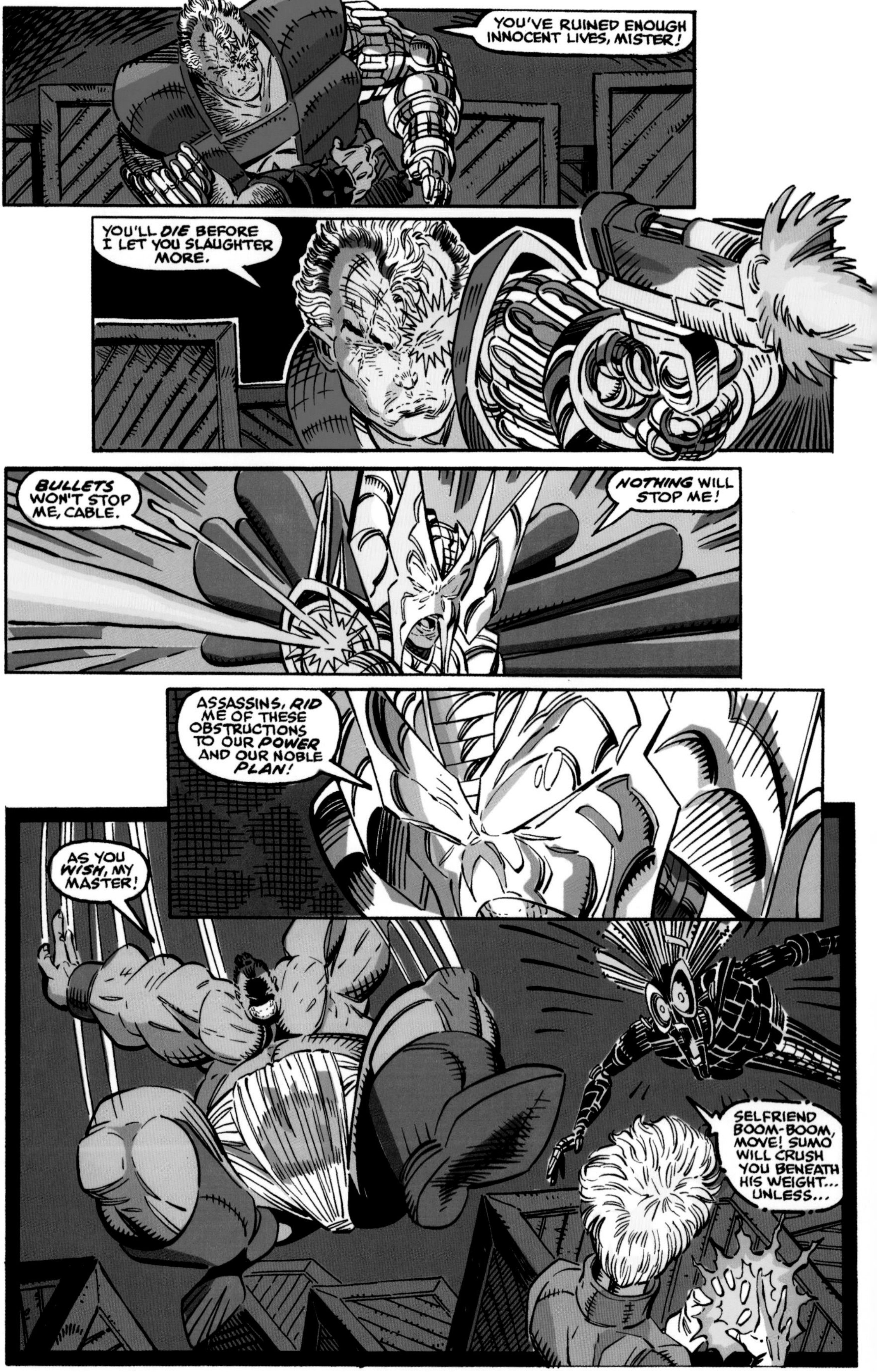
YOU'VE RUINED ENOUGH INNOCENT LIVES, MISTER!
YOU'LL DIE BEFORE I LET YOU SLAUGHTER MORE.
BULLETS WON'T STOP ME, CABLE.
NOTHING WILL STOP ME!
ASSASSINS, RID ME OF THESE OBSTRUCTIONS TO OUR POWER AND OUR NOBLE PLAN!
AS YOU WISH, MY MASTER!
SELFRIEND BOOM-BOOM, MOVE! SUMO WILL CRUSH YOU BENEATH HIS WEIGHT... UNLESS...

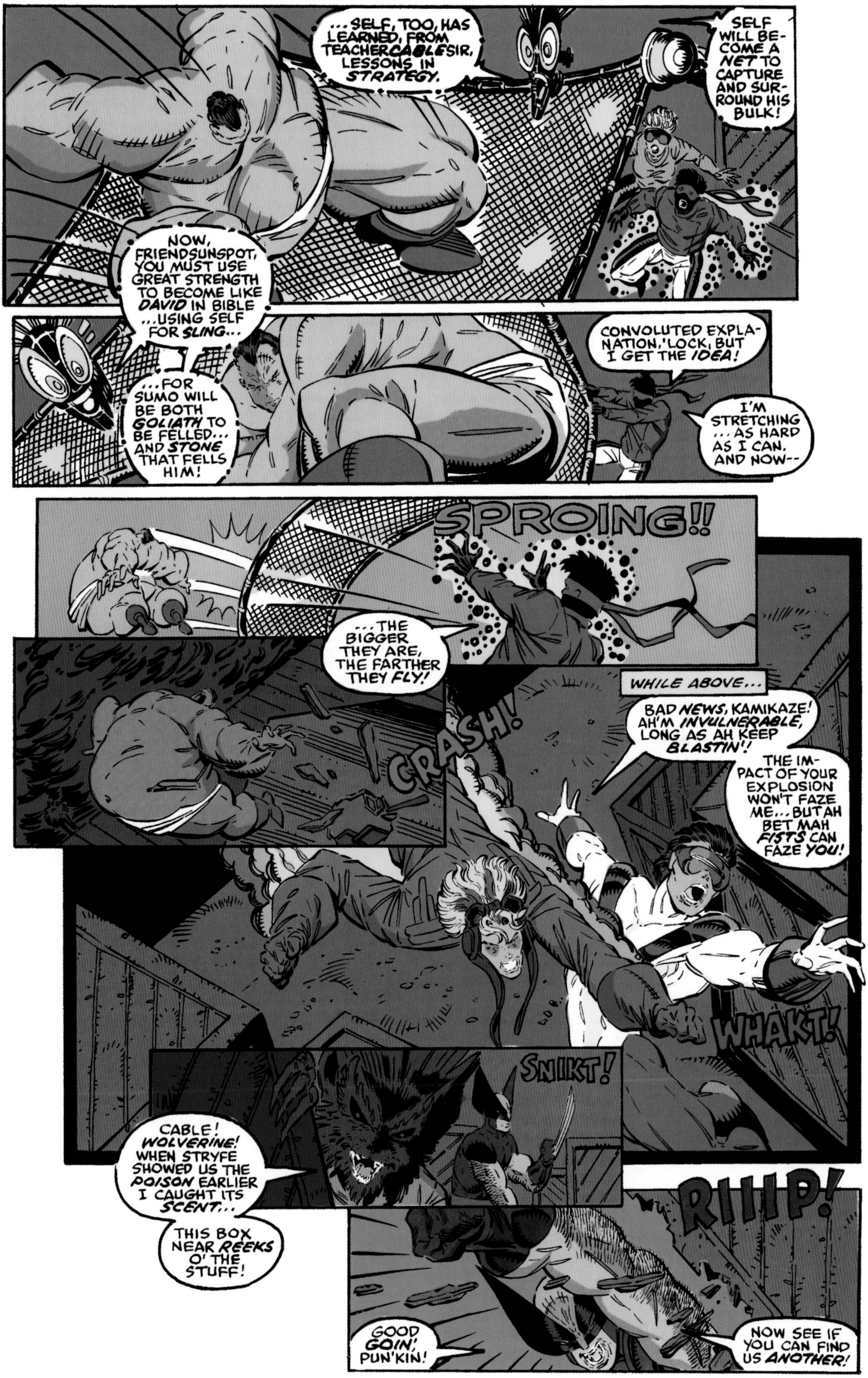
...SELF, TOO, HAS LEARNED, FROM TEACHERCABLESIR, LESSONS IN STRATEGY.
SELF WILL BECOME A NET TO CAPTURE AND SURROUND HIS BULK!
NOW, FRIENDSUNSPOT, YOU MUST USE GREAT STRENGTH TO BECOME LIKE DAVID IN BIBLE ...USING SELF FOR SLING...
...FOR SUMO WILL BE BOTH GOLIATH TO BE FELLED... AND STONE THAT FELLS HIM!
CONVOLUTED EXPLANATION, 'LOCK, BUT I GET THE IDEA!
I'M STRETCHING ...AS HARD AS I CAN. AND NOW--
SPROING!!
...THE BIGGER THEY ARE, THE FARTHER THEY FLY!
CRASH!
WHILE ABOVE...
BAD NEWS, KAMIKAZE! AH'M INVULNERABLE, LONG AS AH KEEP BLASTIN'!
THE IMPACT OF YOUR EXPLOSION WON'T FAZE ME... BUT AH BET MAH FISTS CAN FAZE YOU!
WHAKT!
SNIKT!
CABLE! WOLVERINE! WHEN STRYFE SHOWED US THE POISON EARLIER I CAUGHT ITS SCENT...
THIS BOX NEAR REEKS O' THE STUFF!
RIIIP!
GOOD GOIN', PUN'KIN!
NOW SEE IF YOU CAN FIND US ANOTHER!

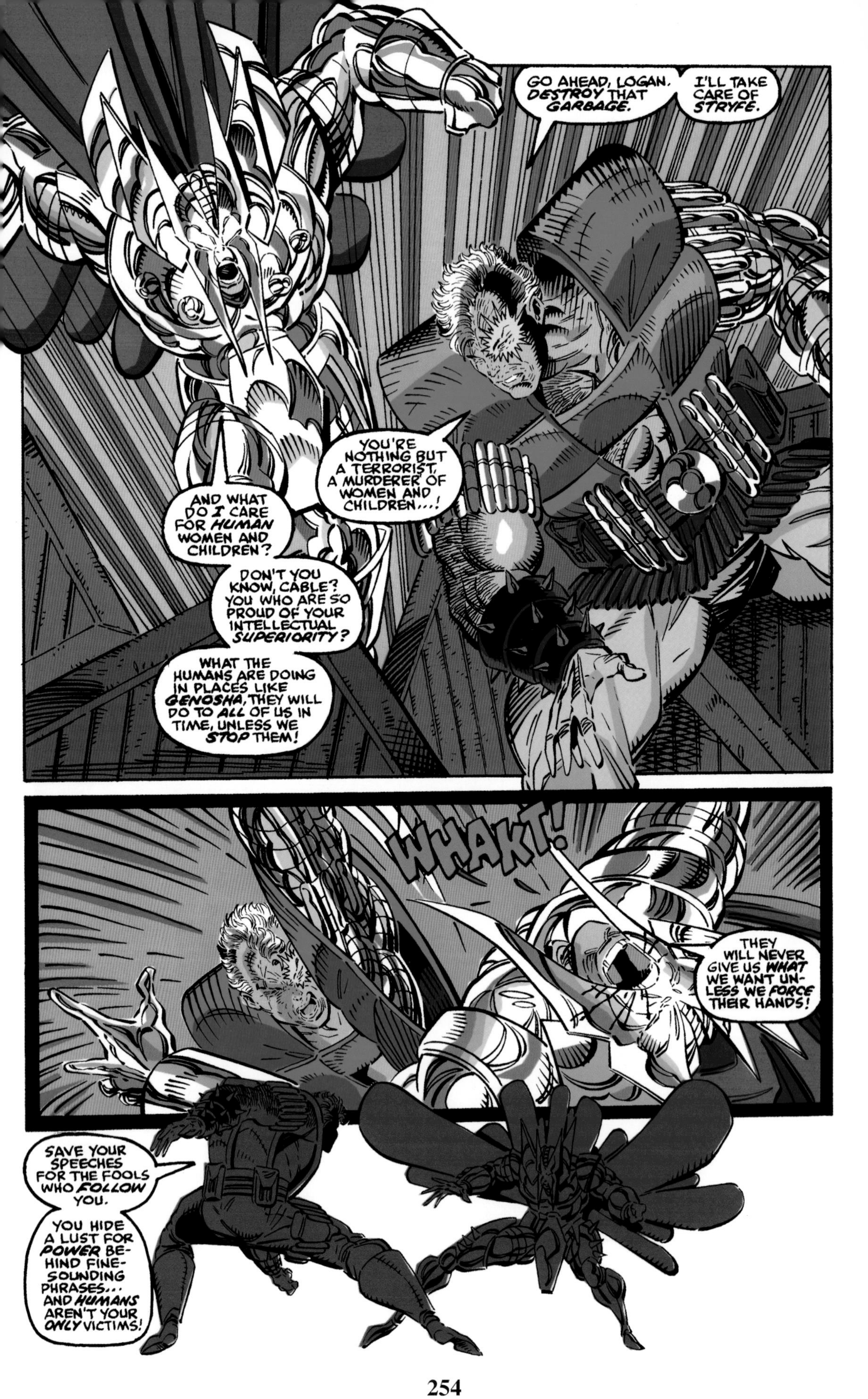
GO AHEAD, LOGAN. DESTROY THAT GARBAGE.
I'LL TAKE CARE OF STRYFE.
YOU'RE NOTHING BUT A TERRORIST, A MURDERER OF WOMEN AND CHILDREN...!
AND WHAT DO I CARE FOR HUMAN WOMEN AND CHILDREN?
DON'T YOU KNOW, CABLE? YOU WHO ARE SO PROUD OF YOUR INTELLECTUAL SUPERIORITY?
WHAT THE HUMANS ARE DOING IN PLACES LIKE GENOSHA, THEY WILL DO TO ALL OF US IN TIME, UNLESS WE STOP THEM!
WHAKT!
THEY WILL NEVER GIVE US WHAT WE WANT UN-LESS WE FORCE THEIR HANDS!
SAVE YOUR SPEECHES FOR THE FOOLS WHO FOLLOW YOU.
YOU HIDE A LUST FOR POWER BE-HIND FINE-SOUNDING PHRASES... AND HUMANS AREN'T YOUR ONLY VICTIMS!

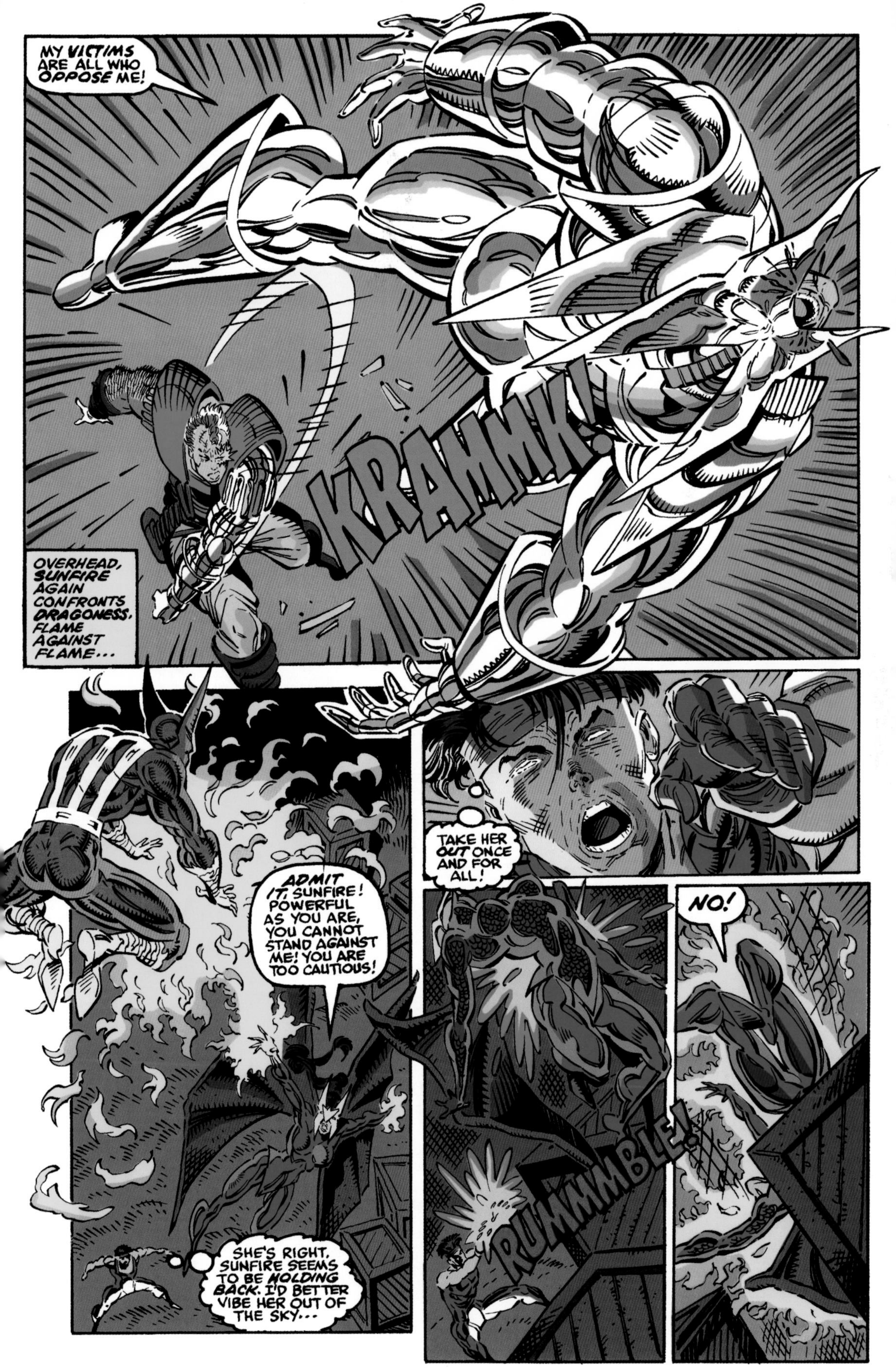
MY VICTIMS ARE ALL WHO OPPOSE ME!
KRAMMK!
OVERHEAD, SUNFIRE AGAIN CONFRONTS DRAGONESS, FLAME AGAINST FLAME...
TAKE HER OUT ONCE AND FOR ALL!
ADMIT IT, SUNFIRE! POWERFUL AS YOU ARE, YOU CANNOT STAND AGAINST ME! YOU ARE TOO CAUTIOUS!
SHE'S RIGHT. SUNFIRE SEEMS TO BE HOLDING BACK. I'D BETTER VIBE HER OUT OF THE SKY...
RUMMMBLE!
NO!

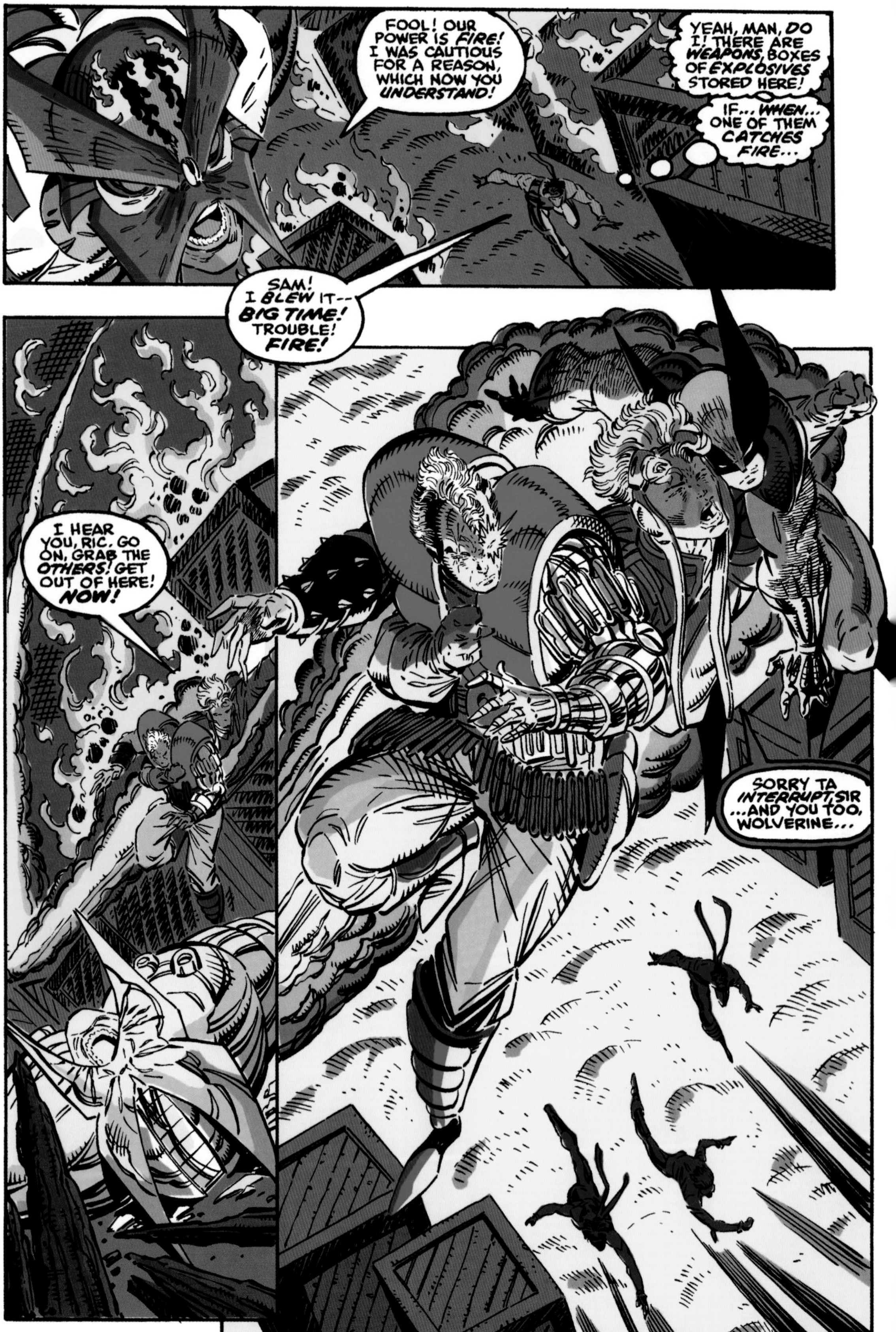
FOOL! OUR POWER IS FIRE! I WAS CAUTIOUS FOR A REASON, WHICH NOW YOU UNDERSTAND!
YEAH, MAN, DO I! THERE ARE WEAPONS, BOXES OF EXPLOSIVES STORED HERE!
IF... WHEN... ONE OF THEM CATCHES FIRE...
SAM! I BLEW IT-- BIG TIME! TROUBLE! FIRE!
I HEAR YOU, RIC. GO ON, GRAB THE OTHERS! GET OUT OF HERE! NOW!
SORRY TA INTERRUPT, SIR ...AND YOU TOO, WOLVERINE...

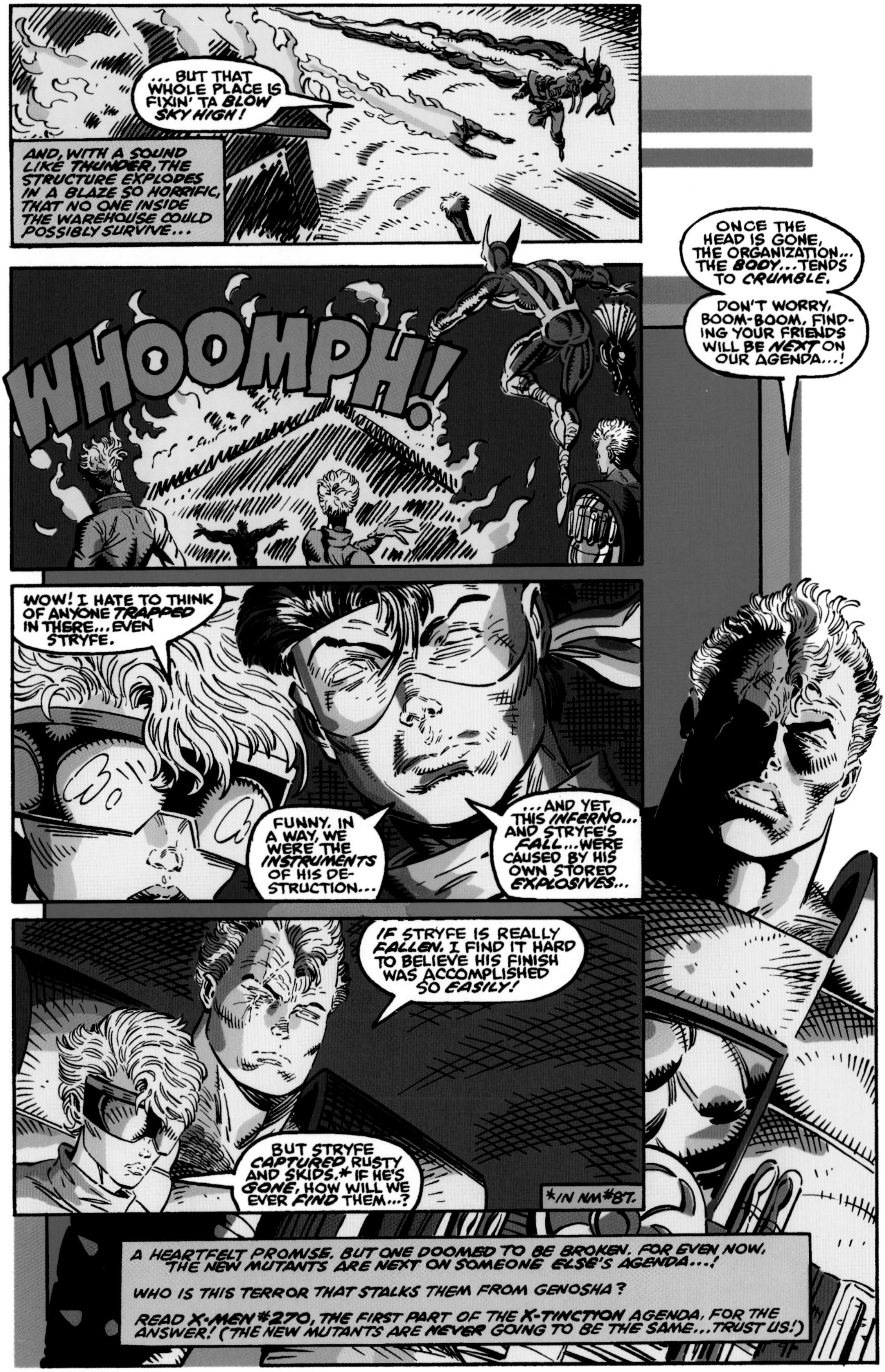

...BUT THAT WHOLE PLACE IS FIXIN' TA BLOW SKY HIGH!
AND, WITH A SOUND LIKE THUNDER, THE STRUCTURE EXPLODES IN A BLAZE SO HORRIFIC, THAT NO ONE INSIDE THE WAREHOUSE COULD POSSIBLY SURVIVE...
WHOOMPH!
ONCE THE HEAD IS GONE, THE ORGANIZATION... THE BODY... TENDS TO CRUMBLE.
DON'T WORRY, BOOM-BOOM. FINDING YOUR FRIENDS WILL BE NEXT ON OUR AGENDA...!
WOW! I HATE TO THINK OF ANYONE TRAPPED IN THERE... EVEN STRYFE.
FUNNY. IN A WAY, WE WERE THE INSTRUMENTS OF HIS DESTRUCTION...
...AND YET, THIS INFERNO... AND STRYFE'S FALL... WERE CAUSED BY HIS OWN STORED EXPLOSIVES...
IF STRYFE IS REALLY FALLEN, I FIND IT HARD TO BELIEVE HIS FINISH WAS ACCOMPLISHED SO EASILY!
BUT STRYFE CAPTURED RUSTY AND SKIDS.* IF HE'S GONE, HOW WILL WE EVER FIND THEM...?
*IN NM #87.
A HEARTFELT PROMISE. BUT ONE DOOMED TO BE BROKEN. FOR EVEN NOW, THE NEW MUTANTS ARE NEXT ON SOMEONE ELSE'S AGENDA...!
WHO IS THIS TERROR THAT STALKS THEM FROM GENOSHA?
READ X-MEN #270, THE FIRST PART OF THE X-TINCTION AGENDA, FOR THE ANSWER! ("THE NEW MUTANTS ARE NEVER GOING TO BE THE SAME... TRUST US!)

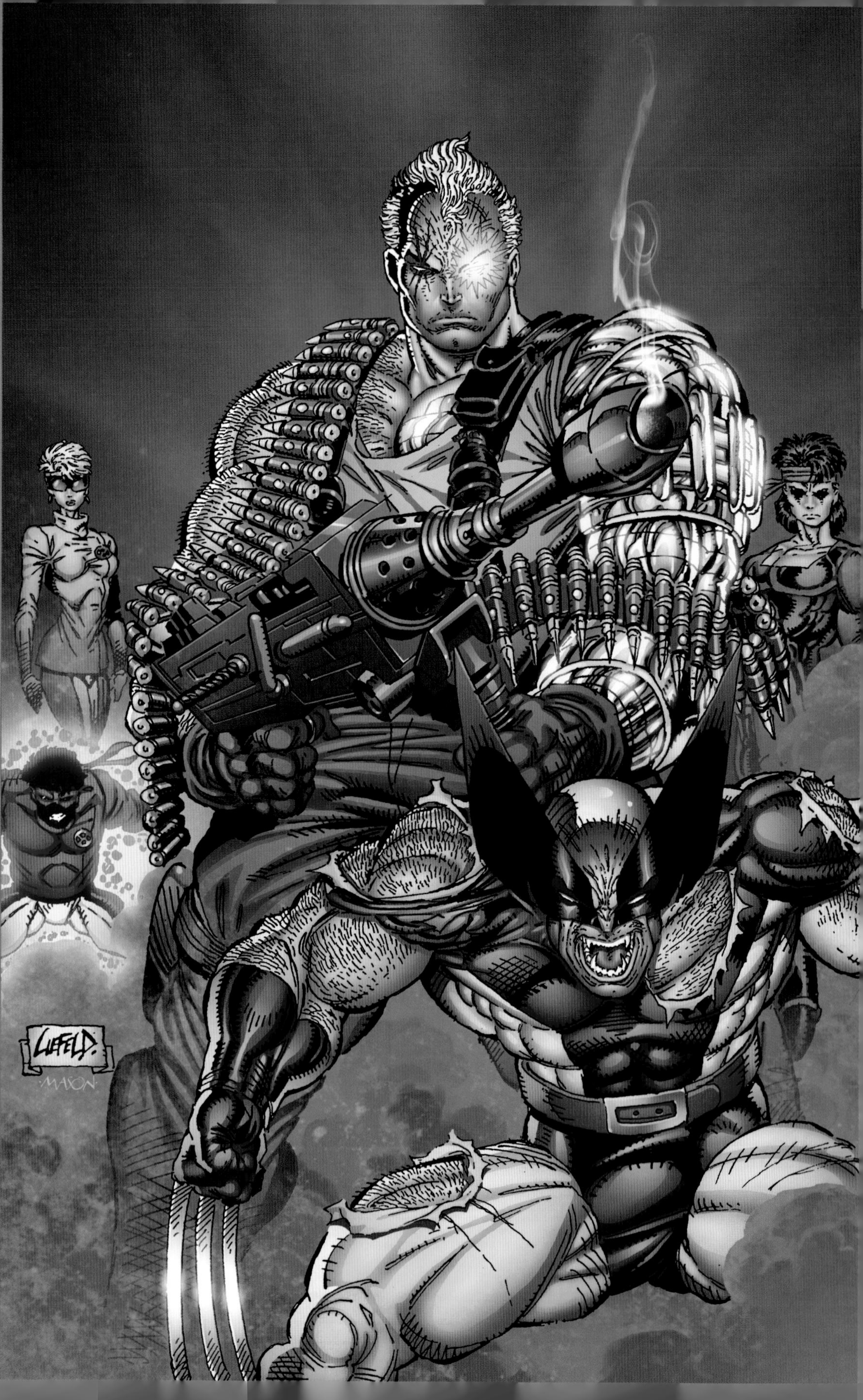
LIEFELD
MASON

CABLE™

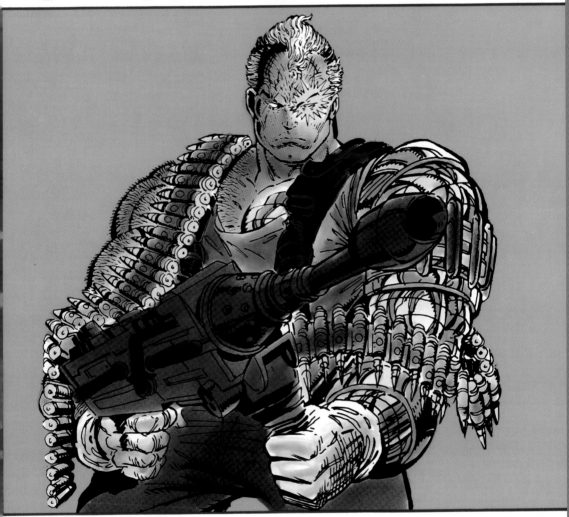

AND THE NEW MUTANTS®

SIMONSON LIEFELD

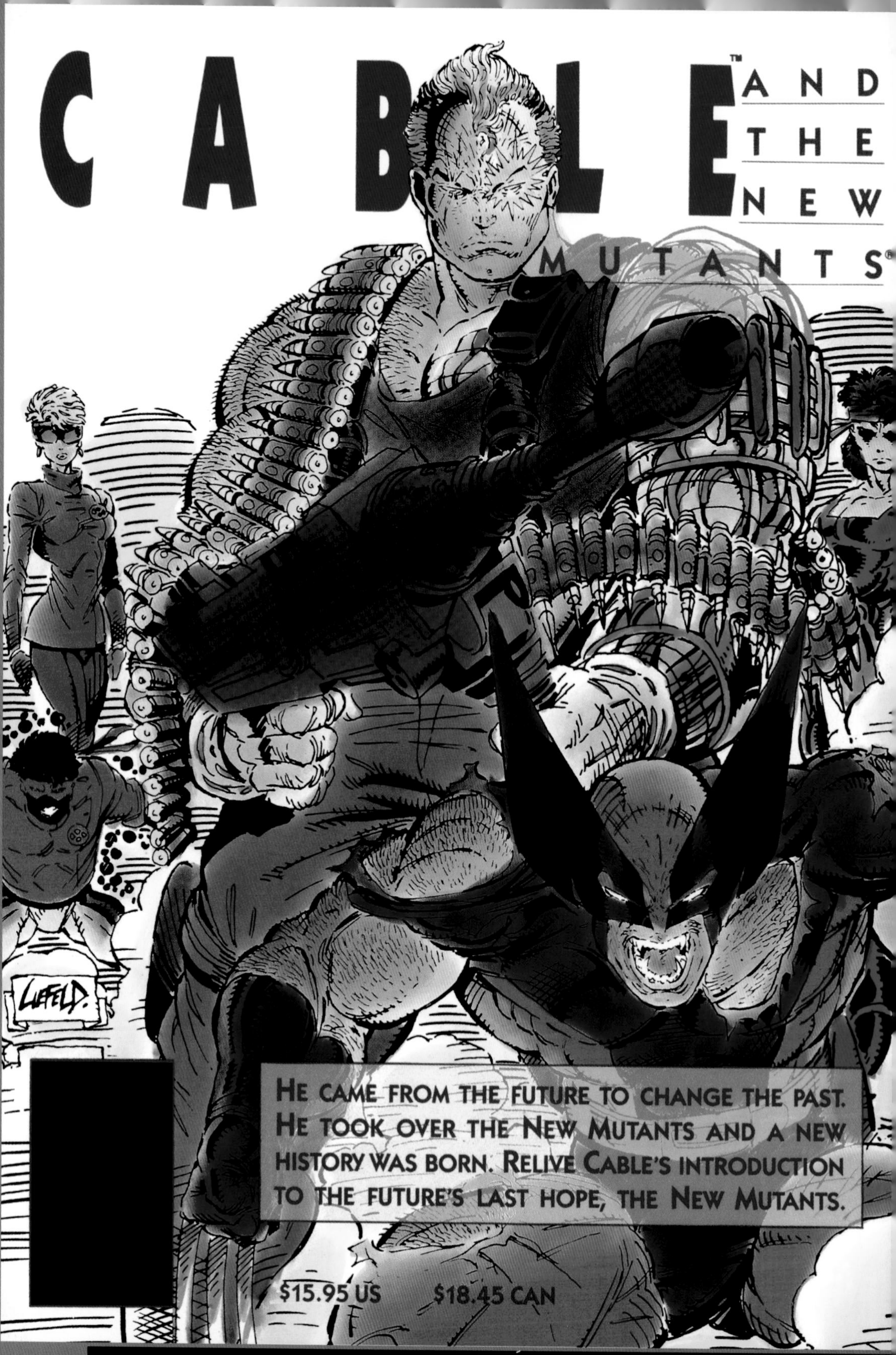
CABLE™ AND THE NEW MUTANTS®
LIEFELD
HE CAME FROM THE FUTURE TO CHANGE THE PAST. HE TOOK OVER THE NEW MUTANTS AND A NEW HISTORY WAS BORN. RELIVE CABLE'S INTRODUCTION TO THE FUTURE'S LAST HOPE, THE NEW MUTANTS.
[redacted]
$15.95 US $18.45 CAN

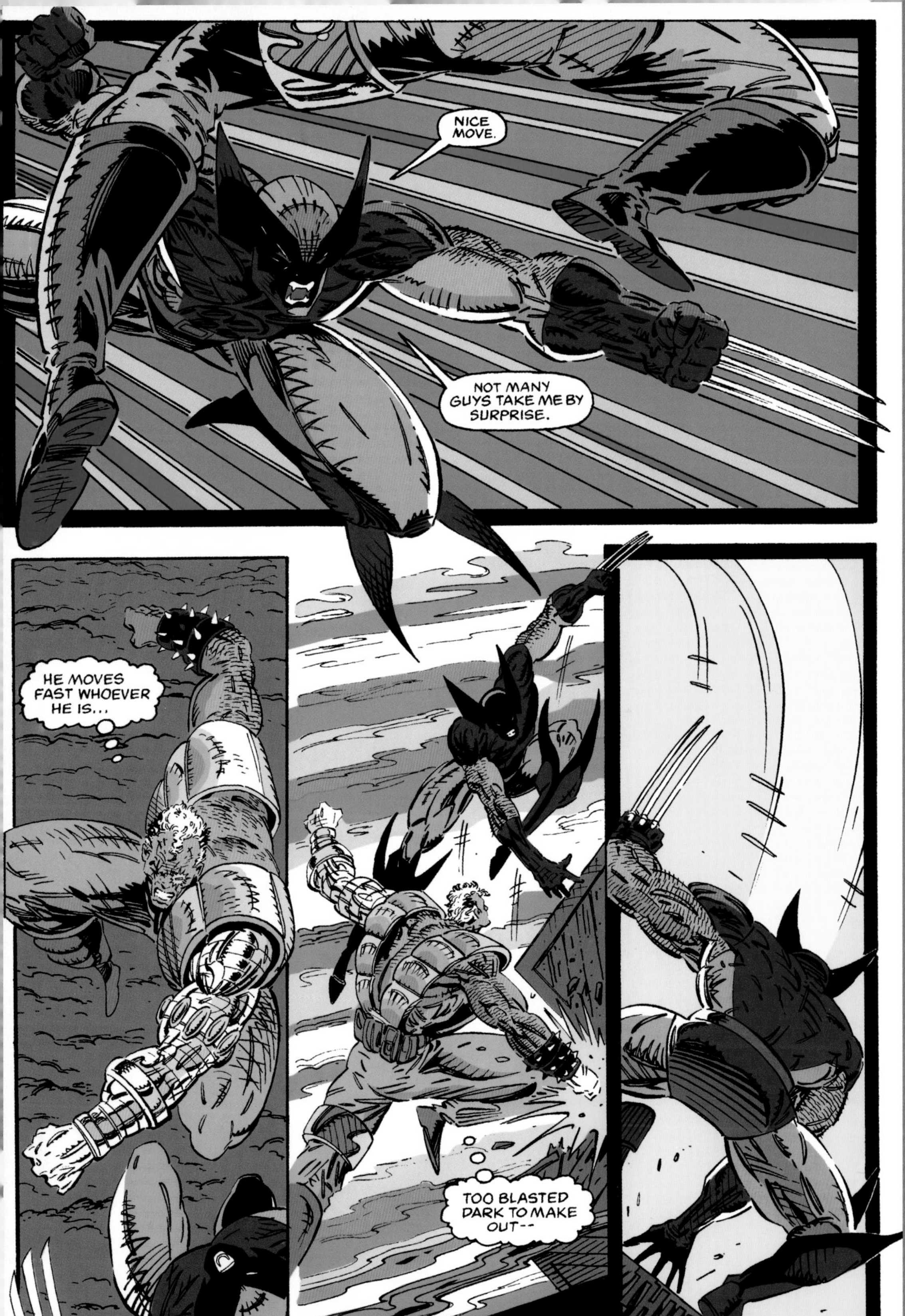
NICE MOVE.
NOT MANY GUYS TAKE ME BY SURPRISE.
HE MOVES FAST WHOEVER HE IS...
TOO BLASTED DARK TO MAKE OUT--

THIS PAGE, DRAWN BY MARK PACELLA, WAS ADDED TO THE **CABLE AND THE NEW MUTANTS** TPB

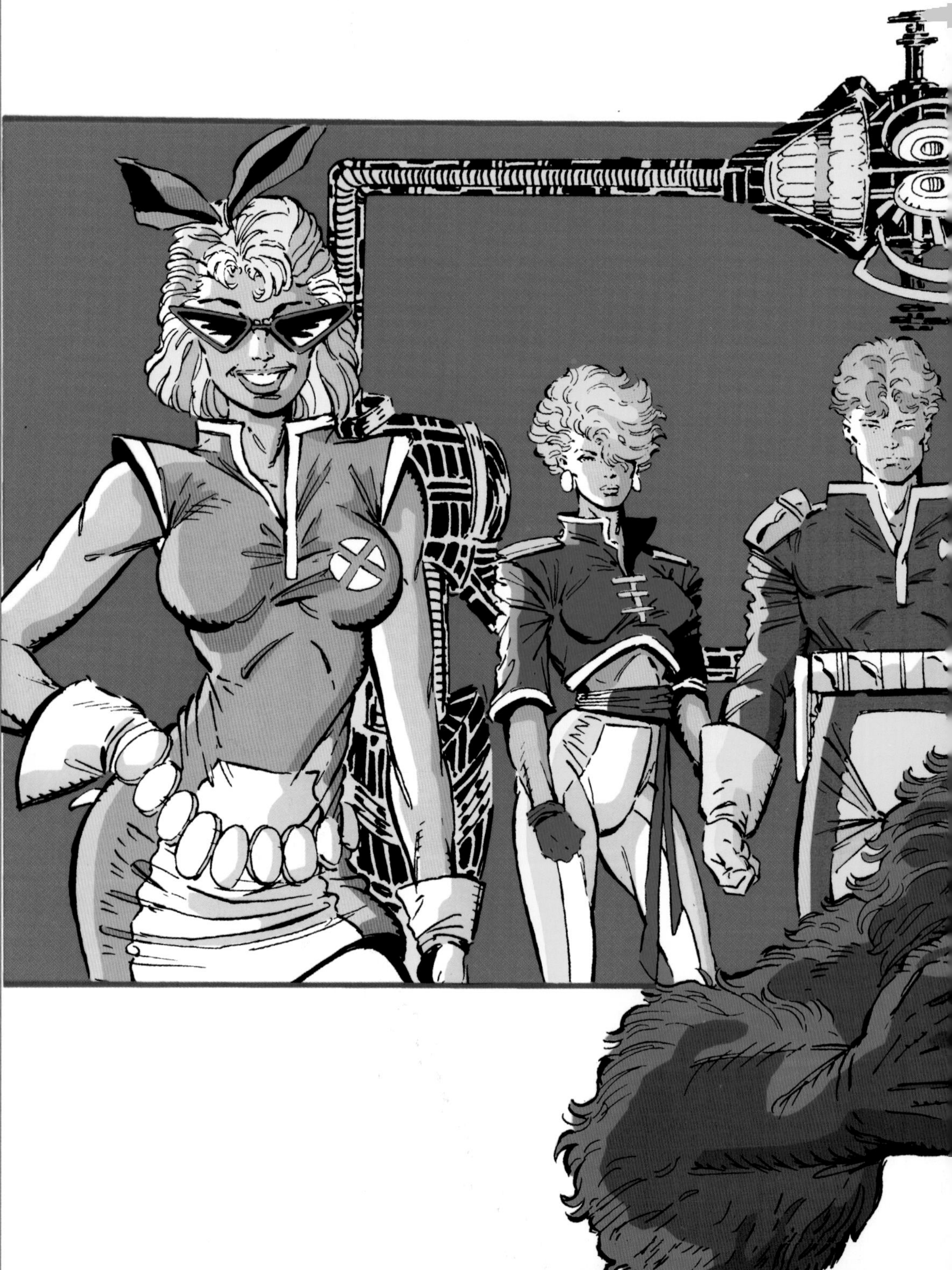

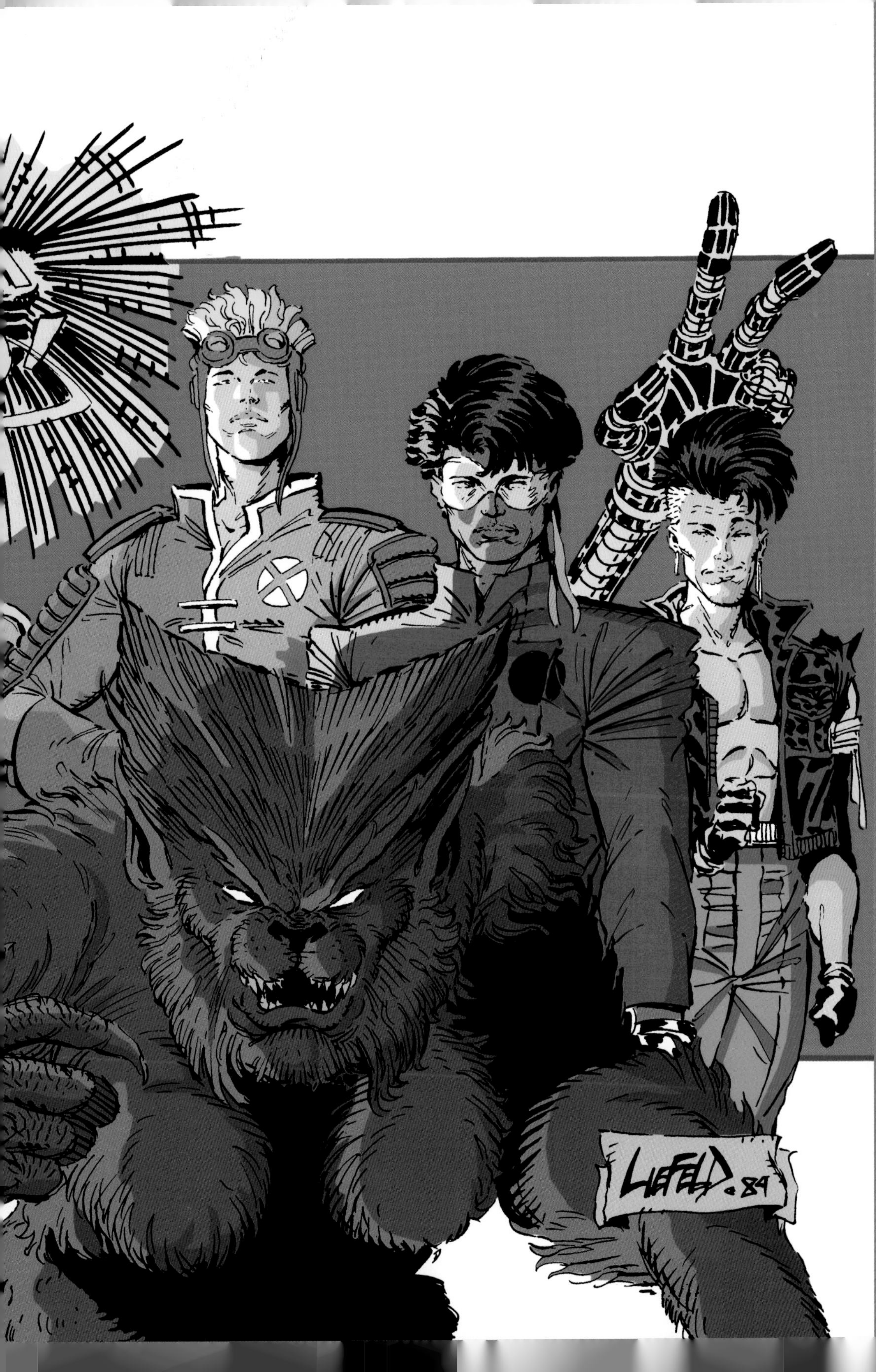
LIEFELD .84

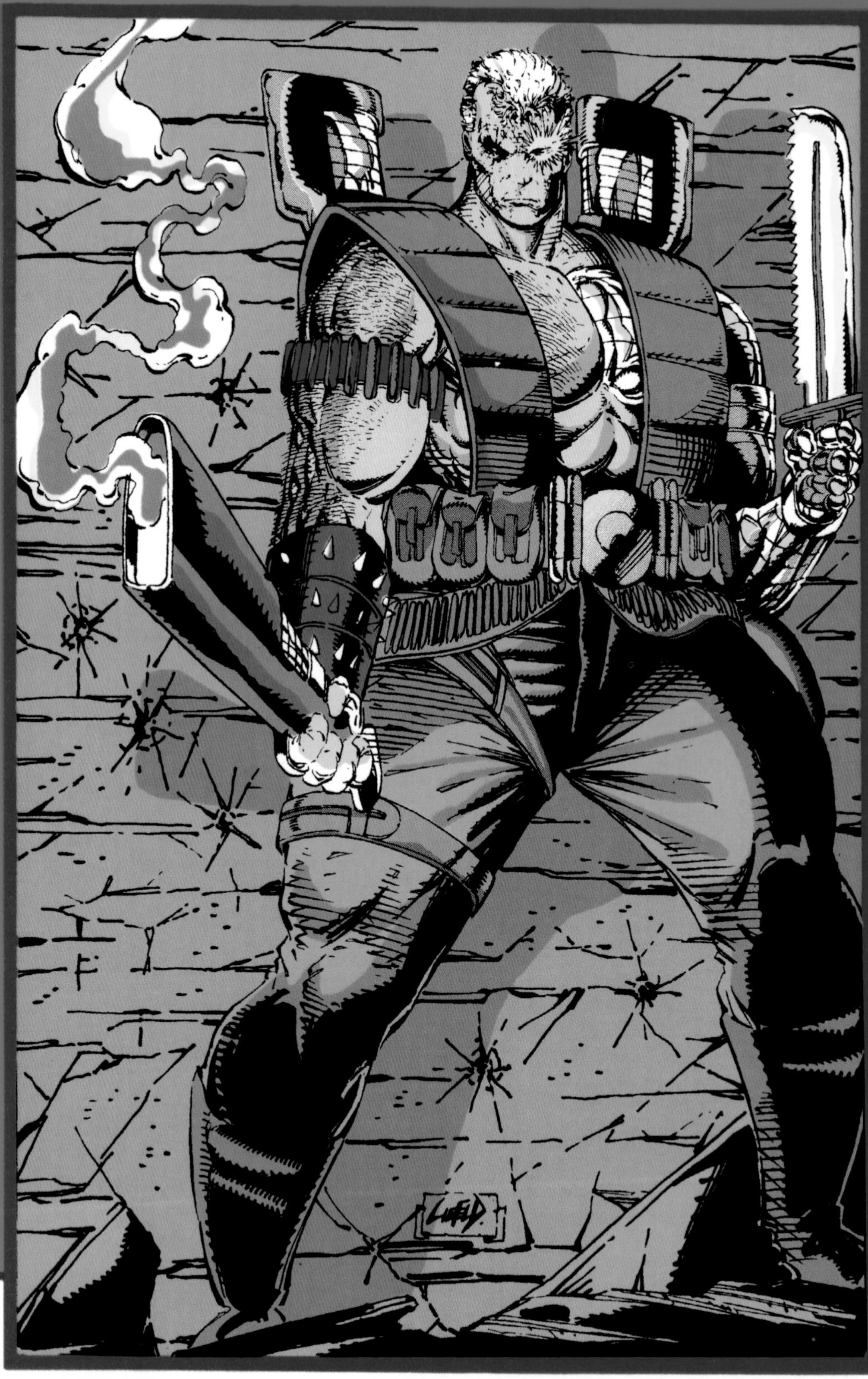